The Clojure Workshop

Use functional programming to build data-centric applications with Clojure and ClojureScript

Joseph Fahey, Thomas Haratyk, Scott McCaughie,
Yehonathan Sharvit, and Konrad Szydlo

The Clojure Workshop

Authors: Joseph Fahey, Thomas Haratyk, Scott McCaughie, Yehonathan Sharvit, and Konrad Szydlo

Technical Reviewers: Cavan David, Kirill Erokhin, Punit Naik, David Parker, Prashant Rathod, Erwin Rooijakkers, and John Stevenson

Managing Editor: Rutuja Yerunkar

Acquisitions Editors: Sarah Lawton, Manuraj Nair, Royluis Rodrigues, and Karan Wadekar

Production Editor: Roshan Kawale

Editorial Board: Shubhopriya Banerjee, Bharat Botle, Ewan Buckingham, Megan Carlisle, Mahesh Dhyani, Manasa Kumar, Alex Mazonowicz, Bridget Neale, Dominic Pereira, Shiny Poojary, Abhishek Rane, Brendan Rodrigues, Erol Staveley, Ankita Thakur, Nitesh Thakur, and Jonathan Wray

First Published: January 2020

Production Reference: 4220221

ISBN: 978-1-83882-548-5

Published by Packt Publishing Ltd.

Livery Place, 35 Livery Street

Birmingham B3 2PB, UK

Why Learn with a Packt Workshop?

Learn by Doing

Packt Workshops are built around the idea that the best way to learn something new is by getting hands-on experience. We know that learning a language or technology isn't just an academic pursuit. It's a journey towards the effective use of a new tool—whether that's to kickstart your career, automate repetitive tasks, or just build some cool stuff.

That's why Workshops are designed to get you writing code from the very beginning. You'll start fairly small—learning how to implement some basic functionality—but once you've completed that, you'll have the confidence and understanding to move onto something slightly more advanced.

As you work through each chapter, you'll build your understanding in a coherent, logical way, adding new skills to your toolkit and working on increasingly complex and challenging problems.

Context is Key

All new concepts are introduced in the context of realistic use-cases, and then demonstrated practically with guided exercises. At the end of each chapter, you'll find an activity that challenges you to draw together what you've learned and apply your new skills to solve a problem or build something new.

We believe this is the most effective way of building your understanding and confidence. Experiencing real applications of the code will help you get used to the syntax and see how the tools and techniques are applied in real projects.

Build Real-World Understanding

Of course, you do need some theory. But unlike many tutorials, which force you to wade through pages and pages of dry technical explanations and assume too much prior knowledge, Workshops only tell you what you actually need to know to be able to get started making things. Explanations are clear, simple, and to-the-point. So you don't need to worry about how everything works under the hood; you can just get on and use it.

Written by industry professionals, you'll see how concepts are relevant to real-world work, helping to get you beyond "Hello, world!" and build relevant, productive skills. Whether you're studying web development, data science, or a core programming language, you'll start to think like a problem solver and build your understanding and confidence through contextual, targeted practice.

Enjoy the Journey

Learning something new is a journey from where you are now to where you want to be, and this Workshop is just a vehicle to get you there. We hope that you find it to be a productive and enjoyable learning experience.

Packt has a wide range of different Workshops available, covering the following topic areas:

- Programming languages
- Web development
- Data science, machine learning, and artificial intelligence
- Containers

Once you've worked your way through this Workshop, why not continue your journey with another? You can find the full range online at http://packt.live/2MNkuyl.

If you could leave us a review while you're there, that would be great. We value all feedback. It helps us to continually improve and make better books for our readers, and also helps prospective customers make an informed decision about their purchase.

Thank you,
The Packt Workshop Team

Table of Contents

Chapter 3: Functions in Depth — 81

Chapter 4: Mapping and Filtering   123

Chapter 6: Recursion and Looping   219

Chapter 9: Host Platform Interoperability with Java and JavaScript   343

Chapter 10: Testing   411

Preface

About

This section briefly introduces the coverage of this book, the technical skills you'll need to get started, and the software requirements required to complete all of the included activities and exercises.

About the Book

The Clojure Workshop is a step-by-step guide to Clojure and ClojureScript, designed to quickly get you up and running as a confident, knowledgeable developer.

Because of the functional nature of the language, Clojure programming is quite different to what many developers will have experienced. As hosted languages, Clojure and ClojureScript can also be daunting for newcomers because of complexities in the tooling and the challenge of interacting with the host platforms. To help you overcome these barriers, this book adopts a practical approach. Every chapter is centered around building something.

As you progress through the book, you will progressively develop the 'muscle memory' that will make you a productive Clojure programmer, and help you see the world through the concepts of functional programming. You will also gain familiarity with common idioms and patterns, as well as exposure to some of the most widely used libraries.

Unlike many Clojure books, this Workshop will include significant coverage of both Clojure and ClojureScript. This makes it useful no matter your goal or preferred platform, and provides a fresh perspective on the hosted nature of the language.

By the end of this book, you'll have the knowledge, skills and confidence to creatively tackle your own ambitious projects with Clojure and ClojureScript.

Audience

The Clojure Workshop is an ideal tutorial for the Clojure beginner who is just getting started. A basic understanding of JavaScript and Java would be ideal but not necessary. *The Clojure Workshop* will guide you well throughout the discussion on the interoperability of these technologies.

About the Chapters

Chapter 1, Hello REPL!, gets you typing code immediately. You'll learn the basics of the language, as well as how to get the most out of Clojure's interactive REPL.

Chapter 2, Data Types and Immutability, provides more building blocks, but these are Clojure building blocks that expose you to one of Clojure's key features: immutability.

Chapter 3, Functions in Depth, is a deeper dive into one of the areas that sets Clojure apart: the functional programming paradigm. These are the tools that will power you through the rest of the book.

Chapter 4, Mapping and Filtering, is the first stop on your exploration of Clojure collections. The patterns and techniques here are all about learning to solve problems. The map and filter functions are two of the foremost Clojure workhorses.

Chapter 5, Many to One: Reducing, will really start getting you thinking in new ways. The data-shaping techniques in this chapter complement those in the previous chapter.

Chapter 6, Recursion and Looping, takes your collection techniques to the next level. This chapter will make you think. By the end of the chapter, you'll be ready to handle tricky problems using advanced functional patterns.

Chapter 7, Recursion II: Lazy Sequences, completes the panorama of Clojure collections with a look at a distinctive Clojure feature. If you can write functions to process complex tree structures, you are ready to use Clojure to solve big problems.

Chapter 8, Namespaces, Libraries, and Leiningen, provides a close look at the tools you need for building real-world Clojure and ClojureScript applications. You have the skills to write good Clojure code; now you need to know how to put your application together.

Chapter 9, Host Platform Interoperability with Java and JavaScript, brings you up to speed on a topic that is one of Clojure's great strengths but can also be daunting. As a hosted language, Clojure gives you access to the underlying platform. Knowing how and when to use that power is a key Clojure skill.

Chapter 10, Testing, is another important step in serious, real-world programming. Understanding Clojure and ClojureScript testing stories is a skill every professional programmer needs.

Chapter 11, Macros, will help you understand a distinctive feature of the Lisp family of languages. Macros allow rich abstraction, but underneath the surface, there are a lot of important practical details.

Chapter 12, Concurrency, reveals another unique Clojure strength. This chapter will give you a taste for building multithreaded applications on the Java Virtual Machine or event-driven ClojureScript single-page applications.

Chapter 13, Database Interaction and the Application Layer, shows you how to leverage Clojure's database libraries. Many real applications require databases, so these skills are essential.

Chapter 14, HTTP with Ring, shows you how to set up and run a Clojure-driven web server. The Ring libraries are the most widely used HTTP technology in the Clojure world.

Chapter 15, The Frontend: A ClojureScript UI, helps put together many of the things you've already learned about ClojureScript, the last layer on a Clojure web stack.

Conventions

Code words in text, database table names, folder names, filenames, file extensions, pathnames, dummy URLs, user input, and Twitter handles are shown as follows: "Please note that this function is in the `clojure.string` namespace, which is not referred to by default."

Words that you see on the screen, for example, in menus or dialog boxes, also appear in the text like this: "When you click on the **Fetch Images** button, the images appear with authors' names."

A block of code is set as follows:

```
(defn remove-large-integers [ints]
  (remove #(and (integer? %) (> % 1000)) ints))
```

In cases where inputting and executing some code gives an immediate output, this is shown as follows:

```
user=> (sort [3 7 5 1 9])
(1 3 5 7 9)
```

In the example above, the code entered is **(sort [3 7 5 1 9])**, and the output is **(1 3 5 7 9)**.

New terms and important words are shown like this: "Welcome to the Clojure **Read Eval Print Loop (REPL)**, a command-line interface that we can use to interact with a running Clojure program."

Key parts of code snippets are highlighted as follows:

```
{:deps {compojure {:mvn/version "1.6.1"}
metosin/muuntaja {:mvn/version "0.6.4"}
        ring/ring-core {:mvn/version "1.7.1"}
        ring/ring-jetty-adapter {:mvn/version "1.7.1"}}}
user=> (require '[muuntaja.middleware :as middleware])
=>nil
```

Long code snippets are truncated and the corresponding names of the code files on GitHub are placed at the top of the truncated code. The permalinks to the entire code are placed below the code snippet. It should look as follows:

`kvitova_matches.clj`

```
 1  (def matches
 2    [{:winner-name "Kvitova P.",
 3      :loser-name "Ostapenko J.",
 4      :tournament "US Open",
 5      :location "New York",
 6      :date "2016-08-29"}
 7     {:winner-name "Kvitova P.",
 8      :loser-name "Buyukakcay C.",
 9      :tournament "US Open",
10      :location "New York",
11      :date "2016-08-31"}
```

The full code can be found at: https://packt.live/2GcudYj

Before You Begin

Each great journey begins with a humble step. Our upcoming adventure in the land of Clojure is no exception. Before we can do awesome things with data, we need to be prepared with a productive environment. In this section, we will see how to do that.

Installing Java

Before installing Clojure, you need to make sure that you have the **Java Developer's Kit (JDK)** installed on your computer. For Mac and Linux users, prebuilt binaries are a few keystrokes away. On Mac, for Homebrew users, you can just type:

```
$ brew install openjdk
```

On Debian-based Linux distributions, you can check which version is available by typing the following:

```
$ apt-get search openjdk
```

Depending on the output, you can then type something like:

```
$ sudo apt-get install openjdk-11-jdk
```

Clojure does not require a particularly recent version of the JDK.

For Windows, you can download the OpenJDK installer here: https://packt.live/3aBu1Qg. Once you have the installer, click on it to run, then follow the instructions.

Installing Clojure

Once you have a working JDK on your system, setting up Clojure is easy with the Leiningen tool.

1. Copy the appropriate version (Windows or Mac/Linux) from the Leiningen home page, here: https://leiningen.org/.

2. Place Leiningen in a directory that is part of your system's **$PATH** and make it executable.

3. On Mac or Linux, this means putting it in a directory such as **~/bin** and calling **chmod**:

```
$ chmod +x ~/bin/lein
```

4. On Windows, to change the **$PATH** variable, go to **Control Panel > User Accounts > User Accounts** and click on **Change My Environment Variables**. In the pane showing the user variables for your personal user account, click on **Path** and then choose **Edit**.

Figure 0.1: User accounts

5. Click on **New** to add a line, then type in the path to your new **bin** directory:

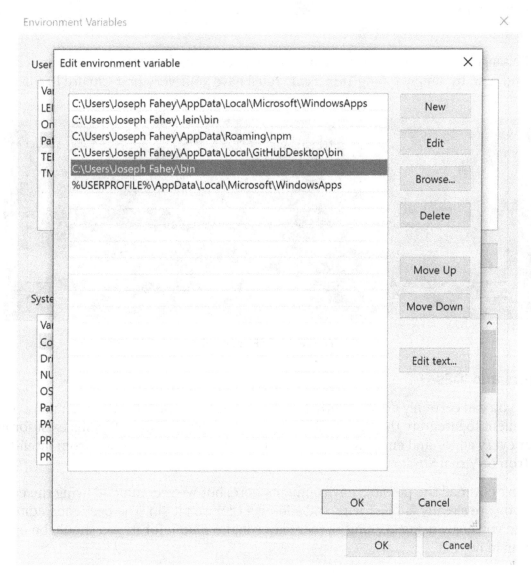

Figure 0.2: Adding the path in bin directory

6. Now that Leiningen is installed and executable, from the command line, simply type:

```
$ lein
```

Leiningen will fetch Clojure and all the libraries it needs to manage Clojure. And now, by simply typing **lein repl**, you'll have your very first Clojure REPL:

```
                                Clojure                                ⌥⌘3
→  ~ lein repl
nREPL server started on port 59082 on host 127.0.0.1 - nrepl://127.0.0.1:59082
REPL-y 0.4.3, nREPL 0.6.0
Clojure 1.10.0
Java HotSpot(TM) 64-Bit Server VM 9.0.1+11
    Docs: (doc function-name-here)
          (find-doc "part-of-name-here")
  Source: (source function-name-here)
 Javadoc: (javadoc java-object-or-class-here)
    Exit: Control+D or (exit) or (quit)
 Results: Stored in vars *1, *2, *3, an exception in *e

user=> █
```

Figure 0.3: REPL started

Editors and IDEs

While you can certainly do a lot with a REPL running in a console, it's much more convenient to integrate the Clojure REPL into your favorite editor. Plugins exist for just about every editor and environment out there, from Vim to Emacs and from IntelliJ to Electron or Visual Studio Code.

We can't cover all the possible environments here, but we recommend using the coding tools you are already familiar with and adding a Clojure plugin. The best code editor is the one you enjoy using. As long as there is a Clojure plugin for it, you should be up and running in no time.

Installing the Code Bundle

Download the code files from GitHub at https://packt.live/2vbksal. Refer to these code files for the complete code bundle.

If you have any issues or questions about installation, please email us at **workshops@packt.com**.

The high-quality color images used in book can be found at https://packt.live/2O5EzNX

1

Hello REPL!

Overview

In this chapter, we explain the basics of creating Clojure programs. We start by getting you familiar with the **Read Eval Print Loop** (**REPL**), where most of the experimentation happens when writing code. The REPL also allows you to explore code and documentation by yourself, so it is an excellent place to start. After the quick dive in the REPL, we describe in more detail how to read and understand simple Lisp and Clojure code, which syntax can sometimes appear unsettling. We then explore fundamental operators and functions in Clojure, which enable you to write and run simple Clojure programs or scripts.

By the end of this chapter, you will be able to use the REPL and work with functions in Clojure.

Introduction

Have you ever ended up entangled in the "spaghetti code" of an object-oriented application? Many experienced programmers would say yes, and at some point in their journey or career would reconsider the foundation of their programs. They might look for a simpler, better alternative to object-oriented programming, and Clojure is an appealing choice. It is a functional, concise, and elegant language of the Lisp family. Its core is small, and its syntax minimal. It shines because of its simplicity, which takes a trained eye to notice and ultimately understand. Employing Clojure's more sophisticated building blocks will allow you to design and build sturdier applications.

Whether you are a seasoned programmer or a novice, hobbyist or professional, C# wizard or Haskell ninja, learning a new programming language is challenging. It is, however, a highly rewarding experience that will make you an overall better programmer. In this book, you will learn by doing and will ramp up your skills quickly.

Clojure is an excellent choice of programming language to learn today. It will allow you to work efficiently using a technology built to last. Clojure can be used to program pretty much anything: from full-blown client-server applications to simple scripts or big data processing jobs. By the end of this book, you will have written a modern web application using Clojure and ClojureScript and will have all the cards in your hand to start writing your own!

REPL Basics

Welcome to the Clojure **Read Eval Print Loop** (**REPL**), a command-line interface that we can use to interact with a running Clojure program. REPL, in the sense that it **reads** the user's input (where the user is you, the programmer), **evaluates** the input by instantly compiling and executing the code, and **prints** (that is, displays) the result to the user. The read-eval-print three-step process repeats over and over again (**loop**) until you exit the program.

The dynamism provided by the REPL allows you to discover and experiment with a tight feedback loop: your code is evaluated instantly, and you can adjust it until you get it right. Many other programming languages provide interactive shells (notably, other dynamic languages such as Ruby or Python), but in Clojure, the REPL plays an exceptional and essential role in the life of the developer. It is often integrated with the code editor and the line between editing, browsing, and executing code blurs toward a malleable development environment similar to Smalltalk. But let's start with the basics.

Throughout these exercises, you may notice some mentions of Java (for example, in the stack trace in the second exercise). This is because Clojure is implemented in Java and runs in the **Java Virtual Machine** (**JVM**). Clojure can, therefore, benefit from a mature ecosystem (a battle-tested, widely deployed execution platform and a plethora of libraries) while still being a cutting-edge technology. Clojure is designed to be a hosted language, and another implementation, called ClojureScript, allows you to execute Clojure code on any JavaScript runtime (for example, a web browser or Node.js). This hosted-language implementation choice allows for a smaller community of functional programmers to strive in an industry dominated by Java, .NET Core, and JavaScript technologies. Welcome to the Clojure party, where we're all having our cake and eating it too.

Exercise 1.01: Your First Dance

In this exercise, we will perform some basic operations in the REPL. Let's get started:

1. Open Terminal and type `clj`. This will start a Clojure REPL:

    ```
    $ clj
    ```

    The output is as follows:

    ```
    Clojure 1.10.1
    user=>
    ```

    The first line is your version of Clojure, which in this example is `1.10.1`. Don't worry if your version is different—the exercises we will go through together should be compatible with any version of Clojure.

    The second line displays the namespace we are currently in (**user**) and prompts for your input. A namespace is a group of things (such as functions) that belong together. Everything you create here will be in the **user** namespace by default. The **user** namespace can be considered your playground.

    Your REPL is ready to **read**.

2. Let's try to evaluate an expression:

    ```
    user=> "Hello REPL!"
    ```

    The output is as follows:

    ```
    "Hello REPL!"
    ```

    In Clojure, *literal* strings are created with double quotes, `""`. A literal is a notation for representing a fixed value in source code.

3. Let's see what happens if we type in multiple strings:

```
user=> "Hello" "Again"
```

The output is as follows:

```
"Hello"
"Again"
```

We have just evaluated two expressions sequentially, and each result is printed onto separate lines.

4. Now, let's try a bit of arithmetic, for example, **1 + 2**:

```
user=> 1 + 2
```

The output is as follows:

```
1
#object[clojure.core$_PLUS_ 0xe8df99a "clojure.core$_PLUS_@e8df99a"]
2
```

The output is not exactly what we expected. Clojure evaluated the three components, that is, **1**, **+**, and **2**, *separately*. Evaluating **+** looks strange because the **+** symbol is bound to a function.

> **Note**
>
> A function is a unit of code that performs a specific task. We don't need to know more for now except that functions can be called (or invoked) and can take some parameters. A function's argument is a term that's used to design the value of a parameter, but those terms are often used interchangeably.

To add those numbers, we need to call the **+** function with the arguments **1** and **2**.

5. Call the **+** function with the arguments **1** and **2** as follows:

```
user=> (+ 1 2)
```

The output is as follows:

```
3
```

You will soon discover that many basic operations that are usually part of a programming language syntax, such as addition, multiplication, comparison, and so on, are just simple functions in Clojure.

6. Let's try a few more examples of basic arithmetic. You can even try to pass more than two arguments to the following functions, so adding 1 + 2 + 3 together would look like **(+ 1 2 3)**:

```
user=> (+ 1 2 3)
6
```

7. The other basic arithmetic operators are used in a similar way. Try and type the following expressions:

```
user=> (- 3 2)
1
user=> (* 3 4 1)
12
user=> (/ 9 3)
3
```

After typing in the preceding examples, you should try a few more by yourself – the REPL is here to be experimented with.

8. You should now be familiar enough with the REPL to ask the following question:

```
user=> (println "Would you like to dance?")
Would you like to dance?
nil
```

Don't take it personally – **nil** was the value that was returned by the **println** function. The text that was printed by the function was merely a *side effect* of this function.

nil is the Clojure equivalent of "null," or "nothing"; that is, the absence of meaningful value. **print** (without a new line) and **println** (with a new line) are used to print objects to the standard output, and they return **nil** once they are done.

9. Now, we can combine those operations and print the result of a simple addition:

```
user=> (println (+ 1 2))
3
nil
```

A value of **3** was printed and the value of **nil** was returned by this expression.

Notice how we have nested those *forms* (or *expressions*). This is how we chain functions in Clojure:

```
user=> (* 2 (+ 1 2))
6
```

10. Exit the REPL by pressing *Ctrl* + D. The function to exit is **System/exit**, which takes the exit code as a parameter. Therefore, you can also type the following:

```
user=> (System/exit 0)
```

In this exercise, we discovered the REPL and called Clojure functions to print and perform basic arithmetic operations.

Exercise 1.02: Getting around in the REPL

In this exercise, we will introduce a few navigational key bindings and commands to help you use and survive the REPL. Let's get started:

1. Start by opening the REPL again.

2. Notice how you can navigate the history of what was typed earlier and in previous sessions by pressing *Ctrl* + P (or the UP arrow) and *Ctrl* + N (or the DOWN arrow).

3. You can also search (case-sensitive) through the history of the commands you have entered: press *Ctrl* + R and then **Hello**, which should bring back the **Hello Again** expression we typed earlier. If you press *Ctrl* + R a second time, it will cycle through the matches of the search and bring back the very first command: **Hello REPL!**. If you press *Enter*, it will bring the expression back to the current prompt. Press *Enter* again and it will evaluate it.

4. Now, evaluate the following expression, which *increments* (adds 1 to) the number 10:

```
user=> (inc 10)
11
```

The returned value is 11, which is indeed 10 + 1.

5. ***1** is a special variable that is bound to the result of the last expression that was evaluated in the REPL. You can evaluate its value by simply typing it like this:

```
user=> *1
11
```

Similarly, ***2** and ***3** are variables bound to the second and third most recent values of that REPL session, respectively.

6. You can also reuse those special variable values within other expressions. See if you can follow and type this sequence of commands:

```
user=> (inc 10)
11
user=> *1
11
user=> (inc *1)
```

```
12
user=> (inc *1)
13
user=> (inc *2)
13
user=> (inc *1)
14
```

Notice how the values of *1 and *2 change as new expressions are evaluated. When the REPL is crowded with text, press *Ctrl + L* to clear the screen.

7. Another useful variable that's available in the REPL is ***e**, which contains the result of the last exception. At the moment, it should be **nil** unless you generated an error earlier. Let's trigger an exception voluntarily by dividing by zero:

```
user=> (/ 1 0)
Execution error (ArithmeticException) at user/eval71 (REPL:1).
Divide by zero
```

Evaluating ***e** should contain details about the exception, including the stack trace:

```
user=> *e
#error {
 :cause "Divide by zero"
 :via
 [{:type java.lang.ArithmeticException
   :message "Divide by zero"
   :at [clojure.lang.Numbers divide "Numbers.java" 188]}]
 :trace
 [[clojure.lang.Numbers divide "Numbers.java" 188]
  [clojure.lang.Numbers divide "Numbers.java" 3901]
  [user$eval1 invokeStatic "NO_SOURCE_FILE" 1]
  [user$eval1 invoke "NO_SOURCE_FILE" 1]
  [clojure.lang.Compiler eval "Compiler.java" 7177]
  [clojure.lang.Compiler eval "Compiler.java" 7132]
  [clojure.core$eval invokeStatic "core.clj" 3214]
  [clojure.core$eval invoke "core.clj" 3210]
  [clojure.main$repl$read_eval_print__9086$fn__9089 invoke "main.clj" 437]
  [clojure.main$repl$read_eval_print__9086 invoke "main.clj" 437]
  [clojure.main$repl$fn__9095 invoke "main.clj" 458]
  [clojure.main$repl invokeStatic "main.clj" 458]
  [clojure.main$repl_opt invokeStatic "main.clj" 522]
  [clojure.main$main invokeStatic "main.clj" 667]
  [clojure.main$main doInvoke "main.clj" 616]
```

```
[clojure.lang.RestFn invoke "RestFn.java" 397]
[clojure.lang.AFn applyToHelper "AFn.java" 152]
[clojure.lang.RestFn applyTo "RestFn.java" 132]
[clojure.lang.Var applyTo "Var.java" 705]
[clojure.main main "main.java" 40]]}
```

> **Note**
>
> Different Clojure implementations may have a slightly different behavior. For example, if you tried to divide by 0 in a ClojureScript REPL, it will not throw an exception and instead return the "infinity value":
>
> **cljs.user=> (/ 1 0)**
>
> **##Inf**
>
> This is to stay consistent with the host platform: the literal number 0 is implemented as an integer in Java (and Clojure) but as a floating-point number in JavaScript (and ClojureScript). The IEEE Standard for Floating-Point Arithmetic (IEEE 754) specifies that division by 0 should return +/- infinity.

8. The **doc**, **find-doc**, and **apropos** functions are essential REPL tools for browsing through documentation. Given that you know the name of the function you want to use, you can read its documentation with **doc**. Let's see how it works in practice. Start by typing **(doc str)** to read more about the **str** function:

```
user=> (doc str)
-------------------------
clojure.core/str
([] [x] [x & ys])
  With no args, returns the empty string. With one arg x, returns
  x.toString().  (str nil) returns the empty string. With more than
  one arg, returns the concatenation of the str values of the args.
nil
```

doc prints the fully qualified name of the function (including the namespace) on the first line, the possible sets of parameters (or "arities") on the next line, and finally the description.

This function's fully qualified name is **clojure.core/str**, which means that it is in the **clojure.core** namespace. Things defined in **clojure.core** are available to your current namespace by default, without you explicitly having to require them. This is because they are fundamental components for building your programs, and it would be tedious to have to use their full name every time.

9. Let's try to use the **str** function. As the documentation explains, we can pass it multiple arguments:

```
user=> (str "I" "will" "be" "concatenated") (clojure.core/str "This" " works "
"too")
"Iwillbeconcatenated"
"This works too"
```

10. Let's inspect the documentation of the **doc** function:

```
user=> (doc doc)
-------------------------
clojure.repl/doc
([name])
Macro
  Prints documentation for a var or special form given its name,
   or for a spec if given a keyword
nil
```

This function is in the **clojure.repl** namespace, which is also available by default in your REPL environment.

11. You can also look at the documentation of a namespace. As its documentation suggests, your final program would typically not use the helpers in the **clojure. repl** namespace (for instance, **doc**, **find-doc**, and **apropos**):

```
user=> (doc clojure.repl)
-------------------------
clojure.repl
  Utilities meant to be used interactively at the REPL
nil
```

12. When you don't know the name of the function, but you have an idea of what the description or name may contain, you can search for it with the **find-doc** helper. Let's try and search for the **modulus** operator:

```
user=> (find-doc "modulus")
nil
```

13. No luck, but there's a catch: **find-doc** is case-sensitive, but the good news is that we can use a regular expression with the **i** modifier to ignore the case:

```
user=> (find-doc #"(?i)modulus")
-------------------------
clojure.core/mod
([num div])
  Modulus of num and div. Truncates toward negative infinity.
nil
```

You don't need to know more about regular expressions for now – you don't even have to use them, but it can be useful to ignore the case when searching for a function. You can write them with the **#"(?i)text"** syntax, where **text** is anything you want to search for.

The function we were looking for was **clojure.core/mod**.

14. Let's make sure it works according to its documentation:

```
user=> (mod 7 3)
1
```

15. Use the **apropos** function to search for functions by name, thereby yielding a more succinct output. Say we were looking for a function that transforms the case of a given string of characters:

```
user=> (apropos "case")
(clojure.core/case clojure.string/lower-case clojure.string/upper-case)
user=> (clojure.string/upper-case "Shout, shout, let it all out")
"SHOUT, SHOUT, LET IT ALL OUT"
```

Please note that this function is in the **clojure.string** namespace, which is not referred to by default. You will need to use its full name until we learn how to import and refer symbols from other namespaces.

Activity 1.01: Performing Basic Operations

In this activity, we will print messages and perform some basic arithmetic operations in the Clojure REPL.

These steps will help you complete this activity:

1. Open the REPL.

2. Print the message "`I am not afraid of parentheses`" to motivate yourself.

3. Add 1, 2, and 3 and multiply the result by 10 minus 3, which corresponds to the following **infix** notation: (1 + 2 + 3) * (10 - 3). You should obtain the following result:

```
42
```

4. Print the message "`Well done!`" to congratulate yourself.

5. Exit the REPL.

> **Note**
>
> The solution to this activity can be found on page 678.

Evaluation of Clojure Code

Clojure is a dialect of Lisp, a high-level programming language that was designed by John McCarthy and first appeared in 1958. One of the most distinctive features of Lisp and its derivatives, or "dialects," is the use of data structures to write the source code of programs. The unusual number of parentheses in our Clojure programs is a manifestation of this as parentheses are used to create lists.

Here, we will focus on the building blocks of Clojure programs, that is, *forms and expressions*, and briefly look at how expressions are evaluated.

> **Note**
>
> The terms "expression" and "form" are often used interchangeably; however, according to the Clojure documentation, an expression is a form type: *"Every form not handled specially by a special form or macro is considered by the compiler to be an expression, which is evaluated to yield a value."*

We have seen how literals are valid syntax and evaluate to themselves, for example:

```
user=> "Hello"
"Hello"
user=> 1 2 3
1
2
3
```

We have also learned how to invoke functions by using parentheses:

```
user=> (+ 1 2 3)
6
```

It is worth noting at this point that comments can be written with ";" at the beginning of a line. Any line starting with ";" will not be evaluated:

```
user=> ; This is a comment
user=> ; This line is not evaluated
```

Functions are invoked according to the following structure:

```
; (operator operand-1 operand-2 operand-3 …)
; for example:
user=> (* 2 3 4)
24
```

Take note of the following from the preceding example:

- The list, denoted by opening and closing parenthesis, (), is evaluated to a function call (or invocation).

- When evaluated, the * symbol resolves to the function that implements the multiplication.

- 2, 3, and 4 are evaluated to themselves and passed as arguments to the function.

Consider the expression you wrote in *Activity 1.01, Performing Basic Operations*: (* (+ 1 2 3) (- 10 3)). It can also help to visualize the expression as a tree:

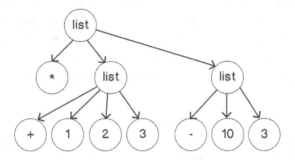

Figure 1.1: Tree representation of the expression, (* (+ 1 2 3) (- 10 3))

Evaluating this expression consists of reducing the tree, starting with the offshoots (the innermost lists): (* (+ 1 2 3) (- 10 3)) becomes (* 6 7), which becomes 42.

The term **s-expression** (or symbolic expression) is often used to designate those types of expressions. You may come across it again, so it is good to know that an s-expression is a data notation for writing data structures and code with lists, as we demonstrated previously.

So far, we have only used literal scalar types as operands to our operators, which hold one value, such as numbers, strings, Booleans, and so on. We've only used lists to invoke functions and not to represent data. Let's try to create a list that represents data but not "code":

```
user=> (1 2 3)
Execution error (ClassCastException) at user/eval255 (REPL:1).
java.lang.Long cannot be cast to clojure.lang.IFn
```

An exception was thrown because the first item of the list (the operator) was not a function.

There is a special syntax to prevent the list from being considered as the invocation of a function: the quote. Creating a literal list is done by adding a quotation ', in front of it, so let's try again:

```
user=> '(1 2 3)
(1 2 3)
user=> '("a" "b" "c" "d")
("a" "b" "c" "d")
```

Great! By preventing the evaluation of the form, we can now write a literal representation of lists.

This concept will help us get ready for what we are going to cover next. It is, however, fascinating to notice at this point that Clojure code is made up of data structures, and our programs can generate those same data structures. "Code is data" is a famous saying in the Lisp world, and a powerful concept that allows your program to generate code (known as **meta-programming**). If you are new to this concept, it is worth pausing for a minute to think and admire the sheer beauty of it. We will explain meta-programming techniques in detail later when explaining *macros* in *Chapter 11, Macros*.

Basic Special Forms

So far, we have been writing code that complies with the simplest rules of evaluating Clojure code, but there are some behaviors that cannot simply be encoded with normal functions. For example, arguments that have been passed to a function will always be resolved or evaluated, but what if we do not want to evaluate all the operands of an operator? That is when special forms come into play. They can have different evaluation rules for functions when the source code is read by Clojure. For example, the special form `if`, may not evaluate one of its arguments, depending on the result of the first argument.

There are a few other special forms that we will go through in this section:

- **when**, which can be used when we are only interested in the case of a condition being *truthy* (a value is *truthy* when considered true in the context of a Boolean expression).

- **do**, which can be used to execute a series of expressions and return the value of the last expression.

- **def** and **let**, which are special forms that are used to create global and local bindings.

- **fn** and **defn**, which are special forms that are used to create functions.

All these special forms have special evaluation rules, all of which we will discover by working through the following three exercises.

Exercise 1.03: Working with if, do, and when

In this exercise, we will evaluate expressions using the **if**, **do**, and **when** forms. Let's get started:

1. Start your REPL and type in the following expression:

    ```
    user=> (if true "Yes" "No")
    "Yes"
    ```

2. The special form **if**, evaluates its first argument. If its value is truthful, it will evaluate argument **2**, otherwise (**else**), it will evaluate argument 3. It will never evaluate both arguments 2 and 3.

3. We can nest expressions and start doing more interesting things:

    ```
    user=> (if false (+ 3 4) (rand))
    0.48331424431072903
    ```

    In this case, the computation of **(+ 3 4)** will not be executed, and only a random number (between 0 and 1) will be returned by the **rand** function.

4. But what if we wanted to do more than one thing in our branch of the condition? We could wrap our operation with **do**. Let's see how **do** works:

    ```
    user=> (doc do)
    --------------------------
    do
      (do exprs*)
    Special Form
      Evaluates the expressions in order and returns the value of
      the last. If no expressions are supplied, returns nil.
      Please see http://clojure.org/special_forms#do
      Evaluates the expressions in order and returns the value of
      the last. If no expressions are supplied, returns nil.
    nil
    ```

5. To use the special form, **do** type the following expression:

    ```
    user=> (do (* 3 4) (/ 8 4) (+ 1 1))
    2
    ```

    All the expressions before the final **(+ 1 1)** expression were evaluated, but only the value of the last one is returned. This does not look very useful with expressions that don't alter the state of the world, and so it would typically be used for side effects such as logging or any other kind of I/O (filesystem access, database query, network request, and so on).

You don't have to take my word for it, so let's experiment with the side effect of printing to the Terminal:

```
user=> (do (println "A proof that this is executed") (println "And this
  too"))
A proof that this is executed
And this too
nil
```

6. Finally, we can combine the use of **if** and **do** to execute multiple operations in a conditional branching:

```
user=> (if true (do (println "Calculating a random number...") (rand)) (+ 1
  2))
Calculating a random number...
0.8340057877906916
```

7. Technically, you could also omit the third argument. Bring back the previous expression in the REPL and remove the last expression, that is, **(+ 1 2)**:

```
user=> (if true (do (println "Calculating a random number...") (rand)))
Calculating a random number...
0.5451384920081613
user=> (if false (println "Not going to happen"))
nil
```

We have a better construct available for this case: the **when** operator. Instead of combining **if** and **do**, when you are only interested in doing work in one branch of the conditional execution, use **when**.

8. Type the following expression to use **when** instead of a combination of **if** and **do**:

```
user=> (when true (println "First argument") (println "Second argument")
  "And the last is returned")
First argument
Second argument
"And the last is returned"
```

By completing this exercise, we have demonstrated the usage of the special forms known as **if**, **do**, and **when**. We can now write expressions that contain multiple statements, as well as conditional expressions.

Bindings

In Clojure, we use the term *bindings* rather than *variables* and *assignments* because we tend to bind a value to a symbol only once. Under the hood, Clojure creates *variables* and so you may encounter this term, but it would be preferable if you don't think of them as classic *variables* or values that can change. We won't use the term variable anymore in this chapter as it can be confusing. You can use **def** to define global bindings and **let** for local bindings.

Exercise 1.04: Using def and let

In this exercise, we will demonstrate the usage of the **def** and **let** keywords, which are used to create bindings. Let's get started:

1. The special form **def** allows you to bind a value to a symbol. In the REPL, type the following expression to bind the value **10** to the **x** symbol:

```
user=> (def x 10)
#'user/x
```

> **Note**
>
> When the REPL returns **#'user/x**, it is returning a reference to the var you have just created. The user part indicates the namespace where the var is defined. The **#'** prefix is a way of quoting the var so that we see the symbol and not the value of the symbol.

2. Evaluate the expression, **x**, which will resolve the **x** symbol to its value:

```
user=> x
10
```

3. Technically, you can change the binding, which is fine when experimenting in the REPL:

```
user=> (def x 20)
#'user/x
user=> x
20
```

It is, however, not recommended in your programs because it can make it hard to read and complicate its maintenance. For now, it would be better if you just consider such a binding as a *constant*.

4. You can use the **x** symbol within another expression:

```
user=> (inc x)
21
user=> x
20
```

5. Wherever **def** is invoked, it will bind the value to the symbol in the current namespace. We could try to define a local binding in a **do** block and see what happens:

```
user=> x
20
user=> (do (def x 42))
#'user/x
user=> x
42
```

The bindings that are created by **def** have an indefinite scope (or dynamic scope) and can be considered as "global." They are automatically namespaced, which is a useful trait to avoid clashing with existing names.

6. If we want to have a binding available only to a local scope or lexical scope, we can use the special form **let**. Type the following expression to create a lexical binding of the **y** symbol:

```
user=> (let [y 3] (println y) (* 10 y))
3
30
```

let takes a "vector" as a parameter to create the local bindings, and then a series of expressions that will be evaluated like they are in a **do** block.

> **Note**
>
> A vector is similar to a list, in the sense that they both are a sequential collection of values. Their underlying data structure is different, and we will shed light on this in *Chapter 2, Data Types and Immutability*. For now, you just need to know that vectors can be created with square brackets, for example, [1 2 3 4].

7. Evaluate the **y** symbol:

```
user=> y
Syntax error compiling at (REPL:0:0).
Unable to resolve symbol: y in this context
```

An error is thrown, that is, **Unable to resolve symbol: y in this context**, because we are now outside of the **let** block.

8. Type the following expression to create a lexical binding of **x** to the value **3**, and see how it affects the indefinite (global) binding of **x** that we created in *step 4*:

```
user=> (let [x 3] (println x))
3
nil
user=> x
42
```

Printing **x** yields the value **3**, which means that the "global" **x** symbol was temporarily overridden or "shadowed" by the lexical context in which **println** was invoked.

9. You can create multiple local bindings at once with **let** by passing an even number of items in the vector. Type the following expression to bind **x** to **10** and **y** to **20**:

```
user=> (let [x 10 y 20]  (str "x is " x " and y is " y))
"x is 10 and y is 20"
```

10. Combine the concepts of this section and write the following expressions:

```
user=> (def message "Let's add them all!")
#'user/message
user=> (let [x (* 10 3)
             y 20
             z 100]
          (println message)
          (+ x y z))
Let's add them all!
150
```

The expression spans over multiple lines to improve readability.

Exercise 1.05: Creating Simple Functions with fn and defn

The special form that's used to define functions is **fn**. Let's jump right into it by creating our first function:

1. Type the following expression in your REPL:

```
user=> (fn [])
#object[user$eval196$fn__197 0x3f0846c6 "user$eval196$fn__197@3f0846c6"]
```

We have just created the simplest anonymous function, which takes no parameters and does nothing, and we returned an object, which is our function with no name.

2. Create a function that takes a parameter named **x** and return its square value (multiply it by itself):

```
user=> (fn [x] (* x x))
#object[user$eval227$fn__228 0x68b6f0d6 "user$eval227$fn__228@68b6f0d6"]
```

3. Remember that, in Clojure, the first item of an expression will be invoked, so we can call our anonymous function by wrapping it with parentheses and providing an argument as the second item of the expression:

```
user=> ((fn [x] (* x x)) 2)
4
```

Now this is great, but not very convenient. If we wanted our function to be reusable or testable, it would be better for it to have a name. We can create a symbol in the namespace and bind it to the function.

4. Use **def** to bind the function returned by the special form, **fn**, to the **square** symbol:

```
user=> (def square (fn [x] (* x x)))
#'user/square
```

5. Invoke your newly created function to make sure that it works:

```
user=> (square 2)
4
user=> (square *1)
16
user=> (square *1)
256
```

6. This pattern of combining **def** and **fn** is so common that a built-in *macro* was born out of necessity: **defn**. Recreate the square function with **defn** instead of **def** and **fn**:

```
user=> (defn square [x] (* x x))
#'user/square
user=> (square 10)
100
```

Did you notice that the **x** argument was passed in a vector? We have already learned that vectors are collections, and so we can add more than one symbol to the argument's vector. The values that are passed when calling the function will be bound to the symbols provided in the vector during the function's definition.

7. Functions can take multiple arguments, and their bodies can be composed of multiple expressions (such as an implicit **do** block). Create a function with the name **meditate** that takes two arguments: a string, **s**, and a Boolean, **calm**. The function will print an introductory message and return a transformation of **s** based on **calm**:

```
user=>
(defn meditate [s calm]
  (println "Clojure Meditate v1.0")
  (if calm
    (clojure.string/capitalize s)
    (str (clojure.string/upper-case s) "!")))
```

> **Note**
>
> Editing multiline expressions in the REPL can be cumbersome. As we start creating lengthier functions and expressions that span multiple lines, it would be preferable to have a window of your favorite editor open next to your REPL window. Keep those windows side by side, edit the code in your editor, copy it to your clipboard, and paste it into your REPL.

The function body contains two main expressions, the first of which is a side effect with **println** and the second of which is the **if** block, which will determine the return value. If **calm** is **true**, it will politely return the string capitalized (with the first character converted into uppercase), otherwise it will shout and return the string with all its characters to uppercase, ending with an exclamation mark.

8. Let's try and make sure that our function works as intended:

```
user=> (meditate "in calmness lies true pleasure" true)
Clojure Meditate v1.0
"In calmness lies true pleasure"
user=> (meditate "in calmness lies true pleasure" false)
Clojure Meditate v1.0
"IN CALMNESS LIES TRUE PLEASURE!"
```

9. If we call the function with only the first parameter, it will throw an exception. This is because the parameters that we have defined are required:

```
user=> (meditate "in calmness lies true pleasure")
Execution error (ArityException) at user/eval365 (REPL:1).
Wrong number of args (1) passed to: user/meditate
```

One last thing to end our initial tour of these functions is the **doc-string** parameter. When provided to **defn**, it will allow you to add a description of your function.

10. Add documentation to your **square** function by adding a doc-string just before the function arguments:

```
user=>
(defn square
  "Returns the product of the number `x` with itself"
  [x]
  (* x x))
#'user/square
```

The doc-string is not only useful when browsing a project's source code – it also makes it available to the **doc** function.

11. Look up the documentation of your **square** function with **doc**:

```
user=> (doc square)
-------------------------
user/square
([x])
  Returns the product of the number `x` with itself
nil
```

It is important to remember that the doc-string needs to come before the function arguments. If it comes after, the string will be evaluated sequentially as part of the function body and won't throw an error. It is valid syntax, but it will not be available in the **doc** helper and other development tools.

It is good practice to document the arguments with backticks, `, like we did with `x`, so that development tools (such as the IDE) can recognize them.

We will take a deeper dive into functions in *Chapter 3, Functions in Depth*, but these few basic principles will get you a long way in terms of writing functions.

Activity 1.02: Predicting the Atmospheric Carbon Dioxide Level

Carbon dioxide (CO_2) is an important heat-trapping (greenhouse) gas, currently rising and threatening life as we know it on our planet. We would like to predict future levels of CO_2 in the atmosphere based on historical data provided by **National Oceanic and Atmospheric Administration (NOAA)**:

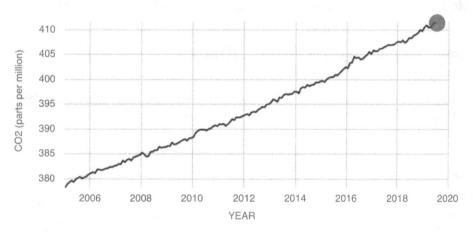

Figure 1.2: CO_2 parts per million (ppm) over the years

> **Note**
>
> The preceding chart was taken from https://packt.live/35kUI7L and the data was taken from NOAA.

We will use the year 2006 as a starting point with a CO_2 level of 382 ppm and calculate the estimate using a simplified (and optimistic) linear function, as follows: *Estimate = 382 + ((Year - 2006) * 2)*.

Create a function called **co2-estimate** that takes one integer parameter called **year** and returns the estimated level of CO_2 ppm for that year.

These steps will help you complete this activity:

1. Open your favorite editor and a REPL window next to it.

2. In your editor, define two constants, **base-co2** and **base-year**, with the values 382 and 2006, respectively.

3. In your editor, write the code to define the **co2-estimate** function without forgetting to document it with the doc-string parameter.

4. You may be tempted to write the function body in a single line but nesting a lot of function calls decreases the readability of the code. It is also easier to reason about each step of the process by decomposing them in a **let** block. Write the body of the function using **let** to define the local binding **year-diff**, which is the subtraction of 2006 from the **year** parameter.

5. Test your function by evaluating **(co2-estimate 2050)**. You should get **470** as the result.

6. Look up the documentation of your function with **doc** and make sure that it has been defined correctly.

The following is the expected output:

```
user=> (doc co2-estimate)
user/co2-estimate
([year])
  Returns a (conservative) year's estimate of carbon dioxide parts per million in
    the atmosphere
nil
user=> (co2-estimate 2006)
382
user=> (co2-estimate 2020)
410
user=> (co2-estimate 2050)
470
```

> **Note**
>
> The solution to this activity can be found on page 679.

Truthiness, nil, and equality

Up until now, we have been using conditional expressions intuitively, possibly on the basis of how they usually work with other programming languages. In this final section, we will review and explain Boolean expressions and the related comparison functions in detail, starting with **nil** and truthiness in Clojure.

nil is a value that represents the absence of value. It is also often called **NULL** in other programming languages. Representing the absence of value is useful because it means that something is missing.

In Clojure, **nil** is "falsey," which means that **nil** behaves like **false** when evaluated in a Boolean expression.

false and **nil** are the only values that are treated as *falsey* in Clojure; everything else is truthy. This simple rule is a blessing (especially if you are coming from a language such as JavaScript) and makes our code more readable and less error-prone. Perhaps it's just that Clojure was not out yet when Oscar Wilde wrote, "The truth is rarely pure and never simple."

Exercise 1.06: The Truth Is Simple

In this exercise, we will demonstrate how to work with Boolean values in conditional expressions. We will also see how to play around with the logical operators in conditional expressions. Let's get started:

1. Let's start by verifying that **nil** and **false** are indeed **falsey**:

```
user=> (if nil "Truthy" "Falsey")
"Falsey"
user=> (if false "Truthy" "Falsey")
"Falsey"
```

2. In other programming languages, it is common for more values to resolve to **false** in Boolean expressions. But in Clojure, remember that only **nil** and **false** are *falsey*. Let's try a few examples:

```
user=> (if 0 "Truthy" "Falsey")
"Truthy"
user=> (if -1 "Truthy" "Falsey")
"Truthy"
user=> (if '() "Truthy" "Falsey")
"Truthy"
user=> (if [] "Truthy" "Falsey")
"Truthy"
user=> (if "false" "Truthy" "Falsey")
```

```
"Truthy"
user=> (if "" "Truthy" "Falsey")
"Truthy"
user=> (if "The truth might not be pure but is simple" "Truthy" "Falsey")
"Truthy"
```

3. If we want to know whether something is exactly **true** or **false**, and not just **truthy** or **falsey**, we can use the **true?** and **false?** functions:

```
user=> (true? 1)
false
user=> (if (true? 1) "Yes" "No")
"No"
user=> (true? "true")
false
user=> (true? true)
true
user=> (false? nil)
false
user=> (false? false)
true
```

The **?** character has no special behavior – it is just a naming convention for functions that return a Boolean value.

4. Similarly, if we want to know that something is **nil** and not just **falsey**, we can use the **nil?** function:

```
user=> (nil? false)
false
user=> (nil? nil)
true
user=> (nil? (println "Hello"))
Hello
true
```

Remember that **println** returns **nil**, and so the last piece of output in the preceding code is **true**.

Boolean expressions become interesting when they are composed together. Clojure provides the usual suspects, that is, **and** and **or**. At this point, we are only interested in *logical* **and** and *logical* **or**. If you are looking to play around with `bitwise` operators, you can easily find them with the `(find-doc "bit-")` command.

and returns the first *falsey* value that it encounters (from left to right) and will not evaluate the rest of the expression when that is the case. When all the values passed to **and** are *truthy*, **and** will return the last value.

5. Experiment with the **and** function by passing a mix of *truthy* and *falsey* values to observe the return value that's been generated:

```
user=> (and "Hello")
"Hello"
user=> (and "Hello" "Then" "Goodbye")
"Goodbye"
user=> (and false "Hello" "Goodbye")
false
```

6. Let's use `println` and make sure that not all the expressions are evaluated:

```
user=> (and (println "Hello") (println "Goodbye"))
Hello
nil
```

and evaluated the first expression, which printed **Hello** and returned **nil**, which is *falsey*. Therefore, the second expression was not evaluated, and **Goodbye** was not printed.

or works in a similar fashion: it will return the first *truthy* value that it comes across and it will not evaluate the rest of the expression when that is the case. When all the values that are passed to **or** are *falsey*, **or** will return the last value.

7. Experiment with the **or** function by passing a mix of *truthy* and *falsey* values to observe the return value that's generated:

```
user=> (or "Hello")
"Hello"
user=> (or "Hello" "Then" "Goodbye")
"Hello"
user=> (or false "Then" "Goodbye")
"Then"
```

8. Once again, we can use **println** to make sure that the expressions are not all evaluated:

```
user=> (or true (println "Hello"))
true
```

or evaluated the first expression **true** and returned it. Therefore, the second expression was not evaluated, and **Hello** was not printed.

Equality and Comparisons

In most imperative programming languages, the = symbol is used for variable assignments. As we've seen already, in Clojure, we have **def** and **let** to bind names with values. The = symbol is a function for equality and will return **true** if all its arguments are equal. As you may have guessed by now, the other common comparison functions are implemented as functions. >, >=, <, <=, and = are not special syntax and you may have developed the intuition for using them already.

Exercise 1.07: Comparing Values

In this final exercise, we will go through the different ways of comparing values in Clojure. Let's get started:

1. First, start your REPL if it is not running yet.

2. Type the following expressions to compare two numbers:

```
user=> (= 1 1)
true
user=> (= 1 2)
false
```

3. You can pass multiple arguments to the = operator:

```
user=> (= 1 1 1)
true
user=> (= 1 1 1 -1)
false
```

In that case, even though the first three arguments are equal, the last one isn't, so the = function returns **false**.

4. The = operator is not only used to compare numbers, but other types as well. Evaluate some of the following expressions:

```
user=> (= nil nil)
true
user=> (= false nil)
false
user=> (= "hello" "hello" (clojure.string/reverse "olleh"))
true
user=> (= [1 2 3] [1 2 3])
true
```

> **Note**
>
> In Java or other object-oriented programming languages, comparing things usually checks whether they are the exact same instance of an object stored in memory, that is, their identity. However, comparisons in Clojure are made by equality rather than identity. Comparing values is generally more useful, and Clojure makes it convenient, but if you ever wanted to compare identities, you could do so by using the **identical?** function.

5. Maybe more surprisingly, but sequences of different types can be considered equal as well:

```
user=> (= '(1 2 3) [1 2 3])
true
```

The list **1 2 3** is equivalent to the vector **1 2 3**. Collections and sequences are powerful Clojure abstractions that will be presented in *Chapter 2, Data Types and Immutability*.

6. It is worth mentioning that the = function can also take one argument, in which case it will always return **true**:

```
user=> (= 1)
true
user=> (= "I will not reason and compare: my business is to create.")
true
```

The other comparison operators, that is, >, >=, <, and <=, can only be used with numbers. Let's start with < and >.

7. `<` returns **true** if all its arguments are in a strictly increasing order. Try to evaluate the following expressions:

```
user=> (< 1 2)
true
user=> (< 1 10 100 1000)
true
user=> (< 1 10 10 100)
false
user=> (< 3 2 3)
false
user=> (< -1 0 1)
true
```

Notice that **10** followed by **10** is not strictly increasing.

8. `<=` is similar, but adjacent arguments can be equal:

```
user=> (<= 1 10 10 100)
true
user=> (<= 1 1 1)
true
user=> (<= 1 2 3)
true
```

9. `>` and `>=` have a similar behavior and return **true** when their arguments are in a decreasing order. `>=` allows adjacent arguments to be equal:

```
user=> (> 3 2 1)
true
user=> (> 3 2 2)
false
user=> (>= 3 2 2)
true
```

10. Finally, the **not** operator is a useful function that returns **true** when its argument is *falsey* (**nil** or **false**), and **false** otherwise. Let's try an example:

```
user=> (not true)
false
user=> (not nil)
true
user=> (not (< 1 2))
false
user=> (not (= 1 1))
false
```

To put things together, let's consider the following JavaScript code:

```javascript
let x = 50;
if (x >= 1 && x <= 100 || x % 100 == 0) {
  console.log("Valid");
} else {
  console.log("Invalid");
}
```

This code snippet prints **Valid** when a number, **x**, is included between 1 and 100 or if **x** is a multiple of 100. Otherwise, it prints **Invalid**.

If we wanted to translate this to Clojure code, we would write the following:

```clojure
(let [x 50]
  (if (or (<= 1 x 100) (= 0 (mod x 100)))
    (println "Valid")
    (println "Invalid")))
```

We may have a few more parentheses in the Clojure code, but you could argue that Clojure is more readable than the imperative JavaScript code. It contains less specific syntax, and we don't need to think about operator precedence.

If we wanted to transform the JavaScript code using an "inline if," we would introduce new syntax with **?** and **:**, as follows:

```javascript
let x = 50;
console.log(x >= 0 && x <= 100 || x % 100 == 0 ? "Valid" : "Invalid");
```

The Clojure code would become the following:

```clojure
(let [x 50]
  (println (if (or (<= 1 x 100) (= 0 (mod x 100))) "Valid" "Invalid")))
```

Notice that there is no new syntax, and nothing new to learn. You already know how to read lists, and that is all you will (almost) ever need.

This simple example demonstrates the great flexibility of **lists**: the building blocks of Clojure and other Lisp languages.

Activity 1.03: The meditate Function v2.0

In this activity, we will improve the **meditate** function we wrote in *Exercise 1.05, Creating Simple Functions with fn and defn*, by replacing the **calm** Boolean argument with **calmness-level**. The function will print a transformation of the string passed as a second argument based on the calmness level. The specifications of the function are as follows:

- **calmness-level** is a number between **1** and **10**, but we will not check the input for errors.

- If the calmness level is strictly inferior to **5**, we consider the user to be angry. The function should return the **s** string transformed to uppercase concatenated with the string **", I TELL YA!"**.

- If the calmness level is between **5** and **9**, we consider the user to be calm and relaxed. The function should return the **s** string with only its first letter capitalized.

- If the calmness level is **10**, the user has reached nirvana, and is being possessed by the Clojure gods. In its trance, the user channels the incomprehensible language of those divine entities. The function should return the **s** string in reverse.

> **Hint**
>
> Use the **str** function to concatenate a string and **clojure.string/reverse** to reverse a string. If you are not sure how to use them, you can look up their documentation with **doc** (for example, **(doc clojure.string/reverse)**).

These steps will help you complete this activity:

1. Open your favorite editor and a REPL window next to it.

2. In your editor, define a function with the name **meditate**, taking two arguments, **calmness-level** and **s**, without forgetting to write its documentation.

3. In the function body, start by writing an expression that prints the string, **Clojure Meditate v2.0**.

4. Following the specification, write the first condition to test whether the calmness level is strictly inferior to **5**. Write the first branch of the conditional expression (the **then**).

5. Write the second condition, which should be nested in the second branch of the first condition (the **else**).

6. Write the third condition, which should be nested in the second branch of the second condition. It will check that **calmness-level** is exactly **10** and return the reverse of the **s** string when that is the case.

7. Test your function by passing a string with different levels of calmness. The output should be similar to the following:

```
user=> (meditate "what we do now echoes in eternity" 1)
Clojure Meditate v2.0
"WHAT WE DO NOW ECHOES IN ETERNITY, I TELL YA!"

user=> (meditate "what we do now echoes in eternity" 6)
Clojure Meditate v2.0
"What we do now echoes in eternity"

user=> (meditate "what we do now echoes in eternity" 10)
Clojure Meditate v2.0
"ytinrete ni seohce won od ew tahw"

user=> (meditate "what we do now echoes in eternity" 50)
Clojure Meditate v2.0
nil
```

8. If you have been using the **and** operator to find whether a number was between two other numbers, rewrite your function to remove it and only use the **<=** operator. Remember that **<=** can take more than two arguments.

9. Look up the **cond** operator in the documentation and rewrite your function to replace the nested conditions with **cond**.

> **Note**
>
> The solution to this activity can be found on page 680.

Summary

In this chapter, we discovered how to use the REPL and its helpers. You are now able to search and discover new functions and look up their documentation interactively in the REPL. We learned how Clojure code is evaluated, as well as how to use and create functions, bindings, conditionals, and comparisons. These allow you to create simple programs and scripts.

In the next chapter, we will look at data types, including collections, and the concept of immutability.

2

Data Types and Immutability

Overview

In this chapter, we start by discovering the concept of immutability and its relevance in modern programs. We then examine simple data types such as strings, numbers and booleans, highlighting subtle differences in different environments like Clojure and ClojureScript. After a first exercise, we move on to more elaborated data types with collections such as lists, vectors, maps and sets, learning along the way which to use in different situations. After touching on the collection and sequence abstractions, we learn new techniques for working with nested data structures, before finally moving on to the final activity: implementing our very own in-memory database.

By the end of this chapter, you will be able to work with the commonly used data types in Clojure.

Introduction

Computer hardware has evolved dramatically in the last few decades. On a typical computer, storage and memory capacity have both increased a millionfold compared to the early 1980s. Nonetheless, standard industry practices in software development and mainstream ways of programming are not that different. Programming languages such as C++, Java, Python, and Ruby still typically encourage you to change things in place, and to use variables and mutate the state of a program, that is, to do things as if we were programming on a computer with a minimal amount of memory. However, in our quest for efficiency, better languages, and better tools, we reach for higher-level languages. We want to get further away from machine code. We want to write less code and let the computers do the tedious work.

We don't want to think about the computer's memory anymore, such as where a piece of information is stored and whether it's safe and shareable, as much as we don't want to know about the order of the instructions in the CPU. It is a distraction to the problems we are trying to solve, which are already complicated enough. If you have ever tried to do some multithreading in the languages cited previously, you will know the pain of sharing data between threads. Although, leveraging multicore CPUs with multithreaded applications is an essential part of optimizing a modern program's performance.

In Clojure, we work almost exclusively with immutable data types. They are safe to share, easy to fabricate, and improve the readability of our source code. Clojure provides the necessary tools to write programs with the functional programming paradigm: first-class citizen functions, which we will discover in the next chapter, and avoiding mutating and sharing the state of an application with immutable data types.

Let's dust off the dictionary and look up the definition of immutable, "*Immutable: that cannot be changed; that will never change.*" It doesn't mean that a piece of information cannot change over time, but we record those modifications as a series of new values. "Updating" an immutable data structure provides a new value derived from the original value. However, the original value remains unchanged – those data structures that preserve previous versions of themselves are called persistent data structures.

Intuitively, we may think that such a persistent data structure would negatively impact performance, but it's not as bad as it seems. They are optimized for performance, and techniques such as structural sharing bring the time complexity of all operations close to classic, mutable implementations.

In other terms, unless you are programming an application that requires extraordinarily high performance, such as a video game, the benefits of using immutable data structures far outweigh the small loss in performance.

Simple Data Types

A data type designates what kind of value a piece of data holds; it is a fundamental way of classifying data. Different types allow different kinds of operations: we can concatenate strings, multiply numbers, and perform logic algebra operations with Booleans. Because Clojure has a strong emphasis on practicality, we don't explicitly assign types to values in Clojure, but those values still have a type.

Clojure is a hosted language and has three notable, major implementations in Java, JavaScript, and .NET. Being a hosted language is a useful trait that allows Clojure programs to run in different environments and take advantage of the ecosystem of its host. Regarding data types, it means that each implementation has different underlying data types, but don't worry as those are just implementation details. As a Clojure programmer, it does not make much difference, and if you know how to do something in Clojure, you likely know how to do it in, say, ClojureScript.

In this topic, we will go through Clojure's simple data types. Here is the list of the data types looked at in this section. Please note that the following types are all immutable:

- Strings
- Numbers
- Booleans
- Keywords
- Nil

Strings

Strings are sequences of characters representing text. We have been using and manipulating strings since the first exercise of *Chapter 1, Hello REPL*.

You can create a string by simply wrapping characters with double quotes ("):

```
user=> "I am a String"
"I am a String"
user=> "I am immutable"
"I am immutable"
```

String literals are only created with double quotes, and if you need to use double quotes in a string, you can escape them with the backslash character (\):

```
user=> (println "\"The measure of intelligence is the ability to change\" - Albert
Einstein")
"The measure of intelligence is the ability to change" - Albert Einstein
nil
```

Strings are not able to be changed; they are immutable. Any function that claims to transform a string yields a new value:

```
user=> (def silly-string "I am Immutable. I am a silly String")
#'user/silly-string
user=> (clojure.string/replace silly-string "silly" "clever")
"I am Immutable. I am a clever String"
user=> silly-string
"I am Immutable. I am a silly String"
```

In the preceding example, calling **clojure.string/replace** on **silly-string** returned a new string with the word "silly" replaced with "clever." However, when evaluating **silly-string** again, we can see that the value has not changed. The function returned a different value and did not change the original string.

Although a string is usually a single unit of data representing text, Strings are also collections of characters. In the JVM implementation of Clojure, strings are of the **java.lang.String** Java type and they are implemented as collections of the **java.lang. Character** Java type, such as the following command, which returns a character:

```
user=> (first "a collection of characters")
\a
user=> (type *1)
java.lang.Character
```

first returns the first element of a collection. Here, the literal notation of a character is \a. The **type** function returns a string representation of the data type for a given value. Remember that we can use *1 to retrieve the last returned value in the REPL, so *1 evaluates to \a.

It is interesting to note that, in ClojureScript, strings are collections of one-character strings, because there is no character type in JavaScript. Here is a similar example in a ClojureScript REPL:

```
cljs.user=> (last "a collection of 1 character strings")
"s"
cljs.user=> (type *1)
#object[String]
```

As with the Clojure REPL, **type** returns a string representation of the data type. This time, in ClojureScript, the value returned by the **last** function (which returns the last character of a string) is of the **#object[String]** type, which means a JavaScript string.

You can find a few common functions for manipulating strings in the core namespace, such as **str**, which we used in *Chapter 1, Hello REPL!*, to concatenate (combine multiple strings together into one string):

```
user=> (str "That's the way you " "con" "ca" "te" "nate")
"That's the way you concatenate"
user=> (str *1 " - " silly-string)
"That's the way you concatenate - I am Immutable. I am a silly String"
```

Most functions for manipulating strings can be found in the **clojure.string** namespace. Here is a list of them using the REPL **dir** function:

```
user=> (dir clojure.string)
blank?
capitalize
ends-with?
escape
includes?
index-of
join
last-index-of
lower-case
re-quote-replacement
replace
replace-first
reverse
split
split-lines
starts-with?
trim
trim-newline
triml
trimr
upper-case
```

As a reminder, this is how you can use a function from a specific namespace:

```
user=> (clojure.string/includes? "potatoes" "toes")
true
```

We will not cover all the string functions, but feel free to try them out now. You can always look up the documentation of a string function from the preceding list with the **doc** function.

Numbers

Clojure has good support for numbers and you will most likely not have to worry about the underlying types, as Clojure will handle pretty much anything. However, it is important to note that there are a few differences between Clojure and ClojureScript in that regard.

In Clojure, by default, natural numbers are implemented as the **java.lang.Long** Java type unless the number is too big for **Long**. In that case, it is typed **clojure.lang.BigInt**:

```
user=> (type 1)
java.lang.Long
user=> (type 1000000000000000000000)
java.lang.Long
user=> (type 10000000000000000000000)
clojure.lang.BigInt
```

Notice, in the preceding example, that the number was too big to fit in the **java.lang.Long** Java type and, therefore, was implicitly typed **clojure.lang.BigInt**.

Exact ratios are represented by Clojure as "Ratio" types, which have a literal representation. 5/4 is not an exact ratio, so the output is the ratio itself:

```
user=> 5/4
5/4
```

The result of dividing **3** by **4** can be represented by the ratio 3/4:

```
user=> (/ 3 4)
3/4
user=> (type 3/4)
clojure.lang.Ratio
```

4/4 is equivalent to **1** and is evaluated as follows:

```
user=> 4/4
1
```

Decimal numbers are "double" precision floating-point numbers:

```
user=> 1.2
1.2
```

If we take our division of 3 by 4 again, but this time mix in a "Double" type, we will not get a ratio as a result:

```
user=> (/ 3 4.0)
0.75
```

This is because floating-point numbers are "contagious" in Clojure. Any operation involving floating-point numbers will result in a float or a double:

```
user=> (* 1.0 2)
2.0
user=> (type (* 1.0 2))
java.lang.Double
```

In ClojureScript, however, numbers are just "JavaScript numbers," which are all double-precision floating-point numbers. JavaScript does not define different types of numbers like Java and some other programming languages do (for example, **long**, **integer**, and **short**):

```
cljs.user=> 1
1
cljs.user=> 1.2
1.2
cljs.user=> (/ 3 4)
0.75
cljs.user=> 3/4
0.75
cljs.user=> (* 1.0 2)
2
```

Notice that, this time, any operation returns a floating-point number. The fact that there is no decimal separation for **1** or **2** is just a formatting convenience.

We can make sure that all those numbers are JavaScript numbers (double-precision, floating-point) by using the **type** function:

```
cljs.user=> (type 1)
#object[Number]
cljs.user=> (type 1.2)
#object[Number]
cljs.user=> (type 3/4)
#object[Number]
```

If you need to do more than simple arithmetic, you can use the Java or JavaScript **math** libraries, which are similar except for a few minor exceptions.

You will learn more about host platform interoperability in *Chapter 9, Host Platform Interoperability with Java and JavaScript* (how to interact with the host platform and its ecosystem), but the examples in the chapter will get you started with doing some more complicated math and with using the `math` library:

Reading a value from a constant can be done like this:

```
user=> Math/PI
3.141592653589793
```

And calling a function, like the usual Clojure functions, can be done like this:

```
user=> (Math/random)
0.25127992428738254
user=> (Math/sqrt 9)
3.0
user=> (Math/round 0.7)
1
```

Exercise 2.01: The Obfuscation Machine

You have been contacted by a secret government agency to develop an algorithm that encodes text into a secret string that only the owner of the algorithm can decode. Apparently, they don't trust other security mechanisms such as SSL and will only communicate sensitive information with their own proprietary technology.

You need to develop an **encode** function and a **decode** function. The **encode** function should replace letters with numbers that are not easily guessable. For that purpose, each letter will take the character's number value in the ASCII table, add another number to it (the number of words in the sentence to encode), and finally, compute the square value of that number. The **decode** function should allow the user to revert to the original string. Someone highly ranked in the agency came up with that algorithm so they trust it to be very secure.

In this exercise, we will put into practice some of the things we've learned about strings and numbers by building an obfuscation machine:

1. Start your REPL and look up the documentation of the **clojure.string/replace** function:

```
user=> (doc clojure.string/replace)
-------------------------
clojure.string/replace
([s match replacement])
  Replaces all instance of match with replacement in s.
```

```
match/replacement can be:

string / string
char / char
pattern / (string or function of match).

See also replace-first.

The replacement is literal (i.e. none of its characters are treated
specially) for all cases above except pattern / string.

For pattern / string, $1, $2, etc. in the replacement string are
substituted with the string that matched the corresponding
parenthesized group in the pattern.  If you wish your replacement
string r to be used literally, use (re-quote-replacement r) as the
replacement argument.  See also documentation for
java.util.regex.Matcher's appendReplacement method.

Example:
(clojure.string/replace "Almost Pig Latin" #"\b(\w)(\w+)\b" "$2$1ay")
-> "lmostAay igPay atinLay"
```

Notice that the **replace** function can take a pattern and a function of the matching result as parameters. We don't know how to iterate over collections yet, but using the **replace** function with a pattern and a "replacement function" should do the job.

2. Try and use the **replace** function with the **#"\w"** pattern (which means word character), replace it with the **!** character, and observe the result:

```
user=> (clojure.string/replace "Hello World" #"\w" "!")
```

The output is as follows:

```
"!!!!! !!!!!"
```

3. Try and use the **replace** function with the same pattern, but this time passing an anonymous function that takes the matching letter as a parameter:

```
user=> (clojure.string/replace "Hello World" #"\w" (fn [letter] (do (println letter)
"!")))
```

The output is as follows:

```
H
e
l
l
o
W
o
r
l
d
"!!!!! !!!!!"
```

Observe that the function was called for each letter, printing the match out to the console and finally returning the string with the matches replaced by the ! character. It looks like we should be able to write our encoding logic in that replacement function.

4. Let's now see how we can convert a character to a number. We can use the **int** function, which coerces its parameter to an integer. It can be used like this:

```
user=> (int \a)
97
```

5. It seems that the "replacement function" will take a string as a parameter, so let's convert our string to a character. Use the **char-array** function combined with **first** to convert our string to a character as follows:

```
user=> (first (char-array "a"))
\a
```

6. Now, if we combine previous steps together and also compute the square value of the character's number, we should be approaching our obfuscation goal. Combine the code written previously to obtain a character code from a string and get its square value using the **Math/pow** function as follows:

```
user=> (Math/pow (int (first (char-array "a"))) 2)
9409.0
```

7. Let's now convert this result to the string that will be returned from our **replace** function. First, let's remove the decimal part by coercing the result to an **int**, and put things together in an **encode-letter** function, as follows:

```
user=>
(defn encode-letter
  [s]
  (let [code (Math/pow (int (first (char-array s))) 2)]
    (str (int code))))
#'user/encode-letter
user=> (encode-letter "a")
"9409"
```

Great! It seems to work. Let's now test our function as part of the **replace** function.

8. Create the **encode** function, which uses **clojure.string/replace** as well as our **encode-letter** function:

```
user=>
(defn encode
  [s]
  (clojure.string/replace s #"\w" encode-letter))
#'user/encode
user=> (encode "Hello World")
"51841020111664116641232 1 756912321129961166410000"
```

It seems to work but the resulting string will be hard to decode without being able to identify each letter individually.

There is another thing that we did not take into account: the **encode** function should take an arbitrary number to add to the code before calculating the square value.

9. First, add a separator as part of our **encode-letter** function, for example, the **#** character, so that we can identify each letter individually. Second, add an extra parameter to **encode-letter**, which needs to be added before calculating the square value:

```
user=>
(defn encode-letter
  [s x]
  (let [code (Math/pow (+ x (int (first (char-array s)))) 2)]
    (str "#" (int code))))
#'user/encode-letter
```

10. Now, test the **encode** function another time:

```
user=> (encode "Hello World")
Execution error (ArityException) at user/encode (REPL:3).
Wrong number of args (1) passed to: user/encode-letter
```

Our **encode** function is now failing because it is expecting an extra argument.

11. Modify the **encode** function to calculate the number of words in the text to obfuscate, and pass it to the **encode-letter** function. You can use the **clojure. string/split** function with a whitespace, as follows, to count the number of words:

```
user=>
(defn encode
  [s]
  (let [number-of-words (count (clojure.string/split s #" "))]
    (clojure.string/replace s #"\w" (fn [s] (encode-letter s number-of-words)))))
#'user/encode
```

12. Try your newly created function with a few examples and make sure it obfuscates strings properly:

```
user=> (encode "Super secret")
"#7225#14161#12996#10609#13456 #13689#10609#10201#13456#10609#13924"
user=> (encode "Super secret message")
"#7396#14400#13225#10816#13689 #13924#10816#10404#13689#10816#14161 #12544#10816#139
24#13924#10000#11236#10816"
```

What a beautiful, unintelligible, obfuscated string – well done! Notice how the numbers for the same letters are different depending on the number of words in the phrase to encode. It seems to work according to the specification!

We can now start working on the **decode** function, for which we will need to use the following functions:

Math/sqrt to obtain the square root value of a number.

char to retrieve a letter from a character code (a number).

subs as in substring, to get a sub-portion of a string (and get rid of our **#** separator).

Integer/parseInt to convert a string to an integer.

13. Write the **decode** function using a combination of the preceding functions, to decode an obfuscated character:

```
user=>
(defn decode-letter
  [x y]
  (let [number (Integer/parseInt (subs x 1))
        letter (char (- (Math/sqrt number) y))]
    (str letter)))
#'user/decode-letter
```

14. Finally, write the **decode** function, which is similar to the **encode** function except that it should use **decode-letter** instead of **encode-letter**:

```
user=>
(defn decode [s]
  (let [number-of-words (count (clojure.string/split s #" "))]
    (clojure.string/replace s #"\#\d+" (fn [s] (decode-letter s number-of-words)))))
#'user/decode
```

15. Test your functions and make sure that they both work:

```
user=> (encode "If you want to keep a secret, you must also hide it from yourself.")
```

The output is as follows:

```
"#7569#13456 #18225#15625#17161 #17689#12321#15376#16900 #16900#15625
#14641#13225#13225#15876 #12321 #16641#13225#12769#16384#13225#1690
0, #18225#15625#17161 #15129#17161#16641#16900 #12321#14884#16641#15625
#13924#14161#12996#13225 #14161#16900 #13456#16384#15625#15129 #18225#15625#17161#16
384#16641#13225#14884#13456."

user=> (decode *1)

"If you want to keep a secret, you must also hide it from yourself."
```

In this exercise, we've put into practice working with numbers and strings by creating an encoding system. We can now move on to learning other data types, starting with Booleans.

Booleans

Booleans are implemented as Java's **java.lang.Boolean** in Clojure or JavaScript's "Boolean" in ClojureScript. Their value can either be **true** or **false**, and their literal notations are simply the lowercase **true** and **false**.

Symbols

Symbols are identifiers referring to something else. We have already been using symbols when creating bindings or calling functions. For example, when using **def**, the first argument is a symbol that will refer to a value, and when calling a function such as **+**, **+** is a symbol referring to the function implementing the addition. Consider the following examples:

```
user=> (def foo "bar")
#'user/foo
user=> foo
"bar"
user=> (defn add-2 [x] (+ x 2))
#'user/add-2
user=> add-2
#object[user$add_2 0x4e858e0a "user$add_2@4e858e0a"]
```

Here, we have created the **user/foo** symbol, which refers to the **"bar"** string, and the **add-2** symbol, which refers to the function that adds 2 to its parameter. We have created those symbols in the user namespace, hence the notation with **/**: **user/foo**.

If we try to evaluate a symbol that has not been defined, we'll get an error:

```
user=> marmalade
Syntax error compiling at (REPL:0:0).
Unable to resolve symbol: marmalade in this context
```

In the *REPL Basics* topic of *Chapter 1, Hello REPL!*, we were able to use the following functions because they are bound to a specific symbol:

```
user=> str
#object[clojure.core$str 0x7bb6ab3a "clojure.core$str@7bb6ab3a"]
user=> +
#object[clojure.core$_PLUS_ 0x1c3146bc "clojure.core$_PLUS_@1c3146bc"]
user=> clojure.string/replace
#object[clojure.string$replace 0xf478a81 "clojure.string$replace@f478a81"]
```

Those gibberish-like values are string representations of the functions, because we are asking for the values bound to the symbols rather than invoking the functions (wrapping them with parentheses).

Keywords

You can think of a keyword as some kind of a special constant string. Keywords are a nice addition to Clojure because they are lightweight and convenient to use and create. You just need to use the colon character, :, at the beginning of a word to create a keyword:

```
user=> :foo
:foo
user=> :another_keyword
:another_keyword
```

They don't refer to anything else like symbols do; as you can see in the preceding example, when evaluated, they just return themselves. Keywords are typically used as keys in a key-value associative map, as we will see in the next topic about collections.

In this section, we went through simple data types such as string, numbers, Boolean, symbols, and keywords. We highlighted how their underlying implementation depends on the host platform because Clojure is a hosted language. In the next section, we will see how those values can aggregate to collections.

Collections

Clojure is a functional programming language in which we focus on building the computations of our programs in terms of the evaluation of functions, rather than building custom data types and their associated behaviors. In the other dominant programming paradigm, object-oriented programming, programmers define the data types and the operations available on them. Objects are supposed to encapsulate data and communicate with each other by passing messages around. But there is an unfortunate tendency to create classes and new types of objects to customize the shape of the data, instead of using more generic data structures, which cascades into creating specific methods to access and modify the data. We have to come up with decent names, which is difficult, and then we pass instances of objects around in our programs. We create new classes all the time, but more code means more bugs. It is a recipe for disaster; it is an explosion of code, with code that is very specific and benefits from little reuse.

Of course, it is not like that everywhere, and you can write clean object-oriented code, with objects being the little black boxes of functionality they were designed for. However, as programmers, whether it's through using other libraries or maintaining a legacy code base, we spend most of our time working with other people's code.

In functional programming, and more specifically, in Clojure, we tend to work with just a few data types. Types that are generic and powerful, types that every other "Clojurian" already knows and has mastered.

Collections are data types that can contain more than one thing and describe how those items relate to each other. The four main data structures for collections that you should know about are **Maps**, **Sets**, **Vectors**, and **Lists**. There are more available, including the data structure offered by your host platform (for example, Java or JavaScript) or other libraries, but those four are your bread and butter for doing things in Clojure.

"Data dominates. If you've chosen the right data structures and organized things well, the algorithms will almost always be self-evident. Data structures, not algorithms, are central to programming." – Rob Pike's Rule #5 of programming.

Maps

A Map is a collection of key-value pairs. Clojure provides – in a persistent and immutable fashion – the usual HashMap but also a SortedMap.

HashMaps are called "Hash" because they create a hash of the key and map it to a given value. Lookups, as well as other common operations (**insert** and **delete**), are fast.

HashMaps are used a lot in Clojure, notably, for representing entities where we need to associate some attributes to some values. SortedMaps are different because they preserve the order of the keys; otherwise, they have the same interface and are used in the same way as HashMaps. SortedMaps are not very common, so let's focus on HashMaps.

You can create a HashMap with the literal notation using curly braces. Here is a Map with three key-value pairs, with the keys being the **:artist**, **:song**, and **:year** keywords:

```
user=> {:artist "David Bowtie" :song "The Man Who Mapped the World" :year 1970}
{:artist "David Bowtie", :song "The Man Who Mapped the World", :year 1970}
```

You might have noticed in the preceding example that key-value pairs in the map are separated by a space, but Clojure evaluates it and returns a Map with key-value pairs separated by a comma. As with other collections, you can choose to use a space or a comma to separate each entry. For maps, there's no best practice and if you think it improves a map's readability, use commas; otherwise, simply omit them. You can also separate entries with new lines.

Here's another map written with comma-separated entries:

```
user=> {:artist "David Bowtie", :song "Comma Oddity", :year 1969}
{:artist "David Bowtie", :song "Comma Oddity", :year 1969}
```

Notice that the values can be of any type, and not only simple values such as strings and numbers, but also vectors and even other maps, allowing you to create nested data structures and structure information as follows:

```
user=>
  {
  "David Bowtie" {
    "The Man Who Mapped the World" {:year 1970, :duration "4:01"}
    "Comma Oddity" {:year 1969, :duration "5:19"}
  }
  "Crosby Stills Hash" {
    "Helplessly Mapping" {:year 1969, :duration "2:38"}
    "Almost Cut My Hair" {:year 1970, :duration "4:29", :featuring ["Neil Young", "Rich
Hickey"]}
  }
}
{"David Bowtie" {"The Man Who Mapped the World" {:year 1970, :duration "4:01"}, "Comma
Oddity" {:year 1969, :duration "5:19"}}, "Crosby Stills Hash" {"Helplessly Mapping"
{:year 1969, :duration "2:38"}, "Almost Cut My Hair" {:year 1970, :duration "4:29",
:featuring ["Neil Young" "Rich Hickey"]}}}
```

Keys can be of different types too, so you could have strings, numbers, or even other types as a key; however, we generally use keywords.

Another way of creating a map is by using the **hash-map** function, passing in pairs of arguments as follows:

```
user=> (hash-map :a 1 :b 2 :c 3)
{:c 3, :b 2, :a 1}
```

Choose to use literal notation with curly braces when possible, but when HashMaps are programmatically generated, the **hash-map** function can come in handy.

Map keys are unique:

```
user=> {:name "Lucy" :age 32 :name "Jon"}
Syntax error reading source at (REPL:6:35).
Duplicate key: :name
```

An exception was thrown because the **:name** key was present twice in the preceding literal map.

However, different keys can have the same value:

```
user=> {:name "Lucy" :age 32 :number-of-teeth 32}
{:name "Lucy", :age 32, :number-of-teeth 32}
```

Notice that both **age** and **number-of-teeth** have the same value, and that is both valid and convenient, to say the least.

Now that you know how to create maps, it is time for a bit of practice.

Exercise 2.02: Using Maps

In this exercise, we will learn how to access and modify simple maps:

1. Start your REPL and create a map:

```
user=> (def favorite-fruit {:name "Kiwi", :color "Green", :kcal_per_100g 61
:distinguish_mark "Hairy"})
#'user/favorite-fruit
```

2. You can read an entry from the map with the **get** function. Try to look up a key or two, as follows:

```
user=> (get favorite-fruit :name)
"Kiwi"
user=> (get favorite-fruit :color)
"Green"
```

3. If the value for a given key cannot be found, **get** returns **nil**, but you can specify a fallback value with a third argument to **get**:

```
user=> (get favorite-fruit :taste)
nil
user=> (get favorite-fruit :taste "Very good 8/10")
"Very good 8/10"
user=> (get favorite-fruit :kcal_per_100g 0)
61
```

4. Maps and keywords have the special ability to be used as functions. When positioned in the "operator position" (as the first item of the list), they are invoked as a function that can be used to look up a value in a map. Try it now by using the **favorite-fruit** map as a function:

```
user=> (favorite-fruit :color)
"Green"
```

5. Try to use a keyword as a function to look up a value in a Map:

```
user=> (:color favorite-fruit)
"Green"
```

As with the **get** function, those ways of retrieving a value return **nil** when the key cannot be found, and you can pass an extra argument to provide a fallback value.

6. Provide a fallback value for a key that doesn't exist in the **favorite-fruit** map:

```
user=> (:shape favorite-fruit "egg-like")
"egg-like"
```

7. We would like to store this value in the map. Use **assoc** to associate a new key, **:shape**, with a new value, **"egg-like"**, in our map:

```
user=> (assoc favorite-fruit :shape "egg-like")
{:name "Kiwi", :color "Green", :kcal_per_100g 61, :distinguish_mark "Hairy", :shape
"egg-like"}
```

The **assoc** operation returns a new map containing our previous key-value pairs as well as the new association we've just added.

8. Evaluate **favorite-fruit** and notice that it remains unchanged:

```
user=> favorite-fruit
{:name "Kiwi", :color "Green", :kcal_per_100g 61, :distinguish_mark "Hairy"}
```

Because a map is immutable, the value bound to the **favorite-fruit** symbol has not changed. By using **assoc**, we have created a new version of the map.

Now, the F3C ("Funny Fruity Fruits Consortium") have reverted their previous ruling and determined during their quarterly review of fruit specifications that the color of the kiwi fruit should be brown and not green. To make sure that your application is F3C compliant, you decide to update your system with the new value.

9. Change the color of **favorite-fruit** by associating a new value to the **:color** key:

```
user=> (assoc favorite-fruit :color "Brown")
{:name "Kiwi", :color "Brown", :kcal_per_100g 61, :distinguish_mark "Hairy"}
```

assoc replaces the existing value when a key already exists, because HashMaps cannot have duplicate keys.

10. If we wanted to add more structured information, we could add a map as a value. Add production information as a nested map in our **Kiwi** map:

```
user=> (assoc favorite-fruit :yearly_production_in_tonnes {:china 2025000 :italy
541000 :new_zealand 412000 :iran 311000 :chile 225000})
{:name "Kiwi", :color "Green", :kcal_per_100g 61, :distinguish_mark "Hairy",
:yearly_production_in_tonnes {:china 2025000, :italy 541000, :new_zealand 412000,
:iran 311000, :chile 225000}}
```

Having nested maps or other data types is commonly used to represent structured information.

New research has found out that the Kiwi contains fewer calories than previously thought, and to stay compliant, the F3C requires organizations to reduce the current value of kcal per 100 g by 1.

11. Decrement **kcal_per_100g** with the **assoc** function, as follows:

```
user=> (assoc favorite-fruit :kcal_per_100g (- (:kcal_per_100g favorite-fruit) 1))
{:name "Kiwi", :color "Green", :kcal_per_100g 60, :distinguish_mark "Hairy"}
```

Great! It works, but there is a more elegant way to deal with this type of operation. When you need to change a value in a map based on a previous value, you can use the **update** function. While the **assoc** function lets you associate a completely new value to a key, **update** allows you to compute a new value based on the previous value of a key. The **update** function takes a function as its third parameter.

12. Decrement **kcal_per_100g** with the **update** function and **dec**, as follows:

```
user=> (update favorite-fruit :kcal_per_100g dec)
{:name "Kiwi", :color "Green", :kcal_per_100g 60, :distinguish_mark "Hairy"}
```

Notice how the value of **:kcal_per_100g** changed from **61** to **60**.

13. You can also pass arguments to the function provided to update; for example, if we wanted to lower **:kcal_per_100g** by 10 instead of 1, we could use the subtract function, **-**, and write the following:

```
user=> (update favorite-fruit :kcal_per_100g - 10)
{:name "Kiwi", :color "Green", :kcal_per_100g 51, :distinguish_mark "Hairy"}
```

Like **assoc**, **update** does not change the immutable map; it returns a new map.

This example illustrates the power of functions being "first-class citizens": we treat them like typical values; in this case, a function was passed as an argument to another function. We will elaborate on this concept in the next chapter while diving into functions in more depth.

14. Finally, use **dissoc** (as in "dissociate") to remove one or multiple elements from a map:

```
user=> (dissoc favorite-fruit :distinguish_mark)
{:name "Kiwi", :color "Green", :kcal_per_100g 61}
user=> (dissoc favorite-fruit :kcal_per_100g :color)
{:name "Kiwi", :distinguish_mark "Hairy"}
```

Well done! Now that we know how to use maps, it is time to move on to the next data structure: sets.

Sets

A set is a collection of unique values. Clojure provides HashSet and SortedSet. Hash Sets are implemented as Hash Maps, with the key and the value of each entry being identical.

Hash Sets are fairly common in Clojure and have a literal notation of a hash with curly braces, **#{}**, for example:

```
user=> #{1 2 3 4 5}
#{1 4 3 2 5}
```

Notice in the preceding expression that when the set is evaluated, it does not return the elements of the sets in the order that they were defined in the literal expression. This is because of the internal structure of the HashSet. The value is transformed in a unique hash, which allows fast access but does not keep the insertion order. If you care about the order in which the elements are added, you need to use a different data structure, for example, a sequence such as a vector (which we will soon discover). Use a HashSet to represent elements that logically belong together, for example, an enumeration of unique values.

As with maps, sets cannot have duplicate entries:

```
user=> #{:a :a :b :c}
Syntax error reading source at (REPL:135:15).
Duplicate key: :a
```

Hash Sets can be created from a list of values by passing those values to the **hash-set** function:

```
user=> (hash-set :a :b :c :d)
#{:c :b :d :a}
```

Hash Sets can also be created from another collection with the **set** function. Let's create a HashSet from a vector:

```
user=> (set [:a :b :c])
#{:c :b :a}
```

Notice that the order defined in the vector was lost.

The **set** function will not throw an error when converting a collection of non-unique values to a set with the **set** function, which can be useful for deduplicating values:

```
user=> (set ["No" "Copy" "Cats" "Cats" "Please"])
#{"Copy" "Please" "Cats" "No"}
```

Notice how one of the duplicate strings, **"Cats"**, was silently removed to create a set.

A Sorted Set can be created with the **sorted-set** function and have no literal syntax as Hash Sets do:

```
user=> (sorted-set "No" "Copy" "Cats" "Cats" "Please")
#{"Cats" "Copy" "No" "Please"}
```

Notice that they are printed in the same way as Hash Sets, only the order looks different. Sorted Sets are sorted based on the natural order of elements they contain rather than the order of the arguments provided upon creation. You could instead provide your own sorting function, but we will focus on Hash Sets as they are far more common and useful.

Exercise 2.03: Using Sets

In this exercise, we will use a Hash Set to represent a collection of supported currencies:

> **Note**
>
> A Hash Set is a good choice of data structure for a list of currencies because we typically want to store a collection of unique values and efficiently check for containment. Also, the order of the currencies probably doesn't matter. If you wanted to associate more data to a currency (such as ISO codes and countries), then you would more likely use nested Maps to represent each currency as an entity, keyed by a unique ISO code. Ultimately, the choice of the data structure depends on how you plan to use the data. In this exercise, we simply want to read it, check for containment, and add items to our set.

1. Start a REPL. Create a set and bind it to the **supported-currencies** symbol:

    ```
    user=> (def supported-currencies #{"Dollar" "Japanese yen" "Euro" "Indian rupee"
    "British pound"})
    #'user/supported-currencies
    ```

2. As with maps, you can use **get** to retrieve an entry from a set, which returns the entry passed as a parameter when present in the set. Use **get** to retrieve an existing entry as well as a missing entry:

    ```
    user=> (get supported-currencies "Dollar")
    "Dollar"
    user=> (get supported-currencies "Swiss franc")
    nil
    ```

3. It is likely that you just want to check for containment, and **contains?** is, therefore, semantically better. Use **contains?** instead of **get** to check for containment:

```
user=> (contains? supported-currencies "Dollar")
true
user=> (contains? supported-currencies "Swiss franc")
false
```

Notice that **contains?** returns a Boolean and that **get** returns the lookup value or **nil** when not found. There is the edge case of looking up **nil** in a set that will return **nil** both when found and not found. In that case, **contains?** is naturally more suitable.

4. As with maps, sets and keywords can be used as functions to check for containment. Use the **supported-currencies** set as a function to look up a value in the set:

```
user=> (supported-currencies "Swiss franc")
nil
```

"Swiss franc" isn't in the **supported-currencies** set; therefore, the preceding return value is **nil**.

5. If you tried to use the **"Dollar"** string as a function to look itself up in the set, you would get the following error:

```
user=> ("Dollar" supported-currencies)
Execution error (ClassCastException) at user/eval7 (REPL:1).
java.lang.String cannot be cast to clojure.lang.IFn
```

We cannot use strings as a function to look up a value in a set or a Map. That's one of the reasons why keywords are a better choice in both sets and maps when possible.

6. To add an entry to a set, use the **conj** function, as in "conjoin":

```
user=> (conj supported-currencies "Monopoly Money")
#{"Japanese yen" "Euro" "Dollar" "Monopoly Money" "Indian rupee" "British pound"}
```

7. You can pass more than one item to the **conj** function. Try to add multiple currencies to our Hash Set:

```
user=> (conj supported-currencies "Monopoly Money" "Gold dragon" "Gil")
#{"Japanese yen" "Euro" "Dollar" "Monopoly Money" "Indian rupee" "Gold dragon"
"British pound" "Gil"}
```

8. Finally, you can remove one or more items with the **disj** function, as in "disjoin":

```
user=> (disj supported-currencies "Dollar" "British pound")
#{"Japanese yen" "Euro" "Indian rupee"}
```

That's it for sets! If you ever need to, you can find more functions for working with sets in the **clojure.set** namespace (such as union and intersection), but this is more advanced usage, so let's move on to the next collection: vectors.

Vectors

A vector is another type of collection that is widely used in Clojure. You can think of vectors as powerful immutable arrays. They are collections of values efficiently accessible by their integer index (starting from 0), and they maintain the order of item insertion as well as duplicates.

Use a vector when you need to store and read elements in order, and when you don't mind duplicate elements. For example, a web browser history could be a good candidate, as you might want to easily go back to the recent pages but also remove older elements using a vector's index, and there would likely be duplicate elements in it. A map or a set wouldn't be of much help in that situation, as you don't have a specific key to look up a value with.

Vectors have a literal notation with square brackets (**[]**):

```
user=> [1 2 3]
[1 2 3]
```

Vectors can also be created with the **vector** function followed by a list of items as arguments:

```
user=> (vector 10 15 2 15 0)
[10 15 2 15 0]
```

You can create a vector from another collection using the **vec** function; for example, the following expression converts a Hash Set to a vector:

```
user=> (vec #{1 2 3})
[1 3 2]
```

As with other collections, vectors also can contain different types of values:

```
user=> [nil :keyword "String" {:answers [:yep :nope]}]
[nil :keyword "String" {:answers [:yep :nope]}]
```

We can now start practicing.

Exercise 2.04: Using Vectors

In this exercise, we will discover different ways of accessing and interacting with vectors:

1. Start a REPL. You can look up values in a vector using their index (that is, their position in the collection) with the **get** function. Try to use the **get** function with a literal vector:

```
user=> (get [:a :b :c] 0)
:a
user=> (get [:a :b :c] 2)
:c
user=> (get [:a :b :c] 10)
nil
```

Because vectors start at 0-index, :a is at index 0 and :c is at index 2. When the lookup fails, **get** returns **nil**.

2. Let's bind a vector to a symbol to make the practice more convenient:

```
user=> (def fibonacci [0 1 1 2 3 5 8])
#'user/fibonacci
user=> (get fibonacci 6)
8
```

3. As with maps and sets, you can use the vector as a function to look up items, but for vectors, the parameter is the index of the value in the vector:

```
user=> (fibonacci 6)
8
```

4. Add the next two values of the Fibonacci sequence to your vector with the **conj** function:

```
user=> (conj fibonacci 13 21)
[0 1 1 2 3 5 8 13 21]
```

Notice that the items are added to the end of the vector, and the order of the sequence is kept the same.

5. Each item in the Fibonacci sequence corresponds to the sum of the previous two items. Let's dynamically compute the next item of the sequence:

```
user=>
(let [size (count fibonacci)
      last-number (last fibonacci)
      second-to-last-number (fibonacci (- size 2))]
    (conj fibonacci (+ last-number second-to-last-number)))
[0 1 1 2 3 5 8 13]
```

In the preceding example, we used **let** to create three local bindings and improve the readability. We used **count** to calculate the size of a vector, **last** to retrieve its last element, **8**, and finally, we used the **fibonacci** vector as a function to retrieve the element at index "size - 2" (which is the value **5** at index **5**).

In the body of the **let** block, we used the local binding to add the two last items to the end of the Fibonacci sequence with **conj**, which returns **13** (which is, indeed, 5 + 8).

Lists

Lists are sequential collections, similar to vectors, but items are added to the front (at the beginning). Also, they don't have the same performance properties, and random access by index is slower than with vectors. We mostly use lists to write code and macros, or in cases when we need a **last-in, first-out** (**LIFO**) type of data structure (for example, a stack), which can arguably also be implemented with a vector.

We create lists with the literal syntax, **()**, but to differentiate lists that represent code and lists that represent data, we need to use the single quote, **'**:

```
user=> (1 2 3)
Execution error (ClassCastException) at user/eval211 (REPL:1).
java.lang.Long cannot be cast to clojure.lang.IFn
user=> '(1 2 3)
(1 2 3)
user=> (+ 1 2 3)
6
user=> '(+ 1 2 3)
(+ 1 2 3)
```

In the preceding examples, we can see that a list that is not quoted with ' throws an error unless the first item of the list can be invoked as a function.

Lists can also be created with the **list** function:

```
user=> (list :a :b :c)
(:a :b :c)
```

To read the first element of a list, use **first**:

```
user=> (first '(:a :b :c :d))
:a
```

The **rest** function returns the list without its first item:

```
user=> (rest '(:a :b :c :d))
(:b :c :d)
```

We will not talk about iterations and recursion yet, but you could imagine that the combination of **first** and **rest** is all you need to "walk" or go through an entire list: simply by calling **first** on the rest of the list over and over again until there's no rest.

You cannot use the **get** function with a list to retrieve by index. You could use **nth**, but it is not efficient as the list is iterated or "walked" until it reaches the desired position:

```
user=> (nth '(:a :b :c :d) 2)
:c
```

Exercise 2.05: Using Lists

In this exercise, we will practice using lists by reading and adding elements to a to-do list.

1. Start a REPL and create a to-do list with a list of actions that you need to do, using the **list** function as follows:

    ```
    user=> (def my-todo (list  "Feed the cat" "Clean the bathroom" "Save the world"))
    #'user/my-todo
    ```

2. You can add items to your list by using the **cons** function, which operates on sequences:

    ```
    user=> (cons "Go to work" my-todo)
    ("Go to work" "Feed the cat" "Clean the bathroom" "Save the world")
    ```

3. Similarly, you can use the **conj** function, which is used because a list is a collection:

    ```
    user=> (conj my-todo "Go to work")
    ("Go to work" "Feed the cat" "Clean the bathroom" "Save the world")
    ```

    Notice how the order of the parameters is different. **cons** is available on lists because a list is a sequence, and **conj** is available to use on lists because a list is a collection. **conj** is, therefore, slightly more "generic" and also has the advantage of accepting multiple elements as arguments.

4. Add multiple elements at once to your list by using the **conj** function:

```
user=> (conj my-todo "Go to work" "Wash my socks")
("Wash my socks" "Go to work" "Feed the cat" "Clean the bathroom" "Save the world")
```

5. Now it's time to catch up with your task. Retrieve the first element in your to-do list with the **first** function:

```
user=> (first my-todo)
"Feed the cat"
```

6. Once done, you can retrieve the rest of your tasks with the **rest** function:

```
user=> (rest my-todo)
("Clean the bathroom" "Save the world")
```

You could imagine then having to call **first** on the rest of the list (if you had to develop a fully blown to-do list application). Because the list is immutable, if you keep calling **first** on the same **my-todo** list, you will end up with the same element, **"Feed the cat"**, over and over again, and also with a happy but very fat cat.

7. Finally, you can also retrieve a specific element from the list using the **nth** function:

```
user=> (nth my-todo 2)
"Save the world"
```

However, remember that retrieving an element at a specific position in a list is slower than with vectors because the list has to be "walked" until the **nth** element. In that case, you might be better off using a vector. One final note about **nth** is that it throws an exception when the element at position n is not found.

That is all you need to know about lists for now and we can move on to the next section about collection and sequence abstractions.

Collection and Sequence Abstractions

Clojure's data structures are implemented in terms of powerful abstractions. You might have noticed that the operations we used on collections are often similar, but behave differently based on the type of the collection. For instance, **get** retrieves items from a map with a key, but from a vector with an index; **conj** adds elements to a vector at the back, but to a list at the front.

A sequence is a collection of elements in a particular order, where each item follows another. Maps, sets, vectors, and lists are all collections, but only vectors and lists are sequences, although we can easily obtain a sequence from a map or a set.

Let's go through a few examples of useful functions to use with collections. Consider the following map:

```
user=> (def language {:name "Clojure" :creator "Rich Hickey" :platforms ["Java"
"JavaScript" ".NET"]})
#'user/language
```

Use **count** to get the number of elements in a collection. Each element of this map is a key-value pair; therefore, it contains three elements:

```
user=> (count language)
3
```

Slightly more apparent, the following set contains no elements:

```
user=> (count #{})
0
```

We can test whether a collection is empty with the **empty?** function:

```
user=> (empty? language)
false
user=> (empty? [])
true
```

A map is not sequential because there is no logical order between its elements. However, we can convert a map to a sequence using the **seq** function:

```
user=> (seq language)
([:name "Clojure"] [:creator "Rich Hickey"] [:platforms ["Java" "JavaScript" ".NET"]])
```

It yielded a list of vectors or *tuples*, which means that there is now a logical order and we can use sequence functions on this data structure:

```
user=> (nth (seq language) 1)
[:creator "Rich Hickey"]
```

A lot of functions just work on collections directly because they can be turned into a sequence, so you could omit the **seq** step and, for example, call **first**, **rest**, or **last** directly on a map or a set:

```
user=> (first #{:a :b :c})
:c
user=> (rest #{:a :b :c})
(:b :a)
user=> (last language)
[:platforms ["Java" "JavaScript" ".NET"]]
```

The value of using sequence functions such as **first** or **rest** on maps and sets seems questionable but treating those collections as sequences means that they can then be iterated. Many more functions are available for processing each item of a sequence, such as **map**, **reduce**, **filter**, and so on. We have dedicated entire chapters to learning about those in the second part of the book so that we can stay focused on the other core functions for now.

into is another useful operator that puts elements of one collection into another collection. The first argument for **into** is the target collection:

```
user=> (into [1 2 3 4] #{5 6 7 8})
[1 2 3 4 7 6 5 8]
```

In the preceding example, each element of the **#{5 6 7 8}** set was added into the **[1 2 3 4]** vector. The resulting vector is not in ascending order because Hash Sets are not sorted:

```
user=> (into #{1 2 3 4} [5 6 7 8])
#{7 1 4 6 3 2 5 8}
```

In the preceding example, the **[5 6 7 8]** vector was added to the **#{1 2 3 4}** set. Once again, Hash Sets do not keep insertion order and the resulting set is simply a logical collection of unique values.

A usage example would be, for example, to deduplicate a vector, just put it into a set:

```
user=> (into #{} [1 2 3 3 3 4])
#{1 4 3 2}
```

To put items into a map, you would need to pass a collection of tuples representing key-value pairs:

```
user=> (into {} [[:a 1] [:b 2] [:c 3]])
{:a 1, :b 2, :c 3}
```

Each item is "conjoined" in the collection, and so it follows the semantic of the target collection for inserting items with **conj**. Elements are added to a list at the front:

```
user=> (into '() [1 2 3 4])
(4 3 2 1)
```

To help you understand **(into '() [1 2 3 4])**, here is a step-by-step representation of what happened:

```
user=> (conj '() 1)
(1)
user=> (conj '(1) 2)
(2 1)
user=> (conj '(2 1) 3)
(3 2 1)
user=> (conj '(3 2 1) 4)
(4 3 2 1)
```

If you want to concatenate collections, **concat** might be more appropriate than **into**. See how they behave differently here:

```
user=> (concat '(1 2) '(3 4))
(1 2 3 4)
user=> (into '(1 2) '(3 4))
(4 3 1 2)
```

A lot of Clojure functions that operate on sequences will return sequences no matter what the input type was. **concat** is one example:

```
user=> (concat #{1 2 3} #{1 2 3 4})
(1 3 2 1 4 3 2)
user=> (concat {:a 1} ["Hello"])
([:a 1] "Hello")
```

sort is another example. **sort** can rearrange a collection to order its elements. It has the benefit of being slightly more obvious in terms of why you would want a sequence as a result:

```
user=> (def alphabet #{:a :b :c :d :e :f})
#'user/alphabet
user=> alphabet
#{:e :c :b :d :f :a}
user=> (sort alphabet)
(:a :b :c :d :e :f)
user=> (sort [3 7 5 1 9])
(1 3 5 7 9)
```

But what if you wanted a vector as a result? Well, now you know that you could use the **into** function:

```
user=> (sort [3 7 5 1 9])
(1 3 5 7 9)
user=> (into [] *1)
[1 3 5 7 9]
```

It is interesting to note that **conj** can also be used on maps. For its arguments to be consistent with other types of collections, the new entry is represented by a tuple:

```
user=> (conj language [:created 2007])
{:name "Clojure", :creator "Rich Hickey", :platforms ["Java" "JavaScript" ".NET"],
 :created 2007}
```

Similarly, a vector is an associative collection of key-value pairs where the key is the index of the value:

```
user=> (assoc [:a :b :c :d] 2 :z)
[:a :b :z :d]
```

Exercise 2.06: Working with Nested Data Structures

For the purpose of this exercise, imagine that you are working with a little shop called "Sparkling," whose business is to trade gemstones. It turns out that the owner of the shop knows a bit of Clojure, and has been using a Clojure REPL to manage the inventory with some kind of homemade database. However, the owner has been struggling to work with nested data structures, and they require help from a professional: you. The shop won't share their database because it contains sensitive data – they have just given you a sample dataset so that you know about the shape of the data.

The shop owner read a blog post on the internet saying that pure functions are amazing and make for good quality code. So, they asked you to develop some pure functions that take their gemstone database as the first parameter of each function. The owner said you would only get paid if you provide pure functions. In this exercise, we will develop a few functions that will help us understand and operate on nested data structures.

> **Note**
>
> A pure function is a function where the return value is only determined by its input values. A pure function does not have any side effects, which means that it does not mutate a program's state nor generate any kind of I/O.

1. Open up a REPL and create the following Hash Map representing the sample gemstone database:

repl.clj

```
1  (def gemstone-db {
2    :ruby {
3      :name "Ruby"
4      :stock 480
5      :sales [1990 3644 6376 4918 7882 6747 7495 8573 5097 1712]
6      :properties {
7        :dispersion 0.018
8        :hardness 9.0
9        :refractive-index [1.77 1.78]
10       :color "Red"
11     }
12   }
```

The complete code for this snippet can be found at https://packt.live/3aD8MgL

One of the most popular questions the shop gets from its customers is about the durability of a gem. This can be found in the properties of a gem, at the **:hardness** key. The first function that we need to develop is **durability**, which retrieves the hardness of a given gem.

2. Let's start by using a function we already know, **get**, with the **:ruby** gem as an example:

```
user=> (get (get (get gemstone-db :ruby) :properties) :hardness)
9.0
```

It works, but nesting **get** is not very elegant. We could use the map or keywords as functions and see how it improves the readability.

3. Use the keywords as a function to see how it improves the readability of our code:

```
user=> (:hardness (:properties (:ruby gemstone-db)))
9.0
```

This is slightly better. But it's still a lot of nested calls and parentheses. Surely, there must be a better way!

When you need to fetch data in a deeply nested map such as this one, use the **get-in** function. It takes a vector of keys as parameters and digs in the map with just one function call.

4. Use the **get-in** function with the **[:ruby :properties :hardness]** vector of parameters to retrieve the deeply nested **:hardness** key:

```
user=> (get-in gemstone-db [:ruby :properties :hardness])
9.0
```

Great! The vector of keys reads left to right and there is no nested expression. It will make our function a lot more readable.

5. Create the durability function that takes the database and the **gem** keyword as a parameter and returns the value of the **hardness** property:

```
user=>
(defn durability
  [db gemstone]
  (get-in db [gemstone :properties :hardness]))
#'user/durability
```

6. Test your newly created function to make sure that it works as expected:

```
user=> (durability gemstone-db :ruby)
9.0
user=> (durability gemstone-db :moissanite)
9.5
```

Great! Let's move on to the next function.

Apparently, a ruby is not simply "red" but "Near colorless through pink through all shades of red to a deep crimson." Who would have thought? The owner is now asking you to create a function to update the color of a gem, because they might want to change some other colors too, for marketing purposes. The function needs to return the updated database.

7. Let's try to write the code to change the color property of a gem. We can try to use **assoc**:

```
user=> (assoc (:ruby gemstone-db) :properties {:color "Near colorless through pink
through all shades of red to a deep crimson"})
{:name "Ruby", :stock 120, :sales [1990 3644 6376 4918 7882 6747 7495 8573 5097
1712], :properties {:color "Near colorless through pink through all shades of red to
a deep crimson"}}
```

It seems to work but, all the other properties are gone! We replaced the existing Hash Map at the key property with a new Hash Map that contains only one entry: the color.

8. We could use a trick. Do you remember the **into** function? It takes a collection and put its values in another collection, like this:

```
user=> (into {:a 1 :b 2} {:c 3})
{:a 1, :b 2, :c 3}
```

If we use the **update** function combined with **into**, we could obtain the desired result.

9. Try to use **update** combined with **into** to change the **:color** property of the ruby gem:

```
user=> (update (:ruby gemstone-db) :properties into {:color "Near colorless through
pink through all shades of red to a deep crimson"})
{:name "Ruby", :stock 120, :sales [1990 3644 6376 4918 7882 6747 7495 8573 5097
1712], :properties {:dispersion 0.018, :hardness 9.0, :refractive-index [1.77 1.78],
:color "Near colorless through pink through all shades of red to a deep crimson"}}
```

That's great, but there are two problems with this approach. First, the combination of **update** and **into** is not very readable or easy to understand. Second, we wanted to return the entire database, but we just returned the **"Ruby"** entry. We would have to add another operation to update this entry in the main database, perhaps by nesting another **into**, reducing readability even further.

As with **get-in**, Clojure offers a simpler way of dealing with nested maps: **assoc-in** and **update-in**. They work like **assoc** and **update**, but take a vector of keys (such as **get-in**) as a parameter, instead of a single key.

You would use **update-in** when you want to update a deeply nested value with a function (for example, to compute the new value with the previous value). Here, we simply want to replace the color with an entirely new value, so we should use **assoc-in**.

10. Use **assoc-in** to change the **color** property of the ruby gem:

```
user=> (assoc-in gemstone-db [:ruby :properties :color] "Near colorless through pink
through all shades of red to a deep crimson")
{:ruby {:name "Ruby", :stock 120, :sales [1990 3644 6376 4918 7882 6747 7495 8573
5097 1712], :properties {:dispersion 0.018, :hardness 9.0, :refractive-index [1.77
1.78], :color "Near colorless through pink through all shades of red to a deep
crimson"}}, :emerald {:name "Emerald", :stock 85, :sales [6605 2373 104 4764 9023],
:properties {:dispersion 0.014, :hardness 7.5, :refractive-index [1.57 1.58], :color
"Green shades to colorless"}}, :diamond {:name "Diamond", :stock 10, :sales [8295
329 5960 6118 4189 3436 9833 8870 9700 7182 7061 1579], :properties {:dispersion
0.044, :hardness 10, :refractive-index [2.417 2.419], :color "Typically yellow,
brown or gray to colorless"}}, :moissanite {:name "Moissanite", :stock 45, :sales
[7761 3220], :properties {:dispersion 0.104, :hardness 9.5, :refractive-index [2.65
2.69], :color "Colorless, green, yellow"}}}
```

Notice how **gemstone-db** was returned entirely. Can you notice the value that has changed? There is a lot of data, so it is not very obvious. You can use the **pprint** function to "pretty print" the value.

Use **pprint** on the last returned value to improve the readability and make sure that our **assoc-in** expression behaved as expected. In a REPL, the last returned value can be obtained with ***1**:

```
                                    1. clj (java)
user⇒ (assoc-in gemstone-db [:ruby :properties :color] "Near colorless through pink through all shades of red to a deep crimson")
{:ruby {:name "Ruby", :stock 480, :sales [1990 3644 6376 4918 7882 6747 7495 8573 5097 1712], :properties {:dispersion 0.018, :hardness 9.0, :ref
ractive-index [1.77 1.78], :color "Near colorless through pink through all shades of red to a deep crimson"}}, :diamond {:name "Diamond", :stock
10, :sales [8295 329 5960 6118 4189 3436 9833 8870 9700 7182 7061 1579], :properties {:dispersion 0.044, :hardness 10, :refractive-index [2.417 2
.419], :color "Typically yellow, brown or gray to colorless"}}, :moissanite {:name "Moissanite", :stock 45, :sales [7761 3220], :properties {:dis
persion 0.104, :hardness 9.5, :refractive-index [2.65 2.69], :color "Colorless, green, yellow"}}}
user⇒ (pprint *1)
{:ruby
 {:name "Ruby",
  :stock 480,
  :sales [1990 3644 6376 4918 7882 6747 7495 8573 5097 1712],
  :properties
  {:dispersion 0.018,
   :hardness 9.0,
   :refractive-index [1.77 1.78],
   :color
   "Near colorless through pink through all shades of red to a deep crimson"}},
 :diamond
 {:name "Diamond",
  :stock 10,
  :sales [8295 329 5960 6118 4189 3436 9833 8870 9700 7182 7061 1579],
  :properties
  {:dispersion 0.044,
   :hardness 10,
   :refractive-index [2.417 2.419],
   :color "Typically yellow, brown or gray to colorless"}},
 :moissanite
 {:name "Moissanite",
  :stock 45,
  :sales [7761 3220],
  :properties
  {:dispersion 0.104,
   :hardness 9.5,
   :refractive-index [2.65 2.69],
   :color "Colorless, green, yellow"}}}
nil
user⇒ ▊
```

Figure 2.1: Printing the output to REPL

That is much more readable. We will not use **pprint** everywhere as it takes a lot of extra space, but you should use it.

11. Create the **change-color** pure function, which takes three parameters: a database, a gemstone keyword, and a new color. This function updates the color in the given database and returns the new value of the database:

```
user=>
(defn change-color
  [db gemstone new-color]
  (assoc-in gemstone-db [gemstone :properties :color] new-color))
#'user/change-color
```

12. Test that your newly created function behaves as expected:

```
user=> (change-color gemstone-db :ruby "Some kind of red")
{:ruby {:name "Ruby", :stock 120, :sales [1990 3644 6376 4918 7882 6747 7495 8573
5097 1712], :properties {:dispersion 0.018, :hardness 9.0, :refractive-index
[1.77 1.78], :color "Some kind of red"}}, :emerald {:name "Emerald", :stock 85,
:sales [6605 2373 104 4764 9023], :properties {:dispersion 0.014, :hardness 7.5,
:refractive-index [1.57 1.58], :color "Green shades to colorless"}}, :diamond
{:name "Diamond", :stock 10, :sales [8295 329 5960 6118 4189 3436 9833 8870 9700
7182 7061 1579], :properties {:dispersion 0.044, :hardness 10, :refractive-index
[2.417 2.419], :color "Typically yellow, brown or gray to colorless"}}, :moissanite
{:name "Moissanite", :stock 45, :sales [7761 3220], :properties {:dispersion 0.104,
:hardness 9.5, :refractive-index [2.65 2.69], :color "Colorless, green, yellow"}}}
```

The owner would like to add one last function to record the sale of a gem and update the inventory accordingly.

When a sale occurs, the shop owner would like to call the **sell** function with the following arguments: a database, a gemstone keyword, and a client ID. **client-id** will be inserted in the **sales** vector and the **stock** value for that gem will be decreased by one. As with the other functions, the new value of the database will be returned so that the client can handle the update themselves.

13. We can use the **update-in** function in combination with **dec** to decrement (decrease by one) the stock. Let's try it with the diamond gem:

```
user=> (update-in gemstone-db [:diamond :stock] dec)
{:ruby {:name "Ruby", :stock 120, :sales [1990 3644 6376 4918 7882 6747 7495 8573
5097 1712], :properties {:dispersion 0.018, :hardness 9.0, :refractive-index [1.77
1.78], :color "Near colorless through pink through all shades of red to a deep
crimson"}}, :emerald {:name "Emerald", :stock 85, :sales [6605 2373 104 4764 9023],
:properties {:dispersion 0.014, :hardness 7.5, :refractive-index [1.57 1.58], :color
"Green shades to colorless"}}, :diamond {:name "Diamond", :stock 9, :sales [8295 329
5960 6118 4189 3436 9833 8870 9700 7182 7061 1579], :properties {:dispersion 0.044,
:hardness 10, :refractive-index [2.417 2.419], :color "Typically yellow, brown or
gray to colorless"}}, :moissanite {:name "Moissanite", :stock 45, :sales [7761
3220], :properties {:dispersion 0.104, :hardness 9.5, :refractive-index [2.65 2.69],
:color "Colorless, green, yellow"}}}
```

The output is not very readable, and it is hard to verify that the value was correctly updated. Another useful command to improve readability in the REPL is the ***print-level*** option, which can limit the depth of the data structure printed to the terminal.

14. Use the ***print-level*** option to set the depth level to **2**, and observe how the result is printed:

```
user=> (set! *print-level* 2)
2
user=> (update-in gemstone-db [:diamond :stock] dec)
{:ruby {:name "Ruby", :stock 120, :sales #, :properties #}, :emerald {:name
"Emerald", :stock 85, :sales #, :properties #}, :diamond {:name "Diamond", :stock
9, :sales #, :properties #}, :moissanite {:name "Moissanite", :stock 45, :sales #,
:properties #}}
```

The diamond stock has indeed decreased by 1, from 10 to 9.

15. We can use the **update-in** function again, this time in combination with **conj** and a **client-id** to add in the **sales** vector. Let's try an example with the diamond gem and **client-id 999**:

```
user=> (update-in gemstone-db [:diamond :sales] conj 999)
{:ruby {:name "Ruby", :stock 120, :sales #, :properties #}, :emerald {:name
"Emerald", :stock 85, :sales #, :properties #}, :diamond {:name "Diamond", :stock
10, :sales #, :properties #}, :moissanite {:name "Moissanite", :stock 45, :sales #,
:properties #}}
```

It might have worked, but we cannot see the **sales** vector as the data has been truncated by the ***print-level*** option.

16. Set ***print-level*** to **nil** to reset the option, and reevaluate the previous expression:

```
user=> (set! *print-level* nil)
nil
user=> (update-in gemstone-db [:diamond :sales] conj 999)
{:ruby {:name "Ruby", :stock 120, :sales [1990 3644 6376 4918 7882 6747 7495 8573
5097 1712], :properties {:dispersion 0.018, :hardness 9.0, :refractive-index [1.77
1.78], :color "Near colorless through pink through all shades of red to a deep
crimson"}}, :emerald {:name "Emerald", :stock 85, :sales [6605 2373 104 4764 9023],
:properties {:dispersion 0.014, :hardness 7.5, :refractive-index [1.57 1.58], :color
"Green shades to colorless"}}, :diamond {:name "Diamond", :stock 10, :sales [8295
329 5960 6118 4189 3436 9833 8870 9700 7182 7061 1579 999], :properties {:dispersion
0.044, :hardness 10, :refractive-index [2.417 2.419], :color "Typically yellow,
brown or gray to colorless"}}, :moissanite {:name "Moissanite", :stock 45, :sales
[7761 3220], :properties {:dispersion 0.104, :hardness 9.5, :refractive-index [2.65
2.69], :color "Colorless, green, yellow"}}}
```

Notice that our diamond **sales** vector now contains the value **999**.

17. Now let's write our pure function, which combines the two operations (updating the stock and the clients):

```
(defn sell
  [db gemstone client-id]
  (let [clients-updated-db (update-in db [gemstone :sales] conj client-id)]
    (update-in clients-updated-db [gemstone :stock] dec)))
```

18. Test your newly created function by selling a `:moissanite` to **client-id 123**:

```
user=> (sell gemstone-db :moissanite 123)
{:ruby {:name "Ruby", :stock 120, :sales [1990 3644 6376 4918 7882 6747 7495 8573
5097 1712], :properties {:dispersion 0.018, :hardness 9.0, :refractive-index [1.77
1.78], :color "Near colorless through pink through all shades of red to a deep
crimson"}}, :emerald {:name "Emerald", :stock 85, :sales [6605 2373 104 4764 9023],
:properties {:dispersion 0.014, :hardness 7.5, :refractive-index [1.57 1.58], :color
"Green shades to colorless"}}, :diamond {:name "Diamond", :stock 10, :sales [8295
329 5960 6118 4189 3436 9833 8870 9700 7182 7061 1579], :properties {:dispersion
0.044, :hardness 10, :refractive-index [2.417 2.419], :color "Typically yellow,
brown or gray to colorless"}}, :moissanite {:name "Moissanite", :stock 44, :sales
[7761 3220 123], :properties {:dispersion 0.104, :hardness 9.5, :refractive-index
[2.65 2.69], :color "Colorless, green, yellow"}}}
```

Notice that the **sales** vector of the moissanite entity now contains the value **123**.

In this exercise, we did not really "update" data but merely derived new data structures from others because of their immutability. Even if we work mostly with immutable data types, Clojure offers simple mechanisms that allow you to persist information. In the following activity, you will create a database that can be read and updated with the techniques acquired in this chapter, and we will even provide a helper function to make the database persistent.

Activity 2.01: Creating a Simple In-Memory Database

In this activity, we are going to create our own implementation of an in-memory database. After all, if the "Sparkling" shop owner was able to do it, then it shouldn't be a problem for us!

Our database interface will live in the Clojure REPL. We will implement functions to create and drop tables, as well as to insert and read records.

For the purposes of this activity, we will provide a couple of helper functions to help you maintain the state of the database in memory:

```
(def memory-db (atom {}))
(defn read-db [] @memory-db)
(defn write-db [new-db] (reset! memory-db new-db))
```

We use an **atom** but you don't need to understand how atoms work for now, as they are explained in great detail later in the book. You just need to know that it will keep a reference to our database in memory, and use two helper functions, **read-db** and **write-db**, to read and persist a Hash Map in memory.

As guidance, we would like the data structure to have this shape:

```
{:table-1 {:data [] :indexes {}} :table-2 {:data [] :indexes {}}
```

For example, if we used our database in a grocery store to save clients, fruits, and purchases, we can imagine that it would contain the data in this manner:

```
{
  :clients {
    :data [{:id 1 :name "Bob" :age 30} {:id 2 :name "Alice" :age 24}]
    :indexes {:id {1 0, 2 1}}
  },
  :fruits {
    :data [{:name "Lemon" :stock 10} {:name "Coconut" :stock 3}]
    :indexes {:name {"Lemon" 0, "Coconut" 1}}
  },
  :purchases {
    :data [{:id 1 :user-id 1 :item "Coconut"} {:id 1 :user-id 2 :item "Lemon"}]
    :indexes {:id {1 0, 2 1}}
  }
}
```

Storing data and indexes separately allows multiple indexes to be created without having to duplicate the actual data.

The **indexes** map stores an association between the index key and its position in the **data** vector for each index key. In the fruits table, "Lemon" is the first record of the **data** vector, so the value in the **:name** index is 0.

These steps will help you perform the activity:

1. Create the helper functions. You can get the Hash Map by executing the **read-db** function with no arguments, and write to the database by executing the **write-db** function with a Hash Map as an argument.

2. Start by creating the **create-table** function. This function should take one parameter: the table name. It should add a new key (the table name) at the root of our Hash Map database, and the value should be another Hash Map containing two entries: an empty vector at the **data** key and an empty Hash Map at the **indexes** key.

3. Test that your **create-table** function works.

4. Create a **drop-table** function such that it takes one parameter as well - the table name. It should remove a table, including all its data and indexes from our database.

5. Test that your **drop-table** function works.

6. Create an **insert** function. This function should take three parameters: **table**, **record**, and **id-key**. The **record** parameter is a Hash Map, and **id-key** corresponds to a key in the record map that will be used as a unique index. For now, we will not handle cases when a table does not exist or when an index key already exists in a given table.

   Try to use a **let** block to divide the work of the **insert** function in multiple steps:

   In a **let** statement, create a binding for the value of the database, retrieved with **read-db**.

   In the same **let** statement, create a second binding for the new value of the database (after adding the record in the **data** vector).

   In the same **let** statement, retrieve the index at which the record was inserted by counting the number of elements in the **data** vector.

   In the body of the **let** statement, update the index at **id-key** and write the resulting map to the database with **write-db**.

7. To verify that your **insert** function works, try to use it multiple times to insert new records.

8. Create a **select-*** function that will return all the records of a table passed as a parameter.

9. Create a **select-*-where** function that takes three arguments: **table-name**, **field**, and **field-value**. The function should use the index map to retrieve the index of the record in the data vector and return the element.

10. Modify the **insert** function to reject any index duplicate. When a record with **id-key** already exists in the **indexes** map, we should not modify the database and print an error message to the user.

On completing the activity, the output should be similar to this:

```
user=> (create-table :fruits)
{:clients {:data [], :indexes {}}, :fruits {:data [], :indexes {}}}
user=> (insert :fruits {:name "Pear" :stock 3} :name)
Record with :name Pear already exists. Aborting
user=> (select-* :fruits)
[{:name "Pear", :stock 3} {:name "Apricot", :stock 30} {:name "Grapefruit", :stock
6}]
user=> (select-*-where :fruits :name "Apricot")
{:name "Apricot", :stock 30}
```

In this activity, we have used our new knowledge about reading and updating both simple and deeply nested data structures to implement a simple in-memory database. This was not an easy feat – well done!

> **Note**
>
> The solution for this activity can be found on page 682.

Summary

In this chapter, we discovered the concept of immutability. We learned about Clojure's simple data types, as well as their implementation on different host platforms. We discovered the most common types of collections and sequences: maps, sets, vectors, and lists. We saw how to use them with generic collections and sequence operations. We learned how to read and update complex structures of nested collections. We also learned about the standard functions for using collection data structures, as well as more advanced usage with deeply nested data structures. In the next chapter, we will learn advanced techniques for working with functions.

3

Functions in Depth

Overview

In this chapter, we will take a deep dive into Clojure's functions. We discover destructuring techniques and advanced call signatures. We take a closer look at the first-class aspect of functions and learn how it enables functional composition, as well as advanced polymorphism techniques. This chapter teaches techniques that will significantly improve the conciseness and readability of your code. It lays down a solid basis to prepare you for the second part of this book about manipulating collections.

By the end of this chapter, you will be able to implement features such as destructuring, variadic functions and multimethods when writing functions.

Introduction

Clojure is a functional programming language, and functions are of primordial importance to the Clojure programmer. In functional programming, we avoid mutating the state of a program, which, as we have seen in the previous chapter, is greatly facilitated by Clojure's immutable data structures. We also tend to do everything with functions, such that we need functions to be able to do pretty much everything. We say that Clojure functions are **first-class citizens** because we can pass them to other functions, store them in variables, or return them from other functions: we also call them first-class functions. Consider an e-commerce application, for example, where a user is presented with a list of items with different search filters and sorting options. Developing such a filtering engine with flags and conditions in an imperative programming way can quickly become unnecessarily complex; however, it can be elegantly expressed with functional programming. Functional composition is a great way to simply and efficiently implement such a filtering engine, for each filter (for example, the price, color, size of an item, and so on), the logic can be contained within a function and those functions could be simply combined or composed as a user interacts with an interface.

In this chapter, you will learn how to master functions. We will start with destructuring techniques, which can notably be used in function parameters, then we will move on to advanced call signatures including functions with multiple arities and a variable number of arguments. Then, we will dive into the first-class aspect of functions and learn how they enable functional composition. Finally, we will explain advanced polymorphism techniques with multimethods and dispatch functions.

Destructuring

Destructuring allows you to remove data elements from their structure or disassemble a structure. It is a technique that improves the readability and conciseness of your code by providing a better tool for a widely used pattern. There are two main ways of destructuring data: sequentially (with vectors) and associatively (with maps).

Imagine that we need to write a function that prints a formatted string given a tuple of coordinates, for example, the tuple [48.9615, 2.4372]. We could write the following function:

```
(defn print-coords [coords]
  (let [lat (first coords)
        lon (last coords)]
    (println (str "Latitude: " lat " - " "Longitude: " lon))))
```

This **print-coords** function takes a tuple of coordinates as a parameter and prints out the coordinates to the console in a nicely formatted string, for example, **Latitude: 48.9615 – Longitude: 2.4372.**

What we are essentially doing when binding the first element to **lat** and the second to **lon** is destructuring: we are taking each element out of their sequential data structure. This use case is very common, and Clojure provides a built-in syntax for destructuring data structures to bind their values to symbols.

We could rewrite the **print-coords** function with a sequential destructuring technique as follows:

```
(defn print-coords [coords]
  (let [[lat lon] coords]
    (println (str "Latitude: " lat " - " "Longitude: " lon))))
```

Observe how the preceding example is shorter and more expressive than the one before. We didn't need to use a function like **first** or **last**, we simply expressed the symbols we wanted to retrieve.

The two functions are equivalent. **lat** is "mapped" to the first element of the vector and **lon** to the second. This other, simpler example might be more visually helpful:

```
user=>(let
;;
;;       [1 2 3]
;;        | | |
      [[a b c] [1 2 3]] (println a b c))
1 2 3
nil
```

Notice how the bindings are created according to both the sequential order of the vector and the order of the symbols defined in vector **[a b c]**. The symbol values are then printed out to the console.

A list, which is a sequential data structure, can be similarly disassembled:

```
user=> (let [[a b c] '(1 2 3)] (println a b c))
1 2 3
nil
```

Consider the same example of printing the coordinates of an airport, but this time we receive the data as a map rather than a tuple. The data has the following shape: **{:lat 48.9615, :lon 2.4372, :code 'LFPB', :name "Paris Le Bourget Airport"}.**

We could write the following function:

```
(defn print-coords [airport]
  (let [lat (:lat airport)
        lon (:lon airport)
        name (:name airport)]
    (println (str name " is located at Latitude: " lat " - " "Longitude: " lon))))
```

This function retrieves the values from the **airport** map by using the keywords as functions in the **let** expression. We can spot the repetitive pattern when binding **lat**, **lon**, and **name**. Similarly, when the data structure we want to disassemble is associative (a **map**), we can use an associative *destructuring* technique. The function can be rewritten using associative destructuring, as follows:

```
(defn print-coords [airport]
  (let [{lat :lat lon :lon airport-name :name} airport]
    (println (str airport-name " is located at Latitude: " lat " - " "Longitude: " lon))))
```

With this technique, we are creating bindings by mapping the symbols to the keys inside the map. The **lat** symbol now contains the value in the airport map at the key :lat, **lon** is mapped to the key :lon, and, finally, the **airport-name** symbol is mapped to the key :name.

When the keys and symbols can all have the same name, there is a shorter syntax available:

```
(defn print-coords [airport]
  (let [{:keys [lat lon name]} airport]
    (println (str name " is located at Latitude: " lat " - " "Longitude: " lon))))
```

The preceding destructuring syntax indicates looking for the **lat**, **lon**, and **name** keys inside the **airport** map and binding them to symbols with the same name. The syntax might look a little bit surprising, but it is a widely used technique in Clojure. We will use it in the next exercise so that you can learn how to use it.

Let's see our final function in action:

```
user=> (def airport {:lat 48.9615, :lon 2.4372, :code 'LFPB', :name "Paris Le Bourget Airport"})
#'user/airport
(defn print-coords [airport]
  (let [{:keys [lat lon name]} airport]
    (println (str name " is located at Latitude: " lat " - " "Longitude: " lon))))
```

```
#'user/print-coords
user=> (print-coords airport)
Paris Le Bourget Airport is located at Latitude: 48.9615 - Longitude: 2.4372
nil
```

In the preceding example, the **print-coords** function destructures the airport **map** in the **let** expression and binds the values **48.9615**, **2.4372**, and **Paris Le Bourget Airport** to the symbols (respectively) **lat**, **lon**, and **name**. Those values are then printed out to the console with the **println** function (which returns **nil**).

Now that we've discovered the basics of destructuring and its utility, we can move on to the REPL, start practicing, and learn even more advanced destructuring techniques.

Exercise 3.01: Parsing Fly Vector's Data with Sequential Destructuring

For the purpose of this exercise, imagine that we are building a flight-booking platform application. For our first prototype, we just want to parse and print flight data that we receive from our partners. Our first partner, Fly Vector, has not yet discovered the power of associative data structures and they send us all their data in the form of Vectors. Luckily, they have comprehensive documentation. I have done the heavy lifting of reading the hundreds of pages of the data format specification for you and here is what it boils down to:

- A coordinate point is a tuple of latitude and longitude, for example: **[48.9615, 2.4372]**.

- A flight is a tuple of two coordinate points, for example: **[[48.9615, 2.4372], [37.742, -25.6976]]**.

- A booking consists of some information followed by one or multiple flights (up to three). The first item is Fly Vector's internal ID for the booking, the second item is the name of the passenger, and the third is some sensitive information that Fly Vector asked us not to parse or even look at (they couldn't update their system to remove the information). Finally, the rest of the vector consists of the flight coordinates data, for example:

```
[
    1425,
    "Bob Smith",
    "Allergic to unsalted peanuts only",
    [[48.9615, 2.4372], [37.742, -25.6976]],
    [[37.742, -25.6976], [48.9615, 2.4372]]
]
```

That should be enough information for us to develop the prototype, so let's get started:

1. Open a REPL and bind the sample booking data to the **booking** symbol:

    ```
    user=> (def booking [1425, "Bob Smith", "Allergic to unsalted peanuts only",
    [[48.9615, 2.4372], [37.742, -25.6976]], [[37.742, -25.6976], [48.9615, 2.4372]]])
    #'user/booking
    ```

2. Start developing our parsing function by experimenting with destructuring. Create a **let** block and define the binding as follows, printing out the result with **println**:

    ```
    user=> (let [[id customer-name sensitive-info flight1 flight2 flight3] booking]
    (println id customer-name flight1 flight2 flight3))
    1425 Bob Smith [[48.9615 2.4372] [37.742 -25.6976]] [[37.742 -25.6976] [48.9615
    2.4372]] nil
    nil
    ```

    Notice that **flight3** was bound to the value **nil**. This is because the data is shorter than the bindings defined, and it is both valid and useful to be able to bind only values that exist.

    Similarly, if the booking vector contained extra data, it would be ignored.

3. Remember that **conj** takes a collection and some elements as arguments and returns a new collection with those elements added to the collection. Add two flights in the booking vector with **conj** and parse the data using the same destructuring expression:

    ```
    user=> (let [big-booking (conj booking [[37.742, -25.6976], [51.1537, 0.1821]]
    [[51.1537, 0.1821], [48.9615, 2.4372]])
            [id customer-name sensitive-info flight1 flight2 flight3] big-booking]
      (println id customer-name flight1 flight2 flight3))
    1425 Bob Smith [[48.9615 2.4372] [37.742 -25.6976]] [[37.742 -25.6976] [48.9615
    2.4372]] [[37.742 -25.6976] [51.1537 0.1821]]
    nil
    ```

    Notice how the last flight was simply ignored and not printed out. That's another useful trait of destructuring and another sign of Clojure's dynamism and practicality.

4. In the data received, we don't really care about the Fly Vector internal ID and we don't want to parse the sensitive information. This can be simply ignored by using an underscore, _, instead of a symbol:

    ```
    user=> (let [[_ customer-name _ flight1 flight2 flight3] booking] (println customer-
    name flight1 flight2 flight3))
    Bob Smith [[48.9615 2.4372] [37.742 -25.6976]] [[37.742 -25.6976] [48.9615 2.4372]]
    nil
    nil
    ```

Great, we now understand how to ignore some parts of the data with destructuring.

Just printing the array of coordinates is not very readable, so until we have a better way of printing out flights, we would like to simply display the number of flights in the booking. Surely, we could test **flight1**, **flight2**, and **flight3** for the presence of a value but there's another aspect of destructuring that we could use: the "remaining" parts of the sequence. By using the **&** character followed by a symbol, we can bind the remaining part of a sequence to a given symbol.

5. Bind the **flights** sequence to a **flights** symbol by using the **&** character, then display the number of flights as follows:

```
user=> (let [[_ customer-name _ & flights] booking]
   (println (str customer-name " booked " (count flights) " flights.")))
Bob Smith booked 2 flights.
nil
```

Notice that **flights** is now a collection and, therefore, we can use the **count** function with it.

Destructuring is very powerful and can also disassemble nested data structures. To parse and print the flight details, let's create a separate function to keep the code clear and readable.

6. Create a **print-flight** function that disassembles a flight path using nested destructuring and print out a nicely formatted flight itinerary:

```
user=>
(defn print-flight [flight]
   (let [[[lat1 lon1] [lat2 lon2]] flight]
      (println (str "Flying from: Lat " lat1 " Lon " lon1 " Flying to: Lat " lat2 "
Lon " lon2))))
#'user/print-flight
user=> (print-flight [[48.9615, 2.4372], [37.742 -25.6976]])
Flying from: Lat 48.9615 Lon 2.4372 Flying to: Lat 37.742 Lon -25.6976
```

Notice how we dug into the nested vectors contained in **flight** to retrieve the coordinate values inside the coordinate tuples, by simply using nested vector literal notation. However, the nested vectors in the **let** bindings can be slightly hard to read.

7. Rewrite the **print-flight** function by decomposing the steps in multiple **let** bindings:

```
user=>
(defn print-flight [flight]
  (let [[departure arrival] flight
        [lat1 lon1] departure
        [lat2 lon2] arrival]
    (println (str "Flying from: Lat " lat1 " Lon " lon1 " Flying to: Lat " lat2 "
Lon " lon2))))
#'user/print-flight
user=> (print-flight [[48.9615, 2.4372], [37.742 -25.6976]])
Flying from: Lat 48.9615 Lon 2.4372 Flying to: Lat 37.742 Lon -25.6976
nil
```

In the preceding example, we have created two intermediate bindings using sequential destructuring: **departure** and **arrival**. Those two bindings contain coordinates tuples that we can destructure further to create the latitude and longitude bindings **lat1**, **lon1**, **lat2**, and **lon2**.

8. Finally, let's write the **print-booking** function by combining the code we have written so far:

```
(defn print-booking [booking]
  (let [[_ customer-name _ & flights] booking]
    (println (str customer-name " booked " (count flights) " flights."))
    (let [[flight1 flight2 flight3] flights]
      (when flight1 (print-flight flight1))
      (when flight2 (print-flight flight2))
      (when flight3 (print-flight flight3)))))
#'user/print-booking
user=> (print-booking booking)
Bob Smith booked 2 flights.
Flying from: Lat 48.9615 Lon 2.4372 Flying to: Lat 37.742 Lon -25.6976
Flying from: Lat 37.742 Lon -25.6976 Flying to: Lat 48.9615 Lon 2.4372
nil
```

Great job! In this exercise, we've successfully used *sequential destructuring* to parse and retrieve data from a vector and improve the readability and conciseness of our code. Now, let's move on to the next exercise, where we will use *associative destructuring*.

Exercise 3.02: Parsing MapJet Data with Associative Destructuring

Let's continue with our flight booking platform application. Now we would like to develop the same parser for another partner called MapJet. You might have guessed, MapJet has discovered the power of associative data structures and are sending us nice and intelligible data structures, which consist of both maps and vectors. Now, the data is self-explanatory and even if MapJet provides very detailed documentation, we won't even bother reading it.

Let's have a look at the data shape of a sample booking:

```
{
  :id 8773
  :customer-name "Alice Smith"
  :catering-notes "Vegetarian on Sundays"
  :flights [
    {
      :from {:lat 48.9615 :lon 2.4372 :name "Paris Le Bourget Airport"},
      :to {:lat 37.742 :lon -25.6976 :name "Ponta Delgada Airport"}},
    {
      :from {:lat 37.742 :lon -25.6976 :name "Ponta Delgada Airport"},
      :to {:lat 48.9615 :lon 2.4372 :name "Paris Le Bourget Airport"}}
  ]
}
```

First, let's agree on the fact that maps are a great way to exchange data. They are very readable for us humans, and simple to parse for our programs. Now, let's get back to the REPL and see how associative destructuring can help us manipulate the data:

1. Bind the sample booking map to the `mapjet-booking` symbol as follows:

```
user=>
(def mapjet-booking
  {
    :id 8773
    :customer-name "Alice Smith"
    :catering-notes "Vegetarian on Sundays"
    :flights [
      {
        :from {:lat 48.9615 :lon 2.4372 :name "Paris Le Bourget Airport"},
        :to {:lat 37.742 :lon -25.6976 :name "Ponta Delgada Airport"}},
      {
```

```
                :from {:lat 37.742 :lon -25.6976 :name "Ponta Delgada Airport"},
                :to {:lat 48.9615 :lon 2.4372 :name "Paris Le Bourget Airport"}}
      ]
   })
#'user/mapjet-booking
```

2. Using associative destructuring, print the booking summary as we did for Fly Vector (the name of the customer and the number of flights):

```
user=> (let [{:keys [customer-name flights]} mapjet-booking] (println (str customer-name " booked " (count flights) " flights.")))
Alice Smith booked 2 flights.
nil
```

By using the shorter and non-repetitive syntax with :**keys**, we were able to fetch the keys inside the map and bind their values to symbols with the same name.

3. Let's write a **print-mapjet-flight** function to print the flight details:

```
user=> (defn print-mapjet-flight [flight]
   (let [{:keys [from to]} flight
         {lat1 :lat lon1 :lon} from
         {lat2 :lat lon2 :lon} to]
      (println (str "Flying from: Lat " lat1 " Lon " lon1 " Flying to: Lat " lat2 " Lon " lon2))))
user=> (print-mapjet-flight (first (:flights mapjet-booking)))
Flying from: Lat 48.9615 Lon 2.4372 Flying to: Lat 37.742 Lon -25.6976
nil
```

Notice that we cannot use the shorter syntax for extracting coordinates because the names **lat** and **lon** would conflict; therefore, we used the normal syntax, allowing us to explicitly declare a new binding to symbols with different names.

As with vectors, we can nest destructuring expressions, and even combine the two techniques.

4. Let's rewrite the **print-mapjet-flight** function, but this time we are going to nest our associative destructuring expressions:

```
user=>(defn print-mapjet-flight [flight]
  (let [{{lat1 :lat lon1 :lon} :from,
         {lat2 :lat lon2 :lon} :to} flight]
    (println (str "Flying from: Lat " lat1 " Lon " lon1 " Flying to: Lat " lat2 "
Lon " lon2))))
#'user/print-mapjet-flight
user=> (print-mapjet-flight (first (:flights mapjet-booking)))
Flying from: Lat 48.9615 Lon 2.4372 Flying to: Lat 37.742 Lon -25.6976
nil
```

The preceding example is slightly complicated to read so don't worry if it looks a bit confusing at first. Think of the key of a destructuring map as the target, and the source as the value, as follows: **{target1 source1 target2 source2}**. The target can either be a symbol, or another destructuring map like this: **{{target3 source3} source1 {target4 source4} source2}**. Notice, in this last expression, how we just bind values to the symbols in the innermost map (**target3** and **target4**). This is what we just did in the **print-mapjet-flight** function: we extracted the nested values of latitude and longitude for both coordinate points.

5. Write the final function for printing MapJet bookings, using the code to print the booking summary to the console. It should produce a similar output to Fly Vector's **print-booking** function, first printing the number of flights and then printing each flight individually with **print-mapjet-flight** as follows:

```
user=>
(defn print-mapjet-booking [booking]
  (let [{:keys [customer-name flights]} booking]
    (println (str customer-name " booked " (count flights) " flights."))
    (let [[flight1 flight2 flight3] flights]
      (when flight1 (print-mapjet-flight flight1)) flights
      (when flight2 (print-mapjet-flight flight2))
      (when flight3 (print-mapjet-flight flight3)))))
user=> (print-mapjet-booking mapjet-booking)
```

The output is as follows:

```
Alice Smith booked 2 flights.
Flying from: Lat 48.9615 Lon 2.4372 Flying to: Lat 37.742 Lon -25.6976
Flying from: Lat 37.742 Lon -25.6976 Flying to: Lat 48.9615 Lon 2.4372
```

It works! We have now finished our first prototype. In this exercise, we have implemented a **Map** parser that prints out data that has been destructured to the console. Well done!

Destructuring techniques are essential because they can make our code more concise and more readable. Additionally, the data that our programs have to deal with often comes from external data sources, and we don't always own the shape of the data we need to handle. Having a powerful tool to dig into various data structures significantly improves our quality of life as programmers.

However, the code we have written in the previous exercise feels somehow repetitive; the two **print-booking** functions, for example, have a lot in common. With what we currently know, it would be difficult to refactor this code. But don't worry, the techniques we are going to learn in the next topics will allow you to write even more elegant code, with less repetition, less code, and therefore fewer bugs.

Advanced Call Signatures

So far, we have been declaring functions with one arity (with only a fixed number of arguments), and simply binding the arguments passed to a function to some parameter names. However, Clojure has a few techniques to allow more flexibility when calling functions.

Destructuring Function Parameters

First, everything we have just learned about destructuring applies to function parameters. Yes, you read that correctly – we can use destructuring techniques right in the function parameter declaration! As promised, here's our first stab at refactoring the **print-flight** functions from the previous exercise. Observe, in the following example, how sequential destructuring is used directly in the function parameters:

```
user=>
(defn print-flight
  [[[lat1 lon1] [lat2 lon2]]]
    (println (str "Flying from: Lat " lat1 " Lon " lon1 " Flying to: Lat " lat2 " Lon "
lon2)))
#'user/print-flight
user=> (print-flight [[48.9615, 2.4372], [37.742 -25.6976]])
Flying from: Lat 48.9615 Lon 2.4372 Flying to: Lat 37.742 Lon -25.6976
nil
```

Notice how we got rid of the **let** expression. Similarly, we can do the same for **print-mapjet-flight**, with associative destructuring used in the function parameters:

```
user=>
(defn print-mapjet-flight
  [{{lat1 :lat lon1 :lon} :from, {lat2 :lat lon2 :lon} :to}]
    (println (str "Flying from: Lat " lat1 " Lon " lon1 " Flying to: Lat " lat2 " Lon "
lon2)))
#'user/print-mapjet-flight
user=> (print-mapjet-flight { :from {:lat 48.9615 :lon 2.4372}, :to {:lat 37.742 :lon
-25.6976} })
Flying from: Lat 48.9615 Lon 2.4372 Flying to: Lat 37.742 Lon -25.6976
```

Once again, we got rid of the **let** expression and destructured the parameter right away from the function arguments. Great – that is one new way of defining function parameters and improving our code even further.

Arity Overloading

Second, Clojure supports "arity overloading," which means that we can *overload* a function with another function of the same name by specifying extra parameters to the new function. Those two functions have the same name but different implementations, and the function body to execute is chosen based on the number of arguments provided upon a function call. Here is an example:

```
user=>
(defn no-overloading []
  (println "Same old, same old..."))
#'user/no-overloading
user=>
(defn overloading
  ([] "No argument")
  ([a] (str "One argument: " a))
  ([a b] (str "Two arguments: a: " a " b: " b)))
#'user/overloading
```

Notice how the different function implementations are defined. In the **no-overloading** function, which is how we are used to creating functions, there are no extra parentheses around the parameter declaration (which comes just after the function name). Whereas in the **overloading** function, each implementation is surrounded by parentheses, starting with the parameter declaration.

Let's see how the multi-arity **overloading** function plays out:

```
user=> (overloading)
"No argument"
```

In the preceding code, no arguments were passed; therefore, the first implementation of the **overloading** function is called.

Consider the following code:

```
user=> (overloading 1)
"One argument: 1"
```

In this case, one argument is passed to the **overloading** function, so the second implementation is called.

```
user=> (overloading 1 2)
"Two arguments: a: 1 b: 2"
user=> (overloading 1 nil)
"Two arguments: a: 1 b: "
```

In the preceding code, two arguments are passed, so the third implementation of the **overloading** function is called.

```
user=> (overloading 1 2 3)
Execution error (ArityException) at user/eval412 (REPL:1).
Wrong number of args (3) passed to: user/overloading
```

Finally, an incorrect number of arguments produce the usual arity exception.

You might (legitimately) wonder how this is useful, and why not just declare different functions? In fact, when defining multiple arities for the same function, you are saying that the functions are essentially the same, that they are doing a similar job, but the execution slightly varies based on the number of arguments. It can also be useful to provide default values.

Consider the following code for a new little fantasy game called **Parenthmazes**, declaring a map of weapons associated with their damage and a **strike** function to compute the new state of an **enemy** entity:

```
user=> (def weapon-damage {:fists 10 :staff 35 :sword 100 :cast-iron-saucepan 150})
#'user/weapon-damage
user=>
(defn strike
  ([enemy] (strike enemy :fists))
  ([enemy weapon]
    (let [damage (weapon weapon-damage)]
      (update enemy :health - damage))))
#'user/strike
```

In the preceding example, we start by defining a **HashMap** and binding it to the **weapon-damage** symbol. The second expression is the definition of the **strike** function, which subtracts damage from an **enemy** entity, retrieving the amount of damage in the **weapon-damage** map. Observe that the **strike** function has two implementations. The first implementation contains only one parameter, **enemy**, and the second implementation has two parameters: **enemy** and **weapon**. Notice how the first implementation is calling the second one by providing an extra parameter. Therefore, when calling the **strike** function with only one argument, the default value, `:fists`, will be provided:

```
user=> (strike {:name "n00b-hunter" :health 100})
{:name "n00b-hunter", :health 90}
```

Observe that the function was called with one parameter only (the **enemy** entity), which therefore went through the one-parameter implementation of the function, using `:fists` as a default value and returning an enemy with 90 points of health left (because fists do 10 points worth of damage):

```
user=> (strike {:name "n00b-hunter" :health 100} :sword)
{:name "n00b-hunter", :health 0}
user=> (strike {:name "n00b-hunter" :health 100} :cast-iron-saucepan)
{:name "n00b-hunter", :health -50}
```

In the preceding example, the **strike** function was called directly with the two-arity implementation, because the second parameter, **weapon**, was explicitly provided.

Variadic Functions

There is a final secret left to reveal regarding function parameters. With what we have learned about function arity, how would you define the parameters of the **str** function, for example?

It seems to take an infinite number of parameters. You might remember using **str** like this:

```
user=> (str "Concatenating " "is " "difficult " "to " "spell " "but " "easy " "to " "use!")
"Concatenating is difficult to spell but easy to use!"
```

But surely, it isn't implemented with overloading like this **(defn str ([s] ...) ([s1 s2] ...) ([s1 s2 s3] ...) ([s1 s2 s3 s4] …))** and so on... Then, what is happening in this case?

This is the destructuring technique coming back into play. Remember that we can use the **&** character to bind the remainder of a sequence to a data structure? It works similarly with function arguments, and we can create a data structure from the arguments passed to a function with the **&** character. This is how you can create variadic functions (functions that take a variable number of arguments), and this is how the **str** function is implemented.

Look at how the documentation describes the **str** function:

```
user=> (doc str)
-------------------------
clojure.core/str
([] [x] [x & ys])
  With no args, returns the empty string. With one arg x, returns
  x.toString().  (str nil) returns the empty string. With more than
  one arg, returns the concatenation of the str values of the args.
nil
```

Notice the declaration of its different arities. It accepts either no element, **[]**, one element, **[x]**, or any number of elements, **[x & ys]**.

Let's try to use this new knowledge to create a function that prints a welcome message to the new player of **Parenthmazes**:

```
user=>
(defn welcome
  [player & friends]
  (println (str "Welcome to the Parenthmazes " player "!"))
  (when (seq friends)
    (println (str "Sending " (count friends) " friend request(s) to the following
players: " (clojure.string/join ", " friends)))))
#'user/welcome
```

Observe how we used the destructuring technique right in the function parameters, binding any arguments that come after **player** to the **friends** collection. Now, let's try to use our function with one and multiple arguments:

```
user=> (welcome "Jon")
Welcome to the Parenthmazes Jon!
nil
user=> (welcome "Jon" "Arya" "Tyrion" "Petyr")
Welcome to the Parenthmazes Jon!
Sending 3 friend request(s) to the following players: Arya, Tyrion, Petyr
nil
```

Notice that when more than one argument is passed to the **welcome** function, the **friends** symbol is bound to a sequence containing the rest of the arguments.

> **Note**
>
> The **seq** function can be used to get a sequence from a collection. In the **welcome** function, we use the **seq** function to test whether a collection contains elements. That's because **seq** returns **nil** when the collection passed as a parameter is empty. **(if (seq (coll))** is a commonly used pattern that you should use instead of **(if (not (empty? coll)))**.

We could improve this function slightly. Instead of testing whether **friends** is empty, we could also take advantage of the multi-arity technique:

```
user=>
(defn welcome
    ([player] (println (str "Welcome to Parenthmazes (single-player mode), " player "!")))
    ([player & friends]
        (println (str "Welcome to Parenthmazes (multi-player mode), " player "!"))
        (println (str "Sending " (count friends) " friend request(s) to the following
players: " (clojure.string/join ", " friends)))))
#'user/welcome
```

Notice how, this time, two **welcome** functions were defined, one with only one **player** parameter, and a second one with an unlimited number of parameters that will be bound to the **friends** symbol. Separating the functions like this improves the clarity of the code by being more explicit about the intent of the function as well as removing the conditional expression with **when**.

Let's try the **welcome** function one last time:

```
user=> (welcome "Jon")
Welcome to Parenthmazes (single-player mode), Jon!
nil
user=> (welcome "Jon" "Arya" "Tyrion" "Petyr")
Welcome to Parenthmazes (multi-player mode), Jon!
Sending 3 friend request(s) to the following players: Arya, Tyrion, Petyr
nil
```

Great – the function call was dispatched to the right function according to the number of parameters.

Exercise 3.03: Multi-arity and Destructuring with Parenthmazes

In this exercise, we will continue working on the **Parenthmazes** game by adding new features, notably improving our **strike** function to implement a healing mechanism. We would also like to add the concept of armor, which can reduce the damage suffered.

Get ready for the great battle between Gnomes and Trolls in this new version of **Parenthmazes**.

1. To begin, start a REPL and your favorite code editor next to it, and create the **weapon-damage** map, which contains damage information for each weapon:

```
user=> (def weapon-damage {:fists 10.0 :staff 35.0 :sword 100.0 :cast-iron-saucepan
150.0})
#'user/weapon-damage
```

We need this map to look up the amount of damage done when a player strikes an enemy.

2. Now, let's create the **strike** function, which will handle healing when the enemy is in the same camp as us (let's assume for now that we picked the Gnomes' side):

```
user=>
(defn strike
  ([target weapon]
    (let [points (weapon weapon-damage)]
      (if (= :gnomes (:camp target))
        (update target :health + points)
        (update target :health - points)))))
#'user/strike
```

In the preceding function, the new code of the **strike** function is to retrieve which side the target is on by looking up the **:camp** key in the **target** entity. If the **target** belongs to the Gnomes camp, we use the **+** function to increase the health in the **target** entity by x number of **points**. Otherwise, we use **-** to decrease the number of health points in the **target** entity.

3. Create an **enemy** entity and test our newly created **strike** function as follows:

```
user=> (def enemy {:name "Zulkaz", :health 250, :camp :trolls})
#'user/enemy
user=> (strike enemy :sword)
{:name "Zulkaz", :health 150.0, :camp :trolls}
```

Health points were subtracted successfully. Let's see what happens with a friendly player.

4. Create an **ally** entity that belongs to the **:gnomes** camp, and test our newly created **strike** function as follows:

```
user=> (def ally {:name "Carla", :health 80, :camp :gnomes})
#'user/ally
user=> (strike ally :staff)
{:name "Carla", :health 115.0, :camp :gnomes}
```

Health points were added successfully!

Now that we have got the shell of our **strike** function, let's amend it to implement the armor functionality. The **target** entity can contain an **:armor** key, which contains a coefficient used to calculate the final amount of damage. The bigger the number, the better the armor. For example, an armor value of 0.8 for a strike of 100 points results in 20 damage points being inflicted. An armor value of 0.1 results in 90 damage points being inflicted, 0 means no armor, and 1 means invincible.

5. Change the amount of damage inflicted on the target by calculating the damage with the **:armor** value in the **target** entity. If the target has no armor value, set it to **0**. To improve readability, we will use a **let** binding to decompose the damage calculation:

```
user=>
(defn strike
  ([target weapon]
    (let [points (weapon weapon-damage)]
      (if (= :gnomes (:camp target))
        (update target :health + points)
        (let [armor (or (:armor target) 0)
              damage (* points (- 1 armor))]
          (update target :health - damage))))))
#'user/strike
```

In the second branching of the **if** expression, we used a **let** expression to assign a default value to **armor** by using **or**. If **(:armor target)** is nil, the value of armor is 0. The second binding contains the reduced damage based on the armor value.

6. Test the **strike** function to see if it still works with no armor:

```
user=> (strike enemy :cast-iron-saucepan)
{:name "Zulkaz", :health 100.0, :camp :trolls}
```

A cast-iron saucepan does 150 damage, and 250 minus 150 is indeed **100**. Great – it works. Let's move on.

7. Redefine the **enemy** binding to add an armor value and test our **strike** function once again:

```
user=> (def enemy {:name "Zulkaz", :health 250, :armor 0.8, :camp :trolls})
#'user/enemy
user=> (strike enemy :cast-iron-saucepan)
{:name "Zulkaz", :health 220.0, :armor 0.8, :camp :trolls}
```

Great – the damage seems to be reduced according to the armor coefficient. Now we would like to use our associative destructuring technique to retrieve the **camp** and **armor** values directly from the function parameters, and reduce the amount of code in the function's body. The only problem we have is that we still need to return an updated version of the **target** entity, but how could we both destructure the **target** entity and keep a reference of the **target** parameter? Clojure has your back – you can use the special key **:as** to bind the destructured map to a specific name.

8. Modify the **strike** function to use associative destructuring in the function's parameters. Use the special key **:as** to bind the map passed as an argument to the symbol target:

```
user=>
(defn strike
  ([{:keys [camp armor] :as target} weapon]
    (let [points (weapon weapon-damage)]
      (if (= :gnomes camp)
        (update target :health + points)
        (let [damage (* points (- 1 (or armor 0)))]
          (update target :health - damage))))))
#'user/strike
```

There is one other useful feature in associative destructuring that we could take advantage of: the special key **:or**. It permits us to provide a default value for when a key that we want to extract isn't found (instead of binding to **nil**).

9. Add the special key **:or** in the destructured map to provide a default value to the armor key in the target map, add an extra arity to make the **weapon** parameter optional, and finally add some documentation, as follows. Don't forget to wrap each function definition with its own set of parentheses:

```
user=>
(defn strike
  "With one argument, strike a target with a default :fists `weapon`. With two
argument, strike a target with `weapon`.
   Strike will heal a target that belongs to the gnomes camp."
  ([target] (strike target :fists))
```

```
      ([{:keys [camp armor], :or {armor 0}, :as target} weapon]
        (let [points (weapon weapon-damage)]
          (if (= :gnomes camp)
            (update target :health + points)
            (let [damage (* points (- 1 armor))]
              (update target :health - damage)))))))
  #'user/strike
```

10. Ensure that your function still works as expected by testing the different scenarios as follows:

```
user=> (strike enemy)
{:name "Zulkaz", :health 248.0, :armor 0.8, :camp :trolls}
user=> (strike enemy :cast-iron-saucepan)
{:name "Zulkaz", :health 220.0, :armor 0.8, :camp :trolls}
user=> (strike ally :staff)
{:name "Carla", :health 115.0, :camp :gnomes}
```

That concludes this exercise. If you look again at the **strike** function you've just written, it is using some advanced Clojure features, including destructuring, multi-arity functions, and reading and updating maps. By passing a function as an argument in the **update** function, we also used the concept of higher-order functions, which we will explain further in the next section.

Higher-Order Programming

Higher-order programming means that programs, and specifically functions, can operate on other programs or functions, as opposed to first-order programming, where functions operate on data elements such as strings, numbers, and data structures. In practice, it means that a function can take some programming logic as a parameter (another function) and/or return some programming logic to be eventually executed. It is a powerful feature that allows us to compose single, modular units of logic in our programs to reduce duplication and promote the reusability of code.

Writing simpler functions increases their modularity. We want to create simple units of functionality that can be used as small bricks to build our programs with. Writing pure functions reduces the complexity of those bricks, and allows us to craft better, sturdier programs. Pure functions are functions that don't alter the state of our program – they produce no side effects; a pure function also always returns the same value when given the exact same parameters. This combination makes pure functions easy to reason about, build upon, and test. Although Clojure offers ways to modify the state of our program, we should write and use pure functions as much as possible.

First-Class Functions

Let's demonstrate the use of functions as parameters. We used functions as parameters in *Exercise 2.01*, *The Obfuscation Machine* of *Chapter 2, Data Types and Immutability*, with the **clojure.string/replace** function, and also in the preceding exercise, with the **update** function. For example, to divide a value by **2** in a **HashMap**, you can pass an anonymous function that does the division as an argument to the **update** function:

```
user=> (update {:item "Tomato" :price 1.0} :price (fn [x] (/ x 2)))
{:item "Tomato", :price 0.5}
```

Even better, you could simply pass the divide function, **/**, with the argument **2**, as follows:

```
user=> (update {:item "Tomato" :price 1.0} :price / 2)
{:item "Tomato", :price 0.5}
```

Notice that **update** will pass the old value as the first argument to the **/** function (here, the old value is **1.0**) as well as all the extra arguments (here, **2**).

You can operate on any kind of value. For example, to invert the value of a Boolean, use the **not** function:

```
user=> (update {:item "Tomato" :fruit false} :fruit not)
{:item "Tomato", :fruit true}
```

As we've just seen, **update** can take a function as a parameter, but we could also define our own function that takes a function and applies it to a given parameter:

```
user=> (defn operate [f x] (f x))
#'user/operate
user=> (operate inc 2)
3
user=> (operate clojure.string/upper-case "hello.")
"HELLO."
```

In the preceding example, **operate** takes a function, **f**, as a parameter and calls it with the second parameter, **x**. Not very useful, but it shows how simple it is to pass and call a function passed as a parameter. If we wanted to pass any number of arguments, we could use the **&** character as we learned in the previous topic about destructuring:

```
user=> (defn operate [f & args] (f args))
#'user/operate
user=> (operate + 1 2 3)
Execution error (ClassCastException) at java.lang.Class/cast (Class.java:3369).
Cannot cast clojure.lang.ArraySeq to java.lang.Number
```

This time, **operate** seems to accept any number of arguments, but the function call fails because **args** is a sequence. That's because we applied the **f** function to the **args** sequence directly, when what we really wanted was to apply **f** using each element of the sequence as an argument. There is a special function to disassemble a sequence and apply a function to that sequence's elements – the **apply** function:

```
user=> (+ [1 2 3])
Execution error (ClassCastException) at java.lang.Class/cast (Class.java:3369).
Cannot cast clojure.lang.PersistentVector to java.lang.Number
user=> (apply + [1 2 3])
6
```

Notice how **+** does not work on a vector, but by using apply, we call **+**, passing each element of the vector as an argument to **+**.

We can, therefore, use **apply** in our **operate** function to have a fully working function that takes a function, **f**, as a parameter and calls **f** with the rest of the parameters, **args**:

```
user=> (defn operate [f & args] (apply f args))
#'user/operate
user=> (operate str "It " "Should " "Concatenate!")
"It Should Concatenate!"
```

It works! The **str** function was applied to the arguments passed to **str**.

The ability to pass a function as a parameter is one aspect of higher-order functions, but another aspect is the ability of functions to *return* other functions. Consider the following code:

```
user=> (defn random-fn [] (first (shuffle [+ - * /])))
#'user/random-fn
```

The **shuffle** function shuffles an array by sorting its elements randomly, and we then take the first element out of it. In other words, the **random-fn** function returns a random function from the [+ - * /] collection. Notice that the **random-fn** function does not take any parameters:

```
user=> (random-fn 2 3)
Execution error (ArityException) at user/eval277 (REPL:1).
Wrong number of args (2) passed to: user/random-fn
```

But the function returned by **random-fn** expects parameters:

```
user=> ((random-fn) 2 3)
-1
```

In the preceding code, **(random-fn)** returned - so **3** was subtracted from **2**, which results in **-1**.

You can use the **fn?** function to check whether a value passed as a parameter is a function:

```
user=> (fn? random-fn)
true
user=> (fn? (random-fn))
true
```

In this case, observe that both **random-fn** and the value returned by **random-fn** are functions. So, we can call the function returned by **random-fn**, and even bind it to a symbol, as in the example that follows, where we bind the function to the **mysterious-fn** symbol:

```
user=>
(let [mysterious-fn (random-fn)]
  (mysterious-fn 2 3))
6
user=>
(let [mysterious-fn (random-fn)]
  (mysterious-fn 2 3))
2/3
user=>
(let [mysterious-fn (random-fn)]
  (mysterious-fn 2 3))
6
user=>
(let [mysterious-fn (random-fn)]
  (mysterious-fn 2 3))
5
```

Notice how every call to **random-fn** returned a different function. On each step, calling **mysterious-fn** with the same arguments is processed by a different function. Based on the returned values, we can guess that the functions are respectively *, /, *, and +.

It is conceivable but not very common to write functions that return other functions. However, you will often use some of Clojure's core utility functions, which return other functions, and which we are going to present next. Those are worth exploring because they enable functional composition, reusability, and conciseness.

Partial Functions

The first of those core utility functions is **partial**, which takes a function, **f**, as a parameter and any number of arguments, **args1**. It returns a new function, **g**, that can take extra arguments, **args2**. When calling **g** with **args2**, **f** is called with **args1** + **args2**. It may sound complicated, but consider the following example:

```
user=> (def marketing-adder (partial + 0.99))
#'user/marketing-adder
user=> (marketing-adder 10 5)
15.99
```

Calling **(partial + 0.99)** returns a new function that we bind to the **marketing-adder** symbol. When **marketing-adder** is called, it will call **+** with **0.99** and any extra arguments passed to the function. Notice that we used **def** and not **defn**, because we don't need to build a new function – **partial** does it for us.

Here is another example:

```
user=> (def format-price (partial str "€"))
#'user/format-price
user=> (format-price "100")
"€100"
user=> (format-price 10 50)
"€1050"
```

Calling **format-price** will call the **str** function with the first parameter, **"€"**, and then the rest of the parameters. Of course, you could write the same function like this: **(fn [x] (str "€" x))**, but using **partial** is a nice and expressive way of defining functions as functions of other functions.

Composing Functions

Another core utility function is **comp**, short for compose. Take, for example, our **random-fn** function. To retrieve a random number from the collection, we call the **shuffle** function and then the **first** function. If we wanted to implement a **sample** function that does exactly that, we could write the following function:

```
user=> (defn sample [coll] (first (shuffle coll)))
#'user/sample
user=> (sample [1 2 3 4])
2
```

But more elegantly, we could implement the **sample** function with the functional composition utility, **comp**:

```
user=> (def sample (comp first shuffle))
#'user/sample
user=> (sample [1 2 3 4])
4
```

comp is a utility that takes any number of functions as a parameter and returns a new function that calls those functions in order, passing the result of each to the other. Observe that the functions are composed from right to left, so in the preceding example, **shuffle** will be applied before **first**. This is important because the number and types of arguments passed to the chain of functions is often meaningful. For example, if you wanted to compose a function that multiplies numbers and increments the result by one, you would need to pass the **inc** function (increment) as a first argument of the function as follows:

```
user=> ((comp inc *) 2 2)
5
user=> ((comp * inc) 2 2)
Execution error (ArityException) at user/eval405 (REPL:1).
Wrong number of args (2) passed to: clojure.core/inc
```

Notice that when providing **inc** as the last argument of the **comp** function, it calls **(inc 2 2)**, which does not work because **inc** takes only one argument.

Now, let's see how we can combine the use of **partial** and **comp** to compose a **checkout** function with the **format-price** and **marketing-adder** functions that we defined previously. The **checkout** function will first add its parameters by reusing **marketing-adder**, then format the price with **format-price** and return the string concatenated with **"Only"** in front of it:

```
user=> (def checkout (comp (partial str "Only ") format-price marketing-adder))
#'user/checkout
user=> (checkout 10 5 15 6 9)
"Only €45.99"
```

In the preceding example, we defined a **checkout** function as a composition of **marketing-adder**, **format-price**, and an anonymous function returned by **partial** to add the text **"Only"** before the price. This example shows the outstanding dynamism and expressivity of composing related functions in Clojure. The programmer's intent is clear and concise, skipping the technicality of defining functions and naming parameters.

Before we jump into the exercise, let's present a new way of writing anonymous functions: the #() literal. #() is a shorter way of writing an anonymous function. Parameters are not named and therefore parameter values can be accessed in order with %1, %2, %3, and so on. When only one argument is provided, you can simply use % (omitting the argument number) to retrieve the value of the argument.

For example, the two following expressions are equivalent:

```
(fn [s] (str "Hello" s))
;; is the same as
#(str "Hello" %)
```

And the two following expressions are equivalent as well:

```
(fn [x y] (* (+ x 10) (+ y 20)))
;; is the same as
#(* (+ %1 10) (+ %2 20))
```

#() literal functions are just functions, called in the same way as other functions:

```
user=> (#(str %1 " " %2 " " %3) "First" "Second" "Third")
"First Second Third"
```

Observe that when more than one argument is provided, we need to use the %1 and %2 to refer to the values passed as a parameter.

> **Note**
>
> The short literal notation of the #() function is convenient but should be used sparingly because numbered parameters can be hard to read. The rule of thumb is to use only short anonymous functions with a single argument and a single function call. For anything else, you should stick with the standard **fn** notation with named parameters to improve readability.

Let's put these new techniques into practice in an exercise with **Parenthmazes** version 3.

Exercise 3.04: High-Order Functions with Parenthmazes

In this exercise, we will demonstrate the benefit of functions being first-class citizens. We will use functions as values and compose them together.

We would like to improve our fantasy game, Parenthmazes, even more, this time by changing weapons' mechanics to allow each weapon to have different behavior. For example, we would like "fists" to inflict damage only if an enemy is weak or has been weakened. Instead of implementing conditional branches in our **strike** function, we are going to implement a *dispatch table* using the **weapon-damage HashMap**, which we are going to rename **weapon-fn-map**, because this time each weapon will have an associated function (rather than a numeric value). A dispatch table is a table of pointers to functions. We can implement it with a **HashMap** where the pointers are keys and the functions are values.

To allow our weapon functions to compose nicely, they will take a numeric value for health as a parameter and return a numeric value for health after the damage has been deducted. For the sake of simplicity, we will leave out the concept of armor this time. Let's start with the **fist** weapon:

1. Start a REPL next to your favorite code editor. Create a new **HashMap** with a **:fists** key and its associated function, which inflicts **10** damage only if the health of the enemy is less than **100**, and otherwise returns the **health** parameter. Bind the newly created function to the **weapon-fn-map** symbol as follows:

```
user=>
(def weapon-fn-map
  {:fists (fn [health] (if (< health 100) (- health 10) health))})
#'user/weapon-fn-map
```

A **HashMap** can have any type of value as a key or parameter, so a function as a value is perfectly fine.

2. Try the function by retrieving it from **weapon-fn-map** and call it with **150** and then **50** as a parameter:

```
user=> ((weapon-fn-map :fists) 150)
150
user=> ((weapon-fn-map :fists) 50)
40
```

Observe that the function returned the new health correctly. It subtracted **10** when the **health** parameter was less than **100**.

3. Now to the **staff** weapon. The **staff** is the only weapon that can be used to heal (**35** health points), so the associated function should simply call **+** instead of **-**. It seems like a good opportunity to generate this function using **partial**:

```
(def weapon-fn-map
  {
    :fists (fn [health] (if (< health 100) (- health 10) health))
    :staff (partial + 35)
  })
```

The value at the **:staff** key is now a function that will call **+** with **35** and any extra argument supplied.

4. Try the function associated with **staff**, as follows:

```
user=> ((weapon-fn-map :staff) 150)
185
```

For the **sword** weapon, we need to simply subtract **100** points from the health points passed as an argument. However, **partial** won't work because the parameters would not be in the correct order. For example, **((partial - 100) 150)** returns **-50**, because the function call is equivalent to **(- 100 150)**, but we need **(- 150 100)**.

5. Create an anonymous function subtracting **100** from its argument and associate it with the **sword** key, as follows:

```
(def weapon-fn-map
  {
    :fists (fn [health] (if (< health 100) (- health 10) health))
    :staff (partial + 35)
    :sword #(- % 100)
  })
```

Notice that we used **%** to retrieve the argument passed to the anonymous function, because we used the short literal syntax, **#()**, expecting only one argument.

6. Test your newly created weapon function as follows:

```
user=> ((weapon-fn-map :sword) 150)
50
```

It works!

The next weapon to add is **cast-iron-saucepan**. To spice things up, let's add a bit of randomness to the mix (a saucepan is not a very accurate weapon anyway).

7. Add the **cast-iron-saucepan** function to the **HashMap** that subtracts **100** health points and a random number between **0** and **50** from the health points, as follows:

```
(def weapon-fn-map
  {
    :fists (fn [health] (if (< health 100) (- health 10) health))
    :staff (partial + 35)
    :sword #(- % 100)
    :cast-iron-saucepan #(- % 100 (rand-int 50))
  })
```

In the preceding example, we used the **rand-int** function, which generates a random integer between **0** and the supplied argument.

8. Test the newly created function as follows:

```
user=> ((weapon-fn-map :cast-iron-saucepan) 200)
77
user=> ((weapon-fn-map :cast-iron-saucepan) 200)
90
```

Two subsequent calls might return a different value because of the **rand-int** function.

9. Finally, we would like to introduce a new weapon (for the unfortunate adventurers) that doesn't do any damage: the sweet potato. For that purpose, we need a function that returns its argument (the health). We don't need to implement it as it already exists: **identity**. First, let's check out the source code of the function identity with the **source** function:

```
user=> (source identity)
(defn identity
  "Returns its argument."
  {:added "1.0"
   :static true}
  [x] x)
Nil
```

Observe how **identity** simply returns its argument. The **source** function is another handy tool to use interactively in the REPL, as it prints out a function definition to the console, which is sometimes more helpful than a function's documentation.

10. Let's redefine our **weapon-fn-map HashMap** one last time by associating the function identity with the **:sweet-potato** key, as follows:

```
(def weapon-fn-map
  {
    :fists (fn [health] (if (< health 100) (- health 10) health))
    :staff (partial + 35)
    :sword #(- % 100)
    :cast-iron-saucepan #(- % 100 (rand-int 50))
    :sweet-potato identity
  })
```

Now that we have our **weapon-fn-map** finalized, we should modify our **strike** function to handle the weapon functions stored as values in our **HashMap**. Remember that the **strike** function takes a **target** entity as a parameter and returns this entity with a new value for the health key. Therefore, updating the entity's health should be as simple as passing a **weapon** function to the **update** function, because our **weapon** functions take the health as a parameter and return the new health value.

11. Rewrite the **strike** function from the previous exercise to use the weapon functions stored in the **weapon-fn-map**, as follows:

```
user=>
(defn strike
  "With one argument, strike a target with a default :fists `weapon`. With two
argument, strike a target with `weapon` and return the target entity"
  ([target] (strike target :fists))
  ([target weapon]
    (let [weapon-fn (weapon weapon-fn-map)]
      (update target :health weapon-fn))))
#'user/strike
```

12. Now test your **strike** function by passing various weapons as a parameter. For convenience, you might want to create an **enemy** entity as well:

```
user=> (def enemy {:name "Arnold", :health 250})
#'user/enemy
user=> (strike enemy :sweet-potato)
{:name "Arnold", :health 250}
user=> (strike enemy :sword)
{:name "Arnold", :health 150}
user=> (strike enemy :cast-iron-saucepan)
{:name "Arnold", :health 108}
```

If we wanted to strike with more than one weapon at a time, instead of nesting a strike call like this:

```
user=> (strike (strike enemy :sword) :cast-iron-saucepan)
{:name "Arnold", :health 42}
```

We could simply compose our weapon functions and just use the core update function.

13. Write an **update** expression to strike with two weapons at a time using **comp**, as follows:

```
user=> (update enemy :health (comp (:sword weapon-fn-map) (:cast-iron-saucepan
weapon-fn-map)))
{:name "Arnold", :health 15}
```

Because the weapon functions that we wrote have a consistent interface (taking **health** as a parameter and returning the health), it is straightforward to compose them with **comp**. To finish this exercise, let's create a **mighty-strike** function that strikes with all of the weapons at once, also known as composing all the weapon functions. The **keys** and **vals** functions can be used on **HashMaps** to retrieve a collection of the map's keys or values. To retrieve all the weapon functions, we can simply retrieve all the values from **weapon-fn-map** using the **vals** function. Now that we have a collection of functions, how do we compose them? We need to pass each function of the collection to the **comp** function. Remember, to pass each element of a collection as a parameter of a function, we can use **apply**.

14. Write a new function named **mighty-strike**, which takes a **target** entity as a parameter and uses all of the weapons on it. It should apply the **comp** function to the values of **weapon-fn-map** as follows:

```
user=>
(defn mighty-strike
  "Strike a `target` with all weapons!"
  [target]
  (let [weapon-fn (apply comp (vals weapon-fn-map))]
    (update target :health weapon-fn)))
#'user/mighty-strike
user=> (mighty-strike enemy)
{:name "Arnold", :health 58}
```

Now, if we pause to reflect on the **mighty-strike** function and think about how we would have to implement that without higher-order functions, we'll realize how simple and powerful the concept of functional composition is.

In this section, we've learned how to use functions as simple values and as parameters or return values of other functions, as well as creating shorter anonymous functions with **#()**. We also explained how to use **partial**, **comp**, and **apply** to generate, compose, and discover new ways of using functions.

Multimethods

Clojure offers a way to implement polymorphism with multimethods. Polymorphism is the ability of a unit of code (in our case, functions) to behave differently in different contexts, for example, based on the shape of the data received by the code. In Clojure, we also call it *runtime polymorphism* because the method to call is determined at runtime rather than at compile time. A multimethod is a combination of a dispatch function and of one or more methods. The two main operators for creating those multimethods are **defmulti** and **defmethod**. **defmulti** declares a multimethod and defines how the method is chosen with the dispatch function. **defmethod** creates the different implementations that will be chosen by the dispatch function. The dispatch function receives the arguments of the function call and returns a dispatch value. This dispatch value is used to determine which function, defined with **defmethod**, to invoke. Those are a lot of new terms but don't worry, the following examples will help you understand the new concepts.

Let's see how we could implement Parenthmazes' **strike** function with multimethods. This time, the weapon is in the **HashMap** passed as a parameter:

```
user=> (defmulti strike (fn [m] (get m :weapon)))
#'user/strike
```

In the preceding code, we've created a multimethod called **strike**. The second argument is the dispatch function, which simply retrieves a weapon in a map passed as a parameter. Remember that keywords can be used as functions of a **HashMap**, so we can simply write **defmulti** as follows:

```
user=> (defmulti strike :weapon)
nil
```

Notice that, this time, the expression returned **nil**. This is because the multimethod was already defined. In that case, we need to **unmap** the **strike** var from the **user** namespace and re-evaluate the same expression again:

```
user=> (ns-unmap 'user 'strike)
nil
user=> (defmulti strike :weapon)
#'user/strike
```

Now that we have our multimethod and our dispatch function defined (which is simply the **:weapon** keyword), let's create our **strike** functions for a couple of weapons, to demonstrate the usage of **defmethod**:

```
user=> (defmethod strike :sword
[{{:keys [:health]} :target}]
(- health 100))
#object[clojure.lang.MultiFn 0xaa549e5 "clojure.lang.MultiFn@aa549e5"]
```

Observe how we called **defmethod** with the function named **strike**, the second argument to **defmethod** is the dispatch value: **:sword**. When **strike** is called with a map containing a weapon key, the weapon value is retrieved from the arguments and then returned by the dispatch function (the **:weapon** keyword). Similarly, let's create another strike implementation for the **:cast-iron-saucepan** dispatch value:

```
user=> (defmethod strike :cast-iron-saucepan
[{{:keys [:health]} :target}]
(- health 100 (rand-int 50)))
#object[clojure.lang.MultiFn 0xaa549e5 "clojure.lang.MultiFn@aa549e5"]
```

This time, **strike** is called with a map containing **:cast-iron-saucepan** at the **:weapon** key. The function defined previously will be invoked. Let's test our newly created multimethod with the two different weapons:

```
user=> (strike {:weapon :sword :target {:health 200}})
100
user=> (strike {:weapon :cast-iron-saucepan :target {:health 200}})
77
```

Notice how calling **strike** with different arguments lets us invoke two different functions.

When the dispatch value doesn't map to any registered function, an exception is thrown:

```
user=> (strike {:weapon :spoon :target {:health 200}})
Execution error (IllegalArgumentException) at user/eval217 (REPL:1).
No method in multimethod 'strike' for dispatch value: :spoon
```

If we need to handle that case, we can add a method with the **:default** dispatch value:

```
user=> (defmethod strike :default [{{:keys [:health]} :target}] health)
#object[clojure.lang.MultiFn 0xaa549e5 "clojure.lang.MultiFn@aa549e5"]
```

In this case, we decided to handle any other weapon by simply returning the unmodified health value, inflicting no damage:

```
user=> (strike {:weapon :spoon :target {:health 200}})
200
```

Notice that, this time, no exception was thrown, and the original health value was returned. The dispatch function can be more elaborate. We could imagine a special behavior when the enemy's health is below 50 points and instantly eliminate it, no matter what weapon was used:

```
user=> (ns-unmap 'user 'strike)
nil
user=> (defmulti strike (fn
  [{{:keys [:health]} :target weapon :weapon}]
  (if (< health 50) :finisher weapon)))
#'user/strike
user=> (defmethod strike :finisher [_] 0)
#object[clojure.lang.MultiFn 0xf478a81 "clojure.lang.MultiFn@f478a81"]
```

The preceding code first unmaps **strike** from the **user** namespace so that it can be redefined. We then redefine the dispatching function by looking in the parameter and dispatching to a **:finisher** function if the health of the enemy is below **50**. We then define the **:finisher** function (the **strike** function with the dispatch value finisher) to return, simply ignore its arguments, and return **0**.

Because we've unmapped **strike**, we must add **defmethods** as they would have been removed too. Let's re-add a sword and the default method:

```
user=> (defmethod strike :sword
[{{:keys [:health]} :target}]
(- health 100))
#object[clojure.lang.MultiFn 0xaa549e5 "clojure.lang.MultiFn@aa549e5"]
user=> (defmethod strike :default [{{:keys [:health]} :target}] health)
#object[clojure.lang.MultiFn 0xaa549e5 "clojure.lang.MultiFn@aa549e5"]
```

Now let's see our multimethod in action:

```
user=> (strike {:weapon :sword :target {:health 200}})
100
```

Great – our function still works as expected. Now let's see what happens when the health is below **50**:

```
user=> (strike {:weapon :spoon :target {:health 30}})
0
```

The **finisher** function has been called and the strike multimethod successfully returned **0**.

Multimethods can do a few more things, such as dispatching on multiple values (using a vector as the dispatch value) or dispatching on types and hierarchies. This is useful but maybe a bit much to take on for now. Let's move on to the exercise and practice using multimethods by dispatching on values.

Exercise 3.05: Using Multimethods

In this exercise, we want to extend our little game, Parenthmazes, with the ability to move a player. The game board is a simple two-dimensional space with the coordinates x and y. We will not implement any rendering or maintain any state of the game at this point as we simply want to practice the use of multimethods, so you will have to use your imagination.

1. Players' entities are now given an extra key, **:position**, which contains a **HashMap** with the coordinates at key x and y as well as the **:facing** key, which contains the direction in which the player is facing. The following code is an example of a player entity:

```
{:name "Lea" :health 200 :position {:x 10 :y 10 :facing :north}}
```

Moving north or south should change the y coordinate, and moving east and west should change the x coordinate. We will implement this with a new **move** function.

2. Start a REPL and create the player entity as follows:

```
user=> (def player {:name "Lea" :health 200 :position {:x 10 :y 10 :facing :north}})
#'user/player
```

3. Create the **move** multimethod. The dispatch function should determine the dispatch value by retrieving the **:facing** value in the **:position** map of a player entity. The **:facing** value could be one of the following values **:north**, **:south**, **:west**, and **:east**:

```
user=> (defmulti move #(:facing (:position %)))
#'user/move
```

You might have noticed that the two successive keyword function calls could be more elegantly expressed with functional composition.

4. Redefine the **move** multimethod by first unmapping the var from the **user** namespace and then using **comp** to simplify its definition:

```
user=> (ns-unmap 'user 'move)
nil
user=> (defmulti move (comp :facing :position))
#'user/move
```

5. Create the first implementation of the **move** function with the **:north** dispatch value. It should increment **:y** in the **:position** map:

```
User=> (defmethod move :north
[entity]
   (update-in entity [:position :y] inc))
#object[clojure.lang.MultiFn 0x1d0d6318 "clojure.lang.MultiFn@1d0d6318"]
```

6. Try your newly created function by calling **move** with the **player** entity and observe the result:

```
user=> (move player)
{:name "Lea", :health 200, :position {:x 10, :y 11, :facing :north}}
```

Observe that the value at **y** successfully increased by 1.

7. Create the other functions for the rest of the dispatch values **:south**, **:west**, and **:east**:

```
User=> (defmethod move :south
[entity]
   (update-in entity [:position :y] dec))
#object[clojure.lang.MultiFn 0x1d0d6318 "clojure.lang.MultiFn@1d0d6318"]
User=> (defmethod move :west
[entity]
   (update-in entity [:position :x] inc))
#object[clojure.lang.MultiFn 0x1d0d6318 "clojure.lang.MultiFn@1d0d6318"]
User=> (defmethod move :east
[entity]
   (update-in entity [:position :x] dec))
#object[clojure.lang.MultiFn 0x1d0d6318 "clojure.lang.MultiFn@1d0d6318"]
```

8. Test your newly created functions by providing **player** entities facing different directions:

```
user=> (move {:position {:x 10 :y 10 :facing :west}})
{:position {:x 11, :y 10, :facing :west}}
user=> (move {:position {:x 10 :y 10 :facing :south}})
{:position {:x 10, :y 9, :facing :south}}
user=> (move {:position {:x 10 :y 10 :facing :east}})
{:position {:x 9, :y 10, :facing :east}}
```

Observe how the coordinates changed correctly when moving the players in different directions.

9. Create an extra function for when the value at :**facing** is different from :**north**, :**south**, :**west**, and :**east**, using the :**default** dispatch value:

```
user=> (defmethod move :default [entity] entity)
#object[clojure.lang.MultiFn 0x1d0d6318 "clojure.lang.MultiFn@1d0d6318"]
```

10. Try your function and make sure it handles unexpected values by returning the original entity map:

```
user=> (move {:position {:x 10 :y 10 :facing :wall}})
{:position {:x 10, :y 10, :facing :wall}}
```

Observe that the multimethod was dispatched to the default function, and that the position remained unchanged when the player was facing a :**wall**.

In this section, we've learned how to use Clojure's polymorphism feature with multimethods.

Activity 3.01: Building a Distance and Cost Calculator

Let's go back to the flight-booking platform application that we worked on in *Exercise 3.01*, *Parsing Fly Vector's Data with Sequential Destructuring*, and *Exercise 3.02*, *Parsing MapJet Data with Associative Destructuring*. In the time it took you to arrive at the end of this chapter, we have now developed the company into a proper start-up called WingIt, with serious investors, a weekly board meeting, and a ping pong table, which means that we now need to build the core services of the app: the itinerary and cost calculations between two locations. However, after looking into routing airways, airport fees, and complicated fuel calculations, we've come to realize that the algorithms that we need to develop might be too complicated for us at this stage. We've decided that for our **Minimal Viable Product (MVP)**, we are just going to "wing it" and offer simpler modes of transportation such as driving and even walking. However, we want to keep the code easily extensible, because we'll eventually need to add flying (some employees even overheard the CEO talking about adding space flights to the roadmap soon!).

The requirement of the WingIt MVP are as follows:

*   For the prototype, we will interact with a Clojure REPL. The interface is an itinerary function taking a **HashMap** as a parameter. For now, the users will have to enter coordinates. It might not be very user-friendly but the user can look up coordinates on their own globe or map!

*   The itinerary function returns a **HashMap** with the keys, :**distance**, :**cost**, and :**duration**. :**distance** is expressed in kilometers, :**cost** in euros, and :**duration** in hours.

- The only parameter to the itinerary function is a **HashMap** containing `:from`, `:to`, `:transport`, and `:vehicle`. `:from` and `:to` contain a **HashMap** with the `:lat` and `:lon` keys, representing the latitude and longitude of a location on our planet.

- `:transport` can be either `:walking` or `:driving`.

- `:vehicle` is only useful when `:transport` is `:driving`, and can be one of `:sporche`, `:sleta`, or `:tayato`.

To compute the distance, we are going to use the "Euclidian distance," which is normally used to calculate the distance between two points on a plan. For flying, we would have to use at least the haversine formula, and technically, for driving, we would need to use routes, but we just want rough estimates on relatively short distances, so the much simpler Euclidian distance should be enough for now. The only complicated bit in this calculation is that the length of a degree of longitude depends on the latitude, so we'll need to multiply the longitude by the cosine of the latitude. The final equation to compute the distance between two points (lat1, lon1) and (lat2, lon2) looks like this:

$$110.25 \cdot \sqrt{(\mathrm{lat2} - \mathrm{lat1})^2 + \cos(\mathrm{lat1}) \cdot (\mathrm{lon2} - \mathrm{lon1})^2}$$

Figure 3.1: Calculating the Euclidean distance

To compute the cost in the case of the transport being `:driving`, we will look at the `:vehicle` chosen by the user in the **HashMap** parameter. The cost of each vehicle should be a function of the distance:

- `:sporche` consumes, on average, 0.12 liters of petrol per kilometer, costing €1.5 per liter.

- `:tayato` consumes, on average, 0.07 liters of petrol per kilometer, costing €1.5 per liter.

- `:sleta` consumes, on average, 0.2 kilowatt hour (kwh) of electricity per kilometer, costing €0.1 per kwh.

- The cost should be 0 when transport is `:walking`.

To compute the duration, we consider an average driving speed of 70 km per hour, and an average walking speed of 5 km per hour.

Here are a couple of examples of calls to the itinerary function, and the expected output:

```
user=> (def paris {:lat 48.856483 :lon 2.352413})
#'user/paris
user=> (def bordeaux {:lat 44.834999  :lon -0.575490})
#'user/bordeaux
user=> (itinerary {:from paris :to bordeaux :transport :walking})
{:cost 0, :distance 491.61380776549225, :duration 122.90345194137306}
user=> (itinerary {:from paris :to bordeaux :transport :driving :vehicle :tayato})
{:cost 44.7368565066598, :distance 491.61380776549225, :duration 7.023054396649889}
```

These steps will help you complete this activity:

1. Start by defining the **walking-speed** and **driving-speed** constants.

2. Create two other constants representing two locations with the coordinates, **:lat** and **:lon**. You can use the previous example with Paris and Bordeaux or look up your own. You will be using them to test your distance and itinerary functions.

3. Create the **distance** function. It should take two parameters representing the two locations for which we need to calculate the distance. You can use a combination of sequential and associative destructuring right in the function parameters to disassemble the latitude and longitude from both locations. You can decompose the steps of the calculation in a **let** expression and use the **Math/cos** function to calculate the cosine of a number and **Math/sqrt** to calculate the square root of a number; for example, **(Math/cos 0)**, **(Math/sqrt 9)**.

4. Create a *multimethod* called **itinerary**. It will offer the flexibility of adding more types of transport in the future. It should use the value at **:transport** as a *dispatch value*.

5. Create the itinerary function for the **:walking** dispatch value. You can use associative destructuring in the function parameters to retrieve the **:from** and **:to** keys from the **HashMap** parameter. You can use a **let** expression to decompose the calculations of the distance and duration. The distance should simply use the **distance** function you created before. To calculate the duration, you should use the **walking-speed** constant that you defined in *Step 1*.

6. For the **:driving** itinerary function, you could use a dispatch table that contains the vehicle associated with the costing function. Create a **vehicle-cost-fns** dispatch table. It should be a **HashMap** with the keys being the types of vehicles, and the values being cost calculation functions based on the distance.

7. Create the itinerary function for the :**driving** dispatch value. You can use associative destructuring in the function parameters to retrieve the :**from**, :**to**, and :**vehicle** keys from the **HashMap** parameter. The driving distance and duration can be calculated similarly to the walking distance and duration. The cost can be calculated by retrieving the cost function from the dispatch table using the :**vehicle** key.

Expected Output:

```
user=> (def london {:lat 51.507351, :lon -0.127758})
#'user/london
user=> (def manchester {:lat 53.480759, :lon -2.242631})
#'user/manchester
user=> (itinerary {:from london :to manchester :transport :walking})
{:cost 0, :distance 318.4448148814284, :duration 79.6112037203571}
user=> (itinerary {:from manchester :to london :transport :driving :vehicle :sleta})
{:cost 4.604730845743489, :distance 230.2365422871744, :duration 3.2890934612453484}
```

> **Note**
>
> The solution for this activity can be found on page 686.

Summary

In this chapter, we took a closer look at Clojure's powerful functions. We learned how to simplify our functions with destructuring techniques, and then discovered the great benefits of higher-order functions: modularity, simplicity, and composability. We also introduced an advanced concept to write code that is more extensible with Clojure's polymorphism mechanism: multimethods. Now that you are familiar with the REPL, data types, and functions, you can move on to learning about tools and functional techniques to manipulate collections.

In the next chapter, we will explore sequential collections in Clojure and take a look at two of the most useful patterns: mapping and filtering.

Mapping and Filtering

Overview

In this chapter, we will begin our exploration of how to use sequential collections in Clojure by taking a look at two of the most useful patterns: mapping and filtering. We will work with the map and filter functions and handle sequential data without using a for loop. We will also use common patterns and idioms for Clojure collections and take advantage of lazy evaluation while avoiding the traps. We will load and process sequential datasets from **Comma-Separated Values (CSV)** files and extract and shape data from a large dataset.

By the end of this chapter, you will be able to parse datasets and perform various types of transformations to extract and summarize data.

Introduction

Dealing with collections of data is one of the most common and powerful parts of programming. Whether they are called lists, arrays, or vectors, sequential collections are at the heart of almost every program. Every programming language provides tools for creating, accessing, and modifying collections, and, often, what you've learned in one language will apply to the others. Clojure is different, however. We are accustomed to setting a variable and then controlling some other part of the system by changing the value of that variable.

This is what happens in a **for** loop in most procedural languages. Say that we have an iterator, **i**, that we increment by calling **i++**. Changing the value of the iterator controls the flow of the loop. By executing **i = i + 3**, we can make the loop skip two iterations. The value of **i** is like a remote control for the loop. In case we increment the iterator by three, what happens if we are just one item away from the end of the array we are looping over? The remote control doesn't prevent us from making mistakes with it.

Clojure has a completely different approach. It may take some practice and some experience to get used to it, depending on what kinds of programming you've done before. With Clojure, it's helpful to think of the functions you write as a way of describing the shape of the data we want to have. Often, you will need to reshape the data in several steps to get it to where you need it to go. Rather than using data, such as the iterator we mentioned previously, to keep track of the internal state of the program, Clojure invites you to write the functions that will be the bridge between the data you have and the data you want. That's at least one way of thinking about it.

From a 30,000-foot perspective, the fundamental pattern of Clojure programs is as follows:

1. Get the data.

2. Shape the data.

3. Do something with the data.

The traditional **for** loop tends to roll these three phases into one. A typical example would be a **for** loop that reads a row of data from a database or a file (*get the data*), does some computations (*shape the data*), and writes data back or sends it somewhere else (*do something*), and then starts over again with the next row. A good design in Clojure usually means separating these three steps and moving as much logic as possible into the middle, which is the data-shaping step.

The techniques that we'll cover in this chapter will help you do that.

> **Note**
>
> Clojure does have a **for** macro, but it is used for list comprehensions, which you can think of as an alternate syntax for many of the patterns in this chapter.

This approach to coding makes Clojure an excellent language for doing complicated things with complex data as simply as possible. Learning a functional approach to data collections is not just for processing large datasets, however. Clojure programs often tend to be data-centric, regardless of how much data they are actually processing. Much of the important work in a Clojure program is done by shaping your data, big or small. The techniques and patterns you'll learn about in this chapter will help you write any kind of Clojure code.

The `map` and `filter` functions are fundamentally quite simple, as you'll soon see. In this chapter, we will focus on how to use them to solve problems. At the same time, learning about `map` and `filter` and, more generally, how to handle sequential data, means learning lots of new things about the Clojure ecosystem – things such as immutability, lazy sequences, or the basics of functional programming. Toward the end of this chapter, we will start to use the techniques we learned along the way to manipulate a larger dataset, composed of the results of years and years of professional tennis matches. In subsequent chapters, we will continue to build on our experience with this data as we learn more and more about Clojure.

map and filter

The `map` and `filter` functions are a key part of a much larger group of functions for dealing with sequences. Of that group, `map` is certainly the one you will use the most, and `filter` is a close second. Their role is to modify sequences.

They accept one or more sequences as input, and return a sequence: *sequence in, sequence out*:

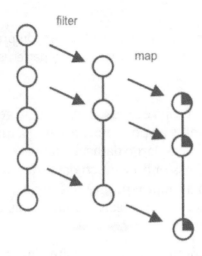

Figure 4.1: A schematic diagram of map and filter working together

In the preceding diagram, we can see `map` and `filter` working together, where `filter` eliminates items from the original list while `map` changes them.

The first question to ask when solving a problem involving collections is: "Do I want to obtain a list of values, or a single value?" If the answer is a list, then `map`, `filter`, or similar functions are what you need. If you need some other kind of value, the solution is probably a reduction of some kind, which we will discuss in the next chapter.
But even then, as you break the problem down, there is a good chance that some component parts of the problem will require sequence-manipulating functions such as `map` and `filter`. If, for example, the problem at hand involves searching in a list of items for sale, perhaps `filter` would allow you to narrow the scope of the search to a certain category or price range. Then, you may use `map` to calculate a derived value for each item – maybe the item's volume in cubic centimeters or the number of commentaries it has received on a website. And then, finally, you may extract the single item you are seeking, or the summary data that you need, from this transformed list.

To get started, let's take a closer look at `map` and `filter` separately, before looking at how we will use them together.

map

Like the majority of Clojure's functions for working with sequences, the first argument of map is always a function. The function we provide will be called on each item in the sequence that we will iterate over. Here is a very simple use of **map** that uses Clojure's **inc** function to add 1 to each value in the input sequence:

```
user> map inc [1 2 3])
(2 3 4)
```

The return value of each call to the **inc** function becomes a value in the new sequence that **map** returns.

> **Note**
>
> The **map** function can take more sequences as arguments, as we'll see shortly. Like many of the sequence-handling functions, there is a single-argument form of **map**. When **map** is called with just one argument, that is, the function, it returns a special function called a **transducer**. You don't need to worry about transducers for now. However, if you forget to provide a third argument to **map**, the Clojure compiler won't complain about not having enough arguments. Instead, you'll see a strange error about a function that you don't remember writing. That function is the transducer you've produced by mistake.

Exercise 4.01: Working with map

Let's get started! In this exercise, we'll use **map** on a list of integers to obtain different kinds of results:

1. Try this in your REPL:

   ```
   user> (map (fn [i] (* i 10)) [1 2 3 4 5])
   ```

   The output is as follows:

   ```
   (10 20 30 40 50)
   ```

This call to **map** simply applied the anonymous function known as **(fn [i] (* i 10))** to the list of integers, multiplying each one by 10. In doing so, we end up with a new list of integers, one for each of the integers in the original input:

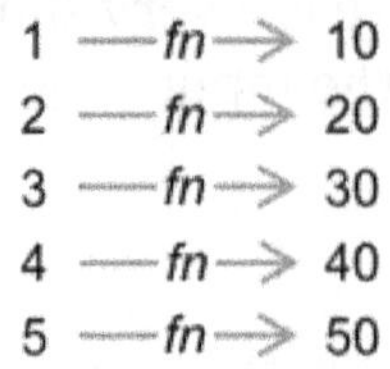

```
1 —fn—> 10
2 —fn—> 20
3 —fn—> 30
4 —fn—> 40
5 —fn—> 50
```

Figure 4.2: Mapping one sequence to another

This one-to-one equivalence is obvious, but it is also a key feature of **map**. With **map**, the sequence of results is always exactly the same length as the input sequence so that each value in the input maps to the corresponding value in the result sequence, hence the name.

2. Let's measure word length now. When working with sequences, Clojure's **count** function is invaluable. Since Clojure considers a string to be a sequence of characters, **count** can also be used to find the length of a string:

```
user> (map count ["Let's" "measure" "word" "length" "now"])
```

You should see the length of each word:

```
(5 7 4 6 3)
```

3. To make our output easier to read, we could add the word along with its length:

```
user> (map (fn [w] (str w ": " (count w))) ["Let's" "measure" "word" "length"
"now"])
```

The output is as follows:

```
("Let's: 5" "measure: 7" "word: 4" "length: 6" "now: 3")
```

This example, of course, just scratches the surface of the different applications of **map**. At the same time, it shows how simple the concept of mapping really is: for each value in a list, produce a new value in a new list.

filter

Unlike **map**, **filter** can, and often does, produce a sequence of results containing fewer items than the input sequence. A call to **filter** looks basically like a call to **map**:

```
user> filter keyword? ["a" :b "c" :d "e" :f "g"])
(:b :d :f)
```

Like in **map**, the function that's supplied as the first argument to **filter** is called on each item in the sequence. The difference is that, in this case, the function is being used as a **predicate**, which means that we only care about whether the value returned is logically **true** or **false**. When a **truthy** value is returned, that item will be included in the sequence of results.

One key difference with **map** is that the predicate that's provided to **filter** only serves to decide whether the given item should be included or not. It does not change the items in any way. The result set of **filter** is always a subset of the input set.

Exercise 4.02: Getting Started with filter

In this exercise, we'll use **filter** on a list of integers to obtain different kinds of results. Let's get started:

1. The **odd?** function is a predicate that returns **true** if a number is **odd**. Try it by itself in the REPL:

   ```
   user> (odd? 5)
   ```

   The output is as follows:

   ```
   true
   ```

2. Now, try passing an even number as input:

   ```
   user> (odd? 6)
   ```

   The output is as follows:

   ```
   false
   ```

3. Now, use **odd?** with **filter**:

   ```
   user> (filter odd? [1 2 3 4 5])
   ```

   The output is as follows:

   ```
   (1 3 5)
   ```

4. We could also use the alter ego of filter, **remove**, which does the exact inverse of **filter**. When the predicate returns **true**, the item is removed:

```
user> (remove odd? [1 2 3 4 5])
```

The output is as follows:

```
(2 4)
```

Here is how we can visualize what **filter** does:

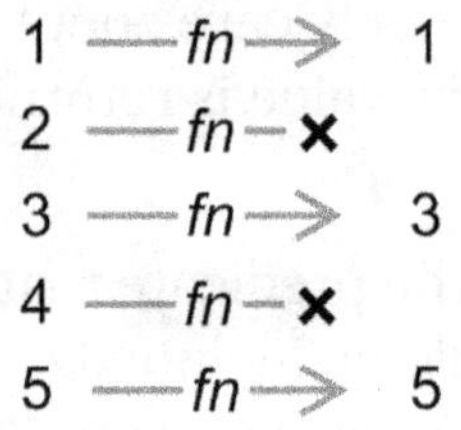

```
1 —— fn —> 1
2 —— fn — ✘
3 —— fn —> 3
4 —— fn — ✘
5 —— fn —> 5
```

Figure 4.3: The filter function uses a predicate to define a new sequence

5. With **filter**, we are limiting the original sequence, but the result is always a sequence. Consider these two extreme cases where each predicate always returns a single value (Clojure's **constantly** function returns a function that does nothing but return a single value, regardless of the number of arguments that are passed to it):

```
user> (filter (constantly true) [1 2 3 4 5])
(1 2 3 4 5)
user> (filter (constantly false) [1 2 3 4 5])
()
```

Whether we keep everything or nothing, **filter** *always* returns a sequence.

Like **map**, **filter** is conceptually very simple: using a predicate, keep some or all of the items in a list. Despite this simplicity, or thanks to it, **filter** is an extremely useful function that can be used in countless circumstances.

Other Members of the filter Family – take-while and drop-while

The **take-while** and **drop-while** functions follow the same logic as **filter** and **remove** – at least as far as their use of a predicate goes. The difference is that they only operate at the beginning of a sequence, much like **take** and **drop**. The **take** function returns the first **n** items of a list, while **drop** returns the original list minus the first **n** items:

```
user> (take 3 [1 2 3 4 5])
(1 2 3)
user> (drop 3 [1 2 3 4 5])
(4 5)
```

Similarly, **take-while** starts at the beginning of the list and returns all the items as long as they satisfy the predicate, while **drop-while** removes those same items from the beginning of the sequence:

```
User> (take-while #(> 10 %) [2 9 4 12 3 99 1])
(2 9 4)
user> (drop-while #(> 10 %) [2 9 4 12 3 99 1])
(12 3 99 1)
```

Perhaps the most obvious application of **take-while** and **drop-while** is to subdivide sorted data. We can even use them together to find the exact point in a sequence where a predicate stops returning **true** and starts returning **false**.

Exercise 4.03: Partitioning a Sequence with take-while and drop-while

We have a sorted list of students that we'd like to separate into two groups: those born before the year 2000 and those born after. Let's get started:

1. In your REPL, define a **students** variable. You can copy the list from this course's GitHub repository at https://packt.live/2sQyVYz:

```
(def students [{:name "Eliza" :year 1994}
               {:name "Salma" :year 1995}
               {:name "Jodie" :year 1997}
               {:name "Kaitlyn" :year 2000}
               {:name "Alice" :year 2001}
               {:name "Pippa" :year 2002}
               {:name "Fleur" :year 2002}])
```

2. Write a predicate that translates the idea **before 2000**:

```
#(< (:year %) 2000)
```

This anonymous function extracts the **:year** value from the student map and compares it to **2000**.

3. Use the predicate with **take-while** to find the students born before 2000:

```
user> (take-while #(< (:year %) 2000) students)
({:name "Eliza", :year 1994}
 {:name "Salma", :year 1995}
 {:name "Jodie", :year 1997})
```

4. Use the same predicate with **drop-while** to find the students born in 2000 or after:

```
user> (drop-while #(< (:year %) 2000) students)
({:name "Kaitlyn", :year 2000}
 {:name "Alice", :year 2001}
 {:name "Pippa", :year 2002}
 {:name "Fleur", :year 2002})
```

You won't use the **take-while** and **drop-while** functions as much as **filter** itself, but they can be very useful in certain circumstances. Like **filter**, they are useful tools for shaping sequences.

Using map and filter Together

Much of the power of Clojure's sequence functions comes from combining them. Let's combine the previous examples. How would we obtain a sequence such as 10, 30, 50 from 1, 2, 3, 4, 5? It's just a question of applying our functions in the right order. If we multiply by 10 first, all the resulting integers will be even. To meaningfully filter out the odd numbers, we have to do this first. Consider the following example:

```
user> (map (fn [n] (* 10 n))
           (filter odd? [1 2 3 4 5]))
```

The output is as follows:

```
(10 30 50)
```

This is a little bit hard to read, especially if you aren't used to reading Lisp code with its nested parentheses. Even though **map** comes first in the source code, the evaluation starts with the call to **filter**. The result is then passed into **map** (we'll show you a better way to write this later in this chapter). First, though, let's look at what is happening.

Conceptually, the computation looks something like this:

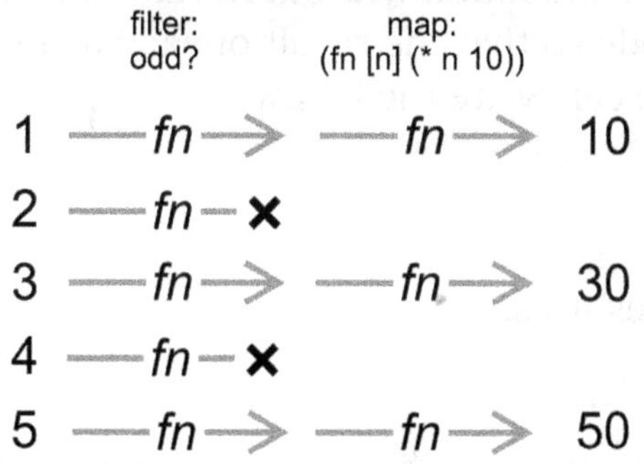

Figure 4.4: Combining the two – filter, then map

It may be helpful to think of this as data flowing through a pipeline. The functional arguments to **map** and **filter** are what shape your data as it flows along.

Threading Macros

It's possible to write the same expression in a way that reflects the logic of what we are doing to the data. If we write this in a very non-idiomatic style, using **def**, it's a little clearer:

```
user> (def filtered (filter odd? [1 2 3 4 5]))
filtered
user> (map (fn [n] (* 10 n)) filtered)
(10 30 50)
```

Alternatively, and much more idiomatically, we can use Clojure's **threading macros** to make it easier to read:

```
user> (->> [1 2 3 4 5]
       (filter odd?)
       (map (fn [n] (* 10 n))))
(10 30 50)
```

> **Note**
>
> A macro is a construct that transforms code before it is executed. In *Chapter 11, Macros*, we will explore macros in much more depth. For now, you can think of Clojure's threading macros as "syntactic sugar" that allows us to write more readable code by avoiding deep nesting.

This is how we will write our code throughout this chapter. Threading allows us to preserve the logical order of execution without having to name the return values. The ->> macro rewrites your code so that the result of each form is inserted at the end of the next form. This way, we can write the following:

```
user> (->> [1 2 3 4 5]
          (filter odd?))
```

And the compiler really "sees" this:

```
user> (filter odd? [1 2 3 4 5])
```

This is an extremely common pattern that helps immensely in writing easy-to-read code, especially when applying many different operations to sequences. In Clojure, when a function takes a sequence as an argument, that argument is generally the last argument. This is quite convenient, or rather, a great design decision, because it allows us to chain together transformations in an intuitive way using the ->> macro, which happens to fill in the last argument in an expression. A complex transformation can be broken down into smaller, composable steps, which are easier to write, test, and understand.

Using Lazy Sequences

Before we move on, it's important to take a closer look at how lazy sequences work in Clojure. When using map and **filter**, lazy evaluation is often an important consideration. In the examples we've looked at so far, we have used a literal vector as input: [1 2 3 4 5]. Instead of typing out each number, we could use the **range** function and write (range 1 6). If we type this in the REPL, we get basically the same thing:

```
user> (range 1 6)
(1 2 3 4 5)
```

So, is this just a shortcut to avoid typing out lots of integers? Well, it is, but **range** has another interesting characteristic: it's lazy.

Before we go further, let's revisit **laziness** briefly. If **(range 100)** is a **lazy sequence**, that means that it is not realized until each element in the sequence has been calculated. Say we define a lazy sequence from 0 to **100**:

```
user> (def our-seq (range 100))
```

> **Note**
>
> The REPL causes lazy sequences to be evaluated. This can be confusing sometimes if the problem you are debugging is caused by a lazy sequence not being fully evaluated: "This code works just fine in the REPL; why doesn't it work correctly in my code?" When debugging in the REPL, if you want to avoid forcing the evaluation of a lazy sequence, assign it to a variable instead.

The **range** function creates a list of integers by calling **inc** as many times as necessary. It's easy enough to guess that the last integer in **our-seq** will be **99**, but the computer doesn't know that until it has performed all the arithmetic. This means that when we look at the first item, only one item is known:

```
user> (first our-seq)
0
```

But if we look at the last item, all the intermediate calculations will be performed:

```
user> (last our-seq)
99
```

Now, the entire sequence has been realized, and for all practical purposes, it's no longer any different from a literal sequence of integers.

Functions such as **map**, **filter**, and **remove** are also lazy. This means that when we call them on a lazy sequence, they do not force the calculation of the entire sequence. Essentially, lazy functions just add new calculations to a virtual backlog of deferred calculations that will realize the sequence when needed. Functions such as **count**, **sort**, or **last**, on the other hand, are not lazy. Obviously, in order to count all the items in the list, we need the entire list first.

Exercise 4.04: Watching Lazy Evaluation

We can observe laziness in action by doing something that we never want to do in production code: introduce a side effect. Let's get started:

1. Define a simple version of **range** in the REPL:

```
user> (defn our-range [limit]
         (take-while #(< % limit) (iterate inc 0)))
```

Here, the **iterate** function creates a lazy sequence by calling **inc** on **0**, then calling **inc** on the result of that, then on the result of that, and so on. **take-while** will stop consuming the sequence when the anonymous function, that is, **#(< % limit)**, stops returning **true**. This will then stop **iterate**.

2. Test the function at the REPL:

```
user> (our-range 5)
(0 1 2 3 4)
```

3. Use **map** to multiply each integer by 10:

```
user> (map #(* 10 %) (our-range 5))
(0 10 20 30 40)
```

4. Now, we'll use a function with side effects to print . each time an integer is multiplied:

```
user> (map (fn [i] (print ".") (* i 10)) (our-range 5))
.(0. 10. 20. 30. 40)
```

As predicted, there is a . operator for each integer. The exact position of the dots may be different when you try this: they may appear before or after the list of integers. They are not part of the result sequence; they are being printed simultaneously, just before each multiplication is executed. There is one dot for each integer because the entire sequence has been realized.

5. This time, use **def** to store the lazy sequence, instead of viewing it in the REPL:

```
user> (def by-ten (map (fn [i] (print ".") (* i 10)) (our-range 5)))
#'user/by-ten
```

The REPL returns the **by-ten** variable, but does not print any dots, so we know that none of the multiplications have been performed yet.

6. Evaluate the variable in the REPL:

```
user> by-ten
.(0. 10. 20. 30. 40)   ;; this looks familiar!
```

What happened here? This is the same output as in *step* 4. The computations weren't performed until we finally decided to consume the lazy sequences in the REPL. This is the essence of laziness in Clojure: deferring evaluation until it is necessary.

Lazy evaluation has some important benefits, both in terms of simplifying our programs and in terms of performance. Deferring computation on a sequence means that we can sometimes avoid the computation altogether, at least on part of the sequence. For now, the important thing to understand is how lazy evaluation can change the way we write and organize our code. Consider this expression:

```
(range)
```

With no arguments, **range** returns all the integers from zero to the biggest number your system can handle. If you type this expression into your REPL, it will fill up the screen with numbers. Because there is a built-in limit regarding the number of items the REPL will display, it won't increment all the way to infinity, or until your JVM blows up – whichever comes first. Now, imagine that we write something like this:

```
(->> (range)
     (map #(* 10 %))
     (take 5))
```

This expression tells the computer to multiply every integer from 1 to infinity by 10, and then, when that calculation is complete, keep the first five values. Without lazy evaluation, this would be crazy. It would fail on the first line. Then, why perform a calculation on a huge set of numbers when we're only interested in the first five values? Yet, in Clojure, this is a perfectly reasonable way to write code. The calls to **range** and **map** are a description of the data that we want: positive integers multiplied by 10. The call to take allows us to select, within that infinite set, the items that we actually need. Lazy evaluation means that only five calculations will be performed, so the preceding code is not only elegant, but perfectly efficient.

There are dangers too, of course. In this example, if we replace **(take 5)** with **last**, it would mean trying to evaluate the entire sequence, with disastrous consequences as your machine tries, and fails, to calculate all the integers to infinity. Lazy evaluation is extremely useful, but it is important to understand how it works.

Exercise 4.05: Creating Our Own Lazy Sequence

From time to time, we need to create sequences of random numbers. This may be for a simulation or for writing tests. In a procedural language such as JavaScript, we may write something like this:

```
var ints = [];
for (var i = 0; i < 20; i++) {
  ints.push(Math.round(Math.random() * 100));
}
```

We could then wrap this in a function and parameterize the length of the array we wanted.

How can we do this in Clojure without a **for** loop? Clojure has a **rand-int** function that returns a single random integer. We can use the **repeatedly** function, which returns a lazy sequence of calls to whatever function we pass it. Let's get started:

1. Create a lazy sequence with **repeatedly** and an anonymous function that calls **rand-int** with a fixed argument:

```
user> (def our-randoms (repeatedly (partial rand-int 100)))
```

The **parse-int** function just takes one argument that defines the upper bound of the value to be returned. It is common to use **partial** in cases like this, but we could have just as well written a literal anonymous function: **#(rand-int 100)**.

2. Use **take** to limit how many integers are returned:

```
user> (take 20 our-randoms)
```

3. Wrap this into a function:

```
user> (defn some-random-integers [size]
        (take size (repeatedly (fn [] (rand-int 100)))))
```

4. Use it as follows:

```
user> (some-random-integers 12)
```

The output is as follows:

```
(32 0 26 61 10 96 38 38 93 26 68 81)
```

When moving from a procedural approach to Clojure's functional approach, this pattern can be useful. First, describe the data you want, and then delimit it or transform it as needed.

Lazy sequences may seem unnecessarily confusing at first: why bother with a data structure that introduces uncertainty about whether something has been calculated or not? There are indeed some edge cases where this can be an issue, and we'll see one of those later in this chapter. Most of the time, however, these problems can be avoided by writing code that does not produce or depend on side effects. And then you will start to reap the benefits of lazy sequences, which allow sequences to be defined in a declarative way that will ultimately simplify your code.

Common Idioms and Patterns

Functions such as `map` and `filter` are two of the most powerful tools in Clojure for extracting, selecting, and transforming data. The key to using them effectively is, of course, knowing what kind of function to use with them. Clojure tries to make writing functions easy, and there are many shortcuts for some of the most common situations. These techniques will help you to start writing code more quickly, and they will also give you some valuable practice in functional programming.

Anonymous Functions

So far, we've been writing functional arguments as anonymous functions using the canonical `fn` form, or by using a named function such as `odd?`. Because sequence-handling functions in Clojure often make use of functions that are passed in as arguments, writing (and reading) anonymous functions is an extremely common task. This is why it's good to know the different shortcuts for writing them.

One of the most common ways to pass a function to `map` or `filter` is by using what's known as a **function literal**. A function literal is a simplified version of the `fn` form. The `fn` symbol and the argument list disappear, leaving only the heart of the function and a `#` operator just before the opening parenthesis.

In *Exercise 4.01, Working with map*, instead of `(fn [n] (* 10 n))`, we could have written `#(* 10 %)`. The leading `#` operator identifies the form that follows as a function. We still don't have an argument list, though, which would be a disastrous omission in a functional language! However, we are saved by a pattern: instead of naming the arguments freely, as in most functions, with function literals, the arguments are automatically named by following a simple pattern. The first argument is named `%` and all the other arguments are named `%2`, `%3`, `%4`, and so forth.

There are some limits to the expressiveness of function literals. The pattern for argument names does not allow anything such as destructuring or any of the other interesting features of Clojure's argument lists. And, of course, not being able to name the arguments does make for inexpressive code. If you have more than two arguments, it may be time to switch back to **fn**. It may seem obvious what you meant by %4 in the complex function literal you wrote this morning, but in a week, you will probably have forgotten. Function literals should be brief and simple.

The final limitation of functional literals is that they cannot be nested. In other words, if you have a function literal that calls **map**, then the function you provide to **map** cannot also be a function literal. The reason why nesting is impossible is quite simple. How would the compiler know which % goes with which function?

As soon as a function literal starts to become even a little bit complex, it's certainly time to switch to the **fn** form. Function literals should be used as simple wrappers for setting up calls to existing functions, rather than as a place to write complex code.

As you become more familiar with some of the more advanced functional techniques in Clojure, you will start to use some of the other options that are now at your disposal. For multiplying by 10, we could have also written the following:

```
(map (partial * 10) [1 2 3 4 5])
```

Notice that there is no # in front of this form. Here, the **partial** function returns a new anonymous function, that is, *, with its first argument "preloaded." This is easier to understand in the REPL:

```
user> (def apart (partial * 10))
#'user/apart
user> (apart 5)
50
```

Here, we've defined **apart**, which is a partially evaluated call to *. By calling that function, it behaves just like *, except that the first argument to * is already filled in. Writing **(partial * 10)** is essentially the same thing as writing **(fn [x] (* 10 x))**.

> **Note**
>
> Any function that's created with **partial** can always be rewritten as a function. The power of functions such as **partial** is their ability to create new functions programmatically. This is where a lot of the power of **functional programming** resides.

This is, in fact, the exact same function we've been writing. For now, you don't need to worry about **partial**. The other ways of writing functions like this are equivalent and sufficient.

Keywords as Functions

By now, you're already familiar with using a **keyword** to get a value in a map, as follows:

```
user> (:my-field {:my-field 42})
42
```

This works because Clojure keywords can be used as functions whose arguments are a map. It is also very useful when extracting a single field from a list of maps, as we'll see in the next exercise.

Exercise 4.06: Extracting Data from a List of Maps

Extracting information from a more complex structure is a common task. We are often presented with a sequence of Clojure maps, where each map has multiple keyword keys. We need a sequence of the values of just one key, one for each map. Let's say we have a vector containing the players in a game. Each player may be represented by a map like this:

```
{:id 9342
 :username "speedy"
 :current-points 45
 :remaining-lives 2
 :experience-level 5
 :status :active }
```

Imagine that the game requires us to get the current points of all the players, maybe to calculate an average or to find the maximum and minimum values.

Copy the **game-users** vector into your REPL from https://packt.live/36tHiI3. It contains a list of maps, with each map containing some information about a user:

```
{:id 9342
 :username "speedy"
 :current-points 45
 :remaining-lives 2s
 :experience-level 5
 :status :active}
```

Let's get started:

1. Use **map** to return a vector of **:current-points** for each user. To do this, we could write something like this:

```
user> (map (fn [player] (:current-points player)) game-users)
(45 67 33 59 12 0…)
```

2. Rewrite this expression using a keyword:

```
user> (map :current-points game-usersplayers)
(45 67 33 59 12 0…)
```

The ability to extract lists of data with so little code is one of the benefits of the fact that Clojure keywords can also be functions. Shortcuts like this are not just convenient or faster to type: they help us write expressive code that says exactly what we want.

Sets as Predicates

Another common task is to filter based on whether an item is a member of a set. Clojure sets are another form of collection that mimic the logic of mathematical sets. As a tool in programming, they have two important characteristics:

* An item is either part of a set or not part of a set. This means that there are never any duplicates in a set. Adding an item to a set more than once has no effect.

* The main job of a set is to tell you whether something belongs or not. This is why sets can be used as functions, and why they can be useful when combined with **filter**.

  Here, we're defining a set with the **set** function, which takes a list as an argument. It can then be used as a function that returns **true** if called on a value that is already part of the set, or **false** otherwise. In this example, **(alpha-set :z)** returns **false** because **alpha-set** does not contain **:z**:

```
user> (def alpha-set (set [:a :b :c]))
#'user/alpha-set
user> (alpha-set :z)
nil
user> (alpha-set :a)
:a
```

The **hash-set** also produces a set. Instead of a sequence, **hash-set** takes zero or more individual items as its arguments:

```
(hash-set :a :b :c)
```

The choice of one over the other will depend on what form of data you have. The resulting sets are identical.

> **Note**
>
> The `clojure.set` library is built into Clojure. This extremely useful library contains functions for performing set arithmetic, such as intersections.

Imagine we have a list of strings that are animal names:

```
user> (def animal-names ["turtle" "horse" "cat" "frog" "hawk" "worm"])
```

Say we want to remove all the mammals from the list. One solution would be to simply test for different values:

```
(remove (fn [animal-name]
          (or (= animal-name "horse")
              (= animal-name "cat")))
        animal-names)
```

This works, but there is a lot of repetitive text. Let's try using a set:

```
user> (remove #{"horse" "cat"} animal-names)
```

The output is as follows:

```
("turtle" "frog" "hawk" "worm")
```

This is brief, clear, and reads almost like an English sentence: remove **horse**, **cat** [from] **animal-names**. There is another advantage, too. Our list of mammals to exclude is fairly limited. What happens if we need to update it? We have to alter the source code to add more tests. The set, on the other hand, is data, so it could be defined once and for all in a variable at the top of our namespace or be calculated at runtime from other data available to our program.

Filtering on a Keyword with comp and a Set

To compose functions means to create a new function out of one to more existing functions. This is what **comp** does. Like **partial**, it is a higher-order function that returns a new function. Functional **composition** with **comp** means that in the returned function, each function provided to **comp** will be called on the results of the previous function.

Let's say we want to normalize an input string by doing two things: trimming whitespace from both ends of the string and converting the string into lowercase. The **clojure.string** library provides functions for both of those tasks: **trim** and **lower-case**. We could, of course, write a function that does what we need:

```
(require '[clojure.string :as string])
(defn normalize [s] (string/trim (string/lower-case s)))
```

> **Note**
>
> The **clojure.string** library is a standard library that provides many familiar string manipulation functions such as **split** and **join**. String behavior depends on how strings are implemented in the underlying platform, so **clojure.string** provides a unified interface that is the same for Clojure and ClojureScript.

With **comp**, we can do exactly the same thing with fewer parentheses:

```
user> (def normalizer (comp string/trim string/lower-case))
user> (normalizer "  Some Information ")
"some information"
```

The functional arguments to **comp** are called from right to left. That might sound confusing. It means that the functions are called in the same order as if they were written out as normal function calls:

```
(comp function-c function-b function-a)
```

The preceding code is equivalent to the following:

```
(fn [x] (function c (function-b (function-a x))))
```

In both of these functions, **function-a** would be called first, then **function-b** on that result, and, finally, **function-c** on the result of that.

Composing functions on the fly can be useful whenever you need to define a function on the fly. With filter, we could use **comp** to quickly build a predicate. Let's say we need to remove any strings from a list that are present in a normalized form set:

```
user> (def remove-words #{"and" "an" "a" "the" "of" "is"})
#'user/remove-words
user> (remove (comp remove-words string/lower-case string/trim) ["February" " THE "
"4th"])
("February" "4th")
```

Using **comp**, we are able to build a function that combines three separate steps.

Exercise 4.07: Using comp and a Set to Filter on a Keyword

Let's go back to **game-users** from the previous exercise. This time, we need to narrow the scope of the users whose scores we want to calculate. In our imaginary game, users can have one of several statuses: **:active**, **:imprisoned**, **:speed-boost**, **:pending**, or **:terminated**. We only want scores for players who have the **:pending** or **:terminated** statuses. To do this, we will combine the techniques we've used so far.

The mapping part will stay the same:

```
(map :current-score game-users)
```

Let's get started:

1. As in the previous exercise, copy the **game-users** vector into your REPL from https://packt.live/36tHil3.

2. Define a set with the statuses we want to keep:

```
(def keep-statuses #{:active :imprisoned :speed-boost})
```

3. Write a function to extract the **:status** field from each map and call the predicate on it.

   There are several ways we could do this. Maybe the first thing that occurs to us would be to write something like this:

```
(filter (fn [player] (keep-statuses (:status player))) game-users)
```

   The difficulty here, compared to our previous examples, is that we need to do two things at the same time: get the field, and then test it. In this case, we could also use the **comp** function, which takes two functions and returns a new function, which is the result of calling the first function on the result of the second function. So, instead of writing **(fn [player] (statuses (:status player)))**, we would write the following:

```
(comp keep-statuses :status)
```

4. Use the **->>** threading macro to put the different pieces back together:

```
user> (->> game-users
        (filter (comp #{:active :imprisoned :speed-boost} :status))
        (map :current-points))
```

The result is uncluttered and easy to read. With a little imagination, it almost reads like an English sentence: start with **game-users**, and filter out the users whose **:status** is not one of **:active**, **:imprisoned**, or **:speed-boost**, and then return the **:current-points** of each of those.

Returning a List Longer than the Input with mapcat

As we've already said, map always returns the same number of items as the original input sequence. Sometimes, you may need to make a new list with more items if, for example, multiple items can be derived from a single input item. This is what mapcat is for.

Here's a simple example. Suppose we have a list of letters of the alphabet, all in lowercase:

```
user> (def alpha-lc [ "a" "b" "c" "d" "e" "f" "g" "h" "i" "j"])
#'user/alpha-lc
```

We'll stop at **"j"** to save space, but you get the idea. The output we want to obtain is a new list where each lowercase letter is followed by its uppercase counterpart. mapcat lets us do that:

```
user> (mapcat (fn [letter] [letter (clojure.string/upper-case letter)]) alpha-lc)
("a" "A" "b" "B" "c" "C" "d" "D" "e" "E" "f" "F" "g" "G" "h" "H" "i" "I" "j" "J")
```

Here, the function we provided returns a two-item vector, such as **["a" "A"]**. mapcat simply unwraps each of these vectors so that, in the end, you have a single, flat list.

> **Note**
>
> Clojure has many interesting, more specialized sequence manipulation functions that you may like to explore. We could have solved this problem with **interleave** as well.

In situations where you have a one-to-many relationship between each item of the input list and the items in the output list, you probably want to consider mapcat first. Later in this book, we will use mapcat in situations where we need to flatten a list that contains a mix of individual items and sublists.

Mapping with Multiple Inputs

Among Clojure's sequence functions, map is unique in that it can accept more than one sequence as input. This can be useful when you need to stitch sequences together in some way or derive a combined value of some kind.

When map has more than one sequence as input, the mapping function must accept as many arguments as there are sequences. The basic pattern looks like this:

```
user> (map (fn [a b] (+ a b)) [5 8 3 1 2] [5 2 7 9 8])
(10 10 10 10 10)
```

Clojure already has a **zipmap** function that takes two sequences and combines them together in a map:

```
user> (defn our-zipmap [xs ys]
         (->> (map (fn [x y] [x y]) xs ys)
              (into {})))
user> (our-zipmap [:a :b :c] [1 2 3])
{:a 1, :b 2, :c 3}
```

> **Note**
>
> The **into** function is extremely useful when moving data from one collection type to another. It can also convert a map into a vector of key-value tuples, any sequence into a set, or the other way around.

The mapping function here, **(fn [x y] [x y])**, simply wraps the value pairs in a vector, which functions as a **tuple**, that is, a fixed-length sequential data structure. The **into** function then converts the sequence of two-item tuples into a Clojure map.

> **Note**
>
> A tuple is not a special Clojure data structure. Generally implemented as a short vector, a tuple is an alternative to a map with named fields. Instead of writing **{:x 5 :y 9}**, it is sometimes simpler to write **[5 9]**. A list is a tuple when the position of the items in the list determines what they mean. In theory, tuples can be of any length; in practice, if they are longer than three or four items, it becomes difficult to remember what each position in the list means.

Another reason to use multiple inputs would be if we needed to know the offset of the item currently being processed. Let's say we have a list of strings for our daily menu:

```
user> (def meals ["breakfast" "lunch" "dinner" "midnight snack"])
```

We may want to add a number in front of each item when presenting the list to the users. We could use **range** to supply an endless supply of integers to match each meal:

```
user> (map (fn [idx meal] (str (inc idx) ". " meal)) (range) meals)
("1. breakfast" "2. lunch" "3. dinner" "4. midnight snack")
```

The lazy sequence produced by **range** starts at zero, which is great inside a computer, but humans prefer lists to start with **1**, so we'll write **(inc idx)**. This pattern is so useful, in fact, that there is already the convenient **map-indexed** function that does exactly the same thing. In the end, all we need to write is the following:

```
(map-indexed (fn [idx meal] (str (inc idx) ". " meal)) meals)
```

In the examples so far, the functions supplied to **map** or **filter** only look at one item at a time. Even when using **map** with multiple sequences, we are still looking at each item separately. With a traditional **for** loop, however, we can look ahead or behind. For example, this is something that we may write in JavaScript if we had an array of values (**ourValues**) and a function that we wanted to call on each value and the next value:

```
for (var i = 0; i++; i < ourValues.length) {
  if (ourValues[i + 1]) {
    myFunction(ourValues[i], ourValues[i + 1]);
  }
}
```

We check to make sure that we aren't at the last value in the array, and then we call **myFunction**. While it would be possible to write more or less the same thing in Clojure (and we'll do some looping in *Chapter 7, Recursion II: Lazy Sequences*), there is a much more elegant way to do this, that is, by using **map** and multiple sequences.

The trick here is to use the same sequence more than once, but with an offset so that the second argument in the mapping function contains the item that follows the first argument:

```
(map (fn [x next-x] (do-something x next-x))
     my-sequence
     (rest my-sequence))
```

The second sequence here is, of course, the same as the first one, except that we start with the second element. The first time the anonymous function is called, its arguments will be the first and second items in **my-sequence**; the second time, the arguments will be the second and third items, and so on.

The following diagram represents this. The list from **0** to **5** is repeated with an offset. Each vertical pair corresponds to the two arguments that the mapping function will receive:

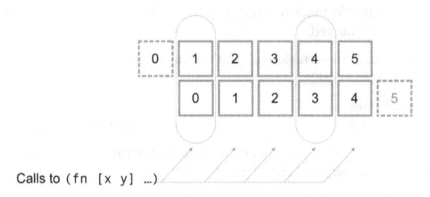

Calls to (fn [x y] ...)

Figure 4.5: A windowing or look-ahead effect with map

When using **map** with multiple collections, **map** stops iterating over them when it reaches the end of the shortest sequence. This ensures that there will always be enough arguments to supply to the mapping function. Depending on the context, when using offsets like this, it may be necessary to append data to the other end of the shortened function if it's important that the last item in the sequence is included in the results.

If the problem you are solving requires looking farther ahead, you can add more offset sequences, and thus more arguments to the mapping function. All sorts of creative possibilities are available. Just remember that the shortest sequence will limit the number of items that will be mapped over.

> **Note**
>
> If you just need to break up a sequence into multiple parts and then map over those, you can just use **partition. (partition 2 my-sequence)** will break your input up into two-item sublists.

Exercise 4.08: Identifying Weather Trends

In this exercise, we'll pretend that we have a list of outdoor temperatures for a series of days. We want to determine whether each day was warmer, colder, or the same as the previous day. This information could then be used to add up or down arrows to a visualization. Let's get started:

1. In your REPL, define a variable with the vector of integers found in https://packt.live/2tBRrnK:

```
(def temperature-by-day
  [18 23 24 23 27 24 22 21 21 20 32 33 30 29 35 28 25 24 28 29 30])
```

2. Write an expression that maps over this vector, starting at the second item, **23**, and outputs either **:warmer**, **:colder**, or **:unchanged**:

```
(map (fn [today yesterday]
          (cond (> today yesterday) :warmer
                (< today yesterday) :colder
                (= today yesterday) :unchanged))
     (rest temperature-by-day)
     temperature-by-day)
```

Instead of looking ahead this time, we are really looking backward, so, for clarity, we've put **(rest temperature-by-day)** before **temperature-by-day** and **today** before **yesterday** in the arguments of the anonymous function. As long as you understand which sequence corresponds to which argument, the order doesn't really matter. Thanks to the offset between the two versions of the same sequence of days, we can compare **yesterday** and **today** to define a trend.

The expression should return the following:

```
(:warmer :warmer :colder :warmer :colder :colder :colder :unchanged :colder :warmer
 :warmer :colder :colder :warmer :colder :colder :colder :warmer :warmer :warmer)
```

Remember that our first day corresponds to the second temperature. 23 is warmer than 18, so we get **:warmer**.

The "windows" that are created by offsetting a sequence against itself can be wider than two items: **map** can accept any number of lists.

The windowing pattern makes **map** even more powerful because it gets around one of its inherent limitations. In its simplest form, **map** is limited to a one-to-one relationship between the input list and the output list. With windowing, more items in the list can participate in each calculation.

Consuming Extracted Data with apply

Often, when **map** and **filter** are used to target and extract data in the form you need, the next step is producing some kind of summary. In *Chapter 7, Recursion II: Lazy Sequences*, we'll go into this in much more depth. For now, though, we can build some simple summary data by calling a single function, such as **min** or **max**, on a list using **apply**.

Functions such as **min**, **max**, and **+** accept an unlimited number of arguments. On the other hand, they don't accept lists. If you have a list of numbers and want to find the highest value, you may find yourself thinking "If only I could take these numbers out of this list and plug them directly into my call to **max**!" Well, with **apply**, you can do just that.

In its simplest form, a call to **apply** takes a function and a list, and calls the function on the list as if it were a simple multiple-arity function call:

```
user> (apply max [3 9 6])
9
```

This would be the same as the following:

```
user> (max 3 9 6)
9
```

There are many situations where this can be useful, even if you do know how many arguments you have:

```
user> (let [a 5
            b nil
            c 18]
        (+ a b c))
Execution error (NullPointerException) at user/eval12115 (REPL:46).
null
```

The **+** function did not appreciate the **nil** that was bound to **b**. With **apply**, we can use **filter** to remove any unwanted arguments:

```
user> (let [a 5
            b nil
            c 18]
        (apply + (filter integer? [a b c])))
23
```

The **apply** function is an important part of any functional programming toolkit. It is especially useful when dealing with sequential data that you can shape with **map** and **filter**.

There is one danger with this technique, however. Many functions that accept multiple arguments do not accept zero arguments. The **+** function can actually be called without any arguments. If you call **(+)**, it will return **0**. On the other hand, **min** and **max** will fail if we **apply** them to an empty list:

```
(apply min [])
Execution error (ArityException) at chapterfive/eval13541 (REPL:103).
Wrong number of args (0) passed to: clojure.core/min
```

In situations like this, it's important to be sure that an empty list is impossible. One way to do that is to supply at least one value. This is made easier by the fact that **apply** can accept non-list items before the list argument. This way, the call to **min** will always at least have a value of **0**:

```
user> (apply min 0 [])
0
```

Exercise 4.09: Finding the Average Weather Temperature

Using the same weather data as in the previous exercise, we'll calculate the average temperature for the days listed. Let's get started:

1. Continue using the REPL from the previous exercise or start a new REPL and copy the data in from https://packt.live/2tBRrnK:

    ```
    user> (def temperature-by-day
        [18 23 24 23 27 24 22 21 21 20 32 33 30 29 35 28 25 24 28 29 30])
    #'user/temperature-by-day
    ```

2. Use **(apply +...)** and **count** to calculate the sum of the temperatures and count them, and then find the average:

    ```
    user> (let [total (apply + temperature-by-day)
                c (count temperature-by-day)]
            (/ total c))
    26
    ```

Activity 4.01: Using map and filter to Report Summary Information

In our imaginary game, we want to create a dashboard where users can compare themselves to other users in the same situation: active users should only be able to see other active users, and so forth. We want to know the maximum and minimum values in each case so that the current user can see how they have been placed relative to the extremes.

This means that we need a function that accepts a field name (whichever field we want to display), a status (the status of the current user), and a list of **game-users**.

Write two functions that report the minimum and maximum values for each of the numeric fields in **game-users** for all the users and for each status category. We want to be able to ask: What is the highest value of **:current-points** for all the **:active** users?

The functions should take three arguments: the field we want, the status we want, and the list of users. They should be called like this:

```
(max-value-by-status :current-points :active game-users)
(min-value-by-status :remaining-lives :imprisoned game-users)
```

The call signature of the function will look like this:

```
(defn max-value-by-status [field status users]
;; TODO: write code
)
```

For simplicity, you should probably structure your code the same way we have done previously, that is, with the threading macro, **->>**, which can chain multiple function calls together.

These steps will help you complete this activity:

1. Use **filter** to narrow down the users who have the status we are looking for.

2. Use **map** to extract the value that you want.

3. Use the **min** and **max** functions with **apply** to find the minimums and maximums. Make sure your code will still work, even if there aren't any users who have the status you are looking for.

The following is the expected outcome:

```
user> (max-value-by-status :experience-level :imprisoned game-users)
5
user> (min-value-by-status :experience-level :imprisoned game-users)
0
user> (max-value-by-status :experience-level :terminated game-users)
12
user> (min-value-by-status :experience-level :terminated game-users)
0
user> (max-value-by-status :remaining-lives :active game-users)
7
user> (min-value-by-status :remaining-lives :active game-users)
0
user> (max-value-by-status :current-points :speed-boost game-users)
2043
```

Figure 4.6: Expected outcome

> **Note**
>
> The solution to this activity can be found on page 689.

Importing a Dataset from a CSV File

Now that we've seen some basic patterns for manipulating data, it's time to be more ambitious! We are going to start using a dataset that we will use in many of the following chapters as we build up our Clojure knowledge: ATP World Tour tennis data, a CSV file that includes, among other things, information about professional tennis matches going back to 1871. Besides learning about new concepts and techniques, we will see that Clojure can be an interesting choice for exploring and manipulating large datasets. And, naturally, most of the datasets that are available to us are CSV files.

> **Note**
>
> This dataset was created and is maintained at https://packt.live/2Fq30kk, and is available under the Creative Commons 4.0 International License. The files that we'll be using here are also available at https://packt.live/37DCkZn.

In the rest of this chapter, we will import tennis match data from a CSV file and use our mapping and filtering techniques to extract interesting data from it.

Exercise 4.10: Importing Data from a CSV File

It's time to imagine that you work for a sports journalism website specializing in data-centric reporting. Your role is to help the journalists analyze data and produce interesting visualizations for the site. In your new job, you need to be able to import large datasets that are usually published as CSV. Let's get started:

1. Create a folder somewhere convenient on your computer.

2. Download the **match_scores_1991-2016_UNINDEXED.csv** file to the folder you created.

3. In your editor, in the same folder, create a **deps.edn** file with the following contents:

```
{:deps
  {org.clojure/data.csv {:mvn/version "0.1.4"}
   semantic-csv {:mvn/version "0.2.1-alpha1"}}}
```

These are references to two libraries that we will use extensively. The first one, **clojure.data.csv**, is lower-level tool and deals with the mechanics of getting data in and out of a **.csv** file. **semantic-csv**, on the other hand, is a higher-level tool that makes it easier to work with **.csv** data.

Still in the same folder, with your editor or IDE, start a Clojure REPL.

4. Verify that everything is working by evaluating the following expression in your REPL:

```
user> (require '[clojure.data.csv :as csv])
nil
user> (require '[clojure.java.io :as io])
nil
user> (with-open [r (io/reader "match_scores_1991-2016_unindexed_csv.csv")]
         (first (csv/read-csv r)))
```

> **Note**
>
> When accessing data files, using the filename without the path will work as long as the data file is in the root directory of your Clojure project, which is the convention we have adopted here. If your data file is somewhere else, you'll need to include the absolute path instead.

Note that we didn't need to include `clojure.java.io` in our `deps.edn` file. That's because `clojure.java.io` is a core Clojure library. We still need to require it into our namespace, though. You should see this as the output:

```
["tourney_year_id"
 "tourney_order"
 "tourney_slug"
 "tourney_url_suffix"
 "tourney_round_name"
 "round_order"
 "match_order"
 "winner_name"
 "winner_player_id"
 "winner_slug"
 "loser_name"
 "loser_player_id"
 "loser_slug"
 "winner_seed"
 "loser_seed"
 "match_score_tiebreaks"
 "winner_sets_won"
 "loser_sets_won"
 "winner_games_won"
 "loser_games_won"
 "winner_tiebreaks_won"
 "loser_tiebreaks_won"
 "match_id"
 "match_stats_url_suffix"]
```

`clojure.data.csv` returns a vector of strings for each line in the file. This is the first line of the file, which is, of course, the column headers.

5. When exploring a new dataset, it's always good to know the size of the data. We can use **count** here to check that:

```
user> (with-open [r (io/reader "match_scores_1991-2016_unindexed_csv.csv")]
          (count (csv/read-csv r)))
91957
```

These are the basics of opening and reading a CSV file in Clojure. All the other data analysis techniques we will examine will use this same basic pattern. But before we go any further, we need to take a look at lazy evaluation.

Real-World Laziness

Did you notice how the code you evaluated in the previous exercise was rather fast? The data file is quite long, and it seems like it would take a long time to parse it. But **parse-csv** is lazy. Because we only asked for the first result, the evaluation stopped after one line. This is convenient because it allows us to process large files without loading them into memory.

Because we are dealing with files, we have to be careful. Remember that lazy evaluation means that evaluation is deferred until it is needed. That is fine for sequences of integers, but with an external resource such as a file reader, if we wait too long, the resource may not be available anymore. To avoid problems, we will do two things:

- Most of our data work will happen inside the scope of the **with-open** macro.

- We won't return any lazy sequences from the **with-open** macro.

In other words, inside the scope of **with-open**, we can use and combine all the lazy evaluation techniques we like. When we return sequences, we'll make sure that they are fully realized, often using the **doall** function. It may be tempting to immediately call **doall** to avoid having to worry about lazy evaluation at all. While there are cases where this may be appropriate, it is best to try to resist this temptation. Reading a large CSV file is a good example of why preserving the laziness of sequences is important. Calling **doall** too soon would force all of the rows of data to be loaded into memory, when maybe we only need a few rows.

Let's look at this in practice.

Exercise 4.11: Avoiding Lazy Evaluation Traps with Files

In the previous exercise, you successfully opened a CSV file and started to play with it a little bit. "It's time," you say to yourself, "to look at some real data." The incoming data appears to be a sequence, since we can use **first** and **count** on it. Let's try to extract some more data:

1. In the same folder as before, open your REPL again.

2. If necessary, load the dependencies again:

```
user> (require '[clojure.data.csv :as csv])
nil
user> (require '[clojure.java.io :as io])
nil
```

3. Let's try to extract the name of the winner of each of the first five matches. Starting from 0, the **winner_name** field is number **7**, so we want to call **#(nth % 7)** on each of the first five lines (after the initial header line). Maybe this will work:

```
(with-open [r (io/reader "match_scores_1991-2016_unindexed_csv.csv")]
  (->> (csv/read-csv r)
       (map #(nth % 7))
       (take 6)))
```

The output is as follows:

```
Error printing return value (IOException) at java.io.BufferedReader/ensureOpen
(BufferedReader.java:122).
Stream closed
```

What happened? As the error message suggests, the file stream is closed when the REPL tries to print the results. **map** and **take** are both lazy. But why? We call **map** and **take** *inside* the scope of **with-open**. Shouldn't the file still be open? The problem is that because the evaluation is deferred, it has not happened yet when we exit the scope of the **with-open** macro. All we have at that point is an unevaluated sequence. When the REPL tried to evaluate the lazy expression returned by **take**, the scope where the file reader was available disappeared. Lazy sequences are not evaluated until they are consumed, and in this case, the sequence is consumed in your REPL.

4. Now, try again with **doall**:

```
user> (with-open [r (io/reader "match_scores_1991-2016_unindexed_csv.csv")]
        (->> (csv/read-csv r)
             (map #(nth % 7))
             (take 6)
             doall))
```

This time, you should see something like this:

```
("winner_name"
 "Nicklas Kulti"
 "Michael Stich"
 "Nicklas Kulti"
 "Jim Courier"
 "Michael Stich")
```

As you can see, **doall** forces the evaluation of the lazy sequence. The closed stream is no longer a problem. The expression returns a simple list.

While working with this dataset, we will use this basic pattern many times, often ending with **doall**. You can also see how it reproduces a familiar pattern: get the information (**csv/read-csv**), shape the information (**map, take**), and hand the information off (**doall**). Lazy evaluation combined with limited external resources, such as file I/O, in this case, does add an extra challenge. Maintaining a clear separation between data acquisition, data manipulation, and data output is not only good design or good practice—in a situation like this, it will really help avoid errors and bugs. Even in this case, however, there is an upside to lazy evaluation: some files may be too large to fit in memory. By evaluating the output from the file "lazily," the entire file doesn't need to be loaded into memory simultaneously.

You've now extracted some real data from the **.csv** file.

> **Note**
>
> Clojure's **mapv** function is a replacement for **map**, with one key difference: instead of returning a lazy sequence, it returns a vector. Because vectors are not lazy, this can be a way of avoiding a call to **doall**. For clarity, however, it is often preferable to use **doall** explicitly.

Convenient CSV Parsing

As you can see from the previous example, **clojure.data.csv** returns a sequence of vectors, where each vector contains, as individual strings, the CSV files in a single line of the original file. There is still some work to do before we can really use that data, however. Because **.csv** is such a common format, there are libraries that can make things a little bit more convenient. We'll be using **semantic-csv**, which we've already included in our **deps.edn** file.

The main functions that we'll use from **semantic-csv** are **mappify** and **cast-with**. With **mappify**, each row becomes a Clojure map, where the keys are the column names from the CSV file, and with **cast-with**, we can transform strings containing numeric values in the source file into the correct types.

Let's see how this works. After that, we'll be ready to do some more interesting things with the data in our **.csv** file.

Exercise 4.12: Parsing CSV with semantic-csv

In this exercise, we'll start by saving our work in a file so that we can come back to it later. Let's get started:

1. In the same folder as before, create a new file, **tennis.clj**, in your text editor.

2. Set up your namespace and use **:require** so that you have access to the necessary libraries:

```clojure
(ns packt-clj.tennis
  (:require
    [clojure.data.csv :as csv]
    [clojure.java.io :as io]
    [semantic-csv.core :as sc]))
```

3. Write a function that returns the first row of data:

```clojure
(defn first-match [csv]
  (with-open [r (io/reader csv)]
    (->> (csv/read-csv r)
         sc/mappify
         first)))
```

4. Evaluate your file, move to the **packt-clj.tennis** namespace in your REPL, and call the function:

```clojure
(in-ns 'packt-clj.tennis)
(first-match "match_scores_1991-2016_unindexed_csv.csv")
```

You should see a map with the data for the first match:

```clojure
{:tourney_slug "adelaide",
 :loser_slug "michael-stich",
 :winner_sets_won "2",
 :match_score_tiebreaks "63 16 62",
 :loser_sets_won "1",
 :loser_games_won "11",
 :tourney_year_id "1991-7308",
 :tourney_order "1",
 :winner_seed "",
 :loser_seed "6",
 :winner_slug "nicklas-kulti",
 :match_order "1",
 :loser_name "Michael Stich",
 :winner_player_id "k181",
 :match_stats_url_suffix "/en/scores/1991/7308/MS001/match-stats",
```

```
:tourney_url_suffix "/en/scores/archive/adelaide/7308/1991/results",
:loser_player_id "s351",
:loser_tiebreaks_won "0",
:round_order "1",
:tourney_round_name "Finals",
:match_id "1991-7308-k181-s351",
:winner_name "Nicklas Kulti",
:winner_games_won "13",
:winner_tiebreaks_won "0"}
```

5. That's a lot of information. We don't need all of those fields, so we'll call **select-keys** on each **map** to keep only the values that interest us. This time, we'll keep the first five rows:

```
(defn five-matches [csv]
  (with-open [r (io/reader csv)]
    (->> (csv/read-csv r)
         sc/mappify
         (map #(select-keys % [:tourney_year_id
                               :winner_name
                               :loser_name
                               :winner_sets_won
                               :loser_sets_won]))
         (take 5)
         doall)))
```

Evaluate your file again, and then call **five-matches** in the REPL:

```
(five-matches "match_scores_1991-2016_unindexed_csv.csv")
```

You should see a list of maps:

```
({:tourney_year_id "1991-7308",
  :winner_name "Nicklas Kulti",
  :loser_name "Michael Stich",
  :winner_sets_won "2",
  :loser_sets_won "1"}
 {:tourney_year_id "1991-7308",
  :winner_name "Michael Stich",
  :loser_name "Jim Courier",
  :winner_sets_won "2",
  :loser_sets_won "0"}
...etc.
```

6. To use the `:winner_sets_won` and `:loser_sets_won` fields in a calculation of some kind, we need to cast them as integers first. Use the **cast-with** function of **semantic-csv**:

```
(defn five-matches-int-sets [csv]
  (with-open [r (io/reader csv)]
    (->> (csv/read-csv r)
         sc/mappify
         (map #(select-keys % [:tourney_year_id
                               :winner_name
                               :loser_name
                               :winner_sets_won
                               :loser_sets_won]))
         (sc/cast-with {:winner_sets_won sc/->int
                        :loser_sets_won sc/->int})
         (take 5)
         doall)))
```

This will return the same data as the previous function, except that the values for `:winner_sets_won` and `:loser_sets_won` won't appear with quotation marks anymore:

```
{:tourney_year_id "1991-7308",
 :winner_name "Nicklas Kulti",
 :loser_name "Michael Stich",
 :winner_sets_won 2, ;; <----- Real integer!
 :loser_sets_won 1}
```

Now, we have enough tools to start performing some interesting queries against our dataset. With **map**, **filter**, and a few simple tools, we are ready to write simple, yet sophisticated, queries. In the next section, we are going to look at some techniques that will be useful in their own right and will help you to think about using functions to describe the data you want.

Exercise 4.13: Querying the Data with filter

If we think of this CSV data as a database, then writing queries is a question of writing and combining predicates. In this exercise, we will use **filter** to narrow our dataset down to the exact information we want. Imagine that the journalists on your team are working on a new project dedicated to famous tennis rivalries. As a first step, they've asked you to produce a list of all the tennis matches won by Roger Federer. Let's get started:

1. Make sure that your project is set up the same way as it was in the previous exercises.

2. Create a function called **federer-wins** that provides the CSV processing steps we've already used. Add the calls to **select-keys** and **doall**, which will be applied to the data once it has been narrowed down:

```
(defn federer-wins [csv]
    (with-open [r (io/reader csv)]
    (->> (csv/read-csv r)
        sc/mappify
        ;; TODO: keep writing code
        (map #(select-keys % [:winner_name
                            :loser_name
                            :winner_sets_won
                            :loser_sets_won
                            :winner_games_won
                            :loser_games_won
                            :tourney_year_id
                            :tourney_slug]))
        doall)))
```

3. Write a predicate that will decide whether Roger Federer won a match. Using the same pattern as in the previous examples, all we need to do is "plug in" a call to **filter** with the right predicate.

    The predicate itself is rather simple. It's just a question of matching one of the fields of each map:

```
#(= "Roger Federer" (:winner_name %))
```

4. Use this predicate with **filter** in the function:

```
(defn federer-wins [csv]
    (with-open [r (io/reader csv)]
      (->> (csv/read-csv r)
        sc/mappify
        (filter #(= "Roger Federer" (:winner_name %)))
        (map #(select-keys % [:winner_name
                              :loser_name
                              :winner_sets_won
                              :loser_sets_won
                              :winner_games_won
                              :loser_games_won
                              :tourney_year_id
                              :tourney_slug]))
        doall)))
```

Try calling **federer-wins**. You will receive the following output:

```
packt-clj.tennis> (take 3 (federer-wins "match_scores_1991-2016_unindexed_csv.csv"))
({:winner_name "Roger Federer",
  :loser_name "Richard Fromberg",
  :winner_sets_won "2",
  :loser_sets_won "0",
  :winner_games_won "13",
  :loser_games_won "7",
  :tourney_year_id "1998-327",
  :tourney_slug "toulouse"}
 {:winner_name "Roger Federer",
  :loser_name "Guillaume Raoux",
  :winner_sets_won "2",
  :loser_sets_won "0",
  :winner_games_won "12",
  :loser_games_won "4",
  :tourney_year_id "1998-327",
  :tourney_slug "toulouse"}
 {:winner_name "Roger Federer",
  :loser_name "Jerome Golmard",
  :winner_sets_won "2",
  :loser_sets_won "1",
  :winner_games_won "20",
  :loser_games_won "19",
  :tourney_year_id "1999-496",
  :tourney_slug "marseille"})
```

Figure 4.7: Printing the details

This seems to work!

This exercise shows how writing a query is as simple as writing a new predicate. You have all the power and flexibility of the Clojure language at hand to describe exactly what results you need. In the next exercise, we will use a higher-order functional technique to write a dedicated query function.

Exercise 4.14: A Dedicated Query Function

Your team is happy with the initial results and now they have started asking you to run new queries all the time. You are tired of writing the same code each time, so you've decided to write a function that can accept any predicate. Let's get started:

1. Use the same environment as in the previous exercise.

2. Rewrite the **federer-wins** function as **match-query**, which takes a second argument, that is, **pred**:

```
(defn match-query [csv pred]
    (with-open [r (io/reader csv)]
    (->> (csv/read-csv r)
         sc/mappify
         (filter pred)
         (map #(select-keys % [:winner_name
                               :loser_name
                               :winner_sets_won
                               :loser_sets_won
                               :winner_games_won
                               :loser_games_won
                               :tourney_year_id
                               :tourney_slug]))
         doall)))
```

3. Write a predicate to search for all of Federer's matches, wins, and losses.

    One possibility would be to simply add an **or** operator:

```
#(or (= "Roger Federer" (:winner_name %))
     (= "Roger Federer" (:loser_name %)))
```

    We could also use a set as a predicate, as we saw earlier:

```
#((hash-set (:winner_name %) (:loser_name %)) "Roger Federer")
```

    First, we define a set that includes the **:winner_name** and **:loser_name** fields and then we ask: is **Roger Federer** a member of that set?

> **Note**
>
> We've written **hash-set** here instead of using the literal notation, **#{…}**, to avoid confusion with the **#(…)** of the anonymous function. **hash-set** and **set** do the same thing, that is, they create Clojure sets, except that **set** takes a single collection as an argument, while **hash-set** takes any number of items.

4. Test this by counting the number of matches played and the number of matches won using the predicate from the previous exercise:

```
packt-clj.tennis> (count (match-query "match_scores_1991-2016_unindexed_csv.csv"
                                       #((hash-set (:winner_name %) (:loser_name %)) "Roger Federer")))
1290
packt-clj.tennis> (count (match-query "match_scores_1991-2016_unindexed_csv.csv"
                                       #(= (:winner_name %) "Roger Federer")))
1050
```

Figure 4.8: Number of matches played and won by Federer

Now, we know that, in our dataset, Federer played **1,290** matches and won **1,050** times!

Providing a predicate as an argument makes writing queries like this very convenient. It becomes easier to write more and more complex queries. In the next exercise, we will continue to build on this.

Exercise 4.15: Using filter to Find a Tennis Rivalry

As your team's deadline approaches, the journalists are asking for more and more specific queries. They've decided to write an article about one of the most famous rivalries in modern tennis, that is, between Roger Federer and Rafael Nadal. They want you to write two queries: the first should return all the matches between the two players, while the second should return only the matches where the score was very close. Let's get started:

1. Use the same environment as the previous exercises.

2. Write a predicate that will select all the matches between the two players. One possibility would be to use **or**, like this:

```
#(and
   (or (= (:winner_name %) "Roger Federer")
       (= (:winner_name %) "Rafael Nadal"))
   (or (= (:loser_name %) "Roger Federer")
       (= (:loser_name %) "Rafael Nadal")))
```

This would work, but you can see that the logic is getting more complex because we have to account for two different possibilities. This is where sets can be very useful:

```
#(= (hash-set (:winner_name %) (:loser_name %))
    #{"Roger Federer" "Rafael Nadal"})
```

Sets are great for these kinds of situations. We don't care about the order, or, unlike the players themselves, which one is the winner or the loser.

Test this predicate using the **match-query** function from the previous exercise:

```
packt-clj.tennis> (take 3 (match-query "match_scores_1991-2016_unindexed_csv.csv"
                           #(= (hash-set (:winner_name %) (:loser_name %))
                              #{"Roger Federer" "Rafael Nadal"})))
({:winner_name "Rafael Nadal",
  :loser_name "Roger Federer",
  :winner_sets_won "2",
  :loser_sets_won "0",
  :winner_games_won "12",
  :loser_games_won "6",
  :tourney_year_id "2004-403",
  :tourney_slug "miami"}
 {:winner_name "Roger Federer",
  :loser_name "Rafael Nadal",
  :winner_sets_won "3",
  :loser_sets_won "2",
  :winner_games_won "27",
  :loser_games_won "23",
  :tourney_year_id "2005-403",
  :tourney_slug "miami"}
 {:winner_name "Rafael Nadal",
  :loser_name "Roger Federer",
  :winner_sets_won "3",
  :loser_sets_won "1",
  :winner_games_won "22",
  :loser_games_won "16",
  :tourney_year_id "2005-520",
  :tourney_slug "roland-garros"})
```

Figure 4.9: Testing the predicate

This seems to work. Now, we need to narrow down the results to the closest matches.

3. Update **match-query** so that we can do arithmetic on the fields. To know whether a match was close, we need to be able to subtract :**loser_sets_won** from :**winner_sets_won**. We have a problem, though: the values are strings here and not integers, so we can't subtract. To fix this, we need to go back to **match-query** and reintroduce the type conversions that we used in the previous exercises. Here's the new version of **match-query**:

```
(defn match-query [csv pred]
    (with-open [r (io/reader csv)]
    (->> (csv/read-csv r)
        sc/mappify
        (sc/cast-with {:winner_sets_won sc/->int
                       :loser_sets_won sc/->int
                       :winner_games_won sc/->int
                       :loser_games_won sc/->int})
        (filter pred)
        (map #(select-keys % [:winner_name
                             :loser_name
```

```
                                      :winner_sets_won
                                      :loser_sets_won
                                      :winner_games_won
                                      :loser_games_won
                                      :tourney_year_id
                                      :tourney_slug]))
          doall)))
```

4. Write a predicate for close matches.

We'll use **and** to combine the Federer-Nadal predicate with a test for the difference in sets won:

```
#(and (= (hash-set (:winner_name %) (:loser_name %))
         #{"Roger Federer" "Rafael Nadal"})
      (= 1 (- (:winner_sets_won %) (:loser_sets_won %))))
```

5. Let's test our new predicate:

```
packt-clj.tennis> (take 3 (match-query "match_scores_1991-2016_unindexed_csv.csv"
                    #(and (= (hash-set (:winner_name %) (:loser_name %))
                             #{"Roger Federer" "Rafael Nadal"})
                          (= 1 (- (:winner_sets_won %) (:loser_sets_won %)))))))
```

```
({:winner_name "Roger Federer",
  :loser_name "Rafael Nadal",
  :winner_sets_won 3,
  :loser_sets_won 2,
  :winner_games_won 27,
  :loser_games_won 23,
  :tourney_year_id "2005-403",
  :tourney_slug "miami"}
 {:winner_name "Rafael Nadal",
  :loser_name "Roger Federer",
  :winner_sets_won 2,
  :loser_sets_won 1,
  :winner_games_won 14,
  :loser_games_won 14,
  :tourney_year_id "2006-495",
  :tourney_slug "dubai"}
 {:winner_name "Rafael Nadal",
  :loser_name "Roger Federer",
  :winner_sets_won 3,
  :loser_sets_won 2,
  :winner_games_won 28,
  :loser_games_won 29,
  :tourney_year_id "2006-416",
  :tourney_slug "rome"})
```

Figure 4.10: Printing the results

The results tell the story of one of the great rivalries in sports!

As long as we are searching for lists of results, **map**, **filter**, and some carefully crafted predicates can accomplish a lot: **map** prepares the data while **filter** finds the items we are looking for.

Activity 4.02: Arbitrary Tennis Rivalries

Your data consultancy team is encouraged by what they could learn by looking at the Federer-Nadal rivalry data and they want to be able to expand the approach. They've asked you to write a function that will find some summary statistics about all the matches between any two players. They would also like to have a list of the most competitive matches between the players.

Using the tennis dataset, write a function that provides information about a tennis rivalry. The call signature should look like this:

```
(defn rivalry-data [csv player-1 player-2])
```

The function should return a map with the following fields:

```
:first-victory-player-1
:first-victory-player-2
:total-matches
:total-victories-player-1
:total-victories-player-2
:most-competitive-matches
```

The values in the :**total-*** fields should be integers. The other fields should be (possibly empty) lists of matches. When displaying matches in the results, limit the fields to those displayed in the previous example, that is, :**winner_name**, :**loser_name**, :**winner_sets_won**, :**loser_sets_won**, :**winner_games_won**, :**loser_games_won**, :**tourney_year_id**, and :**tourney_slug**.

Save your function in the same file that you did for *Exercise 4.12, Parsing CSV with semantic-csv*.

These steps will help you to complete this activity:

1. Don't forget to use the same calls to **sc/mappify** and **sc/cast-with** to make your data easy to work with.

2. Within the scope of a **with-open** macro, use **let** to bind the lazy sequence of all the matches between the two players to a local symbol. Use that binding later whenever you need to match data, rather than rereading from the .**csv** file.

3. To calculate each result field, you will need to filter the list of matches in a different way.

4. For the :**total-*** fields, obtain the correct sequences and then use **count**.

5. For the fields that show matches, use **select-keys** to keep only the fields we are interested in.

The following is the expected outcome:

For any two players who have actually played against each other, your function should produce summary data:

```
packt-clj.tennis> (rivalry-data "/Users/joseph/Documents/Packt/data/atp-world-tour-
tennis-data_zip/data/match_scores_1968-1990_unindexed_csv.csv" "Boris Becker" "Jimmy
Connors"  )
{:first-victory-player-1
  {:winner_name "Boris Becker",
   :loser_name "Jimmy Connors",
   :winner_sets_won 2,
   :loser_sets_won 1,
   :winner_games_won 17,
   :loser_games_won 16,
   :tourney_year_id "1986-411",
   :tourney_slug "chicago"},
  :first-victory-player-2 nil,
  :total-matches 5,
  :total-victories-player-1 5,
  :total-victories-player-2 0,
  :most-competitive-matches
  ({:winner_name "Boris Becker",
   :loser_name "Jimmy Connors",
   :winner_sets_won 2,
   :loser_sets_won 1,
   :winner_games_won 17,
   :loser_games_won 16,
   :tourney_year_id "1986-411",
   :tourney_slug "chicago"}
   {:winner_name "Boris Becker",
   :loser_name "Jimmy Connors",
   :winner_sets_won 2,
   :loser_sets_won 1,
   :winner_games_won 15,
   :loser_games_won 15,
   :tourney_year_id "1986-428",
   :tourney_slug "bolton"}
```

```
{:winner_name "Boris Becker",
 :loser_name "Jimmy Connors",
 :winner_sets_won 2,
 :loser_sets_won 1,
 :winner_games_won 18,
 :loser_games_won 14,
 :tourney_year_id "1987-311",
 :tourney_slug "london"}
{:winner_name "Boris Becker",
 :loser_name "Jimmy Connors",
 :winner_sets_won 2,
 :loser_sets_won 1,
 :winner_games_won 15,
 :loser_games_won 14,
 :tourney_year_id "1987-605",
 :tourney_slug "nitto-atp-finals"})}
```

Note

The solution to this activity can be found on page 691.

Summary

In this chapter, we have looked at how to use two of Clojure's most important and useful functions for handling sequential data. From a practical point of view, you have seen how to use `map` and `filter`, as well as some patterns and idioms for accomplishing common tasks and avoiding some common problems. You are starting to build your mental toolkit for working with collections.

Working with `map` and `filter` means we are working with lazy sequences, and so this chapter explored some of the ins and outs of lazy evaluation, which is one of Clojure's fundamental building blocks.

The techniques for reading and parsing files, extracting, querying, and manipulating data will also be useful right away as we continue to build on these data-handling techniques in the next chapter.

5

Many to One: Reducing

Overview

In this chapter, you will learn new techniques for dealing with sequential data. You will learn how to use the **reduce** function, as well as other reducing techniques that provide greater flexibility for transforming or extracting data from a sequence. We will use the simple form of **reduce**, use **reduce** with an initializer and an accumulator, and solve problems requiring a variable-length "window" over a sequence. We will also reduce sequences with functions other than **reduce**.

By the end of this chapter, you will be able to use **reduce** with complex accumulators.

Introduction

This chapter is about using Clojure's **reduce** function and about *reducing* in general. By that, we mean starting with a sequence and *boiling it down* to a single thing. ("Reducing" is also cooking term, after all.) `map` and `filter` were about taking the sequence you have and turning it into the sequence you want: *sequence in, sequence out*. But that's not always what we want. Even simple operations on a sequence, such as calculating an average, a sum, or a maximum, cannot be directly calculated this way. That's where **reduce**, as well as a wider family of functions and patterns, comes in: *sequence in, something else out*. It's "something else" because the result might be a number, a string, a map, or even another sequence.

In the previous chapter, we saw that functions such as `map` and `filter` only look at one element at a time: how should we transform this item? Should we discard this item, or keep it? This is a powerful approach because it creates a clear scope for the action of the functions we write, which helps us to write simpler code, and it allows lazy evaluation. There is a limit to this approach, however, when we need to look at a sequence as a whole, or at least as more than just the current item. This is why `map` and `filter` are only partial replacements for a `for` loop.

In Clojure, the **reduce** function is not the only way to generate a result from an entire sequence. Even the simple **count** function is a way of reducing a sequence down to a single value. Some core functions actually use **reduce** themselves so that we don't have to. The recursion and looping techniques that we'll discuss in the next chapter can do this as well. The patterns we are going to look at here should, in general, be what you consider first, after you've decided that `map` and `filter` are not enough. **reduce** and other similar functions provide a clear way of solving a certain kind of problem, which is why they are an important part of your mental Clojure toolkit.

The Basics of reduce

To understand how **reduce** works, the best place to start is with a simple example. Let's try to find the sum of a list of integers. In an imperative language such as JavaScript, we might do something like this:

```
var integers = [8, 4000, 10, 300];
var sum = 0;
for (var i = 0; i < integers.length; i++) {
    sum = sum + integers[i];
}
console.log(sum);
```

The **sum** variable here accumulates information found in previous iterations of the loop. This is exactly what **reduce** does. Here's a Clojure version of the same thing:

```
user> (reduce (fn [sum-so-far item] (+ sum-so-far item)) [8 4000 10 300])
4318
```

> **Note**
>
> In the first iteration, **sum-so-far** refers to **0** and **item** refers to **8**. In subsequent iterations, **sum-so-far** refers to the result of evaluating the function with the previous item in the collection and **item** refers to the current item of the collection.

How does this work? This expression looks a lot like some of the uses of `map` or `filter` in the previous chapter. The layout of the s-expression should be very familiar by now:

- A function
- An anonymous function
- A vector of integers

And yet, you can probably already tell that this expression is quite different from using `map` or `filter`. First of all, there is only one sequence supplied, yet the anonymous function takes two arguments, **sum-so-far** and **item**. And, of course, the biggest surprise is the result, which is not a sequence at all, but a single integer. This isn't `map` territory anymore.

Obviously, this expression simply adds up integers in the sequence provided. To do that, it iterates over the integers in the sequence, seemingly like `map` would. The key difference is that with **reduce**, the function *"remembers"* the result of evaluating the previous calculations.

Let's break down the operations here.

The first time **reduce** calls the function we've provided, **(fn [sum-so-far item]** **(+ sum-so-far item))**, the arguments are the first two items in the list:

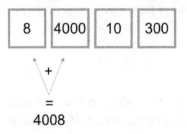

Figure 5.1: sum-so-far and item are the first two items in the list (call 1)

For each of the next calls, **sum-so-far** is the result of the previous calculation, and **item** is the next integer in the list:

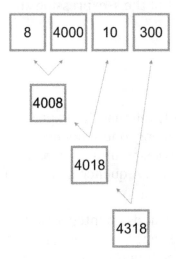

Figure 5.2: Calls 2 and 3: each call builds on the result of the previous calls

We could simplify this expression by replacing the anonymous function with Clojure's **+** function:

```
user> (reduce + [8 4000 10 300])
4318
```

And we could even use **apply** and avoid using **reduce** altogether:

```
user> (apply + [8 4000 10 300])
4318
```

However, with **(apply + …)**, we haven't really escaped from **reduce**: internally, the **+** function, when called with more than two arguments, uses a version of **reduce** to move through the list.

Exercise 5.01: Finding the Day with the Maximum Temperature

Clojure's **max** function is useful when dealing with a list of numbers, but what do you do when the numbers you want to compare are part of a more complex data structure? Suppose we have the following weather data:

```
(def weather-days
  [{:max 31
    :min 27
    :description :sunny
    :date "2019-09-24"}
   {:max 28
    :min 25
    :description :cloudy
    :date "2019-09-25"}
   {:max 22
    :min 18
    :description :rainy
    :date "2019-09-26"}
   {:max 23
    :min 16
    :description :stormy
    :date "2019-09-27"}
   {:max 35
    :min 19
    :description :sunny
    :date "2019-09-28"}])
```

We need to be able to write functions that return the entire map for the day with the highest maximum temperature, the lowest minimum, and so on:

1. Start a REPL and copy the **weather-days** variable from the book GitHub's repository and paste it into your REPL. You'll find the file here: https://packt.live/2SXw372.

2. Use **map** and **max** to find the highest temperature:

```
user> (apply max (map :max weather-days))
35
```

This could be useful, but it doesn't tell us what day had this temperature, or whether it was sunny or cloudy that day, or what the minimum temperature was that day.

3. Find the maximum :max temperature with **reduce**:

```
user> (reduce (fn [max-day-so-far this-day]
                  (if (> (:max this-day) (:max max-day-so-far))
                    this-day
                    max-day-so-far))
              weather-days)
{:max 35, :min 19, :description :sunny, :date "2019-09-28"}
```

If the maximum temperature of a given day is higher than **max-day-so-far**, that day replaces **max-day-so-far** until another day with a higher temperature dethrones it.

4. Find the day that had the lowest maximum temperature:

```
user> (reduce (fn [min-max-day-so-far this-day]
                  (if (< (:max this-day) (:max min-max-day-so-far))
                    this-day
                    min-max-day-so-far))
              weather-days)
{:max 22, :min 18, :description :rainy, :date "2019-09-26"}
```

Returning the *item* with the maximum value, rather than returning the maximum itself, can be useful when working with complex data structures. You will probably never be confronted with this exact problem. The important thing is to be able to quickly write a specialized version of **max**, **min**, a comparator, or whatever other function you need that is adapted to the needs of your particular data. Because of its power and flexibility, knowing how to use **reduce** can be extremely useful in those situations. It's no accident either that, internally, many core Clojure functions use **reduce** themselves. This is true of **take-while**, **set**, **into**, and **map**, for example.

Initializing reduce

Tasks such as adding integers or finding maximum values have a common thread: the input values and the accumulated values are of the same type. When two numbers are added, the result is a number; when a maximum or a minimum is chosen between two numbers, the result is still a number. When we use **reduce** to add numbers together, the running total is a number just like all the other inputs. In the examples so far, the first function call that **reduce** makes takes the first two items in the sequence. We can break a **reduce** call into its successive function calls:

```
(reduce + [1 2 3 5 7])
(+ 1 2)
(+ 3 3)
(+ 6 5)
(+ 11 7)
```

We actually don't need the anonymous function that we used in the previous examples, because + takes numbers as arguments, and returns a number:

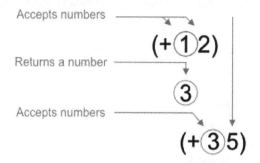

Figure 5.3: The arguments and the return value are all of the same type

In each of our examples so far, three different things are all of the same type:

- The values in the sequence
- Both arguments to +
- The return value of +

In the previous exercise, we returned a map rather than a single number. That was possible because the same kinds of maps were used in these three places: the maps we iterate over as well as the current "best" map that we are comparing the others to.

If this was all we could do with **reduce**, however, it would be rather restrictive. Not all problems can be expressed by this kind of function. Often, we want to compute and accumulate some other kind of value. We might need more complex summary statistics, or to merge individual values together in a specific way, or to divide a sequence into segments based on special criteria. Just because you have a sequence of **matches**, to take up our tennis examples again, doesn't mean that the result you want can also be expressed as a tennis **match**. Maybe we want to iterate over a list of matches and accumulate some other kind of information. At the end of this chapter, in fact, we are going to do just that. At the beginning of this chapter, we said that **reduce** can turn a sequence into *anything* else, but so far, this hasn't really been true.

This is why there is a second form of **reduce** that takes an additional argument. When the additional argument is present, it becomes the first argument to the reducing function. On that initial function call, the first item in the sequence is the second argument. This is a crucial improvement because the reducing function's return value no longer has to be the same kind of thing that is in the sequence.

Consider the following snippet, where we supply an empty map as an initial value for our reduction. As it moves through the sequence, the reducing function updates the :maximum and :minimum fields when new values are discovered. The expression returns a function at the end:

```
user> (reduce (fn [{:keys [minimum maximum]} new-number]
              {:minimum (if (and minimum (> new-number minimum))
                          minimum
                          new-number)
               :maximum (if (and maximum (< new-number maximum))
                          maximum
                          new-number)})
           {}                 ;; <---- The new argument!
           [5 23 5004 845 22])
{:minimum 5, :maximum 5004}
```

The preceding expression finds both the minimum and the maximum value in a sequence. Calling **reduce** like this might be useful if, for some reason, it was difficult to loop over a list twice, if it were very, very long, or perhaps there was a stream that was not being retained. To return two values, we'll place them in a map. Without the initializing argument for **reduce**, this would already have been impossible. This is a case where "numbers in, numbers out" is not sufficient.

Here, we supply an empty map as an initial value for our reduction. As it moves through the sequence, the reducing function updates the :maximum and :minimum fields when new values are discovered. The expression returns a function at the end.

> **Note**
>
> Another common pattern in a case like this would be to return a two-item vector (a tuple) instead of a map: [minimum maximum].

On each call of the reducing function, the first argument is always a map, and the second argument is always an integer from the sequence.

This difference makes **reduce** much more useful. Now, we can extract whatever data we like from each item in the sequence and insert it and carry it forward as the context for the subsequent iterations. Most of the time, we can think of this context as an **accumulator**, a value (often a map) in which we explicitly store whatever we need for the next iteration. We'll often use the name **acc**. Later, when we look at some of Clojure's other looping constructs, the idea of an explicit context will reappear.

Partitioning with reduce

Partitioning a sequence into smaller sequences is a common problem and there are many ways to solve it. When the simpler solutions aren't enough, **reduce** can be a useful alternative.

First, let's take a look at some of the other possibilities. If sub-sequences of a fixed length are required, then there is **partition** or **partition-all**:

```
user> (partition 3 [1 2 3 4 5 6 7 8 9 10])
((1 2 3) (4 5 6) (7 8 9))
user> (partition-all 3 [1 2 3 4 5 6 7 8 9 10])
((1 2 3) (4 5 6) (7 8 9) (10))
```

The difference between the two is that **partition** stops when it has filled its last group, while **partition-all** continues, even if this means the final sub-sequence won't contain the same number of items.

There is also **partition-by**, which offers more flexibility. In addition to the sequence to break apart, **partition-by** takes a function that will be called on each item. **partition-by** will then start a new subsequence whenever the return value changes.

Here, we break a sequence into sub-sequences depending on whether the integers are greater than or less than 10:

```
user> (partition-by #(> % 10) [5 33 18 0 23 2 9 4 3 99])
((5) (33 18) (0) (23) (2 9 4 3) (99))
```

Because **partition-by** allows you to write your own partitioning function, this can be a rather useful function when used creatively.

However, just like **map** and **filter** themselves, none of these functions can look at more than one item at a time. What if, for example, we wanted to partition a sequence of integers into sequences whose sum was less than 20? To solve this kind of problem, we need to be able to consider more than one item at a time.

When using **reduce** for this, the key is to use a map as an initializer and accumulator, with at least two different fields: one for the accumulated sequences and one for the current sequence. The accumulator might look as follows, mid-way through a reduction, if we are trying to make sequences whose sum is less than 20:

```
{:current [5 10]
  :segments [[3 7 8]
             [17]
             [4 1 1 5 3 2]]}
```

The vectors in **segments** are complete: if one more item was added, their sums would exceed 20. The **:current** vector adds up to 15 right now. If the next item in the main sequence is 4 or more, we won't be able to add it to this vector and we'll move **[5 10]** over to **segments**.

Here is how this would work in practice:

```
user> (reduce (fn [{:keys [segments current] :as accum} n]
                (let [current-with-n (conj current n)
                      total-with-n (apply + current-with-n)]
                  (if (> total-with-n 20)
                    (assoc accum
                           :segments (conj segments current)
                           :current [n])
                    (assoc accum :current current-with-n))))
              {:segments [] :current []}
              [4 19 4 9 5 12 5 3 4 1 1 9 5 18])
{:segments [[4] [19] [4 9 5] [12 5 3] [4 1 1 9 5]], :current [18]}
```

Let's take a closer look. For convenience, we start by extracting the segments and current bindings from the accumulator. Then, we set up a couple of useful bindings: **current-with-n** is the current sequence plus the current item, **n**. At this point, we don't know if this is a valid sequence. Its total might go beyond the limit of 20. To check this, we assign another binding (for clarity), **total-with-n**, and we compare that to 20.

If **current-with-n** adds up to more than 20, this means that **current** is a valid sub-sequence. In that case, we add it as is (without **n**) to our list of accumulated segments, and we place **n** as the first item in a brand new **:current** vector. On the other hand, if **current-with-n** does not add up to 20 yet, we just append **n** to **current** and keep going.

You'll notice that the final result is not exactly what we want: the last item, **[18]**, is still stuck in **:current**. To present a clean result, we should probably wrap our call to **reduce** in a function that will take care of this last bit of housekeeping:

```
user> (defn segment-by-sum [limit ns]
        (let [result (reduce (fn [{:keys [segments current] :as accum} n]
                               (let [current-with-n (conj current n)
                                     total-with-n (apply + current-with-n)]
                                 (if (> total-with-n limit)
                                   (assoc accum
                                          :segments (conj segments current)
```

```
                                    :current [n])
                            (assoc accum :current current-with-n))))
                  {:segments [] :current []}
                  ns)]
        (conj (:segments result) (:current result)))))
#'user/segment-by-sum
```

Here, we've made our function a little bit more versatile by adding a **limit** parameter so that we can choose other values besides 20. We also create a binding for the result of the call to **reduce** that we then use, at the last line of the function, to append the final value of **:current** to the accumulated segments. Now we get the result we want:

```
user> (segment-by-sum 20 [4 19 4 9 5 12 5 3 4 1 1 9 5 18])
[[4] [19] [4 9 5] [12 5 3] [4 1 1 9 5] [18]]
```

This common pattern will allow you to do lots of interesting things with **reduce**. In the next two exercises, we will use variations of it to solve two rather different kinds of problems.

Looking Back with reduce

As we saw in the previous chapter, Clojure's **map** function is extremely useful and versatile. The key to understanding **map** is the idea of the one-to-one *mapping* (there's that word!) between each item in the input sequence and each item in the output sequence. Sometimes, this isn't what we need. The windowing pattern we used in *Chapter 4, Mapping and Filtering*, is one way to work around this, but it has its own limitations. Often, we don't know how "wide" the window needs to be. It might depend on the data itself and vary as we move through the input sequence.

We can solve this problem quite easily with **reduce** and an accumulator that retains a certain number of items. To start with a simple example, let's suppose we have a list of integers:

```
(def numbers [4 9 2 3 7 9 5 2 6 1 4 6 2 3 3 6 1])
```

For each integer in the list, we want to return a two-item tuple containing:

- The integer itself

- If the integer is odd, the sum of the consecutive odd integers preceding it; if it's even, the sum of the consecutive even integers

Following this logic, the first **9** in the list should be replaced with **[9 0]**, since it is preceded by an even integer. The second **9**, on the other hand, should be replaced with **[9 10]**, since it is preceded by a **3** and a **7**.

And here is a function that solves this with **reduce**:

```
(defn parity-totals [ns]
  (:ret
   (reduce (fn [{:keys [current] :as acc} n]
             (if (and (seq current)
                      (or (and (odd? (last current)) (odd? n))
                          (and (even? (last current)) (even? n))))
               (-> acc
                   (update :ret conj [n (apply + current)])
                   (update :current conj n))
               (-> acc
                   (update :ret conj [n 0])
                   (assoc :current [n]))))
           {:current [] :ret []}
           ns)))
```

Let's take a closer look, starting with the accumulator, a map with two keys referencing empty vectors: **:current**, for the current series of integers with the same parity; and **:ret**, for the list of values that will be returned. (The entire **reduce** expression is wrapped by a **(:ret…)** expression to extract this value.)

The reducing function starts with some destructuring to give us easy access to **:current**; now, **n**, of course, is the current integer in the list. Inside the function, the structure is quite simple. The **if** expression has a somewhat elaborate set of nested logical operators. First, we use **(seq current)** to check whether **current** is empty, which would be the case on the first iteration. The **seq** function returns **false** if a vector or list is empty. Then, since we know **(last current)** will return an integer, we can test to see whether **n** and the previous value in the list are both odd or both even.

> **Note**
>
> Because we are using vectors here, **conj** appends new items to the end of the vector. To get the most recent item, we use **last**. If we were using lists instead of vectors, **conj** would append to the front of the list and we would have to use **first** to get the most recent item. When using **conj**, it's important to make sure the underlying data structure is what you think it is. Otherwise, your results could easily be backward.

Depending on which branch of the **if** statement we end up in, we update **acc** differently. In the first case, the current integer has the same parity as the contents of **current**. We thread **acc** through two calls to **update**. As you remember from *Chapter 2, Data types and Immutability*, **update** takes a function as its second argument, **conj** in this case, because we are adding to the vector, and applies it to the value associated with the key provided as the first value. We add an additional argument, **[n (apply + current)]**. This will be the second argument to **conj**. Altogether, it's as though we were calling **conj** like this: **(conj (:ret acc) [n (apply + current)])**. The second call to **update** adds **n** to our running list of integers.

In the other case, when we are at the beginning of the list or because of a change from odd to even or even to odd, we know that the current total is zero. Instead of **update**, we can use **assoc** here because we're starting over with a fresh list.

Running the function on our sequence of integers gives us this:

```
user> (parity-totals numbers)
[[4 0]
 [9 0]
 [2 0]
 [3 0]
 [7 3]
 [9 10]
 [5 19]
 [2 0]
 [6 2]
 [1 0]
 [4 0]
 [6 4]
 [2 10]
 [3 0]
 [3 3]
 [6 0]
 [1 0]]
user>
```

Figure 5.4: The original inputs are followed by the sum of the preceding, consecutive integers of the same parity

This would be impossible with **map** because, unlike the windowing technique we used, the **:current** vector in the accumulator here can contain as many items as necessary, depending on the input. This also shows the flexibility of **reduce** when using an accumulator. Now, we can practice using it on a real problem.

Exercise 5.02: Measuring Elevation Differences on Slopes

The organizers of a bicycle race in a mountainous region want to improve the signs they place on the side of the road. Currently, each sign simply indicates the distance from the start of the race. The race organizers would like to add two more numbers:

- The distance to the top or bottom of the current slope, depending on whether that part of the racecourse is gaining or losing elevation

- The remaining elevation gain or loss until the end of the current slope

Here is an example:

Figure 5.5: Racecourse sign indicating the remaining distance and elevation until the top of the current hill

The data you have is a list of tuples: the first value is the distance from the start of the race, and the second is the elevation at that point. You can copy the data from https://packt.live/38IcEvx:

```
(def distance-elevation [[0 400] [12.5 457] [19 622] [21.5 592] [29 615] …])
```

We will solve this problem using **reduce** and the "looking back" pattern. There is, however, a difficulty we need to resolve first. If we are looking *back*, how do we know how far we are from the *next* peak or the *next* valley? Simple: we'll reverse the racecourse data so that when we're looking back, we're actually looking forward!

In the following figure, as we descend the slopes, we can "see" forward and compare our current position with the peaks:

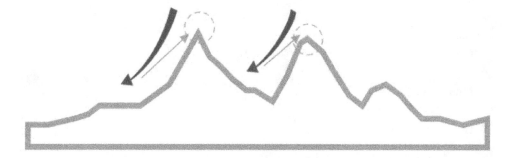

Figure 5.6: The descent slopes

By reversing the direction, we traverse the data; when we look "back," we are looking forward geographically.

Now we can start writing some code:

1. Start a fresh REPL in an empty directory and open a new file, **bike_race.clj**. Add the corresponding namespace declaration:

```
(ns bike-race)
```

> **Note**
>
> Clojure namespaces use hyphens between words (sometimes referred to as "kebab case") but, because of Clojure's Java origins, the corresponding filenames use underscores instead (or "snake case"). That's why the **bike-race** namespace is in a file named **bike_race.clj**. In *Chapter 8, Namespaces, Libraries and Leiningen* you will learn more about namespaces.

2. Copy the **distance-elevation** var from the book's GitHub repository at https://packt.live/38IcEvx.

3. Set up the skeleton for this function:

```
(defn distances-elevation-to-next-peak-or-valley
  [data]
  (->
    (reduce
      (fn [{:keys [current] :as acc} [distance elevation :as this-position]]
        )
      {:current []
       :calculated []}
      (reverse data))
    :calculated
    reverse))
```

There are only a couple of notable differences with the basic "looking back" pattern described above. First of all, there is more destructuring for easy access to the **distance** and **elevation** values inside the incoming tuple. Secondly, the entire call to **reduce** is wrapped inside a -> threading macro. This is, of course, equivalent to **(reverse (:calculated (reduce…)))** but has the advantage of organizing the code according to how the data flows through the function. This is a fairly common idiom with accumulators when only one of the fields will ultimately be returned.

Otherwise, the general approach is the same: the :current field will contain all the points on the path up to the *previous* (but geographically *next*) peak or valley. The :calculated field will store the calculated values so they can be returned at the end.

4. We will need to know whether the new position is on the same slope as the positions stored in **current**. Are we still going up, or down, or have we gone over a peak, or across the lowest part of a valley? To simplify our code, we'll write a helper function, taking **current** and the new elevation. This will return **true** or **false**:

```
(defn same-slope-as-current? [current elevation]
  (or (= 1 (count current))
      (let [[[_ next-to-last] [_ the-last]] (take-last 2 current)]
        (or (>= next-to-last the-last elevation)
            (<= next-to-last the-last elevation)))))
```

First, we check whether there is only one value in **current**. If so, we know the answer to our question because, with only two points, we know we are on the same slope. This also protects our next tests from errors since we can now be sure that there are at least two items in **current**. (We still have to be careful not to call this function with an empty list.)

Now that we know that we have at least two items, we can do some destructuring. This destructuring is doubly nested: first, we take the last two elements in **current**, using the **take-last** function, and then we extract and name the second part of those tuples. To destructure the tuples, we use an underscore, _, as a placeholder to indicate that we are not interested in the first value. This use of an underscore here is simply a Clojure convention that means essentially "don't pay attention to this value."

> **Note**
>
> We named the binding **the-last** instead of simply **last**. This is because of Clojure's **last** function. Since we don't use **last** in this scope, we *could* have named the binding **last** without a problem. However, it is a good practice to avoid using names that coincide with standard Clojure functions. The danger is that your local binding might "shadow" a core Clojure function, resulting in a confusing bug.

Now we have three values and we want to see whether they are either all increasing or all decreasing. This turns out to be quite simple with Clojure's comparison functions, which accept more than two arguments. **(>= next-to-last the-last elevation)** will return **true** if **next-to-last** is greater than or equal to **the-last** , and if **the-last** is greater than or equal to **elevation**.

5. At the REPL, move to the **bike-race** namespace as follows:

```
(in-ns 'bike-race)
```

6. Test the **same-slope-as-current?** function:

```
bike-race> (same-slope-as-current? [[1 5] [2 10]] 15)
true
bike-race> (same-slope-as-current? [[1 5] [2 10]] 5)
false
bike-race> (same-slope-as-current? [[1 5] [2 10]] 10)
true
bike-race> (same-slope-as-current? [[1 5]] 10)
true
bike-race> (same-slope-as-current? [[1 5] [2 10] [3 15]] 20)
true
bike-race> ▮
```

Figure 5.7: Testing the program

It seems to work as expected, including when there is only one value in **current**.

7. The rest of the function will be structured around a **cond** expression with three branches to handle the three possible cases: the initial case where **current** is empty; the continuing case, when we are on the same slope as what is in **current**; and the slope change case, when we have passed a peak or a valley and we need to reset **current**.

Here is the reducing function:

bike_race.clj

```
42 (fn [{:keys [current] :as acc} [distance elevation :as this-position]]
43    (cond (empty? current)
44          {:current [this-position]
45           :calculated [{:race-position distance
46                         :elevation elevation
47                         :distance-to-next 0
48                         :elevation-to-next 0}]}
49          (same-slope-as-current? current elevation)
50          (-> acc
51              (update :current conj this-position)
52              (update :calculated
53                      conj
54                      {:race-position distance
55                       :elevation elevation
56                       :distance-to-next (- (first (first current)) distance)
57                       :elevation-to-next (- (second (first current)) elevation)}))
```

The complete code for this step can be found at https://packt.live/2sTxk4m

In what we referred to above as the "continuing case," when we are at a position that prolongs the slope in **current**, we simply subtract the current elevation and distance from the first item in **current**. The "slope change" case is slightly more complex because we have to reset **current**, taking care to include the latest "peak-or-valley." A figure might make this clearer:

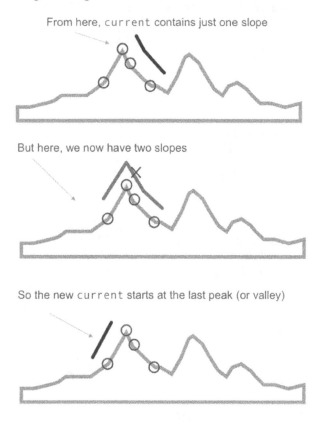

Figure 5.8: The new current starts at the top of the previous peak

To "reset" **current**, therefore, we use the previous peak and our position:

```
(assoc :current [peak-or-valley this-position])
```

Because we are starting over with a new value in **:current**, instead of **update**, we use **assoc**, which replaces the old value entirely.

8. Test the function using the following command:

```
(distances-elevation-tp-next-peak-or-valley distance-elevation)
```

The output is as follows:

```
bike-race> (distances-elevation-to-next-peak-or-valley distance-elevation)
({:race-position 0,
  :elevation 400,
  :distance-to-next 19,
  :elevation-to-next 222}
 {:race-position 12.5,
  :elevation 457,
  :distance-to-next 6.5,
  :elevation-to-next 165}
 {:race-position 19,
  :elevation 622,
  :distance-to-next 2.5,
  :elevation-to-next -30}
 {:race-position 21.5,
  :elevation 592,
  :distance-to-next 21.5,
  :elevation-to-next 885}
 {:race-position 29,
  :elevation 615,
  :distance-to-next 14,
  :elevation-to-next 862}
 {:race-position 35.5,
  :elevation 892,
  :distance-to-next 7.5,
  :elevation-to-next 585}
 {:race-position 39,
  :elevation 1083,
  :distance-to-next 4,
  :elevation-to-next 394}
 {:race-position 43,
  :elevation 1477,
  :distance-to-next 19.5,
  :elevation-to-next -747}
 {:race-position 48.5,
  :elevation 1151,
  :distance-to-next 14.0,
  :elevation-to-next -421}
```

Figure 5.9: A partial view of the results

In this problem, the most important part of the data is the relationship between the items. Problems like this require an approach that allows us to "see" more than one item at a time. Unlike the windowing technique we used with map in the last chapter, in this problem, we don't know beforehand how far we need to look. This is where **reduce** can really shine, because it allows us to shape the accumulator to suit the needs of the problem.

Exercise 5.03: Winning and Losing Streaks

In this exercise, we will start with a vector of all the matches that Serena Williams played in 2015. Each match is represented by a map:

```
{:loser-sets-won 0,
 :winner-sets-won 2,
 :winner-name "Williams S.",
 :loser-name "Williams V.",
 :tournament "Wimbledon",
 :location "London",
 :date "2015-07-06"}
```

> **Note**
>
> You don't need this data to perform this exercise, but if you'd like to play around with the data, it is available here: https://packt.live/37HKOyC.

The goal is to add a `:current_streak` field to each match that would say "Lost 3," if Williams was struggling and had lost her last three matches, or "Won 5":

1. In a convenient directory, open a REPL and a file called **tennis_reduce.clj** with the corresponding namespace definition:

   ```
   (ns tennis-reduce)
   ```

   In Clojure, when a namespace contains more than one word, the words are joined by hyphens. The corresponding file, however, must use underscores instead.

   > **Note**
   >
   > We'll use this file and namespace for the rest of the tennis-related exercises in this chapter.

2. From the course's GitHub repository, in https://packt.live/2sPo4hv, copy the **serena-williams-2015** var into your file.

3. Set up the skeleton of a function based on a call to **reduce**, and provide an initializer map:

```
(defn serena-williams-win-loss-streaks [matches]
  (reduce (fn [acc match]
            ;; TODO: solve problem
            )
          {:matches []
           :current-wins 0
           :current-losses 0}
          matches))
```

The map that we provide as an initial value here shows us the form of the data we need for each iteration. The counters for current wins and current losses are self-explanatory: we'll just need to update those values depending on what happens in each successive match. :**matches** may seem strange at first, though. It is there because we want to return the entire sequence of matches, decorated with the new :**current-streak** field. Because of Clojure's immutability, we can't just modify the matches "in place" as we go along. As we move through the items in the **matches** list, we add some data to each match and then place it in the :**matches** vector in the accumulator.

4. Extract the matches from the call to **reduce**:

```
(defn serena-williams-win-loss-streaks [matches]
  (:matches
    (reduce (fn [acc match]
              ;; TODO: solve problem
              )
            {:matches []
             :current-wins 0
             :current-losses 0}
            matches)))
```

The :**current-wins** and :**current-losses** fields aren't useful outside of the function, so we want to only return the newly decorated matches.

5. Write a helper function that formats a string for presenting the current streak:

```
(defn streak-string [current-wins current-losses]
  (cond (pos? current-wins) (str "Won " current-wins)
        (pos? current-losses) (str "Lost " current-losses)
        :otherwise "First match of the year"))
```

There are three possible situations: a winning streak (at least one win, zero losses), a losing streak (at least one loss, zero wins) or no matches played yet (zero wins, zero losses). This is a good time to use **cond**, which allows us to have multiple conditions without using nested **if** statements. The test for the final catch-all condition could be anything at all, except **false** or **nil**. We use the **:otherwise** keyword because it is easy to read. And finally, **pos?** is a handy and commonly used predicate for determining whether a number is above zero, rather than writing `(> current-wins 0)`.

This logic could have been part of the main reducing function. Breaking it out into its own, very simple function makes for easier-to-read code.

6. Write a skeleton for the reducing function. As usual, it takes two arguments: the accumulator, **acc**, and the current match. All we do here is some destructuring so that we'll have easy access to this context inside the function. We also keep references to the original maps, **acc** and **match**, because our function will end up returning modified versions of them:

```
(fn [{:keys [current-wins current-losses] :as acc}
     {:keys [winner-name] :as match}]
  ;; TODO: do something
  )
```

7. Introduce a **let** binding for the current match and insert it into the **:matches** vector in the accumulator:

```
(fn [{:keys [current-wins current-losses] :as acc}
     {:keys [winner-name] :as match}]
        (let [this-match (assoc match :current-streak (streak-string current-
wins current-losses))]
            (update acc :matches #(conj % this-match))))
```

Even though our function isn't complete yet, this is the most important part of the data flow. The **match** argument is "decorated" with the current streak information formatted by the **streak-string** helper function and then inserted into the **:matches** vector that the function will return at the end. We don't have the contextual information yet, so that is the next step.

8. The final step here is to produce the contextual information: we need to update **:current-wins** and **:current-losses** in the accumulator so that we're ready for the next iteration. The logic here is that if Williams won the current match, then we need to add 1 to the current streak and set the losing streak to zero. These will be used for calculating the winning and losing streaks for the next match. Conversely, if Williams lost the previous match, we set the current winning streak to zero and add 1 to the losing streak.

To translate this logic into code, we'll start by adding another **let** binding, **serena-victory?**, that we will refer to later:

```
serena-victory? (= winner-name "Williams S.")
```

Now all that remains is updating **:current-wins** and **:current-losses** in **acc**. We'll use the **->** threading macro because there are several things that need to be done to our accumulator:

```
(-> acc
    (update :matches #(conj % this-match))
    (assoc :current-wins (if serena-victory?
                           (inc current-wins)
                           0))
    (assoc :current-losses (if serena-victory?
                             0
                             (inc current-losses))))
```

The calls to **assoc** just apply the conditional logic discussed above, incrementing the counters or resetting them to zero. Here is the complete function when we put all the parts back together:

```
(defn serena-williams-win-loss-streaks [matches]
  (:matches
    (reduce (fn [{:keys [current-wins current-losses] :as acc} match]
              (let [this-match (assoc match :current-streak (streak-string current-
wins current-losses))
                    serena-victory? (= (:winner-name match) "Williams S.")]
                (-> acc
                    (update :matches #(conj % this-match))
                    (assoc :current-wins (if serena-victory?
                                           (inc current-wins)
                                           0))
                    (assoc :current-losses (if serena-victory?
                                             0
                                             (inc current-losses))))))
            {:matches []
             :current-wins 0
             :current-losses 0}
            matches)))
```

Try the function on the data. You should see something like this:

```
tennis-reduce> (serena-williams-win-loss-streaks serena-williams-2015)
[{:loser-sets-won 0,
  :winner-sets-won 2,
  :winner-name "Williams S.",
  :loser-name "Van Uytvanck A.",
  :tournament "Australian Open",
  :location "Melbourne",
  :date "2015-01-20",
  :current-streak "First match of the year"}
 {:loser-sets-won 0,
  :winner-sets-won 2,
  :winner-name "Williams S.",
  :loser-name "Zvonareva V.",
  :tournament "Australian Open",
  :location "Melbourne",
  :date "2015-01-22",
  :current-streak "Won 1"}
 {:loser-sets-won 1,
  :winner-sets-won 2,
  :winner-name "Williams S.",
  :loser-name "Svitolina E.",
  :tournament "Australian Open",
  :location "Melbourne",
  :date "2015-01-24",
  :current-streak "Won 2"}
 {:loser-sets-won 1,
  :winner-sets-won 2,
  :winner-name "Williams S.",
  :loser-name "Muguruza G.",
  :tournament "Australian Open",
  :location "Melbourne",
  :date "2015-01-26",
  :current-streak "Won 3"}
 {:loser-sets-won 0,
  :winner-sets-won 2,
  :winner-name "Williams S.",
  :loser-name "Cibulkova D.",
  :tournament "Australian Open",
  :location "Melbourne",
  :date "2015-01-28",
  :current-streak "Won 4"}
```

Figure 5.10: Using the function on data

This example shows us a couple of different interesting things about using **reduce**. The first point is that we are free to create whatever kind of context we would like to pass on to each successive iteration of the reducing function. To make things simple in this case, we just counted the number of wins or losses, but the context can be just as complex as you need it to be.

The second point is that the ultimate return value can also be whatever we need it to be. The function in this example actually looks like something you might do with **map**: it takes a sequence and returns a sequence of the same length. Yet, by building up data from previous calls to the reducing function, it does something that **map** would be unable to do.

Reducing without reduce

Before we go any further, it's important to point out that sometimes there are other, better options than **reduce** for taking a sequence and turning it into something non-sequential. Often, this is because Clojure provides functions that do the hard work for us. Sometimes, clever use of Clojure's "sequence-to-sequence" functions can get you the data you need.

As a general rule, it is usually preferable to do as much as possible with functions that can handle lazy sequences before turning to **reduce**. In some cases, this can be for performance reasons, and in nearly all cases, your code will be easier to write, and, more importantly, *to read*, if you can stay in the realm of sequences. That said, most solutions will require a little of both. Knowing how to combine the two is an important skill.

zipmap

Clojure's **zipmap** function is a tool for building a map from two sequences. The first sequence becomes the keys for the new map and the second becomes the values. This is often useful for building a lookup table. Lookup tables can be convenient when you need to repeatedly access data in a sequence based on its content rather than its position in the list.

It's easy to imagine a scenario where this would be useful. Maybe at one step in a program, you have a list of maps, each one containing contact data for a person. Later, you discover that you often have a telephone number and need to find the corresponding user. If you have a lookup table where the keys are telephone numbers, you can find a user with a simple **(get users-by-phone "+44 011 1234 5678")**. Maps provide easy access, as long as you have meaningful and unique keys.

The basic operation of **zipmap** is to align two sequences, one for the keys and one for the values, which **zipmap** will "zip" together:

```
user> (zipmap [:a :b :c] [0 1 2])
{:a 0, :b 1, :c 2}
```

Often, you will only have the second list, the values. You will derive values from the list and use them as the keys. Just be careful that the keys are unique to avoid collisions.

Exercise 5.04: Creating a Lookup Table with zipmap

Maps are an extremely useful and flexible way to quickly access data. Often, however, the data you have is sequential and you find that you would like to be able to access an individual item without having to walk the entire sequence. If you know the criteria that you'll use to look up the item you need, building a lookup table from your data can be an interesting solution.

In this exercise, you have a list of some of the matches that Petra Kvitova played in 2014. Let's suppose you need to be able to quickly access the matches by date, perhaps to be able to plug them into a calendar of some kind or to test which players were playing on the same day. Whatever the reason, you need to build a map where the keys are dates and the values are the individual matches. Because the same player never plays two matches on the same day, we can be sure that the date keys are unique. Here's how to build the lookup table:

1. Copy the following var into your REPL from the book's GitHub repository: https://packt.live/39Joc2H:

kvitova_matches.clj

```
1  (def matches
2    [{:winner-name "Kvitova P.",
3      :loser-name "Ostapenko J.",
4      :tournament "US Open",
5      :location "New York",
6      :date "2016-08-29"}
7     {:winner-name "Kvitova P.",
8      :loser-name "Buyukakcay C.",
9      :tournament "US Open",
10     :location "New York",
11     :date "2016-08-31"}
```

The complete code for this step can be found at https://packt.live/2Ggpsgs

2. Use **map** to create a sequence with a date from each match:

```
user> (map :date matches)
("2016-08-29"
 "2016-08-31"
 "2016-09-02"
 "2016-09-05"
 "2016-09-20"
 "2016-09-21")
```

3. Combine both sequences into a single map:

```
user> (def matches-by-date (zipmap (map :date matches) matches))
#'user/matches-by-date
```

4. Use the map to look up a match by date:

```
user> (get matches-by-date "2016-09-20")
{:winner-name "Kvitova P.",
 :loser-name "Brengle M.",
 :tournament "Toray Pan Pacific Open",
 :location "Tokyo",
 :date "2016-09-20"}
```

In a single line of code, you've created a way to quickly find a match for a given day. Because it's so concise, this pattern can easily be integrated into a more complex function.

> **Note**
>
> Building a lookup table like this might seem wasteful in terms of memory resources. Aren't we doubling the amount of data in memory? Actually, we aren't. Clojure's immutable data structures efficiently share data, which is possible without conflict because the data cannot be modified. This means that, in this example, the original sequence and the lookup table we've created are basically two ways of accessing the same data.

Maps to Sequences, and Back Again

One of the most useful techniques is one that we mentioned briefly in the last chapter: using **into** to build a map from a list of paired items. This pattern is so versatile that it's worth taking a closer look.

In its simplest form, the pattern looks like this:

```
user> (into {} [[:a 1] [:b 2]])
{:a 1, :b 2}
```

Maps, after all, are really just data pairs, and Clojure knows how to convert between the two. It's just as easy to make a sequence of tuples from a map:

```
user> (seq {:a 1 :b 2})
([:a 1] [:b 2])
```

Use a map as a map when that makes sense, but don't hesitate to use it as a sequence whenever that's easier.

When you need to "modify" a map (in the Clojure sense of not actually modifying, but creating a new map with modified data), you may be tempted to use the **keys** function to iterate through the values in the map:

```
user> (def letters-and-numbers {:a 5 :b 18 :c 35})
#'user/letters-and-numbers
user> (reduce (fn [acc k]
                (assoc acc k (* 10 (get letters-and-numbers k))))
              {}
              (keys letters-and-numbers))
{:a 50, :b 180, :c 350}
```

Here, we've used **reduce** to multiply each of the values by 10. This works, but it adds complexity and mental overhead to a problem that can be solved more easily:

```
user> (into {} (map (fn [[k v]] [k (* v 10)]) letters-and-numbers))
{:a 50, :b 180, :c 350}
```

We simply interpret the map, **letters-and-numbers**, as a list of key-value pairs. In the function supplied to **map**, we've used destructuring to assign **k** and **v** to the key and value inside the tuple, which we then wrap up again in a two-item vector. Thanks to **into**, we get a map back again in the end.

> **Note**
>
> For convenience, there is another version of **reduce** specifically for iterating through the key-value pairs in a map, called **reduce-kv**. The main difference is that with **reduce-kv**, the reducing function that you provide takes three arguments, instead of two: the first is the same as **reduce**, but the next two are the key and the corresponding value in the map.

group-by

Summarizing data in Clojure doesn't always mean calling **reduce** directly. The language provides functions that are built on top of **reduce** that are sometimes more convenient. **group-by** is one of those functions.

The **group-by** function takes a sequence, calls a function on each item, and uses whatever the function call returns as a key in a map. The value of the key will be a list of all the items that returned the same key.

Let's say that we have a list of maps where each map represents a dish, with a **:name** key for the dish's name, and a **:course** field that tells us what part of the meal the dish is served at:

```
(def dishes
  [{:name "Carrot Cake"
    :course :dessert}
   {:name "French Fries"
    :course :main}
   {:name "Celery"
    :course :appetizer}
   {:name "Salmon"
    :course :main}
   {:name "Rice"
    :course :main}
   {:name "Ice Cream"
    :course :dessert}])
```

With **group-by**, we can organize this list by category. The function we call on each item will just be the **:course** keyword, to extract the corresponding value:

> **Note**
>
> For most of our examples, we use keywords as map keys. This is usually more readable and provides the convenience of using keywords as functions. However, Clojure allows us to use any value as map keys. Just like we've been using strings for the names of tennis players, you can also use any Clojure value as a map key: integers, vectors, maps, even functions!

```
user> (group-by :course dishes)
         {:dessert
           [{:name "Carrot Cake", :course :dessert}
            {:name "Ice Cream", :course :dessert}],
          :main
           [{:name "French Fries", :course :main}
            {:name "Salmon", :course :main}
            {:name "Rice", :course :main}],
          :appetizer
           [{:name "Celery", :course :appetizer}]}
```

With *very* little coding, we have a nicely organized map. **group-by** uses **reduce** under the hood and really just encapsulates a fairly simple pattern. We could write a simplified version of **group-by** like this:

```
user> (defn our-group-by [f xs]
         (reduce (fn [acc x]
                   (update acc (f x) (fn [sublist] (conj (or sublist []) x))))
                {}
                xs))
#'user/our-group-by
```

If we call **our-group-by** on the list of dishes, we get the same results:

```
user> (our-group-by :course dishes)
{:dessert
 [{:name "Carrot Cake", :course :dessert}
  {:name "Ice Cream", :course :dessert}],
 :main
 [{:name "French Fries", :course :main}
  {:name "Salmon", :course :main}
  {:name "Rice", :course :main}],
 :appetizer [{:name "Celery", :course :appetizer}]}
```

The official version will have better performance, but the real advantage of a function like **group-by** is that it frees us from thinking about the details. Any time you have a list and some categories, **group-by** is ready to help.

Exercise 5.05: Quick Summary Statistics with group-by

In this exercise, we'll use **group-by** to quickly count the number of matches played in different tournaments in our tennis match data:

1. In the same directory as *Exercise 5.03, Winning and Losing Streaks*, create a **deps. edn** file with the following content:

```
{:deps
 {org.clojure/data.csv {:mvn/version "0.1.4"}
  semantic-csv {:mvn/version "0.2.1-alpha1"}}}
```

2. Change the namespace declaration in **tennis_reduce.clj** so that it references these two new libraries:

```
(ns packt-clj.tennis-reduce
  (:require
            [clojure.java.io :as io]
            [clojure.data.csv :as csv]
            [semantic-csv.core :as sc]))
```

3. Start a REPL in the same directory as the previous exercise, with the same **deps. edn**, and then open and evaluate **tennis_reduce.clj**.

4. In your REPL, move to the **packt-clj.tennis-reduce** namespace as follows:

```
user> (in-ns 'packt-clj.tennis-reduce)
```

5. Make sure that you have the **match_scores_1968-1990_unindexed_csv.csv** file in the same directory. This is the same data file we used in *Chapter 4, Mapping and Filtering*. You can find it here: https://packt.live/36k1o6X.

6. Set up the now familiar **with-open** macro that we've used before, and give your function an expressive name:

```
(defn tennis-csv->tournament-match-counts [csv]
  (with-open [r (io/reader csv)]
    (->> (csv/read-csv r)
         sc/mappify
         ;;....
         )))
```

7. Write a call to **group-by** that builds a map where the keys are the **:tourney_slug** instances and the values are the lists of matches played there. To make the output more manageable, temporarily remove all but a few keys in the match maps by mapping over the list with **select-keys**:

```
(defn tennis-csv->tournament-match-counts [csv]
  (with-open [r (io/reader csv)]
    (->> (csv/read-csv r)
         sc/mappify
         (map #(select-keys % [:tourney_slug :winner_name :loser_name]))
         (group-by :tourney_slug))))
```

8. Evaluate the source file and then try calling this function. Define a var so that your screen doesn't fill up with tennis match data:

```
packt-clj.tennis-reduce> (def tournaments (tennis-csv->tournament-match-counts
"match_scores_1991-2016_unindexed_bcsv.csv"))
#'user/tournaments
```

9. Examine some of the data, first by using the **keys** function, to see all the tournament names:

```
packt-clj.tennis-reduce> (keys tournaments)
("chicago"
 "bologna"
 "munich"
 "marseille"
 "dubai"
 "milan"
 "buzios"
 "miami"
 "warsaw"
 "bucharest"
 "wimbledon"
 "umag"
 "besancon"
;; ....etc.
)
```

10. Look at a single tournament. Once again, limit the data returned, this time by using **take**:

```
packt-clj.tennis-reduce> (take 5 (get tournaments "chicago"))
({:tourney_slug "chicago",
  :winner_name "John McEnroe",
  :loser_name "Patrick McEnroe"}
 {:tourney_slug "chicago",
  :winner_name "John McEnroe",
  :loser_name "MaliVai Washington"}
 {:tourney_slug "chicago",
  :winner_name "Patrick McEnroe",
  :loser_name "Grant Connell"}
 {:tourney_slug "chicago",
  :winner_name "John McEnroe",
  :loser_name "Alexander Mronz"}
 {:tourney_slug "chicago",
  :winner_name "Patrick McEnroe",
  :loser_name "Richey Reneberg"})
```

11. Use **count** to obtain the number of matches played in a single tournament:

```
packt-clj.tennis-reduce> (count (get tournaments "chicago"))
31
```

12. Calculate the total number of matches played in each tournament using **count** in the original function:

```
(defn tennis-csv->tournament-match-counts [csv]
  (with-open [r (io/reader csv)]
    (->> (csv/read-csv r)
         sc/mappify
         (group-by :tourney_slug)
         (map (fn [[k ms]] [k (count ms)]))
         (into {}))))
```

Notice that **select-keys** is gone. Since we are reducing the lists of matches to a single integer, there is no point in removing any fields. Here, we use a pattern that you have seen before: the call to **map** treats the Clojure map as if it were a sequence of key-value pairs. The function passed to **map** then returns a two-item vector with the keyword and the newly calculated total. And finally, **into** repackages the sequence back into a map.

13. Evaluate the file again and call **tennis-csv→tournament-match-counts** again:

```
packt-clj.tennis-reduce> (def tournament-totals (tennis-csv->tournament-match-counts
"match_scores_1991-2016_unindexed_csv.csv"))
#'user/tournament-totals
```

14. Inspect the data:

```
packt-clj.tennis-reduce> (get tournament-totals "chicago")
31
packt-clj.tennis-reduce> (get tournament-totals "wimbledon")
4422
packt-clj.tennis-reduce> (get tournament-totals "roland-garros")
4422
packt-clj.tennis-reduce> (get tournament-totals "australian-open")
4422
packt-clj.tennis-reduce> (get tournament-totals "us-open")
4422
```

Here we see that the Grand Slam tournaments have the exact same number of matches over the same period, because these seven-round tournaments are structured identically.

In this exercise, we were able to extract the data we wanted in a few short lines of code. Beyond illustrating the power of **group-by**, this is a good example of how mapping and reducing can work together. We used **group-by** to structure our data, and then **map** to shape it some more. It's easy to imagine using **filter** as well, if we wanted to limit the scope of our inquiry to certain players or certain tournaments, for example.

Summarizing Tennis Scores

In the previous chapter, we were able to generate some summary data from the tennis scores, using **filter**. If we wanted to know how many matches a particular player had won, we could filter out that player's victories and call **count**. While this approach works well when we are only interested in one player, it becomes cumbersome if we want more complete data. For example, if we needed to know the number of matches played or won by *each* of the players in the dataset, we would have to filter, for each query, the entire history of all the matches. The **map** and **filter** functions are extremely useful in many situations, but reducing a large collection down into a more compact report is not what they are best for.

Let's suppose that for each player, we need to know the number of matches played, won, and lost. We'll walk through two different ways to solve the problem in Clojure, the first using **reduce** and the second using **group-by**, one of Clojure's many convenient **reduce**-based functions.

In the first exercise, we will use a common reducing pattern to build up our data, row by row, from the CSV file. Of course, we'll use the three-argument version of **reduce** with a map as the accumulator.

Exercise 5.06: Complex Accumulation with reduce

For each row of CSV in the tennis dataset we've been using, the work we need to do is rather simple: count the wins and losses. In an imperative language, the most common approach would be to loop over the results, and for each line do something like this:

```
var matches = [{winner_slug: 'Player 1',
                loser_slug: 'Player 2'},
               {winner_slug: 'Player 2',
                loser_slug: 'Player 1'}];
var players = {}
for (var i = 0; i < matches.length; i++) {
  var winnerSlug = matches[i].winner_slug;
  var loserSlug = matches[i].loser_slug;
  if (!players[winnerSlug]) {
    players[winnerSlug] = {wins: 0, losses: 0};
  }
  players[winnerSlug].wins = players[winnerSlug].wins + 1;

  if (!players[loserSlug]){
    players[loserSlug] = {wins: 0, losses: 0};
  }
  players[loserSlug].losses = players[loserSlug].losses + 1;
}
console.log(players);
```

We will do essentially the same thing in Clojure, but within the scope of a function passed to **reduce**:

1. Open **tennis_reduce.clj**, start your REPL, evaluate the file, and move to the **packt**-Copy in the **with-open** pattern that we've used before and prepare the skeleton
    of a call to **reduce**. We'll call this function **win-loss-by-player**:

```clojure
(defn win-loss-by-player [csv]
  (with-open [r (io/reader csv)]
    (->> (csv/read-csv r)
         sc/mappify
         (reduce (fn [acc row]


                   )
                 {}                        ; an empty map as an accumulator
                 ))))
```

We won't need the call to **sc/cast-with** this time, since the only values we need are strings. And we don't need to call **doall** either, because **reduce** is not lazy.

2. Write the function to pass to **reduce**:

```clojure
(fn [acc {:keys [winner_slug loser_slug]}]
  (-> acc
      (update-in [winner_slug :wins]
                 (fn [wins] (inc (or wins 0))))
      (update-in [loser_slug :losses]
                 (fn [losses] (inc (or losses 0))))))
```

Here, we use **->** to thread the accumulator, **acc**, through two calls to **update-in**. This function, like **assoc-in**, allows us to access the content of a nested data structure by providing a vector as a second argument. Each call in this example would look like this:

```clojure
(update-in acc ["roger-federer" :wins] (fn [wins] (inc (or wins 0))))
```

By repeatedly calling this on the accumulator as **reduce** moves through the list of matches, we end up with a large map of player "slugs" mapped to small maps each containing a **:wins** key and a **:losses** key:

```
{
  ...
  "player" {:wins 10 :losses 5}
  "another-player" {:wins 132 :losses 28}
  ...
}
```

3. Evaluate your file and try running the function on the CSV data. Put the results in a var to avoid filling up your screen with all the data:

```
packt-clj.tennis-reduce> (def w-l (win-loss-by-player "match_scores_1991-2016_
unindexed_csv.csv"))
#'user/w-l
```

4. Look up a player, using the "slug":

```
packt-clj.tennis-reduce> (get w-l "roger-federer")
{:losses 240, :wins 1050}
```

> **Note**
>
> We need to use **get** here because the keys in our map are strings. If we had used the **keyword** function to convert the player "slugs" when building up the map, we could access a player's data with **(:roger-federer w-l)** instead.

Introduction to Elo

In the rest of this chapter, and in some of the following chapters, we are going to be working with the Elo Rating System to develop player ratings and predict match outcomes. The algorithm itself is quite simple and it will allow us to demonstrate how Clojure can be used as a data analysis tool. Since we'll be referring to it a lot, it's worth taking a closer look at how it works. The Elo Rating System was developed by Arpad Elo to rate chess players. The United States Chess Federation began using it in 1960.

Elo ratings work by establishing a score for each player. This score is used to calculate the probable outcome of a match. When the real outcome of the match is known, a player's rating is raised or lowered depending on their performance relative to the probable outcome. In other words, if a beginner with a low rating loses to a higher-rated player, the beginner's rating will not suffer by much, since that outcome was expected. If they defeat the higher-rated player, on the other hand, their rating will increase by a much greater margin, and the higher-rated player's rating will be diminished accordingly.

The obvious question is, of course, how do we know a player's rating to start with? This requires looking at their previous matches, and the rating of their opponents, which, in turn, are determined by the ratings of *their* opponents, and so on. If that sounds recursive, it's because it is. Our strategy will take the form of a complex reduction: starting at the earliest match, we will accumulate player ratings, which we will then use to calculate the scores for each successive match:

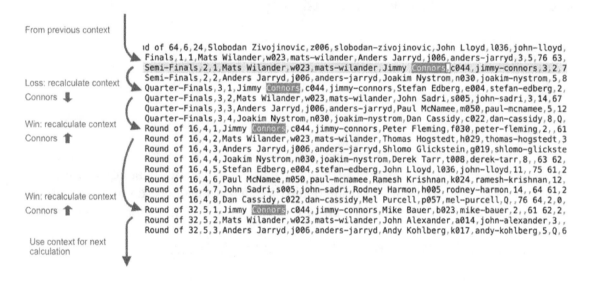

Figure 5.11: Reducing from match to match: each result improves the ratings for the next match

Does this look familiar? It might, because we are doing the same thing as in the previous reductions: calculating a context, moving it forward, and using it again for the next calculation. The difference with this project is that the context is much more complex. Our method for moving through the data is fundamentally the same.

Before we can perform this reduction, we need to build a few key pieces of the Elo implementation. At the heart of the Elo system is a simple formula for determining the probability of a player winning a given match. It looks like this:

$$P_1 = \frac{1}{1 + 10^{\frac{R_2 - R_1}{400}}}$$

$$P_2 = \frac{1}{1 + 10^{\frac{R_1 - R_2}{400}}}$$

Figure 5.12: Calculating the probability of outcomes for a given match

P_1 and P_2 here are the probabilities of winning for player one and player two. R_1 and R_2 are their respective ratings before the match.

If we fill in the values for a match between a player, rated at 700, and a stronger player, rated at 1,000, we get the following results:

$$P_1 = \frac{1}{1 + 10^{\frac{1000 - 700}{400}}} \qquad P_2 = \frac{1}{1 + 10^{\frac{700 - 1000}{400}}}$$

$$P_1 = 0.15 \qquad P_2 = 0.85$$

Figure 5.13: Example Elo calculation for a single match

The P_1 value indicates that there is a 15% chance that the weaker player will win the match and an 85% chance that the stronger player will win. The reliability of these percentages depends, of course, on the quality of the ratings. Before we look at how the ratings are calculated, though, let's translate these equations into Clojure functions.

Exercise 5.07: Calculating Probabilities for a Single Match

In this exercise, we'll set up one of the building blocks for our implementation of the Elo system, the formula for calculating the probabilities of victory for each of the two players in a match, based on their current ratings:

1. In the same folder as in the previous exercises, add **math.numeric-tower**, which is Clojure's standard **math** library, to your **deps.edn** file. It should look like this now:

```
{:deps
 {org.clojure/data.csv {:mvn/version "0.1.4"}
  semantic-csv {:mvn/version "0.2.1-alpha1"}
  org.clojure/math.numeric-tower {:mvn/version "0.0.4"}}}
```

In **tennis_reduce.clj**, update the namespace declaration:

```
(ns packt-clj.tennis-reduce
  (:require
            [clojure.java.io :as io]
            [clojure.data.csv :as csv]
            [semantic-csv.core :as sc]
            [clojure.math.numeric-tower :as math]))
```

2. Open a REPL session, evaluate **tennis_reduce.clj**, and move to the **packt-clj. tennis-reduce** namespace.

3. Write a function implementing the formula for calculating the probability of a player defeating another player:

```
packt-clj.tennis-reduce> (defn match-probability [player-1-rating player-2-rating]
    (/ 1
       (+ 1
          (math/expt 10 (/ (- player-2-rating player-1-rating) 400)))))
```

4. Try your function with players of different strengths:

```
packt-clj.tennis-reduce> (match-probability 700 1000)
0.15097955721132328
packt-clj.tennis-reduce> (match-probability 1000 700)
0.8490204427886767
packt-clj.tennis-reduce> (match-probability 1000 1000)
1/2
packt-clj.tennis-reduce> (match-probability 400 2000)  ;; beginner vs. master
1/10001
```

When the match is finally played, if the strong player wins, their rating will increase modestly (and their opponent's rating will go down slightly) because the result was not a surprise. If the weaker player wins, on the other hand, the change to the ratings will be much more significant.

This equation shows how the player's score is updated after a match:

$$R' = R + K(S - ES)$$

Figure 5.14: Equation to calculate the player's score

A player's new rating (R') is based on their previous rating (R), the match score (S), the expected score (ES), and the K factor.

The score (S) of a tennis match is either 0, for a loss, or 1, for a victory. If a player is expected to win by a probability of 0.75 and they go on to win their match, then the (S - ES) part of the equation works out to 1 - 0.75 = 0.25. This result gets multiplied by what the Elo system calls the "K factor." The K factor determines the impact of a match result on a player's overall rating. A high K factor means ratings will move around a lot; a low K factor means they will be more stable. If we use a K factor of 32, that gives us 32 * 0.25 = 8, so the player's rating in this example would go up by eight points. If the player had lost instead, we would get 32 * (0 - 0.75) = -24. Once again, unexpected results thus have a much greater impact on ratings.

Exercise 5.08: Updating Player Ratings

In this exercise, we will update the player ratings:

1. In the same file and REPL session as the previous exercise, define a **k-factor** var and a function that encapsulates the equation for updating a player's rating after a match:

```
packt-clj.tennis-reduce> (def k-factor 32)
#'packt-clj.tennis-reduce/k-factor
packt-clj.tennis-reduce> (defn recalculate-rating [previous-rating expected-outcome
real-outcome]
        (+ previous-rating (* k-factor (- real-outcome expected-outcome))))
#'packt-clj.tennis-reduce/recalculate-rating
```

Now, let's test the equation with some outputs from the **match-probability** function that we defined earlier.

2. A player rated 1,500 loses to a slightly weaker player (1,400):

```
packt-clj.tennis-reduce> (match-probability 1500 1400)
0.6400649998028851
packt-clj.tennis-reduce> (recalculate-rating 1500 0.64 0)
1479.52
```

The player's rating has gone down by almost 21 points.

3. A player with a low rating, 400, scores an upset victory against a strong player (1,000):

```
packt-clj.tennis-reduce> (match-probability 400 1000)
0.0306534300031715508
packt-clj.tennis-reduce> (recalculate-rating 400 0.03 1)
431.04
```

In this example, the supposedly weaker player gains 31 points, which is close to the maximum possible gain per match when K is 32. This shows how K determines the importance of a single match.

These two equations are all the math we need. That's it! The beauty of the Elo system is that the actual calculations are quite simple. Now, it's time to start using the functions we've written on some real data.

Activity 5.01: Calculating Elo Ratings for Tennis

A sports journalism website has asked you to provide improved ratings for the men's professional tennis circuit. They want to know the relative strengths of current players, as well as the strength of a given player during a given year in the past. Most of all, the journalists want high-quality predictions for future matches.

Your assignment is to build the prototype for this new system. A REPL-based implementation is fine for now, but it's important to be able to demonstrate the accuracy of your results based on past match data.

To do this, you'll need to write a function that parses the CSV file that we've been working with, using **reduce**. The function will not only calculate player ratings. It will also keep track of its own success rate in predicting match results. This will allow you to show the journalists how well your algorithm works, and before that, it will allow you to tweak your code to obtain the best possible predictions.

Your accumulator map will need to build up the following information:

- **Player ratings**: This is the most important part: a huge map linking each player to his rating. The map will be updated with the new ratings for the two players in the match being analyzed.

- **Success count**: For each match where one of the two players has a better than 50% chance of winning, did the expected winner actually win? By counting successes, you'll be able to divide by the total number of match predictions to determine the precision of your predictions.

- **Total match count**: The total number of matches that have been considered.

- **Prediction count**: The number of matches where a winner could be predicted – that is, matches where the forecast was not 50-50. Since we're excluding those matches from the success count, we need to exclude them from the prediction count.

These steps will help you complete the activity:

1. Set up your project with a **deps.edn** file containing the necessary references to the Clojure libraries you will use and include the tennis data files from https://packt.live/37DCkZn.

2. Place your work in a new file and namespace. Include the **recalculate-rating** and **match-probability** functions from the previous exercises.

3. Write the skeleton for a new function. It should accept two arguments: the path to the CSV file and a K factor.

4. Adapt the pattern based around **with-open** used in previous activities and exercises for reading the file, mappifying each line and converting useful fields to integers.

5. Prepare a call to **reduce** that will encompass most of the remaining logic you need to write.

6. Design an initializer/accumulator map as the second argument to **reduce** that will adequately keep track of all the information you need to pass on from one iteration to the next.

7. Write the code to update the accumulator after each match. Use the functions you already have to predict a winner and adjust the ratings according to the actual result of the match.

8. Test your function on the tennis datasets.

9. When testing, the results will be huge, so remember to assign them to a var. Check your results in the REPL by querying the result map.

10. You should be able to query your results like this:

```
elo-world> (def ratings (elo-world "match_scores_1991-2016_unindexed_csv.csv" 32))
#'elo-world/ratings
elo-world> (get-in ratings [:players "roger-federer"])
1119.6561580920807
elo-world> (get-in ratings [:players "rafael-nadal"])
969.5294559130078
elo-world> (get-in ratings [:players "andre-agassi"])
744.2950294510404
elo-world> (get-in ratings [:players "jimmy-connors"])
429.38371383476505
elo-world>
```

Figure 5.15: Expected query results

You should also be able to check how often the match predictions were correct:

```
elo-world> (:predictable-match-count ratings)
95356
elo-world> (:correct-predictions ratings)
61991
elo-world> (double (/ (:correct-predictions ratings) (:predictable-match-count ratings)))
0.6501006753638995
elo-world>
```

Figure 5.16: Checking the match prediction

> **Note**
>
> The solution for this activity can be found on page 693.

Summary

With this chapter, we've taken another important step forward in our exploration of Clojure's collections and how to use them to solve problems. Techniques involving collections will always be at the heart of your Clojure programming experience: they will inform how you organize your code, as well as how you choose and design your data structures.

In the next chapter, we will take a look at flexible ways to work with the collections in Clojure.

6

Recursion and Looping

Overview

In this chapter, you will learn more flexible ways to work with collections. When the problem you need to solve does not fit the patterns that we've looked at so far. We will also use **doseq** for loops with side effects and see how you can avoid writing some loops by using specialized repetition functions such as **repeat** and **iterate**. You will use **recur** for recursive looping and identify when this is possible, work with the **loop** macro, and solve complex problems with recursion.

By the end of this chapter, you will be able to implement different aspects of recursion and see how they can replace traditional loops.

Introduction

Data in our programs doesn't always take the nice, linear form for which functions such as **map** or **reduce** are particularly adapted. None of the techniques we've discussed in the last two chapters will work for traversing non-linear structures such as trees or graphs. And while it's possible to do a lot by being creative with **reduce**, the strong guard rails that **reduce** provides can sometimes get in the way of writing expressive code. There are situations that call for tools that give the programmer more control. Clojure has other resources for these kinds of problems and that is what we are going to look at in this chapter.

Recursion plays a major role when functions such as **map** and **reduce** are no longer adapted to the task at hand. Thinking recursively is an important Clojure skill to learn. Because functional programming languages tend to emphasize recursion, this might seem unfamiliar if your background is in more procedural languages. Most programming languages do actually support recursion, so the concept is not necessarily that foreign. Additionally, some of the things that we have already done with **reduce** are actually recursive, so even if you've never used recursion very much before, the learning curve should not be that steep.

Having said that, there are some aspects of recursion that may require you to think in new ways if you do not have much experience with functional programming. Compared to **map** and **filter**, or even **reduce**, recursive approaches are far more flexible. And by "flexible," we mean powerful but easy to get wrong. When trying to get a recursive function to do just what we want, we make mistakes and end up in infinite loops, blowing the call stack (we'll discuss what that means shortly) or getting other kinds of errors that would simply not be possible otherwise. This is why "looping," whether it's with the **loop** macro or with recursive functions, should always be what you turn to when the other options just won't work.

Clojure's Most Procedural Loop: doseq

Before we get started with recursion, let's take a look at the **doseq** macro. It is arguably the most procedural of Clojure's looping alternatives. At least, it looks a lot like the **foreach** loop found in other languages. Here's a very simple use of **doseq**:

```
user> (doseq [n (range 5)]
    (println (str "Line " n)))
Line 0
Line 1
Line 2
Line 3
Line 4
nil
```

Translated into English, we might say: "For each integer from 0 to 5, print out a string with the word 'Line' and the integer." You might ask: "*What is that nil doing there?*" Good question. **doseq** always returns **nil**. In other words, **doseq** doesn't collect anything. The sole purpose of **doseq** is to perform side effects, such as printing to the REPL, which is what **println** does here. The strings that appear in your REPL—**Line 0**, **Line 1**, and so on—are not returned values; they are side effects.

> ### Note
>
> In Clojure, like in many languages in the Lisp family, functions that produce side effects often have names that end with an exclamation point. While it's not a firm rule, this convention does make code easier to read and helps to remind us to be careful of side effects. Clojure developers often use an exclamation point to indicate that a function modifies a mutable data structure, writes to a file or a database, or performs any kind of operation that produces a lasting effect outside the scope of the function.

So, why not just use **map**? Well, there are a couple of good reasons. The first is that **map** does not guarantee that the entire sequence will be executed. The **map** function is lazy, and **doseq** is not.

Generally, with **map**, **filter**, **reduce**, and all the other sequence-manipulating functions, you should always try to use **pure functions**, that is, functions without side effects. The exception to this rule is debugging, in which case a carefully placed **println** statement can be a lifesaver. (Remember, though, that **println** returns **nil**, so you have to be careful not to place it at the end of a function where it would mask the return value). With sequential data of some sort, it's important to use **doseq** when you want to produce side effects, and only then. By being strict about this, you also make your code easier to read and maintain. **doseq** is a flag in your source code that says: "Be careful, there are side effects here!" It is also a clear signal that we are not interested in the return value, since **doseq** always returns **nil**. This practice encourages developers to isolate code with side effects in specific parts of a program.

But what if we only wanted to print something on odd-numbered lines in the previous example? Here's one way we could do that:

```
(doseq [n (range 5)]
  (when (odd? n)
    (println (str "Line " n))))
```

There is nothing wrong with this code per se. As a general rule, though, it would be preferable to remove as much logic as possible from the body of **doseq**, perhaps doing something like this:

```
(doseq [n (filter odd? (range 5))]
    (println (str "Line " n)))
```

By enforcing the separation between the place where we shape our data and the place where the data is consumed, not only have we removed a conditional, but we've also organized our code in a way that opens the door to better practices. Maybe in the future, we will need to choose differently which lines to print. If that happens, our code is already in the right place, written in the clear vocabulary of Clojure sequence handling, and possibly benefiting from lazy evaluation. Remember: shape the data, and then use the data.

Looping Shortcuts

Generally, it is best to avoid writing real loops. Clojure provides some interesting functions that can help in some simple cases where what you really want is just a **repetition** of some kind. Unlike most of the techniques in this chapter, these functions return lazy sequences. We mention them here because many times, when a loop might seem necessary at first, these functions provide a simpler solution.

The simplest possible example is the **repeat** function, which is so simple that it barely qualifies as a looping construct. However, it can still come in handy from time to time. **repeat** simply repeats whatever value it is called with, returning a lazy sequence of that value. Here's an easy way to repeat yourself:

```
user> (take 5 (repeat "myself"))
("myself" "myself" "myself" "myself" "myself")
```

Yes, it's that simple. Still, it can be useful if you need to quickly load default values into a map. Imagine a game where each player is represented by a map. You need to initialize the player with default values for various counters and most of them have a default of **0**. One way to do this is to use **repeat**. Since **repeat** returns a lazy sequence, it will supply just as many zeros as you need:

```
user> (zipmap [:score :hits :friends :level :energy :boost] (repeat 0))
{:score 0, :hits 0, :friends 0, :level 0, :energy 0, :boost 0}
```

The next step beyond **repeat** is the **repeatedly** function. Instead of taking a value, **repeatedly** takes a function and returns a lazy sequence of calls to that function. The function provided to **repeatedly** cannot take any arguments, which limits its usefulness to **impure functions**, that is, functions whose return values do not depend on inputs, perhaps consulting some kind of external data store or sensor. Otherwise, if the function always returned the same value, **repeatedly** would return a list of identical values just like **repeat**.

Probably the most common use of **repeatedly** is producing a sequence of random values. A call to **rand-int** potentially varies every time we call it (unless, of course, you call **(rand-int 1)**, which can only ever return **0**.) Here's a good way of producing a list of random integers from 0 to 100, where **repeatedly** simply calls **rand-int** 10 times. The output from **rand-int** is different nearly every time it's called, so the resulting sequence is a series of random integers:

```
user> (take 10 (repeatedly (partial rand-int 100)))
(21 52 38 59 86 73 53 53 60 90)
```

As a convenience, **repeatedly** can take an integer argument that limits the number of values returned. We could write the previous expression without calling **take**, like this:

```
user> (repeatedly 10 (partial rand-int 100))
(55 0 65 34 64 19 21 63 25 94)
```

In the next exercise, we'll try a more complex scenario using **repeatedly** to generate random test data.

The next step beyond **repeatedly** is a function called **iterate**. Like **repeatedly**, **iterate** calls a function over and over again, returning the resulting lazy sequence. Unlike **repeatedly**, though, the function provided to **iterate** takes arguments, and the result of each call is passed on to the next iteration.

Let's say we have a bank account that returns an annual rate of 1% and we want to project what the balance will be each month for the next year. We could write a function like this:

```
user> (defn savings [principal yearly-rate]
    (let [monthly-rate (+ 1 (/ yearly-rate 12))]
      (iterate (fn [p] (* p monthly-rate)) principal)))
```

To predict the balances over the next 12 months, we have will ask for 13 months, since the first value returned is the starting balance:

```
user> (take 13 (savings 1000 0.01))
(1000
 1000.8333333333333
 1001.667361111111
 1002.5020839120368
 1003.3375023152968
 1004.1736169005594
 1005.0104282479765
 1005.847936938183
 1006.6861435522981
 1007.5250486719249
 1008.3646528791514
 1009.2049567565506
 1010.045960887181)
```

By compounding the interest every month, you have already earned almost 5 cents more than the annual rate!

Functions such as **repeatedly** and **iterate** can be used in very specific situations where they perfectly match what you need. The real world is often just a little bit more complicated though. Sometimes, the task at hand will require writing customized ways of moving through your data. It's time to move on to recursion.

Exercise 6.01: An Endless Stream of Groceries

Your employer is building a system to automatically handle groceries coming down a conveyor belt. As part of their research, they want you to build a simulator. The goal is to have an endless stream of random groceries. Your job is to write a function to do this:

1. Create a new directory in a convenient place; add a **deps.edn** file containing just an empty map and start a new REPL.

2. Open a new file with an expressive name such as **groceries.clj** and include the corresponding namespace declaration:

    ```
    (ns groceries)
    ```

Before we start, we need to build our grocery store simulator. The first step is to define all the possible articles. (This store doesn't offer a lot of choices, but at least it has them in infinite supply.) Copy the **grocery-articles** variable from https://packt.live/2tuSvd1 into your REPL and evaluate it:

grocery_store.clj

```
3   (def grocery-articles [{:name "Flour"
4                           :weight 1000    ; grams
5                           :max-dimension 140 ; millimeters
6                           }
7                          {:name "Bread"
8                           :weight 350
9                           :max-dimension 250}
10                         {:name "Potatoes"
11                          :weight 2500
12                          :max-dimension 340}
13                         {:name "Pepper"
14                          :weight 85
15                          :max-dimension 90}
```

The full file is available at https://packt.live/35r3Xng.

3. Define a function that will return long lists of randomly ordered grocery articles:

```
(defn article-stream [n]
  (repeatedly n #(rand-nth grocery-articles)))
```

rand-nth returns a randomly selected item from **grocery-articles** each time it is called. **repeatedly** creates a lazy sequence of calls to **rand-nth**. The **n** argument tells **repeatedly** how many random articles to return.

4. Test the function by asking for some articles:

```
groceries> (article-stream 12)
({:name "Olive oil", :weight 400, :max-dimension 280}
 {:name "Potatoes", :weight 2500, :max-dimension 340}
 {:name "Green beans", :weight 300, :max-dimension 120}
 {:name "Potatoes", :weight 2500, :max-dimension 340}
 {:name "Flour", :weight 1000, :max-dimension 140}
 {:name "Ice cream", :weight 450, :max-dimension 200}
 {:name "Potatoes", :weight 2500, :max-dimension 340}
 {:name "Green beans", :weight 300, :max-dimension 120}
 {:name "Potatoes", :weight 2500, :max-dimension 340}
 {:name "Ice cream", :weight 450, :max-dimension 200}
 {:name "Pepper", :weight 85, :max-dimension 90}
 {:name "Bread", :weight 350, :max-dimension 250})
```

5. Try again to make sure that the results are random:

```
groceries> (article-stream 5)
({:name "Potatoes", :weight 2500, :max-dimension 340}
  {:name "Green beans", :weight 300, :max-dimension 120}
  {:name "Bread", :weight 350, :max-dimension 250}
  {:name "Olive oil", :weight 400, :max-dimension 280}
  {:name "Pepper", :weight 85, :max-dimension 90})
```

It seems to work. This shows how functions can be combined in cases where, in other languages, it might seem more natural to write a **for** loop. In JavaScript once again, we might write a function like this (assuming that **groceryArticles** is an array of objects):

```
function randomArticles (groceryArticles, n) {
  var articles = [];
  for (var i = 0; i < n.length; i++) {
   articles.push(
   groceryArticles[Math.random(groceryArticles.length - 1)]
   );
  }
  return articles;
}
```

A function such as **repeatedly** provides a concise way to express this and saves us the trouble of writing all this iterative logic.

Recursion at Its Simplest

As we said before, a recursive function is a function that, as part of its execution, calls itself. Visually, recursion can be imagined as something like one of those pictures you've probably seen, where, inside the main picture, there is a smaller version of the original picture. Since the second picture is identical to the first, it also contains a very small, third version of the picture. After that, any further pictures are usually hard to represent as something bigger than a tiny dot. However, even if we can't see them, we can imagine the process going on for basically forever... or at least down to the molecular level. Recursion works in a similar way. And the problem of a recursive process that just keeps going on and on, like in the picture, is also a very real issue. However, before we look at the pitfalls of recursion, let's take a look at some simple examples.

To start out, we'll do something you already know how to do: find the sum of a collection of numbers. In real life, you would never use recursion for this, but the problem is deliberately simple so that we can point out some of the mechanisms of recursion:

```clojure
(defn recursive-sum [so-far numbers]
  (if (first numbers)
    (recursive-sum
     (+ so-far (first numbers))
     (next numbers))
    so-far))
```

A call to this function would look like this:

```clojure
user> (recursive-sum 0 [300 25 8])
333
```

This probably looks familiar to you because this is quite similar to the functions we passed to **reduce**. This isn't too surprising. We could even think of **reduce** as a framework for "controlled recursion," or "recursion with guardrails," which is why it's generally best to use **reduce** when you can, and recursion only when you must.

There are some important differences here though, so let's take a closer look at how this function works. The first thing to notice is the conditional with two branches: **(if (first numbers))**. When we first call the function, **(first numbers)** returns 300. That's truthy, so we keep going, and right away our functions call **recursive-sum** again (we warned you, there's going to be a lot of this in recursion.) The function gets called again but with different arguments: **(first numbers)** gets added to **so-far**, our accumulator, and instead of using numbers again as the second argument, we have **(next numbers)**.

With each call to **recursive-sum**, one more integer is shifted from the input sequence to the output integer:

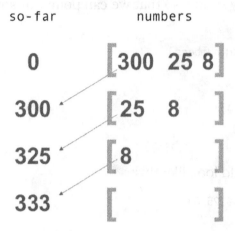

Figure 6.1: Recursively moving items from the input sequence to the output integer

With **reduce**, we don't need to think about how to advance through the sequence. The **reduce** function itself takes care of the mechanics of the iterations: moving from one item to the next and stopping when there are no more items. With a recursive function, it's up to us to make sure that each function call receives the right data and that the function stops when the data has been consumed. When you need it, recursion is extremely powerful because, as the programmer, you have complete control over the iteration. You get to decide what the arguments of each successive call will hold. You also get to decide how and when the recursion will stop.

So, how do we move through the sequence? On each call to **recursive-sum**, the input sequence is split between the first item and all the following items. The call to **first** gives us the current item, and the call to **next** helps set up the argument for the next function call. Repeating this splitting action moves us down the sequence.

There is one more problem, though: when do we stop? This is why our function, like the vast majority of recursive functions, is organized around a condition. Ours is simple: stop adding or keep going? The **next** function is important here too. When called on an empty list, **next** returns **nil**:

```
user> (next '())
nil
```

In this case, **nil** reliably means that it is time to stop iterating and just return the value that we have accumulated. More complex situations will require more complicated branching, but the basic idea generally remains the same.

Exercise 6.02: Partitioning Grocery Bags

In this exercise, we'll go back to the grocery conveyor belt simulation from the previous exercise. Now that we can simulate an endless stream of random articles, we need to be able to place the food items into grocery bags as they arrive at the end of the belt. If the bag gets too full, it will break or start to overflow. We need to know when to stop before it gets too full. Luckily, a barcode reader can tell us the weight and longest dimension of the items. If either of these gets beyond a certain number, the bag is removed and replaced with an empty bag:

1. Use the same environment as in the previous exercise.

2. Our grocery bags will be modeled as lists of articles. Define a **full-bag?** predicate so that we'll know when to stop filling a bag:

```
(defn full-bag? [items]
  (let [weight (apply + (map :weight items))
     size (apply + (map :max-dimension items))]
   (or (> weight 3200)
     (> size 800))))
```

3. Test **full-bag?** with the output from grocery streams of different lengths:

```
groceries> (full-bag? (article-stream 10))
true
groceries> (full-bag? (article-stream 1))
false
groceries> (full-bag? (article-stream 1000))
true
groceries> (full-bag? '())
false
```

4. Set up two functions, **bag-sequences** and its recursive helper function, **bag-sequences***. Define **bag-sequences*** first, since **bag-sequences** will call it:

```
(defn bag-sequences* [{:keys [current-bag bags] :as acc} stream]
  ;; TODO: write code
)
(defn bag-sequences [stream]
  (bag-sequences* {:bags []
          :current-bag []} stream))
```

As you can see from the arguments to the helper function, we've defined an accumulator, this time with two fields: :bags will hold the list of all the completed bags and :current-bag will hold the items we are testing. When :current-bag fills up, we will place it in :bags and start off with a fresh, empty vector in :current-bag.

The second function, without the asterisk, will be the public-facing function. Users of our library won't have to worry about supplying the accumulator; bag-sequences* will be the truly recursive function and do all the work.

5. Inside the **bag-sequences*** function, we will use a **cond** expression to react to the state of the articles as they arrive. Write the first, negative condition of the **cond** expression:

```
(defn bag-sequences* [{:keys [current-bag bags] :as acc} stream]
  (cond
    (not stream)
    (conj bags current-bag)
    ;; TODO: the other cond branches
    ))
```

Here, we decide what happens if there are no more articles in **stream**. If there's nothing left to put in the bag, then it's time to add **current-bag** to the list and return everything we've accumulated so far.

> **Note**
>
> In recursive functions, it's common practice to test whether the end of the input sequence has been reached as early as possible. This test is often a simple one, so it's good to get it out of the way. More importantly, if we know that the input sequence is not empty, we don't have to guard against **nil** values in the tests that follow. This helps eliminate some possible errors in the subsequent test clauses and allows us to write simpler, more readable code.

6. Add the condition for when the current bag is full:

```
(defn bag-sequences* [{:keys [current-bag bags] :as acc} stream]
  (cond
    (not stream)
    (conj bags current-bag)
    (full-bag? (conj current-bag (first stream)))
    (bag-sequences* (assoc acc
```

```
          :current-bag [(first stream)]
          :bags (conj bags current-bag))
      (next stream))
;; TODO: one more branch, for when the bag is not full yet
))
```

Thanks to the convenient **full-bag?** function, we know that the current bag is full. This means we need to move some data around inside **acc** when we make the next call to **bag-sequences***. Both of the arguments to **bag-sequences*** need to be updated. Our call to **assoc** may look strange at first glance, but **assoc** can accept multiple pairs of keys and values.

The most recent article in **stream** is going to become the first article in a new "bag" vector, so we assign that to the **:current-bag** key in **acc**. At this point, the **current-bag** binding (from the destructuring in the function's parameters) still refers to the bag we decided is full. We are going to add it to the list of bags we are maintaining in the **:bags** key in **acc**.

And since we want to keep advancing through **stream**, we use **next** to move on to the next article: **(next stream)**.

7. Write the final, default condition. If we've made it past the two previous conditions, we know that **stream** is not empty and that the current bag is not full. In this case, all we need to do is add the current article to the current bag. With this condition, our function is complete:

```
(defn bag-sequences* [{:keys [current-bag bags] :as acc} stream]
  (cond
    (not stream)
    (conj bags current-bag)
    (full-bag? (conj current-bag (first stream)))
    (bag-sequences* (assoc acc
                :current-bag [(first stream)]
                :bags (conj bags current-bag))
          (next stream))
    :otherwise-bag-not-full
    (bag-sequences* (update acc :current-bag conj (first stream))
          (next stream))))
```

This time, we'll use **update** instead of **assoc** to "modify" the **:current-bag** key in **acc**. This form of the **update** function takes, as its third argument, a function that will be applied to the value corresponding to the key provided and any further arguments. That means that, in this case, **conj** will be called as if we had written **(conj (:current-bag acc) (first stream))**.

8. Test the function using the **article-stream** function that we wrote in the previous exercise:

```
groceries> (bag-sequences (article-stream 12))
[[{:name "Pepper", :weight 85, :max-dimension 90}
 {:name "Pepper", :weight 85, :max-dimension 90}
 {:name "Green beans", :weight 300, :max-dimension 120}
 {:name "Flour", :weight 1000, :max-dimension 140}
 {:name "Olive oil", :weight 400, :max-dimension 280}]
 [{:name "Bread", :weight 350, :max-dimension 250}
 {:name "Pepper", :weight 85, :max-dimension 90}
 {:name "Green beans", :weight 300, :max-dimension 120}
 {:name "Olive oil", :weight 400, :max-dimension 280}]
  [{:name "Potatoes", :weight 2500, :max-dimension 340}
 {:name "Bread", :weight 350, :max-dimension 250}]]
```

This seems to work! Each bag appears as a vector of items. The length of the vectors varies depending on the size and weight of the items.

We've solved one of the problems we mentioned at the beginning of the chapter: traversing a sequence in steps of different lengths. In this example, we've partitioned the input sequence into chunks whose size depends on the properties of the underlying data.

When to Use recur

Now, **bag-sequence** worked fine for relatively short **grocery-stream** sequences, but when we moved it into production in our multimodal grocery mega-platform, the entire system ground quickly to a halt. Here's the message that appeared on all the technicians' consoles:

```
packt-clj.recursion> (def production-bags (bag-sequences (article-stream 10000)))
Execution error (StackOverflowError) at packt-clj.recursion/article-stream$fn (recursion.
clj:34).
null
```

So, what happened? What's a **StackOverflowError**?

The **stack** is how the JVM keeps track of nested function calls. Each function call requires a little bit of bookkeeping to maintain some contextual information, such as the value of local variables. The runtime also needs to know where the results of each call should go. When a function is called within another function, the outer function waits for the inner function to complete. If the inner function also calls other functions, it too must wait for those to complete, and so on. The job of the stack is to keep track of these chains of function calls.

We can use a very simple function as an illustration. This one takes two integers and performs two different operations on them:

```
user> (defn tiny-stack [a b]
    (* b (+ a b)))
#'user/tiny-stack
user> (tiny-stack 4 7)
77
```

Here's a simplified version of what happens when we call **tiny-stack**:

We call **tiny-stack** and an initial stack frame is produced. It waits for the contents of the function to be evaluated.

While **tiny-stack** waits, the * function is called. A new stack frame is produced. The **b** binding evaluates right away, but it can't return yet because of the call to +.

+ is finally called, producing a new, short-lived stack frame. The two integers are added together, the value is returned, and the stack frame of + is erased.

The call to * can now complete. It passes its return value back up to **tiny-stack** and then its stack frame is erased.

tiny-stack returns **77** and its stack frame is erased:

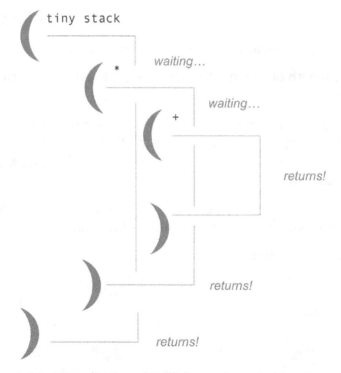

Figure 6.2: A visualization of stack frames in nested function calls

This is how the stack frame is supposed to work. Most of the time, we don't have to think about it at all. However, when we use recursion to walk the length of a sequence, we are actually using the stack, through nesting, to move along the sequence. Because there are limits to how many stack frames the runtime can handle, if we have a very long sequence, we will eventually run out of stack frames and our program will explode:

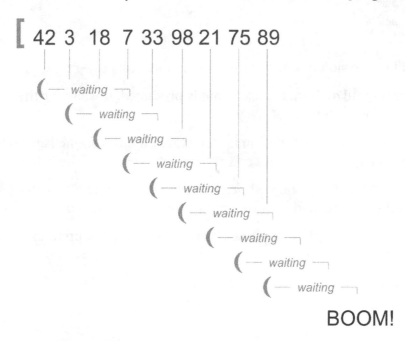

Figure 6.3: Representation of recursion

With recursion, the length of the input vector is translated into depth in the call stack until it goes too far

At this point, you're probably thinking that recursion doesn't sound like such a great pattern after all. This is actually due to a limitation that is built into the JVM. Other Lisps, not based on the JVM, do not have this limitation, and, in those languages, the preceding code would work just fine.

There is, however, a solution in Clojure, and it is called **recur**. Let's take another look at the **recursive-sum** function that we wrote in the last section:

```
(defn recursive-sum [so-far numbers]
  (if (first numbers)
   (recursive-sum
    (+ so-far (first numbers))
    (next numbers))
  so-far))
```

First, let's watch this explode on a long input sequence:

```
user> (recursive-sum 0 (range 10000))
Execution error (StackOverflowError) at user/recursive-sum (REPL:53).
null
```

To use **recur**, we simply replace the call to **recursive-sum** with the **recur** in our original equation:

```
user> (defn safe-recursive-sum [so-far numbers]
    (if (first numbers)
     (recur
      (+ so-far (first numbers))
      (next numbers))
     so-far))
#'user/safe-recursive-sum
user> (safe-recursive-sum 0 (range 10000))
49995000
```

Why does this work? Well, with **recur**, a function becomes tail recursive. **Tail recursion** means that successive calls don't add to the call stack. Instead, the runtime treats them as repetitions of the current frame. You can think of this as a way of staying in the same frame rather than waiting for all the nested calls to resolve. In this way, the looping can continue without adding to the stack. This allows us to process large amounts of data without running into the dreaded stack overflow.

A function can only be tail recursive if it returns a complete call to itself and nothing more. This is a little hard to understand at first, but it should become clearer as we work through some examples. In the next exercise, we'll look at a straightforward use of **recur** in a tail recursive function.

Exercise 6.03: Large-Scale Grocery Partitioning with recur

As we mentioned before, our previous experiment with **bag-sequences** did not scale well once the input stream became too long because we ran into stack overflow exceptions. Maybe we can improve on the previous design by using **recur**:

1. Set up the same environment as in the previous exercise.

2. Make a copy of the **bag-sequences** and **bag-sequences*** functions with new names, such as **robust-bag-sequences** and **robust-bag-sequences***.

3. In **robust-bag-sequences***, use **recur** instead of calling **bag-sequences***:

```
(defn robust-bag-sequences* [{:keys [current-bag bags] :as acc} stream]
 (cond
  (not stream)
  (conj bags current-bag)
  (full-bag? (conj current-bag (first stream)))
  (recur (assoc acc
          :current-bag [(first stream)]
          :bags (conj bags current-bag))
     (next stream))
  :otherwise-bag-not-full
  (recur (assoc acc :current-bag (conj current-bag (first stream)))
     (next stream))))
```

The only difference with the previous version of **bag-sequences*** is that we've replaced the recursive calls (where we wrote out the function name, **bag-sequences***) with **recur**. This function is tail recursive. Why? Well, let's look at the three possible outputs that correspond to the three branches of the **cond** expression. The first branch simply returns data, so there is no recursion at all there. The other two return calls to **recur** that are the last things to be evaluated in the function. This fits our definition of tail recursion, which is that the function must return a call to itself *and nothing else.*

4. In the public-facing **robust-bag-sequences** function, don't forget to update the call to **bag-sequences*** to the new function name:

```
(defn robust-bag-sequences [stream]
 (robust-bag-sequences* {:bags []
             :current-bag []} stream))
```

5. Evaluate your namespace and test the new function on a very long **article-stream**. Don't forget to assign the result to a variable, otherwise it will fill your REPL!

Here, we put 1 million articles into 343,091 bags:

```
groceries> (def bags (robust-bag-sequences (article-stream 1000000)))
#'packt-clj.recursion/bags
groceries> (count bags)
343091
groceries> (first bags)
[{:name "Olive oil", :weight 400, :max-dimension 280}
 {:name "Potatoes", :weight 2500, :max-dimension 340}]
```

Because the contents of **article-stream** are random, your results will be slightly different.

This example shows the basics of using **recur** to easily improve the performance of the recursive function. The **robust-bag-sequences*** function is indeed tail recursive because it returns a complete call to itself and nothing more.

What about loop?

As you may already know, Clojure does, in fact, have a **loop** macro. If, on hearing that, you're suddenly thinking "Great, I can just use **loop** instead!," you are probably going to be disappointed. The **loop** macro can indeed be useful, but the terrible secret of **loop** is that it is almost identical to writing a recursive function with **recur**.

The advantage of the **loop** macro is that it can be contained inside a function. This removes the need to write a public function that sets up the recursion and possibly does some "post-production" on the result, and a helper function that does the actual recursion. There is nothing wrong with that pattern, of course, but using **loop** can make a namespace easier to read by limiting the number of functions that need to be defined.

> **Note**
>
> Clojure provides another mechanism for avoiding public functions. Functions defined with **defn-** instead of **defn** are only available inside the namespace where they are defined.

The basic logic and structure of **loop** is really quite similar to that of a function with **recur**: a call to **loop** starts with one or more bindings and, just like a recursive function, starts over again thanks to **recur**. Just like with a recursive function, the parameters to **recur** must be modified on each iteration to avoid looping infinitely. And calls to **loop** must also be tail recursive, just like functions using **recur**.

Here is a simple skeleton for a function that uses **loop** to do something to the articles in our imaginary grocery store. Let's suppose that the **process** function does something important with each article, such as sending an API call to a different service. For now, we'll define it as a stub function aliased to **identity**, which is the Clojure function that simply returns whatever arguments it is provided with:

```
(def process identity)
(defn grocery-verification [input-items]
  (loop [remaining-items input-items
         processed-items []]
    (if (not (seq remaining-items))
      processed-items
      (recur (next remaining-items)
             (conj processed-items (process (first remaining-items)))))))
```

Obviously, the basic pattern is very similar to the recursive functions that we've already looked at: the conditionals to detect whether to continue iterating, and the call to **recur** at the end, are starting to become very familiar to you. It's important to remember that the initial bindings are just that: initial. Just like arguments to a function, they are assigned at the beginning of the loop and then reassigned by the calls to **recur**. Making sure that the iteration continues smoothly and not infinitely is up to you.

Exercise 6.04: Groceries with loop

Use **loop** to rewrite the **robust-bag-sequences** function from the previous exercise:

1. Use the same environment as the previous exercises.

2. Write the outline for a function with the same call signature as **robust-bag-sequences**:

```
(defn looping-robust-bag-sequences [stream]
  )
```

3. Set up a loop inside the function with the same arguments as **robust-bag-sequences***:

```
(defn looping-robust-bag-sequences [stream]
  (loop [remaining-stream stream
         acc {:current-bag []
              :bags []}]
    ;;TODO: the real work
    ))
```

As you can see, the initial setup of our accumulator is going to happen in the bindings.

4. Fill in the rest of the logic by reusing the code from **robust-bag-sequences*** in the previous exercise:

```
(defn looping-robust-bag-sequences [stream]
(loop [remaining-stream stream
    acc {:current-bag []
      :bags []}]
  (let [{:keys [current-bag bags]} acc]
   (cond (not remaining-stream)
      (conj bags current-bag)
      (full-bag? (conj current-bag (first remaining-stream)))
      (recur (next remaining-stream)
         (assoc acc
           :current-bag [(first remaining-stream)]
           :bags (conj bags current-bag)))
    :otherwise-bag-not-full
    (recur (next remaining-stream)
        (assoc acc :current-bag (conj current-bag (first remaining-stream)))))))))
```

This version is almost the same as the original. The primary difference is that, because of the way the variables are bound, we end up using a **let** binding to destructure the accumulator in order to have the **current-bag** and **bags** bindings. Other than that, the code is the same.

5. Test the new version of the function:

```
groceries> (looping-robust-bag-sequences (article-stream 8))
[[{:name "Bread", :weight 350, :max-dimension 250}
 {:name "Potatoes", :weight 2500, :max-dimension 340}]
 [{:name "Potatoes", :weight 2500, :max-dimension 340}]
 [{:name "Potatoes", :weight 2500, :max-dimension 340}
 {:name "Olive oil", :weight 400, :max-dimension 280}]
 [{:name "Flour", :weight 1000, :max-dimension 140}
 {:name "Green beans", :weight 300, :max-dimension 120}
 {:name "Pepper", :weight 85, :max-dimension 90}]]
```

This version of the code illustrates how similar **loop** and a recursive function can be. Choosing one form or the other depends mostly on which version will make your code easier to understand. Thinking of **loop** as a form of recursion will also make it easier to remember to write tail recursive code inside the loop.

Tail Recursion

As we said earlier, **recur** tells the JVM to expect the function to be tail recursive. What does that mean exactly, though? Replacing the function name with **recur** is not, in fact, enough to make a recursive function call tail recursive.

Let's start with an example of what happens when a recursive function is *not* tail recursive. So far, we've done a lot of adding of sequences of integers. Here's a new twist: suppose the integers are not in a simple sequence, but in nested sequences, perhaps like this:

```
(def nested [5 12 [3 48 16] [1 [53 8 [[4 43]] [8 19 3]] 29]])
```

Nested vectors like this are a common way of representing trees in Clojure. The vectors themselves are the branch nodes and the integers, in this case, are the leaves:

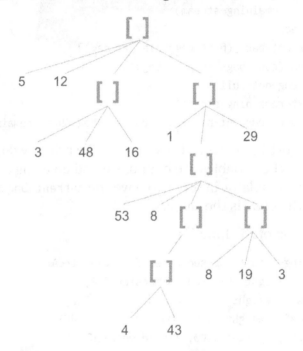

Figure 6.4: Nested vectors are a common way of representing tree structures

We haven't seen this kind of problem yet. It happens to be the kind of problem for which recursion is possibly the best or even the only solution. It's also an important kind of problem: these nested vectors actually define a tree structure. Trees are, of course, one of the most useful ways of representing data, so this is a fairly important subject.

Essentially, to solve this problem, we need a recursive function that adds when it sees a number and calls itself when it sees a list. Here's a start that looks a lot like some of the other functions we've written so far:

```
(defn naive-tree-sum [so-far x]
  (cond (not x) so-far
    (integer? (first x)) (recur (+ so-far (first x)) (next x))
    ; TODO: more code
    ))
```

The first condition in the **cond** form is pretty standard: if we're at the end of the input, we just return whatever is in **so-far**, our accumulator. The next condition should also seem pretty straightforward by now: if we have a number, add it to our running total and keep going by splitting the input sequence between the first item and the next items.

Now, let's write that last condition for when **(first x)** is a vector. The new call to **recur** will need to calculate **(first x)** so that it can be an integer. Here's what that would have to look like:

```
(defn naive-tree-sum [so-far x]
  (cond (not x) so-far
    (integer? (first x)) (recur (+ so-far (first x)) (next x))
    (or (seq? (first x)) (vector? (first x)))
    (recur (recur so-far (first x)) (next x)))) ;; Warning!!!
```

If you type this into your REPL and evaluate it, you'll get an error:

```
1. Caused by java.lang.UnsupportedOperationException
   Can only recur from tail position
```

What's going on? Why doesn't this work?

On the surface, we're just respecting the established pattern. The nested call to **recur** does look a little strange. But if **(first x)** is a vector or a list, we can't just add it to **so-far**. Our function needs an integer as the **so-far** argument. We need to transform the vector at **(first x)** into an integer by evaluating that entire part of the tree. And when that's done, and we have a nice, simple integer instead of a subtree, we can finally move on to the rest of the sequence, with **(next x)**.

The reason that the compiler refuses to compile our code, though, is that, because of the final line, the function is not tail recursive. In the last line of the function, the first **recur** has to wait for the second one to finish before moving on. That is a violation of the tail position requirement of **recur**: simultaneous calls to **recur** are forbidden. As we said before, to be tail recursive, a function must return only a call to itself, and nothing more. But in this case, one **recur** is waiting for the other to return.

We could also think about this in terms of stack frames. Tail recursion means that when the recursive function is called again (through **recur**), a new frame is not produced: the previous function call is "forgotten," or "erased," by the new one. The only trace of the previous calls is in the changes made to the arguments to the current call. The problem with this function is that the first call to **recur** can't be "forgotten." It's waiting for the result of the second call. It's only when the second call is resolved that the first will be able to continue. If we're in a situation where two stack frames need to coexist, we can't use **recur**. When treating linear data, this is generally not a problem. Tree structures, on the other hand, usually can't be handled in the linear way required by **recur**.

Let's try rewriting the same function without using **recur**:

```
user> (defn less-naive-tree-sum [so-far x]
         (cond (not x) so-far
            (integer? (first x)) (less-naive-tree-sum (+ so-far (first x)) (next x))
            (or (seq? (first x)) (vector? (first x)))
            (less-naive-tree-sum (less-naive-tree-sum so-far (first x)) (next x))))
#'user/less-naive-tree-sum
user> (less-naive-tree-sum 0 nested)
252
```

This works! We might have a new problem, though. Without **recur**, this version of the function will explode the stack when run on a tree with too many items. This may, or may not, be a problem, depending on what kind of data needs to be processed. If we did have many thousands of items and sub-vectors, we would need to find another solution. For that, you'll need to wait until the next chapter, where we'll learn about producing our own **lazy sequences**, which will permit us to use recursion on large, complex trees.

Recursion without **recur** and without lazy sequences can work just fine in many cases, though. When the input data is not in the thousands or millions of items, "normal" non-lazy recursion will probably be all you need. For now, the important thing is to understand that there are limits to when **recur** can be used. Luckily, many of the tasks you'll need to accomplish with recursion fit nicely into a tail recursive pattern. And don't worry: if you forget, the compiler is always there to remind you.

Solving Complex Problems with Recursion

When we talk about recursion, there are really two categories of use cases that are quite different from each other. This is particularly true of Clojure. On the one hand, recursion is the primary, low-level way to build loops where other languages would use **for**, **foreach**, or **with**. On the other hand, functional languages such as Clojure generally make it easier for programmers to find elegant, recursive solutions to complex problems.

Tail recursion and functions, or loops, built around **recur** are suited for problems where the data, input, and output, is essentially linear. Because tail recursive functions can only return one call at a time, they cannot handle problems where it is necessary to follow multiple, forking paths through the data. Clojure provides the tools you need. Using them may require some practice in approaching the problem in a recursive style.

To help build this skill, the remaining exercises in this chapter will be dedicated to solving a complex problem: finding the most efficient path through a network of nodes. Or, to put it differently: how to travel cheaply between European capitals. These exercises will show you how to break a problem down and resolve it recursively.

Exercise 6.05: Europe by Train

In this exercise, we need to find the least expensive way for a traveler to get from one European city to another. All we have is a list of city-to-city connections and an amount in euros. For the sake of this exercise, we will pretend that these are the only routes available and that the price of train tickets is constant for a given route. Here are our routes:

train_routes.clj

```
1   (def routes
2     [[:paris :london 236]
3      [:paris :frankfurt 121]
4      [:paris :milan 129]
5      [:milan :rome 95]
6      [:milan :barcelona 258]
7      [:milan :vienna 79]
8      [:barcelona :madrid 141]
9      [:madrid :lisbon 127]
10     [:madrid :paris 314]
```

The full code for this step is available at https://packt.live/2FpIjVM

And here is a visual representation:

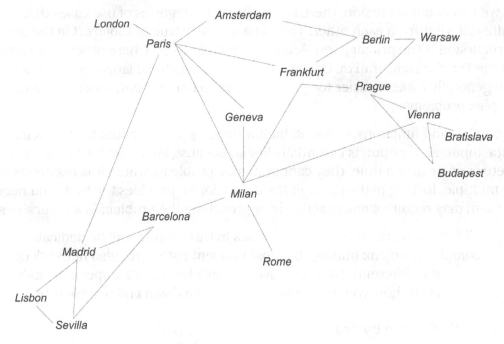

Figure 6.5: Train routes across Europe

> **Note**
>
> The list of paths between cities and the visual map are two ways of representing a graph, which is the computer science term for a system of nodes. A tree is one kind of graph in which there are no "cycles": you can't go from point A, to point B, to point C, and then back to point A. The European railroad network, on the other hand, has plenty of cycles. In graph theory, each city would be called a node and the paths between cities would be called an edge.

The goal is to write a function that takes two cities and returns a list of cities that represents the best route. To solve this problem, we will use recursion, as well as many of the techniques from the last two chapters.

In this exercise, we will set up the project and transform the list of routes into a table that we'll be able to query to see 1) if City A is connected to City B and, if so, 2) the cost of travel between cities A and B.

Thus, the table would look like this:

```
{:paris {:london 236
         :frankfurt 121
         :milan 129
         ;;...etc...
         }
 :milan {:paris 129
         :vienna 79
         :rome 95
         ;;...etc...
         }}
```

We also have to make sure that all of the routes are represented in both directions. In the initial list, we have `[:paris :milan 129]`. We also need to represent the reverse route, that is, Milan to Paris. In the preceding example, we have `:milan` in the `:paris` section, as well as `:paris` in the `:milan` section:

1. Create a new project directory with a **deps.edn** file containing just an empty map, **{}**, and start a new REPL.

2. Open a new file called **train_routes.clj** with just a **(ns train-routes)** namespace declaration.

3. Copy the **routes** variable from https://packt.live/39JOFit into the new namespace.

4. The first step is to group all the routes together by origin city. Use **group-by** to do this. Start by defining a function called **grouped-routes**:

```
(defn grouped-routes
  [routes]
  (->> routes
       (group-by first)))
```

5. Run this early version of the function on the route list and look at the results for just one city:

```
train-routes> (:paris (grouped-routes routes))
[[:paris :london 236]
 [:paris :frankfurt 121]
 [:paris :milan 129]
 [:paris :amsterdam 139]]
```

With the call to **group-by**, we have a list of all the **:paris** routes. We now need a way to change this sub-list into a map.

6. Write a function that accepts one of these sub-lists and returns a map:

```
(defn route-list->distance-map [route-list]
  (->> route-list
    (map (fn [[_ city cost]] [city cost]))
    (into {})))
```

This function uses the **map-into** pattern to create a list of two-item vector tuples. We don't need the first item because it's the same as the key associated with the sub-list, so we use destructuring to place **city** and **cost** in a new vector.

7. Test **route-list->distance-map** in the REPL with some sample data:

```
train-routes> (route-list->distance-map [[:paris :milan 129]
                                          [:paris :frankfurt 121]])
{:milan 129, :frankfurt 121}
```

8. Continue building the **grouped-routes** function. Use the **map-into** pattern again to apply **route-list->distance-map** to all the sub-lists returned by the call to **group-by**:

```
(defn grouped-routes
  [routes]
  (->> routes
    (group-by first)
    (map (fn [[k v]] [k (route-list->distance-map v)]))
    (into {})))
```

The call to **map** treats the key-value pairs of the top-level map as a series of two-item vectors and runs **route-list->distance-map** on each value. The call to **into** converts the sequence back into a map.

9. Test this version of **grouped-routes** in the REPL:

```
train-routes> (:paris (grouped-routes routes))
{:london 236, :frankfurt 121, :milan 129, :amsterdam 139}
```

Perfect! This kind of map will make it easy to look up a route between an origin (**:paris**) and a destination (**:amsterdam**).

We still need to produce the reverse routes. We'll use **mapcat**, in a pattern we mentioned back in *Chapter 4*, *Mapping and Filtering*, to produce two routes for each input route. This can go before the call to **group-by**:

```
(defn grouped-routes
  [routes]
  (->> routes
       (mapcat (fn [[origin-city dest-city cost :as r]]
                 [r [dest-city origin-city cost]]))
       (group-by first)
       (map (fn [[k v]] [k (route-list->distance-map v)]))
       (into {})))
```

The anonymous function in the **mapcat** call returns a vector containing two sub-vectors. The first of these is the original route, and the second is the same route with the origin and destination cities reversed. Thanks to **mapcat**, the result is a flattened list with twice as many elements as the input list.

10. Test this in the REPL again:

```
train-routes> (:paris (grouped-routes routes))
{:london 236,
 :frankfurt 121,
 :milan 129,
 :madrid 314,
 :geneva 123,
 :amsterdam 139}
```

Now, the **[:madrid :paris 34]** route is also included as a **:paris** to **:madrid** route.

11. Define a **lookup** variable with the lookup table:

```
train-routes> (def lookup (grouped-routes routes))
#'train-routes/lookup
```

We'll need this variable later.

12. Test the lookup table. First, we'll ask for a route from Paris to Madrid:

```
train-routes> (get-in lookup [:paris :madrid])
314
```

Can we go back to Paris?

```
train-routes> (get-in lookup [:madrid :paris])
314
```

Let's try a route that we know does not exist:

```
train-routes> (get-in lookup [:paris :bratislava])
nil
```

Our lookup table answers two important questions: Is there a route between City A and City B? How much does it cost?

We now have a data store that we can consult when we need to find which cities are available from any given point in the European rail graph. Rearranging data into an easy-to-query form can be an important step when dealing with a complex problem like this one. The next steps will be easier thanks to this easy access to our data.

Pathfinding

If we are in a city that is not directly connected to the city we want to travel to, we need to choose intermediate cities. To get from City A to City F, maybe we can go to City C first; or, maybe we'll need to go to City B and then City D before reaching City F. To find the best path, we first need to find all the possible paths.

This is why a recursive approach is a good fit. The basic strategy is to test whether City A and City F are connected. If so, we've already found the answer. If not, we look at all the cities we can reach directly from City A. We go through the same process on each of those, and so on and so forth, until finally we find a city that is connected directly to City F. The process is recursive because we repeat the same process on each node until we find what we are looking for.

Let's try to visualize this process, using a small part of the network. In this example, we'll start in Paris and search for Berlin. The first step is to test the cities we can reach from Paris. In London, Amsterdam, and Frankfurt, we ask: are you Berlin?

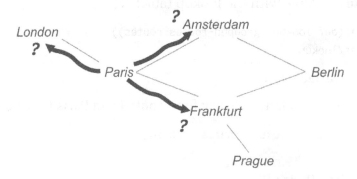

Figure 6.6: Starting in Paris, we query all the available cities

Since none of the cities is the one that we are looking for, we repeat the process from London, Amsterdam, and Frankfurt:

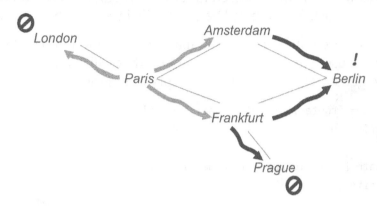

Figure 6.7: Searching again from the previously found cities

From London, we have nowhere left to go. But from Amsterdam and Frankfurt, we can reach Berlin. Success! Not only have we found Berlin, but we've found two paths to get there.

We could represent these paths as Clojure vectors:

```
[:paris :london nil]
[:paris :amsterdam :berlin]
[:paris :frankfurt :berlin]
[:paris :frankfurt :prague nil]
```

Notice that the paths going through Prague and London end with **nil**. This is how we will represent paths that do not lead to our destination and must be removed from the result set.

There is one more issue that we haven't dealt with yet. What prevents us from going from Amsterdam back to Paris? This would create infinite loops where we search from Paris, then search Amsterdam, then search Paris again, and so on. To get around this problem, we will need to "remember" where we've been.

This is our general approach. Now, let's write some more code!

Exercise 6.06: The Search Function

The next step is to write the main search function, a recursive function that we'll call **find-path***. The **find-path** function will be the public interface that calls **find-path***:

1. At this point, we are ready to write the main search function. The **find-path** function can be used for the wrapper function that will serve as the public interface. To get started, let's write the empty functions:

    ```
    (defn find-path* [route-lookup destination path]
      ;; TODO: write code
      )
    (defn find-path [route-lookup origin destination]
      ;; TODO: write code
      )
    ```

    We've written the "private" function, **find-path***, first since the "public" function, **find-path**, will refer to it.

    There are already some design decisions here in the function arguments. Both functions accept the **route-lookup** argument. This will be the lookup table generated by **grouped-routes**. They both accept the destination argument as well. Since we want to build up a list of cities, a path, the private function, **find-path***, doesn't take an origin argument like **find-path** does. Instead, it will take whatever the current path is. Since it's a recursive function, the current "origin" will always be whatever the last city in the path is.

    In other words, if we're testing a path, the value of **path** might be [:paris :milan]. That means that on the next iteration, **find-path*** will try all the cities available from :milan, making :milan the temporary origin. The next cities are tested in the same way and the path gets lengthened by one city on each successive call.

2. Call **find-path*** from **find-path**:

    ```
    (defn find-path [route-lookup origin destination]
      (find-path* route-lookup destination [origin]))
    ```

    This is simple. We package the initial **origin** in a vector to pass off to **find-path***. This way, we know that we will always have at least one city in the **path** parameter.

3. Set up the basic conditional structure of the recursive function:

```
(defn find-path* [route-lookup destination path]
 (let [position (last path)]
  (cond
   (= position destination) path
   (get-in route-lookup [position destination])
   (conj path destination)
   ;; TODO: still not there
 )))
```

This part does two things. We are going to need to refer to the current position a lot, so it's a good idea to create a **let** binding immediately. As we mentioned earlier, our current position is always the last item in the **path** argument. The whole process is about adding cities on to the end of this list.

The next thing we do is to start setting up the different checks we'll use. The two conditions we add here both end the recursion and return a value. These are the "Are we there yet?" tests. The second one is the one that will be called the most, so let's look at it first.

If you remember how our lookup table is structured, there is a top-level set of keys, one for each city in our system. The value of each of those keys is a map of reachable cities. That's why we can use **get-in** here. Say our lookup table looks something like this:

```
{:paris {:frankfurt 121
      :milan 129
      ;; etc.
      }
 ;; etc.
 }
```

If we call (**get-in routes-lookup [:paris :milan]**), we will get **129**. If our current position is **:paris** and our destination is **:milan**, then this call will return truthy. In that case, we add **:milan** to the current path and we return the path. We've arrived.

So, why do we need the first condition then? In what circumstances would the destination city already be in the path? There is only one way that could happen, but we do have to take care of it. Someday, a user will call your function and ask the best route from **:paris** to **:paris** and we don't want to blow up the stack on such a simple request.

4. Test the simple cases. We already have enough code for two cases, so let's see whether our functions work. Try **find-path*** first with a one-city path:

```
train-routes> (find-path* lookup :sevilla [:sevilla])
[:sevilla]
```

Now, let's try the same thing with **find-path**:

```
train-routes> (find-path lookup :sevilla :sevilla)
[:sevilla]
```

The current code should also work if the destination city is only one "hop" away from the origin:

```
train-routes> (find-path* lookup :madrid [:sevilla])
[:sevilla :madrid]
```

So far so good. Onward!

5. Start building the recursive logic to **find-path***:

```
(defn find-path* [route-lookup destination path]
  (let [position (last path)]
   (cond
     (= position destination) path
     (get-in route-lookup [position destination])
     (conj path destination)
     :otherwise-we-search
     (let [path-set (set path)
           from-here (remove path-set (keys (get route-lookup position)))]
      (when-not (empty? from-here)
       (->> from-here
            (map (fn [pos] (find-path* route-lookup destination (conj path pos))))
            (remove empty?)))))))
```

For the final condition, we use an expressive Clojure keyword such as **:otherwise-we-search** as a condition, but anything that isn't **false** or **nil** will do. If we get this far, we know that we haven't reached the destination yet, so we have to keep searching.

6. Let's look at this line by line. The first thing we do is define **path-set**, which will allow us to test whether a city is already in our path. You can try building and using a set in the REPL:

```
train-routes> (set [:amsterdam :paris :milan])
#{:paris :milan :amsterdam}
train-routes> ((set [:amsterdam :paris :milan]) :berlin)
nil
train-routes> ((set [:amsterdam :paris :milan]) :paris)
:paris
```

The reason this is important becomes apparent in the next line. We bind **from-here** to this:

```
(remove path-set (keys (get route-lookup position)))
```

We can't use **get-in** like we did earlier because this time, we don't want just one city reachable from **position**, we want all of them. So, we grab the entire sub-map for the current city, with **(get route-lookup position)**, and then extract a list of keywords. Now, the **path-set** binding from the previous line becomes useful. We use it to remove any cities that we've already visited. This is how we avoid recursively going back and forth between **:paris** and **:amsterdam** forever.

The **from-here** binding now contains all the cities we still need to test. First, though, we check to see whether **from-here** is empty, using Clojure's well-named **empty?** predicate. Let's say our destination is **:berlin** and our current path is **[:paris :london]**. The only way out of **:london** is to go back to **:paris**, but we've already been there. This means it's time to give up, so we return **nil**. As you'll soon see, paths that resolve to **nil** will be ignored.

7. After this, we start threading **from-here** through a series of s-expressions. The first one is where the actual recursion is going to happen:

```
(map (fn [pos] (find-path* route-lookup destination (conj path pos))))
```

8. We're mapping over the cities that we can reach from our current position. Say we've arrived in **:paris** from **:london**. In the lookup table, the value for **:paris** is as follows:

```
train-routes> (:paris lookup)
{:london 236,
 :frankfurt 121,
 :milan 129,
 :madrid 314,
 :geneva 123,
 :amsterdam 139}
```

9. We can't go back to :london, so that means **from-here** is [:frankfurt :milan :madrid :geneva :amsterdam]. The anonymous function provided to **map** will be called once for each of these cities as **pos**. Each city will thus be appended to the path argument in the recursive calls to **find-path***. The following values will be tried as the **path** argument to **find-path***:

```
[:london :paris :frankfurt]
[:london :paris :milan]
[:london :paris :madrid]
[:london :paris :geneva]
[:london :paris :amsterdam]
```

Remember that **map** returns a list. The list returned here will be the result of calling **find-path*** on each city. Each of those calls will produce a list as well, until the search finds the destination city or runs out of places to look.

Now, we can start to visualize the recursive structure of our path search:

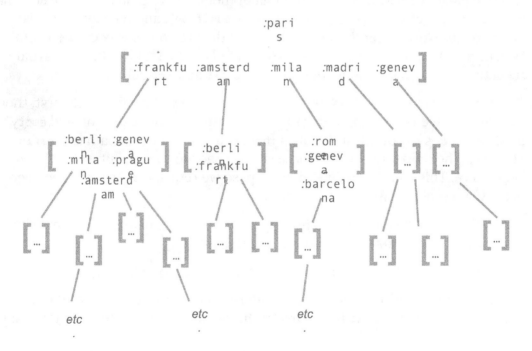

Figure 6.8: Each city resolves to a new list of cities, each of which resolves to a new list

Eventually, the search will either find the destination or run out of options, at which point the lists will all be resolved. If there are no more options and the destination still hasn't been found, **nil** is returned. Otherwise, a list of resolved paths is returned. This simple call to **map** ends up walking the entire city graph until all the possible routes are found.

Before returning, though, the call to map gets threaded through one last s-expression: (remove empty?). This is how we filter out the nil paths that never find the destination.

10. Test the current state of the function on a short path.

To make this easier to test, we'll use a smaller rail network. Start by defining a new variable for the lookup table:

```
train-routes> (def small-routes (grouped-routes [[:paris :milan 100][:paris :geneva
100][:geneva :rome 100][:milan :rome 100]]))
#'train-routes/small-routes
train-routes> small-routes
{:paris {:milan 100, :geneva 100},
 :milan {:paris 100, :rome 100},
 :geneva {:paris 100, :rome 100},
 :rome {:geneva 100, :milan 100}}
```

There should be precisely two paths between :paris and :rome:

```
train-routes> (find-path* small-routes :rome [:paris])
([:paris :milan :rome] [:paris :geneva :rome])
```

11. Test the current state of the function with a slightly bigger network. We'll add another route between :paris and :milan:

```
train-routes> (def more-routes (grouped-routes [[:paris :milan 100]
                                                 [:paris :geneva 100]
                                                 [:paris :barcelona 100]
                                                 [:barcelona :milan 100]
                                                 [:geneva :rome 100]
                                                 [:milan :rome 100]]))
#'train-routes/more-routes
```

12. With this set of routes, our result is not quite what we expect:

```
train-routes> (find-path* more-routes :rome [:paris])
([:paris :milan :rome]
 [:paris :geneva :rome]
 ([:paris :barcelona :milan :rome]))
```

13. The data looks good, but where did those extra parentheses come from? This is a consequence of using **map** in a recursive way. **map** always returns a list. The **:barcelona** route requires an extra level of recursion because it is one item longer than the others. As a result, it is wrapped in a list. We can verify this by adding another possible route:

```
train-routes> (def even-more-routes (grouped-routes [[:paris :milan 100]
                                                     [:paris :geneva 100]
                                                     [:paris :barcelona 100]
                                                     [:barcelona :madrid 100]
                                                     [:madrid :milan 100]
                                                     [:barcelona :milan 100]
                                                     [:geneva :rome 100]
                                                     [:milan :rome 100]]))
#'train-routes/even-more-routes
train-routes> (find-path* even-more-routes :rome [:paris])
([:paris :milan :rome]
 [:paris :geneva :rome]
 (([:paris :barcelona :madrid :milan :rome])
 [:paris :barcelona :milan :rome]))
```

As you can see, the five-city path that goes through **:madrid** is wrapped in an extra set of parentheses.

14. Unnest the nested lists. To solve this problem, use **mapcat** to strip away the containing lists. Here is the final version of **find-path***:

```
(defn find-path* [route-lookup destination path]
(let [position (last path)]
 (cond
  (= position destination) path
  (get-in route-lookup [position destination])
  (conj path destination)
  :otherwise-we-search
  (let [path-set (set path)
        from-here (remove path-set (keys (get route-lookup position)))]
   (when-not (empty? from-here)
    (->> from-here
        (map (fn [pos] (find-path* route-lookup destination (conj path pos))))
        (remove empty?)
        (mapcat (fn [x] (if (keyword? (first x))
                 [x]
                 x)))))))))
```

The last addition is the call to `mapcat`. It might look strange at first, but remember: `mapcat` removes the outer parentheses from the items in the list that it returns. That's why we have the conditional: if **x** is just a path, like `[:prague :bratislava]`, we don't want it to be directly concatenated, which is why we return `[x]` instead. The new wrapper is instantly removed when the items are concatenated together, and the original vector remains intact. In the other cases though, when the underlying vector is wrapped in a list, `mapcat` "removes" it.

15. Test this version on the small and large railroad networks. First, we'll test it with **even-more-routes**:

```
train-routes> (find-path* even-more-routes :rome [:paris])
([:paris :milan :rome]
 [:paris :geneva :rome]
 [:paris :barcelona :madrid :milan :rome]
 [:paris :barcelona :milan :rome])
```

Much better!

16. Now, try it with the full-sized lookup table. We won't print the full results here because they're quite long:

```
train-routes> (find-path* lookup :rome [:paris])
([:paris :frankfurt :milan :rome]
 [:paris :frankfurt :berlin :warsaw :prague :vienna :milan :rome]
 [:paris :frankfurt :berlin :warsaw :prague :bratislava :vienna :milan :rome]
 [:paris :frankfurt :berlin :warsaw :prague :budapest :vienna :milan :rome]
 [:paris :frankfurt :geneva :milan :rome]
 [:paris :frankfurt :prague :vienna :milan :rome]
 [:paris :frankfurt :prague :bratislava :vienna :milan :rome]
 [:paris :frankfurt :prague :budapest :vienna :milan :rome]
 ;; etc. )
```

Now, we can walk the entire network. Our **find-path** function returns all the possible routes between any two cities.

Once again, Clojure has helped us write a concise solution to a fairly complex problem. A recursive algorithm such as this depends on a design that combines two elements. On the one hand, the recursive function treats each new node as if it were the first node. Recursive solutions are often perceived as "elegant" because of this. By solving the problem for one item, it can be solved for an entire network of items. To work, however, this requires the second design element: a way of accumulating the results from one node to another. In this example, we built up our knowledge by adding cities to one of the parameters. In the next exercise, we'll use different techniques for bringing the data together.

This exercise also shows the value of using small, sample inputs at the REPL. The interactive programming experience allows you to quickly try things and verify your hypotheses.

Exercise 6.07: Calculating the Costs of the Routes

There's just one more problem to solve. In our original problem description, we didn't ask for all the possible routes, but just the least expensive one! We need a way to evaluate the cost of all the paths and choose one. To accomplish this, we will use the lookup table from the two previous exercises to calculate the cost of each path returned by **find-path***. Then, we can use a reducing pattern from *Chapter 5, Many to One: Reducing*, for finding the path with the lowest cost:

1. Write a **cost-of-route** function.

    To do this, we'll use a pattern from *Chapter 4, Mapping and Filtering*, **map**, with two input lists. The first will be the path, and the second will be the path offset by one item so that each call can evaluate the cost of going from one city to the next. It should look like this:

    ```
    (defn cost-of-route
     [route-lookup route]
     (apply +
         (map (fn [start end]
             (get-in route-lookup [start end]))
           route
           (next route))))
    ```

    By now, this should look familiar. **(next route)** provides the offset version of **route**. For each pair of cities, we use **get-in** the same way we did earlier. That call gives us the cost of a given segment in the path. Then, we use the **(apply +)** pattern to find the grand total.

2. Test the new function:

    ```
    train-routes> (cost-of-route lookup [:london :paris :amsterdam :berlin :warsaw])
    603
    ```

    And it even works with the edge cases:

    ```
    train-routes> (cost-of-route lookup [:london])
    0
    ```

3. Write a **min-route** function to find the least expensive route.

   Now, we'll leverage another familiar pattern, this time using **reduce**. We want to find the route with the lowest total cost and we need a function like **min**, except that it will return the *item* that has the minimum cost, and not just the minimum cost itself:

   ```
   (defn min-route [route-lookup routes]
     (reduce (fn [current-best route]
           (let [cost (cost-of-route route-lookup route)]
             (if (or (< cost (:cost current-best))
                 (= 0 (:cost current-best)))
               {:cost cost :best route}
             current-best)))
         {:cost 0 :best [(ffirst routes)]}
         routes))
   ```

   The only slightly tricky aspect of this function is the initialization value in the call to **reduce**: **{:cost 0 :best [(ffirst routes)]}**. We start with a default cost of **0**. So far so good. The default **:best** route should be the route corresponding to a distance of zero, which means that we're not going anywhere. That's why we use **ffirst**, which is not a typo but a convenience function for nested lists. It is a shortcut for **(first (first my-list))**, so it returns the first element of the first element of the outer list.

4. Now, put it all together. Add a call to **min-route** to the public-facing **find-path** function:

   ```
   (defn find-path [route-lookup origin destination]
     (min-route route-lookup (find-path* route-lookup destination [origin])))
   ```

5. Test this out on several pairs of cities:

   ```
   train-routes> (find-path lookup :paris :rome)
   {:cost 224, :best [:paris :milan :rome]}
   train-routes> (find-path lookup :paris :berlin)
   {:cost 291, :best [:paris :frankfurt :berlin]}
   train-routes> (find-path lookup :warsaw :sevilla)
   {:cost 720,
    :best [:warsaw :prague :vienna :milan :barcelona :sevilla]}
   ```

Working through this code involved a lot of different steps, but, in the end, it was worth it. We've actually solved a somewhat difficult problem in about 50 lines of code. Best of all, the solution involved many techniques that we've already seen, which shows, one more time, how important and powerful they can be when used together.

A Brief Introduction to HTML

In many of the remaining chapters of this book and starting with the activity at the end of this chapter, we will be working in one way or another with **Hypertext Markup Language (HTML)**, which holds together just about every web page you've ever seen. Producing HTML from data is an extremely common programming task. Just about every mainstream programming language has multiple templating libraries for generating web pages. Even before Clojure, Lisps have used nested s-expressions for this. S-expressions are a particularly good fit for HTML documents, which are structured like logical trees.

In case you're not familiar with the essentials of producing HTML, it's worth briefly reviewing the basics. HTML is the content of the text file that provides the structure for other kinds of content (that is, images, audio, and video resources) on a web page. The fundamental unit of HTML is called an element. Here is a simple paragraph element, using the **<p>** tag:

```
<p>A short paragraph.</p>
```

The HTML standard, of which there are several versions, contains many, many kinds of elements. The **<html>** element contains a web page in its entirety. In turn, this contains the **<head>** and **<body>** elements. The first of these contains various kinds of metadata for displaying the page; the second contains the actual content that will be shown to the user. The **<body>** element can contain both text and more elements.

We'll only use a small handful of elements here:

- **<div>**: Perhaps the most widely used element of all, **<div>** is a generic container for anything from the size of the paragraph up to an entire document. It can't be used for content below the size of a paragraph, however, because the end of a **<div>** causes a break in the text flow.

- **<p>**: The paragraph element.

- **<ul>** and **<li>**: "UL" stands for "unordered list," that is, a list without numbers. A **<ul>** should only contain "list items," that is, **<li>** elements.

- **<span>**, **<em>**, and **<strong>**: These elements are part of the text; they are for wrapping single words or single letters. They do not cause breaks in text flow. **<span>** is a generic element. **<em>** (for emphasis) generally produces italicized text, while **<strong>** generally produces bold text.

- **<a>**: A hypertext link element. This is also a text-level element. The **href** attribute (we'll explain attributes in a second) of an **<a>** element tells the browser where to go when you click on a link.

- **<img>**: The **<img>** tag inserts an image, referenced by its **src** attribute.

- **<h1>**, **<h2>**, and **<h3>**: These are the heading elements, for page titles, section titles, subsection titles, and more.

These few elements are enough to get started producing web content. You can learn about others as needed by consulting, for example, the Mozilla Developers Network's MDN web documentation.

> **Note**
>
> The MDN web docs can be referred to at https://packt.live/2s3M8go.

Since we will be producing HTML, there are only a few things you need to know in order to produce well-formed HTML:

- Most HTML tags have three parts: a start tag, a closing tag, and some content.

- A start tag consists of a short string wrapped in angle brackets: **<h1>**.

- A closing tag is similar, except that there is a slash, **/**, in front of the tag name, **</h1>**.

- Opening tags can contain attributes, which are key-value pairs, with the values in quotes: **<h1 class="example-title">Example</h1>**.

- Certain attributes, known as "Boolean attributes", don't need to have a value. The presence of a key is enough:

```
<input type="checkbox" checked>
```

- Some tags do not have any content. They can be written as a single element containing a slash after the tag name: **
**.

- In some dialects of HTML, certain tags without content can be written without a slash: **<img>**.

- If an element begins inside another element, its end tag must occur before the end of the containing element.

The last point is important. This means that it would be invalid to write something like this:

```
<div>Soon a paragraph <p>will start</div>, then end too late.</p>
```

The **<p>** element here should be a child element of **<div>**. A child element must be contained completely by its parent element. This is a very good thing when manipulating HTML because it means that correctly formed HTML is always a tree structure, with a root note, the **<html>** element that contains nodes that contain other nodes, and so on. As you'll see, this matches well with the kinds of tree structures that we've already looked at here.

Now, you know enough to write a system that will produce well-formed HTML. (To become a renowned web designer, however, you'll need to learn a little bit more.)

In Clojure, vectors are generally used for representing the structure of an HTML document. One of the more popular libraries that does this is called **Hiccup**. With **Hiccup**, a short paragraph containing a link would look like this:

```
[:p "This paragraph is just an "
 [:a {:href "http://example.com"} "example"] "."]
```

The output would be as follows:

```
<p>This paragraph is just an <a href="http://example.com">example</a>.</p>
```

The syntax for this is quite simple. Besides using vectors, it uses keywords to identify HTML tags and maps to add attributes such as **href** or **class**.

Some tags, such as **<link>**, **<meta>**, **
, **<input>, and **<img>**, are generally not closed, so they should receive special handling. All other tags should be explicitly closed even if they don't have any content.

> **Note**
>
> More information on Hiccup can be found at https://packt.live/36vXZ5U.

Activity 6.01: Generating HTML from Clojure Vectors

The company you work for is building a new web application. Generating and serving HTML pages is, quite logically, a key part of the operation. Your team has been asked to write a library for generating HTML from Clojure data.

Producing HTML from data is an extremely common programming task. Just about every mainstream programming language has multiple templating libraries for generating web pages. Even before Clojure, Lisps have used nested s-expressions for this. S-expressions are a particularly good fit for HTML documents that are structured like logical trees.

Goal

In this activity, you are going to write your own system for generating HTML from nested vectors, using this format. The goal is to be able to take any vector written with this syntax, including an arbitrary number of descendant vectors, and produce a single string containing correctly structured HTML.

Your code should also handle "Boolean attributes." Clojure maps don't allow keys to have no value to do this of course. You'll need to invent a convention so that users of your library can assign some non-string value to these attributes and get a Boolean attribute in the output string.

Steps

The following steps will help you to complete the activity:

1. Set up a new project directory with an empty **deps.edn** file. You don't need any external dependencies for this activity. Make your own namespace with a catchy name for this new library.

2. If you decide to use the **clojure.string** library, now is the time to reference it in the **:require** part of your namespace.

3. It's often a good idea to start by writing some of the smaller functions. Simple functions that take a keyword and output a string containing either an opening tag or a closing tag would be convenient, for example. You'll need the **name** function for converting a keyword into a string.

   A good choice for this would be the function that will accept a map, such as **{:class "my-css-class"}**, and return a properly formatted set of HTML attributes: **class="my-css-class"**. Don't forget to handle the case of Boolean attributes too. Remember that a Clojure map can be read as a sequence of key-value pairs. And don't forget to put quotes around the values. A string containing a single escaped quotation mark looks this: **"\""**.

   It might be useful to have a predicate function to determine whether the second element in a vector is an attribute map.

   When parsing a vector, you'll know that the first element is a keyword. The second element might be a map if there are attributes, but it might not. Use the **map?** predicate to test that.

4. The fun part will be writing the recursive function. We won't say much about that, except that the basic tree walking pattern that we used in the "Europe by train" example should provide you with a rough base. You won't be able to use **recur** because you need to handle a real tree.

There are a lot of different kinds of elements that you need to handle, in addition to string content. In cases like this, it is often a good idea to write very clear predicates that you will use when deciding how to handle an element, such as **singleton-with-attrs?**, for example. These will be useful when writing the conditional part of your recursive function.

Upon completing the activity, you will be able to test your code with an input of your choice. You should see an output similar to the following:

```
packt-clj.my-hiccup> (my-hiccup
                       [:html
                        [:head
                         [:title "HTML output from vectors!"]]
                        [:body
                         [:h1 {:id "page-title"} "HTML output from vectors!"]
                         [:div {:class "main-content"}
                          [:p "Converting nested lists into HTML is an old Lisp trick"]
                          [:p "But Clojure uses vectors instead."]]]])
 "<html><head><title>HTML output from vectors!</title></head><body><h1 id=\"page-title\">HTM
 L output from vectors!</h1><div class=\"main-content\"><p>Converting nested lists into HTML
  is an old Lisp trick</p><p>But Clojure uses vectors instead.</p></div></body></html>"
 packt-clj.my-hiccup> []
```

Figure 6.9: Expected output

> **Note**
>
> The solution to this activity can be found on page 696.

Summary

We've covered a lot of ground in this chapter. Recursion in Clojure, as in many functional languages, is a central concept. On the one hand, it can be necessary for some fairly simple looping situations. In those cases, **recur**, whether used with **loop** or in a recursive function, can almost be seen as just "Clojure's syntax for looping." Understanding tail recursion is important for avoiding mistakes, but otherwise, it is relatively simple. On the other hand, recursion can be an extremely powerful way of solving complex problems. If it makes your head spin from time to time, that's normal: recursion is more than just a technique. It's a way of thinking about problem solving. Don't worry, though. In the next chapter, you are going to be able to practice your recursion skills some more!

In the next chapter, we will continue exploring the recursive techniques and focus on lazy evaluation.

Recursion II: Lazy Sequences

Overview

In this chapter, as we continue our exploration of recursive techniques, we will focus on lazy evaluation. We will write functions that safely produce potentially infinite lazy sequences, use lazy evaluation to consume linear data, produce lazily evaluated tree structures from linear data, and write functions that consume tree structures.

By the end of this chapter, you will be able to think about new ways of understanding and solving problems.

Introduction

At its simplest, a **lazy sequence** is a hybrid of two things:

- A *list* (not a vector!) of zero or more items

- A *reference* to possible future items of the list that can be computed if necessary

In other words, there's a real part and a virtual part. Most of the time, you don't need to think about this distinction. That's the whole point of lazy sequences: the virtual part becomes real when you need it, if you need it. When you can stay away from the edge cases, you don't need to worry about the virtual part because as soon as it's needed, it will become real.

Over the last few chapters, we've already used lazy sequences in many different ways. They are an important, distinctive feature of Clojure and they are something that you'll use every day as a Clojure programmer. You've seen by now that they are list-like structures with a twist: while you are using the first elements of the list, the rest of the list may not exist during runtime. Remember that in a lazy sequence, the individual items are not computed until they are needed. Or, to use the vocabulary of Clojure, they are not realized until they are consumed. You can define a potentially infinite lazy sequence and then only use, and compute, the first three items.

Up to now, the lazy sequences we've used were returned by core Clojure functions, such as `iterate`, which we looked at briefly in *Chapter 6, Recursion and Looping*, or familiar functions such as `map` and `filter`, which we saw in *Chapter 4, Mapping and Filtering*. The next step forward in this path is learning to write your own functions to produce lazy sequences.

When working in Clojure, lazy sequences are used all the time, as you've already seen by now. Writing functions to build your own lazy sequences is an advanced step and is more prone to errors. It should be considered the final option when dealing with sequences. Here is a rough guide to when deciding which techniques to use for solving a sequence-related problem:

- **Option 1**: Often, functions such as `map`, `filter`, and `remove` that accept and return sequences will be all you need when working with sequential data.

- **Option 2**: Sometimes, it will be necessary to combine the techniques in option 1 with `reduce`, because your calculation needs to take into account the relationships between items in your data, or because you need to produce an aggregate result.

- **Option 3**: In a much smaller number of cases, you'll need to use some form of recursion, either because you need to customize the iteration (`recur`), or because your data is non-linear, such as a `tree` or a `graph`.

- **Option 4**: In a subset of the cases in *Option 3*, the input data is extremely vast, or your calculation produces too many branches. The result is a blown call stack. In such cases, lazy sequences are a solution.

Each step down this list incurs a higher cost in terms of programmer effort and code complexity. When you stay closer to the beginning of the list, Clojure provides more help and protection from potential mistakes. As you move further down the list, you have to pay more attention to how you implement your solution. Part of being an effective Clojure developer is knowing how to avoid options 3 and 4 when you can, and then using them effectively when you really need to. For certain kinds of problems, such as parsing deeply nested data structures, lazy sequences are a very good fit, and may be the only practical solution in Clojure. That's why it's an important skill to have. There is another benefit too. Knowing how lazy sequences are produced will give you a deeper understanding of how they work.

In this chapter, we will start by using lazy sequences to deal with linear data before moving on to more complex tree structures.

A Simple Lazy Sequence

To start with, let's consider the simplest possible producer of lazy sequences, the **range** function, which simply returns a possibly infinite series of consecutive integers. The easiest way to write this is to use **iterate**:

```
(defn iterate-range [] (iterate inc 0))
```

Here, **iterate** returns a sequence that starts with the initializer value, zero, and then continues with the result of calling **inc** on zero, then on the result of that and so on. Each intermediate value becomes an item in the returned lazy sequence. It works just fine:

```
user> (take 5 (iterate-range))
(0 1 2 3 4)
```

The **iterate** function is doing all the work. We could stop here, but we wouldn't have learned much about how lazy sequences are built. Here's a more low-level version that performs the same task. It uses the **lazy-seq** macro, which is the base of all lazy sequences:

```
user> (defn our-range [n]
        (lazy-seq
          (cons n (our-range (inc n)))))
#'user/our-range
```

This function might look strange to you. We're going to break it down in detail. Before we do that, let's make sure it works:

```
user> (take 5 (our-range 0))
(0 1 2 3 4)
```

There are three things that stand out here.

- The use of **lazy-seq**. This is what makes the "magic" happen. Notice that **lazy-seq** wraps the entire body of the function.

- The use of **cons**. The name of the **cons** function goes back to Lisp, which is much, much older than Clojure. **cons** is a function that connects two things. In most Lisp dialects, a list is constructed by using **cons** to connect an item to the rest of the list. Using **cons** here means that we are returning a list like this.

- The use of recursion. Without **lazy-seq**, this recursive call would execute immediately, and continuously, until the stack blew up. With **lazy-seq**, the next call does not happen; instead, a reference to that future call is returned.

The structure of the function mirrors the data structure that it produces:

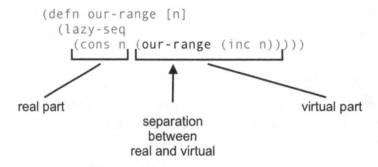

Figure 7.1: Structure of functions

Thanks to **lazy-seq**, the recursive call becomes a reference.

On the left, we have the real part; on the right, the virtual part. As the sequence is consumed, more and more virtual calls to **our-range** become real. The reference to further virtual calls remains at the end of the list, ready when more integers are needed.

> **Note**
>
> The future, unrealized calculation is often called a **thunk**. The word makes it sound like something that has already been thought, but it is something that hasn't been "**thunk**" yet.

This is just about the simplest possible version of a lazy sequence, but it is enough to provide an idea of the basic pattern that we will continue to expand upon.

Consuming a Sequence

An iterative sequence such as **our-range** takes a single input and builds a sequence by calling a function on the input, then on the result of the first function call, then on the result of that call, and so on. While this kind of computation can be useful sometimes, more often than not our code needs to accept incoming data of some kind.

The pattern for doing this is a blend of the iterative style of lazy sequence and the recursive functions from the previous chapter. As with other forms of recursion, these functions will be built around conditionals, **if** or **cond** usually, and they will advance through the input sequence by working on the first item and then calling themselves again on the rest of the input. And like **our-range**, they will generally build their output with **cons**, attaching the current item onto a list that points to future possible calculations.

Exercise 7.01: Finding Inflection Points

In this exercise, we are building a tool to analyze data from users' GPS watches. Runners and hikers want to know how much of the time they are going uphill or downhill. The incoming data is a potentially endless sequence of tuples containing an elevation in meters, and a timestamp, the number of milliseconds since the user started their exercise.

Each tuple looks as follows:

```
[24.2 420031]
```

We need to iterate through the input sequence looking for local peaks or valleys, that is, the points where the elevation is greater than the preceding and following points (peak), or less than the preceding and following points (valley). We could use **reduce** instead, as we did for the bicycle race problem in *Chapter 5, Many to One: Reducing*. However, the input stream might be very, very long, so we don't want to force evaluation, which is what would happen with **reduce**.

1. Define some sample data in the required format. You can find this var at https://packt.live/2Rhcbu6:

```
(def sample-data
  [[24.2 420031]
   [25.8 492657]
   [25.9 589014]
   [23.8 691995]
   [24.7 734902]
   [23.2 794243]
   [23.1 836204]
   [23.5 884120]])
```

2. A peak or a valley can be detected by comparing three consecutive items. Write a predicate for detecting peaks or valleys.

   As we move through the list of elevation-time tuples, we will look at the current item and the next two items in order to identify peaks and valleys. In a sub-sequence of three items, if the middle item is greater than the first and the last, it's a peak; if it is less than both, it is a valley. In all other cases, the middle item is neither a peak nor a valley. We'll write two functions, **local-max?** and **local-min?**, which will translate this logic into functions:

```
(defn local-max? [[a b c]]
  (and (< (first a) (first b)) (< (first c) (first b))))
(defn local-min? [[a b c]]
  (and (> (first a) (first b)) (> (first c) (first b))))
```

   If we wanted to clean up our code with some destructuring, we could avoid all those **first** calls. The functions would take a single, three-item list. Each item is a two-item tuple. With two levels of destructuring, we can extract the elements we need without calling any functions:

```
(defn local-max? [[[a _] [b _] [c _]]]
  (and (< a b) (< c b)))
(defn local-min? [[[a _] [b _] [c _]]]
  (and (> a b) (> c b)))
```

> **Note**
>
> As with many minor stylistic optimizations like this, the important thing is to use the one that you think is the easiest to understand. Clojure's destructuring will seem more and more intuitive as you learn the language, but there's nothing wrong with repeating **first** several times if it makes more sense to you.

We can already test these on the sample data. The first three values are [24.2 420031], [25.8 492657], and [25.9 589014]. Each value is greater than the next so we don't expect this to be either a peak or a valley:

```
user> (local-max? (take 3 sample-data))
false
user> (local-min? (take 3 sample-data))
false
```

If we move forward by two items in **sample-data**, we find a valley. The third, fourth, and fifth items are [25.9 589014], [23.8 691995], and [24.7 734902]. The middle value is less than the first and last:

```
user> (local-min? (take 3 (drop 2 sample-data)))
true
```

3. Outline the recursive function. As we discussed, our function will have the same basic shape as most of the recursive functions we've seen so far. For our conditional, there are four cases we need to deal with. Before that, though, we must create a local binding to **current-series**, which will be the first three items in **data**.

Since we are just laying out the function, we will return different keywords instead of real values for the moment:

```
(defn inflection-points [data]
  (lazy-seq
    (let [current-series (take 3 data)]
      (cond (< (count current-series) 3)
              :no-more-data-so-stop
            (local-max? current-series)
              :peak
            (local-min? current-series)
              :valley
            :otherwise
              :neither-so-keep-moving))))
```

In the first test in the **cond** expression, we check to see whether we've run out of data, which we can do by checking the length of **current-series**. If **current-series** does not contain three items, then we know that we'll never find a peak or a valley, so it's time to stop. As usual, we place this condition first so that in the subsequent tests we can be sure to have at least some data. The next two tests use the predicates we defined earlier: **local-max?** and **local-min?**. In these cases, we will add the current value to the accumulated **data**. The last possibility is that the current item is neither a minimum nor a maximum. In this case, we aren't interested in that particular item, so we will continue without placing it in the accumulated data.

4. Now we can start deciding what will happen in each of these four cases. The first case, when we've run out of data, is the simplest, but perhaps the most surprising as well. Here, we just return an empty list:

```
(< (count current-series) 3)
'()
```

With **recur** based recursion, this wouldn't make any sense: returning an empty list on reaching the end of the input data would mean that the function always returns... an empty list. Not very useful, really.

With a lazy sequence, however, this last item is simply the end of the list that will be returned. In many cases, the entire list will not be consumed, and the end of the input sequence will never be reached. If we think of a lazy sequence as a series of pointers toward potential calculations, the empty list here is simply the result of the very last potential calculation.

It is also important that this be an empty list, and not, for example, an empty vector. Vectors are do not support laziness.

5. The next two cases are where **local-max?** or **local-min?** have decided that the second item in **current-series** is indeed a peak or a valley. When that happens, we need to do two things. First, we need to mark the tuple as either a peak or a valley by appending the appropriate keyword; secondly, we need to make sure that the tuple becomes part of the output sequence.

Appending the keyword is easy:

```
(conj (second current-series) :peak)
```

Since each item is a two-value tuple, **conj** will make it into a three-value tuple:

```
[24.7 734902 :peak]
```

> **Note**
>
> When using **conj**, always be careful of what type of sequence you are using. When called on a vector, **conj** will append the new item to the end of the vector. When called on a list, it will append to the beginning. This may seem surprising, but there is a reason: **conj** always adds the new item in the most efficient way possible, depending on the data structure used. For vectors, this means adding to the end; for lists, this means adding to the beginning.

6. Next, we need to incorporate this new value into the sequence that will be returned. Rather than placing it in an accumulator of some kind, as we might if we were using **recur**, the current item becomes the head of the list of all the remaining items to be calculated. This is what the **cons** function does. And that "list of all the remaining items to be calculated" is represented here as the recursive call to **inflection-points**:

```
(local-max? current-series)
(cons
  (conj (second current-series) :peak)
  (inflection-points (rest data)))
(local-min? current-series)
(cons
  (conj (second current-series) :valley)
  (inflection-points (rest data)))
```

Think of it this way. To the right, you have all the remaining items. The call to **inflection-points** is going to return them, eventually, or at least potentially. The current item, like we said, is the head of that list. To the left, there are the items that have already been calculated. The last one of those, just to the left of the current item, is going to be the head of a list where the second item is the current item. And so on, all the way to the start of the list. An item is linked to the right by calling a function, and to the left because a function is being called on it.

> **Note**
>
> Recursion can be hard to grasp. Don't worry! It will get easier with practice.

When using **recur**, we tend to place the results in an argument to the next call to the recursive function. And we will be doing that with the **current-series** parameter. Because this function will return a lazy sequence, we'll use **cons** and place the current item in front of the potential result set. Each call to the function returns part of a list that the parent call can integrate into what it returns.

7. The last condition is the least interesting: ignore the current item and move on to the next. We do this in the now-familiar way of removing one item from data in the next recursive call to **inflection-points**:

```
:otherwise
(inflection-points (rest data))
```

Here's the complete function:

```
(defn inflection-points [data]
  (lazy-seq
    (let [current-series (take 3 data)]
      (cond (< (count current-series) 3)
            '()
            (local-max? current-series)
            (cons
              (conj (second current-series) :peak)
              (inflection-points (rest data)))
            (local-min? current-series)
            (cons
              (conj (second current-series) :valley)
              (inflection-points (rest data)))
            :otherwise
            (inflection-points (rest data)))))))
```

8. Test the function using the **sample-data** var we defined at the beginning:

```
user> (inflection-points sample-data)
([25.9 589014 :peak]
 [23.8 691995 :valley]
 [24.7 734902 :peak]
 [23.1 836204 :valley])
```

9. Use Clojure's **cycle** function to transform **sample-data** into a circuit that our jogger runs over and over again:

```
user> (take 15 (inflection-points (cycle sample-data)))
([25.9 589014 :peak]
 [23.8 691995 :valley]
 [24.7 734902 :peak]
```

```
        [23.1 836204 :valley]
        [25.9 589014 :peak]
        [23.8 691995 :valley]
        [24.7 734902 :peak]
        [23.1 836204 :valley]
        [25.9 589014 :peak]
        [23.8 691995 :valley]
        [24.7 734902 :peak]
        [23.1 836204 :valley]
        [25.9 589014 :peak]
        [23.8 691995 :valley]
        [24.7 734902 :peak])
   It just keeps going and going!
```

cycle returns a lazy sequence that repeats a **seq** forever.

This exercise introduced the fundamental structure that you will find in most functions that produce lazy sequences. Making the current the head of the list of future calculations by using **cons** it onto the next recursive call is lazy sequence recursion in a nutshell. The surrounding code may become more complex as we move forward, but this operation will be the building block of all the lazy sequence-producing functions that we write.

Exercise 7.02: Calculating a Running Average

To put this into practice, let's imagine a scenario similar to the grocery conveyor belt in the previous chapter. This time, though, we're doing quality control on the potatoes that are delivered to our mega-store. The potatoes are weighed as they pass a gate. We want to keep accepting potatoes as long as the average stays within certain bounds. It's all right to have a few small potatoes, or a few huge ones, as long as most of them are within the limits. If the average gets too high or too low, then something must be wrong, so we'll stop accepting potatoes.

1. Start up a fresh REPL.

2. First, we need to simulate a potato source. We need to define a randomized potato-generating function. We'll use the same technique for producing an infinite sequence of random values as we did for the grocery store, using **repeatedly** and **rand-int**. In this version, we add **10**, which will act as an extreme minimum potato size. This way our generator will produce potatoes between **10** and **400** grams:

```
user> (def endless-potatoes (repeatedly (fn [] (+ 10 (rand-int 390)))))
#'user/endless-potatoes
```

3. Test this lazy sequence with **take**. You will naturally get different random numbers:

```
user> (take 5 endless-potatoes)
(205 349 97 250 18)
user> (take 10 endless-potatoes)
(205 349 97 250 18 219 68 186 196 68)
```

Notice how the first five elements are the same both times. Those items have been realized. New potato generation will only occur when more items are computed further along in the sequence.

Now we arrive at our first design challenge. We need a way of representing the current average for each item in the list. Beyond just the weight of the current potato, we need the potato count at that point in the sequence and the accumulated weight so far. We could use a three-item tuple to hold those three values. If the fifth potato in the list weighs **200** grams, and the total weight of the first five potatoes was **784**, that potato could be represented like this:

```
[200 5 784]
```

Since we have the item count and the total, this design allows us to easily calculate the average at any point in the sequence.

4. To find the average after three items, we would take three items from the sequence, if our function returns something like this:

```
([59 1 59] [134 2 193] [358 3 551])
```

Dividing **551**, the total weight so far, by **3**, the number of potatoes, would give us the current average, which is **179.33333** in this case.

We have our design, but we still need to implement it. Let's go through our options for selecting a sequence-handling technique. **map** won't work here because we need to accumulate data. The **map** windowing pattern from *Chapter 4, Mapping and Filtering*, sounds like it might do the job, but it cannot accumulate data from one end of the sequence. The "window" is local to a few list items. So then maybe **reduce** is the answer? Unfortunately, **reduce** is not lazy: the entire sequence would be realized immediately. In some cases that would be acceptable, but in this case we don't know how long the input will be.

That leaves us with recursion. We can't use **recur** for the same reason we can't use **reduce**: we might be processing a nearly infinite stream. That also means that standard recursion without **recur** will blow the stack well before we get through our first ton of potatoes. Therefore, we'll use **lazy-seq** to produce different computations.

5. Start with a skeleton for a function that returns a lazy sequence, using the **lazy-seq** macro to wrap the contents of the recursive function:

```
(defn average-potatoes [prev arrivals]
  (lazy-seq
    ))
```

The **prev** parameter will start as an empty vector. We will use it to pass the current total on to the next calculation.

6. Fill in the contents of the recursive function using the patterns learned in the previous chapter, starting with the conditional that stop the recursion when we've exhausted the input. Unlike functions that are designed to continue infinitely, such as **range, average-potatoes** only continues as long as it has input, so we do need to check if there is anything left:

```
(defn average-potatoes [prev arrivals]
  (lazy-seq
    (if-not arrivals
      '()
      )))
```

Here, we see the same pattern as in the previous exercise. When we reach the end of the list, we return an empty list.

> **Note**
>
> It would be possible to return **nil** here instead because **cons** treats **nil** here just like the empty list. Try **(cons 5 nil)** in your REPL. The empty list does a better job of telling us what is happening here.

7. Calculate the current item before performing the recursion. We'll use a **let** binding here because we need the current item twice: once as an item in the list, and once as the **prev** argument that will be the basis for calculating the total weight when we get the next potato:

```
(defn average-potatoes [prev arrivals]
  (lazy-seq
    (if-not arrivals
      '()
      (let [[_ n total] prev
            current [(first arrivals)
                     (inc (or n 0))
                     (+ (first arrivals) (or total 0))]]
        ;; TODO: the actual recursion
        ))))
```

The first part of the **let** binding uses some destructuring to get the current count and the total so far from the **prev** argument. We don't need the weight of the previous potato since it is already included in the running total, which is why we've used an underscore for that value.

With the next binding, we build the actual tuple that will become an item in the sequence. The only complexity here is that **n** and **total** might be nil, so we have to check for that and supply **0** if they are. The first item in the tuple is just the weight of the current potato; the second item is the count we'll use calculating the average; the last is the total weight of all the potatoes counted so far.

8. Add the recursive logic:

```
(defn average-potatoes [prev arrivals]
  (lazy-seq
    (if-not arrivals
      '()
      (let [[_ n total] prev
            current [(first arrivals)
                     (inc (or n 0))
                     (+ (first arrivals) (or total 0))]]
        (cons
          current
          (average-potatoes
            current
            (next arrivals)))))))
```

All we've done in this last step is attach the current item to the list that will be created by the subsequent recursive calls to **average-potatoes**. We've supplied **current** as the **prev** argument for the next call.

Note also that we use **next** instead of **rest**: this way, arrivals will be **nil** when we get to the end of the sequence, which is what we are expecting when we test with **if-not** at the beginning of this function. The **next** function is very similar to **rest**, which we used in the previous example. Both functions take a list and return all but the first item of that list. The difference between the two is visible when there are no more items in the list. In that case, **rest** returns an empty list, while **next** returns **nil**. Choosing one or the other depends on the circumstances. The advantage of **next** is that it is easy to test for truthiness as we did here, instead of calling **empty?** as we did with **rest** in the previous exercise. Because **rest** never returns **nil**, there is no risk of a null pointer exception.

9. Test your new lazy function. Let's start by looking at a few individual items:

```
user> (take 3 (average-potatoes '() endless-potatoes))
([321 1 321] [338 2 659] [318 3 977])
```

The third element of each tuple correctly indicates the accumulated weight. That part seems correct.

Now let's try working with a large number of items. We'll take the last element from a long list of potatoes:

```
user> (last (take 500000 (average-potatoes '() endless-potatoes)))
[43 500000 102132749]
```

At **500,000** potatoes, everything seems to still be working as expected.

In this example, it's important to note the difference between the preceding examples of lazy evaluation using **rand-int** and **inc**. With **rand-int**, each call is independent of all the other calls. Lazy evaluation is only useful here because it's useful to have a potentially infinite sequence. With **inc**, when we implemented our version of **range**, the situation is slightly more complex because each call, and thus each item in the sequence, relies on the results of the call before. This is also true of the **average-potatoes** function: each call relies on the total and the count established in the previous call, and it relays this information onto the next call. At the same time, it does something more, because each calculation also consumes an item from the input sequence.

The core **map** and **filter** functions do this as well: their results are no longer than their inputs. This adds one more reason to use write functions that consume and produce lazy sequences: they can be chained together with other lazy functions without forcing evaluation.

Lazy Consumption of Data

Lazy evaluation is an interface that, most of the time, hides from the user whether a calculation has already been performed, or is about to be performed. This is what it means when we say that a lazy sequence contains possibly differed computations. "Possibly," because we don't know, and we don't need to know, whether or not the computation has already happened.

To be useful though, lazy evaluation has to be passed from one function call to the next. If we pass a lazy sequence to function A, and the result of that to function B, and so on, the evaluation only remains lazy if A and B are designed to return lazy sequences.

For example, say we have a lazy sequence called **xs**. If it gets passed to **map**, then to **filter**, and then to **take-while**, it will remain "lazy" the whole time. If instead we insert a **reduce** into that chain of function calls, or if we use **mapv** instead of **map**, the laziness disappears.

In the end, potential evaluation isn't enough. You do actually want some real data at some point! However, there is generally an advantage in preserving laziness until the very end. That means avoiding something like this:

```
(->> xs
     (map some-func)
     (reduce some-reducing-func)
     (filter some-predicate?))
```

Here, we take some a sequence and use **map** to apply a function to each item. The call to **map** is lazy but the call to **reduce** is not, so the entire sequence is realized. Then some of those results are discarded by **filter**. Depending on what the functions are doing, this may be the only way to write this code. However, ideally, we would try to use **filter** first to narrow the data as much as possible before calling **reduce**, or any other function that does not preserve laziness:

```
(->> xs
     (map some-func)
     (filter some-predicate?)
     (take-while another-predicate?)
     (reduce +))
```

The first advantage with this pattern is that your code becomes simpler. **filter** and **take-while** may have removed some types of data that the **reduce** call will not need to deal with at all. By waiting until the very last minute before forcing the sequence to be completely realized, there may actually be less computational work to do.

To see how this might work, let's look at this simple expression:

```
(nth (filter even? (range)) 3)
```

The evaluation starts with (range), which, if range were not lazy, would return all the integers from zero to infinity. In other words, CPU usage would go to 100% and evaluation would stop when something broke.

Instead of that horrible outcome, though, we can imagine the return value of (range) as looking something like this:

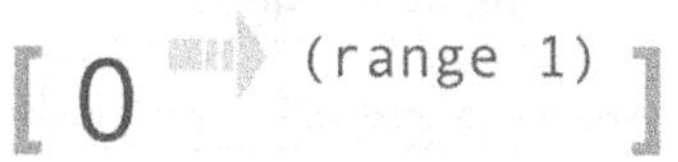

Figure 7.2: Representation of range value

An unrealized lazy sequence: a starting point and a pointer to future calculations.

This is a lot less work than counting from zero to infinity. It's essentially 0 and a pointer toward instructions for calculating the rest of the sequence, if necessary.

However, we don't want all the integers, just the even ones:

```
(filter even? (range))
```

With this call to filter, we've created a second lazy sequence built upon the first:

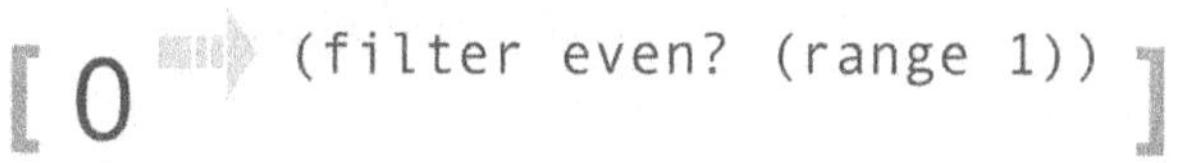

Figure 7.3: Creating the second lazy sequence

By adding filter, we've created a new lazy sequence that still only has one real piece of data.

The only concrete data we have so far is still zero. All we've done is add to the instructions for getting the rest of the sequence. Everything is still virtual at this point.

And then, finally, we call nth and ask for the fourth item in the sequence:

```
user> (nth (filter even? (range)) 3)
6
```

Now everything changes. We need the real values of the first four items. nth causes the first four items of the filter sequence to be evaluated. To do this, filter needs the first seven items of the range sequence to be evaluated. Suddenly, (range) looks like this:

Figure 7.4: Current values in the range

The first seven items are realized. The rest of the sequence is still virtual.

And **(filter even? (range))** looks as follows:

Figure 7.5: Filtering even numbers from the range

The fourth value in the list can now be consumed just like any other value.

The important thing to understand here is this: the last element in each of these sequences is a pointer to further potential calculations. **filter** and **range** worked together to provide just enough data to **nth**, and no more. By passing pointers (or "instructions for future computations") from function to function, the ultimate consumer can send a signal back up the chain, from pointer to pointer, to obtain the necessary data.

> **Note**
>
> Lazy sequences in Clojure are actually implemented as **chunked sequences**. This is an implementation detail: as an optimization, Clojure sometimes realizes a few more items than are actually necessary. While this is good to know, it should never matter. It just means that you can't count on an item *not* being realized.

The capacity to avoid performing certain calculations until the last millisecond, or to avoid them entirely, is an important feature of lazy computation. There is another aspect that can be equally important: the ability to "forget" some of the calculations that have already been performed.

Consider a non-lazy Clojure collection, such as a vector. Whatever size the vector is, the entire vector is available in memory at the same time. When the program no longer needs the vector, the platform on which the program is running, the JVM or a JavaScript engine, has a garbage collector that will free up the memory occupied by the vector. But if the program still needs even just one item from that vector, the garbage collector will keep waiting until it can safely reclaim that memory space.

A lazy sequence behaves in a totally different manner. Instead of being a single entity, it is a series of linked entities, each one referring to the next. As we've seen, this is how a lazy sequence can even reference items that don't exist yet, and maybe never will. There is another important part of the equation, though. Lazy sequences also the first part of the sequence to be garbage collected if it is no longer needed.

In the last example, we were looking for the fourth even number in the range. Instead, what if we were looking for the seven millionth even number?

```
user> (nth (filter even? (range)) 7000000)
14000000
```

There is no reason, in this situation, to keep a reference to those first 13,999,999 integers that were produced by (range). That means that they can be safely garbage collected.

This feature of lazy sequences means that they can be used to process datasets that would be too big to fit in the computer's memory all at once. By "forgetting" the first part and not immediately computing the last part, Clojure can process extremely long sequences while using only a fraction of the memory it would take to contain them all at once. There is, however, a limitation.

If a program maintains a reference to the beginning of a sequence, then it can no longer be garbage collected. Often, this won't matter, but with very long sequences, it becomes an important consideration. Throughout this chapter, you may notice that we often repeat expressions such as (first my-seq) inside a function when it might be tempting to use a local let binding instead. This is a way of avoiding references that would prevent a sequence from being garbage collected.

Lazy Trees

So far, we've seen that the "laziness" of lazy sequences is that they can point to future computations that will only be performed if they become necessary. There is another important advantage that is equally important, and that is what we are going to explore now. Remember from *Chapter 6*, *Recursion and Looping*, how recursive functions in Clojure need to use recur to avoid blowing up the stack? And remember how recur only works with a specific kind of recursion, tail recursion, where the next call to the recursive function can totally replace the previous call? The problem, you'll recall, is that only a limited number of stack frames are available. The function call on the root node of the tree needs to wait until all the calls have completed on all the child and grandchild and great-grandchild nodes, and so on. Stack frames are a limited resource but the data we need to operate on is often vast. This mismatch is a problem.

This is where lazy evaluation comes in. With lazy evaluation, Clojure itself handles the link to the next calculation, not the call stack. This way, when we use a recursive function to walk an entire tree, we are no longer trying to use the stack to map the structure of the tree. Instead, the lazy sequence itself does all the work of keeping track of which results need to be returned to which functions.

Exercise 7.03: A Tennis History Tree

In this exercise, we return to the world of tennis. As you remember, in *Chapter 5*, *Many to One: Reducing*, we built a system for establishing Elo ratings for tennis players based on historical data. These predictions have become popular on the sports journalism website you work for. Some readers have asked for more information about Elo predictions. In response to this new interest in your prediction engine, your employer wants the frontend team to build a visualization that shows the evolution of a player's rating over their last few matches. Your job will be to provide the necessary data.

We can reuse most of the work we did in *Chapter 5*, *Many to One: Reducing*, for importing the data and generating the ratings. One modification will be necessary, though. In *Chapter 5*, *Many to One: Reducing*, we were only interested in the final rating. We'll need to modify our previous code to append, line by line, the current ratings for the players in each match.

1. Set up a project identical to the one in *Activity 5.01*, *Calculating Elo Ratings for Tennis* and copy the functions you wrote for the activity into a new file. You'll need **match-probability**, **recalculate-rating**, and **elo-world-simple**. Copy **match_scores_1968-1990_unindexed_csv.csv** from https://packt.live/36k1o6X into the new project as well. The **deps.edn** file looked like this:

    ```
    {:paths ["src" "resources"]
     :deps
     {org.clojure/data.csv {:mvn/version "0.1.4"}
      semantic-csv {:mvn/version "0.2.1-alpha1"}
      org.clojure/math.numeric-tower {:mvn/version "0.0.4"}}}
    ```

    The namespace declaration should look as follows:

    ```
    (ns packt-clojure.lazy-tennis
      (:require [clojure.math.numeric-tower :as math]
                [clojure.java.io :as io]
                [clojure.data.csv :as csv]
                [semantic-csv.core :as sc]))
    ```

2. Modify **elo-world-simple** so that each line (each match) is retained and that the ratings of both players are recorded.

    Adding the ability to store the ratings of players of each match, at the time they played the match, is rather simple. All the changes occur toward the end of the function. Start with the initialization map for the call to **reduce**.

In **elo-world-simple**, the call to reduce looks like this (without the contents of the reducing function, for brevity):

```
(reduce (fn [{:keys [players] :as acc} {:keys [winner_name winner_slug
                                              loser_name loser_slug] :as match}]
          ;; TODO: content temporarily unavailable
          )
        {:players {}
         :match-count 0
         :predictable-match-count 0
         :correct-predictions 0})
```

3. In the new version, we'll replace the **:match-count** field with a **:matches** field, whose initial value will be an empty vector:

```
(reduce (fn [{:keys [players] :as acc} {:keys [winner_name winner_slug
                                              loser_name loser_slug] :as match}]
          ;; TODO: your content will be restored shortly
          )
        {:players {}
         :matches []})
```

4. To count the matches in the **elo-world-simple** version, for each line in the CSV file, we'll simply increment **:match-count field** in the accumulator as follows:

```
(-> acc
    ;; TODO: more missing code
    (update :match-count inc))
```

5. In this version, we need to append the current match, decorated with the **winner-rating** and the **loser-rating** that have already been calculated, to the growing list of matches. Here's the complete series of modifications made to **acc**. The new part is the anonymous function supplied to **update**:

```
(-> acc
    (assoc-in [:players winner_slug] (recalculate-rating k winner-rating winner-
probability 1))
    (assoc-in [:players loser_slug] (recalculate-rating k loser-rating loser-
probability 0))
    (update :matches (fn [ms]
                       (conj ms (assoc match
                                       :winner_rating winner-rating
                                       :loser_rating loser-rating)))))
```

6. Put the function back together again. For clarity, let's rename it **elo-db**. Since we only care about the list of matches, we can remove all the code dedicated to counting the number of correct predictions. Finally, after the call to **reduce**, we'll add two more calls to the **->** threading macro:

```
(->>
  ;; calls to reduce, etc.
  :matches
  reverse)
```

The **:matches** keyword, acting as a function, extracts the list of matches from the map returned by **reduce**. We also need to **reverse** the order of the matches because the queries we intend to run start at the present and go toward the past.

This gives us the final state of our function:

tennis_history.clj

```
16 (defn elo-db
17   ([csv k]
18    (with-open [r (io/reader csv)]
19      (->> (csv/read-csv r)
20           sc/mappify
21           (sc/cast-with {:winner_sets_won sc/->int
22                          :loser_sets_won sc/->int
23                          :winner_games_won sc/->int
24                          :loser_games_won sc/->int}
```

The full code for this step can be found at https://packt.live/2GffSKv

In the REPL, run this function on the CSV file and store the matches in a var:

```
packt-clojure.lazy-tennis> (def ratings (elo-db "match_scores_1991-2016_unindexed_
csv.csv" 35))
#'packt-clojure.lazy-tennis/db
```

We can verify that the ratings are available:

```
packt-clojure.lazy-tennis> (map #(select-keys % [:winner_rating :loser_rating])
(take 5 ratings))
({:winner_rating 985.2418497337458, :loser_rating 927.9839328429639}
 {:winner_rating 1265.3903009991964, :loser_rating 875.8644912132612}
 {:winner_rating 1012.6267015729657, :loser_rating 969.5966741618663}
 {:winner_rating 1311.801159776237, :loser_rating 1002.1872608853402}
 {:winner_rating 853.6200747439426, :loser_rating 950.2283493122825})
```

With this data in place, we're ready to write functions to search for and extract information from it.

7. Write a function that tests whether a player is either the winner or loser in a given match.

We need to be able to skip over the matches we aren't interested in, so this is a common test. Making it into its own predicate function will make our code easier to read. You might recognize the pattern, using a Clojure set, from *Chapter 4, Mapping and Filtering*:

```
(defn player-in-match? [{:keys [winner_slug loser_slug]} player-slug]
  ((hash-set winner_slug loser_slug) player-slug))
```

> **Note**
>
> Previously, we used a literal set. The **hash-set** function does the same thing, but in a more robust way. If **Winner** and **Loser** were identical for some reason, bad data for example, the program would crash. A literal set expects that you will provide a correct set without any duplicate items. The **hash-set** and **set** functions build sets from the arguments they receive and therefore handle duplicates gracefully. **set** takes a collection of items, whereas **hash-set** takes multiple arguments. It's basically **(apply set …)**.

We can test it in the REPL with some real data from our "database":

```
packt-clojure.lazy-tennis> (player-in-match? (first ratings) "gael-monfils")
"gael-monfils"
packt-clojure.lazy-tennis> (player-in-match? (first ratings) "boris-becker")
nil
```

8. Now we're ready to write our recursive function that will search through the list of matches. Start with a simple skeleton:

```
(defn match-tree-by-player [m player-name]
  (lazy-seq
    (cond (empty? m)
          ;; No more matches
          (player-in-match? (first m) player-name)
          ;; Build the tree!
          ::otherwise
          ;; Keep walking through the tree
          )))
```

Like all of our recursive functions that consume another sequence, this one is structured around a conditional. Here we have the tests without the corresponding code. All we need to do now is fill in the blanks!

9. Start with the last condition, when the current match does not contain the player we're looking for.

   In this case, we forget about the current record and continue moving along the input list, recursively calling **match-tree-by-player** on the remaining items:

   ```
   (match-tree-by-player (rest m) player-slug)
   ```

10. Once again, the basic pattern should be somewhat familiar: **cons** will connect the current item—the current match—to the rest of whatever is to be calculated later. This time, however, we have a new problem: we need to continue our search for matches played by the winner and the loser of the current match. That's two separate searches, which means two separate recursive calls to **match-tree-by-player**. Since we have two things, we need to put them into something. A vector is often a good choice in this kind of situation. Here's the code:

    ```
    (cons (first ms)
          (cons
            [(match-tree-by-player (rest ms) (:Winner (first ms)))
             (match-tree-by-player (rest ms) (:Loser (first ms)))]
            '()))
    ```

    Surprised by that second call to **cons**? It is there because we need to add more than just one item to our output. We add the current match, then the vector that will hold the heads of the two new trees. Inside the vector, the two calls to **match-tree-by-player** will only be made when needed.

    The final '() is necessary because **cons** need a collection as a second argument.

11. Add the code for when **m** is empty.

    As in the previous example, we provide an empty list so that the lazy sequence can finally end somewhere.

Now we can see the complete function:

```
(defn match-tree-by-player [m player-slug]
  (lazy-seq
    (cond (empty? m)
            '()
          (player-in-match?  (first m) player-slug)
          (cons (first m)
                (cons
                  [(match-tree-by-player (rest m) (:winner_slug (first m)))
                   (match-tree-by-player (rest m) (:loser_slug (first m)))]
                  '())))
          ::otherwise
          (match-tree-by-player (rest m) player-slug))))
```

12. Test the function. Let's start with a player we know is not in the match records:

```
packt-clojure.tennis> (match-tree-by-player ratings "non-tennis-player")
()
```

We get an empty list, which is exactly what we want.

Now let's try a player from the "database" (this is one of those times where you really want to attach the results to a var rather than trying to print everything to your REPL!):

```
packt-clojure.tennis> (def federer (match-tree-by-player ratings "roger-federer"))
#'packt-clojure.lazy-tennis/federer
packt-clojure.lazy-tennis> (type federer)
clojure.lang.LazySeq
```

We can check the first item to see if our data is really there:

```
packt-clojure.lazy-tennis> (:winner_rating (first federer))
1129.178155312036
```

So far so good!

Let's step back and think about what we've created here. If we try to see how many items are in the list, we get this:

```
packt-clojure.lazy-tennis> (count federer)
2
```

That seems strange. We know that Roger Federer has played a lot more matches than that. The **count** function doesn't work as we expect here because it doesn't understand the structure of this hierarchal return value. All **count** can see is the first item, which is one match, **cons** onto a vector. All the other results are nested inside that vector. Each item in the hierarchy shares this same structure. Conceptually, it looks something like this:

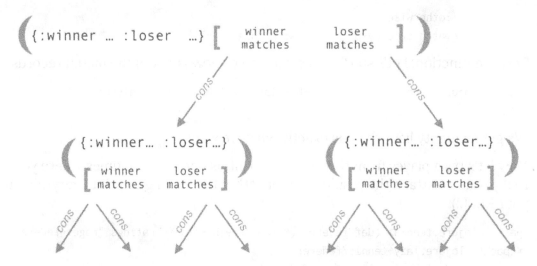

Figure 7.6: A hierarchical data structure where cons arrows contained in the vectors are lazy

In this diagram, the laziness occurs inside the vector. Those two lazy sequences are not yet realized. We can check this by carefully drilling down into the structure:

```
packt-clojure.lazy-tennis> (realized? (first (second federer)))
false
```

This is a good thing, because the entire structure, if realized, would be huge. Really, really huge. Hiding behind the fast response time is a tree that, if fully realized, would end up repeating thousands of times over the data in the original list. Try removing the **lazy-seq** wrapper from inside **match-tree-by-player**. The result will look something like this:

```
Show: Project—Only All
Hide: Clojure Java REPL Tooling Duplicates   (0 frames hidden)

2. Unhandled clojure.lang.Compiler$CompilerException
   Error compiling NO_SOURCE_FILE at (63417:35)
   #:clojure.error{:phase :compile-syntax-check,
                   :line 63417,
                   :column 35,
                   :source "NO_SOURCE_FILE"}
1. Caused by java.lang.StackOverflowError
   (No message)

                    REPL:   75  packt-clojure.tennis/match-tree-by-player
                    REPL:   74  packt-clojure.tennis/match-tree-by-player
                    REPL:   84  packt-clojure.tennis/match-tree-by-player
                    REPL:   74  packt-clojure.tennis/match-tree-by-player
                    REPL:   84  packt-clojure.tennis/match-tree-by-player
                    REPL:   74  packt-clojure.tennis/match-tree-by-player
                    REPL:   84  packt-clojure.tennis/match-tree-by-player
                    REPL:   74  packt-clojure.tennis/match-tree-by-player
                    REPL:   84  packt-clojure.tennis/match-tree-by-player
                    REPL:   74  packt-clojure.tennis/match-tree-by-player
                    REPL:   84  packt-clojure.tennis/match-tree-by-player
                    REPL:   74  packt-clojure.tennis/match-tree-by-player
                    REPL:   84  packt-clojure.tennis/match-tree-by-player
                    REPL:   74  packt-clojure.tennis/match-tree-by-player
                    REPL:   84  packt-clojure.tennis/match-tree-by-player
                    REPL:   74  packt-clojure.tennis/match-tree-by-player
                    REPL:   84  packt-clojure.tennis/match-tree-by-player
                    REPL:   74  packt-clojure.tennis/match-tree-by-player
                    REPL:   84  packt-clojure.tennis/match-tree-by-player
                    REPL:   74  packt-clojure.tennis/match-tree-by-player
                    REPL:   84  packt-clojure.tennis/match-tree-by-player
                    REPL:   74  packt-clojure.tennis/match-tree-by-player
                    REPL:   84  packt-clojure.tennis/match-tree-by-player
```

Figure 7.7: Overflowing the stack—too many recursive calls

Let's look briefly at this error message. Clojure stack traces are not always that easy to read, but this one does contain some interesting information. The most part is the "`Caused by java.lang.stackOverflowError`" statement. That's what caused the compiler exception and stopped our code. Below this, the repeated lines mentioning `match-tree-by-player` are telling us that `match-tree-by-player` kept calling itself over and over again. This is just a small part of the entire stack trace, which goes on and on for several screens. Earlier, we talked about stack frames. Here, each line is a frame. Each call to the function is waiting for the next one to resolve. After a certain point, there are too many functions waiting on one another, and the stack finally overflows.

Once again, lazy evaluation saves us from this and allows us to traverse data in complex ways and to build, in a few lines of code, very complex data structures.

Exercise 7.04: A Custom take Function

The previous exercise gave us a way to extract a tree from our linear dataset. It still doesn't allow you to do what your employer is asking, namely to display a limited tree that shows just a few levels in the hierarchy. Once we have that, we'll be able to as many levels as the design team wants to show.

What we really need is a specialized version of Clojure's **take** function that understands the structure of our data. We want to be able to write **(take-matches 4 federer)** and get a four-level tree.

To do this, we need to solve two problems. First, we need to be able to traverse the tree we've created. Secondly, we need a way to count the number of levels we've traversed.

1. This exercise builds on the previous one. Use the **tennis_history.clj** files from https://packt.live/38Dzp3H or make a complete copy.

2. Start with a version of the function that only works when called with zero as its first argument:

```
(defn take-matches [limit tree]
  (cond (zero? limit)
        '()))
```

Check if it works. To do this, you'll need the **federer** var from the previous exercise:

```
packt-clojure.lazy-tennis> (take-matches 0 federer)
()
```

3. Let's add the possibility of asking for either zero or one items:

```
(defn take-matches [limit tree]
  (cond (zero? limit)
        '()
        (= 1 limit)
        (first tree)))
```

This behavior duplicates our tests in the last exercise. We simply return the first match in the lazy sequence.

It's still a good idea to test though. We'll use **select-keys** to avoid lots of extra output data:

```
packt-clojure.lazy-tennis> (select-keys (take-matches 1 federer) [:winner_slug
:loser_slug])
{:winner_slug "roger-federer", :loser_slug "guido-pella"}
```

4. Add an **:otherwise** condition when the **limit** is more than one:

```
(defn take-matches [limit tree]
  (cond (zero? limit)
        '()
        (= 1 limit)
        (first tree)
        :otherwise-continue
        (cons
          (first tree)
          (cons
            [(take-matches (dec limit) (first (second tree)))
             (take-matches (dec limit) (second (second tree)))]
            '()))))
```

This part should look familiar, because it mirrors the structure of the function we wrote to build this structure to begin with, with two levels of **cons**, the second of which attaches a vector containing two more calls to **take-matches**.

By saying **(dec limit)** each time, the future calls to **take-matches** will eventually reach zero and stop traversing the tree.

5. Test the complete function:

```
(take-matches 3 federer)
```

The results will be too long to print here because there are so many fields in each match map. They should have this basic structure:

```
({}
  [({}
    [{} {}])
  ({}
    [{} {}])])
```

In the next exercise, we will make it easier to see these results.

Knowing When to Be Lazy

You may have noticed that we did not use **lazy-seq** this time. Should we have? Obviously, it would be easy enough to wrap the function body with the **lazy-seq** macro. Whether we do that or not depends mostly on how and where the **take-matches** function is going to be used inside our application. If **take-matches** is the final step before passing off our data to the frontend, there is no point in making it lazy. We are certain that the data is of a reasonable size and that we need all of it to produce the visual we are going to show. Making the function eager (the opposite of lazy) seems like a good choice in this case.

On the other hand, if **take-matches** is going to be used for other tasks, then making it lazy might make sense. If, for example, we wanted to extract a larger number of levels and then perform some other kind of operation on the result, the benefits of lazy evaluation might be important.

We are getting very close to satisfying our employer's requirements. We can retrieve the tree as a lazy sequence and now we can limit how many levels of match history we want to include. Our only remaining problem is that the results are hard to visualize, even in the REPL. We need to be able to format each match map. However, because of the tree structure, we can't just use **map** to transform each match. This is what we'll accomplish in the next exercise.

Exercise 7.05: Formatting the Matches

We need a way to reach every map in the tree. Rather than writing a specialized **map** function, we'll add an extra argument to **take-matches** that will be called on each match before it is returned. This will allow us to eliminate some of the keys we don't need for presenting the data to users. Likewise, it would be nice to display the ratings as integers rather than floats. We'll also add a feature: since we have the rating for each player before the match, we can also use the **match-probability** function to show the Elo prediction.

1. In the same file as the previous exercise (or in a copy of the project), add a function argument to **take-matches** and call it on the matches before they're returned:

```clojure
(defn take-matches [limit tree f]
  (cond (zero? limit)
        '()
        (= 1 limit)
        (f (first tree))
        :otherwise-continue
        (cons
          (f (first tree))
          (cons
            [(take-matches (dec limit) (first (second tree)) f)
             (take-matches (dec limit) (second (second tree)) f)]
            '())))))
```

This is really quite simple. Just be careful not to forget to pass the **f** argument to the two recursive calls at the end. The formatting function is needed at every level of the tree.

Now we can call the function with **select-keys**, or any other formatting function we want.

To test this, we'll reuse the **federer** var from the two previous exercises. You can rebuild it if necessary like this, where **matches** is the output from **elo-db**:

```clojure
(def federer (match-tree-by-player matches "roger-federer"))
```

Let's look at a few values:

```clojure
packt-clojure.lazy-tennis> (take-matches 3 federer #(select-keys % [:winner_slug
:loser_slug]))
({:winner_slug "roger-federer", :loser_slug "guido-pella"}
 [({:winner_slug "roger-federer", :loser_slug "marcus-willis"}
   [{:winner_slug "roger-federer", :loser_slug "daniel-evans"}
    {:winner_slug "pierre-hugues-herbert",
     :loser_slug "marcus-willis"}])
  ({:winner_slug "benjamin-becker", :loser_slug "guido-pella"}
   [{:winner_slug "dudi-sela", :loser_slug "benjamin-becker"}
    {:winner_slug "guido-pella", :loser_slug "diego-schwartzman"}])])
```

Our data visualization could probably use some polish, but even in this form, we can see not only the actual structure of the tree, but the win-loss history of the players involved in Roger Federer's recent matches!

> **Note**
>
> If we wanted to make the **f** parameter optional, we could supply the **identity** function as a default formatting function. The **identity** function simply returns whatever argument it is called with, which makes it the ideal placeholder function.

2. Write a **matches-with-ratings** function with a more sophisticated formatting function that changes the rating floats to integers and only shows the players' names and ratings:

```
(defn matches-with-ratings [limit tree]
  (take-matches limit
                tree
                (fn [match]
                  (-> match
                      (update :winner_rating int)
                      (update :loser_rating int)
                      (select-keys [:winner_name :loser_name :winner_rating :loser_
rating])
                      (assoc :winner_probability_percentage
                             (->> (match-probability (:winner_rating match)
                                                     (:loser_rating match))
                                  (* 100)
                                  int))))))
```

Because **match-probabilty** returns a long decimal, we've made it more user friendly by turning it into a percentage.

3. Test the new function:

```
packt-clojure.lazy-tennis> (matches-with-ratings 3 federer)
({:winner_name "Roger Federer",
  :loser_name "Guido Pella",
  :winner_rating 1129,
  :loser_rating 625,
  :winner_probability 94}
 [({:winner_name "Roger Federer",
    :loser_name "Marcus Willis",
    :winner_rating 1128,
    :loser_rating 384,
    :winner_probability 98}
   [{:winner_name "Roger Federer",
     :loser_name "Daniel Evans",
     :winner_rating 1127,
     :loser_rating 603,
     :winner_probability 95}
    {:winner_name "Pierre-Hugues Herbert",
     :loser_name "Marcus Willis",
     :winner_rating 587,
     :loser_rating 392,
     :winner_probability 75}])
  ({:winner_name "Benjamin Becker",
    :loser_name "Guido Pella",
    :winner_rating 638,
    :loser_rating 643,
    :winner_probability 49}
   [{:winner_name "Dudi Sela",
     :loser_name "Benjamin Becker",
     :winner_rating 560,
     :loser_rating 661,
     :winner_probability 35}
    {:winner_name "Guido Pella",
     :loser_name "Diego Schwartzman",
     :winner_rating 623,
     :loser_rating 665,
     :winner_probability 43}])])
packt-clojure.lazy-tennis>
```

Figure 7.8: Matches with ratings

Now our results tell a real story! Beyond showing who won and who lost, they show whether the result was expected, or a surprise. It's easy to see which matches were upsets, like when Dudi Sela won despite only having 35% chance and which victories were nearly inevitable, such as Roger Federer's 98% chance of defeating Marcus Willis.

This exercise is also a good illustration of the power of using functions as arguments. With this minor change to our **take-matches** function, it has become something like a custom **map** function that could be used for many different purposes.

Activity 7.01: Historical, Player-Centric Elo

The data visualization team at the sports journalism website loves your work. The readers are more and more curious about how Elo scores evolve over time. Emails pour in asking for more information. As a result, the journalists have a new request for a visualization. They found that it is difficult to present, on a single web page, more than four levels of tennis history. After that, there are too many branches and the readers stop reading.

In the new project, the journalists would like to show the evolution of a single player over many matches. For a given match, they would like to show a relatively long history for the player they're focused on, and much shorter histories for each of their opponents.

This is the kind of graphic that the team wants to be able to make:

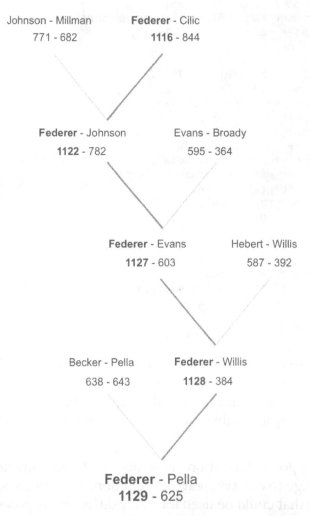

Figure 7.9: The focus player has a long history, but the opponents are displayed with truncated histories

The journalists don't know yet how long the histories will have to be, so both lengths need to be parameterized. If opponent histories are longer than one level, the function should not focus only on the opponent but should return a full sub-tree that includes the opponent, and their opponent, and so on.

Your job is to adapt the existing code to this new use case.

1. As a starting point, you will need the `match-probability`, `recalculate-rating`, `elo-world-db`, and `match-tree-by-player` functions from the code in *Exercise 7.03, A Tennis History Tree*. You will also need to include their dependencies in your `deps.edn` file.

2. The recursive function you will write will be a specialized version of the `take-matches` function from Exercise 7.04. It will operate on the output of `match-tree-by-player`, which in turn uses the output from `elo-world-db`.

3. The new function will have different behavior depending on whether a match involves the "focus player" or not. You will need to have separate parameters for both of these behaviors (in place of the `limit` parameter in `take-matches`, for example).

4. Like `take-matches`, your new function should accept a functional argument that will be called on individual matches.

> **Hint**
>
> Don't forget that you can call `take-matches` from inside your new function, if you need to.

5. The fact that you have two separate behaviors for different kinds of matches will shape how your function moves recursively through the tree.

> **Note**
>
> The solution for this activity can be found on page 701.

Summary

Lazy sequences and recursion can be rather challenging. By now, you should know how to safely consume lazy sequences, how to produce them, and how to use them to build tree structures from linear data sources, all without blowing the stack of your runtime.

As we've said before, writing functions to produce your own recursion-based lazy sequences should be something that you reach for only when all the other options won't work. Start with `map` and `filter`. If that's not enough, try `reduce`. Maybe the other forms of recursion will work. If none of those solve your problem, you have lazy sequences, an extremely powerful and efficient tool.

Lazy sequences and recursion always make us think. Being able to write your own lazy sequences will also make you a more enlightened consumer of lazy sequences. In Clojure, this is very valuable because lazy sequences are everywhere. Techniques like the ones we've explored here can also help you start thinking about new ways of understanding and solving problems.

By now, you are well on your way to being able to code effectively in Clojure. To be an effective developer, you also need to know the tooling necessary to manage a Clojure project. That's what we will explore now. In the next chapter, you will learn about namespaces and how to use Leiningen to organize and run your projects.

8

Namespaces, Libraries and Leiningen

Overview

In this chapter, we learn how to organize Clojure code. We start by looking at namespaces—a way to group Clojure functions together. We will see how to create our own namespaces and how to import namespaces written by others. Namespaces are building blocks of Clojure libraries. We will learn how to import and use Clojure libraries. After learning about namespaces and libraries, we investigate how to structure a Clojure project. We then look at Leiningen project template and how it helps developers to create applications.

By the end of this chapter, you will be able to use Leiningen to organize and run your projects.

Introduction

In the previous chapter, we learned about sequences in Clojure and how working with them helps us to build Clojure programs. Now that you're familiar with using Clojure to implement various pieces of functionality, it's time to become more comfortable with accomplishing the basic tasks of creating, building, testing, deploying, and running projects in Clojure and ClojureScript.

Clojure was designed to be a very practical language from the beginning. Getting things done means interacting with the outside world, building projects, using libraries, and deploying your work. As a developer, you will need to organize written code in a structure. In this chapter, you will see how namespaces can help you structure code and how build tools such as Leiningen help you put together a whole application.

In a real-world project, you won't write all the code. External dependencies are a crucial part of any project, and we'll learn here how to bring them into your project and your code.

The first step is to understand how Clojure namespaces work in general. Then we'll look at the project level and using Leiningen and your `project.clj` file to pull everything together into a Java executable. Finally, we'll take a look at some of the conveniences that Leiningen provides throughout the life cycle of a project.

Namespaces

Namespaces are a way to organize Clojure functions; you can think of a namespace as being a directory (or file) that stores a particular group of functions. Each directory is independent of other directories; this helps to keep different groups of functions separate and gives a clear structure to your code. It also helps to avoid the confusion that can come with naming clashes.

Consider a situation where you have written a function called `calculate-total`, and as part of your project, you're using a library (*more on libraries later in this chapter*) that also contains a function called `calculate-total`. Although these functions have the same name, they work differently, produce slightly different outputs, and are intended to be used in different situations. When you come to use `calculate-total` in your code, how does the system know which `calculate-function` you actually want? That's where namespaces come in. The two functions will exist in different namespaces, so you can state the appropriate namespace when calling the function in order to specify which one you want to use.

In more technical terms, namespaces provide a mapping between a symbol (which makes sense to a human reader) and a var or class. Namespaces can be compared to packages in Java or modules in Ruby and Python. We will first explore the concept of namespaces in Clojure using REPL.

Exercise 8.01: Investigating Namespaces Started by Default in REPL

In this exercise, we will investigate how namespaces are handled in REPL:

1. Open Terminal or Command Prompt and add the following command to start REPL using Leiningen:

```
lein repl
```

This will start REPL using Leiningen. It might take several seconds to start REPL. Once REPL is started, you should see something similar to the following:

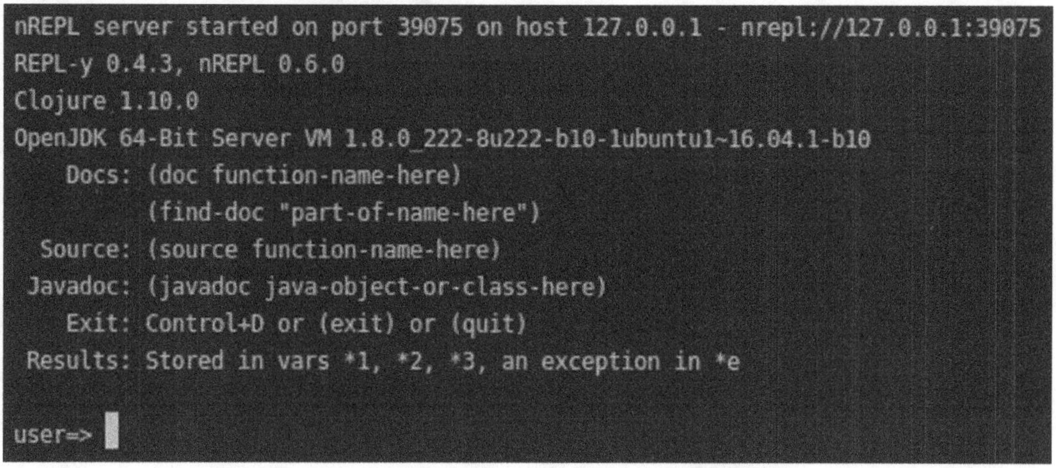

```
nREPL server started on port 39075 on host 127.0.0.1 - nrepl://127.0.0.1:39075
REPL-y 0.4.3, nREPL 0.6.0
Clojure 1.10.0
OpenJDK 64-Bit Server VM 1.8.0_222-8u222-b10-1ubuntu1~16.04.1-b10
    Docs: (doc function-name-here)
          (find-doc "part-of-name-here")
  Source: (source function-name-here)
 Javadoc: (javadoc java-object-or-class-here)
    Exit: Control+D or (exit) or (quit)
 Results: Stored in vars *1, *2, *3, an exception in *e

user=>
```

Figure 8.1: Starting REPL

The last line, **user=>**, tells us that we are in the default **user** namespace. In this namespace, functions from the **clojure.core** namespace are available to us. Let's explore a few functions.

2. In REPL, type the following code to calculate the sum of two numbers:

```
(+ 1 2)
```

This simple code should return:

```
3
```

3. Let's try Clojure's **filter odd** function to return the odd numbers:

```
(filter odd? [1 2 3 4 5 6])
```

This will return the following:

```
(1 3 5)
```

We see that in the default user namespace, we have access to core Clojure functions. But what if we want to access functions that are defined in some other namespaces? Clojure provides us with the **in-ns** function, which switches to the requested namespace. This function will also create a new namespace if the requested namespace does not exist. In the next exercise, we will use the **in-ns** function to access data from a different namespace than the one currently being used.

Exercise 8.02: Navigating Namespaces

In the previous exercise, we used functions in the default user namespace. In this exercise, we will have a look at accessing data from other namespaces:

1. In Terminal, call the **in-ns** function to create a new namespace:

    ```
    (in-ns 'new-namespace)
    ```

    In REPL, we will see that a new namespace has been created:

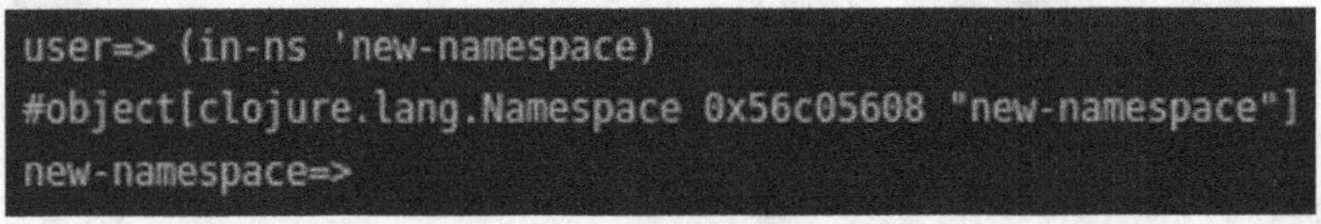

    ```
    user=> (in-ns 'new-namespace)
    #object[clojure.lang.Namespace 0x56c05608 "new-namespace"]
    new-namespace=>
    ```

    Figure 8.2: New namespace created

    You should notice that the REPL prompt has changed to **new-namespace=>**.

    This visual cue tells us that we have successfully switched to a new namespace. Anything you declare inside this namespace will be available in it.

2. We will declare a variable in our new namespace. Type the following declaration:

    ```
    (def fruits ["orange" "apple" "melon"])
    ```

    REPL lets us know that a new variable has been created:

    ```
    #'new-namespace/fruits
    ```

3. To check its content, we will access it from REPL as follows:

    ```
    fruits
    ```

    As expected, REPL gives us back the vector:

    ```
    ["orange" "apple" "melon"]
    ```

4. We will switch the namespace now using the **in-ns** function:

```
(in-ns 'other-namespace)
```

REPL lets us know that the change has happened:

```
#object[clojure.lang.Namespace 0x2f2b1d3c "other-namespace"]
```

REPL's prompt has also changed:

```
other-namespace=>
```

5. Now access the **fruits** vector as follows:

```
fruits
```

We will see an unpleasant surprise:

```
CompilerException java.lang.RuntimeException: Unable to resolve symbol: fruits in
this context, compiling:(null:0:0)
```

We have declared the **fruits** vector in **new-namespace** but we tried to access it from another namespace. To access vars from one namespace in another namespace, we need to explicitly state which namespace the var comes from.

6. Type the fully qualified name in REPL to access the data as follows:

```
new-namespace/fruits
```

This time, we get our **fruits** vector:

```
["orange" "apple" "melon"]
```

Using fully qualified names can become tedious. In the next exercise, we will see how Clojure helps us with managing multiple namespaces.

Importing Clojure Namespaces Using the refer Function

Clojure provides the **refer** function, which aims to help developers write compact code. This is achieved by importing the contents of a specific namespace into the current namespace, thereby allowing those contents to be accessed easily. In the previous example, we used **new-namespace/fruits** to access the **fruits** vector from a different namespace outside **new-namespace**. What **refer** allows us to do is reference **new-namespace** once and then use **fruits** as many times as we need, without having to state the full namespace every time.

In the previous section, we used the **in-ns** function. In this section, we will use **refer** function. Although both functions help us to work with namespaces, we use them for different purposes. The **in-ns** function creates a scope for our code. We place data and functions inside a namespace. When we want to create a new namespace and thus a new scope for code, we use **in-ns**. Now, **refer**, on the other hand, will allow us to work within the scope of the current namespace and import data from a different namespace. We can import one or more namespaces and still work in one namespace scope.

Exercise 8.03: Using the refer Function to Import a Namespace

In this exercise, we will use the **refer** function to import Clojure namespaces. This will help us understand how the **refer** function is used.

Using **refer** allows us to reference functions or objects from other namespaces:

1. In REPL, type the following command to import a new namespace using the **refer** function:

```
(clojure.core/refer 'new-namespace)
```

We used **refer** here to import data from **new-namespace**. If we'd used the **in-ns** function, we would have changed the scope of the code. We would be able to access data from **new-namespace** but because the scope changed, we would lose access to **other-namespace** that we worked at before switching to **new-namespace**. Our aim is to write code within the scope of **other-namespace** and only access functions from **new-namespace**.

2. After this, we can use the **fruits** vector directly by calling it in REPL:

```
fruits
```

The output is as follows:

```
["orange" "apple" "melon"]
```

Using **refer** allowed us to include all objects from the specified namespace in the current one. The **refer** function allows us to use optional keywords to control importing namespaces. We will see them in action now.

Advanced Use of the refer Function

In *Chapter 2, Data Types and Immutability*, we learned about keywords in Clojure. The basic usage of the **refer** function that we learned in the previous section can be altered or expanded using keywords. They are optional as we can use them but do not have to.

The keywords that we can use with **refer** are:

- **:only**: The **:only** keyword allows us to import only the functions that we specify. This means that any functions not specified are not imported.

- **:exclude**: The **:exclude** keyword allows us to exclude certain functions from being imported. We would import all but the ones that we want to exclude.

- **:rename**: The **:rename** keyword allows us to rename functions that we import. This sets an alias—a new name for a function—and we would refer to the function using that new name.

We now know three keywords that can modify the importing of namespaces using the **refer** function. In the next three exercises, we will use each keyword to import namespaces and use data from them.

Exercise 8.04: Using the :only Keyword

The aim of this exercise is to show how we can extend the basic use of the **refer** function by using the **:only** keyword. We will import namespaces using the **refer** function with the **:only** keyword. Then, we will access data from the imported namespace:

1. In REPL, type the following command to use the **in-ns** function to create the **garden** namespace:

```
(in-ns 'garden)
```

REPL creates a new namespace for us:

```
#object[clojure.lang.Namespace 0x6436be0 "garden"]
```

2. We can define two variables in this namespace:

```
(def vegetables ["cucumber" "carrot"])
(def fruits ["orange" "apple" "melon"])
```

REPL informs us that vars have been created:

```
#'garden/vegetables
#'garden/fruits
```

3. After that, we switch to a new namespace using the **in-ns** function:

```
(in-ns 'shop)
```

> **Note**
>
> With the **:only** keyword, we can refer to another namespace but import only selected parts.

4. Import the **garden** namespace using the **refer** function together with the **:only** keyword:

```
(clojure.core/refer 'garden :only '(vegetables))
```

This will return the following:

```
nil
```

We can access the **vegetables** var directly in the new **shop** namespace.

5. Call the **vegetables** var to access its content:

```
vegetables
```

REPL returns the expected vector as follows:

```
["cucumber" "carrot"]
```

6. If, however, we want to access another var, **fruits**, call the **fruits** vector as follows:

```
fruits
```

We get an exception in REPL:

```
CompilerException java.lang.RuntimeException: Unable to resolve symbol: fruits in
this context, compiling:(null:0:0)
```

Because when we imported the namespace, we used the **:only** keyword to import the **vegetables** var. The other var needs to be fully qualified with a namespace if we want to use it.

7. Call the **fruits** vector using the fully qualified name:

```
garden/fruits
```

This time, we get the expected vector as follows:

```
["orange" "apple" "melon"]
```

In this exercise, we created vars in one namespace and then we imported this namespace using the **refer** function. During the import, we used the **:only** keyword, which allowed us to import only the selected data.

In the next exercise, we will import a namespace using the **refer** function and the **:exclude** keyword.

Exercise 8.05: Using the :exclude Keyword

In the previous exercise, we imported content from one namespace to another using the **refer** function. We restricted importing using the **:only** keyword to import only selected data. Now we will use a second keyword that allows us to control the importing of namespaces with the **refer** function.

Using the **:exclude** keyword allows us to import some parts from a namespace but exclude parts that we do not need:

1. First, we will switch to a new namespace using the **in-ns** function:

    ```
    (in-ns 'market)
    ```

    REPL tells us that we successfully switched to a new namespace:

    ```
    #object[clojure.lang.Namespace 0x177c36c4 "market"]
    ```

2. The next step is to import the **garden** namespace but exclude the **vegetables** var. We use the **refer** function with the **:exclude** keyword:

    ```
    (clojure.core/refer 'garden :exclude '(vegetables))
    ```

    This will return the following:

    ```
    nil
    ```

3. We test the import by trying to access the **fruits** var:

    ```
    fruits
    ```

    So far, so good, as REPL returns us the vector:

    ```
    ["orange" "apple" "melon"]
    ```

4. We will try accessing the excluded var, **vegetables**:

    ```
    vegetables
    ```

    We immediately see an exception message in REPL:

    ```
    CompilerException java.lang.RuntimeException: Unable to resolve symbol: vegetables
    in this context, compiling:(null:0:0)
    ```

5. We need to use the fully qualified name to access the **vegetables** var:

```
garden/vegetables
```

This time, REPL shows us the expected vector:

```
["cucumber" "carrot"]
```

In this exercise, we imported a namespace using the **refer** function. During the import, we used the **:exclude** keyword, which allowed us to restrict the data to be imported.

In the next exercise, we will import a namespace using the **refer** function and the **:rename** keyword.

Exercise 8.06: Using the :rename Keyword

In the previous exercise, we imported content from one namespace to another using the **refer** function. We restricted importing using the **:exclude** keyword to import only data that we wanted. Now we will use a third keyword that allows us to control the importing of namespaces with the **refer** function.

We will see the **:rename** keyword in use. It allows us to import from one namespace and rename certain symbols:

1. We will switch to a new namespace using the **in-ns** function:

```
(in-ns 'shops)
```

2. While we import the **garden** namespace, we want to rename the **fruits** var to **owoce** (Polish for fruits). We will use the **refer** function with the **:rename** keyword:

```
(clojure.core/refer 'garden :rename '{fruits owoce})
```

3. We access the **vegetables** var in the REPL:

```
vegetables
```

This returns the vector in the REPL:

```
["cucumber" "carrot"]
```

4. Trying to access the **fruits** var:

```
fruits
```

It tells us that it is not accessible:

```
CompilerException java.lang.RuntimeException: Unable to resolve symbol: fruits in
this context, compiling:(null:0:0)
```

Because we renamed the **fruits** var, we need to access **fruits** with a new name, which we defined when we used the **refer** function.

5. Now type **owoce** in the REPL:

```
owoce
```

This time, we get the expected vector:

```
["orange" "apple" "melon"]
```

In this exercise, we imported a namespace using the **refer** function. During the import, we used the **:rename** keyword, which allowed us to restrict what data should be imported.

We now know how to use **refer**. First, we imported a namespace using the **refer** function. Then we saw how we can modify importing with the **refer** function when we use three keywords: **:only**, **:exclude**, and **:rename**.

We use the **:only** keyword when we want to import from one namespace to certain other functions. The **:only** keyword allows us to limit the functions that we import.

We use the **:exclude** keyword when we want to import from one namespace to another but without certain functions. The **:only** keyword allows us to exclude functions that we do not want to import.

We use the **:rename** keyword when we want to import from one namespace to another and change the names of some functions during the import.

In the next section, we will learn how **require** and **use** help us with managing namespaces.

Importing Clojure Functions with require and use

In the previous section, we learned how to import Clojure functions using **refer**. In this section, we will learn how we can import Clojure functions with **require** and **use**.

While **refer** allows us to literally refer to other namespaces' vars without fully qualifying them, often we need more than that. In the previous exercise, we imported a namespace and accessed vars such as **fruits** from it without using the namespace name as a prefix to the **garden/fruits** var. Often, we want to load functions from a namespace and use those functions. If we want to read the file, we need to import code from the Clojure I/O library (the library for input-output operations such as reading and writing files).

With the **require** function, we will load a namespace that we'll specify. This way, functions from the loaded namespace are available in our namespace for use. This is a great way to write Clojure code, reuse existing functions, and make them available in our code. Although we loaded new functions with **require**, we still need to fully qualify them.

While the **require** function allows us to load a designated namespace, the **use** function goes a little bit further and implicitly uses **refer** to allow code to refer to other namespaces' vars without fully qualifying them.

refer, **require**, and **use** all serve different purposes:

- **refer** allows us to call functions from a different namespace (functions are not imported).

- **require** imports functions from a different namespace but we have to qualify them when using them.

- **use** loads functions from a different namespace and we do not have to qualify them.

Exercise 8.07: Importing Clojure Functions with require and use

In this exercise, we will learn how the **require** and **use** functions can help us to import Clojure namespaces. We will import Clojure namespaces using both methods. This will help us understand the difference between both methods.

By using **require**, we ensure that the namespaces provided are fully loaded whenever we need to use them.

Clojure provides a number of namespaces, such as **clojure.edn** or **clojure.pprint**, that help developers to create programs. EDN stands for extensible data notation. It is a system for representing objects. It provides a rich set of features such as functionality for specifying the date and time. The **clojure.edn** namespace allows us to use the **edn** format. Imagine that you want to send a date from one program to another. If you send the date as a string, "Monday 7.10.2019," there is no information about time zone. The program receiving this date string does not know whether this time is in London or New York. With **edn**, we can send a date object that contains information about the time zone.

The **clojure.print** namespace contains utility functions that help to print data from programs in an easy-to-understand and easy-to-read format.

Consider printing a hash as shown in the following figure:

Figure 8.3: Printing a hash

Instead of printing a hash as shown in *Figure 8.3*, functions from the **clojure.pprint** namespace allow us to print a hash like this:

```
user=> (clojure.pprint/pprint big-map)
{:a {:a 0, :b 1, :c 2, :d 3, :e 4},
 :b {:a 0, :b 1, :c 2, :d 3, :e 4},
 :c {:a 0, :b 1, :c 2, :d 3, :e 4},
 :d {:a 0, :b 1, :c 2, :d 3, :e 4},
 :e {:a 0, :b 1, :c 2, :d 3, :e 4}}
```

Figure 8.4: Printing a hash using the functions from the namespace

By default, when we start a new session, only **clojure.core** is available. The **clojure.core** namespace contains the main Clojure functions, such as **filter**, **map**, **reduce**, and **count**. These are core functions that are used very often when working in Clojure. That is why they are available by default when working in Clojure. The other namespaces need to be added by us:

1. We will require a new namespace in our REPL session that will help us pretty print some content:

```
(require 'clojure.pprint)
```

2. We can use functions from this namespace now. We call the **print-table** function to print a table in REPL:

```
(clojure.pprint/print-table [{:text "Clojure"}{:text "is"}{:text "fun"}])
```

This prints a table in REPL:

```
user=> (clojure.pprint/print-table [{:text "Clojure"}{:text "is"}{:text "fun"}])

|   :text |
|---------|
| Clojure |
|      is |
|     fun |
```

Figure 8.5: Printing a table in REPL

Using fully qualified names can become tedious because every time we want to call any function, we have to provide its full name, including the namespace. This results in verbose code and a lot of repetition of namespace names. Fortunately, Clojure allows us to set an alias for a namespace. In order to set an alias, we use the **:as** keyword. With the **:as** keyword, we shorten how we call functions. We do not need to write the full namespace but simply an alias that we choose.

3. Call the **require** function with the **:as** keyword to simplify importing the function:

```
(require '[clojure.pprint :as pprint])
```

4. Now we can use the alias to call the **print-table** function:

```
(pprint/print-table [{:text "Clojure"}{:text "is"}{:text "fun"}])
```

We have just seen how the **require** function is used. Next, we will see how the **use** function helps us to import namespaces.

5. We call the **use** function to import namespaces in REPL:

```
(use 'clojure.pprint)
```

The preceding statement will load the **clojure.pprint** namespace and refer to the namespace.

We can use functions from this namespace without fully qualifying them.

6. Call the **print-table** function without the namespace name to print a table:

```
(print-table [{:text "Clojure"}{:text "is"}{:text "fun"}])
```

This will print a table for us:

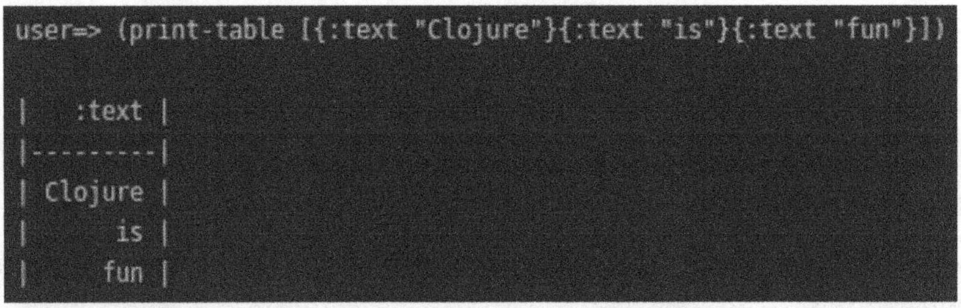

Figure 8.6: Calling the print-table function

We have just seen how **use** works. Next, we will look into using keywords such as **:only** and **:rename** with **use**.

7. Import a function from the **clojure.string** namespace:

```
(use '[clojure.string :only [split]])
```

This will import the **split** function from the **string** namespace and return the following:

```
nil
```

We can use the **split** function without a namespace name:

```
user=> (split "Clojure workshop" #" ")
["Clojure" "workshop"]
```

Figure 8.7: Using the split function

8. Rename the function from the **clojure.edn** namespace when importing with **use**:

```
(use '[clojure.edn :rename {read-string string-read}])
```

This will return the following:

```
nil
```

9. We renamed the **read-string** function from the **clojure.end** namespace to **string-read**. We can call the **string-read** function without a namespace name now:

```
(class (string-read "#inst \"1989-02-06T13:20:50.52Z\""))
```

The output is as follows:

```
java.util.Date
```

We have a string that represents a date from 1989. We pass this string to the **edn** function, which converts a string to a **Date** object. When we call the **class** function, it tells us that we have a **Date** object.

We have seen how to import namespaces with **refer** and **use**. In the following activity, we will put this knowledge into practice.

Activity 8.01: Altering the Users List in an Application

In this activity, we will apply our knowledge about importing namespaces to solve a real-world problem. Imagine that we work in an IT company and we are responsible for designing a backend application. One of the functions in our backend returns a list of users. A new frontend feature needs this list in a different format. The aim of this activity is to alter the list of users.

The two alterations required are:

- Capitalizing usernames
- Checking whether the users John, Paul, and Katie belong to an admin group

The application currently displays a list of users, their honorifics, their first names, and their last names. The honorifics and first names are separated by _ (an underscore). In this activity, we will add a space between the honorifics and the first names. Then, we will take the first and last names and capitalize the first letter of the honorifics, first names, and last names. Finally, we will check whether our users belong to the admin group.

These steps will help you complete the activity:

1. Import the **clojure.string** namespace with **use** and the **:rename** keyword for the **replace** and **reverse** functions.

2. Create a set of users.

3. Replace the underscore between the honorifics and the first names.

4. Use the **capitalize** function to capitalize each person's initials in the user group.

5. Update the user list by using the string **replace** and **capitalize** functions.

6. Import only the **print-table** function from the **clojure.pprint** namespace.

7. Print a table with users.

8. Import the **clojure.set** namespace, excluding the **join** function.

9. Create a set of admins.

10. Call the **subset?** function on two sets of users and admins.

The initial list of users and admins will look as follows:

```
#{"mr_john blake" "miss_paul smith" "dr_katie hudson"}
```

The admin list will look as follows:

```
#{"Mr Paul Smith" "Dr Mike Rose" "Miss Katie Hudson" "Mrs Tracy Ford"}
```

The final list of users will look as follows:

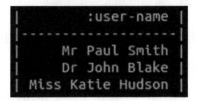

Figure 8.8: Expected outcome

Note

The solution for this activity can be found on page 706.

When You Want use versus When You Want require

Although **use** and **require** may seem very similar at first glance, with some practice you will understand when to use each one.

If we want to import a namespace using **require**, we will call it as follows:

```
(require 'clojure.pprint)
```

Importing a namespace with **use** is done as follows:

```
(use 'clojure.pprint)
```

If we compare both statements, we see that the only difference is the importing function, either **require** or **use**. The syntax of using them is the same. We call a function and then the namespace that we want to import. The reason to use both importing functions is different, though, as we will see in this topic.

When in doubt, choose **require**. It allows you to add an alias for the namespace and makes the code more readable than having to use fully qualified names:

```
(require '[clojure.string :as str])
```

This way, we can call functions very easily. Consider the following example:

```
(str/reverse "palindrome")
```

When choosing **use**, advised to add an alias and import only required functions:

```
(use '[clojure.string :as str :only (split)])
```

When you import only required functions, you can easily add more later on. Importing only the functions that we require at the moment helps us to maintain the code. The developers dealing with the code will not spend time searching for the usage of functions that we imported.

There are two potential problems with using **use** without the `:only` keyword:

- Inspecting the code does not tell us quickly from which namespace a certain function comes. With aliased namespaces, we can establish this more easily.

- We avoid any name collisions in the future if we add a new library or if an existing library introduces a new function with a name that we are already using.

Now that we've looked at namespaces, we will go a level higher and investigate how to structure projects using Leiningen.

Leiningen—A Build Tool in Clojure

With namespaces, we put our functions into files and group related functions together. This helps to keep code separated into units. Consider a situation where utility functions are separated from frontend functions. This helps us navigate code and find functions. We know that frontend functions responsible for creating HTML will not be in a backend namespace responsible for connecting to the database. Build tools serve a different purpose. As the name suggests, these are tools that help us build. With them, we automate the creation of an executable application. An alternative would be to compile all the code ourselves and put it on a server. Even in applications with only a few features, we run the risk of forgetting to compile a namespace. The more namespaces there are and the more complicated an application is, the bigger the risk of making a mistake in manual code compilation. Build tools compile our code and package it into a usable form. Developers specify parts of the application that need to be compiled and the build tool automatically compiles the parts for them. This helps to minimize compilation mistakes. Some build tools are Maven, Gradle, Webpack, and Grunt.

Leiningen is a very popular build tool in the Clojure community. Its popularity comes from the rich set of features it has. It provides a lot of templates that allow developers to start writing code without much of a project setup. Often, the type of application that a developer wants to create has already been created by someone else. This way, we can reuse what developers before us created instead of writing so much code ourselves. We have a web application template that provides us with a common structure for a web page. There is a template for a backend server with a file structure and configuration that is common in backend servers. In the next exercise, we will create a new project.

Exercise 8.08: Creating a Leiningen Project

The aim of this exercise is to learn about the standard structure in Leiningen projects. We will create a sample project based on a template from Leiningen. This will allow us to explore the files that Leiningen creates and the purpose of each file.

In order to create a new Leiningen project, we will use the command line:

1. Call a new **lein** task with the **app** template. To create a new project, execute the following:

    ```
    lein new app hello-leiningen
    ```

    In the preceding command, the **lein** command takes three parameters:

    new: A **lein** task telling Leiningen what type of task to execute. Task **new** will create a project based on a template.

    app: The name of the template to use when creating a project. Leiningen will create a project using a specified template.

    hello-leiningen: The name of the project.

    We should see that our new project has been created:

    ```
    Generating a project called hello-leiningen based on the 'app' template.
    ```

2. After creating a project, we will navigate to the project's directory:

    ```
    cd hello-leiningen
    ```

3. Now, inspect the project as follows:

```
find  .
```

We will see that Leiningen has created a number of files for us already:

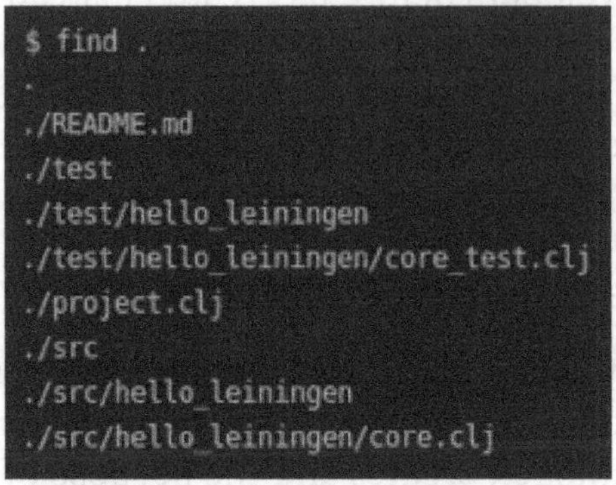

```
$ find .
.
./README.md
./test
./test/hello_leiningen
./test/hello_leiningen/core_test.clj
./project.clj
./src
./src/hello_leiningen
./src/hello_leiningen/core.clj
```

Figure 8.9: Inspecting the project

There are a few important things to notice here:

- We have a source directory, **src**, where we will put our code.

- The **project.clj** file contains a description of our project.

- **README.md** is an entry point with information about our application.

- We have a **test** directory for our tests.

We will have a closer look at these points in the following sections. Testing will be covered in *Chapter 10, Testing*. In the next section, we will look at the **project.clj** file.

Investigating project.clj

The **project.clj** file that you have created will look similar to this one:

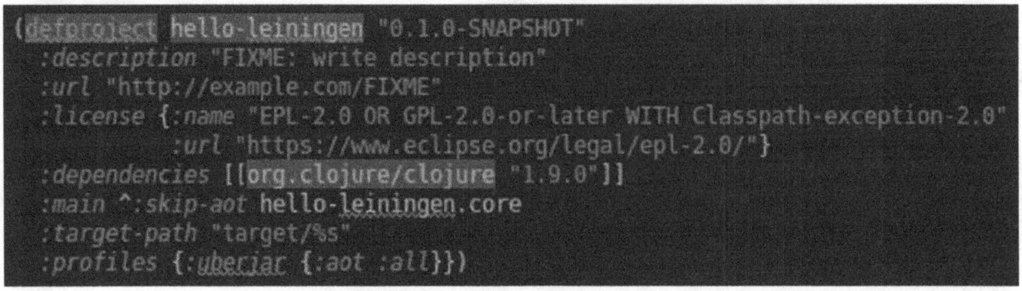

```clojure
(defproject hello-leiningen "0.1.0-SNAPSHOT"
  :description "FIXME: write description"
  :url "http://example.com/FIXME"
  :license {:name "EPL-2.0 OR GPL-2.0-or-later WITH Classpath-exception-2.0"
            :url "https://www.eclipse.org/legal/epl-2.0/"}
  :dependencies [[org.clojure/clojure "1.9.0"]]
  :main ^:skip-aot hello-leiningen.core
  :target-path "target/%s"
  :profiles {:uberjar {:aot :all}})
```

Figure 8.10: The project.clj file

Let's take a look at each parameter:

- **Project version**: We see that our `hello-leiningen` project has got a SNAPSHOT version. This means that it is not yet a stable production-tested version but rather a development version. When you are ready to publish your project, be sure to add a proper version. A good guide is to use semantic versioning. There are times when using a snapshot version is necessary, such as with a bug fix before the fix gets included in the next release. The rule of thumb is to use stable versions unless a bug fix is needed.

- **Description**: Adding a description is a good starting point for people looking at understanding the purpose of a project. Also, when the project is published in project repositories such as Maven or Clojars, it is easier to search for the project.

- **URL**: While the description is limited, the `url` parameter allows us to place a web URL for our project. On our web page, we can add much more information about our project. Most project websites would have:

  A rationale: Why the project was created

  Documentation: A description of its usage

  Tutorials: Examples of using the project

- **License**: The license is used as you might expect. It is a legal instrument governing the use of software. Essentially, it is an agreement between the owner of software and its user, allowing the user to use software under certain conditions.

  There are many types of software licenses. Examples of licenses include:

  MIT license: This allows the distribution and modification of source code.

  Apache License 2.0: Like the MIT license, this allows the distribution and modification of code but requires the preservation of copyright notices.

  GNU AGPLv3: Like the MIT license, this allows the distribution and modification of code but requires the stating of changes compared to the original version of the software.

- **Dependencies**: Java or JVM projects are distributed as `jar` files. They are basically `zip` files (compressed files) with some metadata about the project. When we specify dependencies in our `project.clj`, Leiningen will search the local repository. If dependencies are not already stored locally, then it will search the Maven and Clojars websites and download the dependencies. Such dependencies are then available for our project.

- **Main namespace**: In the `:main` keyword, we specify the namespace that is the entry point for our project and application. It gets called when we run our project.

- **Ahead of time (AOT)**: Clojure compiles all our code on the fly into JVM bytecode. AOT compilation allows us to compile code before we run it. This speeds up application startup. We can see that under the `:profiles` keyword, we have an `uberjar` profile where we want AOT compilation. On the other hand, we would like our `:main` namespace to be without AOT. We create an uberjar with AOT because we want to compile the code before we run it. We do not want AOT for `:main` as we want to defer compilation until we start an application. For example, `:main` can use symbols such as environment settings, parameters that are not available at AOT compilation. They are only available when we start an application. If we compile too fast, the application will not have access to parameters that we passed when we start an application.

- **Profiles**: Leiningen allows us to set up various profiles in our projects. Thanks to profiles, we can customize projects depending on our needs.

  For example, a development version could require a testing suite and we might want testing dependencies. On the other hand, when creating a production jar, we do not need testing dependencies.

  We will look at Leiningen's profiles at the end of this chapter.

Now that we have looked at `project.clj`, we will see what the `README.md` file has to offer for us.

A README file is a Markdown file that provides information about our project that we consider important for users to know. Markdown is a markup language that allows us to style documents.

Typically, a README file will have the following sections:

- **Project name**: Where we put a short description of what the project does

- **Installation**: Where we inform users of the steps necessary to install our application

- **Usage**: Where we let users know how to use our project

- **Examples**: A section with code samples showing how to use our project

- **Bugs**: Any known bugs

- **Changelog**: Where we document any changes between versions

- **License**: Where we inform users of our project's license type

Here's a sample README file:

```
# hello-leiningen

FIXME: description

## Installation

Download from http://example.com/FIXME.

## Usage

FIXME: explanation

    $ java -jar hello-leiningen-0.1.0-standalone.jar [args]

## Options

FIXME: listing of options this app accepts.

## Examples

...

### Bugs

...

### Any Other Sections
### That You Think
### Might be Useful

## License

Copyright © 2019 FIXME

This program and the accompanying materials are made available under the
terms of the Eclipse Public License 2.0 which is available at
http://www.eclipse.org/legal/epl-2.0.
```

Figure 8.11: Sample README file

You can add more sections. It all depends on what you think is important for users of your project to know. In the next topic, we will modify source files and run our application.

Exercise 8.09: Executing the Application on the Command Line

The aim of this exercise is to create a Leiningen application and explore how applications are run.

This will help us understand the different options that Leiningen provides in the **project.clj** file.

As we will see at the end of this exercise, in order to run our application from the command line, we need to call Leiningen's **run** task. Leiningen's **run** task will search the **project.clj** file for the **:main** keyword and corresponding namespace.

In our case, the **:main** keyword in **project.clj** will look like this:

```
:main ^:skip-aot hello-leiningen.core
```

^:skip-aot instructs Leiningen to skip AOT for the namespace that we specify. Here, the namespace is **hello-leiningen.core**. When we explored the **project.clj** file, we talked about why we want to skip AOT for the **:main** namespace.

By default, Leiningen will search for the namespace that we specified in the **:main** keyword. In our case, it will search for the **hello-leiningen.core** namespace. In this namespace, if we have the **-main** function, it will be called:

1. After creating a new project, the content of the **hello-leiningen.core** namespace is the following:

```
(ns hello-leiningen.core
  (:gen-class))
(defn -main
  "I don't do a whole lot ... yet."
  [& args]
  (println "Hello, World!"))
```

When we create an application using Leiningen, it will autogenerate code in the **core** namespace. **(:gen-class)** instructs Leiningen to generate a Java class from the namespace. Build tools such as Leiningen execute Java bytecode so we need to compile Clojure to bytecode in order to run the **core** namespace.

Next, we have the **-main** function. By default, when an application is started, Leiningen will search for a method with that name and execute it. As such, **-main** is an entry point to our application.

Like all functions in Clojure, **-main** can be supplied with an optional documentation string. Here, it tells us that the function does not do a whole lot... yet. This function takes optional arguments. We can pass arguments when we start an application. Often, applications are started for various environments by passing an environment type, such as test or production, as a command-line argument.

When Leiningen calls the **-main** function, it will execute the body of this function. In this case, the function will print the string **Hello World!** to the console.

2. To run the application from the command line, we use Leiningen's **run** task:

```
lein run
```

This will print the following to the console:

```
Hello, World!
```

This exercise showed us how to run a Leiningen application as defined in **project.clj** file.

In the next exercise we will extend the application to take arguments from the command line.

Exercise 8.10: Executing Application on the Command Line with arguments

In this exercise we will write a small command line application that takes a string as input, parses that input and replaces the contents of that string.

1. After creating a new project, the content of the **hello-leiningen.core** namespace is the following:

```
(ns hello-leiningen.core
  (:gen-class))
(defn -main
  "I don't do a whole lot ... yet."
  [& args]
  (println "Hello, World!"))
```

2. When we create an application using Leiningen, it will autogenerate code in the core namespace. (**:gen-class**) instructs Leiningen to generate a Java class from the namespace. Build tools such as Leiningen execute Java bytecode so we need to compile Clojure to bytecode in order to run the core namespace.

3. Next, we have the **-main** function. By default, when an application is started, Leiningen will search for a method with that name and execute it. As such, -main is an entry point to our application.

4. Like all functions in Clojure, **-main** can be supplied with an optional documentation string. Here, it tells us that the function does not do a whole lot... yet. This function takes optional arguments. We can pass arguments when we start an application. Often, applications are started for various environments by passing an environment type, such as test or production, as a command-line argument.

5. When Leiningen calls the -main function, it will execute the body of this function. In this case, the function will print the string Hello World! to the console.

6. To run the application from the command line, we use Leiningen's run task:

```
lein run
```

7. This will print the following to the console:

```
Hello, World!
```

8. Import the **clojure.string**. We want to manipulate strings in our **-main** function. In order to do that we need to import string namespace.

```
(ns hello-leiningen.core
  (:require [clojure.string :as str]))
```

After importing **clojure.string** namespace we can use functions from this namespace.

9. Updating **-main** function to replace certain words when the **-main** function is run:

```
(defn -main
  "I don't do a whole lot ... yet."
  [& args]
    (-> (str/join " " args)
        (str/replace "melon" "banana")
        (str/replace "apple" "orange")
        println))
```

This code will replace words "**melon**" and "**apple**" with other fruits.

10. We run the application as follows:

```
lein run "apple" "melon" "grapes"
```

11. This will print the following in the REPL:

```
orange banana grapes
```

We know now how to run an application from the command line and pass arguments. In the following activity, you will use this knowledge to create a new application.

Activity 8.02: Summing Up Numbers

Often, applications that are created by developers need to run in different environments and business contexts. This requires the applications to be flexible. One way to achieve this is by using command-line parameters that change how applications behave.

In this activity, you will create an application that takes integers as input parameters from the command line and sums them up to print the result to the console. Depending on the integers passed, the results will differ. This shows the flexibility of the application.

These steps will help you complete the activity:

1. Create a Leiningen application.

2. Alter the **-main** function to convert string arguments to integers, add integers, and print the result.

The output will look like the following:

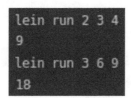

Figure 8.12: Expected output

> **Note**
>
> The solution for this activity can be found on page 708.

Working with External Libraries

Libraries are packaged programs that are ready to be used in other projects. External libraries are libraries that come from other developers. In Clojure, examples of such libraries include Ring, an HTTP library; **clojure.java-time**, a library for time and date manipulation; and **hiccup**, a library for writing HTML code using Clojure-style syntax.

Most projects will require developers to use existing code packaged as libraries. This is a good thing. We do not want to write code over and over again if the problem at hand has been already solved and someone has created a library for it that we can use.

In this section, we will use the **clojure.Java-time** library to display the current time.

Exercise 8.11: Using an External Library in a Leiningen Project

The aim of this exercise is to show you how to add a library to a Leiningen project and demonstrate how this library is used in code:

1. The first thing to do is add a dependency to the **time** library in the **project.clj** file. The **dependencies** section should look like this:

```
:dependencies [[org.clojure/clojure "1.9.0"]
               [clojure.java-time "0.3.2"]]
```

2. The next step is to import the library to our **core** namespace. Alter **hello-leiningen.core** to look like this:

```
(ns hello-leiningen.core
    (:require [java-time :as time]))
```

3. Finally, we will change the **-main** function to print the local time using a function from the **clojure.java-time** library:

```
(defn -main
  "Display current local time"
  [& args]
  (println (time/local-time)))
```

4. We run the application from the command line using the **run** task:

```
lein run
```

   This will show us output similar to the following:

```
#object[java.time.LocalTime 0x2fa47368 23:37:55.623]
```

We now know how to add and use external libraries. We are ready to package our application to a jar and run it.

Creating and Executing a jar with Leiningen

When we discussed project structure in Clojure, we mentioned that projects are packaged as jar files. To remind you, a jar file is a zipped (packed) file that is an executable application. Leiningen has tasks for creating jars.

Leiningen provides two tasks that can create a jar:

- jar
- uberjar

Both will create a zipped file with our code. The difference is that a jar task will package only our code while an uberjar task will also package dependencies. If you run one application on your server and want one standalone file, then an uberjar is your go-to option. If you have a number of applications on your server and they share libraries, then packaging each application as a jar will take less space overall than packaging them as uberjars. This is because libraries are shared on servers between your applications.

If we want to run a jar, we need to generate a named class from our core namespace.

Exercise 8.12: Creating a Jar File

In this exercise, we will show how to create a jar file using Leiningen tasks:

1. Alter the **hello-leiningen.core** namespace declaration to include a (**:gen-class**) function call:

```
(ns hello-leiningen.core
  (:require [java-time :as time])
  (:gen-class))
```

The **:gen-class** directive is an important concept in Clojure. This directive will generate a Java class corresponding to the target namespace. The result of generating a Java class is a **.class** file. A Java **.class** file contains Java bytecode that can be executed on the JVM. Such a file can be executed by build tools such as Leiningen.

Running Leiningen tasks for both a jar and uberjar is the same. In our case, we will create an uberjar.

2. Call Leiningen's **uberjar** task in the command line:

```
lein uberjar
```

This task will create **hello-leiningen-0.1.0-SNAPSHOT.jar** and **hello-leiningen-0.1.0-SNAPSHOT-standalone.jar** jar files inside the target directory.

When we compare the files, we will see that their sizes differ greatly:

```
$ ls -lh
937K paź 12 14:39 hello-leiningen-0.1.0-SNAPSHOT.jar
5,2M paź 12 14:39 hello-leiningen-0.1.0-SNAPSHOT-standalone.jar
```

Figure 8.13: Comparing the files

The **hello-leiningen-0.1.0-SNAPSHOT.jar** file is less than 1 MB, while **hello-leiningen-0.1.0-SNAPSHOT-standalone.jar** is 5.2 MB. There is a good reason why the size differs. The standalone version is meant to include all the dependencies necessary for running the jar. We can check what is actually included in the jar file by listing its content:

```
jar -tvf target/uberjar/hello-leiningen-0.1.0-SNAPSHOT-standalone.jar
```

Running this command will give us the output similar to the following:

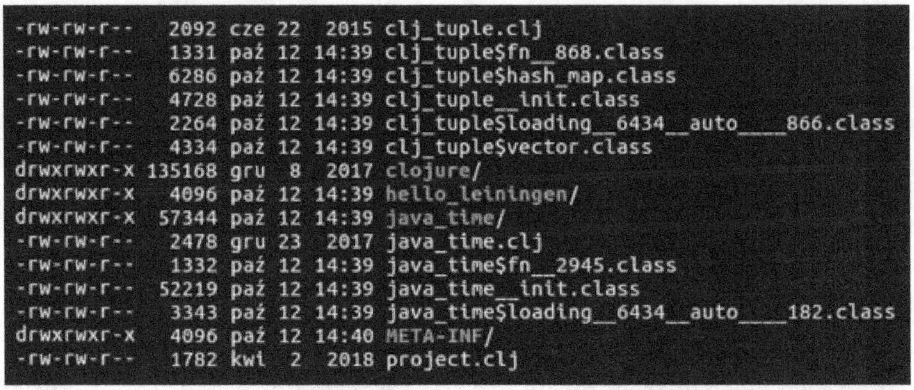

```
-rw-rw-r--    2092 cze 22  2015 clj_tuple.clj
-rw-rw-r--    1331 paź 12 14:39 clj_tuple$fn__868.class
-rw-rw-r--    6286 paź 12 14:39 clj_tuple$hash_map.class
-rw-rw-r--    4728 paź 12 14:39 clj_tuple__init.class
-rw-rw-r--    2264 paź 12 14:39 clj_tuple$loading__6434__auto____866.class
-rw-rw-r--    4334 paź 12 14:39 clj_tuple$vector.class
drwxrwxr-x  135168 gru  8  2017 clojure/
drwxrwxr-x    4096 paź 12 14:39 hello_leiningen/
drwxrwxr-x   57344 paź 12 14:39 java_time/
-rw-rw-r--    2478 gru 23  2017 java_time.clj
-rw-rw-r--    1332 paź 12 14:39 java_time$fn__2945.class
-rw-rw-r--   52219 paź 12 14:39 java_time__init.class
-rw-rw-r--    3343 paź 12 14:39 java_time$loading__6434__auto____182.class
drwxrwxr-x    4096 paź 12 14:40 META-INF/
-rw-rw-r--    1782 kwi  2  2018 project.clj
```

Figure 8.14: Inspecting the standalone version of the file

We would notice a **clojure** directory. When inspecting the first file, however, there would be no Clojure directory:

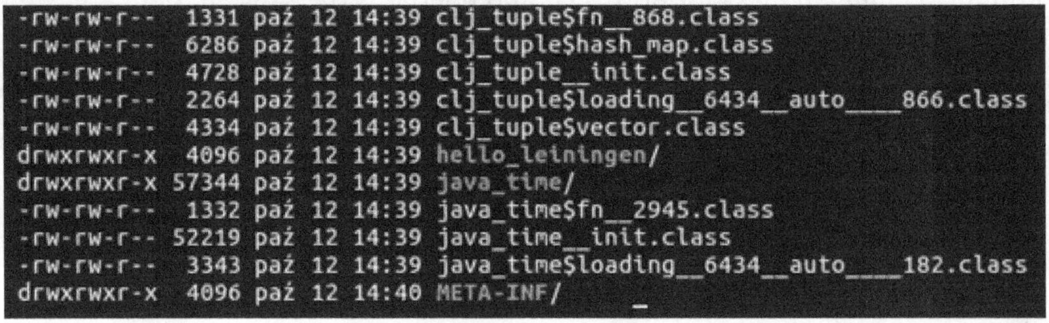

```
-rw-rw-r--    1331 paź 12 14:39 clj_tuple$fn__868.class
-rw-rw-r--    6286 paź 12 14:39 clj_tuple$hash_map.class
-rw-rw-r--    4728 paź 12 14:39 clj_tuple__init.class
-rw-rw-r--    2264 paź 12 14:39 clj_tuple$loading__6434__auto____866.class
-rw-rw-r--    4334 paź 12 14:39 clj_tuple$vector.class
drwxrwxr-x    4096 paź 12 14:39 hello_leiningen/
drwxrwxr-x   57344 paź 12 14:39 java_time/
-rw-rw-r--    1332 paź 12 14:39 java_time$fn__2945.class
-rw-rw-r--   52219 paź 12 14:39 java_time__init.class
-rw-rw-r--    3343 paź 12 14:39 java_time$loading__6434__auto____182.class
drwxrwxr-x    4096 paź 12 14:40 META-INF/
```

Figure 8.15: Checking for the Clojure directory

The first jar (**hello-leiningen-0.1.0-SNAPSHOT.jar**) contains only application code, while the second file (**hello-leiningen-0.1.0-SNAPSHOT-standalone.jar**) also contains core Clojure code. The standalone file is intended to be used when we have one Clojure application. In such cases, we want to have all the dependencies in one place. When we run more than one Clojure application on a server, having each application containing core Clojure functions takes more space than needed. In such cases, having core Clojure code once and allowing all applications to access it saves disk space.

3. In order to run a jar, we will call the following:

```
java -jar target/uberjar/hello-leiningen-0.1.0-SNAPSHOT-standalone.jar
```

This will display the current local time for us, as follows:

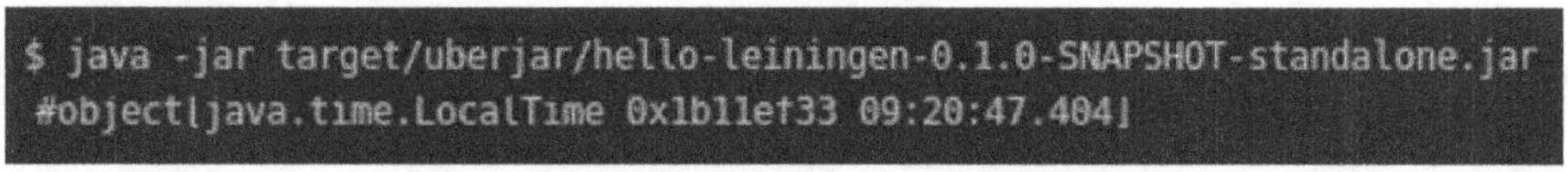

Figure 8.16: Print the local time

In the next section, we will look at Leiningen profiles—a powerful feature that allows us to customize our projects.

Leiningen Profiles

Profiles are a Leiningen tool that allows us to change the configuration of our projects. A profile is a specification that influences how a project behaves. For example, during development or testing, say that we would like to include testing frameworks in our builds but the production build does not need testing dependencies. Using profiles is a great way to separate different development setups that should be run against one code base.

Leiningen allows us to define profiles in a few places depending on our needs:

- In the **project.clj** file

- In the **profiles.clj** file

- In the **~/.lein/profiles.clj** file

Leiningen profiles defined in **project.clj** are specific to that particular project. Such profiles will not affect other projects. This allows separation between projects and the ability to customize them independently. We could have one application that uses the newest version of Clojure and requires different libraries to another application relying on an older Clojure version.

Leiningen profiles defined in **profiles.clj** are also specific to a project. Such profiles will not affect other projects. The difference between putting a profile in **project.clj** and **profiles.clj** is that profiles in **project.clj** will be committed in version control. Profiles defined in **profiles.clj** are independent of the project configuration in **project.clj** and do not need to be committed to version control. Profiles from both files are merged together by Leiningen. Profiles with the same name in **profiles.clj** take precedence over profiles in **project.clj**.

Now that we know what Leiningen profiles are and the places that they can be defined, we will look at the syntax of creating profiles. First, we will define a profile in a **project.clj** file.

Exercise 8.13: Adding Leiningen Profiles to a Project

The aim of this exercise is to add a new development profile inside a **project.clj** file. This will allow us to customize a project for the development phase of the software development life cycle.

If we wanted to add a dependency on a testing framework, such as **expectations**, we would alter the **project.clj** file to look like this:

```
(defproject hello-leiningen "0.1.0-SNAPSHOT"
 ;;; skipped irrelevant content
  :profiles {:uberjar {:aot :all}
                :dev {:dependencies [[expectations "2.1.10"]]}})
```

Inside the **:profiles** hash, we have a **:dev** hash with a dependency on the **expectations** framework. With this change, the **dev** profile is available for us. We can check this by listing available profiles:

1. Calling Leiningen's **show-profiles** task will display the available profiles:

    ```
    lein show-profiles
    ```

    The output is as follows:

Figure 8.17: Printing the available profiles

The profiles available in this example are:

base: A profile that provides basic REPL functionality.

debug: When Leiningen tasks are run with this profile, they print more information to the console, such as the names of the dependencies used.

default: The default profile run when no profiles are selected. Unless overridden, the profile defaults to the **leiningen/default** profile.

dev: The development profile as set up in the **project.clj** file by a developer.

leiningen/default: The default profile that runs when no profile is selected.

leiningen/test: A test profile that runs test files.

offline: Profiles where stored dependencies are used offline without downloading new ones.

uberjar: Profiles that create uberjar files.

update: Profiles that update dependencies.

user: A profile defined for a Linux user.

whidbey/repl: A profile where results in the REPL are printed in a formatted way.

As you can see, the **dev** profile is listed among other profiles.

2. If we wanted to run this profile, we would call the **with-profiles** task:

```
lein with-profile dev test
```

Calling this task would run the tests with the **dev** profile. In *Chapter* 10, *Testing*, we will explore testing in Clojure and this task will be used often.

In this exercise, we have added a new Leiningen profile to the **project.clj** file. This allows us to have a configuration for a particular project. This configuration is independent of configurations in other projects.

In the next exercise, we will add user-wide profile configuration.

User-Wide Profiles

Leiningen allows us to define user-wide profiles that will affect all Leiningen projects. This is a great place to put common code that we want for all our projects. The most common examples would be including libraries for testing or pretty printing output. Once we include a testing library in a user-wide profile, that library can be used to write tests for all our projects. This also benefits us when it comes to upgrading the library. We only need to upgrade its version in one place.

User-wide profiles allow us to add dependencies that we would like to be included in all our projects. One such dependency would be Ultra, which gives developers working in REPL features such as colorization and pretty printing.

Exercise 8.14: Using User-Wide Profiles

The aim of this exercise is to add a new library to the **profiles.clj** file. This will allow us to access the added library on all Leiningen projects, reducing the need to manually add a dependency every time we create a new project. Additionally, if a new version of the library is available, we need to update only one **profiles.clj** file and the update will be available in all our Leiningen projects.

If we often work with input that we need to display in a way that's accessible to users, we can use the **humanize** library. This library pluralizes nouns, shows dates in a friendly manner, and converts numbers to strings.

In order to use the humanize library for all of our projects, we add it to the **:user** keyword in **~/.lein/profiles.clj**:

```
{:user {:dependencies [[clojure-humanize "0.2.2"]]}}
```

Quite often, you will have more libraries and plugins defined in **profiles.clj**. It could look like this with the **humanize** library and two plugins, **ultra** and **localrepo**:

```
{:user {:plugins [[lein-localrepo "0.5.4"]
                  [venantius/ultra "0.6.0"]]
        :dependencies [[clojure-humanize "0.2.2"]]}}
```

1. Start the REPL using Leiningen:

   ```
   lein repl
   ```

2. Import the humanize library:

   ```
   (require 'clojure.contrib.humanize)
   ```

   Although we did not have the **humanize** library in the **project.clj** file, we could import this library:

   ```
   hello-leiningen.core=> (require 'clojure.contrib.humanize)
   nil
   ```

   Figure 8.18: Importing the humanize library

3. Convert numbers to strings as follows:

   ```
   (clojure.contrib.humanize/numberword 4589)
   ```

   humanize will convert passed numbers to strings as follows:

   ```
   "four thousand five hundred and eighty-nine"
   ```

4. Convert the number of milliseconds to time values:

```
(clojure.contrib.humanize/duration 500)
```

500 milliseconds is not even a second and hence the output will be as follows:

```
"less than a second"
```

This concludes our tour of namespaces in Clojure and Leiningen project structure. In the following activity, we will use our new knowledge of libraries and profiles in Leiningen.

Useful Clojure Libraries

The Clojure ecosystem has a number of great libraries. As we have learned in this chapter, using libraries helps us to create Clojure applications. Libraries provide features that we can use in our code. We do not need to write code ourselves as we can instead reuse code written by others. This saves us time and means we can focus on developing features specific to our application. There are a number of Clojure libraries. Clojure provides a central place to search for available libraries on https://clojars.org. We will learn about two useful Clojure libraries, **cheshire** and **lein-ancient**. The **cheshire** library allows us to work with the JSON format. **JavaScript Object Notation (JSON)** is a data format from JavaScript. The JSON format defines what data types, such as strings or numbers, are allowed. It is a very popular format. Using a common format allows applications to exchange data. With the **cheshire** library, we can change Clojure data to JSON format and back. This is a very powerful feature. Imagine that we have a holiday-booking application. In the application, we want to display current weather information. There are national services providing such information. The weather services allow the downloading of data in a common JSON format. When we download weather data, we need to turn JSON into Clojure data. The **cheshire** library helps us with data conversion. **lein-ancient** is a useful Leiningen plugin. This plugin allows us to check our Leiningen projects for outdated dependencies. Often, a new version of a library that we use is released. New releases introduce errors or security fixes. Using updated libraries helps our applications to stay secure. In the following activity, we will create a Leiningen project using useful Clojure libraries.

Activity 8.03: Building a Format-Converting Application

The aim of this activity is to create a Leiningen project that will convert between JSON format and Clojure data. JSON is a popular transfer format often used to send data between various backend applications. Using a common format increases the operability between different applications and reduces the development cost of building and maintaining applications.

Like most applications used in production, our application will have development and default production profiles. Leiningen profiles will be used to create a testing profile that will use testing libraries to make sure our application is running correctly.

As our application matures, newer versions of the libraries used will be released. We will use a plugin that will let us know whether any libraries that we use are outdated.

Once you complete this activity, the application will have the following features:

- Converting between JSON and Clojure data
- A testing profile for checking code before releasing to production
- Checking for outdated libraries

These steps will help you complete the activity:

1. Include the **cheshire** "3.0.0" library as a dependency.
2. Create a function to convert from hash to JSON.
3. Create a function to convert from JSON to hash.
4. Add the **expectations** library to the testing profile defined for the project.
5. Add the **lein-expectations** plugin to the project.
6. Write a test for the JSON functions.
7. Add **lein-ancient** to the user-wide profiles.

The latest versions of libraries can be found on the https://clojars.org website.

After creating the application and running it, you should have output similar to the following.

Converting from hash to JSON format should return the following:

```
json-parser.core=> (generate-hash-from-json "{\"name\":\"Mike\",\"occupation\":\"carpenter\"}")
{"name" "Mike", "occupation" "carpenter"}
```

Figure 8.19: Converting from hash to JSON

Generating JSON from hash should return the following:

```
json-parser.core=> (in-ns 'json-parser.core)
#object[clojure.lang.Namespace 0x164d1490 "json-parser.core"]
json-parser.core=> (generate-json-from-hash {:name "John" :occupation "programmer"})
"{\"name\":\"John\",\"occupation\":\"programmer\"}"
```

Figure 8.20: Generating JSON from hash

Running the testing profile should return the following:

```
$ lein with-profile qa expectations

Ran 2 tests containing 2 assertions in 3 msecs
0 failures, 0 errors.
```

Figure 8.21: Executing the test profile

Checking for outdated dependencies should return the following:

```
$ lein ancient
[org.clojure/clojure "1.10.1"] is available but we use "1.10.0" (use :check-clojure to upgrade)
[cheshire "5.9.0"] is available but we use "3.0.0"
```

Figure 8.22: Checking for outdated dependencies

> **Note**
>
> The solution for this activity can be found on page 709.

Summary

In this chapter, we learned about namespaces in Clojure. Namespaces are key Clojure concepts. We organize code into namespaces. We investigated various ways in which we can import namespaces in Clojure by using **refer**, **require**, and **use**. With each option to import, we learned the syntax of importing functions and when to use each type of function. We went into depth and investigated the `:only`, `:exlude`, and `:rename` keywords, which help us to fine-tune importing.

Then, we learned about Leiningen–a popular Clojure build tool. We created a Leiningen application and explored how Clojure projects are structured. We added dependencies on libraries. Finally, we saw how we can customize Leiningen projects using profiles. We created an application that accepted command-line arguments that were used by the application to customize the output.

In the next chapter, we will investigate host platform interop–accessing Java and JavaScript from Clojure.

Host Platform Interoperability with Java and JavaScript

Overview

In this chapter, we will look at interoperability between Clojure and both Java and JavaScript. Clojure runs on top of platforms provided by Java and JavaScript. Clojure was designed to use libraries provided by Java or JavaScript. We will learn how to access Java and JavaScript objects and methods in Clojure. We will also learn how to convert data between Clojure and Java or JavaScript and back. After learning how to access Java and JavaScript from Clojure, we will investigate how to perform Input-Output (I/O) operations like reading and writing to files using Java classes. We will then learn how to deal with errors and exceptions in our code.

By the end of this chapter, you will be able to work with the appropriate syntax and semantics to access Java and JavaScript objects and methods from Clojure, and deal with Java exceptions and JavaScript errors.

Introduction

In the previous chapter, we learned how to create a Leiningen project. A project gives a structure for organizing our code. We structure our project around namespaces. We created new namespaces and we imported external Clojure libraries in order to use them in our code.

Now that you are familiar with using namespaces and creating Clojure projects, it is time to become more comfortable with working on projects that use Java and JavaScript.

As we learned in *Chapter 1, Hello REPL!*, Clojure compiles to Java bytecode and operates on the **Java Virtual Machine (JVM)**. The JVM is a host platform. Any programming language that compiles to Java bytecode can run on the JVM. Because Clojure compiles to Java bytecode and runs on the JVM, we call it a hosted language. Java dates from the 1990s and is now one of the most popular backend languages. We can leverage existing Java libraries instead of writing a lot of code on our own. This helps us deliver new features faster.

As we will see, importing Java classes in Clojure is a bit different than using Clojure libraries. In this chapter, we will learn how to import and call Java classes in Clojure by writing an application that performs I/O operations—reading and writing from a file.

In the second part of this chapter, we will look into ClojureScript and JavaScript interoperability. JavaScript is a scripting language that runs in browsers. It is the most popular frontend language at the moment. ClojureScript compiles to JavaScript. In ClojureScript, we can use JavaScript libraries. This gives us access to a huge amount of code written by other developers. A great boost to our productivity.

Using Java in Clojure

Any code written by a developer needs to be converted to code that is understood by a machine. An interpreter uses code from a developer and compiles it into machine code. Each operating system is different, hence the need for platform-specific compilers and interpreters. One of the reasons why Java is so successful is that it provides the JVM, which takes human-understandable code and converts it into machine code. Developers are not usually interested in the JVM. They can focus on writing code in Java without interacting with the underlying operating system. This job is done by the JVM.

Clojure is a hosted language. It means that it uses the JVM instead of creating a new runtime environment. Clojure cleverly reuses facilities provided by the JVM. This is a very powerful approach. Things such as garbage collection, threading, concurrency, IO operations (all of which will be explained in the following paragraphs) are JVM battle-tested technologies that Clojure relies on.

Java garbage collection is the process by which Java programs perform automatic memory management. Java programs compile to bytecode that can be run on a JVM. When Java programs run on a JVM, objects are created on the heap, which is a portion of memory dedicated to the program. Eventually, some objects will no longer be needed. The garbage collector finds these unused objects and deletes them to free up memory. We could have a vector with usernames in our program. The usernames are strings. Each string will occupy some space in memory. When we display a list of users on a page, we need this list. When we click on a user and display her profile, we do not need information about other users. We could remove this information from memory so the memory is available for other data.

In concurrent computing several computations and operations are executed during overlapping time periods. This is in contrast with sequential programming, where one operation must finish before other operations can start. In sequential computing, an operation to capitalize a vector of usernames must finish before the second operation that finds only admin users can start. In concurrent computing, execution of both operations overlaps. We do not need to wait for one to finish before the second can start.

A thread is a lightweight process on the JVM. When a computing program uses two or more threads, it runs concurrently. Each part of a program is a separate thread. In our usernames example, one thread will filter usernames for admins while the other thread will capitalize names.

IO operations are processes that deal with reading from a source, such as a keyboard, and writing to a destination, such as a monitor. Java provides support for a number of sources and destinations. We can read from a text file and write to a printer. Java IO will be covered in this chapter.

As Clojure developers, we have access to an ecosystem of JVM libraries. Because Java is one of the most popular languages, by targeting JVM, we join a big community. This gives us the benefit of using many well-tested and optimized libraries.

In order to use existing Java code, we need to import it to our project. Clojure gives us tools to import and operate with Java.

In the next sections, we will explore tasks such as:

- Importing Java classes
- Creating new instances of Java classes

We will start with importing Java classes. Clojure provides an **import** function to do this job. This function can import a single class or a number of classes.

Exercise 9.01: Importing a Single Java Class in Clojure

As we learned in the previous chapter, Clojure code is organized into namespaces. Java organizes its code into packages that contain classes. In this exercise, we will learn how to import packages and Java classes.

We will explore Java interoperability using a REPL.

1. Open a Terminal and add the following command to start the REPL:

```
lein repl
```

In order to use a Java class, we need to import it. First, we will import a single class. We will start with **BigDecimal** class, which allows us to store very large decimal numbers.

2. Call the **import** function with the **BigDecimal** class:

```
(import 'java.math.BigDecimal)
```

This will let us know that the class has been imported:

```
java.math.BigDecimal
```

In Java, we construct an instance of a class using the **new** keyword:

```
BigDecimal big_number = new BigDecimal("100000");
```

Similarly, in Clojure, we can construct an object from the **BigDecimal** class.

3. Call the **new** function on the **BigDecimal** class to create an instance of it:

```
(new BigDecimal "100000")
```

Executing the preceding statement in the REPL returns a **BigDecimal** value:

```
100000M
```

4. Often, we want to use a value many times. Storing the value in a variable is a good choice:

```
(def big-num (new BigDecimal "100000"))
```

Calling an instance of the variable in the REPL will give us the value stored in **BigDecimal**:

```
user=> (def big-num (new BigDecimal "100000"))
#'user/big-num
user=> big-num
100000M
user=>
```

Figure 9.1: Printing the value stored in BigDecimal

Clojure provides a special shorthand symbol for constructing class instances using a dot, .. We place a dot after a class name. In these cases, Clojure assumes that we want to construct an instance of a class.

The preceding example with **BigDecimal** could have been written using dot notation.

5. Construct a **BigDecimal** instance using dot notation:

```
(def big-num (BigDecimal. "100000"))
```

Notice the dot after the **BigDecimal** class name:

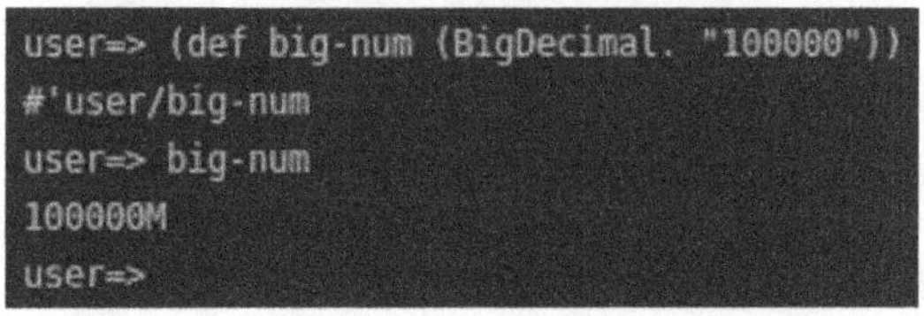

```
user=> (def big-num (BigDecimal. "100000"))
#'user/big-num
user=> big-num
100000M
user=>
```

Figure 9.2: Printing the BigDecimal value

We have seen how to import a class and create an instance of it. Very often, you would want to import more than one class. In the next exercise, we will investigate how to import more than one Java class.

Working with Time in Java

The Java standard library provides the **java.time** and **java.util** packages, which contain classes that are useful for working with time. Two useful classes are:

- **Locale**: A class representing a specific geographical region such as **US** (United States), **FR** (France).

- **LocalTime**: A class representing time in the current locale. The local time for Eastern Europe is two hours ahead of Universal time (London).

In this chapter, we will see examples of manipulating time in Java and Clojure.

Exercise 9.02: Importing Multiple Java Classes in Clojure

Importing more than one class can be divided into two actions:

- Importing classes from the same package
- Importing classes from different packages

In order to import more than one class from the same Java package, we will use a vector import:

1. Call the **import** function with two classes in a vector:

```
(import '[java.math BigDecimal BigInteger])
```

Once they are imported, we can use both classes like we have.

2. Create an instance of the **BigInteger** class:

```
(BigInteger. "10000")
```

We will see a new **BigInteger** instance created in the REPL:

```
10000
```

3. Create an instance of the **BigDecimal** class:

```
(BigDecimal. 100000.5)
```

We will see a new **BigInteger** instance created in the REPL:

```
100000.5M
```

If we want to import classes from different packages, we specify their full names, including the package names.

4. Import the **LocalTime** class from the **time** package and the **Locale** class from the **util** package:

```
(import 'java.time.LocalTime 'java.util.Locale)
```

Once they are imported, we can construct these classes as we did before.

5. Create an instance of the **Locale** class using dot notation:

```
(Locale. "pl")
```

The output is as follows:

```
#object[java.util.Locale 0x50e7be4d "pl"]
```

The **LocalTime** class provides static methods to obtain the current time. A static method is a class method. We call it on a class and not on an instance of the class that we create. In Java, we call the class name followed by the method name when we want to use a static method. The static **now** method returns the current time:

```
LocalTime time = LocalTime.now();
System.out.println(time);
```

Here, the static **now** method is called on the **LocalTime** class. The **now** method is a static method in the **LocalTime** class. The **now** method returns the current time. The time is in the format **hour:minutes:seconds.miliseconds**. Since we can run the code at any time, the output will differ in each execution of the code:

```
/usr/lib/jvm/java-8-openjdk-amd64/bin/java ...
23:02:40.960

Process finished with exit code 0
```

Figure 9.3: Printing the local time

We can also access static methods from the **LocalTime** class in Clojure. This is done by stating the class followed by a slash and a method name.

6. Call the static **now** method from the **LocalTime** class using slash notation:

```
(LocalTime/now)
```

The output is similar to the following:

```
#object[java.time.LocalTime 0x355f5f59 "23:10:29.761"]
```

A Java class can have static fields—fields that belong to a class and not an instance of a class. In Java, we access class fields using a dot. The **LocalTime** class has class fields corresponding to the times of the day: the **NOON** field indicates the middle of the day, 12:00, and the **MIDNIGHT** field indicates the middle of the night, 00:00.

In order to get the **NOON** field for **LocalTime**, we would write the following:

```
LocalTime.NOON
```

This would give us the following

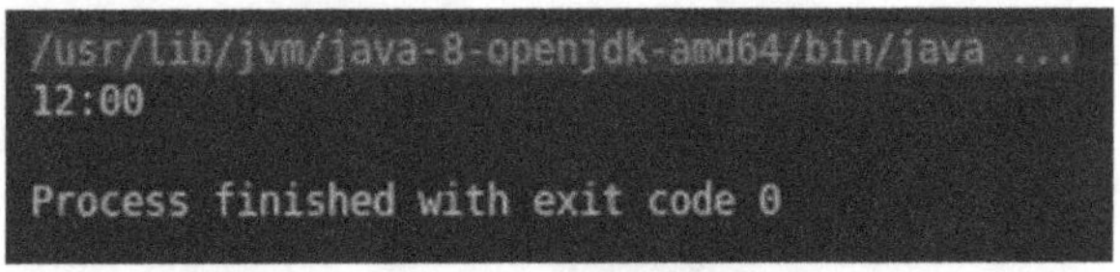

```
/usr/lib/jvm/java-8-openjdk-amd64/bin/java ...
12:00

Process finished with exit code 0
```

Figure 9.4: Printing the NOON value

When we run the code, we are accessing the **NOON** field. In the output, we see that noon is at **12:00**. In Clojure, we use the form with a slash, as we have just seen when we accessed the static **now** method.

7. Access the static **MIDNIGHT** field from the **LocalTime** class using slash notation:

```
(LocalTime/MIDNIGHT)
```

The output is as follows:

```
#object[java.time.LocalTime 0x2712e99d "00:00"]
```

When we run the code, we are accessing the **MIDNIGHT** field. In the output, we see that midnight is at **00:00**.

As we have just seen, accessing static fields and methods with a slash uses the same syntax as the dot.

If we want to access instance methods, we use the dot operator with a function name. In the following example, we will use the **negate** method on **BigDecimal**, which negates the value of **BigDecimal**.

8. Call the **negate** function on the **BigDecimal** instance:

```
(.negate big-num)
```

The output is as follows:

```
-100000M
```

This was an example of calling a function without any arguments. In the following example, we will see how to call an instance method that accepts arguments. The **BigDecimal** class provides an exponentiation method, **pow**, that raises the base to the specified power. In order to calculate the product of the exponentiation of a **BigDecimal** instance, we pass to the power method an integer.

In Java, we use the **pow** method, as shown in the next step.

9. First, we will create a **BigDecimal** instance:

```
BigDecimal big_num = new BigDecimal("100000");
```

10. Then, we will call the **pow** method:

```
big_num.pow(2);
```

If we printed the call to **pow** method, we would get the following output:

```
10000000000
```

In Clojure, we can also use the **pow** method.

11. Call the **pow** method on a **BigDecimal** instance:

```
(.pow big-num 2)
```

This gives us the following:

```
10000000000M
```

In this exercise, we imported a number of classes from Java packages. We also saw how to call static and instance methods. This allows us to import and use any Java classes that we might need.

In the next exercise, we will learn about macros, which help us use Java classes in Clojure. Syntax in Clojure is very concise. Code written in Clojure is shorter than code written in Java. One common pattern in Java is calling multiple methods on class instances. The methods are chained together, each operating on the result of the previous method call. Clojure provides macros that simplify this method chaining. We will learn more about macros in *Chapter 11, Macros*. For the purpose of this chapter and learning about Java interoperability, we can think about macros as functions on steroids. One macro that we have used a lot so far is **let**. With **let**, we can create a local variable:

```
(let [num 2]
  (+ 3 num))
```

In this example, **let** allows us to define a variable, **num**, with a value of **2**. The plus function adds **3** to our variable. Both **let** and **+** are the first elements in their lists. We can see that the use of the **let** macro and the plus function is similar.

Clojure macros help us simplify code. We will learn about macros in depth in *Chapter 11, Macros*. In the meantime, we will see what macros we can use to simplify Java interoperability.

Exercise 9.03: Macros That Help Us Use Java in Clojure

In this exercise, we will find out the difference in seconds between our time zone and the target zone in London (UTC). In order to do this, we will use two Java classes from the **time** package. We will chain method calls to get the result.

The **ZonedDateTime** class contains information about the date and time in specific time zones. If we live in India, this class allows us to get the current date and time in India as opposed to the current time in London (UTC).

1. Import the **ZonedDateTime** class:

    ```
    (import 'java.time.ZonedDateTime)
    ```

2. Get an instance of **ZonedDateTime**:

    ```
    (ZonedDateTime/now)
    ```

    The output is as follows:

    ```
    #object[java.time.ZonedDateTime 0x1572c67a "2019-10-05T18:00:27.814+02:00[Europe/
    Warsaw]"]
    ```

    In this example, the time zone is in Central Europe in Warsaw.

3. Use **getOffset** from **ZonedDateTime**. This will tell us the time difference between our time zone and the UTC zone:

    ```
    (. (ZonedDateTime/now) getOffset)
    ```

    The output is as follows:

    ```
    #object[java.time.ZoneOffset 0x362c5bf1 "+02:00"]
    ```

    Please note that the preceding statement can be written as follows:

    ```
    (.getOffset (ZonedDateTime/now))
    ```

    The statements are equivalent. It is a matter of preference regarding which one to use. Most Clojure code uses the **.getOffset** function call, though it is good to know the other form in case you ever see it. The time difference between Central Europe and London (UTC) is two hours (+2).

4. Now that we know the time difference between the zones, we can get this value in seconds:

    ```
    (. (. (ZonedDateTime/now) getOffset) getTotalSeconds)
    ```

    The output is as follows:

    ```
    7200
    ```

In the output, we see that the time difference between Central Europe and London is 7,200 seconds. Depending on where you live, the output might differ. What is important here is that the method chaining looks verbose. We have two dot operators and some parentheses. This already looks confusing, and with more method chaining, it will be even more confusing. Luckily, Clojure provides a convenience .. (dot-dot) macro for method chaining.

This example can be rewritten using the dot-dot macro.

5. Get the time difference in seconds from **ZonedDateTime** using the dot-dot macro:

```
(.. (ZonedDateTime/now) getOffset getTotalSeconds)
```

The output is as follows:

```
7200
```

The output is the same. The method calls are much easier to read. Whenever you need to chain methods on Java objects, the dot-dot macro will simplify the code.

This was an example of calling methods on different objects. Clojure provides a **doto** macro for situations where we want to call methods on the same instance of a Java class.

It is common in Java to write a code where it is necessary to make a lot of modifications to strings of characters. Consider a situation where we have an auto finder on a website. Whenever we type a new character, we need to create a new string. With constant typing, this would mean creating many string objects. Such objects would occupy lots of memory space. With **StringBuffer**, we create one instance and we can add characters to this instance. This saves a lot of memory compared to having string objects.

In Java, we could use **StringBuffer** in the following way:

```
StringBuffer string = new StringBuffer("quick");
        string.append("brown");
        string.append("fox");
        string.append("jumped");
        string.append("over");
        string.append("the");
        string.append("lazy");
        string.append("dog");
```

6. In Clojure, a sentence can be constructed by calling the append method on the **StringBuffer** class as follows:

```
(let [string (StringBuffer. "quick")]
      (.append string " brown")
      (.append string " fox")
      (.append string " jumped")
      (.append string " over")
      (.append string " the")
      (.append string " lazy")
      (.append string " dog")
      (.toString string))
```

The output we get is a sentence:

```
"quick brown fox jumped over the lazy dog"
```

There is a repetition of the word **string**. The **doto** macro eliminates this duplication. The **doto** macro will implicitly call functions on instances that we specify. The preceding code can be rewritten using **doto**.

7. Construct a sentence using **StringBuffer** and the **doto** macro:

```
(let [string (StringBuffer. "quick")]
    (doto string
          (.append " brown")
          (.append " fox")
          (.append " jumped")
          (.append " over")
          (.append " the")
          (.append " lazy")
          (.append " dog"))
    (.toString string))
```

The output is the following sentence:

```
"quick brown fox jumped over the lazy dog"
```

In this example, we eliminated code duplication. With the **doto** macro, we called methods on an instance of **StringBuffer**. Once we were done, we converted the instance to a string.

In this exercise, we looked at two helpful macros for situations when we need to work with Java classes. Often, we call many methods. The **doto** and **dot-dot** macros allow us to simplify code that has multiple method calls.

In the next topic, we will use our new knowledge of calling Java classes in Clojure. We will look into Java IO operations. Then, we will create a coffee-ordering application that performs file manipulations.

Working with Java I/O

I/O deals with reading data from a source and writing data to a destination. These are some of the most common activities that programs do. Source and destination are very broad concepts. You could read from a file or a keyboard and display data on a monitor. You could read from a database and write to an API serving data. Java provides classes for many sources and destinations for reading and writing data.

In this topic, we will look at the most common I/O cases:

- Reading and writing to a file
- Reading from a keyboard and writing to a monitor

We have already worked with I/O without realizing it. Whenever we start the REPL and type on the keyboard, we perform write operations. Similarly, all function calls in the REPL print to the monitor, performing output operations.

I/O is a huge and difficult topic. Even the people that created Java did not get it right in the beginning, as we can see from the number of classes and packages for I/O. We have the **java.io** package and the **java.nio** (new IO) package. The **java.io** package contains classes for working with input and output in Java. This package has methods for reading from sources such as the keyboard and displaying to destinations such as a printer or a screen. While the **java.io** package contains many useful classes, it is considered complicated. In order to write I/O code, we have to use many classes. The newer package, **java.nio** (new I/O), introduces new I/O classes that simplify working with input and output in Java.

Java has many I/O classes because there are many scenarios for using input and output. We will see the **PushbackReader** class in action. This class allows us to read ahead a few characters to see what is coming, before we determine how to interpret the current character. This is useful when we want to read and interpret data by taking into account what other data is in the file.

Luckily for us, Clojure is a very pragmatic language and provides tools to work with I/O. Clojure has a `with-open` macro that helps us to work with files. Opening a file, or, to be more precise, any stream of data, uses computer resources such as CPU and RAM. After finishing reading from a file, we want to free these resources so they are available for other tasks. The `with-open` macro closes the opened stream, thus freeing up the resources. Closing resources is done automatically, and we do not need to think about closing resources ourselves. This prevents our application from slowing down or even crashing if we have many opened resources that are not used.

Immutability in Clojure

In *Chapter 2, Data Types and Immutability*, we learned about immutability. Clojure defaults to immutability. We do not alter data structures but create new structures based on existing data. For example, information about employees that is stored in a map is updated by creating a new map of employees with the necessary changes. The original map of employees is intact and available if we need it. As we have learned, this approach prevents many bugs in Clojure when we want to access one data structure from many places.

There are times, however, when we want to mutate data. We want to run an application by default and stop it when the user selects the exit option. Ref is one of Clojure's concurrency primitives. We will learn more about concurrency in Clojure in *Chapter 12, Concurrency*. Now, all we need to know is that with **ref** we can change the value of data. We will use ref to control the state of an application that we will shortly create.

In the next two exercises, we will create a coffee-ordering app. During the development process, we will have the opportunity to work with I/O operations such as file reading and writing. We will start by creating a new Leiningen project for the frontend part of the application. We will display the coffee menu and handle user choices.

Exercise 9.04: Coffee-Ordering Application – Displaying a Menu

In this chapter, we have seen how to use Java classes in Clojure. The aim of this exercise is to extend our knowledge of Clojure and Java. We will create a coffee-ordering app.

The app will have the following features:

- Display the coffee menu
- Be able to order coffee (type and quantity)
- Display order confirmation

Once we finish the application, we will be able to place orders and display them:

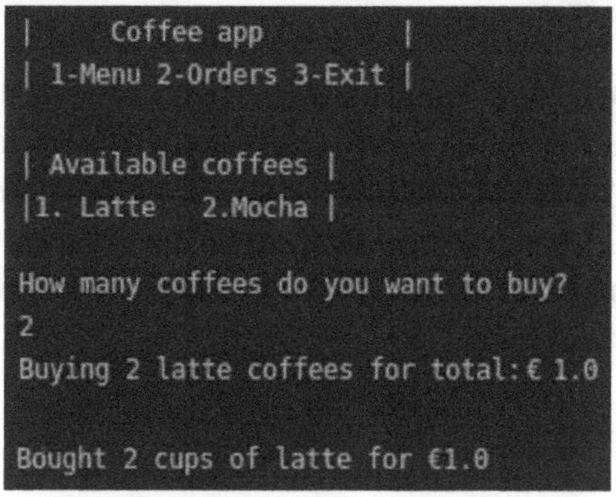

Figure 9.5: The coffee application

1. Open the Terminal and create a new Leiningen project:

```
lein new app coffee-app
```

This will create a Leiningen project that's similar to the one we investigated in the previous chapter.

In this application, we will get user input from a keyboard. To help us, we will use a Java class called **Scanner** from the **java.util** package.

2. Import namespaces to the **core.clj** file:

```
(ns coffee-app.core
    (:require [coffee-app.utils :as utils])
    (:import [java.util Scanner])
    (:gen-class))
```

We have imported the **Scanner** class. This class allows us to get input from a keyboard. In order to use methods from **Scanner**, we need to create an instance of this class.

We also imported the **coffee-app.utils** namespace, where we will have utility functions.

3. We will store the menu in a hash. A hash is a Clojure collection that we learned about in *Chapter 1, Hello REPL !* In the hash, we use a coffee type such as **:latte** as the key. The value of the key is the price:

```
(def ^:const price-menu {:latte 0.5 :mocha 0.4})
```

In the price menu, the price for **mocha** is **0.4**.

4. Create an instance of the **Scanner** class:

```
(def input (Scanner. System/in))
```

We will call methods on this class instance when we want to get input from a user. The **Scanner** class needs to know the source of the input. In our case, we use the default in source from the **System** class – keyboard. When a user runs the application, they should see a menu with options. The options are displaying and ordering coffees, listing orders, and exiting the application:

Figure 9.6: Options of the coffee application

5. Add the code for displaying the menu and handling user choices:

```
(defn- start-app []
        "Displaying main menu and processing user choices."
        (let [run-application (ref true)]
            (while (deref run-application)
                    (println "\n|      Coffee app           |")
                    (println "| 1-Menu 2-Orders 3-Exit |\n")
                    (let [choice (.nextInt input)]
                        (case choice
                                1 (show-menu)
                                2 (show-orders)
                                3 (dosync (ref-set run-application false)))))))
```

6. In the **start-app** function, we set the application to run by default:

```
run-application (ref true)
(while (deref run-application)
```

Concurrency primitives are special. In order to get the values stored in them, we use the **deref** function.

7. Inside the **while** block, the application runs until the user chooses the exit option. In this case, we will update the value of **ref**:

```
(dosync (ref-set run-application false))
```

After updating, **ref** is false. The **while** block will stop when the value of ref is **false** and our application will exit.

8. When our application runs, the user can choose options from the menu:

```
(println "\n|      Coffee app          |")
(println "| 1-Menu 2-Orders 3-Exit |\n")
```

This will display the following menu:

Figure 9.7: Choosing the options

We are able to display the initial menu. We can work on handling user choices from the menu.

9. In order to get the user response, we call the **nextInt** method from the **Scanner** instance:

```
choice (.nextInt input)
```

10. Finally, once we get the user input, we check which option from the menu should be executed:

```
(case choice
        1 (show-menu)
        2 (show-orders))
```

We now know the logic in the main application menu when we start the app. It is time to dig deeper and see the code for the **show-menu** function.

11. Display the menu:

```
(defn- show-menu []
        (println "| Available coffees |")
        (println "|1. Latte    2.Mocha |")
        (let [choice (.nextInt input)]
            (case choice
                  1 (buy-coffee :latte)
                  2 (buy-coffee :mocha))))
```

12. In the **show-menu** function, we let the user know about the two available coffees, latte and mocha:

```
(println "| Available coffees |")
(println "|1. Latte    2.Mocha |")
```

This will display the coffee menu:

```
| Available coffees |
|1. Latte    2.Mocha |
```

Figure 9.8: Displaying the coffee menu

We need to respond to the user's coffee choice now.

13. We use a **Scanner** instance to get the user input:

```
choice (.nextInt input)
```

14. Finally, we proceed to buying the coffee that the user chose:

```
(case choice
      1 (buy-coffee :latte)
      2 (buy-coffee :mocha))
```

The **show-menu** function is not long. Its purpose is to display the available coffees and get the user input. Once the user has chosen, we call the **buy-coffee** function to handle buying the selected coffee.

15. Ask the user how many coffees they want:

```
(defn- buy-coffee [type]
       (println "How many coffees do you want to buy?")
       (let [choice (.nextInt input)
             price (utils/calculate-coffee-price price-menu type choice)]
            (utils/display-bought-coffee-message type choice price)))
```

The **buy-coffee** function asks how many coffees user wants to buy. Again, we use an instance of the Scanner class – **input** – to get the user's choice. Next, the function calls two utility functions to process buying. The functions are responsible for calculating the coffee price and displaying a feedback message to the user.

All the functions will be placed in the **utils.clj** file. Instead of having all the functions in one big file, it is a good practice to split functions into various namespaces. A common namespace name is **utils**. We can keep any useful functions that operate on data there.

16. Create the **utils** namespace:

```
(ns coffee-app.utils)
```

Because the methods that we place in this namespace perform I/O operations, we could have called this namespace **coffee-app.io**. In our case, both names for namespaces, **utils** and **io**, are valid. In much bigger applications, it is common to split the **utils** namespace into different namespaces.

17. Calculate the coffee price:

```
(defn calculate-coffee-price [coffees coffee-type number]
    (->
      (get coffees coffee-type)
      (* number)
      float))
```

Our first utility function calculates the coffee price. It uses the get function to check the **coffees** hash for the passed coffee type. The hash was defined in the core namespace. The value obtained from the hash is then multiplied by the number of coffee cups that the user ordered. Finally, we convert the number to a float. This allows us to convert numbers such as **1.2000000000000002** to **1.2**.

The last utility function used when we handle buying coffee is the **display-bought-coffee-message** function.

18. Display a message to the user after buying coffee:

```
(ns coffee-app.utils)
(defn display-bought-coffee-message [type number total]
    (println "Buying" number (name type) "coffees for total:€" total))
```

The **display-bought-coffee-message** function takes an order map and constructs a string message for a user based on the data from a map. The user is informed that they have bought a certain number of coffee cups for a specified price.

With this function, we can control the information passed back to the user after completing the order:

```
Buying 2 latte coffees for total:€ 1.0
```

The second option from the main menu allows us to see placed orders:

Figure 9.9: Option 2 to see placed orders

The function responsible for displaying orders is **show-orders** from the **coffee-app. core** namespace.

19. Display placed orders:

```
(ns coffee-app.core)
(defn- show-orders []
       (println "\n")
       (println "Display orders here"))
```

This function displays the coffee orders placed. In this exercise, we inform the user that orders will be displayed here. In the following exercise, we will implement saving and displaying orders:

```
Display orders here
```

When we run the application and buy two cups of latte, we will see the following output:

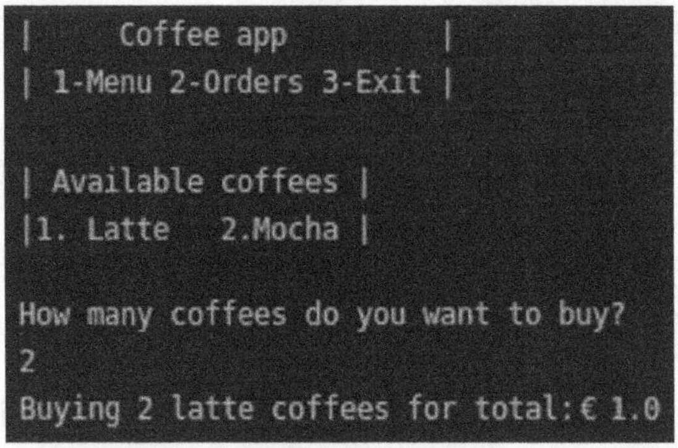

Figure 9.10: Output displaying placed orders

In this exercise, we learned how to work with I/O and Java in Clojure. We created a coffee-ordering application that allowed us to see the coffee menu and order coffees.

In the next exercise, we will extend this application and implement saving coffee orders and retrieving orders.

Exercise 9.05: Coffee-Ordering Application – Saving and Loading Orders

The aim of this exercise is to extend our I/O knowledge. We will learn how to save and read from files. We will extend the coffee-ordering application to save data to a file and read data from a file.

The application will have the following features:

- Saving orders
- Retrieving orders
- Displaying saved orders

Once we finish the application, we will be able to display orders:

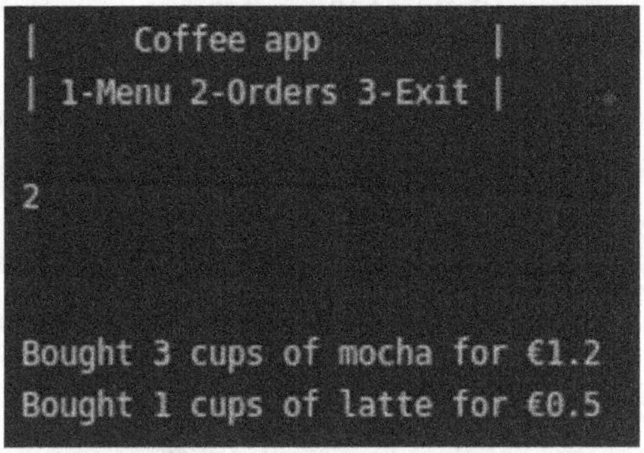

Figure 9.11: Output for placed orders

The main features of this application are saving and loading orders. We will create utility functions for this purpose:

1. In order to work with file I/O, we need to import I/O namespaces:

```
(ns coffee-app.utils
    (:require [clojure.java.io :as io])
    (:import [java.io PushbackReader]))
```

We will use the **PushbackReader** Java class to read a file. We will also use utilities from the Clojure I/O library.

2. The first function that we will implement will save data to a file:

```
(defn save-to [location data]
    (spit location data :append true))
```

The **spit** function is a Clojure I/O function that writes to a specified file location. With the :append keyword set to true, data that we want to store will be appended to existing data. Otherwise, every time we save data, new data will override the existing file content. After saving a file, we want to retrieve data from it.

3. In order to retrieve data from a file, we need to make sure that the file exists:

```
(defn file-exists? [location]
    (.exists (io/as-file location)))
```

The **file-exists?** function calls an I/O function, **as-file**, that returns **java.io.File**. Then, we call the **exists** function to check whether we have a file in the requested location. The return value of the **file-exists** function is a Boolean value. If a file exists, we get **true**:

```
coffee-app.core=> (file-exists? "/etc/bash.bashrc")
true
```

Figure 9.12: Function output as true for file_exists?

If the file does not exist, we get **false**:

```
coffee-app.core=> (file-exists? "/bash.bashrc")
false
```

Figure 9.13: Function output as false for file_exists?

Once we know that a file exists, we can load the saved orders.

4. We will need to load orders from a file:

```
(defn load-orders
  "Reads a sequence of orders stored in file."
  [file]
  (if (file-exists? file)
    (with-open [r (PushbackReader. (io/reader file))]
                  (binding [*read-eval* false]
                    (doall (take-while #(not= ::EOF %) (repeatedly #(read-one-
order r))))))
    []))
```

The **load-orders** function takes a filename as a parameter. We call the **file-exists?** function to check whether we have a file in the requested location. The return value of the **file-exists?** function is used in an **if** block in the **load-orders** function. If we do not have a file, we return an empty vector. If we have a file, we will read its content.

We use the **with-open** macro to read from a file. The macro will automatically handle closing a file once we finish reading. This will free up computer resources for us. We use the **PushbackReader** class to read from a file. This class allows us to read ahead a few characters to see what is coming before you can determine how to interpret the current character. Our plan is to read orders until we reach the end of the file, marked by the **::EOF** keyword. We repeatedly read one order.

We have changed the binding for **read-eval** to **false**. It is not secure to read from a file that we do not know. By default, **read-eval** is set to **true**. This means that any data that we read can be evaluated. User data or files sent over a network should never be trusted. The data that we work with can contain malicious code. When we manipulate data in Clojure, the data should always be read without evaluating the content of the data.

5. We will use the **read** function from the **clojure.java.io** namespace to read each line in the orders file:

```
(defn read-one-order [r]
 (try
   (read r)
 (catch java.lang.RuntimeException e
   (if (= "EOF while reading" (.getMessage e))
     ::EOF
   (throw e)))))
```

Once we reach the end of the file, a Java error is thrown and we catch this error. Upon catching the error, we return the **::EOF** keyword, which instructs our while loop to stop reading from the file. We will learn more about exceptions in Java later on in this chapter. We have our utility functions to save and load data to a file. We are ready to use these functions.

6. Save the coffee order. The **save-to** function is used to save a coffee order:

```
(defn save-coffee-order [orders-file type number price]
 (save-to orders-file {:type type :number number :price price}))
```

The **save-coffee-order** function takes the names of files in which to save data, the coffee type, the number of cups of coffee, and the price of the order as parameters.

Using this data, we construct a map that we pass to the **save-to** function. The **save-to** function will save data to the file that we specify.

After implementing the ability to save coffee orders, we can use this function when we handle buying coffee.

7. Handle buying coffee. The **buy-coffee** function will be responsible for calculating the coffee price, saving the coffee order, and displaying the feedback message to the user:

```
(ns coffee-app.core)
(defn buy-coffee [type]
        (println "How many coffees do you want to buy?")
        (let [choice (.nextInt input)
               price (utils/calculate-coffee-price price-menu type choice)]
            (utils/save-coffee-order orders-file type choice price)
            (utils/display-bought-coffee-message type choice price)))
```

In the **buy-coffee** function, we ask how many coffees the user wants to buy. We use an instance of the Scanner class – **input** – to get the user's choice. Next, the function calls three utility functions to process buying.

After we calculate the order price, we save the order and finally display information to the user about the order placed. After placing an order, we are ready to load orders in order to display them in the menu.

8. We will show orders using the **show-orders** function:

```
(def ^:const orders-file "orders.edn")
(defn show-orders []
        (println "\n")
        (doseq [order (utils/load-orders orders-file)]
              (println (utils/display-order order))))
```

In the **show-orders** function, we get orders from the orders file. We iterate over a sequence of orders using **doseq**. With **doseq**, for each order, we will call the **display-order** function.

9. Data for displaying an order is constructed from an order passed as a parameter to the **display-order** function:

```
(defn display-order [order]
        (str "Bought " (:number order) " cups of " (name (:type order)) " for €"
(:price order)))
```

The **display-order** function creates a string from an order map. We access information about the number of cups bought, the type of coffee bought, and the price of the order.

After ordering two coffees, we will have the following output:

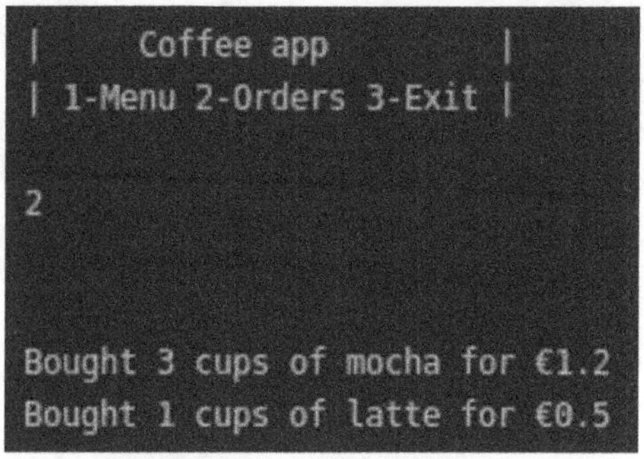

Figure 9.14: Output for the display-order function

In this exercise, we extended our coffee-ordering application. We added functionality to save orders to a file and load data from the file. While implementing these features, we learned more about Java I/O. These features improved our coffee-ordering application.

Working with Java Data Types

A data type refers to how data is classified. Any variable or object in Java has a specific type. In this book, we have seen types such as strings (**"Paris"**), Booleans (**true**, **false**), numbers (**1**, **2**) and collections (**[:one :two :three]**).

Clojure reuses some of the most common Java data types, such as strings and numbers. This is a good approach because Java types have been tested by many developers in their code since Java was created in the 90s. This gives us confidence when using Java data types. There are some types that are not directly present in Clojure. In such cases, we use Java interoperability in Clojure to access Java data types.

When writing applications in Clojure, we can use the data types that we have learned about in this book. We can also use data types if we know them from Java. In the previous exercises, we learned how to use access methods in Java classes. We know how to work with classes now.

In the next exercise, we will learn how to work with Java collections in Clojure. Java provides collections such as **ArrayList** and **HashMap**:

- **ArrayList** is like a Clojure vector. Elements in an **ArrayList** are stored in sequential order.

- **HashMap** is like a Clojure hash. Elements in a **HashMap** are stored as key/value pairs.

Exercise 9.06: Java Data Types

The aim of this exercise is to learn how to work with Java data types in Clojure. Often, when we work in Clojure we rely on external libraries. There are many Java libraries. Knowing how to use Java data types will help us to use Java libraries efficiently. In this exercise, we will work on a part of a geography application. The application stores information such as countries, capitals, and rivers as Java collections. We will write code to convert between Java and Clojure collections:

1. Start the REPL using the following command:

```
lein repl
```

It will start as follows:

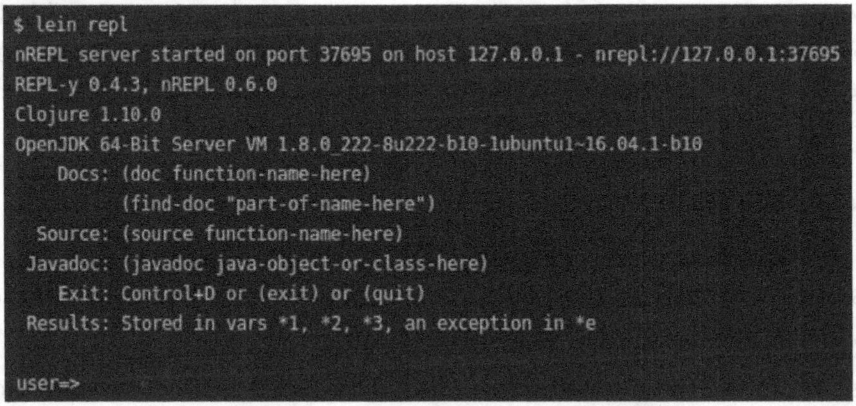

```
$ lein repl
nREPL server started on port 37695 on host 127.0.0.1 - nrepl://127.0.0.1:37695
REPL-y 0.4.3, nREPL 0.6.0
Clojure 1.10.0
OpenJDK 64-Bit Server VM 1.8.0_222-8u222-b10-1ubuntu1~16.04.1-b10
    Docs: (doc function-name-here)
          (find-doc "part-of-name-here")
  Source: (source function-name-here)
 Javadoc: (javadoc java-object-or-class-here)
    Exit: Control+D or (exit) or (quit)
 Results: Stored in vars *1, *2, *3, an exception in *e

user=>
```

Figure 9.15: Output for the REPL

2. We will create a vector containing some capitals:

```
(def capitals ["Berlin" "Oslo" "Warszawa" "Belgrad"])
```

3. Check the **capitals** vector:

```
capitals
```

The output is as follows:

```
["Berlin" "Oslo" "Warszawa" "Belgrad"]
```

4. We can check the class of our **capitals** vector:

```
(class capitals)
```

The output is as follows:

```
clojure.lang.PersistentVector
```

We see that **capitals** is a **PersistentVector** from Clojure.

5. Using Clojure's vector, we can create an **ArrayList** in Java:

```
(def destinations (java.util.ArrayList. capitals))
```

We created an **ArrayList** from a vector. We can check it as follows:

```
destinations
```

The output is as follows:

```
["Berlin" "Oslo" "Warszawa" "Belgrad"]
```

6. We can check the class for our **destinations** array:

```
(class destinations)
```

The output is as follows:

```
java.util.ArrayList
```

The destinations variable has the **ArrayList** class from Java. We just converted from Clojure to Java. We converted the **capitals** vector to the **destinations ArrayList**.

7. We can also convert the other way. We can convert from Java to Clojure as follows:

```
(vec destinations)
```

The **vec** function from the Clojure core library allows us to convert from **ArrayList** to a vector.

8. We can check the class of our newly converted data:

```
(class (vec destinations))
```

The output is as follows:

```
clojure.lang.PersistentVector
```

When we convert from **ArrayList** to a vector, we get the **PersistentVector** class in Clojure.

9. We were able to convert back and forth from Java to Clojure using an ArrayList and a vector. Clojure has another collection type that stores data. A hash stores data in a key/value pair:

```
(def fluss {"Germany" "Rhein" "Poland" "Vistula" })
```

10. We defined a hash containing countries and rivers (fluss in German) in those countries:

```
fluss
```

The output is as follows:

```
{"Germany" "Rhein" "Poland" "Vistula" }
```

11. We can check the **fluss** variable's class:

```
(class fluss)
```

The output is as follows:

```
clojure.lang.PersistentArrayMap
```

The **fluss** variable is a **PersistentArrayMap** from Clojure.

12. Using Clojure's hash, we can create a HashMap using Java:

```
(def rivers (java.util.HashMap. fluss))
```

13. We create a HashMap from Java using a hash from Clojure.

```
rivers
```

The output is as follows:

```
{"Poland" "Vistula" "Germany" "Rhein"}
```

The **rivers** variable contains countries and the rivers in those countries.

14. We can check the class of the **rivers** variable as follows:

```
(class rivers)
```

The output is as follows:

```
java.util.HashMap
```

We can see that **rivers** is a HashMap from Java.

15. Using HashMap from Java, we can create a hash in Clojure:

```
(into {} rivers)
```

The output is as follows:

```
{"Poland" "Vistula" "Germany" "Rhein"}
```

In the preceding code we used the **into** function from Clojure's core library. The **into** function takes the destination collection and the source collection as the two arguments.

Our destination collection is a hash from Clojure. Remember that we define a hash in Clojure using curly brackets, **{}**. We put the content of the **rivers** HashMap from Java into a hash **{}** from Clojure.

16. We can check the class of our newly converted hash:

```
(class (into {} rivers))
```

The output is as follows:

```
clojure.lang.PersistentArrayMap
```

The class of our converted data is a **PersistentArrayMap** from Clojure.

In this exercise, we extended our knowledge of Java's interoperability with Clojure. We learned how to convert data from Java to Clojure and back again. In the following activity, you will use your knowledge of Java interoperability to create an application that performs I/O operations.

Activity 9.01: Book-Ordering Application

In this activity, we will apply our new knowledge about I/O and Java to create a book-ordering application. A media company has decided to create an app that allows users to order books. A user can select a year and titles from a list in the application. Once a book order has been placed, we should be able to see the orders grouped by year.

Once you complete the activity, you should have output similar to the following.

Initial menu:

Figure 9.16: Menu display

Listing years:

Figure 9.17: Available books by year

Books in one year:

```
| Books in 2019 |
| 1.  Hands-On Reactive Programming with Clojure  2.  Go Cookbook |
```

Figure 9.18: Books purchased in 2019

Asking how many books the user wants to buy:

```
How many books do you want to buy?
```

Figure 9.19: Asking for the number of books to be bought

Order confirmation message:

```
Buying 2 Hands-On Reactive Programming with Clojure for total:€ 40.0
```

Figure 9.20: Order confirmation message

Listing purchased books:

```
Bought 2: Hands-On Reactive Programming with Clojure published in 2019 for €40.0
Bought 3: Go Cookbook published in 2019 for €54.0
```

Figure 9.21: List of purchased books

These steps will help you complete the activity:

1. Create a new project.

2. Import the necessary namespace.

3. Create a map to hold books by year.

4. Create a variable for a file that stores orders.

5. Create an initial menu with options to order a book and list orders.

6. Create a menu to display books by year.

7. Create the application's `main` method.

8. Create a function to save data to a file.

9. Create a function to save an order.

10. Create a function to calculate the `book price`.

11. Create a function to display an order confirmation message.

12. Create a function to display the bought order.

13. Create a function to read a single order.

14. Create a function to check whether a file exists.

15. Create a function to load orders from a file.

16. Create a submenu to order a book.

17. Create a function to buy a book by year.

18. Create a function to show orders by year.

19. Create a submenu to list orders.

> **Note**
>
> The solution for this activity can be found on page 712.

Using JavaScript in ClojureScript

ClojureScript allows us to use JavaScript constructs. We can call JavaScript methods and functions like any other in ClojureScript. When we called Java from Clojure we used operators such as . dot or \ slash. Using JavaScript in ClojureScript will also require us to learn a new syntax.

While Java operates on classes a lot, in JavaScript we operate on objects. Two JavaScript constructs that we want to use on objects are:

- Methods

- Fields

In order to access a method from a JavaScript object, we place . (a dot) followed by a method name. Accessing a field of an object is very similar. We use .- (a dot and a hyphen) before the field name. You might wonder why accessing a function uses slightly different syntax than accessing a field. In JavaScript, an object can have a method and a field with the same name. In ClojureScript, we need a way to distinguish between a function call and a field access.

In JavaScript, the code looks as follows:

```
var string = "JavaScript string"
var string_length = string.length;
var shout = string.toUpperCase();
```

In ClojureScript, the code looks as follows:

```
(def string "JavaScript string")
(def string_length (.-length string))
(def shout (.toUpperCase string))
```

Let's take a minute to appreciate the design of ClojureScript. We learned at the beginning of the book about ClojureScript functions and how to call them. Essentially, it is the same syntax as in Clojure. Unless we have a sequence, the first position in a list is treated as a function:

```
(range 1 10)
```

Calling **range** will return a sequence of numbers from 1 to 10:

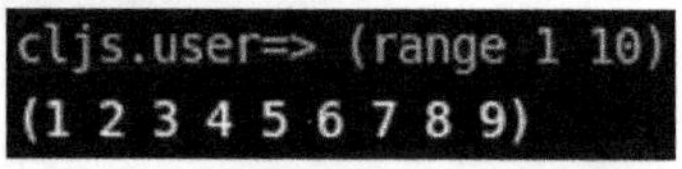

```
cljs.user=> (range 1 10)
(1 2 3 4 5 6 7 8 9)
```

Figure 9.22: Output for calling range

Here, **range** is in the first position and the ClojureScript compiler rightly treats **range** as a function. We have just seen how to call JavaScript methods and fields. With the addition of a dot or a hyphen, nothing changes in the syntax. This uniformity of placing method calls in the first position in ClojureScript reduces the mental burden on developers. We do not need to learn a lot of special syntax for JavaScript interoperability.

We will see this uniformity when we compare using the **range** function and checking the length of a string.

We call the **range** function in this way:

```
(range 1 10)
```

It will work as follows:

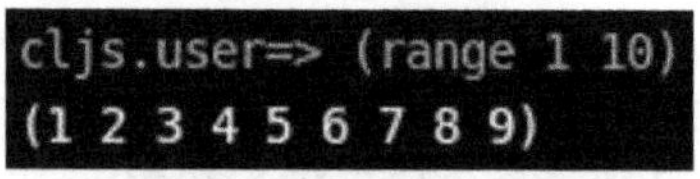

```
cljs.user=> (range 1 10)
(1 2 3 4 5 6 7 8 9)
```

Figure 9.23: Calling the range function

Checking the length of a string is done in the following way:

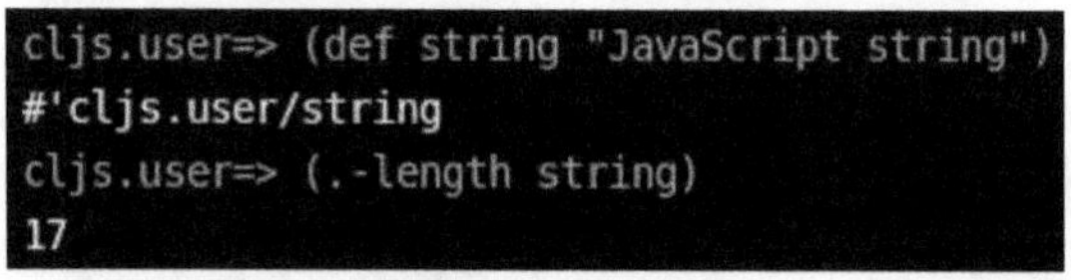

```
cljs.user=> (def string "JavaScript string")
#'cljs.user/string
cljs.user=> (.-length string)
17
```

Figure 9.24: Checking the length of a string

The **range** function and accessing the length field of a JavaScript string are both placed in the first position in a statement.

What is even more amazing is that ClojureScript improves on JavaScript. In JavaScript, there is no concept of a namespace. When we define a function or a variable, it belongs to a global namespace. This poses a problem when two or more libraries use the same name for a variable or a method. This causes a conflict and gives us errors. Library designers use JavaScript objects as modules/namespaces and place functions in their objects. This is, however, only a workaround and not a language design. In ClojureScript, namespaces are first-class citizens designed in the language.

We should pay attention to one namespace. ClojureScript uses the **js** namespace to refer to the global scope of a program. Core JavaScript objects such as **Number**, **String**, and **Date** are accessed in ClojureScript using the **js** namespace. In this namespace, we will also find browser-defined objects such as **window**.

In order to construct a JavaScript object, we use the object's name followed by a dot. This is the same syntax we used to construct an instance of a Java class in Clojure.

In JavaScript, the code looks as follows:

```
var num = new Number(123);
```

In ClojureScript, the code looks as follows:

```
(def num (js/Number. 123))
```

Notice that we use the **js** namespace. As was mentioned in this section, core JavaScript objects such as Number are accessed through this namespace.

ClojureScript takes advantage of JavaScript data types. ClojureScript does not invent new data types but reuses existing JavaScript data types. The following table presents ClojureScript data types and their JavaScript origin:

ClojureScript	JavaScript
strings	String
numbers	Number
nil	null
regular expressions	RegExp instance
collections	objects

Figure 9.25: ClojureScript data types with their origins

As we can see, data types often used in ClojureScript are based on JavaScript data types.

We have seen how to access JavaScript in ClojureScript. In the next exercise, we will learn how to work with JavaScript data types in ClojureScript.

Exercise 9.07: Working with JavaScript Data Types

The aim of this exercise is to learn how to work with JavaScript data types in ClojureScript. We will learn how to convert ClojureScript data to JavaScript objects. Later, we will learn the reverse process of how to convert JavaScript objects to ClojureScript data:

1. We will create a new project for our code:

```
lein new mies js-interop
```

This command creates a basic ClojureScript project called **js-interop**.

2. We will start the REPL with the following command.

```
scripts/repl
```

The output is as follows:

```
/js-interop$ scripts/repl
ClojureScript 1.10.339
cljs.user=>
```

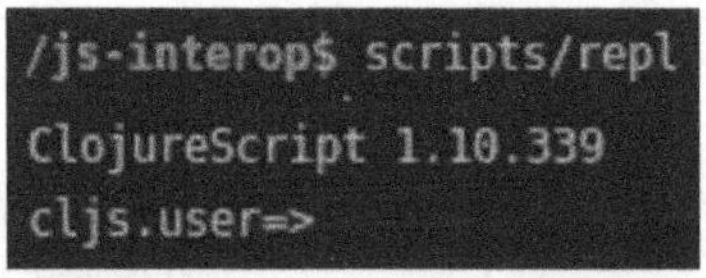

Figure 9.26: Output of the REPL

3. ClojureScript provides the **js-obj** function for creating a JavaScript object from ClojureScript data:

```
(js-obj "Austria" "Donau")
```

The output is as follows:

```
#js {:Austria "Donau"}
```

Calling the **js-obj** function created a new JavaScript object. Notice the **#js** in the REPL. This symbol in the REPL informs us that the following expression is a JavaScript object.

4. Frequently, we use nested structures where one object contains another object:

```
(def rivers-map-js (js-obj "country" {"river" "Donau"}))
```

The output is as follows:

```
cljs.user=> (def rivers-map-js (js-obj "country" {"river" "Donau"}))
#'cljs.user/rivers-map-js
cljs.user=> rivers-map-js
#js {:country {"river" "Donau"}}
```

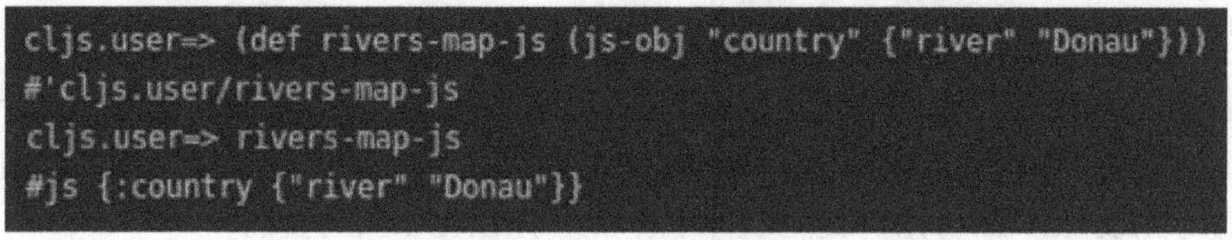

Figure 9.27: Nested structures

The **rivers-map-js** object is a nested structure. It contains a country key, the value of which is another object with some river details.

5. We can access fields in the **rivers-map-js** object:

```
(.-country rivers-map-js)
```

The output is as follows:

```
{"river" "Donau"}
```

6. After accessing country, we got nested data about rivers. We will try to access this nested data:

```
(.-river (.-country rivers-map-js))
```

The output is as follows:

```
nil
```

When we try to get information about a river, we get **nil**. It turns out that we cannot access data using JavaScript interoperability. The reason is because the **js-obj** function is shallow. It does not transform nested data structures to JavaScript objects. If we want to transfer nested ClojureScript data to JavaScript objects we need to use some other method.

7. In order to transform all nested data, we need to use the **clj->js** function:

```
(def rivers-map-js-converted (clj->js {"country" {"river" "Donau"}}))
```

The output is as follows:

```
#cljs.user/rivers-map-js-converted
```

8. With the **clj->js** function, we are able to convert nested ClojureScript data:

```
rivers-map-js-converted
```

The output is as follows:

```
#js {:country #js {:river "Donau"}}
```

Notice the two **#js** symbols. Each symbol informs us that we have a JavaScript object. The first object contains the name of a country. Inside this country object, we have another JavaScript object with the name of a river.

9. When we have nested JavaScript objects, we can access data from them using JavaScript interoperability:

```
(.-river (.-country rivers-map-js-converted))
```

The output is as follows:

```
"Donau"
```

We were able to access nested JavaScript objects using JavaScript interoperability.

10. So far, we have converted from ClojureScript to JavaScript. It is possible to convert the other way, from JavaScript to ClojureScript:

```
(js->clj #js {:river "Donau"})
```

The output is as follows:

```
{"river" "Donau"}
```

Using the **#js** symbol, we converted a JavaScript object to ClojureScript data.

11. Convert nested JavaScript objects to ClojureScript data:

```
(js->clj #js {:country #js {:river "Donau"}})
```

The output is as follows:

```
{"country" {"river" "Donau"}}
```

Using the **js->clj** function, we again converted from JavaScript objects to ClojureScript data. Notice that we used the **#js** symbol twice. Every time we have a JavaScript object, we have to mark it using the **#js** symbol. This instructs ClojureScript to treat the following data as a JavaScript object.

In this exercise, we learned how to convert ClojureScript data to JavaScript objects. Then we saw how to reverse the process and convert from JavaScript objects to ClojureScript data.

We are ready to start building ClojureScript applications. In *Chapter 8, Namespaces, Libraries, and Leiningen*, we learned about structuring projects and using Leiningen to create Clojure projects. We can use Leiningen to create ClojureScript projects as well. Using Leiningen templates to create ClojureScript applications will create the necessary configuration for working in ClojureScript. One of the most common ClojureScript templates is the Figwheel template. We will learn about this template in the next topic.

Figwheel Template

Figwheel is a tool that compiles ClojureScript code. One of the selling points of Figwheel is hot-code reloading. When we make changes to ClojureScript files, the code will be recompiled and a page in a browser will be updated. This helps to speed up the development process by giving quick feedback to programmers.

Figwheel not only reloads our code, but is intelligent with code reloading. Figwheel gives us compiler errors when we make changes in our code that result in faulty code.

If we try to use a function that is not declared, Figwheel will inform us:

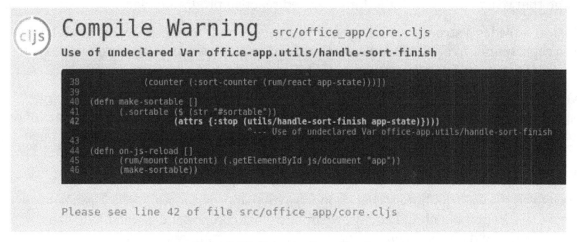

Figure 9.28: Message from Figwheel

Figwheel informed us that on line 42 in the **core.cljs** file we tried to call a **handle-sort-finish** function without declaring it.

With this concise and high-quality feedback from Figwheel, we can develop ClojureScript applications faster than if we had to dig through errors in stack traces. Or worse, our application runs but gives unexpected results.

Figwheel supports an interactive programming style. Changes made in our code base are recompiled and displayed in a web browser. We learned in *Chapter 1, Hello REPL!*, that Clojure uses immutable data structures by default. You can reload function definitions all day long. They are side-effect free and not tied to the local state of a running system. This means that running the same function many times does not change the state of an application. Recompiling and reloading is thus safe.

Figwheel encourages using React to develop applications. React is a web tool that allows us to manipulate elements on a page. React allows you to write functions that express what the state of such elements should be given the current application state.

In the next section, we will learn about Rum. Rum is a library used to create HTML elements on a page using application state.

Reactive Web Programming Using Rum

Many websites allow users to interact with web pages. Users can click, drag, and sort elements. These pages are dynamic – they respond to user actions. A programming page that reacts to user interactions is called reactive programming.

HTML provides a structure of elements on a page. The **Document Object Model (DOM)** is a representation of HTML in JavaScript. JavaScript allows us to operate on DOM elements that are finally displayed as HTML elements on a web page.

One way to make a page react to user actions is to render (display) that whole page again. Rendering a whole page consumes computer resources. If only a small part of the page needs re-rendering, we waste precious resources re-rendering the entire page. Fortunately for us, there is a solution that allows us to re-render only the parts of a page that have changed.

React.js is a JavaScript library that supports reactive programming. The basic block of React.js is a component. In React.js, we define what components should look like and how they should behave. With React.js, we can create components based on the current application state. Changes in state result in re-rendering components that require a change. React internally checks which parts of the application state have changed and which components rely on these parts of state. As a result, React re-renders only those components that used parts of the application state that have changed.

Rum is a Clojure library for creating HTML elements on a web page. Rum is based on React.js. We often have some state in a ClojureScript application. A state could be a list of users. We can manipulate a list of users by adding or removing users, and based on our actions a web page should update. In Rum, it is possible to define page elements such as a user entry that will react to changes to the list of users. Adding a new user will result in a page displaying an updated list of users.

In the next exercise, we will create a Figwheel project that uses Rum and explore what benefits Figwheel and Rum provide for developers.

Exercise 9.08: Investigating Figwheel and Rum

The aim of this exercise is to learn about Figwheel and Rum. Figwheel will create a ClojureScript project structure for us. Rum will allow us to build HTML components that respond to user actions:

1. Create the Figwheel and Rum project:

```
lein new figwheel-main hello-clojurescript.core -- --rum
```

We use Leiningen to call the **fighwheel-main** template. This template will create a new ClojureScript project with a main namespace called **hello-clojuresript.core**.

We want to use Rum, so we pass the **--rum** command-line parameter to add Rum support to the project:

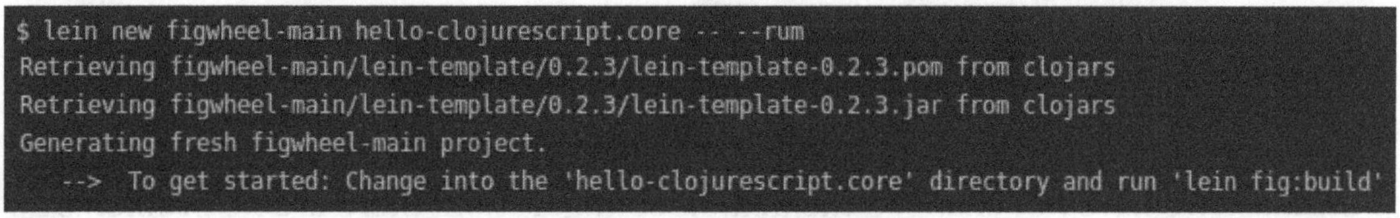

```
$ lein new figwheel-main hello-clojurescript.core -- --rum
Retrieving figwheel-main/lein-template/0.2.3/lein-template-0.2.3.pom from clojars
Retrieving figwheel-main/lein-template/0.2.3/lein-template-0.2.3.jar from clojars
Generating fresh figwheel-main project.
  --> To get started: Change into the 'hello-clojurescript.core' directory and run 'lein fig:build'
```

Figure 9.29: Creating a Figwheel and Rum project

Leiningen downloads the template and creates a ClojureScript project for us.

2. We will move to the project to the command line:

```
cd hello-clojurescript.core/
```

This will change the directory to **hello-clojurescript.core**:

```
$ cd hello-clojurescript.core/
hello-clojurescript.core$
```

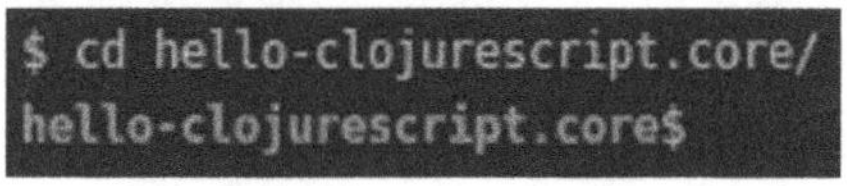

Figure 9.30: Changing directory

We are ready to run our application. In order to run our ClojureScript application, we need to build it.

3. Figwheel provides an automatic build configuration that allows us to run a newly-created ClojureScript application:

```
lein fig:build
```

Calling this command will build a ClojureScript application. First, Figwheel will download any necessary dependencies:

```
$ lein fig:build
Retrieving rum/rum/0.11.2/rum-0.11.2.pom from clojars
Retrieving com/bhauman/figwheel-main/0.2.3/figwheel-main-0.2.3.pom from clojars
Retrieving org/clojure/clojurescript/1.10.339/clojurescript-1.10.339.pom from central
```

Figure 9.31: Building a ClojureScript application

Here, Figwheel downloads three dependencies:

- Rum

- **Figwheel-main** library

- ClojureScript

Second, Figwheel will check our configuration:

```
[Figwheel] Validating figwheel-main.edn
[Figwheel] figwheel-main.edn is valid \(ツ)/
```

Figure 9.32: Figwheel checking configuration

Because we have not changed the default configuration, there are no problems with our project's configuration. We will see what the default configuration looks like shortly.

Third, Figwheel will compile our code and output a main file that is run:

```
[Figwheel] Compiling build dev to "resources/public/cljs-out/dev-main.js"
[Figwheel] Successfully compiled build dev to "resources/public/cljs-out/dev-main.js" in 10.052 seconds.
[Figwheel] Outputting main file: resources/public/cljs-out/dev-main-auto-testing.js
```

Figure 9.33: Compiling code

4. After Figwheel builds our application, it will launch a server that will serve our application:

```
[Figwheel] Starting Server at http://localhost:9500
```

Figure 9.34: Starting the server

The server runs locally. If we navigate to **http://localhost:9500**, we will see an initial page created by Figwheel:

Hello world!

Edit this in src/hello_clojurescript/core.cljs and watch it change!

Figure 9.35: Initial page created by Figwheel

The page contains welcome information. We can also see that we can edit the **core.clsj** file and see the changes on the web page. Seeing the changes is possible because Figwheel is set up to watch both the source and test directories for any changes.

```
[Figwheel] Watching paths: ("test" "src") to compile build - dev
```

Any changes that we make in source files will result in recompilation of the code and our application being updated in the web browser.

We will investigate the core source file now.

5. Figwheel will import two namespaces for us in the **core.cjs** file:

```
(ns ^:figwheel-hooks hello-clojurescript.core
  (:require [goog.dom :as gdom]
            [rum.core :as rum]))
```

The first namespace is the Google **dom** namespace, which allows us to manipulate DOM elements. The second namespace is **rum**, which was imported because we set our application to use Rum. Remember that we passed the **--rum** command-line parameter when we created the application.

In the namespace, we have defined the **^:figwheel-hooks** keyword. This is autogenerated by Figwheel and instructs Figwheel that it needs to auto-compile this file.

6. The Google DOM namespace allows us to manipulate DOM elements on the page:

```
(defn get-app-element []
  (gdom/getElement "app"))
```

The **getElement** function will search a page for an element with an ID of **app**. By default, Figwheel will create an index page with a **div**. This **div** will have an ID of **app**.

7. Figwheel creates a default index file in the **resources/public** folder:

```html
<!DOCTYPE html>
<html>
  <head>
    <link href="css/style.css" rel="stylesheet" type="text/css">
  </head>
  <body>
    <div id="app"></div>
    <script src="cljs-out/dev-main.js" type="text/javascript"></script>
  </body>
</html>
```

The main things that interest us in the index file are importing styles from the **css/style.css** file, creating the **div** with app **id** where we will mount our application, and adding our compiled code as a script from the **dev-main.js** file.

8. Reactive applications need to manage state to react to user interactions. The state is defined as an atom:

```clojure
(defonce app-state (atom {:text "Hello world!" :counter 0}))
```

n the state, we store a hash with a **:text** key that has a value of **"Hello world!"** and a **:counter** key with a value of zero. The state is defined using **defonce**. This is because we do not want to redefine the state when Figwheel reloads the code. This way, we preserve application state during page reload.

9. Rum components are defined using the **defc** macro:

```clojure
(rum/defc hello-world []
  [:div
   [:h1 (:text (deref app-state))]
   [:h3 "Edit this in src/hello_clojurescript/core.cljs and watch it change!"]])
```

The **hello-world** component constructs an HTML **div** element. Inside the **div**, we have an **h1** HTML element and an **h3** HTML element.

The **h1** element will display text stored in the application state. Because the application state is an atom, if we want to access values, we need to dereference it. Dereferencing is an action that returns a value stored in an atom.

The **h3** element informs us that we can edit the **core.cljs** file and see the changes on the web page.

Defined components need to be mounted on the page.

10. In order to see the components on the page, we need to mount them:

```
(defn mount [el]
  (rum/mount (hello-world) el))

(defn mount-app-element []
  (when-let [el (get-app-element)]
    (mount el)))
```

The **rum/mount** function will mount the **hello-world** component to the DOM element. This element is returned by the **get-app-element** function that we investigated earlier.

Once the component is mounted to the DOM element, it will be displayed on the page:

Hello world!

Edit this in src/hello_clojurescript/core.cljs and watch it change!

Figure 9.36: Initial page after mounting the component to the DOM element

Our **hello-world** component displays two headers. First is an **h1** header with saying **Hello world!**. Then is an **h3** header with information about editing the **core.cljs** file.

11. Rum allows us to define reactive components. A reactive component is a component that reacts to changes in the application state. When a change happens, the component is re-rendered on the page with a new value taken from the application state:

```
(rum/defc hello-world < rum/reactive []
        [:div {}
          (band "Metallica" (:counter (rum/react app-state)))])
```

We marked the component to be reactive by using Rum's **< rum/reactive** syntax. The **<** symbol tells Rum that a component is a special type. In our case, it is a reactive component. Rum will react to changes to **app-state**.

The **hello-world** component will call a band component and pass the band name together with **:counter**, which is defined in the application state.

Whenever the **app-state** is updated, Rum will react to the change and re-render the band component.

12. In the **hello-world** component, we will display a band:

```
(rum/defc band [name likes]
        [:div {:class "band"
               :on-click #(increment-likes)}
         (str name " is liked " likes " times")]])
```

The **band** component takes two band names and the number of likes as the parameters.

The component will display the band name and the number of likes:

Metallica is liked 0 times

Figure 9.37: Displaying the band name in the hello-world component

Inside the component, we use the **:on-click** DOM attribute.

The **on-click** attribute allows us to attach a function that is called when a user clicks on an element on a web page:

```
(defn increment-likes []
      (swap! app-state update-in [:counter] inc))
```

The function updates a **:counter** key inside the **app-state** hash. The update is done by incrementing the value of the counter using Clojure's **inc** function:

Metallica is liked 3 times

Figure 9.38: Incrementing likes for the band name

Clicking three times on the page element will update the counter. Updating the counter will trigger the re-rendering of the component with a new value.

In this exercise, we updated the `hello-world` component. After code changes, the component was displayed in the browser. We did not have to recompile the code. The code was recompiled by Figwheel. When we run Figwheel, it starts to watch our files for changes:

```
[Figwheel] Watching paths: ("test" "src") to compile build - dev
```

Thanks to Figwheel, we were able to focus on coding without worrying about recompiling our code. This is done automatically by Figwheel.

In this section, we learned about Figwheel. It creates a template for ClojureScript projects. The main feature of Figwheel is hot-code reloading. Changes in our source files are automatically recompiled and re-displayed in the browser.

We also learned about Rum. Rum is a library that helps to create reactive components. The components react to changes in application state and are redisplayed on the web pages.

In the next topic, we will delve deeper into JavaScript interoperability.

Drag and Drop

One of the most common use cases in web pages is using drag and drop. It is so common that we rarely even notice it nowadays. The jQuery UI library provides functions to code drag and drop functionality. With this library, we can mark HTML elements as draggable and droppable.

The library has a number of options that allow us to alter how dragging and dropping behaves. We can:

- Constrain the movement of draggable elements to certain areas on a web page
- Specify if the element returns to the original position after dragging
- Specify if the element auto-aligns to other elements
- Give visual aids while dragging, such as transparency or animation
- Accept only one droppable element in a page area
- Allow or deny reverting after dropping
- Give visual feedback once an element has been dropped

Using jQuery's draggable and droppable functionality, we can create a truly interactive page.

We have seen the syntax for JavaScript interoperability. It is now time to put our knowledge into practice. In the next exercise, we will create a drag and drop application using JavaScript interoperability. The application will be based on the Figwheel template and use Rum for reactive behavior.

Exercise 9.09: JavaScript Interoperability with Drag and Drop

The aim of this exercise is to get comfortable with JavaScript interoperability in ClojureScript. We will create a frontend application that allows users to drag and drop elements. When coding dragging and dropping behavior, we will use objects and functions from JavaScript. JavaScript's jQuery UI library has drag and drop methods. We will use methods from this library.

The application will be based on a Figwheel template that helps build ClojureScript applications. One of its main features is hot-code reloading. Any changes in source files are recompiled and updated in a browser. This helps to speed up the development process by giving quick feedback to programmers:

1. Create a new ClojureScript application based on the **figwheel** template:

```
lein new figwheel-main hello-drag-and-drop -- --rum
```

The REPL will display information saying that a new project based on the **figwheel** template has been created:

```
$ lein new figwheel-main hello-drag-and-drop -- --rum
Generating fresh figwheel-main project.
  --> To get started: Change into the 'hello-drag-and-drop' directory and run 'lein fig:build'
```

Figure 9.39: REPL output

In the project, we will use the **jayq** external library. **jayq** is a ClojureScript wrapper for jQuery.

2. Add external ClojureScript dependencies in **project.clj**. In **project.clj**, add the **jayq** library in the **:dependencies** section:

```
[jayq "2.5.4"]
```

The **dependencies** section in **project.clj** should look like the following:

```
:dependencies [[org.clojure/clojure "1.9.0"]
               [org.clojure/clojurescript "1.10.520"]
               [jayq "2.5.4"]
               [rum "0.11.2"]]
```

Figure 9.40: Output for dependencies

3. Now that we have dependencies configured in **project.clj**, we can import them in the **hello-drag-and-drop.core** namespace:

```
(ns ^:figwheel-hooks hello-drag-and-drop.core
  (:require [jayq.core :as jayq :refer [$]]
            [goog.dom :as gdom]
            [rum.core :as rum]))
```

The libraries will help us create drag and drop elements on a page. Drag and drop implementation will be based on a component from jQuery UI. We need to import these JavaScript libraries in the **index.html** file.

4. Open the **resources/public/index.html** file and, inside the **<head>** tag, add imports for jQuery and jQuery UI:

```
<script src="https://code.jquery.com/jquery-3.4.1.min.js" integrity="sha256-CSXorXvZ
cTkaix6Yvo6HppcZGetbYMGWSFlBw8HfCJo=" crossorigin="anonymous"></script>
  <script src="https://code.jquery.com/ui/1.12.1/jquery-ui.min.js" integrity="sha256-
VazP97ZCwtekAsvgPBSUwPFKdrwD3unUfSGVYrahUqU=" crossorigin="anonymous"></script>
```

5. After importing the necessary libraries, we will launch Figwheel. In Terminal, type the following:

```
lein fig:build
```

This will launch Figwheel for us:

```
$ lein fig:build
2019-11-10 15:34:56.017:INFO::main: Logging initialized @5129ms to org.eclipse.jetty.util.log.StdErrLog
[Figwheel] Validating figwheel-main.edn
[Figwheel] figwheel-main.edn is valid \(ツ)/
[Figwheel] Compiling build dev to "resources/public/cljs-out/dev-main.js"
[Figwheel] Successfully compiled build dev to "resources/public/cljs-out/dev-main.js" in 2.905 seconds.
[Figwheel] Outputting main file: resources/public/cljs-out/dev-main-auto-testing.js
[Figwheel] Watching paths: ("test" "src") to compile build - dev
[Figwheel] Starting Server at http://localhost:9500
```

Figure 9.41: Launching Figwheel

Figwheel will compile ClojureScript code and launch a server for us. The server will automatically open a web browser displaying the content from the **index.html** file:

Hello world!

Edit this in src/hello_clojurescript/core.cljs and watch it change!

Figure 9.42: Content from index.html

One of the selling points of Figwheel is code reloading. When we make changes to ClojureScript files, the code will be recompiled and a page in the browser will be updated.

In our app, we will implement drag and drop functionality. We will move draggable cards into droppable tiles. We start by defining a tile component.

6. Inside **hello-clojurescript.core**, add a definition for a tile:

```
(rum/defc tile [text number]
  [:div {:class "tile" :id number} text])
```

Here, a tile is a **rum** component that is basically an HTML block. We define a component using the **defc** method from **rum**. A tile accepts two arguments: text and a number. Inside it, a hash that allows us to set properties on an element number parameter is used to set an ID for the tile div. Text will be displayed inside the div element. We also set a "**tile**" class for styling.

7. Inside **resources/public/css/styles.css**, add a CSS definition. CSS stands for Cascading Style Sheets. Style sheets allow us to style HTML elements on a web page. Cascading means that if an HTML element has some styles, any HTML elements inside this element will inherit the same styling:

```
.tile {
    border: 1px solid green;
    display: inline-block;
    height: 100px;
    width: 200px;
}
```

Here, we define the style for a tile component with a solid green border. The border's width should be 1 pixel, the height should be 100 pixels, the width should be 200 pixels, and the component is displayed inline, meaning that it is on the same line as other elements. When we render the tiles, they will look as follows:

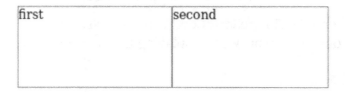

Figure 9.43: Defining the tile component

We have two tiles on the same line. Each tile has a green border.

8. This styling will help us to see each tile clearly. We have a solid green line to distinguish between the tiles. We are going to create a component that holds tiles:

```
(rum/defc tiles []
  [:.tiles {}
    (tile "first" 1)
    (tile "second" 2)])
```

We create a component that is a **div** holding two **tile** components. We mark them as first and second. Notice that we did not write a **div** tag directly. When we omit the **div** tag and provide a class or an ID, Rum will implicitly create a **div** element. Here, we used a shorthand notation for a class and gave the component class **tiles**.

9. We want to inform a user that an element was dropped. We will store information about dropping elements in an **atom**:

```
(defonce is-element-dropped? (atom false))
```

When the application starts, we set the value to **false**. We do not want Figwheel to redefine the atom when it reloads the page, so we define it once.

10. The component will display information if an element was dropped:

```
(rum/defc dropped-message < rum/reactive []
          [:div {}
           (str "Was element dropped? " (rum/react is-element-dropped?))])
```

We use the **reactive** directive from Rum. This directive instructs Rum that the component will **react** to changes in **application state**. In our case, any changes to the **is-element-dropped?** atom will cause the component to be rerendered with a new value. We have three components already, but they are not visible in the web browser yet. We need to write code that will mount our components on the page. We will have a top-level component that will contain all the HTML for our application.

11. We will put all our components into one **main** component. This **main** component will contain cards that we drag and tiles where we drop elements:

```
(rum/defc content []
  [:div {}
    (tiles)
    (dropped-message)])
```

12. After defining our **main** component, we are ready to tell Rum how to mount this component:

```
(defn mount [el]
  (rum/mount (content) el))
```

We tell Rum that we want to mount a component called **content**. The mount point is an element with an ID of **app**. When we check the web browser, we can see the changes applied:

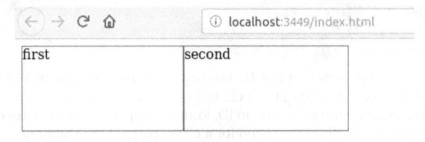

Figure 9.44: Changes in the tile component

We did not have to compile the code ourselves. All this was done by Figwheel. After creating droppable elements, it is time to create elements that we can drag.

13. We will create a new **rum** component – a **card**:

```
(rum/defc card [number]
  [:.card {:data-number number :id number}])
```

The card component will accept one argument, a number. This argument is used twice inside the properties hash. We will set an ID for this component using the number. We will also set a data property with the number.

14. Once we have the card component, we can create a component that will hold a number of cards:

```
(rum/defc cards []
  [:.cards {}
    (card 1)
    (card 2)])
```

15. In this example, we create two cards. Finally, we need to place our cards somewhere. A good place is our **main** component. It should look like this now:

```
(rum/defc content []
  [:div {}
        (tiles)
        (cards)
        (dropped-message)])
```

16. The main content consists of cards and tiles. Even if we went to the web browser, we would not see any cards yet. We have to add some styling:

```
.card {
    border: 1px solid red;
    display: inline-block;
    height: 50px;
    width: 50px;
}
```

After adding styling for a card, the web browser will show us new content:

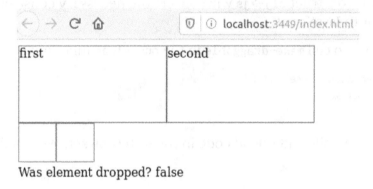

Figure 9.45: Styled cards

Besides two big green tiles, we have two small red cards. The draggable and droppable elements are now placed. We are ready to implement the dragging and dropping behavior.

17. We will add dragging to cards. We will use the **draggable** function from jQuery UI. Add code for dragging cards to **hello-clojurescript.core**:

```
(defn make-draggable []
  (.draggable ($ ".card") (attrs {:revert true :cursor "move"})))
```

18. We find HTML elements with the **card** class and use the **$** function from the **jayq** library that we imported at the beginning of the section. The **$** function will create a jQuery object. We call the **draggable** method on this object, passing attributes. Attributes are constructed using a new function, **attrs**:

```
(defn attrs [a]
  (clj->js (sablono.util/html-to-dom-attrs a)))
```

The **attrs** function takes attributes as arguments. We use **sablono**'s **html-to-dom-attrs** function to convert all HTML attributes to their DOM equivalents. We convert from HTML attributes to DOM attributes because jQuery manipulates the DOM, not HTML.

19. We need to import the **sablono** library to the **hello-drag-and-drop.core** namespace:

```
(ns ^:figwheel-hooks hello-drag-and-drop.core
  (:require [goog.dom :as gdom]
            [jayq.core :as jayq :refer [$]]
            [rum.core :as rum]
            [sablono.util]))
```

The **clj->js** function will recursively transform ClojureScript values to JavaScript. Sets/vectors/lists become arrays, keywords and symbols become strings, and maps become objects. We can code in ClojureScript, and when we need to use JavaScript construct **clj->js** will convert the necessary constructs from ClojureScript to JavaScript.

20. The last step is to call **make-draggable** in the **on-reload** function:

```
(defn ^:after-load on-reload []
  (mount-app-element)
  (make-draggable))
```

Figwheel will compile and reload code in the web browser. We can drag the red cards now:

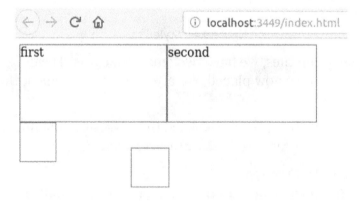

Figure 9.46: Dragging the red cards

The last piece in our application is implementing the dropping behavior for tiles. A **tile** should accept a dragged card.

21. For the dropping behavior, we will use the **droppable** function from the jQuery UI library:

```
(defn make-droppable []
  (.droppable ($ (str ".tile"))
                    (attrs {:hoverClass "hovered-tile" :drop handle-drop :activate
start-dragging}))))
```

Similar to the **make-draggable** function, we use the **$** function to construct jQuery objects using the **tile** CSS class. Next, we call the **droppable** function from the jQuery UI library passing attributes as arguments.

22. We set two attributes. The first one is **:hoverClass**, which takes a value of **hovered-tile**. This attribute allows us to add styling when an element is hovered over with the mouse. In **styles.css**, add the following declaration:

```
.hovered-tile {
    background-color: cornflowerblue;
}
```

When we hover over a tile during dragging, its background color will change to a shade of blue.

23. For the second attribute, **:drop**, we assign the **handle-drop** function:

```
(defn handle-drop [event ui]
  (let [draggable-id (jayq/data (.-draggable ui) "number")]
    (println "Dropping element with id" draggable-id)
    (reset! is-element-dropped? true)
    (.draggable (.-draggable ui) "disable")
    (.droppable ($ (str "#" (.-id (.-target event)))) "disable")
    (.position (.-draggable ui)
                     (attrs {:of ($ (str "#" (.-id (.-target event)))) :my "left top"
:at "left top"}))))
```

Inside the **handle-drop** function, we specify the behavior when an element is dropped. There are a few things happening in the function. We access the **draggable** field on the **ui** element using JavaScript interoperability with **.-** (dot and hyphen). This field is passed to the **data** function from the **jayq** library to access the **data-number** HTML attribute. We print the ID of the dragged element. We reset the atom informing that an element has been dropped. We disable the dragged element. This will add the **ui-draggable-disabled** CSS class to the element. We disable the element into which we dropped, preventing dropping more elements. Finally, we set the position of the dropped element to the top left of the droppable container

The **handle-drop** function is a good example of using JavaScript interoperability. We call functions on JavaScript objects and access fields from these objects.

24. The droppable widget allows us to add a function that is called when an element is being dragged:

```
(defn start-dragging [event ui]
    (reset! is-element-dropped? false))
```

In our implementation, we set the **is-element-dropped?** atom to **false**.

25. We need to add styling to the element that we dropped. In **styles.css**, add the following declaration:

```
.card.ui-draggable-disabled {
    background-color: yellow;
}
```

This will set the background color of dropped elements to yellow.

26. Finally, we will call the **make-droppable** function on **on-js-reload**. It should look as follows:

```
(defn ^:after-load on-reload []
  (mount-app-element)
  (make-draggable)
  (make-droppable))
```

When we drop an element in the web browser, we will see the following result:

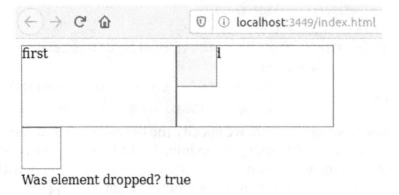

Was element dropped? true

Figure 9.47: Dropping an element

In this exercise, we have created a drag and drop application. We used JavaScript interoperability to access functions, objects, and fields from JavaScript.

We did not have any problems when coding this application. There are situations when our application does not operate as expected. In the next section, we will look at exception and error handling in Clojure.

Exceptions and Errors in Clojure

In an ideal world, every program runs without any problems. In the real world, mistakes happen and programs do not run as planned. Errors and exceptions in Java and Clojure are a mechanism for informing developers when such unexpected situations occur.

An error indicates a serious problem that an application should not try to catch or handle. An exception indicates conditions that an application might want to catch. To put it another way, errors are situations from which an application cannot recover. Such conditions could be running out of disk space or memory. If an application runs out of disk space to save data, there is no possibility that this application can serve its purpose. Unless we provide more disk space, the application cannot run successfully. Exceptions are conditions from which an application can recover. Such a condition could be trying to access a list from a database before a connection to the database has been established, or trying to use arithmetic operations on strings instead of numbers.

Both errors and exceptions are subclasses of the **Throwable** class. This class indicates a Java object that can be thrown. Throwing means raising an alert such as an error or an exception. Java provides four constructs to deal with errors and exceptions:

- `throw`
- `try`
- `catch`
- `finally`

`throw` allows a developer to raise an exception. We could have a web application that accepts user input such as their age. In this application, we could have a feature where we check for the user's age before showing age-restricted content. When we perform an arithmetic operation on input, we expect a number from a user. If a user puts a string instead, the application cannot carry out such calculations. Throwing an error in such a situation will alert the application of an input that is not correct. Once we raise an exception or throw an error, we can deal with them using the remaining three Java constructs.

`try` is a Java reserved word that allows a developer to write a block of code that can potentially result in a **Throwable** object appearing. This code is scoped within a `try` block and guarded against errors. Going back to our application, an age check will be placed inside a `try` block. When we encounter an error or exception, we can handle it. The third construct will help us with that.

catch is a reserved word in Java that allows a developer to handle and deal with exceptions and errors. The block of code under catch is executed when the specified exception or error is encountered. In our example, when we try to manipulate an age string such as a number, an exception is thrown and the **catch** block is executed. In this block, we could return a message to the user that they need to input numbers.

finally is the last reserved word for dealing with exceptions and errors in Java. The block of code under **finally** is always executed. There are situations when we want to execute code regardless of whether we have encountered an exception or not. An example is I/O operations. Opening a file could raise an error if a file is not present. If a file is present, an error is not thrown. Opening a file uses computer resources such as RAM that we want to free up after we finishing reading the file. Closing a file after reading the **finally** block is a common practice. It is so common that Clojure provides the **with-open** macro that we saw in action in the I/O section of this chapter.

The most common example of a **try-catch-finally** block is reading or writing to a file. Inside the **try** block, we have an operation to read or write to a file. The **catch** block would guard against IO exceptions such as file not present. In the **finally** block, we would have code to close the file. Closing the file releases computer resources for other tasks.

The following table presents the most common exceptions and errors in Java:

Exception name	Description
FileNotFoundException	Raised when we try to access a file that does not exist.
OutOfMemoryError	Raised when the JVM runs out of RAM.
IndexOutOfBoundsException	Raised when accessing an element in an array that does not exist.
ClassCastException	Thrown to indicate that the code has attempted to cast an object to a subclass of which it is not an instance.

Figure 9.48: Common exceptions and errors in Java

In the next exercise, we will learn how to use **throw**, **try**, **catch**, and **finally** in Clojure.

Exercise 9.10: Handling Errors and Exceptions in Clojure

The aim of this exercise is to learn how exceptions and errors in Clojure are handled. It is common that in Clojure we work with data from Java. In this exercise, we will create a function that takes a Java **ArrayList** instance and an index. The **ArrayList** class is like a vector in Clojure, which we saw in *Chapter 2, Data Types and Immutability*. The **ArrayList** class stores data. We can access elements from the **ArrayList** class using the index, the same as we do with vectors in Clojure. Accessing elements from **ArrayList** can cause exceptions. While designing our function, we will handle the exceptions raised:

1. Open Terminal and start the REPL:

    ```
    lein repl
    ```

    After opening the REPL, we will define an **ArrayList** instance.

2. We will create an **ArrayList** containing three numbers:

    ```
    (def three-numbers-array (java.util.ArrayList. [0 1 2]))
    ```

3. We have an array that contains three numbers, zero to two:

    ```
    three-numbers-array
    ```

    The output is as follows:

    ```
    [0 1 2]
    ```

    We will create a function that allows us to access elements from an array.

4. The **array-list-getter** function will allow us to access elements from an array:

    ```
    (defn array-list-getter [array index]
        (.get array index))
    ```

    The **array-list-getter** function takes two arguments: an array and an index. We access an element from the array using the passed index.

5. When we access the element that is present in the array, we get it back:

    ```
    (array-list-getter three-numbers-array 1)
    ```

The output is as follows:

```
1
```

We wanted to get the element at index 1, and we got it back.

6. When we try to access an element that is not present, Clojure complains:

```
(array-list-getter three-numbers-array 5)
```

The output is as follows:

```
IndexOutOfBoundsException Index: 5, Size: 3 java.util.Arraylist.rangeCheck
(ArrayList.java:657)
```

Our array has only three elements. When we try to access the element at index **5**, Clojure raises **IndexOutOfBoundsException**.

7. We can catch errors thrown by our code:

```
(defn array-list-getter [array index]
    (try
        (.get array index)
        (catch IndexOutOfBoundsException ex
            (str "No element at index " index))))
```

8. The new definition of **array-list-getter** catches the **IndexOutOfBoundsException**:

```
(array-list-getter three-numbers-array 5)
```

The output is as follows:

```
"No element at index 5"
```

In the **catch** block, we specify what error or exception we want to catch and how to handle it. Here, we return information that the array does not have an element in the passed index.

9. If our code does not throw an exception, the **catch** block is not executed:

```
(array-list-getter three-numbers-array 1)
```

The output is as follows:

```
1
```

We have an element at index **1**. The **array-list-getter** function returns this number for us. No exception is thrown.

10. Code in the **finally** block is always executed just before the **try** block finishes. This happens even if no exception has been thrown:

```
(defn array-list-getter [array index]
  (try
    (.get array index)
    (catch IndexOutOfBoundsException ex
      (str "No element at index " index))
    (finally (println "Login usage of array-list-getter"))))
```

11. Executing this correct code returns the expected result and prints a message that this code always gets executed:

```
(array-list-getter three-numbers-array 1)
```

The output is as follows:

```
Login usage of array-list-getter:
1
```

We see that when code does not throw any errors or exceptions, only the **finally** block is executed and not the **catch** block.

12. When our code will throw an error situation, the **catch** and **finally** blocks are executed:

```
(array-list-getter three-numbers-array 5)
```

This time, we try to access an element that is not present. This code will raise an exception and execute the **finally** block. Instead of getting a number, we see two messages in the REPL. One is from the **catch** block and the other from the **finally** block.

In this exercise, we have learned about errors and exceptions. Clojure reuses these constructs from Java. Code that can throw errors or exceptions is protected by a **try** block. When exceptions are thrown, code in the **catch** block is executed. For situations when some code needs to be run regardless of exceptions raised, the **finally** block is used.

Like in Java, errors happen in JavaScript as well. In the final section of this chapter, we will learn about errors in JavaScript and how to deal with them in ClojureScript.

Errors in JavaScript

In the previous section, we learned about errors and exceptions in Java and how to handle them in Clojure. Unexpected situations that lead to problems in JavaScript applications also happen. This results in a need to handle errors. JavaScript does not distinguish between errors and exceptions, so any situations in which code causes the application not to run as expected are errors.

Like in Java, in JavaScript, we have tools to deal with errors. JavaScript provides four constructs:

- `throw`

- `try`

- `catch`

- `finally`

They are the same as we saw in the previous section. JavaScript reuses error handling concepts known from other languages, such as Java. Because JavaScript is not Java, the way we deal with errors in ClojureScript is not 100% the same as in Clojure. It's very close, but code pasted from Clojure to ClojureScript will not work straight away. In the next exercise, we will see how to deal with JavaScript errors in ClojureScript and examine the small syntax differences with error handling in Clojure.

ClojureScript Leiningen Templates

We have used Leiningen to create projects for us. When we create a new project, we use a project template. Template developers can publish project templates on the internet and other developers (like us) can create projects using such templates.

So far, we have used Figwheel to create ClojureScript projects. As we have learned, Figwheel provides a lot of default configuration for us. A new Figwheel project comes with features such as hot-code reloading, a REPL, and tests.

There are situations where we do not need all these nice things from Figwheel. We want a simple ClojureScript setup. For such cases, we can use a `mies` project template. The `mies` template creates a basic project structure for ClojureScript.

To reiterate, for most situations when we want to develop a website application, we would use Figwheel. On rare occasions when we want a minimal ClojureScript project setup, we will use `mies`.

Exercise 9.11: Handling Errors in ClojureScript

The aim of this exercise is to learn how ClojureScript handles JavaScript errors. In this exercise, we will write a function that abbreviates programming language names. When a programming language is not supported, we will throw an error to inform the user that this language is not supported:

1. Create the project:

```
lein new mies error-handling
```

This command will create a new project for us.

2. We will run the ClojureScript REPL from the command line:

```
scripts/repl
```

This launches the REPL.

```
/error-handling$ scripts/repl
ClojureScript 1.10.339
cljs.user=>
```

Figure 9.49: Output for the REPL

With REPL launched, we can investigate error handling in ClojureScript.

3. In our code, we will support the following languages:

```
(def languages {:Clojure "CLJ"
                :ClojureScript "CLJS"
                :JavaScript "JS"})
```

4. We will implement a function that abbreviates a programming language name:

```
(defn language-abbreviator [language]
  (if-let [lang (get languages language)]
        lang
        (throw (js/Error. "Language not supported"))))
```

The function will try to get a short version of a language from a language hash defined earlier.

If the language is not found, we will throw an error. The syntax of **throw** in ClojureScript is very similar to syntax that we have seen in Clojure. Here, instead of Java classes, we have an **Error** object that we access from the **js** namespace.

5. When a function is called with a valid argument, it returns the abbreviated name of a programming language:

```
(language-abbreviator :JavaScript)
```

The output is as follows:

```
"JS"
```

We see that a short name for JavaScript is **JS**.

6. When we call a function with an invalid argument, it will throw an error:

```
(language-abbreviator :Ruby)
```

This will return an error as follows:

```
Execution error (Error) at (<cljs repl>:1)
Language not supported
```

We see that Ruby is not a supported language and calling the **language-abbreviator** function with Ruby as the argument throws an error. We know how to throw errors in ClojureScript. We will see how to catch them now.

7. We will create a function that returns the language of the week:

```
(defn get-language-of-the-week [languages]
       (let [lang-of-the-week (rand-nth languages)]
            (try
                (str "The language of the week is: " (language-abbreviator lang-of-the-
week))
                (catch js/Error e
                  (str lang-of-the-week " is not a supported language")))))
```

The function uses Clojure's **rand-nth** function to randomly pick an element from a sequence. Using this language, we try to get an abbreviated version of a language. If the language is not supported and an error is thrown, we catch the error and inform the user that the language is not supported.

8. Calling the **get-language-of-the-week** function with unsupported languages will result in errors:

```
(get-language-of-the-week [:Ruby :Kotlin :Go])
```

The output is as follows:

```
"Go is not a supported language"
```

The **Go** language was picked as the language of the week. Sadly, we do not have an abbreviated name for **Go**. The **language-abbreviator** function threw an error that was caught by the **catch** block in the **get-language-of-the-week** function.

9. We will call the **get-language-of-the-week** function with supported languages:

```
(get-language-of-the-week [:Clojure :JavaScript :ClojureScript])
```

The output is as follows:

```
"The language of the week is: CLJS"
```

When we call the **get-language-of-the-week** function with supported languages, we get an abbreviated name for the picked language.

10. We will extend our language of the week function to include the **finally** block:

```
(defn get-language-of-the-week [languages]
      (let [lang-of-the-week (rand-nth languages)]
           (try
              (str "The language of the week is: " (language-abbreviator lang-of-the-
week))
              (catch js/Error e
                (str lang-of-the-week " is not a supported language"))
              (finally (println lang-of-the-week "was chosen as the language of the
week")))))
```

With the **finally** block, we can execute any code we want to run regardless of errors thrown in our code.

11. We will choose a language of the week from the supported languages:

```
(get-language-of-the-week [:Clojure :JavaScript :ClojureScript])
```

The output is as follows:

```
ClojureScript was chosen as the language of the week
"The language of the week is: ClojureScript"
```

ClojureScript was chosen as the language of the week. The **get-language-of-the-week** function returned the abbreviated name of the chosen language and a message from the **finally** block.

12. We will choose the language of the week from the languages that are not supported:

```
(get-language-of-the-week [:Ruby :Kotlin :Go])
```

The output is as follows:

```
:Kotlin was chosen as the language of the week
":Kotlin is not a supported language"
```

Kotlin was chosen as the language of the week. The `get-language-of-the-week` function returned two messages: the message from the `catch` block that Kotlin is not a supported language and the message from the `finally` block.

We have just seen how `try-catch-finally` blocks are used in ClojureScript. Using these constructs will help us write code that can deal with many unexpected situations.

We now know how to handle exceptions in Clojure and ClojureScript. We have seen how to use interoperability between JavaScript and ClojureScript. It is time to put our knowledge to use. We will write a ClojureScript application that uses JavaScript interoperability.

Activity 9.02: Creating a Support Desk

The aim of this activity is to write a web application that uses external JavaScript libraries. We will create a support desk application that manages issues raised in the support desk. The application allows us to sort issues and resolve them when they are done. By sorting the issues, we can raise the priority of individual issues.

The application will have the following features:

- Display how many times the list has been sorted:

  less than three: few times

  less than six: medium times

  more than six: many times

- Filter the list of issues by priority, such as only displaying issues above priority 3.
- Sort the list of issues.
- Resolve an issue.

The following steps will help you complete the activity:

1. Create a new project.
2. Add the `jayq` and `cuerdas` libraries as dependencies in `project.clj`.
3. Create the `utils` function to filter the issues list by priority.
4. Create the `utils` function to get the sorted issues list.

5. Create the **utils** function to get the sorted messages by issue count.

6. Create the **utils** function to delete issues from a list.

7. Create the **utils** function that's called when sorting is finished.

8. Add jQuery and jQuery UI to **index.html**.

9. Import **jayq** ,**cuerdas** and **utils** to the core namespace.

10. Define the priorities list.

11. Define app state.

12. Define the counter Rum component.

13. Create the issue on **click** function.

14. Define the issue item Rum component.

15. Define the reactive issue items component.

16. Define the reactive page content component.

17. Make item components sortable.

18. Mount the page component.

19. Call the mount function.

20. Call the sortable function.

21. Run the application.

The initial issues list will look as follows:

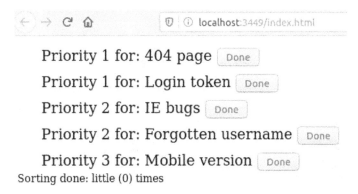

Figure 9.50: Initial issue list

The issues list after sorting will look as follows:

Figure 9.51: Issue list after sorting

The issues list after resolving three issues will look as follows:

Figure 9.52: Issue list after resolving issues

Note

The solution for this activity can be found on page 718.

Summary

In this chapter, we have learned about the interoperability of Clojure and Java. We saw how to import Java classes in Clojure. We constructed instances of Java classes and called methods on these instances. We have also learned about macros that help us use Java in Clojure.

Next, we learned about input/output (I/O) operations in Java. We accessed files from a disk, both reading and writing content. We saw how to get input from a user using a keyboard and how to display information back to the user.

After that, we learned about interoperability in ClojureScript. We created a drag and drop application using objects and methods from JavaScript libraries.

Finally, we learned about exceptions and errors in Clojure and ClojureScript. We saw how errors are thrown and how to guard against errors using **try-catch** blocks. We investigated the **finally** block and when to use it.

We finished the chapter by working on a help desk application that allows users to sort a list of items in order of priority.

In the next chapter, we will investigate testing in Clojure and ClojureScript. We will see why testing is important, what libraries both languages provide for testing, and how to use testing libraries in Clojure and ClojureScript.

10

Testing

Overview

In this chapter, we look at testing in Clojure. We start by learning about different types of tests. We then explore the most common unit testing libraries in order to test our Clojure functions. We see how to do test-driven development. We dive into property-based testing that helps us to generate a vast amount of testing data. We then learn how to integrate testing with Clojure and ClojureScript projects.

By the end of this chapter, you will be able to test programs in Clojure and ClojureScript using their respective standard test libraries.

Introduction

In the previous chapter, we learned about host platform interoperability (inter-op) in Clojure. We explored how to use Java code in Clojure and JavaScript in ClojureScript. During our inter-op adventure, we created a coffee-ordering application. The application has various features, such as displaying a menu with coffee choices and ordering a coffee. We ran the code and we saw the application working. It is now time to learn about testing in Clojure.

Clojure was designed from the beginning to be a very practical language. Getting things done means interacting with the outside world, building projects, using libraries, and deploying your work. We need to be confident that the code that we write does what it is supposed to do. As a developer, you will need to test your applications. In this chapter, we will see what types of tests can be used. We will look at unit tests as they are the most common type of test written by developers.

Consider a situation where we have an air-ticket ordering application. This application allows users to search for flights and book flights. One of its features is searching for flights. A user should be able to enter search dates. The end date should be after the start date – it does not make much sense to fly back before we have even flown out. Testing allows us to ensure that the code handling start and end dates are in order.

Similarly, we would want to make sure that when many customers enter our site, it does not slow down. User experience elements such as website speed are also tested in software.

The first step is to understand why testing is important and what types of tests can be done in Clojure and ClojureScript. Then, we will look at testing libraries in Clojure and ClojureScript. Finally, we will look at a special type of testing called **generative testing** and how it helps developers to write tests.

Why Testing Is Important

At the beginning of this chapter, we saw that software testing is important. Why? In order to answer that, we will need to understand what software testing is. It can be defined as a process that ensures that a particular piece of software is bug-free. A software bug is a problem that causes a program to crash or produce invalid output. In *Chapter 9, Host Platform Interoperability with Java and JavaScript*, we learned about errors in Clojure and ClojureScript. Testing is a step-by-step process that ensures that software passes expected standards of performance, set by customers or the industry. These steps can also help to identify errors, gaps, or missing requirements. Bugs, errors, and defects are synonyms. They all mean problems with our software.

The benefits of software testing are as follows:

- Providing a high-quality product with low maintenance costs
- Assuring the accuracy and consistency of the product
- Discovering errors that are not recognized during the developmental phase
- Checking whether the application produces the expected output
- Providing us with knowledge of customers' satisfaction with the product

There are a number of software testing methodologies, depending on the angle from which we look at the software. The most common distinction is between functional testing and non-functional testing. We will now discuss what makes tests functional or non-functional, and when it is appropriate to use one type or the other.

Functional Testing

Functional tests try to capture the functional requirements of the software being tested. The requirements are taken from the specifications of the software.

Consider the air-ticket ordering application, which allows users to buy airline tickets. As mentioned, one of its features is searching for flights. Users would want to search using different criteria. One criterion could be searching for direct flights. Functional tests would ensure that when a user searches for a direct flight, they do not see connecting flights.

Typically, functional testing involves the following steps:

1. Identifying what functions and features a software component has, based on the requirements specification document
2. Creating input data based on the requirements
3. Determining the expected output
4. Executing the tests
5. Comparing the expected results with the actual output

While functional testing has advantages, there are some testing areas that are not covered by functional tests. In such cases, so-called non-functional tests are performed.

Non-Functional Testing

Non-functional tests check things that are not directly related to the functional requirements. To put it another way, non-functional tests are concerned with the way that software operates as a whole, rather than with the specific behaviors of the software or its components.

With non-functional tests, we are concerned with areas such as security, how a system behaves under various load conditions, whether it is user-friendly, and whether it provides localization to run in different countries.

Consider the air-ticket ordering application again. This application allows users to buy airline tickets. Users should be able to pay with their credit cards. The application should handle payments securely. This means that transactions should be encrypted. Encryption is the process of encoding a message or information in such a way that only authorized parties can access it and those who are not authorized cannot. Someone who is not authorized should not be able to see transaction details.

Another non-functional test for the air-ticket ordering application would be load testing. With load testing, we would test that our application can handle a very high page load. During the festive period, many customers will enter our website. We need to make sure that thousands of users can use the application at the same time. The application should be responsive and not slow down when many customers use it.

Functional tests ensure that our applications are secure. While we have discussed functional and non-functional testing separately, they should not be seen as opposing testing methodologies, but rather, complementary approaches. They are often performed together to provide assurance that software has a high standard of quality and can operate under various conditions.

Testing and catching bugs in software are not free. It requires time and resources from developers and testers. Having said that, fixing bugs late in development is more expensive than catching them early in the development phase. Unit testing allows us to catch many bugs early on, while not requiring too many resources from developers.

In the next topic, we will examine what unit testing is, and the most popular unit testing frameworks in Clojure.

Clojure Unit Testing

Unit testing is the testing of an individual software component or module. In Clojure, a function is a good candidate for unit testing. A function is intended to perform one task at a time. Otherwise, a change in logic in one job would influence a second job. When a function has one responsibility, we can reason about the function much more easily than if it performed more than one thing. Clojure provides a number of testing frameworks for unit testing. When we use testing libraries, we often call them frameworks. A framework is a structure that supports and encloses testing. With testing frameworks, we support testing our code. Our code is enclosed in a number of tests written for our code.

There are a number of concepts in testing, two of which are as follows:

- **Assertion**: A Boolean (true or false) expression. An assertion is a statement about a specific part of our program, which will be true or false. For example, we can state that a function in our program will throw an error when we pass a string instead of a number as a parameter. The assertion will be: Does this function throw an error? The answer is either yes (true) or no (false).

- **Stub**: A temporary replacement for a part of a code or a concept. A stub simulates the behavior of the replaced software component. In the flight-ticket ordering application, we could have a payment component that takes card details and contacts the bank to withdraw money for the plane ticket. After taking payment through the bank, we would display ticket details. A stub would simulate contacting the bank without actually contacting the bank. When we use a stub, we can focus on testing displaying ticket details without handling contacting the bank and all card transactions. This keeps the test focused on a single task, in this case, displaying a ticket after taking payment via a bank.

The `clojure.test` framework is the default Clojure unit testing framework that comes with the Clojure standard library. The purpose of `clojure.test` is to provide developers with a number of testing functions. In our first exercise, we will write unit tests for the coffee app from the previous chapter using the clojure.test library.

Exercise 10.01: Unit Testing with the clojure.test Library

The aim of this exercise is to learn how to perform unit testing with the **clojure.test** library. This is the default testing library in Clojure. It is included in Clojure so we do not need to import this library as an external dependency. In the previous chapter, we created a coffee-ordering application that allowed us to display a coffee menu and order coffees. In this exercise, we will write unit tests for the functions created in the coffee-ordering application.

First, we will create the application, then we will write tests:

1. Create the coffee-ordering application:

```
lein new app coffee-app
```

Leiningen created the project for us. By default, we have one source file called **core.clj**. Inside this file, we will add the code responsible for displaying the menu options and processing them.

2. Import the **java.util.Scanner** class in the **core** namespace:

```
(ns coffee-app.core
    (:require [coffee-app.utils :as utils])
    (:import [java.util Scanner])
    (:gen-class))
```

We have imported the **Scanner** class. This class allows us to get input from a keyboard. In order to use methods from Scanner, we need to create an instance of this class.

3. Create an instance of the **Scanner** class.

We will call methods on this class instance when we want to get input from a user. The **Scanner** class needs to know what the source of the input is. In our case, we use the default **in** source of the **System** class – the keyboard.

```
(def input (Scanner. System/in))
```

When a user runs the application, they should see a menu with options. The options are displaying and ordering coffees, listing orders, and exiting the application.

Figure 10.1: Menu of the application showing all the options

4. Add the code for displaying the menu and handling user choices:

```
(defn- start-app []
        "Displaying main menu and processing user choices."
        (let [run-application (ref true)]
            (while (deref run-application)
                    (println "\n|     Coffee app |")
                    (println "| 1-Menu 2-Orders 3-Exit |\n")
                    (let [choice (.nextInt input)]
                        (case choice
                                1 (show-menu)
                                2 (show-orders)
                                3 (dosync (ref-set run-application false)))))))
```

5. In the **start-app** function, we set the application to running by default:

```
run-application (ref true)
(while (deref run-application)
```

In order to get the values stored in **run-application**, we use the **deref** function.

6. Inside the **while** block, the application runs until the user chooses the exit option. In such cases, we will update the value of **ref**:

```
(dosync (ref-set run-application false))
```

7. After updating, **ref** is no longer true but false. The **while** block will stop when the value of **ref** is false and our application will exit. When our application runs, the user can choose options from the menu:

```
(println "| 1-Menu 2-Orders 3-Exit |\n")
```

This will display the following menu:

Figure 10.2: Menu of the coffee ordering application

We are able to display the initial menu. We can work on handling user choices from the menu.

8. In order to get the user response, we call the **nextInt** method from
    the **Scanner** instance:

```
choice (.nextInt input)
```

Finally, once we get the user input, we check which option from the menu should
be executed:

```
(case choice
   1 (show-menu)
     2 (show-orders))
```

We now know about the logic in the main application menu when we start the app.
It is time to dig deeper and look at the code for the **show-menu** function.

9. Display the menu for the available coffees:

```
(defn- show-menu []
       (println "| Available coffees |")
       (println "|1. Latte   2.Mocha |")
       (let [choice (.nextInt input)]
           (case choice
                 1 (buy-coffee :latte)
                 2 (buy-coffee :mocha))))
```

In the **show-menu** function, we let the user know about two available coffees – **Latte**
and **Mocha**:

```
(println "| Available coffees |")
(println "|1. Latte   2.Mocha |")
```

This will display the coffee menu:

Figure 10.3: Coffee menu display

The user can choose numbers **1** or **2**. We need to respond to the user's coffee
choice now.

10. We use the **Scanner** instance to get the user input:

```
choice (.nextInt input)
```

11. Finally, we proceed to buy the coffee that the user chose:

```
(case choice
      1 (buy-coffee :latte)
      2 (buy-coffee :mocha))
```

The **show-menu** function is not long. Its purpose is to display the available coffees and get the user input. Once the user has chosen their coffee, we call the **buy-coffee** function to handle buying the selected coffee.

12. Ask the user how many coffees they'd like to buy:

```
(defn- buy-coffee [type]
       (println "How many coffees do you want to buy?")
       (let [choice (.nextInt input)
             price (utils/calculate-coffee-price price-menu type choice)]
            (utils/display-bought-coffee-message type choice price)))
```

The **buy-coffee** function asks how many coffees the user wants to buy. Again, we use an instance of the **Scanner** class – **input** – to get the user's choice. Next, the function calls two utility functions to process the purchase. The functions are responsible for calculating the coffee price and displaying the feedback message to the user.

All the functions will be placed in the **utils.clj** file. Instead of having all functions in one big file, it is good practice to split functions into various namespaces. A common namespace name is **utils**. We can keep any useful functions that operate on data there.

13. Create a **utils** namespace:

```
(ns coffee-app.utils
```

14. Calculate the coffee price:

```
(defn calculate-coffee-price [coffees coffee-type number]
      (->
        (get coffees coffee-type)
        (* number)
        float))
```

Our first utility function calculates the coffee price. It uses the **get** function to check the **coffees** hash for the passed-in coffee type. The hash is defined in the core namespace:

```
(ns coffee-app.core
    (:require [coffee-app.utils :as utils])
    (:import [java.util Scanner])
    (:gen-class))
(def ^:const price-menu {:latte 0.5 :mocha 0.4})
```

The value obtained from the hash is then multiplied by the number of coffee cups that the user ordered. Finally, we coerce the number to float. This allows us to convert a number such as 1.2000000000000002 to 1.2.

The last utility function used when we handle buying coffee is the **display-bought-coffee-message** function.

15. Display the message to the user after buying the coffee:

```
(ns coffee-app.utils)
(defn display-bought-coffee-message [type number total]
      (println "Buying" number (name type) "coffees for total:€" total))
```

The **display-bought-coffee-message** function takes the order map and constructs a string message for the user based on the data from the map. The user is informed that they bought a certain amount of cups of coffee for the specified price.

With this function, we can control the information passed back to the user after completing their order:

```
Buying 2 latte coffees for total:€ 1.0
```

Figure 10.4: Displaying the message for the coffee bought

The second option from the main menu allows us to see the placed orders:

```
|        Coffee app        |
| 1-Menu 2-Orders 3-Exit |
```

Figure 10.5: Orders allows the user to see their orders

The function responsible for displaying orders is **show-orders** from the **coffee-app. core** namespace.

16. Display the placed orders:

```
(ns coffee-app.core)
(defn- show-orders []
       (println "\n")
       (println "Display orders here"))
```

This function will display the coffee orders made. In this exercise, we informed the user that orders will be displayed here. In the following exercise, we will implement saving and displaying orders:

```
Display orders here
```

When we run the application and buy two cups of latte, we will see the following output:

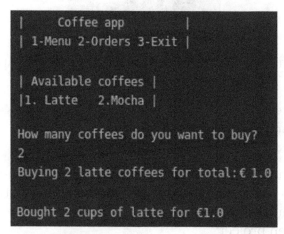

Figure 10.6: Output when the user buys two cups of coffee

17. Add the main function as follows:

```
(defn -main
      "Main function calling app."
      [& args]
      (start-app))
```

18. In order to run the application, we will use the following:

```
lein run
```

Once we run the application, we can see the available coffees and order them, similar to what we saw in *Figure 10.6*.

We have our application running successfully. We will create tests for our application now.

19. Check the testing directory. We use the **tree** command to display a list of folders and files within the test directory:

```
tree test
```

When we created the application, Leiningen created the **test** directory for us. There are a number of ways to check the project's structure. We check the project structure using the preceding **tree** command.

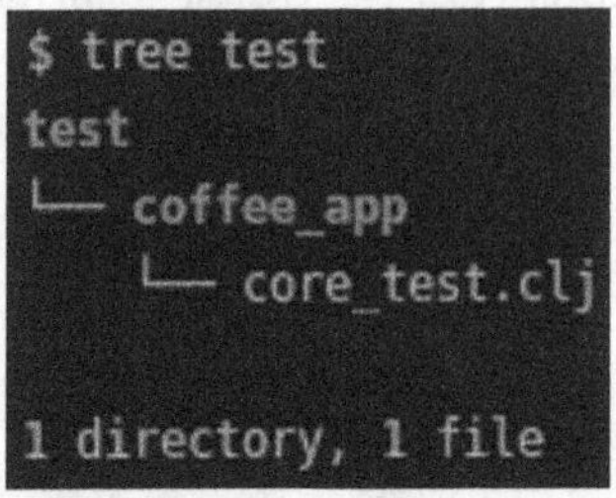

```
$ tree test
test
└── coffee_app
    └── core_test.clj

1 directory, 1 file
```

Figure 10.7: Project structure

We have one test file, **core.clj**. Inside this file, there is a sample test created by Leiningen:

```
(ns coffee-app.core-test
  (:require [clojure.test :refer :all]
            [coffee-app.core :refer :all]))
```

This file imports the Clojure testing namespace, as well as the core file from the source directory. The file contains one test method. This method is called **a-test**. Because we have autogenerated the **a-test** test function, we can run tests after creating a Leiningen project:

```
(deftest a-test
  (testing "FIXME, I fail."
    (is (= 0 1))))
```

When we create a new project with Leiningen, it will create one test function. This function is called **a-test** and is inside the **core_test.clj** file.

20. In order to run tests, we need to call Leiningen's **test** task. The **test** task is a task that will run the tests within the test directory:

```
lein test
```

The output is as follows:

```
$ lein test

lein test coffee-app.core-test

lein test :only coffee-app.core-test/a-test

FAIL in (a-test) (core_test.clj:7)
FIXME, I fail.
expected: (= 0 1)
  actual: (not (= 0 1))

Ran 1 tests containing 1 assertions.
1 failures, 0 errors.
Tests failed.
```

Figure 10.8: Running the test task

The **a-test** test fails, as we have not yet implemented the **a-test** test from the `core_test.clj` file. Leiningen informed us that it tested the `coffee-app.core-test` namespace. We have information that the test failed, including which line in the test file (line 7) caused the test to fail.

Leiningen even provided us with information about what the test expected and what the actual result was. In this case, the default test tried to compare the numbers one and zero. In order to make the test pass, let's change the **a-test** function.

21. To fix the default **test** function from the Leiningen project, we will change the implementation of the default **a-test** function that we have just seen:

```
(deftest a-test
  (testing "FIXME, I fail."
    (is (= 1 1))))
```

We changed the test to state that 1 is equal to 1. This will make our **a-test** pass.

22. We run the test using the following:

```
lein test
```

We can run the tests again:

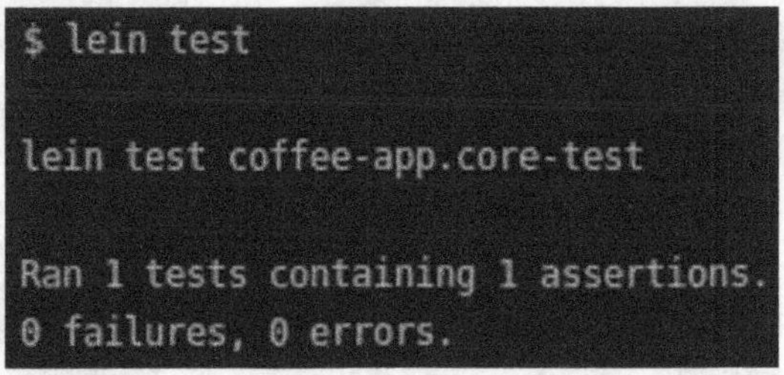

```
$ lein test

lein test coffee-app.core-test

Ran 1 tests containing 1 assertions.
0 failures, 0 errors.
```

Figure 10.9: Running the test after fixing the default a-test function

This time, Leiningen informs us that it ran one test with one assertion (test condition). There were zero failures and zero errors. We now know how to run tests. It is time to write tests for the **utils** namespace. We will create a testing file for the **utils** namespace.

23. Create a test file for the **utils** namespace. Inside the file, we will write code to test functions in the **utils** namespace:

```
touch test/coffee_app/utils_test.clj
```

After creating **utils_test.clj**, we will have two test files:

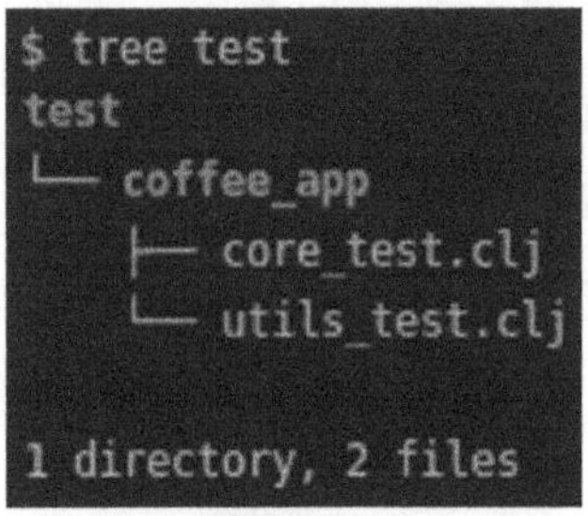

```
$ tree test
test
└── coffee_app
    ├── core_test.clj
    └── utils_test.clj

1 directory, 2 files
```

Figure 10.10: We now have two test files after creating utils_test.clj

In **utils_test.clj**, we want to test functions from the **utils** namespace. We will add the necessary dependencies to the testing namespace. Inside **core_test.clj**, we will keep tests for functions that are defined in the **core.clj** file. The **utils_test.clj** file will contain tests for functions defined in the **utils.clj** file.

24. We will import the **clojure.test** library and namespaces from the source directory that we will test:

```
(ns coffee-app.utils-test
    (:require [clojure.test :refer [are is deftest testing]]
                  [coffee-app.core :refer [price-menu]]
                  [coffee-app.utils :refer :all]))
```

The **clojure.test** namespace has a number of testing functions. We import them using the **:refer** keyword, which we learned about in *Chapter 8, Namespaces, Libraries, and Leiningen*. We import four functions:

are: Allows you to test multiple testing scenarios

is: Allows you to test a single testing scenario

deftest: Defines a Clojure test

testing: Defines an expression that will be tested

We import the **coffee-app.core** and **coffee-app.utils** namespaces from the source directory. From the **core** namespace, we import **price-menu**, which contains a list of available coffees and the price for each coffee. Finally, we import the **utils** namespace, which contains the functions that we want to test.

25. The **clojure.test** object provides the **is** macro for testing. We will learn about macros in *Chapter 11, Macros*. For the purpose of this exercise, you can think of macros as special functions. Macros are used in the same way as we have used functions.

The **is** macro takes a test and an optional assertion message. Add the following code to **utils_test.clj**:

```
(deftest calculate-coffee-price-test-with-single-is
  (testing "Single test with is macro."
    (is (= (calculate-coffee-price price-menu :latte 1)
           0.5))))
```

The **deftest** macro allows us to define tests. Each test is defined using the **testing** macro. The **testing** macro can be supplied with a string to provide a testing context. Here, we inform you that this is a single test using the **is** macro. In this test, we call the **calculate-coffee-price** function, passing **price-menu**, which contains information about the available coffees.

The second argument that we pass is the number of cups of coffee that we want to buy. In our case, we want to buy one cup. For the test, the result of calling the **calculate-coffee-price** function for one latte should be 0.5.

We will run the test now:

```
lein test
```

The output is as follows:

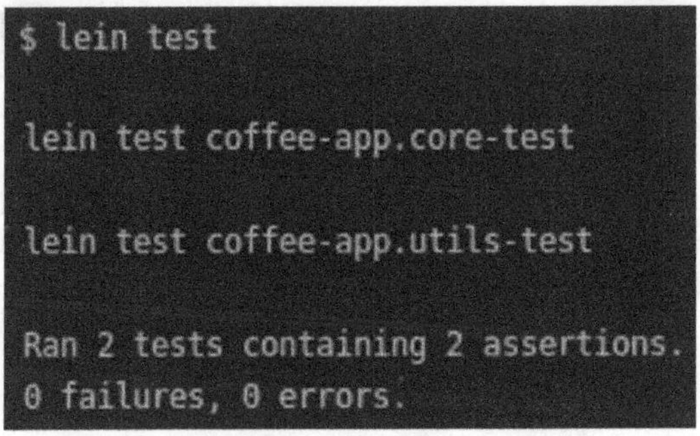

```
$ lein test

lein test coffee-app.core-test

lein test coffee-app.utils-test

Ran 2 tests containing 2 assertions.
0 failures, 0 errors.
```

Figure 10.11: Running the test after using the is macro

We can see that the newly added test passes.

26. While we can write tests with the **is** macro, testing multiple times with the **is** macro results in the unnecessary duplication of code. Consider the next test, where we run through three scenarios:

Buying one coffee – a user decides to buy one cup of coffee

Buying two coffees – a user decides to buy two cups of coffee

Buying three coffees – a user decides to buy three cups of coffee

```
(deftest calculate-coffee-price-test-with-multiple-is
  (testing "Multiple tests with is macro."
    (is (= (calculate-coffee-price price-menu :latte 1) 0.5))
    (is (= (calculate-coffee-price price-menu :latte 2) 1.0))
    (is (= (calculate-coffee-price price-menu :latte 3) 1.5))))
```

Inside the **calculate-coffee-price-test-with-multiple-is** test, we have three single tests using the **is** macro. We test three different scenarios: buying one coffee, buying two coffees, and buying three coffees.

27. Run multiple **is** tests. We run the tests for the **calculate-coffee-price-test-with-multiple-is** test:

```
lein test
```

The output is as follows:

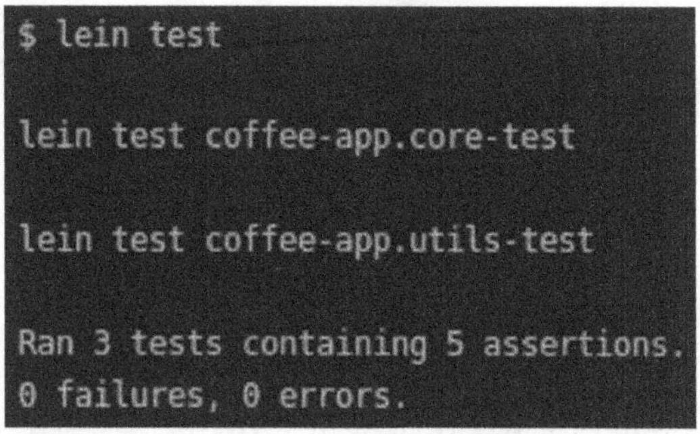

Figure 10.12: Running multiple is tests

The new test has been run and passes. In the preceding code, we see that we duplicate a lot of calls to the **calculate-coffee-price** function. There should be a more efficient way to write tests for multiple scenarios.

28. The **are** macro is a convenience macro when we plan to write multiple tests using the **is** macro. The **are** macro is a test macro used for testing multiple testing scenarios. It differs from the **is** macro in a number of scenarios that we can test.

The **is** macro allows us to test one scenario. It is singular. The **are** macro allows us to test more than one scenario. It is plural. We use the **is** macro when we want to test a single scenario and the **are** macro when we want to test more than one scenario. The previous test with multiple **is** macro calls can be rewritten as:

```
(deftest calculate-coffee-price-test-with-are
  (testing "Multiple tests with are macro"
    (are [coffees-hash coffee-type number-of-cups result]
         (= (calculate-coffee-price coffees-hash coffee-type number-of-cups)
  result)
         price-menu :latte 1 0.5
         price-menu :latte 2 1.0
         price-menu :latte 3 1.5)))
```

The **are** macro checks multiple tests against the assertion written by us.

In the preceding test, we wrote an assertion:

```
(= (calculate-coffee-price coffees-hash coffee-type number-of-cups) result)
```

The result of calling **calculate-coffee-price** with **coffees-hash coffee-type number-of-cups** should be equal to the result.

Inside the vector, we specify four arguments that we need to run our test:

```
price-menu :latte 1 0.5
```

The arguments include coffee-hash with information about coffees, coffee-type, number-of-cups, and result – the result of calculating the coffee price.

Again, we use the **equals (=)** function to check the result of calling the **calculate-coffee-price** function against the result that we expect.

29. When we run the tests again, we get the following:

```
lein test
```

The output is as follows:

```
$ lein test

lein test coffee-app.core-test

lein test coffee-app.utils-test

Ran 4 tests containing 8 assertions.
0 failures, 0 errors.
```

Figure 10.13: Output for tests run after using the are macro

Our new test passes. We used the **are** macro to simplify writing multiple test assertions. Whenever we need to write multiple tests with the **is** macro, using the **are** macro will make our code shorter and more readable.

In this exercise, we have seen how to write tests using the **clojure.test** library. In the next exercise, we will look at another Clojure library for testing.

Using the Expectations Testing Library

The main philosophy in the **Expectations** library revolves around an expectation. The **expectation** object is built with the idea that unit tests should contain one assertion per test. A result of this design choice is that expectations have very minimal syntax, and reduce the amount of code needed to perform tests.

Minimal syntax helps to maintain the code as it is easier to read and reason about code that is short and focused on testing one feature. Another benefit relates to testing failing code. When a test fails, it is easy to check which test failed and why because the test is focused on one feature and not multiple features.

The **Expectations** library allows us to test things like the following:

- Errors thrown by the code: We can test whether a part of our code throws an error. Imagine a function that calculates a discount. This function takes numbers as input and multiplies them. If we pass a string such as **"text"** and a number **5**, we will get an error because Clojure cannot multiply a number and a string. We can write tests to check whether an error is thrown in this scenario.

- The function's return value: We can test whether a function returns the expected value. Imagine a function that calculates a discount. This function takes numbers as input and multiplies them. After the multiplication, it should return a number. We can write tests to check that our function returns a number instead of a collection or a string.

- Elements in a collection: We can write tests to check whether a collection contains expected elements. Imagine a function checking a list of users for children. This function takes a list of users as input. We can write tests checking the age of users.

In order to use **Expectations**, we need to import it into a Leiningen project:

- We add a dependency for the **expectations** library [**expectations "2.1.10"**].

- **lein-expectations** is a Leiningen plugin that runs expectations tests from the command line [**lein-expectations "0.0.8"**].

We will write tests for the **calculate-coffee-price** function. This will allow us to compare how we compose tests in the **Expectations** library against tests written using the **clojure.test** library.

Exercise 10.02: Testing the Coffee Application with Expectations

The aim of this exercise is to learn how to write unit testing in Clojure using the **Expectations** library. We will write tests for the **calculate-coffee-price** function:

1. Add **expectations** to the **project.clj** file. After adding the **Expectations** library to **project.clj**, the file should look as follows:

```
(defproject coffee-app "0.1.0-SNAPSHOT"
  ;;; code omitted
  :dependencies [[org.clojure/clojure "1.10.0"]
                 [expectations "2.1.10"]]
  :plugins [[lein-expectations "0.0.8"]]
  ;;; code omitted
)
```

2. Create a file for the **utils** tests.

   In order to use the Expectations library, we need to import functions first. The **utils** namespace should look like the following:

```
(ns coffee-app.utils-test
    (:require [coffee-app.core :refer [price-menu]]
              [coffee-app.utils :refer :all]
              [expectations :refer [expect in]]))
```

3. Test the **calculate-coffee-price** function. Buying three cups of latte should cost us 1.5. The following test will check this condition:

```
(expect 1.5 (calculate-coffee-price price-menu :latte 3))
```

   We are ready to run the test.

4. Run the **expectations** test with the Leiningen task. In order to run tests on the command line, we need to use the Leiningen task from the **lein-expectations** plugin:

```
lein expectations
```

   This task will execute the **expectations** tests.

```
$ lein expectations

Ran 1 tests containing 1 assertions in 2 msecs
0 failures, 0 errors.
```

Figure 10.14: Output after running the expectations test

As we expected, for three lattes, we need to pay 1.5. What will happen if we pass a string instead of a number for a number of cups? We would expect an error. With **expectations**, we can test for errors.

5. The **expectations** library allows us to test whether a function throws an error. The **calculate-coffee-price** function requires a number. Passing a string should result in an error:

```
(expect ClassCastException (calculate-coffee-price price-menu :latte "1"))
```

The output is as follows:

```
$ lein expectations

Ran 2 tests containing 2 assertions in 2 msecs
0 failures, 0 errors.
```

Figure 10.15: Testing the calculate-coffee-price function using the Expectations library

After running the test, we see that all tests pass. Tests do not always pass. With **expectations**, we are informed when tests fail.

6. When we run a test that fails, **Expectations** will let us know. Testing for an error when the error is not thrown will fail the test:

```
(expect ClassCastException (calculate-coffee-price price-menu :latte 2))
```

The output is as follows:

```
$ lein expectations

failure in (utils_test.clj:10) : coffee-app.utils-test
(expect ClassCastException (calculate-coffee-price price-menu :latte 2))

          (calculate-coffee-price price-menu :latte 2) did not throw ClassCastException

Ran 2 tests containing 2 assertions in 24 msecs
1 failures, 0 errors.
```

Figure 10.16: Running a test that fails using the Expectations library

The Expectations library informed us that one test failed. We also know in which namespace we have a failing test and which line of code caused the test to fail. This allows us to quickly find the failing test.

We know that passing a string to **calculate-coffee-price** will result in an error. With Expectations, we can also check what the return type from the function is.

7. In Clojure code, we often compose functions. One function operates on the result of running other functions. It is common to check that functions that we call return the types of values that we expect. With **Expectations**, we can check the return type from a function:

```
(expect Number (calculate-coffee-price price-menu :latte 2))
```

We expect that **calculate-coffee-price** will return a number:

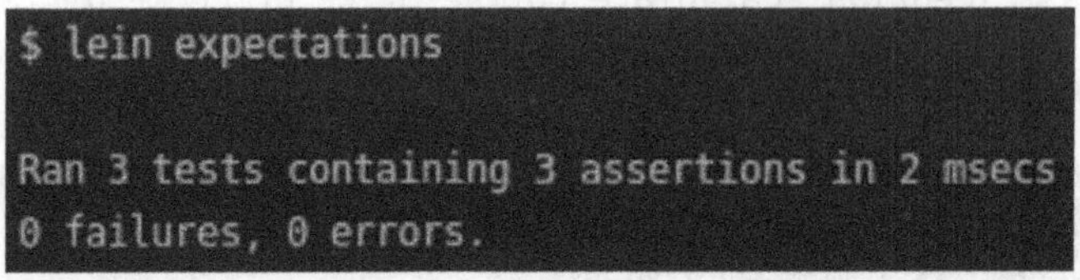

```
$ lein expectations

Ran 3 tests containing 3 assertions in 2 msecs
0 failures, 0 errors.
```

Figure 10.17: Using Expectations

Running the tests confirms that the number is the correct return type of the **calculate-coffee-price** function. With **Expectations**, we also can test whether a collection contains requested elements.

8. The **price-menu** hash contains information about the available coffees, such as type and price. With **Expectations**, we can test whether elements belong to a collection:

```
(expect {:latte 0.5} (in price-menu))
```

We expect that, on the menu, we have latte and that its price is **0.5**.

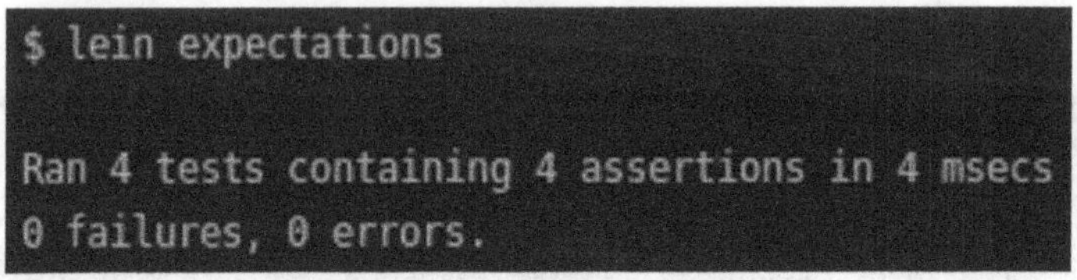

```
$ lein expectations

Ran 4 tests containing 4 assertions in 4 msecs
0 failures, 0 errors.
```

Figure 10.18: Testing whether latte belongs to the menu

As expected, on our menu, we have a latte. We now know two testing libraries in Clojure: **clojure.test** and Expectations. The third testing library that we will learn about is **Midje**.

Unit Testing with the Midje Library

Midje is a testing library in Clojure that encourages writing readable tests. **Midje** builds on top of the bottom-up testing provided by **clojure.test** and adds support for top-down testing. Bottom-up testing means that we write tests for a single function first. If this function is used by some other function, we write tests after finishing the implementation for the other function.

In the coffee-ordering application, we have the **load-orders** function:

```
(defn load-orders
    "Reads a sequence of orders in file at path."
    [file]
    (if (file-exists? file)
      (with-open [r (PushbackReader. (io/reader file))]
                 (binding [*read-eval* false]
                          (doall (take-while #(not= ::EOF %) (repeatedly #(read-one-
order r))))))
      []))
```

The **load-orders** function uses the **file-exists?** function. Functions in Clojure should not perform many things. It is good practice to have small functions focusing on single tasks. The **file-exist** function checks a file. The **load-orders** function loads orders. Because we cannot load orders from a file that does not exist, we need to use the **file-exist** function to check for a file with saved orders:

```
(defn file-exists? [location]
    (.exists (io/as-file location)))
```

With bottom-up testing, we have to write the implementation for **file-exists** first. After we have a working implementation of **file-exist**, then we can write the implementation for **load-orders**. This way of writing tests forces us to think about implementation details for all functions instead of focusing on a feature that we want to implement. Our original goal was to load data from a file but we are focusing now on checking whether a file exists.

With a top-down approach, we can write working tests for the main tested function without implementing functions that are used by the tested function. We state that we want to test the **load-orders** function and that it uses the file-exist function but we do not need to have a full implement of file-exist. We merely need to say that we will use this function. This allows us to focus on a feature that we want to test without worrying about implementing all sub-steps.

In order to use **Midje**, add it as a dependency (**[midje "1.9.4"] to project.clj**) to the **project.clj** file.

Exercise 10.03: Testing the Coffee Application with Midje

The aim of this exercise is to learn how to use the **Midje** library and write top-down tests. We will write tests for **calculate-coffee-price**. We will use a top-down approach to write tests for the load-orders function:

1. We will import the **Midje** namespace to the **utils** namespace:

```
(ns coffee-app.utils-test
    (:require [coffee-app.core :refer [price-menu]]
              [coffee-app.utils :refer :all]
              [midje.sweet :refer [=> fact provided unfinished]]))
```

After importing the **Midje** namespace, we are ready to use the **fact** macro from the **Midje** namespace.

2. **Midje** uses the **fact** macro, which states certain facts about a future version of our test. The macro takes a single argument on both sides of the **=>** symbol. The **fact** macro states that the result from the left-hand side is to be expected on the right-hand side of the symbol:

```
(fact (calculate-coffee-price price-menu :latte 3) => 3)
```

We wrote a test where we expect that the price for three cups of latte is **3**.

Midje supports autotesting in the REPL.

3. With autotesting, we do not need to run tests every time we make changes. The autotester will run the tests anytime it detects changes. In order to use autotesting in **Midje**, we enable autotesting in the REPL:

```
lein repl
```

4. After starting the REPL, we import the **Midje** namespace and enable the autotester:

```
user=> (use 'midje.repl)
user=> (autotest)
```

After starting the REPL, we imported the **Midje** namespace.

The second step was calling the **autotest** function. This function will run the tests automatically when our code changes.

After enabling autotesting, our tests are run thanks to the **autotest** function that
we used in the REPL:

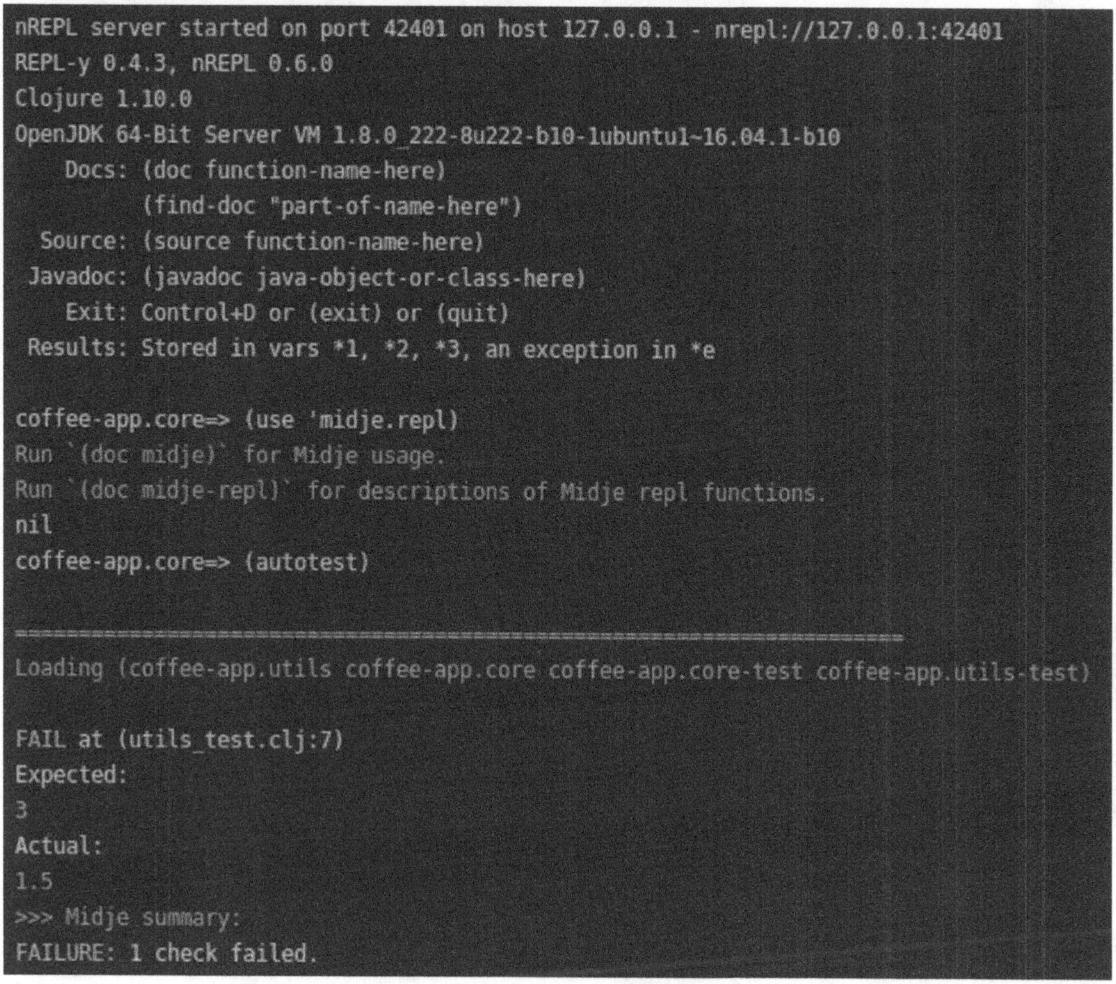

```
nREPL server started on port 42401 on host 127.0.0.1 - nrepl://127.0.0.1:42401
REPL-y 0.4.3, nREPL 0.6.0
Clojure 1.10.0
OpenJDK 64-Bit Server VM 1.8.0_222-8u222-b10-1ubuntu1~16.04.1-b10
    Docs: (doc function-name-here)
          (find-doc "part-of-name-here")
  Source: (source function-name-here)
 Javadoc: (javadoc java-object-or-class-here)
    Exit: Control+D or (exit) or (quit)
 Results: Stored in vars *1, *2, *3, an exception in *e

coffee-app.core=> (use 'midje.repl)
Run `(doc midje)` for Midje usage.
Run `(doc midje-repl)` for descriptions of Midje repl functions.
nil
coffee-app.core=> (autotest)


======================================================================================
Loading (coffee-app.utils coffee-app.core coffee-app.core-test coffee-app.utils-test)

FAIL at (utils_test.clj:7)
Expected:
3
Actual:
1.5
>>> Midje summary:
FAILURE: 1 check failed.
```

Figure 10.19: Executing the tests

5. **Midje** informs us that our tests failed. The price for three cups of latte is not **3** but
    1.5. When we change the implementation of the test, the autotest runs again:

```
(fact (calculate-coffee-price price-menu :latte 3) => 1.5)
```

The autotest runs as follows:

```
Loading (coffee-app.utils-test)
nil
All checks (1) succeeded.
[Completed at 15:37:51]
```

Figure 10.20: Running autotest after changing the implementation

This time, we are informed that our tests pass. We know now how to run autotests and how to write tests using **Midje**. It is time now to explore top-down testing in **Midje**.

6. In the **utils** namespace, we have the **display-bought-coffee-message** function, which displays a message about the number of coffee types bought. This function has a hardcoded currency symbol:

```
(defn display-bought-coffee-message [type number total]
    (str "Buying" number (name type) "coffees for total:€" total))
```

It would be nice to obtain the currency code from a utility function and not hardcode it. As some countries use the same currency, just as the euro is used in many European countries, it is a good idea to encapsulate the logic of getting the currency into a function.

7. We will keep the information about the currencies in a hash. Remember from *Chapter 1, Hello REPL!*, that a hash is a Clojure collection where we store data using keys and values:

```
(def ^:const currencies {:euro {:countries #{"France" "Spain"} :symbol "€"}
                             :dollar {:countries #{"USA"} :symbol "$"}})
```

This allows us to check the currencies that different countries use and currency symbols.

8. As we do not plan to write the implementation for the functions of currencies, we will provide a stub (substitution) for it.

    We saw an explanation of a stub at the beginning of this chapter:

```
(unfinished get-currency)
```

9. This tells **Midje** that we plan to use the **get-currency** function but we have not implemented it yet. We will test against the euro, so we will add the **helper** var:

```
(def test-currency :euro)
```

10. The function for displaying information about bought coffees will initially look like this:

```
(defn get-bought-coffee-message-with-currency [type number total currency]
    (format "Buying %d %s coffees for total: %s%s" number (name type) "€" total))
```

11. The test for the **get-bought-coffee-message-with-currency** function looks as follows:

```
(fact "Message about number of bought coffees should include currency symbol"
    (get-bought-coffee-message-with-currency :latte 3 1.5 :euro) => "Buying 3
latte coffees for total: €1.5"
    (provided
        (get-currency test-currency) => "€"))
```

In the test, we use the **Midje** **=>** symbol. We expect the result of calling **get-bought-coffee-message-with-currency** to equal the string message.

We use the provided function from **Midje** to stub call to the **get-currency** function. When the **Midje** test calls this function, it should return the euro symbol, €.

If we check autorun in the REPL, we will see the following:

```
Loading (coffee-app.utils-test)

FAIL at (utils_test.clj:21)
These calls were not made the right number of times:
    (get-currency test-currency) [expected at least once, actually never called]
nil
FAILURE: 1 check failed.  (But 2 succeeded.)
[Completed at 18:25:09]
```

Figure 10.21: Testing the get-bought-coffee-message-with-currency function using Midje

12. **Midje** informs us that one test failed. The **get-currency** function should have been called but was not called at all. We just wrote a test that compiled and ran. We did not get a compilation error. We focused on the logic for displaying a message and this part was a success. Once we have a test for **get-bought-coffee-message-with-currency**, it is time now to think about using **get-currency** to display messages:

```
(defn get-bought-coffee-message-with-currency [type number total currency]
    (format "Buying %d %s coffees for total: %s%s" number (name type)
(get-currency test-currency) total))
```

This implementation of the **get-bought-coffee-message-with-currency** function uses the **get-currency** function:

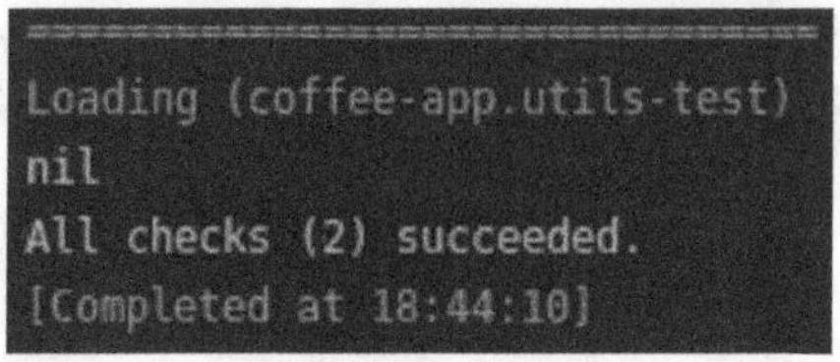

Figure 10.22: Testing again after using the get-currency function

When we check the autotest in the REPL, we see that all tests pass now.

In this exercise, we were able to write tests using the **Midje** library. This library allows us to write tests using a top-down approach where we think about testing the main function and any other functions called by it are stubbed first. This helps us to focus on the behavior of the main function under test without worrying about implementing all of the used functions.

While we wrote tests using various libraries, all tests are limited. When we tested **calculate-coffee-price**, we tested it a few times. If we could test it more times, we could be more confident that the **calculate-coffee-price** function is performing as expected. Writing a few tests can be quick but writing 100 or 200 tests takes time. Luckily, with property-based testing, we can generate lots of test scenarios very quickly.

Property-Based Testing

Property-based testing, also known as generative testing, describes properties that should be true for all valid test scenarios. A property-based test consists of a method for generating valid inputs (also known as a generator), and a function that takes a generated input. This function combines a generator with the function under test to decide whether the property holds for that particular input. With property-based testing, we automatically generate data across a wide search space to find unexpected problems.

Imagine a room-booking application. We should allow users to search for rooms suitable for families. Such rooms should have at least two beds. We could have a function that returns only those rooms that have at least two beds. With unit testing, we would need to write scenarios for the following:

- Zero beds
- One bed
- Two beds

- Three beds

- Four beds

- Five beds

- And other scenarios

If we wanted to test rooms with 20 beds, it would mean creating over 20 tests that are very similar. We would only change the number of beds. We can generalize such tests by describing what a family room is in general terms. As we said, a family room would have at least two beds. Property-based testing allows us to generalize inputs and generate them for us. Because inputs are generated automatically, we are not limited to manually typing tests and we could create 1,000 test scenarios easily. For our family room example, the input is a number of rooms. Testing would involve specifying that a room number is a number. With property-based tests, integer inputs would be automatically generated for us.

Clojure provides the **test.check** library for property-based testing. Property-based testing has two key concepts:

- **Generators**: A generator knows how to generate random values for a specific type. One generator could create strings, another generator could create numbers. The **test.check.generators** namespace has many built-in generators, as well as combinator functions for creating your own new generators from the built-in generators.

- **Properties**: Properties are characteristics of inputs. An input to any function can be described in general terms. In our family room example, the input is a number of rooms. So, the property is a number.

In the next exercise, we will write property-based tests for the coffee-ordering application.

Exercise 10.04: Using Property-Based Testing in the Coffee-Ordering Application

The aim of this exercise is to learn how to create tests using property-based testing. We will describe inputs for the **calculate-coffee-price** function and this will allow us to generate tests automatically.

In order to use the **test.check** library, we need to add **[org.clojure/test.check "0.10.0"]** as a dependency in the **project.clj** file:

1. Before we can use **test.check** in the utils namespace, we need to import the necessary namespaces:

```
(ns coffee-app.utils-test
    (:require    [clojure.test.check :as tc]
                 [clojure.test.check.generators :as gen]
                 [clojure.test.check.properties :as prop]
                 [clojure.test.check.clojure-test :refer [defspec]]
                 [coffee-app.core :refer [price-menu]]
                 [coffee-app.utils :refer :all]))
```

We import three **test.check** namespaces:

clojure.test.check.generators: Will generate inputs

clojure.test.check.properties: Will allow us to describe inputs in a general form

clojure.test.check.clojure-test: Will allow us to integrate with clojure.test

If we wanted to import these namespaces in the REPL, we would do the following:

```
(require '[clojure.test.check :as tc]
         '[clojure.test.check.generators :as gen]
         '[clojure.test.check.properties :as prop])
```

Once we have the necessary namespaces imported, we can look at how to generate inputs.

2. In order to generate inputs for tests, we will use generators. The **calculate-coffee-price** function takes a number of cups as an argument. A generator creating numbers such as **small-integer** is what we need:

```
(gen/sample gen/small-integer)
```

The **small-integer** function from the generators' namespace returns an integer between **-32768** and **32767**. The **sample** function returns a sample collection of the specified type. In the preceding example, we have a sample collection of small integers:

```
coffee-app.core=> (gen/sample gen/small-integer)
(0 1 -1 1 1 2 6 4 -5 -9)
```

Figure 10.23: Creating a sample of small integers

3. With generator combinators, we can obtain new generators. The **fmap** generator allows us to create a new generator by applying a function to the values created by another generator. The **fmap** generator works like the **map** function, which we know about from the first chapter. It allows us to map a function to a value created by the following generator. In this example, each integer created by the **small-integer** generator is incremented using the **inc** function:

```
(gen/sample (gen/fmap inc gen/small-integer))
```

This will return the following:

```
(1 2 1 -1 -3 4 -5 -1 7 -6)
```

We were able to increase the numbers generated by the **small-integer** generator by applying the **inc** function using the **fmap** combinator.

We now know how to create inputs using generators. It is time to learn how to describe the properties of inputs.

4. A property is an actual test – it combines a generator with a function you want to test, and checks that the function behaves as expected given the generated values.

Properties are created using the **for-all** macro from the **clojure.test.check. properties** namespace:

```
(defspec coffee-price-test-check 1000
         (prop/for-all [int gen/small-integer]
                       (= (float (* int (:latte price-menu))) (calculate-coffee-price
price-menu :latte int))))
```

The **defspec** macro allows you to run **test.check** tests like standard **clojure.test** tests. This allows us to extend test suits to include property-based testing together with standard unit tests. In the **for-all** macro, we use a small-integer generator to create a number of small integers. Our test passes when the number of coffee cups value created by the generator is multiplied by the price of the coffee. The result of this calculation should equal the result of running the **calculate-coffee-price** function. We intend to run the test 1,000 times. This is amazing that with three lines of code we were able to create 1,000 tests.

5. We can run **test.check** tests using Leiningen:

```
lein test
```

The output is as follows:

```
$ lein test

FAIL in (coffee-price-test-check) (utils_test.clj:9)
expected: {:result true}
  actual: {:shrunk {:total-nodes-visited 1, :depth 0, :pass? false, :result false, :result-data nil, :
time-shrinking-ms 1, :smallest [-1]}, :failed-after-ms 4, :num-tests 5, :seed 1574172768285, :fail [-2
], :result false, :result-data nil, :failing-size 4, :pass? false, :test-var "coffee-price-test-check"
}

Ran 2 tests containing 2 assertions.
1 failures, 0 errors.
Tests failed.
```

Figure 10.24:Testing test.check using Leiningen

After running tests with **lein test**, we will quickly get a result similar to the following:

```
{:num-tests 5,
 :seed 1528580863556,
 :fail [[-2]],
 :failed-after-ms 1,
 :result false,
 :result-data nil,
 :failing-size 4,
 :pass? false,
 :shrunk
 {:total-nodes-visited 5,
  :depth 1,
  :pass? false,
  :result false,
  :result-data nil,
  :time-shrinking-ms 1,
  :smallest [[-1]]}}
```

Our test failed. The original failing example **[-2]** (given at the **:fail** key) has been shrunk to **[-1]** (under **[:shrunk :smallest]**). The test failed because in the implementation of **calculate-coffee-price**, we return only absolute, non-negative values. The current implementation of **calculate-coffee-price** is as follows:

```
(defn calculate-coffee-price [coffees coffee-type number]
    (->
        (get coffees coffee-type)
        (* number)
        float
        Math/abs))
```

In the last line, we have the **Math/abs** function call. **calculate-coffee-price** should return only absolute numbers. Yet in our tests we allowed negative numbers to be generated. We need to use a different generator to match the expected result from the **calculate-coffee-price** function.

6. **test.check** provides a **nat** generator that can create natural numbers (non-negative integers).

   The test for **calculate-coffee-price** should be updated to the following:

```
(defspec coffee-price-test-check 1000
        (prop/for-all [int gen/nat]
                            (= (float (* int (:latte price-menu))) (calculate-coffee-price
price-menu :latte int))))
```

   When we run tests with this generator, the tests pass:

```
lein test
```

   The output is as follows:

```
$ lein test

lein test coffee-app.core-test

lein test coffee-app.utils-test
{:result true, :num-tests 1000, :seed 1571601121823, :time-elapsed-ms 57, :test-var "coffee-price-test-check"}

Ran 2 tests containing 2 assertions.
0 failures, 0 errors.
```

Figure 10.25: Using nat to create non-negative integers and running tests

We were able to test the **calculate-coffee-price** function 1,000 times. We generated an integer each time and used the integer as a number of cups. With **test.check**, we can truly check parameters against generated inputs. We have tested only the number of cups parameter. It is time to write generators and test all of the parameters.

7. In order to generate all of the remaining parameters for the **calculate-coffee-price** function, we will use some new generators. The code for creating all parameters is as follows:

```
(defspec coffee-price-test-check-all-params 1000
  (prop/for-all [int (gen/fmap inc gen/nat)
                 price-hash (gen/map gen/keyword
                                          (gen/double* {:min 0.1 :max 999
 :infinite? false :NaN? false})
                                  {:min-elements 2})]
                (let [coffee-tuple (first price-hash)]
                  (= (float (* int (second coffee-tuple)))
                     (calculate-coffee-price price-hash (first coffee-
tuple) int)))))
```

The coffee hash that stores the coffee menu contains information about the coffee type as a key and its value as a double:

```
{:latte 0.5 :mocha 0.4}
```

The **gen/map** generator allows us to create a hash. In the hash, we want to generate a keyword as a key and a double for a value. We limit the value to be between 0.1 and 999. We are only interested in numbers. We do not want to get an infinite value. With generators, we could create an infinite value if we wanted. We also do not want a NaN (not a number) to be generated. Lastly, our hash should have at least two elements – two tuples to be precise. Each tuple is a pair of a key and a value.

In the **let** block, we take the first tuple and assign it to **coffee-tuple**. This will help us to test and pass appropriate arguments to the **calculate-coffee-price** function.

We will run the tests again:

```
lein test
```

The output is as follows:

```
$ lein test

lein test coffee-app.core-test

lein test coffee-app.utils-test
{:result true, :num-tests 1000, :seed 1571691849346, :time-elapsed-ms 6937, :test-var "coffee-price-test-check-all-params"}
{:result true, :num-tests 1000, :seed 1571691856294, :time-elapsed-ms 20, :test-var "coffee-price-test-check"}

Ran 3 tests containing 3 assertions.
0 failures, 0 errors.
```

Figure 10.26: Running the tests after generating all parameters for the calculate-coffee-price function

We see that both **test.check** tests pass. With a few lines of code, we were able to test 2,000 scenarios. This is amazing.

So far, we have tested the **calculate-coffee-price** function. In the following activity, you will write tests for other functions from the coffee-ordering application.

Activity 10.01: Writing Tests for the Coffee-Ordering Application

In this activity, we will apply knowledge about unit testing to write a test suite. Many applications running in production are very complex. They have lots of features. Developers write unit tests in order to increase their trust in the application. The features coded should fulfill business needs. A well written and maintained test suite gives confidence to developers and people using such applications that the applications' features perform as expected.

The coffee-ordering application that we wrote in the previous chapter allowed us to display the coffee menu and order some coffees. In this chapter, we have learned about unit testing libraries in Clojure by testing the **calculate-coffee-price** function. In the coffee-ordering application, there are still functions that have not been tested.

In this activity, we will write unit tests for the following functions:

- **display-order**: Displays information about the order
- **file-exist**: Checks whether a given file exists
- **save-coffee-order**: Saves the coffee order to a file
- **load-orders**: Loads coffee orders from a file

These steps will help you complete the activity:

1. Import the testing namespace.

2. Create tests using the **clojure.test** library to display orders messages:

   Tests using **is** macro

   Tests using **are** macro

3. Create tests using the **clojure.test** library to test if the file exists or if the file does not exist

4. Create tests using the **clojure.test** library to save orders, load empty orders, load coffee orders.

5. Create tests using the **expectations** library to save data to file, save coffee orders, save coffee data, and load orders

6. Create tests using the **expectations** library to check whether the file exists.

7. Create tests using the **expectations** library to save and load orders.

8. Create tests using the **Midje** library to display the orders messages.

9. Create tests using the **Midje** library to check whether the file exists.

10. Create tests using the **Midje** library to load orders.

11. Create tests using **test.check** to display the orders messages:

    Import the **test.check** namespace

    Test the displayed orders

12. Create tests using **test.check** to check whether the file exists.

13. Create tests using **test.check** to load orders.

The output of the **clojure.test** and **test.check** tests will look as follows:

```
$ lein test

lein test coffee-app.utils-test

lein test coffee-app.utils-test-expectations

Ran 9 tests containing 26 assertions.
0 failures, 0 errors.

Ran 13 tests containing 13 assertions in 15 msecs
0 failures, 0 errors.
```

Figure 10.27: Expected output for the clojure.test and test.check tests

The output of the **expectations** tests will look as follows:

```
$ lein expectations

Ran 13 tests containing 13 assertions in 13 msecs
0 failures, 0 errors.
```

Figure 10.28: Expected output for the expectations test

The output of the **Midje** tests will look as follows:

```
$ lein repl
nREPL server started on port 35131 on host 127.0.0.1 - nrepl://127.0.0.1:35131
coffee-app.core=> (use 'midje.repl)
Run (doc midje) for Midje usage.
Run (doc midje-repl) for descriptions of Midje repl functions.
nil
coffee-app.core=> (autotest)

===================================================================
Loading (coffee-app.utils coffee-app.core coffee-app.utils-test-midje coffee-app.utils-test)
>>> Midje summary:
All checks (11) succeeded.

>>> Output from clojure.test tests:

Ran 9 tests containing 26 assertions.
0 failures, 0 errors.
[Completed at 19:33:21]
```

Figure 10.29: Output for the Midje tests

The output of the **test.check** tests will look as follows:

```
$ lein test

lein test coffee-app.utils-test

lein test coffee-app.utils-test-check
{:result true, :num-tests 1000, :seed 1571837004058, :time-elapsed-ms 262, :test-var "load-orders-test-check"}
{:result true, :num-tests 1000, :seed 1571837004324, :time-elapsed-ms 214, :test-var "display-order-test-check"}
{:result true, :num-tests 1000, :seed 1571837004539, :time-elapsed-ms 221, :test-var "file-exists-test-check"}

Ran 12 tests containing 29 assertions.
0 failures, 0 errors.

Ran 0 tests containing 0 assertions in 0 msecs
0 failures, 0 errors.
```

Figure 10.30: Output for the test.check tests

> **Note**
>
> The solution for this activity can be found on page 723.

We now know how to write unit tests in Clojure using four libraries. In the next section, we will look at testing in ClojureScript.

Testing in ClojureScript

In Clojure, we used the **clojure.test** library for testing. In ClojureScript, we have a port of **clojure.test** in the form of **cljs.test**. In **cljs.test**, we have functionality that we used when we wrote tests using the **clojure.test** library. We can use the **is** and **are** macros to write our tests. **cljs.test** provides facilities for asynchronous testing. Asynchronous testing is a type of testing that tests asynchronous code. We will see shortly why it is important that **cljs.test** allows us to test asynchronous code.

Synchronous code is what developers write most of the time, even without realizing this. In synchronous code, code is executed line by line. For example, the code defined in line 10 needs to finish executing before the code on line 11 can start executing. This is step-by-step execution. Asynchronous coding is a more advanced concept.

In asynchronous programming, executing code and completing the execution of code cannot happen in a line-by-line fashion. For example, we could schedule downloading a song on line 10 and then on line 11 we could have code to let the user know that downloading has finished. In synchronous code, we would have to wait for the download to finish before we can show information to the user or perform some other actions. This is not what we would really want. We would like to inform the user about the progress as we download the song. In asynchronous code, we would schedule downloading a song and start showing the progress bar before the song is downloaded.

In Java and Clojure, we would use threads to write asynchronous code. A thread is a process on a JVM that consumes little computer resources. One thread would handle downloading a song and the other would display the progress bar.

As we learned in *Chapter 1*, *Hello REPL*, ClojureScript runs on top of JavaScript. JavaScript provides a single-thread environment. This is in contrast to Java, which allows creating many threads. Writing code for one thread is simpler as we do not need to coordinate resource-sharing between many threads. ClojureScript applications requiring asynchronous code need to use some other facilities than threads.

JavaScript provides callbacks to manage writing asynchronous code. Callbacks are functions that we define to be run once certain conditions are met. In our downloading example, a callback would let us know when downloading is finished so we can inform the user.

ClojureScript provides the **core.async** library for working with asynchronous code. The **core.async** library has a number of functions and macros:

- **go**: Creates a block that marks the code as asynchronous. The result from the block is put on a channel.

- **<!**: Takes a value from a channel.

Why do we need a go block and channels?

Asynchronous code is by definition asynchronous. We do not know when we will get a return value from an asynchronous call. When we use channels for asynchronous calls, our code becomes simpler. This happens because return values are put on a channel. We do not need to manage this channel. **core.async** does this management for us. When we are ready, we just take value from this channel. Without explicit channel management, our code is shorter as the code can focus on simpler tasks that we program.

In the following exercise, we will see how to set up and use testing libraries in ClojureScript.

Exercise 10.05: Setting Up Testing in ClojureScript

The aim of this exercise is to learn how to set up testing libraries in ClojureScript and how to use those libraries. We will use **cljs.test** for testing.

In this exercise, we will create a number of folders and files. There are many ways to create folders and files. Readers are welcome to use any methods they are most comfortable with. The following steps will use the command line.

Command	Meaning
mkdir	Create a directory (make a directory)
touch	Create a file
tree	Show the content of a directory

Figure 10.31: Command and it's description

1. Create a project named **hello-test**, as follows:

```
mkdir hello-test
```

This will create a project where we will keep our code. Once we finish setting up, the project structure should look like the following screenshot. We can see the project structure using the **tree** command or your preferred way to check directories:

```
tree
```

The output is as follows:

```
├── package-lock.json
├── project.clj
├── README.md
├── src
│   └── hello_test
│       └── core.cljs
└── test
    └── hello_test
        ├── runner.cljs
        └── core_test.cljs
```

Figure 10.32: Project structure

2. Inside the source folder, we will keep our code:

```
mkdir -p src/hello_test
```

Executing this command will create the **src** and **hello_test** folders.

3. Create a source file. In the source file, we will keep our code:

```
touch src/hello_test/core.cljs
```

This command creates an empty core file.

4. Create a core namespace. Inside the **core.cljs** file, add a namespace:

```
(ns hello-test.core)
```

5. Inside the **core.cljs** file, put a function for adding numbers:

```
(defn adder [x y ]
      (+ x y))
```

6. Create a testing folder.

We will create a folder for our testing files:

```
mkdir -p test/hello_test
```

This command will create the **test** and **hello_test** folders.

7. Create the configuration.

We will keep the project configuration in the **project.clj** file. The file should look like the following:

```
(defproject hello-test "0.1.0-SNAPSHOT"
            :description "Testing in ClojureScript"
            :dependencies [[org.clojure/clojure "1.10.0"]
                           [org.clojure/clojurescript "1.10.520"]
                           [cljs-http "0.1.46"]
                           [org.clojure/test.check "0.10.0"]
                           [funcool/cuerdas "2.2.0"]]])
```

This is a standard **project.clj** file like we created in *Chapter 8, Namespaces, Libraries and Leiningen*. Inside the project.clj file, we have the **:dependencies** key where we put the libraries that we need for testing.

The **cljs-http** library will allow us to make HTTP calls. We will use **GET** requests to make asynchronous calls that will be tested.

The **cuerdas** library has many string utility functions. Some of the functions are as follows:

capital: Uppercases the first character of a string. The string "john" becomes "John".

Clean: Trims and replaces multiple spaces with a single space. The string " a   b " becomes "a b."

Human: Converts a string or keyword into a human-friendly string (lowercase and spaces). The string "DifficultToRead" becomes "difficult to read."

Reverse: Returns a reverted string. The string "**john**" becomes "**nhoj**."

We will write unit tests manipulating strings.

8. Add a test plugin dependency. We will use the **lein-doo** plugin to run ClojureScript tests. Add the following line in **project.clj**:

```
:plugins [[lein-doo "0.1.11"]]
```

The **lein-doo** plugin will be used to run ClojureScript tests. This plugin will autorun tests and display test results. We will run **lein-doo** against a web browser environment. **lein-doo** relies on the JavaScript **Karma** library to run tests in a JavaScript environment. Karma is a JavaScript tool that helps to run JavaScript tests. We need to install the necessary dependencies for **Karma**.

9. Install Karma. Karma is distributed using **Node Package Manager** (**NPM**). **npm** is an equivalent of Maven that we learned about in *Chapter 8, Namespaces, Libraries, and Leiningen*. Basically, it is a repository of projects. While Maven hosts Java projects, npm hosts JavaScript projects.

We will use npm to install Karma:

```
npm install karma karma-cljs-test –save-dev
```

With the **–save-dev** flag, we install the **karma** packages in the current directory. The purpose of using the **–save-dev** flag is to allow us to separate different test configurations between projects. One legacy project could still rely on an old version of Karma while a new project could use a newer version of Karma.

10. We will install the Chrome Karama launcher. Our tests will be run (launched) in the Chrome browser:

```
npm install karma-chrome-launcher –save-dev
```

The preceding command searches **npm** for **karma-chrome-launcher** projects. When **npm** finds this project, it will download the Chrome launcher and install it. With the **–save-dev** flag, we install the karma-chrome-launcher in the current directory.

11. Install the Karma command-line tool.

The final step to install the Karma libraries is to install command-line tools that allow executing Karma commands:

```
npm install -g karma-cli
```

We install Karma command-line tools globally as the ClojureScript plugin running the tests needs to access Karma commands.

12. We need to set the build configuration for the test task in the **project.clj** file:

```
:cljsbuild {:builds
                    {:test {:source-paths ["src" "test"]
                                            :compiler {:output-to "out/tests.js"
                                                        :output-dir "out"
                                                        :main hello-test.
  runner
                                                        :optimizations
  :none}}}}
```

ClojureScript build configurations are set under the **:cljsbuild** key in the project. clj file. We specify one **:browser-test** build. This build will access files from the **src** and **test** directories. The code will be compiled to the **out** directory to the **tests.js** file. The **:main** entry point for tests is the **hello-test.runner** namespace. For testing, we do not need any optimizations for compilation so we set the optimizations parameter to **:none**.

13. Create a core test file:

```
touch test/hello_test/core_test.cljs
```

This command creates the **core_test.cljs** file.

14. Import the testing namespaces.

The **core_test.cljs** file will contain the tests. We need to import the necessary namespaces:

```
(ns hello-test.core-test
  (:require [cljs.test :refer-macros [are async deftest is testing]]
            [clojure.test.check.generators :as gen]
            [clojure.test.check.properties :refer-macros [for-all]]
            [clojure.test.check.clojure-test :refer-macros [defspec]]
            [cuerdas.core :as str]
            [hello-test.core :refer [adder]]))
```

We import the testing macros from the **cljs.test** namespace. We will use them for testing our code. We also import the namespace from the **test.check** namespace. We will write property-based tests for our functions. The **cuerdas** namespace will be used to manipulate strings. Finally, we import test functions from the **hello-test.core** namespace.

15. Create a test runner.

   A test runner is a file that runs all the tests. We will test our code using the browser engine from Karma:

   ```
   touch test/hello_test/runner.cljs
   ```

16. Import the namespaces for the test runner.

   Inside **hello_test.runnerfile**, we import the core testing namespace and the **lein-doo** namespace:

   ```
   (ns hello-test.runner
     (:require [doo.runner :refer-macros [doo-tests]]
               [hello-test.core-test]))
   (doo-tests 'hello-test.core-test)
   ```

   We let **lein-doo** know that it needs to run tests from the **hello-test.core-test** namespace.

17. Once we install Karma and create all the files, the project structure should look like this:

   ```
   tree
   ```

   The output is as follows:

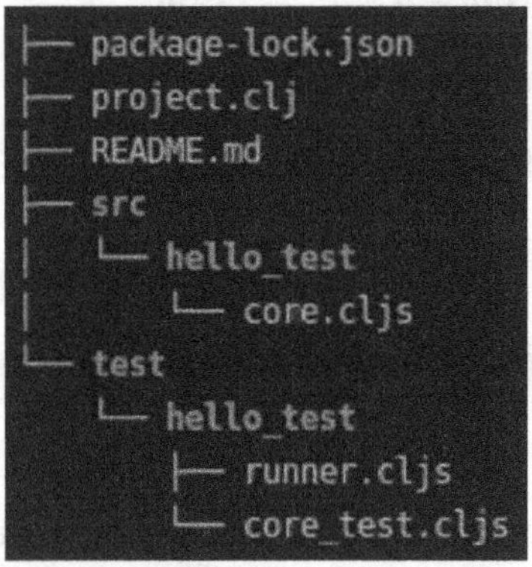

   ```
   ├── package-lock.json
   ├── project.clj
   ├── README.md
   ├── src
   │   └── hello_test
   │       └── core.cljs
   └── test
       └── hello_test
           ├── runner.cljs
           └── core_test.cljs
   ```

   Figure 10.33: Project structure after installing Karma and creating all the files

   We are ready to launch the test runner.

18. Launch the test runner:

```
lein doo chrome test
```

We call the **lein doo** plugin to run tests using the Chrome browser. Remember that JavaScript is a language that runs in browsers.

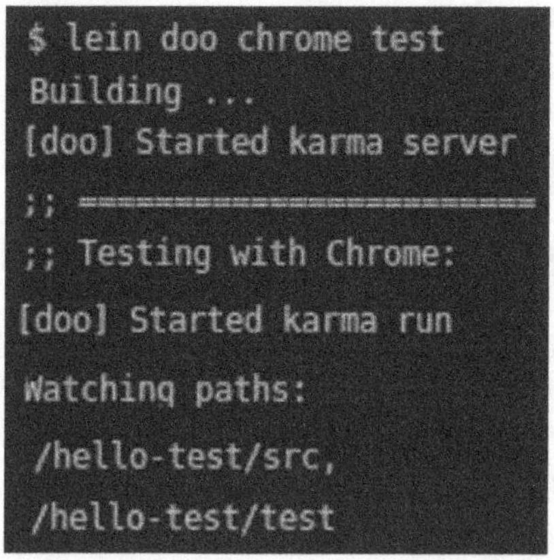

```
$ lein doo chrome test
Building ...
[doo] Started karma server
;; ============================
;; Testing with Chrome:
[doo] Started karma run
Watching paths:
 /hello-test/src,
 /hello-test/test
```

Figure 10.34: Launching the test runners

The **lein doo** plugin launched a Karma server for us. The server is watching the source and test directories for us. When we make changes in our ClojureScript files, the tests will run against our code.

In this exercise, we learned how to set up testing in ClojureScript. In the next exercise, we will learn how to write ClojureScript tests.

Exercise 10.06: Testing ClojureScript Code

In the previous exercise, we configured a project for ClojureScript testing. In this exercise, we will write ClojureScript tests. We will use functions from the **cuerdas** library that allow us to manipulate strings. We will also test the asynchronous ClojureScript code.

We will implement and test three functions:

- **profanity-filter**: It is common to filter certain words in chat applications or web forums. A profanity filter will remove words that we consider inappropriate.

- **prefix-remover**: This function will use string functions and will remove prefixes from words.

- **http-caller**: This function will make a HTTP call to a web address. This will help us test asynchronous code.

1. Import namespaces for the core file.

   Inside the **core.cljs** file, add the necessary namespaces:

   ```
   (ns hello-test.core
     (:require [cuerdas.core :as str]))
   ```

   We import the **cuerdas** namespace for string manipulation.

2. Create a profanity filter. The first function that we will write in the **hello_test. core.cljs** file is a profanity filter:

   ```
   (defn profanity-filter [string]
          (if (str/includes? string "bad")
            (str/replace string "bad" "great")
            string))
   ```

   In this function, we test whether a passed string contains the word **bad**. If it does, we replace it with the word **great**.

3. Import the test namespaces.

   Inside the **hello_test.core_test.cljs** file, import the necessary test namespaces:

   ```
   (ns hello-test.core-test
     (:require [cljs.test :refer-macros [are async deftest is testing]]
               [cuerdas.core :as str]
               [hello-test.core :refer [profanity-filter]]))
   ```

4. Write a test for the **profanity-filter** functions.

   Inside the **hello_test.core_test.cljs** file, add a test for the profanity filter function:

   ```
   (deftest profanity-filter-test
          (testing "Filter replaced bad word"
                  (is (= "Clojure is great" (profanity-filter "Clojure is bad"))))
          (testing "Filter does not replace good words"
                  (are [string result] (= result (profanity-filter string))
                       "Clojure is great" "Clojure is great"
                       "Clojure is brilliant" "Clojure is brilliant")))
   ```

The tests look similar to the ones we wrote using the **clojure.test** library. We use **is** and **are** macros to set testing scenarios. We are ready to run the tests.

5. In order to run the tests, we call the **lein doo** task from the command line. If you have a **lein doo** running from the previous exercise, it will watch file changes and run the tests for us:

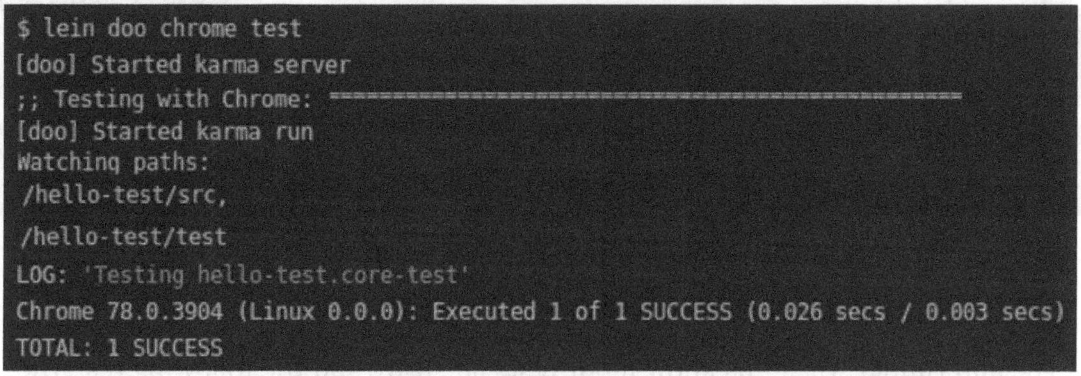

```
$ lein doo chrome test
[doo] Started karma server
;; Testing with Chrome: =========================================
[doo] Started karma run
Watching paths:
/hello-test/src,
/hello-test/test
LOG: 'Testing hello-test.core-test'
Chrome 78.0.3904 (Linux 0.0.0): Executed 1 of 1 SUCCESS (0.026 secs / 0.003 secs)
TOTAL: 1 SUCCESS
```

Figure 10.35: Calling the lein doo task from the command line

The profanity filter test was run. The output informs us that one test was successful.

6. If you do not have **lein doo** running, you need to start **lein doo**:

```
lein doo chrome test
```

Starting the **lein doo** task will start watching our ClojureScript files for changes:

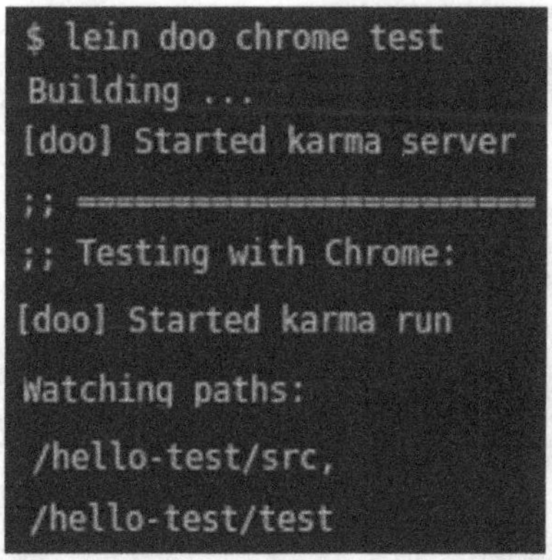

```
$ lein doo chrome test
Building ...
[doo] Started karma server

;; =======================
;; Testing with Chrome:
[doo] Started karma run

Watching paths:
/hello-test/src,
/hello-test/test
```

Figure 10.36: Starting the lein doo task

Once the **lein doo** is watching the changes in our file, we are ready. We are informed that the **karma** server has been started. The autorunner is watching for changes in the **src** and **test** directories. Any changes in these directories will result in **lein doo** running the tests again.

Go to **hello_test.core_test.cljs**, save the file, and watch the tests being executed:

```
$ lein doo chrome test
[doo] Started karma server
;; Testing with Chrome: =================================================
[doo] Started karma run
Watching paths:
/hello-test/src,
/hello-test/test
LOG: 'Testing hello-test.core-test'
Chrome 78.0.3904 (Linux 0.0.0): Executed 1 of 1 SUCCESS (0.026 secs / 0.003 secs)
TOTAL: 1 SUCCESS
```

Figure 10.37: Executing the tests

We are informed that one test has been successfully executed.

7. The autorunner will let us know if our tests fail. If we add the following test, the autorunner informs us that one test failed:

```
(deftest capitalize-test-is
        (testing "Test capitalize? function using is macro"
                (is (= "katy" (str/capitalize "katy")))
                (is (= "John" (str/capital "john")))
                (is (= "Mike" (str/capitalize "mike")))))
```

The test fails as follows:

```
LOG: 'Testing hello-test.core-test'
Chrome 78.0.3904 (Linux 0.0.0) hello-test.core-test capitalize-test-is FAILED
        FAIL in   (capitalize-test-is) (cljs/test.js:433:14)
        "Test capitalize? function using is macro"
        expected: (=
                        "katy"
                        (str/capitalize "katy"))
          actual: (=
                        "katy"
                        "Katy")
            diff: - "katy"
                  + "Katy"

Chrome 78.0.3904 (Linux 0.0.0): Executed 2 of 2 (1 FAILED) (0.044 secs / 0.007 secs)
TOTAL: 1 FAILED, 1 SUCCESS
```

Figure 10.38: The autorunner informs us when a test fails

We see that we expected lowercase **katy** but the **capitalize** function returned **Katy** instead.

We will fix the test as follows:

```
(is (= "Katy" (str/capitalize "katy")))
```

In the test, we pass the lowercase string "**katy**" to the capitalize function from the **cuerdas** library. The **capitalize** function will uppercase the first letter, "k," and return a new string, "**Katy**". This new string is compared to the string **Katy** in a test.

As both strings, **Katy** and **Katy**, are equal, the tests will pass.

The autorunner tells us that all of the tests passed now:

```
LOG: 'Testing hello-test.core-test'
Chrome 78.0.3904 (Linux 0.0.0): Executed 2 of 2 SUCCESS (0.012 secs / 0.002 secs)
TOTAL: 2 SUCCESS
```

Figure 10.39: All of the tests passed after we fixed the string case

8. We can check for errors being thrown by our code:

```
(deftest error-thrown-test
        (testing "Catching errors in ClojureScript"
                (is (thrown? js/Error (assoc ["dog" "cat" "parrot"] 4 "apple")))))
```

In the preceding code, we wanted to insert an apple in the fourth index, which does not exist as we have only three elements. Remember that, in Clojure, the first index is zero so the third element in a list has an index of two. Trying to add an element at index 4 generates an error in ClojureScript. In our test, we caught this error:

```
LOG: 'Testing hello-test.core-test'
Chrome 78.0.3904 (Linux 0.0.0): Executed 3 of 3 SUCCESS (0.018 secs / 0.005 secs)
TOTAL: 3 SUCCESS
```

Figure 10.40: The third test passes because we caught the error in our code

The autorunner tests our code and the third test passed.

9. In ClojureScript, we can make requests to websites. These requests are asynchronous. We will import ClojureScript namespaces that help us to make asynchronous calls:

```
(ns hello-test.core
  (:require-macros [cljs.core.async.macros :refer [go]])
  (:require [cljs.core.async :refer [<!]]
            [cljs-http.client :as http]))
```

The **cljs-http.client** namespace will allow us to make HTTP calls. Functions from the **core.async** namespace will manage asynchronous calls for us.

10. Our HTTP function will take three arguments, a website address, HTTP parameters, and a callback function to call after we finish sending the request to the website address:

```
(defn http-get [url params callback]
      (go (let [response (<! (http/get url params))]
            (callback response))))
```

11. We have our function making asynchronous calls. We need to import this function:

```
(ns hello-test.core-test
  (:require [hello-test.core :refer [http-get]]))
```

12. HTTP calls happen asynchronously in ClojureScript. A **GET** request will run a callback function when the request finishes. This is ideal for testing asynchronous code:

```
(deftest http-get-test
        (async done
                (http-get "https://api.github.com/users" {:with-credentials? false
                                                           :query-
params       {"since" 135}}
                        (fn [response]
                            (is (= 200 (:status response)))
                            (done)))))
```

The **async** macro allows us to write an asynchronous block of code for testing. In our block, we make a GET request to GitHub API to access the list of current public users. The **http-get** function takes a callback function as the last parameter. In the callback, we check the response. A successful response will have the status **200**.

The final function call in the callback is **done**. **done** is a function that is invoked when we are ready to relinquish control and allow the next test to run:

```
LOG: 'Testing hello-test.core-test'
Chrome 78.0.3904 (Linux 0.0.0): Executed 4 of 4 SUCCESS (0.473 secs / 0.46 secs)
TOTAL: 4 SUCCESS
```

Figure 10.41: The fourth test is passed

Our request was successful and the fourth test passed.

13. Import the namespaces for property-based testing. ClojureScript allows us to use property-based testing to check our functions:

```
(ns hello-test.core-test
  (:require [clojure.test.check.generators :as gen]
            [clojure.test.check.properties :refer-macros [for-all]]
            [clojure.test.check.clojure-test :refer-macros [defspec]]))
```

We already know about generators and the properties used for property-based testing. With generators, we can create various types of function inputs such as numbers or strings. Properties allow us to describe the characteristics of the inputs.

The **defspec** macro allows us to write tests that can be run with the **clsj.test** library.

14. With property-based tests, we can check 1,000 scenarios against our profanity filter. The structure of property-based tests in ClojureScript is the same as in Clojure:

```
(defspec simple-test-check 1000
         (for-all [some-string gen/string-ascii]
                  (= (str/replace some-string "bad" "great") (profanity-filter some-
string))))
```

With the **for-all** macro, we specify what properties our function parameters should have. For the profanity filter, we generate ASCII strings. ASCII, abbreviated from American Standard Code for Information Interchange, is a character encoding standard for electronic communication:

```
LOG: 'Testing hello-test.core-test'
LOG: '{:result true, :num-tests 1000, :seed 1572125478055, :time-elapsed-ms 914, :test-var "simple-test-check"}'
Chrome 78.0.3904 (Linux 0.0.0): Executed 5 of 5 SUCCESS (1.439 secs / 1.419 secs)
TOTAL: 5 SUCCESS
```

Figure 10.42: The fifth test is passed

Our fifth test passed. Furthermore, the **test.check** informed us that 1,000 test scenarios were executed.

In this exercise, we have seen how to set up testing in ClojureScript. We wrote functions and tested them using the **cljs.test** and **test.check** libraries. In the next section, we will see how to integrate tests with existing projects.

Testing ClojureScript Applications with Figwheel

In *Chapter 9, Host Platform Interoperability with Java and JavaScript*, we learned about Figwheel. Figwheel allows us to create ClojureScript applications. Most developers use Figwheel because it provides hot-code reloading. It means that any changes in our code are recompiled and the application running in the web browser is updated.

In the previous exercise, we learned how to add testing to a ClojureScript project. Figwheel comes with a testing configuration. Any Figwheel application is ready to add tests to after creating the application. Because the testing configuration is included in each project, developers save time. Developers do not need to install external tools or create the configuration; they can start writing tests straight away.

In *Chapter 9, Host Platform Interoperability with Java and JavaScript*, we talked about Figwheel projects in detail. As a reminder, in Figwheel, we use two concepts:

- Reactive components

- Application state management

For reactive components – HTML elements that react to user actions – we will use the Rum library. The state of the application will be kept inside an atom. Concurrency is a topic covered in *Chapter 12, Concurrency*. For our purposes, an atom is a data structure like a collection. We learned about collections in *Chapter 1, Hello REPL!*. The main difference between collections and atoms is that we can alter the value of an atom, while collections are immutable.

Exercise 10.07: Tests in Figwheel Applications

In the previous section, we learned that Figwheel supports testing ClojureScript applications. We revised the benefits of using Figwheel to create ClojureScript applications. We also reminded ourselves about important concepts in Figwheel applications, such as reactive components and application state management.

In this exercise, we will investigate how Figwheel configures projects to support testing in ClojureScript. Figwheel aims to support developers creating applications. Figwheel sets up default testing configuration for us. In *Exercise 10.5, Setting Up Testing in ClojureScript*, we saw how much setup is needed to configure testing in ClojureScript. With Figwheel, we do not need to write this configuration; we can focus on writing our code.

In order to write tests in Figwheel, we need to understand how Figwheel sets up the default testing configuration:

1. Create a Figwheel application:

```
lein new figwheel-main test-app -- --rum
```

We created a new Figwheel project using Rum.

2. Test the configuration in the project.clj file.

Figwheel puts some testing configuration in the **project.clj** file:

```
:aliases {"fig:test"  ["run" "-m" "figwheel.main" "-co" "test.cljs.edn" "-m" "test-
app.test-runner"]}
```

Inside the **project.clj** file, Figwheel defines aliases to help run tasks on the command line. An alias is a shortcut for commands that we use often. Using aliases saves developers typing. Figwheel defines the **fig:test** task.

This task runs on a command line with a number of parameters:

-m: Search a file for the main function. Remember from *Chapter 8, Namespaces, Libraries, and Leiningen*, that the main function in Leiningen projects is an entry point in an application. We start applications in main functions.

-co: Load options from a given file.

3. Test the configuration in the **test.cljs.edn** file. Inside the **test.cljs.edn** file, we have the testing configuration:

```
{
  ;; use an alternative landing page for the tests so that we don't launch the
application
  :open-url "http://[[server-hostname]]:[[server-port]]/test.html"
}
{:main test-app.test-runner}
```

When the Figwheel application is run, it launches a web page. Figwheel provides two web pages. There is one web page for the actual application that we are developing. Also, there is a different web page for testing.

Figwheel also provides a main method inside the **test-app.test-runner** namespace.

4. Test the runner namespace. Inside the **test/test_app/test_runner.cljs** file, we have code for running ClojureScript tests:

```
(ns test-app.test-runner
  (:require
    ;; require all the namespaces that you want to test
    [test-app.core-test]
    [figwheel.main.testing :refer [run-tests-async]]))

(defn -main [& args]
  (run-tests-async 5000))
```

First, in the file, we require the namespaces that we want to test. Initially, the only namespace to test is a **test-app.core-test** namespace created by default by Leiningen. If we add more files for testing, we need to import namespaces in those files. The second namespace that is required is a Figwheel namespace with a utility function.

Second, we have the **-main** function. This function is called by Leiningen to run tests. Figwheel provides a **run-tests-async** function. This means that tests are run in an asynchronous manner. This allows the tests to run faster than if run in a synchronous manner. They run faster because the tests do not need to wait for other tests to finish before they can be started.

5. Inside the **test/test_app/core_test.cljs** file, we have autogenerated tests by Figwheel:

```
(ns test-app.core-test
    (:require
    [cljs.test :refer-macros [deftest is testing]]
    [test-app.core :refer [multiply]]))
```

Figwheel first requires the **cljs.test** namespace with macros that we are familiar with. The tests will use macros such as **deftest**, **is**, and **testing**.

The second namespace required is the **test-app.core** namespace. This namespace, from the source directory, contains the implementation for a **multiply** function.

6. Inside the **core_test.cljs** file, we have two autogenerated tests:

```
(deftest multiply-test
  (is (= (* 1 2) (multiply 1 2))))

(deftest multiply-test-2
  (is (= (* 75 10) (multiply 10 75))))
```

Both tests use the familiar **is** macro. With the **is** macro, we test whether calling the **multiply** function is equal to the expected output. Multiplying 1 by 2 should equal calling the **multiply** function with two arguments: 1 and 2.

7. Run the default tests. When we create a new application based on Figwheel, the application has some default tests. Straight after creating the application, we can run the default tests:

```
lein fig:test
```

The output is as follows:

```
$ lein fig:test
2019-11-19 23:12:29.505:INFO::main: Logging initialized @5506ms to org.eclipse.jetty.util.log.StdErrLog
[Figwheel] Validating figwheel-main.edn
[Figwheel] figwheel-main.edn is valid \(ツ)/
[Figwheel] Compiling build test to "resources/public/cljs-out/test-main.js"
[Figwheel] Successfully compiled build test to "resources/public/cljs-out/test-main.js" in 0.959 seconds.
Opening URL http://localhost:9500/test.html

Testing test-app.core-test

Ran 2 tests containing 2 assertions.
0 failures, 0 errors.
:figwheel.main.testing/success
```

Figure 10.43 Using the fig:test command to run tests

We use Leiningen to launch Figwheel. In order to run tests, we use the `fig:test` command-line task. This task will read the Figwheel configuration from the `project.clj` file and run tests according to the configuration.

We saw two default tests in the previous steps. Both tests pass and we are informed about the tests passing.

8. The selling point of Figwheel is hot-code reloading. In order to get an interactive development environment, run the following:

```
lein fig:build
```

This will launch Figwheel, which autocompiles code for us:

```
$ lein fig:build
2019-11-20 00:09:31.869:INFO::main: Logging initialized @4965ms to org.eclipse.jetty.util.log.StdErrLog
[Figwheel] Validating figwheel-main.edn
[Figwheel] figwheel-main.edn is valid \(ツ)/
[Figwheel] Compiling build dev to "resources/public/cljs-out/dev-main.js"
[Figwheel] Successfully compiled build dev to "resources/public/cljs-out/dev-main.js" in 13.849 seconds.
[Figwheel] Outputting main file: resources/public/cljs-out/dev-main-auto-testing.js
[Figwheel] Watching paths: ("test" "src") to compile build - dev
```

Figure 10.44: Figwheel validates the configuration on the figwheel-main.edn file

Figwheel reads and validates the configuration on the `figwheel-main.edn` file. Then, **if** compiles our source code to the `dev-main.js` file. The test code is compiled to the `dev-auto-testing.js` file.

9. With Figwheel, we can see a summary of our tests in a browser. Go to `http://localhost:9500/figwheel-extra-main/auto-testing`:

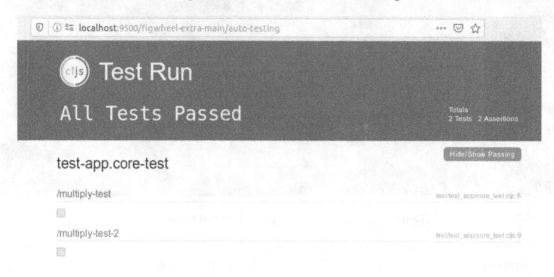

Figure 10.45: All tests passed

Figwheel informs us that all tests have passed. We have a summary displaying which tests were run.

In this exercise, we learned how Figwheel supports testing in ClojureScript. We saw the default testing configuration provided by Figwheel. In the next exercise, we will see how to add tests to a Figwheel application.

Exercise 10.08: Testing a ClojureScript Application

The aim of this exercise is to learn how to test ClojureScript applications. Often, front-end code is complex. The state of an application in the browser changes. User interactions result in many unpredictable scenarios. Having ClojureScript tests for frontend applications helps us to catch bugs early.

In the previous chapter, we learned about the Figwheel application template. It is a very common template for writing frontend applications in ClojureScript. We will create an application that will react to user actions. When a user clicks on the action button, we will increment a counter.

Initially, the count will be zero:

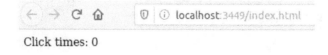

Figure 10.46: The initial number of clicks is zero

After six clicks the count will change:

Click times: 6

Figure 10.47: The count changes to six

We know what our application will do. We are ready to implement the functionality now.

1. Create a Figwheel application:

```
lein new figwheel-main test-app -- --rum
```

   We created a new Figwheel project using Rum.

2. In the previous section, we learned that Figwheel supports testing. After creating a project, we are already set to run tests:

```
lein fig:test
```

   The output is as follows:

```
$ lein fig:test
2019-11-19 23:12:29.505:INFO::main: Logging initialized @5506ms to org.eclipse.jetty.util.log.StdErrLog
[Figwheel] Validating figwheel-main.edn
[Figwheel] figwheel-main.edn is valid \(ツ )/
[Figwheel] Compiling build test to "resources/public/cljs-out/test-main.js"
[Figwheel] Successfully compiled build test to "resources/public/cljs-out/test-main.js" in 0.959 seconds.
Opening URL http://localhost:9500/test.html

Testing test-app.core-test

Ran 2 tests containing 2 assertions.
0 failures, 0 errors.
:figwheel.main.testing/success
```

Figure 10.48: Two tests containing two assertions are passed

   Figwheel compiles our code and runs the tests. We test the tet-app.core-test namespace. The two tests pass.

3. We will implement a function to handle user clicks inside the **src/test_app/core.cljs** file:

```
(ns test-app.core)
(defn handle-click [state]
      (swap! state update-in [:counter] inc))
```

The **handle-click** function has one parameter. The parameter is the current application state. We increment the value stored in the atom under the :**counter** key.

4. We will store the state application in an atom in the **core.cljs** file:

```
(ns test-app.core)
(defonce state (atom {:counter 0}))
```

The atom is a hash with the :**counter** key. The initial value of the key is zero.

5. Create the counter component.

We create a Rum component that will display the number of mouse clicks:

```
(rum/defc counter [number]
          [:div {:on-click #(handle-click state)}
           (str "Click times: " number)])
```

The component displays the number of clicks, which is passed as an argument. Inside the component, we use the **handle-click** function to respond to :**on-click** actions. Whenever a user clicks on the component, the **handle-click** function is called.

6. Create a page component. We will put the **counter** component inside the **page-content** component. It is good practice to have a main component on the page where we will put all our components. In our example, we have one component:

```
(rum/defc page-content < rum/reactive []
          [:div {}
           (counter (:counter (rum/react state)))])
```

The container uses Rum's **reactive** directive. This directive instructs Rum to handle the component in a special manner. Reactive components will **react** to changes to the application state. Whenever there is a change to the application state, the component will be updated and redisplayed in the browser using the new application state. We learned about reactive components in *Chapter 9, Host Platform Interoperability with Java and JavaScript*, and refreshed our memory in the section preceding this exercise.

7. Finally, we need to attach our **page-component** to a web page. As we did in *Chapter 9, Host Platform Interoperability with Java and JavaScript*, we use the **mount** method from Rum:

```
(defn mount [el]
  (rum/mount (page-content) el))
```

The **page-content** component is mounted to the web page.

8. Run the application.

    We will run our Figwheel application:

    ```
    lein fig:build
    ```

    This command will launch Figwheel for us:

    ```
    $ lein fig:build
    2019-11-20 00:09:31.869:INFO::main: Logging initialized @4965ms to org.eclipse.jetty.util.log.StdErrLog
    [Figwheel] Validating figwheel-main.edn
    [Figwheel] figwheel-main.edn is valid \(ツ)/
    [Figwheel] Compiling build dev to "resources/public/cljs-out/dev-main.js"
    [Figwheel] Successfully compiled build dev to "resources/public/cljs-out/dev-main.js" in 13.849 seconds.
    [Figwheel] Outputting main file: resources/public/cljs-out/dev-main-auto-testing.js
    [Figwheel] Watching paths: ("test" "src") to compile build - dev
    ```

    Figure 10.49: Launching the Figwheel

    Figwheel successfully launches our application. We can see the page in the browser. It will look as follows:

    Click times: 0

    Figure 10.50: The number of clicks at the start of the application

    When the application starts, the number of clicks is zero. After six clicks, the state is updated and a new value is displayed on the page:

    Click times: 6

    Figure 10.51: The updated number of clicks

    We see that the component on the page reacts to our actions. It is time to write tests for the **handle-click** function.

9. We will create fixtures for our tests. A test fixture is a fixed state of a set of objects used as a baseline for running tests. The purpose of a test fixture is to ensure that there is a well-known and fixed environment in which tests are run so that results are repeatable.

Because we will manipulate the state of an application, we want the state to be the same every time we run our tests. We do not want previous tests to influence subsequent tests.

The **handle-click** function takes a state atom as an argument. In order to test the handle-click function, we need a state atom. **cljs.test** provides the **use-fixtures** macro, which allows us to preset tests to the required state before tests are run. This is a good place to create a state atom for further manipulation.

We will put our tests inside the **core_test.cljs** file:

```
(ns test-app.core-test
    (:require
    [cljs.test :refer-macros [are deftest is testing use-fixtures]]
    [test-app.core :refer [handle-click multiply]]))


(use-fixtures :each {:before (fn [] (def app-state (atom {:counter 0})))
                                 :after (fn [] (reset! app-state nil))})
```

With the **:each** keyword, we specify that we want the fixtures to be run for each test. This way, we can set the state for each test. An alternative would be to use the **:only** keyword, which would set up fixtures only once per test.

In the fixtures, we have two keys:

:before: Runs a function before the test is executed

:after: Runs a function after the test is executed

In **:before** and **:after**, we set the state of the application's atom. Before each test, we set **:counter** to zero. After each test, we reset the application state to **nil**. Setting the counter to zero resets it. This way, every time we run a new test, the counter is started from zero. Previous tests will not influence subsequent tests.

After setting up fixtures, we are ready to launch the test runner.

10. Test the **handle-click** function.

We will test handling multiple clicks:

```
(deftest handle-click-test-multiple
        (testing "Handle multiple clicks"
                (are [result] (= result (handle-click app-state))
                        {:counter 1}
                        {:counter 2}
                        {:counter 3})))
```

We use the **are** macro to simplify testing. We compare the expected result to the return value of calling the **handle-click** function. Calling **handle-click** three times should increase the counter to three.

11. We will run the tests now:

```
lein fig:test
```

The output is as follows:

```
$ lein fig:test
2019-11-20 11:22:23.416:INFO::main: Logging initialized @5747ms to org.eclipse.jetty.util.log.StdErrLog
[Figwheel] Validating figwheel-main.edn
[Figwheel] figwheel-main.edn is valid \(ツ)/
[Figwheel] Compiling build test to "resources/public/cljs-out/test-main.js"
[Figwheel] Successfully compiled build test to "resources/public/cljs-out/test-main.js" in 3.102 seconds.
Opening URL http://localhost:9500/test.html

Testing test-app.core-test

Ran 3 tests containing 5 assertions.
0 failures, 0 errors.
:figwheel.main.testing/success
```

Figure 10.52: Running the tests

As we see in the summary, the tests pass. The **handle-click** test used **app-state**, which we set up using the **use-fixtures** macro. Before each test, the fixtures created an application state. After each test, the fixtures should reset the state to zero. We will write a new test to check whether the application state is reset.

12. In the following test, we will test a single click:

```
(deftest handle-click-test-one
        (testing "Handle one click"
                (is (= {:counter 1} (handle-click app-state))))))
```

In this test, we use the **is** macro to test a single click.

13. We will run the tests again:

```
lein fig:test
```

The output is as follows:

```
$ lein fig:test
2019-11-20 11:22:23.416:INFO::main: Logging initialized @5747ms to org.eclipse.jetty.util.log.StdErrLog
[Figwheel] Validating figwheel-main.edn
[Figwheel] figwheel-main.edn is valid \(ツ)/
[Figwheel] Compiling build test to "resources/public/cljs-out/test-main.js"
[Figwheel] Successfully compiled build test to "resources/public/cljs-out/test-main.js" in 3.102 seconds.
Opening URL http://localhost:9500/test.html

Testing test-app.core-test

Ran 4 tests containing 6 assertions.
0 failures, 0 errors.
:figwheel.main.testing/success
```

Figure 10.53: Running the tests again

Running the new test tells us that the state has been reset. We see that our test passed as the application state has been reset successfully.

In this exercise, we learned how to integrate testing into ClojureScript applications. We created a project using the Figwheel template. This template allowed us to create a web application. In the application, we added user interaction. The application counted the number of clicks. We wrote tests to make sure that our functions perform as expected.

You are ready to start writing web applications and adding tests to them. In the following activity, you will put your new knowledge to use.

Activity 10.02: Support Desk Application with Tests

The aim of this activity is to add a testing suite to a web application. Many applications require complex functionality and many features. While manual testing can catch many bugs, it is time-consuming and requires many testers. With automated testing, checking applications are faster and more features can be tested. ClojureScript provides tools to help with unit testing.

In the previous chapter, we wrote a support desk application that allowed us to manage issues raised with the help desk (https://packt.live/2NTTJpn). The application allows you to sort issues and resolve them when they are done. By sorting the issues, we can raise the priority of the issue. In this activity, we will add unit tests using **clsj.test** and **test.check** for property-based testing.

You will write tests for the following:

- A function displaying the sort message status
- A function filtering the list of issues by priority

- A function sorting the list of issues
- A function deleting an item from the issues list

These steps will help you complete the activity:

1. Add the testing dependencies to the **project.clj** file.
2. Import the namespaces to the **core_test.cljs** file.
3. Create fixtures with issues in the application state.
4. Write tests for the sort message function, **cljs.test**.
5. Write tests for the sort message function using **test.check**.
6. Write tests to filter issues by priority function using **cljs.test**.
7. Write tests to sort the issues list using **cljs.test**.
8. Write tests to delete issues from the list using **cljs.test**.
9. Write tests to handle the sort function using **cljs.test**.

The initial issues list will look as follows:

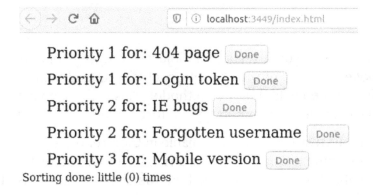

Figure 10.54: List of initial issues

The issues list after sorting will look as follows:

Figure 10.55: List after sorting

When the tests are run, the output should look like the following:

```
$ lein fig:test
2019-11-20 12:12:55.301:INFO::main: Logging initialized @5773ms to org.eclipse.jetty.util.log.StdErrLog
[Figwheel] Validating figwheel-main.edn
[Figwheel] figwheel-main.edn is valid \(ツ )/
[Figwheel] Compiling build test to "resources/public/cljs-out/test-main.js"
[Figwheel] Successfully compiled build test to "resources/public/cljs-out/test-main.js" in 4.577 seconds.
Opening URL http://localhost:9500/test.html

Testing support-desk.utils-test
{:result true, :num-tests 10, :seed 1574248386648, :time-elapsed-ms 18, :test-var "get-sort-message-test-check"}

Ran 6 tests containing 20 assertions.
0 failures, 0 errors.
:figwheel.main.testing/success
```

Figure 10.56: Output after running the tests

> **Note**
>
> The solution for this activity can be found on page 730

Summary

In this chapter, we learned about testing in Clojure. First, we explored why testing is important. We looked at some of the benefits, such as reduced maintenance costs and bug fixing. We also learned what testing methodologies are available. We focused on unit testing as this is the most common type of test written by developers.

Next, we explored four testing libraries available in Clojure. We started with the standard clojure.test library, which provides a rich set of testing features. The second library we learned about was Expectations. It allows us to write concise tests as it focuses on readability.

The `Midje` library allowed us to explore top-down test-driven development (TDD). We created a test for the main function and stubs for functions that would be implemented in the future. TDD allows us to focus on testing functions' features without worrying about implementing all of the subfunctions used.

The last library used was `test.check`, which introduced us to property-based testing. With property-based tests, we describe the properties of function arguments in a general form. This allows tests to generate input based on such properties. With this type of test, we can run thousands of test scenarios with a few lines of code. There's no need to enumerate every single test case.

In the second part of this chapter, we learned about testing in ClojureScript. We saw that the cljs.test library provides us with features comparable to the **clojure. test** library. With **clsj.test**, we were able to test ClojureScript code. We also looked at macros, allowing us to test asynchronous ClojureScript code. We also set up an autorunner to run ClojureScript tests automatically when our code changes.

Finally, we worked through two activities that allowed us to use our testing knowledge in projects. We wrote tests using libraries we learned about for applications developed in previous chapters.

In the next chapter, we will learn about macros. Macros are a powerful feature that allows us to influence the Clojure language.

11
Macros

Learning objectives

In this chapter, you will learn how Clojure macros work and how to write them. Macros are a very powerful feature of Clojure that simply does not exist in many other non-Lisp languages. Writing macros requires learning some new concepts and some new skills. This chapter will take you through the basic concepts: distinguishing between compile-time and run-time execution, quoting strategies and macro hygiene.

By the end of this chapter, you will be able to automatically generate functions and craft custom environments to streamline your code.

Introduction

Macros have been a distinctive feature of Lisps for decades. They are sometimes presented as a superpower native to the world of Lisp. While macros do exist in other languages, for many decades, Lisps have had the most complete macro systems. Why is this? Languages from the Lisp family share the ability to write code that modifies itself. People often talk about "code as data": Lisp programs, with their nested sets of parentheses called **s-expressions**, are in fact lists. And Lisps, as languages, are good at manipulating lists. The name "Lisp" originally came from "LISt Processor" when the language was first invented in 1958. As a result, Lisps can be made to operate on the code of Lisp programs. Usually, this means that a program modifies its own code.

> **Note**
>
> The term **homoiconicity** is often applied to Lisps. While the exact meaning of this term depends on who is talking, it generally means that Lisps are written in forms that they can manipulate themselves and that these same structures are more or less mirrored inside the Lisp interpreter or compiler.

Sometimes, this is called **metaprogramming**: writing a program that will write your program for you. If that sounds too good to be true, it's because it is. Macros can't do everything for you, of course. They can write parts of your program, though, and make your code easier to write by removing some of the boilerplate and other forms of repetition, or by transforming the language's syntax to better fit the problem at hand.

Has this ever happened to you? You're working on a large project and you find yourself writing function after function, method after method, and they are almost identical. You know the DRY principle: *Don't Repeat Yourself*. "Maybe I'm missing an abstraction here, maybe I could simplify this," you think to yourself. Yet when you try, there is always *one* piece of code that needs to be different and can't be abstracted away. It might be some conditional logic that is different each time. So, you give up on a cleaner solution and keep typing away. Macros might have helped.

Here's a slightly more concrete scenario. You're writing code with a lot of Boolean logic. After a few days, it starts to feel as though just about every function in your code base has a few of these:

```
(and
  (or (> x 23) (> y 55))
  (or (= c d) (= e f))
  (or (> a 55) (> b 55)))
```

The logic is slightly different each time, so you can't write a function, yet the logic is so similar each time that you feel like you're constantly repeating yourself. What if you could just write this instead?

```
(and-ors (> x 23) (> y 55) | (= c d) (= e f) | (> a 55) (> b 55))
```

Well, you can. With a macro.

This eliminates one level of nested parentheses, so it's easier to type. It might even be easier to read.

There are a couple of reasons this would be impossible with a function. The most important reason is that a macro such as **and-ors** preserves the "short-circuiting" property of **and** (which is a macro itself). As soon as one of the conditions fails, evaluation stops and the remaining conditions are ignored, with possible performance benefits, or to avoid possible side effects. The other reason is that we're able to use **|** as a separation symbol without having to define it before using the macro. It's like being able to define our own language operators.

This kind of "magic" is possible because macros are executed before your code is compiled. Their purpose is to transform your source code before it goes to the compiler. If this sounds complicated and confusing, well, sometimes, it is. By building on concrete examples, however, you'll quickly realize that though macros aren't magical, they can be useful. And though they can be very complex, they don't always have to be. Understanding how they work will also help you avoid using them when they are not the best solution.

Clojure provides a modern macro system that is largely based on – and improves – the Common Lisp macro system, and as such, it is an extremely powerful tool. In spite of this power, Clojure programmers generally write far fewer macros than Common Lisp programmers, or Scheme or Racket programmers. The reasons for this are probably varied. Most books about macros, in any Lisp, start out by warning that macros should only be used when you're absolutely sure that a function will not work. Often, Clojure's functional programming is useful and powerful enough that writing a macro isn't really necessary.

Sometimes, though, a macro can be the best solution to a problem or can help simplify code that would otherwise be complicated and/or repetitive. Learning to write macros is also a rite of passage for any self-respecting Clojure programmer. So, let's go!

What is a Macro?

A macro is a piece of code that is executed before your code is compiled. The code contained inside a macro call is transformed into something different and then passed on to the compiler. In Clojure, macros are defined by calling **defmacro**. A call to **defmacro** looks fairly similar to a call to **defn**:

```
(defmacro my-macro
  "Macro for showing how to write macros"
  [param]
  ;;TODO: do something
  )
```

Despite this apparent similarity, there is a huge difference between macros and functions. Unlike functions, macros are not called at runtime. When your program finally starts running, the macros have already been called. The code they produce has already been included in your program *as if you had typed it in yourself*:

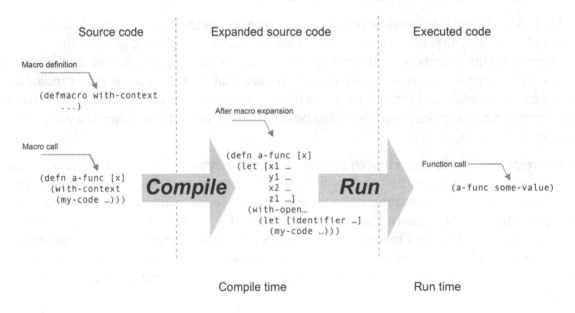

Figure 11.1: Separating compile time from runtime is the key to understanding macros

Keep this idea in mind while you think about and work with macros: any macro in your code could, in principle, be replaced by code that you type out yourself. Some macros are very complex and it would be extremely difficult and painstaking to replace them with hand-written code, but with enough time, patience, and expertise, it would theoretically be possible. Just as you write your code before you run it, macros are expanded before your code is run.

A Very Minimal Macro

Let's start with a very simple, and not very useful, macro:

```
(defmacro minimal-macro []
  '(println "I'm trapped inside a macro!"))
```

This looks a lot like a function definition. We could just as easily write this:

```
(defn minimal-function []
  (println "I'm trapped inside a function!"))
```

If we run both of these at the REPL, the results are also identical:

```
user> (minimal-macro)
I'm trapped inside a macro!
nil
user> (minimal-function)
I'm trapped inside a function!
nil
```

There is only one meaningful difference between these two definitions, and it is a very small one. Do you see it? It's the ', which is shorthand for the **quote** special form. Despite its small size, it makes a huge difference.

When we run **minimal-function**, the Clojure runtime simply executes the call to **println**. When we run **minimal-macro**, the macro actually inserts the **(println "I'm trapped inside a macro!")** statement into your source code before the Clojure runtime reads it. To be more precise, we say that Clojure **expands** the macro.

The best way to appreciate the difference between **minimal-macro** and **minimal-function** is to use Clojure's **macroexpand** function, which translates a call to a macro into actual code.

Here's the result of calling **macroexpand** on a call to **minimal-function**:

```
user> (macroexpand '(minimal-function))
(minimal-function)
```

This seems a little redundant, and for good reason: **(minimal-function)** is not a macro, and so only expands into itself.

> **Note**
>
> When calling **macroexpand**, it's important to quote the form you are expanding. Otherwise, **macroexpand** will try to expand the results of the call to **minimal-function**. Because **println** returns **nil**, the result would be **nil**, and there would be nothing to expand. Whenever you get surprising results from **macroexpand**, make sure that you haven't forgotten to quote the macro.

Expanding **(minimal-macro)** is quite different, though:

```
user> (macroexpand '(minimal-macro))
(println "I'm trapped inside a macro!")
```

When we type **(minimal-macro)** at the REPL, it is expanded into the **println** expression, exactly as if you had typed it out yourself. Notice that the expanded form is no longer quoted. (As you're probably starting to guess, quoting is an important part of macro writing.)

Compile Time and Run Time

To see the importance of quoting, let's try writing a macro without the ' at the beginning:

```
(defmacro mistaken-macro []
  (println "I'm trapped... somewhere!"))
```

Calling this macro in the REPL yields the same results:

```
user> (mistaken-macro)
I'm trapped... somewhere!
nil
```

What's wrong with that? **mistaken-macro** seems to work just as well as the others... Or does it? Let's try expanding it:

```
user> (macroexpand '(mistaken-macro))
I'm trapped... somewhere!
nil
```

That's strange! The output is the same as when we call the macro directly, yet it is totally different from both `minimal-function`, which just expanded to itself, and `minimal-macro`, which expanded into the `println` expression. So, what is really going on here? And why did removing the `quote` apostrophe make such a difference?

The fact that calling `(mistaken-macro)` produces the same output as the other forms could almost be called a coincidence. The call to `println` happens, but it happens at compile time. And because `println` returns nil, `(mistaken-macro)` expands to exactly that: `nil`. This is also why we see the `"I'm trapped…"` message when we call `macroexpand`: that message is a side effect of the macro expansion!

The difference between `minimal-macro` and `mistaken-macro` is that the former, by quoting the form, actually returns a **list** that is not executed until runtime. The list that is returned contains the `println` symbol and the message string. `mistaken-macro`, on the other hand, expands to `nil` because it calls `println` immediately, at expansion time.

There are several important points here that we will build on in the rest of this chapter:

- Code is actually run when macros are expanded, and when the code is run. This is why `mistaken-macro` actually prints out a message.

- Understanding the difference between compile time and runtime is important.

- Quoting is important because it is one of the ways that you, as a programmer, control which code is executed when the macro is expanded, and which code is run at runtime.

Remember: a macro is code that writes code. Let's write a slightly more sophisticated macro that will expand to an arbitrary number of `println` calls. Our goal is for the macro to expand to this if we provide **3** as a parameter:

```
(do
  (println "Macro")
  (println "Macro")
  (println "Macro"))
```

> **Note**
>
> When working with macros, it is always a good idea to start by thinking about the code you want the macro to produce and then work back to how you will produce it.

Rather than thinking of this as a series of steps to execute, it's best to think of it as a list containing a symbol (do) and a series of sub-lists, each containing a symbol and a string. Thinking of **do** and **println** as symbols rather than a special form and a function is a good approach because, at expansion time, we just want to make sure that the form we end up producing has the correct symbols in the right order. Thinking of **println** as "just a symbol" is how the macroexpansion code "thinks" about it too if it is quoted.

To produce a list of lists, we might use **repeat**:

```
user> (repeat 3 '(println "Macro"))
((println "Macro")
 (println "Macro")
 (println "Macro"))
```

There's that single quotation mark again. If we left it out, we would get **(nil nil nil nil nil)**. And thanks to quoting, none of those calls to **println** are ever called. We are getting close to our target code and we haven't even called **defmacro** yet.

The only thing missing is the initial **do** symbol. Adding a value to the front of a list is fairly easy too, as long as we quote it:

```
user> (cons 'do (repeat 3 '(println "Macro")))
(do
 (println "Macro")
 (println "Macro")
 (println "Macro"))
```

There's our code! All that's left is to wrap this up as a macro:

```
user> (defmacro multi-minimal [n-times]
         (cons 'do (repeat n-times '(println "Macro"))))
```

When we call the macro directly, it seems to work:

```
user> (multi-minimal 3)
Macro
Macro
Macro
nil
```

And **macroexpand** confirms it:

```
user> (macroexpand '(multi-minimal 3))
(do
 (println "Macro")
 (println "Macro")
 (println "Macro"))
```

The point here is to show that a macro is code that writes code. The contents of `multi-minimal` don't look very much like the output. We could even go further and wrap them in a function:

```
user> (defn multi-min [n-times]
        (cons 'do (repeat n-times '(println "Macro"))))
#'user/multi-min
user> (defmacro multi-minimal-two [n-times]
        (multi-min n-times))
#'user/multi-minimal-two
user> (multi-minimal-two 3)
Macro
Macro
Macro
nil
```

As we'll see later, some macros look a little bit like templates, but there is nothing that requires their definitions to resemble the code that is output. Breaking the code-building code out into a separate function can be a useful pattern, especially for debugging.

Runtime Parameters

Obviously, we can't expect this particular macro to be very useful. Still, it would be nice if it would print something besides "macro." What if we gave it a second parameter – a string to be passed on to all those `println` calls? There's already one parameter; adding a second one should be easy enough... right?

Let's try just adding a parameter and passing that to `println`:

```
user> (defmacro parameterized-multi-minimal [n-times s]
        (cons 'do (repeat n-times '(println s))))
#'user/parameterized-multi-minimal
```

Unfortunately, this doesn't work:

```
user> (parameterized-multi-minimal 3 "My own text.")
Syntax error compiling at (Chapter11:localhost:58838(clj)*:49:36).
Unable to resolve symbol: s in this context
```

What's wrong? As always, when we don't understand what is wrong with a macro, we reach for `macroexpand`:

```
user> (macroexpand '(parameterized-multi-minimal 3 "My own text."))
(do (println s) (println s) (println s))
```

By the time the macro has been expanded, the **s** parameter has disappeared. Where did it go? Unlike **defn**, **defmacro** does not provide a context for runtime variable bindings. The original **n-times** parameter is available while the macro is being expanded, but afterward, the macro itself has been replaced by the code it produced. There is no trace left of **n-times**, or **s**.

Of course, there must be a way around this, since macros would be rather useless if they didn't accept parameters. If we want there to be a context, we just need to create that context explicitly ourselves in quoted code that will still be present at runtime. In a case like this, the simplest solution would be a **let** binding. We need to change our target code to something like this:

```
(let [string-to-print "My own text."]
  (println string-to-print)
  (println string-to-print)
  (println string-to-print))
```

Why is the **let** binding called **string-to-print** and not **s**? Remember that when the code is finally run, **s** and **n-times** are no longer present as symbols. **n-times** is present in a way since it is what determined how many **println** calls end up in the expanded expression. The **s** parameter from the call to the macro needs to live on, not as **string-to-print**, but as the string bound to **string-to-print**. In other words, in the preceding target code, **s** is there: it's **"My own text"**.

We can do this by using some of Clojure's list-manipulating power to carefully build the exact code that we need, that is, a **let** binding containing a sub-list of **println** expressions:

```
(defmacro parameterized-multi-minimal [n-times s]
  (concat (list 'let ['string-to-print s])
          (repeat n-times '(println string-to-print))))
```

We'll check to make sure it works:

```
user> (parameterized-multi-minimal 3 "My own text.")
My own text.
My own text.
My own text.
nil
```

This time, **s** is not quoted when we bind it to **string-to-print**. When the macro is expanded, the value of **s** will be inserted into the list that the macro is going to return. Items such as **let** and **string-to-print** are quoted, because we don't want their values in the macro expansion; we want them to appear as symbols.

To achieve this, we've had to do some tricky quoting, applying a single quote to some items and not to others. This is why we used **list** instead of **'()**. The single quote is a shortcut for writing **(quote…)**. **quote** is a special form and its effect is to quote everything inside the parentheses, including sub-lists. Sometimes, this is exactly what we want, as with **'(println string-to-print)**. We need both items in that list to appear as symbols, not as values. **list** simply returns a list. By using **list**, we can choose which items should be quoted or not.

This is not an optimal quoting solution. Shortly, we'll see that Clojure proposes another more sophisticated syntax that makes this easier. The underlying principles are the same, however, so it's good to see how the mechanics of quoting work.

There is one more noteworthy (or simply strange) thing in this version of the macro. Why are we using **concat** to join the list and the results of the call to **repeat**? Previously, we wrapped all the **println** calls inside a **do** expression. Now that we have a **let** block, this isn't necessary anymore. At the same time, we still need to make sure that the **println** calls aren't wrapped in a list. Using **concat** solves the immediate problem but it is not an elegant solution. In the next section, the new quoting syntax will make this easier as well.

Syntax Quoting

A lot of the art of writing macros lies in mastering the separation between expansion code and output code. A lot of the control over that separation depends on deciding what gets quoted when the macro is expanded and what does not get quoted. The previous example started to reveal the limits of the standard **quote** special form. Once a list has been quoted, all its symbols and sub-lists are **quote**d as well. As such, **quote** is a fairly heavy-handed tool.

For this reason, Clojure, like many Lisps, provides a more sophisticated quoting mechanism called **syntax quoting**. Syntax quoting uses ', the backtick character, instead of the standard single quote. When used by itself, the backtick has more or less the same behavior as **quote**: all symbols and sub-lists are quoted by default. The difference is that syntax quoting allows us to mark certain forms, sub-lists, or symbols that should not be quoted.

With syntax quoting, we can simplify our macro from the previous section:

```
(defmacro parameterized-with-syntax [n-times s]
        `(do ~@(repeat n-times '(println ~s))))
```

How does this work? There are three new things here:

- The **syntax-quote** backtick, in front of the **do** form and the **println** form
- The **~**, the tilde, in front of the **s** symbol
- The **~@** in front of the **repeat** form

The **syntax-quote** backticks initiate syntax quoting. Then, we can see two different ways of preventing quoting on child elements. The simplest of the two is the tilde in `'(println ~s)`: the **println** symbol, where the list itself will be quoted when the macro is expanded, but **~s** will evaluate to the value of **s**. The tilde is called **unquote**. Thanks to **unquote**, we can now insert the value of **s** into each **println** call and we no longer need to wrap the entire expression in a **let** expression.

~@ is called **unquote-splicing** and does two things at once. Like **unquote**, it prevents quoting on the expression it is attached to. Unlike **unquote**, though, it only works on lists because its role is to splice the contents of the list into the containing list. Before, we had to use **cons** or **concat** to avoid ending up with all the **(println "String!")** expressions wrapped inside a list.

Expanded, a call to the new macro looks like this:

```
user> (macroexpand '(parameterized-with-syntax 3 "Syntax quoting!"))
(do
 (clojure.core/println "Syntax quoting!")
 (clojure.core/println "Syntax quoting!")
 (clojure.core/println "Syntax quoting!"))
```

You may notice a slight difference relative to some of the previous macro expansions: the **println** symbols are namespaced! This is an important feature for writing robust macros that we will explore shortly when we get to the topic of macro hygiene. First, though, let's practice using our new macro skills.

Exercise 11.01: The and-ors Macro

At the beginning of this chapter, to whet your appetite for macro magic, we showed you a macro called **and-ors**. Its purpose was to make it easier to write nested Boolean logic when you have lots of expressions with or contained in an overarching **and** expression.

Consider this function (hopefully, real code would have more descriptive parameter names!):

```
(defn validate-params
  [a b c d]
  (and
    (or (> a 5) (> a b))
    (or (= b a) (> b 5))
    (or (> a c) (> c 5) (= c b))
    (or (= a d) (> d 5))))
```

Logic like this is inherently hard to read, especially when there are lots of conditions.

Let's suppose that you are writing a library that will contain lots of important business logic that is mostly expressed with a long series of Boolean operators, as in the preceding function. Anything we can do to make it simpler will help the overall readability of your code base. The **and-ors** macro would be a welcome improvement. Instead of the nested **or** expressions in the preceding function, you could write this:

```
(defn validate-params
  [a b c d]
  (and-ors
    (> a 5) (> a b) |
    (= b a) (> b 5) |
    (> a c) (> c 5) (= c b) |
    (= a d) (> d 5)))
```

This is an admittedly minor improvement, but it does remove some parentheses and generally helps put the accent on the logical expressions themselves. Now, we just need to figure out how to make this work:

1. Start with a skeleton for **defmacro**:

    ```
    (defmacro and-ors [& or-exps]
      ;; TODO: write a macro
      )
    ```

    Just like with functions, macros can be variadic and accept an unknown number of arguments. This is exactly what we need here since we don't know how many **or** expressions there will be.

2. Write the logic that will split the list of **or-exps** each time there is a **|** symbol:

```
(defmacro and-ors [& or-exps]
  (let [groups (remove (partial = '(|)) (partition-by (partial = '|) or-exps))]
    ;; TODO: do something finally
    ))
```

Breaking the list of arguments in **or-exps** into sub-lists is a simple sequence operation. There are several ways to do this, including writing a small external function. Here, we've chosen to use **partition-by**. Remember, **partition-by** takes a function that it uses to decide where to break a list. The list is broken every time the function returns a different response. We only care about whether the current item is **|** or something else, which is exactly what **(partial = '|)** will do. The only trick here is that we need to quote the **|** symbol to make sure that we are talking about the symbol itself and not its value. (Which is good, since it doesn't have a value.)

Splitting on the **|** symbols leaves the symbols as sub-lists. You can try this in the REPL if you quote the **|** symbol in the input:

```
user> (partition-by (partial = '|) [1 2 '| 3 4])
((1 2) (|) (3 4))
```

We need to remove the **(|)** sublist from the results. We'll use **remove** for this:

```
(remove #(= '(|) %) (partition-by (partial = '|) or-exps))
```

> **Note**
>
> The **|** symbol has now disappeared from our code. It will not be present in any way in the compiled code. This is why we don't have to worry about it being defined or namespaced. From the point of view of the compiled code, it's like it was never there in the first place.

Now, we have our **groups** binding, which contains a list of lists.

3. Prepare to output the outer **and** expression.

    The structure we want to create is that of an **and** expression containing zero or more expressions. So first, we need the **and** expression:

```
(defmacro and-ors [& or-exps]
  (let [groups (remove (partial = '(|)) (partition-by (partial = '|) or-exps))]
    '(and
       ;; TODO: the ors
       )))
```

Here, the important thing is the quoting. The backtick in front of **(and...)** starts the syntax quoting. This ensures, first of all, that the **(and...)** form will be output, and secondly that we will be able to use **splice-insert** to include the new **or** expressions.

4. Convert each sub-list into an **or** expression.

    Here is the complete macro:

```
(defmacro and-ors [& or-exps]
  (let [groups (remove (partial = '(|)) (partition-by (partial = '|) or-exps))]
    '(and
       ~@(map (fn [g] '(or ~@g)) groups))))
```

The call to **map** will return a list. Since we don't want an extra set of parentheses inside the **(and...)** expression, we use **insert-splice** here. Inside the anonymous mapping function, we need to start syntax quoting again since it was suspended by the ~@ in front of **(map...)**. That's why we've put the backtick in front of **(or...)**. The same process is more or less repeated since each element in **groups** is a list of items to be placed inside an **(or...)** expression.

5. Test and macroexpand your new macro:

```
user> (and-ors (> 5 3) (= 6 6) | (> 6 3) | (= 5 5 5))
true
```

It seems to work. Let's try it with nested **and-ors**:

```
user> (and-ors
         (and-ors (= 3 3) | (= 5 5) (= 6 8))
         |
         (> 5 3) (= 6 6)
         |
         (> 6 3)
         |
         (= 5 5 5))
true
```

Macroexpansion will show us whether we are getting exactly what we originally wanted. To avoid expanding the **and** and **or** macros, we'll use a different version of **macroexpand** here, called **macroexpand-1**. The difference between the two is that, when a macro expansion contains other macros, **macroexpand** will continue, recursively, to expand all of the nested macros, while **macroexpand-1** will stop after the first macro. When writing your own macros, **macroexpand-1** is often more intuitive because it prevents us from seeing the details of built-in macros, such as **let** or, as in this example, **and** or **or**:

```
user> (macroexpand-1 '(and-ors (> 5 3) (= 6 6) | (> 6 3) | (= 5 5 5)))
(clojure.core/and
  (clojure.core/or (> 5 3) (= 6 6))
  (clojure.core/or (> 6 3))
  (clojure.core/or (= 5 5 5)))
```

This exercise shows how even a four-line macro can allow you to introduce what could be a useful syntactical improvement. The decision to write a macro such as **and-ors** would be based on whether or not it was starting to be painful to write all those repetitive Booleans in your code base.

Exercise 11.02: An Automatic HTML Library

In this exercise, you will write a macro that, given a list of items, automatically creates a function for each item. This can be useful in situations where you need a large number of very similar functions.

Back in *Chapter 6, Recursion and Looping*, you built a library that translated Clojure vectors into HTML, using keywords to identify the HTML tags. In that system, an HTML element would be written like this:

```
[:h1 "First things first"]
```

The output would be as follows:

```
<h1>First things first</h1>
```

Recently, a co-worker decided to rewrite the library using functions rather than vectors. With this new approach, an HTML element would be written as a function:

```
(h1 {:class "intro"} "First things first")
```

Functions can be nested so that developers can write entire HTML pages in their source code.

Unfortunately, your co-worker left before they could finish the project and you've been asked to take over.

You can view what the new library looks like at https://packt.live/2Gf4bn9.

As you read through the code, you start to see how the library was supposed to work, and also why it was abandoned. You realize that, like your former colleague, you don't feel like writing out a separate function for every element in the HTML spec! It would be a long, buggy process of copying and pasting hard-to-maintain code. Looking closer, you start to suspect that your former colleague had the same idea. The last function, **tag-fn**, looks suspiciously like an attempt to generalize the approach. It also includes a rather clever use of **mapcat**, similar to the wrap-unwrap technique from *Chapter 4, Mapping and Filtering*, so that a list of items can be spliced into a containing list. Unfortunately, the file ends there.

Using **tag-fn** to produce a function for each element seems like a good idea. It still means defining a **var** for each kind of HTML element. Your code would look like this:

```
(def p (tag-fn "p"))
(def ul (tag-fn "ul"))
(def li (tag-fn "li"))
(def h1 (tag-fn "h1"))
(def h2 (tag-fn "h2"))
(def h3 (tag-fn "h3"))
(def h4 (tag-fn "h4"))
;; etc. etc. etc.
```

This is a lot better than typing out all those functions, but it still seems too repetitive. Maybe a macro could help?

With the right macro, we could just copy a list of elements from the HTML specification, wrap them in quotes, and run our macro once while loading the source file:

```
(define-html-tags "p" "ul" "li" "h1" "h2" "h3" "h4")
```

The output would be a series of **def** expressions, just like what we have in the preceding code. Let's have a look:

1. Set up a new project directory with an empty **deps.edn**. Copy the **htmlgen.clj** file from this book's GitHub repository (https://packt.live/2Gf4bn9). You will add your code to the bottom of the file.

2. First, sketch out the code you want to produce. Because we need to be able to produce an arbitrary number of functions, our macro will return a list of **def** forms. It will be simpler to enclose those forms in a **do** expression:

```
(do
  (def h1 (tag-fn "h1"))
  (def h2 (tag-fn "h2"))
  (def h3 (tag-fn "h3"))
  (def h4 (tag-fn "h4")))
```

3. Write the skeleton for the macro with syntax quoting applied to the **do** expression:

```
(defmacro define-html-tags [& tags]
  '(do
      ;; TODO: macro code
      ))
```

> **Note**
>
> We give the macro a **variadic** call signature: **[& tags]**. We'll come back to this later.

4. Map over the arguments in **tags** to produce a series of **def** expressions:

```
(defmacro define-html-tags [& tags]
  '(do
      ~@(map (fn [tagname]
                '(def ~(symbol tagname) (tag-fn ~tagname)))
            tags)))
```

There are several things to note here. Look carefully at what is quoted and what is not: the use of **unquote-splice** (~@) ensures that the elements returned by **map** are the direct children of the **do** expression. Then, with **syntax-quote** ('), we quote the entire **def** expression, except for what is going to become the name of the var we are defining, which we protect from quoting with **unquote** (~). Finally, the **tag-fn** expression inherits its quoting from the backtick in front of **def**. We still need to use **unquote** so that the **tagname** value, something like **"h1"**, is inserted rather than just the **tagname** symbol itself.

The **symbol** function is needed here because the input is a string. **tag-fn** takes a string, but its name needs to be a symbol.

5. Test the new macro. Evaluate the macro definition and then use it to define some HTML element functions:

```
(define-html-tags "h1" "h2" "h3" "h4" "h5" "p" "div" "span")
```

By copying an official list of HTML tags, you can quickly implement the entire standard. From inside the **packt-clojure.htmlgen** namespace, you are now able to generate HTML elements with your new functions:

```
packt-clj.htmlgen> (div
                    (h1 "First things first")
                    (p {:class "intro"} "What's the best way to get started?"))
"<div><h1>First things first</h1><p class=\"intro\">What's the best way to get
started?</p></div>"
```

It works. You've fulfilled the requirements of the assignment and management is satisfied... for now, at least.

Automatically producing a large number of functions is a task that macros are well adapted for. A macro like this one is little more than a template for a function. Macros can do much more, of course, but sometimes, mass-producing simple functions is exactly what you need.

In this exercise, the macro we wrote was variadic. It accepts a variable number of arguments and its parameter list looks like this: **[& tag]**. It might be tempting to rewrite the macro so that it accepts a list or a vector of tag names. That way, we could define our list and then call the macro on it separately. Here's our macro, rewritten to accept a list instead:

```
(defmacro define-html-tags-from-list [tags]
  '(do
     ~@(map (fn [tagname]
              '(def ~(symbol tagname) (tag-fn ~tagname)))
            tags)))
```

Unfortunately, this doesn't work:

```
user> (def heading-tags ["h1" "h2" "h3" "h4"])
#'user/heading-tags
user> (define-html-tags-from-list heading-tags)
Execution error (IllegalArgumentException) at refactor_nrepl.ns.slam.hound.regrow$wrap_cloj
sure_repl$fn__10248/doInvoke (regrow.clj:18).
Don't know how to create ISeq from: clojure.lang.Symbol
user> []
```

Figure 11.2: At compile time, a symbol such as heading-tags is just a symbol, not a list

The macro fails because, at compile time, **heading-tags** is not a list yet. The macro only "sees" a symbol and, just like the error says, it doesn't know how to create a sequence from a symbol. The macro code in the exercise needs access to the actual tag name at compile time.

This is one reason why **apply** can't be used on macros:

```
packt-clj.htmlgen> (apply define-html-tags ["br" "p" "a"])
Syntax error compiling at (Exercise01:localhost:52997(clj)*:116:24).
Can't take value of a macro: #'packt-clojure.htmlgen/define-html-tags
```

By the time the call to **apply** is made, the code is already running and it's too late for the macro to be expanded. For the same reason, a macro cannot be passed as an argument to a function such as **map** or **filter**. While macros bring great flexibility to a language, there is always a cost to using a macro instead of a function.

Exercise 11.03: Expanding the HTML Library

Your team was impressed with how quickly you implemented all the known HTML elements as functions and now, the HTML generating library is becoming more popular inside your organization. As often happens with successful libraries, the developers using it are starting to run into problems. One of the most common frustrations that's expressed by members of your team is that it is awkward to wrap a list of elements inside a containing element.

Here is a simple example of a common use case: creating an unordered list (**<ul>**) by mapping over a list of strings, transforming each string into a list item (**<li>**). Thanks to how the original **tag-fn** was written to handle sequences as well as strings, the code for creating an HTML list from a vector of items is fairly simple:

```
(ul (map li ["item 1" "item2"]))
```

However, this pattern arises so often in your co-workers' code that they are starting to complain that your library forces them to be redundant. "Why," they ask, "can't this be simpler? We know that a **ul**, when given a list, will result in a **(map li…)** call. Can't that be automatic?"

"Well," you reply, "of course it can." After some thought, you decide that you want your colleagues to be able to write this instead:

```
(ul->li ["item 1" "item 2"])
```

And this won't just apply to **ul**. **ol->li** would be just as useful. Some of the table elements could use the same thing: **table->tr** and **tbody->tr** would be quite useful for lists of table rows (**<tr>**), as would **tr->td** for table rows (**<tr>**) containing lists of table cells (**<td>**). You decide to write a second, specialized macro called **define-html-list-tags** that will take tag name pairs and define the corresponding functions:

1. In the same file as the previous exercise, define a helper function to build the new functions. It will be called **subtag-fn** and will be simpler than **tag-fn** because it doesn't need to handle as many different cases:

```
(defn subtag-fn [tagname subtag]
  (fn [content]
    (str
      (->opening-tag tagname nil)
      (apply str (map subtag content))
      (->end-tag tagname))))
```

The contents of the function should appear relatively familiar. The only new piece of code here is **(map subtag content)**. For a function such as ul→li, the **li** function (which we assume is already defined – make sure **define-html-tags** is called first!) is called on each item in the **content** argument.

2. Test the helper function. The helper function will be called at runtime, so it is easy to test:

```
packt-clj.htmlgen> ((subtag-fn "ul" li) ["Item 1" "Item 2"])
"<ul><li>Item 1</li><li>Item 2</li></ul>"
```

Note again that this works because the **li** function has already been defined. We pass it in as a symbol – **li**, without quotes – and not as a string like **"ul"**. The **ul** function won't be defined until after the macro has been run.

There is one small problem here, however: we can't optionally pass in a map of attributes. This breaks the interface we've established for the other functions, so we need to fix that before moving on.

3. Add a second arity to the anonymous function returned by **subtag-fn**:

```
(defn subtag-fn [tagname subtag]
  (fn subtag-function-builder
    ([content]
     (subtag-function-builder nil content))
    ([attrs content]
       (str
         (->opening-tag tagname attrs)
         (apply str (map subtag content))
         (->end-tag tagname)))))
```

This code highlights two interesting features of anonymous functions. First of all, they support multiple arities, which makes them just as flexible as their **defn** defined counterparts. Secondly, despite being anonymous, they can have names. This feature exists in other languages, such as JavaScript, and can be useful for debugging purposes. When reading error messages, having a function name can be a big help. Naming an anonymous function in Clojure has another advantage, in that the function can refer to itself this way. Thus, in the preceding code, the single version of the function can fill in the **attrs** argument with **nil** and then call the double argument version. This way, we don't have to write the function's logic twice.

4. Test the new **subtag-fn**:

```
packt-clj.htmlgen> ((subtag-fn "ul" li) {:class "my-class"} ["Item 1" "Item 2"])
"<ul class=\"my-class\"><li>Item 1</li><li>Item 2</li></ul>"
```

This works. Now, let's try the single-argument form:

```
packt-clj.htmlgen> ((subtag-fn "ul" li) ["Item 1" "Item 2"])
"<ul><li>Item 1</li><li>Item 2</li></ul>"
```

It still works too!

5. Write the macro that will define functions such as **ul->li**.

As always, the first step in designing a macro is to decide how it should be called. A call to this macro should look like this:

```
(define-html-list-tags ["ul" "li"] ["ol" "li"])
```

> **Note**
>
> We use two item vectors here to group tags together. As we mentioned earlier, it would be impossible to define these inputs elsewhere and replace them with a symbol in the call to **define-html-list**.

We can use the same variadic form as in the previous version:

```
(defmacro define-html-list-tags [& tags-with-subtags]
  '(do
     ~@(map (fn [[tagname subtag]]
              '(do
                 (def ~(symbol tagname) (tag-fn ~tagname))
                 (def ~(symbol (str tagname "->" subtag)) (subtag-fn ~tagname
~(symbol subtag)))))
            tags-with-subtags)))
```

To understand what is happening here, let's start from inside the anonymous function that's been passed to **map**. The first line should look familiar:

```
(def ~(symbol tagname) (tag-fn ~tagname))
```

This is exactly the same as in the **define-html-tags** macro from the previous exercise. Even though we're going to define **ul->li**, we still need to define the **ul** function.

The next line is where we define functions such as **ul->li**:

```
(def ~(symbol (str tagname "->" subtag)) (subtag-fn ~tagname ~(symbol subtag)))
```

This definition follows the same pattern as in the preceding code, except that we use **str** to build the symbol that will be the name of the function and we turn the subtag string into a symbol as well.

Both of these definitions are wrapped in a **do** expression, and the output from **map** is, in turn, wrapped in a single **do**. Expanded, it looks like this:

```
packt-clj.htmlgen> (macroexpand '(define-html-list-tags ["ul" "li"] ["ol" "li"]))
(do
  (do
    (def ul (packt-clj.htmlgen/tag-fn "ul"))
    (def ul->li (packt-clj.htmlgen/subtag-fn "ul" li)))
  (do
    (def ol (packt-clj.htmlgen/tag-fn "ol"))
    (def ol->li (packt-clj.htmlgen/subtag-fn "ol" li))))
```

6. Test the new macro:

```
packt-clj.htmlgen> (define-html-list-tags ["ul" "li"] ["ol" "li"])
#'packt-clj.htmlgen/ol->li
packt-clj.htmlgen> (ol->li ["Item 1" "Item 2"])
"<ol><li>Item 1</li><li>Item 2</li></ol>"
packt-clj.htmlgen> (ol->li {:class "my-class"} ["Item 1" "Item 2"])
"<ol class=\"my-class\"><li>Item 1</li><li>Item 2</li></ol>"
```

It works.

In the previous exercise, it may seem inelegant to use nested **do** expressions. We would certainly never write code this way by hand! For code produced by a macro, however, it really isn't a problem. This doesn't mean that macros should expand into convoluted code. Simple is always better. However, most of the time, no human will need to read this code. Someone (probably you) might have to read and debug the code of your macro, so keeping it as simple as possible will generally be worth it, even at the cost of a few extra nested **do** expressions or some other repetitive code oddity.

We could, of course, use **mapcat** to create a flat list:

```
(defmacro define-html-list-tags-with-mapcat [& tags-with-subtags]
  '(do
     ~@(mapcat (fn [[tagname subtag]]
                 ['(def ~(symbol tagname) (tag-fn ~tagname))
                  '(def ~(symbol (str tagname "->" subtag)) (subtag-fn ~tagname ~(symbol
subtag)))])
               tags-with-subtags)))
```

There is a subtle difference here, in that the syntax-quoting has been moved from the containing **(do...)** expression to the **(def...)** expressions themselves. At runtime, the vector will no longer exist, so we don't want to quote it.

This version produces nicer code when expanded:

```
packt-clj.htmlgen> (macroexpand '(define-html-list-tags-with-mapcat ["ul" "li"] ["ol"
"li"]))
(do
  (def ul (packt-clj.htmlgen/tag-fn "ul"))
  (def ul->li (packt-clj.htmlgen/subtag-fn "ul" li))
  (def ol (packt-clj.htmlgen/tag-fn "ol"))
  (def ol->li (packt-clj.htmlgen/subtag-fn "ol" li)))
```

Your mileage may vary, but in general, simplifying your macro code is more important than producing elegant expansions. The macro is the code you will need to debug.

In this and the previous exercise, we used **def**, along with helper functions that built new functions. Nothing prevents you from writing macros that define new functions with **defn**.

Macros in ClojureScript

The distinction between **compile time** and **runtime** is perhaps the most important concept to grasp when learning about macros. Before going further into the consequences of this distinction, it's worth looking at how it affects macros in ClojureScript, where compilation and execution have a slightly more complex relationship than they do in JVM Clojure.

ClojureScript runs in a JavaScript runtime, like the browser or Node.js. This is possible because ClojureScript code is first compiled by the ClojureScript compiler, which is a program written in Clojure and runs on the JVM. This means that ClojureScript programs, once they're compiled and running, no longer have access to the compilation phase.

This has several consequences for working with macros in ClojureScript, the most important of which is that ClojureScript macros cannot be defined in `.cljs` files alongside other ClojureScript code. Instead, they are defined in separate files with either the `.clj` file extension or the cross-compiling `.cljc` extension.

In the GitHub repository accompanying this book, there is a minimal **ClojureScript project** that illustrates this. It contains two namespaces: **minmacros/core.cljs** and **minmacros/macros.cljc**.

The **minmacros/core.cljs** namespace uses special syntax to require the macros in **minmacros/macros.cljc**. Here's the entire content:

```
(ns minmacros.core
  (:require-macros [minmacros.macros :as mm]))


(println "Hello from clojurescript")
(mm/minimal-macro)
```

This is the only situation where specifying **:require-macros** is necessary. It does not exist in JVM Clojure, only in ClojureScript. If **minmacros/macros.cljc** contained functions that we also wanted to import, we would have to require the namespace separately:

```
(ns minmacros.core
  (:require-macros [minmacros.macros :as mm])
  (:require [minmacros.macros :as mm]))
```

Note that we can use the same namespace alias in both cases. This is because the macroexpansion phase is totally separate from the code execution phase.

To see these macros in action, copy the complete **Chapter11/minmacros** directory from GitHub (https://packt.live/2TQHTjQ). In your Terminal, change to the **minmacros** directory. From there, you can run this from the command line:

```
$ clj --main cljs.main --compile minmacros.core --repl
```

If you're on Windows, you'll need to download a copy of **cljs.jar** from https://packt.live/36m0O8q. Then, assuming that **cljs.jar** is in your working directory, you can run this command:

```
$ java -cp "cljs.jar;src" cljs.main --compile minmacros.core --repl
```

In your Terminal, the output from **println** should appear before the REPL prompt:

```
$ clj --main cljs.main --compile minmacros.core --repl
Hello from clojurescript
I'm trapped inside a Clojurescript macro!
ClojureScript 1.10.520
cljs.user=>
```

Figure 11.3: Output on the Terminal

The second of these, **minmacros/macros.cljc**, is written just like any other Clojure namespace. This is, in fact, a requirement, since it will be compiled on the JVM. Even if the macros here target a JavaScript *runtime*, the macroexpansion code can't contain any JavaScript-specific code. However, the expanded code can contain ClojureScript-specific code, since it will be run in the browser or in an environment such as Node.js.

For example, using JavaScript's native string functions inside your macro would not work. Consider this (admittedly contrived) example, where we try to use the JavaScript string method called **includes** as a test in the macroexpansion code:

```
(defmacro js-macro [symbol-name]
  '(def ~(symbol symbol-name)
     ~(if (.includes symbol-name "b")
        "Hello"
        "Goodbye")))
```

Java strings do not have an **includes** method, so when we try to invoke this macro at the REPL, we get an error:

```
cljs.user=> (minmacros.macros/js-macro "hello")
Unexpected error (IllegalArgumentException) macroexpanding minmacros.macros/js-macro at
(<cljs repl>:1:1).
No matching method includes found taking 1 args for class java.lang.String
```

The Java-based ClojureScript compiler cannot use a JavaScript string method; thus, the macroexpansion fails.

While using JavaScript-specific code during macroexpansion is impossible, it is perfectly fine to use a macro to create code that will only *run* on a JavaScript platform. Here's an equally contrived macro that does just that:

```
(defmacro runtime-includes [function-name character]
  '(defn ~(symbol function-name) []
     (if (.includes "Clojurescript macros" ~character)
       "Found it!"
       "Not here...")))
```

In the REPL, we can define and call a function that returns either **"Found it!"** or **"Not here..."**:

```
cljs.user=> (load-file "minmacros/core.cljs")
nil
cljs.user=> Hello from clojurescript
I'm trapped inside a Clojurescript macro!
cljs.user=> (minmacros.macros/runtime-includes "hello" "m")
#'cljs.user/hello
cljs.user=> (hello)
"Found it!"
cljs.user=>
```

In practice, this kind of issue will rarely arise. It would be extremely rare for macroexpansion code to require some kind of help from the underlying platform. If you find yourself doing this, on either platform, it's probably a sign that you need to rethink what you're trying to accomplish with your macro. The point of these examples is to help illustrate how the details of the ClojureScript compilation process can be important when writing macros. When writing macros, it's always very important to distinguish between compile time and runtime; with ClojureScript, the distance between the two is much greater. Once these issues are accounted for, though, the actual process of writing macros in ClojureScript is identical to writing Clojure macros.

Macro Hygiene

Like most programming languages, Clojure provides a lot of resources for avoiding name collisions. Namespaces, **let** bindings, and lexical scope, all help to make it fairly difficult to override variables by choosing the wrong name. Because they operate in a different space, and at a different time, macros have the potential to go around some of those guardrails. **Macro hygiene** is the art of writing macros that avoid **variable capture**. Variable capture is what happens when a symbol produced by a macro coincides with a macro in the surrounding environment.

> **Note**
>
> The term **variable capture** has its origins in other languages of the Lisp family. Unlike Clojure, most Lisps do not have immutable data structures, so the word "variable" is perfectly appropriate. We'll continue to say "variable capture," even though most Clojure "variables" aren't really variables.

Here's a quick example. Earlier in this chapter, we tried to write a macro like this:

```
user> (defmacro parameterized-multi-minimal [n-times s]
          (cons 'do (repeat n-times '(println s))))
#'user/parameterized-multi-minimal
```

This macro didn't work. It produced this error:

```
user> (parameterized-multi-minimal 5 "error?")
Syntax error compiling at (Exercise01:localhost:52997(clj)*:121:36).
Unable to resolve symbol: s in this context
```

The reason for this was that the **s** parameter disappears after expansion. As a result, **(println s)** fails because, at runtime, there is no **s**. What if **s** is already defined, though? We can do the following:

```
user> (let [s "Wrong"]
        (parameterized-multi-minimal 2 "Right"))
Wrong
Wrong
nil
```

Even though there is no syntax error, this really is *wrong*. Depending on the context, this macro will not behave the same way. The real argument, **"Right"**, is obscured by a variable in the environment, **"Wrong"**. It's easy to imagine how code like this could produce wildly unpredictable results. The macro writer has no knowledge of or control over whatever **s** might be bound to in the environment where the macro is called.

The Clojure macro system provides some protection against this kind of problem. We've already seen one of them. The **syntax-quote** backtick causes symbols to be assigned to the namespace where the macro is defined:

```
user> '(my-symbol 5)
(user/my-symbol 5)
```

This provides an initial degree of protection against variable capture since a namespaced symbol can't be confused with core Clojure functions or with local **let** bindings. The **let** macro, in fact, won't allow a namespaced symbol to be used as a binding.

> **Note**
>
> When looking at the expansion of a macro you are working on, if you see symbols that have been assigned to the current namespace, it's probably a sign that those symbols are vulnerable to variable capture.

Let's try a slightly more realistic example. Here's a macro that defines a **let**-like environment where the **body** parameter can be evaluated. This is a common structure for macros, where the macro sets up and possibly tears down a specialized environment. The environment might be a database connection, an open file or, like in this example, just a series of bindings that make it easier to write your code. This macro will take an integer and symbol and then provide an environment with automatic bindings for the integer as a string, as an integer, and as a Java **double**. The symbol parameter is then used to define the **-as-string**, **-as-int**, and **-as-double** bindings, which can be used in the code provided as the **body**:

```
(defmacro let-number [[binding n] body]
  '(let [~(symbol (str binding "-as-string"))  (str ~n)
         ~(symbol (str binding "-as-int")) (int ~n)
         ~(symbol (str binding "-as-double")) (double ~n)]
    ~body))
```

In a simple case, the **let-int** macro could be used like this:

```
user> (let-number [my-int 5]
        (type my-int-as-string))
java.lang.String
```

This result just shows that **my-int-as-string** is indeed defined and that the integer **5** has been coerced into a string.

Look what happens, though, when one of the internal bindings is already defined and is used in the macro parameter:

```
user> (let [my-int-as-int 1000]
        (let-number [my-int (/ my-int-as-int 2)]
        (str "The result is: " my-int-as-double)))
"The result is: 250.0"
```

Even when working with macros, 1,000 divided by 2 should be 500 and not 250! What happened? The problem here is that with a macro, the **(/ my-int-as-int 2)** parameter is not evaluated before being passed to the macro. The macro doesn't "know" about the value 500. It only "sees" the code that is present at compile time. The expanded version of this macro call provides a better view of what is happening:

```
user> (macroexpand-1 '(let-number [my-int (/ my-int-as-int 2)]
                        (str "The result is: " my-int-as-double)))
(clojure.core/let
 [my-int-as-string
  (clojure.core/str (/ my-int-as-int 2))
  my-int-as-int
```

```
  (clojure.core/int (/ my-int-as-int 2))
  my-int-as-double
  (clojure.core/double (/ my-int-as-int 2))]
 (str "The result is: " my-int-as-double))
```

The first thing to notice is that **(/ my-int-as-int 2)** appears three times. When **my-int-as-double** is defined, the local binding, **my-int-as-int**, supersedes the original binding. If the original binding was 1,000, the local **my-int-as-int** is defined as 500. When **my-int-as-double** is defined, **my-int-as-int** becomes 500, which is then divided by two one more time.

This is a subtle variable capture bug that could have disastrous consequences. Most of the time, everything would work correctly. Then, from time to time, the results would be inexplicably incorrect. Staring for hours at the source code would not help since the actual bug is only visible when the code is expanded. While it may seem like a strange edge case, a bug like this could actually occur fairly easily with nested **let-number** macros.

Avoiding Variable Capture with Automatic Gensyms

Luckily, there is a solution for a macro such as **let-number**, which is to evaluate the argument only once and then store the result in a local binding that can then be used for further calculations:

```
(defmacro let-number [[binding n] body]
  '(let [result# ~n
         ~(symbol (str binding "-as-string"))  (str result#)
         ~(symbol (str binding "-as-int")) (int result#)
         ~(symbol (str binding "-as-double")) (double result#)]
     ~body))
```

In the first line of the **let** bindings, the calculation represented by **n** is performed and bound to **result#**. All of the following bindings then use **result#** to produce their particular versions: **string**, **integer**, **double**. This is a very good habit to have when writing macros: avoid calculating things twice.

First, let's make sure this works:

```
user> (let [my-int-as-int 1000.0]
        (let-number [my-int (/ my-int-as-int 2)]
          (str "The result is: " my-int-as-double)))
"The result is: 500.0"
```

That's better. The (/ my-int-as-int 2) expression is only evaluated once and the result is correct now. Multiple evaluations of code inside a macro could have other unintended consequences if the repeated code has side effects.

There is one remaining question, though: why do we write result# instead of just result? This is an example of Clojure's macro system helping us avoid other kinds of errors. The suffix on the result symbol has a special meaning when it's used in a syntax-quoted expression. In those cases, Clojure's syntax quoting transforms result into what is called a **gensym**, a *generated symbol* with a name that is guaranteed to be unique. In the code produced by the let-number macro, you won't see a binding to a symbol named result or even result#. Instead, there will be something like result__15090__auto__. That's a generated, unique symbol. Gensyms are a key component in Clojure's macro system because, when used effectively, they prevent name collisions between symbols that have been produced by a macro and symbols present in the environment where the macro is called, or in code that is a macro argument. In the REPL, you can produce your own gensyms:

```
user> '(result#)
(result__15099__auto__)
user> '(result#)
(result__15103__auto__)
```

Each time, a different symbol is produced, unless the symbols are in the same syntax-quoted expression:

```
user> '(= result# result#)
(clojure.core/= result__15111__auto__ result__15111__auto__)
```

This is what allows gensyms to be used to refer to the same thing. It can also be a limitation since, often, you need to use more than one syntax-quoted expression inside a macro. We'll show you how to deal with those cases a little later.

To understand the importance of this, imagine a version of let-number where the result of n was assigned to result without the # suffix. Because of this, the result binding would be available inside the code in the body parameter. Most of the time, this would not be a problem, as long as the body code did not use a value named result. If there was a collision, though, the direct consequence would be a very nasty bug.

Consider this use of the macro while using **result** without the protection afforded by the **#** suffix. To do that, we need to insert the literal result symbol into the expanded code. This will require using a little macro trick where we unquote and then quote the symbol, like this ~'**result**. The initial unquote suspends the syntax quoting and then the single quotation mark applies a standard quote that does not use namespacing.

> **Note**
>
> The unquote-quote pattern should generally be avoided because gensyms are much safer. However, a simple quoted symbol can be useful in certain cases, especially when a symbol is supposed to have a special syntactical meaning inside the macro, as we saw with the | in *Exercise 11.01, The and-ors Macro*.

We get the following macro code:

```
user> (defmacro bad-let-number [[binding n] body]
        '(let [~'result ~n
               ~(symbol (str binding "-as-string")) (str ~'result)
               ~(symbol (str binding "-as-int")) (int ~'result)
               ~(symbol (str binding "-as-double")) (double ~'result)]
           ~body))
```

Using this macro could be dangerous:

```
(let [result 42]
  (bad-let-number [my-int 1000]
    (= result 1000)))  ;; Would return "true"
```

This would be extremely confusing. We expect the **result** in the initial **let** binding to be the same as the **result** in the **let-number** binding. Debugging this error would require exploring the inner workings of the macro and would probably be a long, painful process. Gensyms protect against this kind of problem and Clojure makes them easy to use.

> **Note**
>
> Not all Lisps have automatic gensyms. In Common Lisp, macro writers have to call the **gensym** function explicitly. Clojure also has a **gensym** function, which can be used to create gensyms outside of a syntax-quoted environment. We'll use the **gensym** function ourselves a little later

As a general rule, any bindings in a macro that are not part of the exposed interface should be defined with gensyms. In the **let-number** macro, bindings such as **my-int-as-string** are an exposed part of the interface and, as such, require real symbol names. Bindings such as **result#**, which only are used "behind the scenes" (at compile time), should be protected with gensyms.

Exercise 11.04: Monitoring Functions

In this exercise, we will write a macro for creating functions. The functions will be wrapped inside logic that adds some extra behavior to an otherwise ordinary function.

These days, you're working for a company that provides Software as a Service to other companies. Management wants to rethink the prices that are charged to customers. They want to know, at a very fine-grained level, which services are the most expensive to provide and which customers are consuming the most resources.

Your job is to develop a system for logging the computation time of some of the important, high-level functions in the code base. At first, you thought that you would have to go through the entire code base and add timing and reporting logic every time one of these high-level functions is called. Then, you remembered macros. You've decided to write a proof-of-concept macro to show to your boss.

The high-level functions you want to measure all have, among others, a **client-id** parameter. You'll use that parameter to provide feedback to the monitoring framework. One requirement is that the data will be sent, even if an exception is thrown. Collecting detailed error statistics will be useful for monitoring and diagnostics.

The macro will be invoked instead of **defn** when defining the functions. In addition to the standard arguments to **defn**, the macro will also take a function that will be called to send data to the monitoring system. Let's get started:

1. In a REPL, set up an outline for the macro:

```
(defmacro defmonitored
  [fn-name tx-fn args & body-elements]
  ;; TODO: everything
  )
```

This means that, when defining a function that needs to be monitored, we'll write something like this, assuming that **send-to-framework** is a function that has already been defined:

```
(defmonitored my-func send-to-framework
              [an-arg another-arg client-id]...)
```

Calling the function will be no different from calling any other function, as long as there is a `client-id` argument:

```
(my-func an-arg another-arg 42)
```

2. Establish the basic layout of the macro's internals. There will be two parts: on the outside, some compile-time **let** bindings, and on the inside, a syntax-quoted **(defn...)** expression:

```
(defmacro defmonitored
  [fn-name tx-fn & args-and-body]
  (let [
        ;; TODO: compile time let bindings
        ]
    '(defn ~fn-name ~[]
       ;; TODO: the defn template
       )))
```

The outer **let** bindings will set up some of the values that will be used in the more "template"-like **defn** part.

We've placed the **fn-name**, unquoted, and an empty parameter list inside the call to **defn**. Even if it doesn't do anything yet, the macro should already compile, and you should be able to use it to define a function:

```
user> (defmonitored my-func identity [])
#'user/my-func
user> (my-func)
nil
```

3. As you already know, the Clojure **defn** macro allows us to define multiple arities for the same function. This really means that there are two different structures that a function definition can have. First there is the single arity that we use most of the time:

```
(defn a-func [arg1 arg2]
  (+ arg1 arg2))
```

Multiple arity functions have several "bodies." Each "body" is a list that starts out with the argument list, which is specific to that arity, and then includes the corresponding code:

```
(defn b-func
  ([arg1] arg1)
  ([arg1 arg2]
   (+ arg1 arg2))
  ([arg1 arg2 arg3]
   (* (+ arg1 arg2) arg3)))
```

Because we want **defmonitored** to act as a replacement for **defn**, we need to be able to handle these two different structures.

Much of what we are going to do now requires us to have access to the code inside each of the function bodies, if there are multiple arities. To avoid having to deal with two separate cases, that is, single and multiple arities, we are going to check to see which kind we have. If we have just one arity, we will wrap the argument list and the function body in a list so that it has the same structure as the multiple arity variety.

A function like this is correct, even if it only has one arity:

```
(defn a-func
  ([arg] (println arg)))
```

To do this, we add a **vector?** check:

```
(defmacro defmonitored
  [fn-name tx-fn & args-and-body]
  (let [pre-arg-list (take-while (complement sequential?) args-and-body)
        fn-content (drop-while (complement sequential?) args-and-body)
        fn-bodies (if (vector? (first fn-content))
                    '(~fn-content)
                    fn-content)]
    '(defn ~fn-name ~@pre-arg-list
       ;; TODO: more magic
       ~@fn-bodies)))
```

When the first item in **fn-content** is an argument list, we use syntax quoting, and then **unquote**, to enclose the function body in a list.

4. To handle the multiple arities, we need to deal with each function body separately. This sounds like a good time to write a function that can be called on each one.

    We'll call the **wrap-fn-body** function to deal with this. Even though this is a function and not a macro, it will be called at compile time, so all our macro-writing skills are still applicable here.

    The function will repeat the basic structure of the macro: **let** bindings on the outside and a syntax-quoted "template" on the inside. This time, we'll start with the bindings:

```
(defn wrap-fn-body [fn-name tx-fn b]
  (let [arg-list (first b)
        client-id-arg (first (filter #(= 'client-id %) arg-list))
        fn-body (rest b)]
    ;; TODO: the body
    ))
```

    We know that the first item in a function body is the argument list. That's easy to extract, just like **fn-body**, which is everything that's not the argument list.

5. Add a check for the **client-id** parameter in the argument list. Our goal is to be able to measure function use per client, so we absolutely need a **client-id** argument. If it's missing, the code should fail. To do this, we'll simply check the **arg-list** binding:

```
(defn wrap-fn-body [fn-name tx-fn b]
  (let [arg-list (first b)
        client-id-arg (first (filter #(= 'client-id %) arg-list))
        fn-body (rest b)]
    (when-not (first (filter #(= % 'client-id) arg-list))
      (throw (ex-info "Missing client-id argument" {})))
    ;; TODO: the body
    ))
```

    We can safely use the "unquote/quote" pattern here on the **client-id** symbol, rather than a gensym, because we know the **client-id** will not be picked up accidentally from the surrounding code, precisely because it will be in the argument list.

6. It's finally time to write the "template" part. This is a longer block of code, but it is really quite simple. We'll come back and explain some of the quoting strategies here later:

```
'(~arg-list
  (let [start-time# (System/nanoTime)]
    (try
      (let [result# (do  ~@fn-body)]
        (~tx-fn {:name ~(name fn-name)
                 :client-id ~'client-id
                 :status :complete
                 :start-time start-time#
                 :end-time (System/nanoTime)})
        result#)
      (catch Exception e#
        (~tx-fn {:name ~(name fn-name)
                 :client-id ~'client-id
                 :status :error
                 :start-time start-time#
                 :end-time (System/nanoTime)})
        (throw e#)))))
```

The overall pattern is fairly simple. The heart of the function is in the inner **let** binding, where, in the expanded code, we will bind the **result#** gensym to the output resulting from calling the actual code, which is still in **fn-body**.

Once we have that result, we send off some information to **tx-fn** by using **System/nanoTime** as our **:end-time**. This "heart" of the function is then wrapped in two things, the first of which is a **try/catch** form. If there's an exception, we send a slightly different message via **tx-fn**. And finally, the outer **let** binding is where we establish the **start-time#** binding so that we can also report when the function started.

Note that we were required to use several automatic gensyms: **start-time#**, **end-time#**, **results#**, and even **e#**, the exception.

7. Put it all back together.

Here's the complete **wrap-fn-body** function:

```
(defn wrap-fn-body [fn-name tx-fn b]
  (let [arg-list (first b)
        fn-body (rest b)]
    (when-not (first (filter #(= % 'client-id) arg-list))
      (throw (ex-info "Missing client-id argument" {})))
```

```
    '(~arg-list
      (let [start-time# (System/nanoTime)]
        (try
          (let [result# (do  ~@fn-body)]
            (~tx-fn {:name ~(name fn-name)
                     :client-id ~'client-id
                     :status :complete
                     :start-time start-time#
                     :end-time (System/nanoTime)})
            result#)
          (catch Exception e#
            (~tx-fn {:name ~(name fn-name)
                     :client-id ~'client-id
                     :status :error
                     :start-time start-time#
                     :end-time (System/nanoTime)})
            (throw e#)))))))
```

Now, call **wrap-fn-body** from the final **defmonitored** macro. You can do this by mapping over the list of function bodies. Naturally, **map** will wrap them in a list, which we don't want, so we "unquote-splice" (**~@**) the list:

```
(defmacro defmonitored
  [fn-name tx-fn & args-and-body]
  (let [pre-arg-list (take-while (complement sequential?) args-and-body)
        fn-content (drop-while (complement sequential?) args-and-body)
        fn-bodies (if (vector? (first fn-content))
                    '(~fn-content)
                    fn-content)]
    '(defn ~fn-name ~@pre-arg-list
       ~@(map (partial wrap-fn-body fn-name tx-fn) fn-bodies))))
```

8. Test the macro, using **println** as the reporting function. First, define a simple function:

```
user> (defmonitored my-func println [client-id m]  (assoc m :client client-id))
#'user/my-func
```

The **my-func** function seems to work:

```
user> (my-func 32 {:data 123})
{:client-id 32, :name my-func, :start-time 770791427794572, :end-time
770791428448202, :status :complete}
{:data 123, :client 32}
```

Let's try some problematic cases. We'll start by throwing an exception:

```
user> (defmonitored exception-func println [client-id] (throw (ex-info "Boom!" {})))
```

The output is as follows:

```
user> (exception-func 5)
{:client-id 5, :name exception-func, :start-time 772295578435009, :end-time 772295579255183
i, :status :error}
Execution error (ExceptionInfo) at user/exception-func (REPL:75).
Boom!
```

Figure 11.4: An exception, timed, recorded, and reported

What about if we try to define a function that doesn't have a **client-id** argument?

```
user> (defmonitored no-client-func println [no-client-id] (+ 1 1))
```

The output is as follows:

```
user> (defmonitored no-client-func println [no-client-id] (+ 1 1))
Syntax error macroexpanding clojure.core/defn at (Chapter11:localhost:64419(clj)*:69:7).
Missing client-id argument
```

Figure 11.5: The exception we threw during macroexpansion appears as a syntax error

The **defmonitored** macro shows how macros can be used to modify Clojure itself. The situation called for a **defn** with extra capabilities, so that is what we wrote. It would, of course, be possible to accomplish the same thing by wrapping functions inside a "timing and reporting" function. But this would be much more intrusive than simply writing **defmonitored** instead of **defn**.

When to Use Manual gensyms

When using Clojure's automatic gensyms, such as **result#**, it's important to remember that they are a feature of syntax quoting. Writing **result#** outside of a syntax-quoted expression won't throw an exception, but none of the magic happens:

```
user> (macroexpand '(def my-number# 5))
(def my-number# 5)
```

On the other hand, if we syntax-quote **my-number#**, the "magic" comes back:

```
user> (macroexpand '(def `my-number# 5))
(def `my-number__14717__auto__ 5)
```

This will usually not be a problem. It's easy to remember that automatic gensyms only work inside syntax quoting. There is another important thing to remember, though: an automatic gensym is only valid inside the scope of the syntax-quoted expression where it was originally defined. This means that, with nested syntax-quoted expressions, a **result#** in the outer expression will not expand to the same gensym as a **result#** in the inner expression. Let's try an example.

Consider this little macro:

```
(defmacro fn-context [v & symbol-fn-pairs]
  '(let [v# ~v]
     ~@(map (fn [[sym f]]
              '(defn ~sym [x#]
                 (f v# x#))) (partition 2 symbol-fn-pairs))))
```

This macro is supposed to allow us to define multiple functions inside a **let** block so that each function refers, via a **closure**, to the same binding. We want it to produce code that, conceptually, at least, looks roughly like this:

```
(let [common-value 5]
  (defn adder [n] (+ common-value 5))
  (defn subtractor [n] (- common-value 5))
  (defn multiplier [n] (* common-value 5)))
```

To define those functions, we would write this:

```
(fn-context 5 adder + subtractor - multiplier *)
```

The **symbol-fn-pairs** argument is expected to be an alternating series of symbols that will become the names of the functions, and some will become functions as well. We then use **partition-by** in the body of the macro to organize this list into pairs. (In production code, we would probably want to check that **symbol-fn-pairs** contains an even number of items, just as **let** complains if there is an odd number of items in its bindings.)

Let's see if this macro works as advertised:

```
user> (fn-context 5 adder + subtractor - multiplier *)

Syntax error compiling at (Activity:localhost:52217(clj)*:246:15).
Unable to resolve symbol: v__14896__auto__ in this context
```

Oh no! What happened?

Before we use **macroexpand** to start debugging, we can tell that the problem is related in some way to the **v#** binding because the **v__14896__auto__** gensym is prefixed with a **v**.

Macro expansions are hard to read, especially when there are a lot of gensyms, which are, let's face it, hardly things of beauty when expanded. Start by trying to find the symbol mentioned in the syntax error message. We'll use `macroexpand-1` here, to avoid expanding the `let` and `defn` macros:

```
user> (macroexpand-1 '(fn-context 5 adder + subtractor - multiplier *))
(clojure.core/let
 [v__14897__auto__ 5]
 (clojure.core/defn
  adder
  [x__14895__auto__]
  (+ v__14896__auto__ x__14895__auto__))
 (clojure.core/defn
  subtractor
  [x__14895__auto__]
  (- v__14896__auto__ x__14895__auto__))
 (clojure.core/defn
  multiplier
  [x__14895__auto__]
  (* v__14896__auto__ x__14895__auto__)))
```

The problem here is that, in the initial `let` binding, `v#` becomes `v__14897__auto__`. Later, inside each of the function definitions, we want to use that binding, but unfortunately, in each of the functions, `v#` has been replaced with a slightly different gensym, which is `v__14896__auto__`. Suddenly, the syntax error makes more sense: in each function, we're trying to use a non-existent binding.

Why did `v#` fail in this case? The problem here is that we have two separate syntax-quoted expressions. The first is the top-level `let`, where `v#` is used initially. Then, we use `unquote-splice` to splice the list of functions into the `let` expression. Inside the anonymous function that's passed to `map`, we use the syntax-quoting backtick one more time to return the `defn` form. And this is where we get into trouble. Because we are no longer in the same syntax-quoted expression, `v#` does not expand to the same gensym. As a result, the two symbols are treated as totally separate values and we get a syntax error.

This is a time when we can't use automatic gensyms. Instead, we'll have to do this the old-fashioned way and use the **gensym** function ourselves. Here's how:

```
(defmacro fn-context [v & symbol-fn-pairs]
  (let [common-val-gensym (gensym "common-val-")]
    '(let [~common-val-gensym ~v]
       ~@(map (fn [[sym f]]
                '(defn ~sym [x#]
                   (~f ~common-val-gensym x#))) (partition 2 symbol-fn-pairs)))))
```

The primary difference here is that we've wrapped the body of the first version of the macro in a separate **let** expression that is not quoted. This means that it will be present at compile time but will disappear at runtime in the expanded code. In this outer **let** expression, we call **gensym** and assign its value to **common-val-gensym**. At compile time, we'll refer to the gensym with this symbol. Because our **let** expression wraps the entire body of the macro, **common-val-gensym** will have the same value throughout the entire macro.

Let's test it:

```
user> (fn-context 5 adder + subtractor - multiplier *)
#'user/multiplier
user> (adder 5)
10
user> (subtractor 12)
-7
user> (multiplier 10)
50
```

Any reasonably complex macro will likely have more than one syntax-quoted expression, so knowing when to manually create and assign gensyms can be important. This knowledge can help avoid some hard-to-debug situations where your code looks correct but just doesn't work.

As a side note, the **fn-context** macro could easily be replaced with a functional solution by using the **partial** function. Remember, **partial** takes a function and one or more arguments and returns a function identical to the original, except that the first one or more arguments are already "filled in." Thus, instead of using a macro and **defn** forms, we can simply define new functions using **def** and **partial**:

```
user> (let [x 100]
         (def adder (partial + x))
         (def subtractor (partial - x))
         (def multiplier (partial * x)))
#'user/multiplier
user> (adder 5)
105
```

The possibilities offered by functional programming in Clojure are such that it is fairly rare to find a problem, in day-to-day coding, that can only be expressed as a macro. Authors of libraries will tend to use macros slightly more often, for those times when it is important to have a very clear interface for some code. Perhaps the greatest advantage of Clojure macros is that most of the time, we don't need to write them: either library authors have already done so or there is a solution on the functional side. And then, of course, if we really must write a macro, Clojure provides some excellent tools for doing so.

In this chapter, we've taken a close look at several of the most common traps in macro writing. By taking these into consideration, you should be able to write effective macros. They should also serve as a reminder of why macros should be avoided when it is convenient to do so: writing and debugging macros can be a difficult and error-prone task. In the right circumstances, macros can be an extremely powerful tool for removing boilerplate and other forms of repetition from source code.

Activity 11.01: A Tennis CSV Macro

In some of the earlier chapters, we worked with tennis data contained in CSV files. Each time, we used a standard Clojure macro called **with-open**, and each time, we followed an almost identical pattern where the file's contents are threaded (with the ->> macro) through a series of transformations:

1. Read the contents using the **clojure.data.csv** library's **read-csv** function.

2. Transform each line from the input file into a map using the **semantic-csv** library's **mappify** function.

3. Cast some of the fields to numeric values using **semantic-csv**'s **cast-with** function.

4. Remove some of the unnecessary data fields by using **map** to call **select-keys** on each item in the dataset.

5. End with a call to **doall** to make sure we avoid returning a lazy sequence that would not be able to be completed once the file had been closed.

Each of these steps added some repetitive boilerplate to your code. The result is that each time you want to write a function that analyzes one of these CSV files, you end up repeating the same code over and over again, which is tedious and error-prone to write, and hard to read because the important logic in your code is buried in boilerplate.

Due to the success of the tennis data on the data-driven sports journalism website you work for, you now write a lot of functions with this identical pattern. You've decided it's time to make your life easier by cleaning up this code with a nice macro called **with-tennis-csv**.

Your goal is to write a macro called **with-tennis-csv** that will encapsulate most or all of the repetitive steps for accessing the CSV data.

Interface Design

The macro should accept the following as arguments:

- The CSV filename (a string).

- The mappings from field names to types for **cast-with** (a map of keywords to functions).

- A list of keywords to keep. If an empty list is supplied, all the keywords will be kept.

- An arbitrary number of Clojure forms. These forms must accept and return a list of maps.

The Clojure forms will be inserted in the middle of the **->>** chain of expressions:

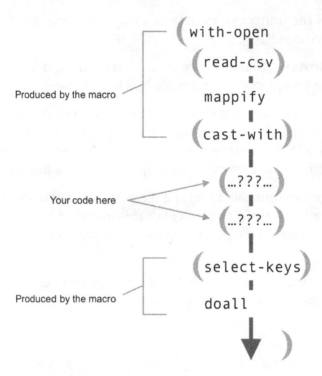

Figure 11.6: Inserting the Clojure form

The macro caller will supply the forms that will be placed inside the chain of transformations.

Because the Clojure forms will be used inside a double-arrow threading macro, **->>** their final argument must be omitted.

The following **blowout** function illustrates a possible use of the macro you want to write. The function takes a CSV file path and a threshold and then returns a list of matches where the winner won by more than **threshold** games. The results are narrowed to three fields: the names of the two players and the number of games by which the winner defeated the loser:

```
(defn blowouts [csv threshold]
  (with-tennis-csv csv
    {:winner_games_won sc/->int :loser_games_won sc/->int}
    [:winner_name :loser_name :games_diff]
    (map #(assoc % :games_diff (- (:winner_games_won %) (:loser_games_won %))))
    (filter #(> (:games_diff %) threshold))))
```

Implementation

The central challenge here is making sure that the forms are correctly inserted into the `->>` threading macro.

Make sure that none of the arguments are evaluated more than once inside the macro:

1. Start by determining what the call to **with-tennis-csv** should expand to in the preceding example.

2. Set up your project with the necessary dependencies in a **deps.edn** file and require the necessary libraries in a **tennis-macro** namespace.

3. Determine what the arguments to your macro will be. Don't forget that it should accept an arbitrary number of forms to be threaded.

4. In your macro, as a syntax-quoted "template," insert all the parts of the target code that will always be present, no matter how the macro is called.

5. Insert the expressions to be threaded.

6. Find a way to only apply **select-keys** if keys have been supplied and can be selected.

To test your macro, you can use the CSV files we've been using all along: https://packt.live/2Rn7PSx.

> **Note**
> The solution for this activity can be found on page 733.

Summary

In this chapter, we've explored Clojure's macro system, as well as many of the issues surrounding macros. By now, you should have a grasp of the fundamental concepts of macros, starting with the difference between compile-time and runtime evaluation, and have a mental model that will allow you to move on to writing your own macros if necessary, or to understand macros that have been written by others. The problems of macro hygiene, variable capture, and double evaluation are at the heart of the macro writing process. Knowing all of this will help you write macros, read macros, and, most of all, decide when to write a macro and when not to.

Regardless of whether or not you go on to use macros to write your own **Domain-Specific Languages** (**DSL**) in Clojure, you'll already benefit from Clojure macros. The flexibility they provide allows Clojure to be extended by library authors in ways that would simply be impossible without macros. Many commonly used Clojure libraries, such as the Ring HTTP server, which you'll learn about in *Chapter 14, HTTP with Ring*, make extensive use of macros to make life simpler for developers.

In the next chapter, we are going to explore another one of Clojure's strong points: dealing with concurrency.

12

Concurrency

Overview

In this chapter we will explore Clojure's concurrency features. On the JVM, you will learn the basics of programming with multiple processor threads: starting a new thread and using the results. To coordinate your threads, we will use Clojure's innovative reference types. One of these, the atom, can also be used in a JavaScript environment.

By the end of this chapter, you will be able to build simple browser games and manage their state using atoms.

Introduction

Ever since the Clojure language was first introduced, its concurrency model has been one of its major selling points. In programming, the word "concurrency" can apply to a lot of different situations. To start with a simple definition, any time your program or your system has more than one simultaneous flow of operations, you are dealing with concurrency. In multithreaded Java programs, that would mean code running simultaneously in separate processor threads. Each processor thread follows its own internal logic, but to work properly your program needs to coordinate the communication between the different threads. Even though JavaScript runtimes are single-threaded, both the browser and Node.js environments have their own ways of dealing with simultaneous logical flows. While the roots of Clojure's concurrency are definitely in Java, some of the ideas and tools apply equally in **ClojureScript**.

In this chapter, you will learn the basics of concurrent programming. Some of Clojure's features, such as **Software Transactional Memory (STM)**, are mostly useful in large, complex systems. While we can't simulate all of that complexity in a single chapter, we will explore the basic concepts and tools that Clojure provides. To demonstrate the techniques and get you up to speed on concurrency, we'll use two different environments. On the JVM, you'll learn how to create threads that communicate with each other. In the browser, you'll learn how to coordinate events that occur in different parts of the web page.

Concurrency in General

Modern computers use **threads** to distribute execution between multiple processor cores. There are many reasons for this, including the physics of microchip design and the need for user environments that remain responsive even when one program is performing an intensive computation in the background. Everyone wants to be able to check their email, listen to music, and run their Clojure REPL at the same time! Inside a program, this kind of multitasking can also represent a significant performance gain. While one thread is waiting for data from the disk drive, another for the network, two other threads can be processing data. When done correctly, this can represent a significant gain in performance and overall efficiency. The operative phrase here, though, is "when done correctly." Concurrency can be tricky.

Most computer code is written in a linear manner: do this, do that, then do this. The source code for a method or a function reads from top to bottom. We think about code linearly when we are writing it. In a multithreaded system, that's not how your code will be executed. Some parts of your program will run in one thread, and other parts in other threads, simultaneously. Coordination becomes a new problem. Experience shows that multithreaded applications are harder to write and tend to be more error-prone than single-threaded applications. Most of all, they are harder for us to understand. So, while there is a potential for better performance, there is also a potential for greater complexity. Like many aspects of programming, it's all about trade-offs.

Clojure's most important concurrency feature is actually one that you've been using from the beginning: immutability. Clojure's immutable data types provide a special kind of protection throughout your system. Values are locked down once and for all; if a separate thread needs to "modify" your data, it will actually use an efficient copy that won't interfere with the other threads. And because this feature is a fundamental part of the Clojure language, you get it for "free": data is immutable by default, so there is no extra procedure to prepare it for concurrency.

When a new thread is created, we say that the current thread has been forked. The parent thread shares its state with the new thread but loses control of the execution flow. Let's take a look at how things can go wrong when values are mutable:

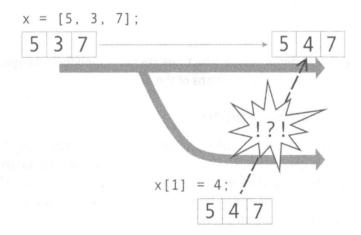

Figure 12.1: Shared state in a language with mutable data structures can lead to problems

In this diagram, we can see a main thread that creates a fork. In the original thread, the variable, **x**, is an array: **[5, 3, 7]**. The fork then modifies the array. Because it is shared between the two threads, the array is also modified in the main thread. From the point of view of the main thread, the value of **x** seems to change suddenly for no reason, as if modified by some external force. This is an oversimplification, of course, since languages such as Java do allow programmers to protect themselves from problems like this. However, shared mutable state does create a risk of this kind of problem.

Immutability in Clojure largely solves this part of the problem. Here's a similar diagram representing a Clojure version of the same thing:

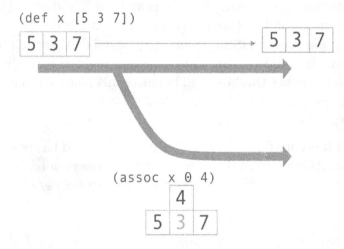

Figure 12.2: Clojure's immutable data structures are never modified: changes create new versions of the data

Automatic Parallelization with pmap

Nearly every kind of concurrency involves some additional complexity for the programmer. There is an exception to this rule though: Clojure's **pmap** function. The name is the abbreviation of **parallel map**. Just like **map**, **pmap** calls a function on each item in a list. The difference is that each function call runs on a separate thread so that some of the calculations can be run simultaneously.

In this diagram, we map an imaginary function, **pfn**, over a simple vector. For each item, **pmap** calls **pfn** in a new thread:

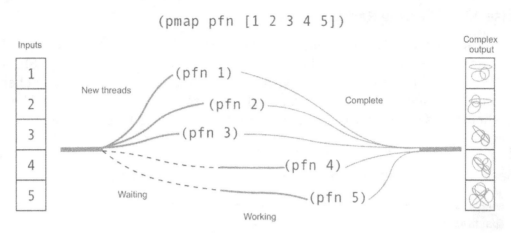

Figure 12.3: pmap spawns new threads so that calculations can occur simultaneously

This might seem like great news. In certain cases, it might be. But if you're thinking "I'll use **pmap** all the time and my program will run faster," you'll be disappointed most of the time. The problem is that there is a lot of behind-the-scenes work that must occur for **pmap** to spawn new threads. It turns out that **pmap** is only more efficient than the single-threaded **map** function when the calculation is particularly time-consuming. We can compare the relative speed of **map** and **pmap** on a trivial **map** operation. We'll use Clojure's **time** macro to compare execution times. The **time** macro wraps an expression, evaluates it normally, and prints out the time it took to evaluate:

```
user> (time (doall (map inc (range 10))))
"Elapsed time: 0.081947 msecs"
(1 2 3 4 5 6 7 8 9 10)
user> (time (doall (pmap inc (range 10))))
"Elapsed time: 2.288832 msecs"
(1 2 3 4 5 6 7 8 9 10)
```

Incrementing 10 integers is not a resource-intensive task. With the ordinary **map** function, it takes less than a tenth of a microsecond. Performing the same operation with **pmap** takes almost 30 times longer! What took so long? Creating threads consumes resources. Obviously, **pmap** should only be used when it's clear that the additional overhead is worth it.

> **Note**
>
> We need to use **doall** here; otherwise, we would just be timing the speed of the creation of an unrealized lazy sequence.

Exercise 12.01: Testing Randomness

Back on your job at the data journalism website, one of the analysts is concerned that the random number generator used in your programs is not random enough. She wants you to test it by generating a very long sequence of random integers and then checking a few numbers to see whether they are equally represented. In doing this, you'll be able to see whether it's faster to use **map** or **pmap** thanks to Clojure's **time** function.

Open a **REPL**. This is a one-off test, so there's no need to create a project:

1. Generate a very long sequence of integers between **0** and **1000**:

```
user> (def random-ints (doall (take 10000000 (repeatedly
(partial rand-int 1000)))))
#'user/random-ints
```

   Note that we use **doall** to make sure that the lazy sequence returned by **repeatedly** is fully realized.

2. Define a function that counts the number of occurrences of an integer in a list:

```
user> (defn int-count [i xs]
    (count (filter #(= % i) xs)))
#'user/int-count
```

3. Use **map** to count the number of occurrences of some integers in **random-ints**:

```
user> (map #(int-count % random-ints) [0 1 2 45 788 500 999 ])
(1034 1009 971 1094 968 1029 908)
```

4. This seems to work, but it is fairly slow. To discover how slow it is, we can use Clojure's **time** function to provide a quick benchmark. Don't forget to wrap the output from **map** in **doall**. Otherwise, you're just timing the creation of an unrealized lazy sequence:

```
(time (doall (map #(int-count % random-ints) [0 1 2 45 788 500
999])))
"Elapsed time: 7307.28571 msecs"
(9808 10027 9825 10090 9963 10096 9984)
```

   Your time will be longer or shorter, of course.

5. Now try using **pmap** instead:

```
user> (time (doall (pmap #(int-count % random-ints) [0 1 2 45
  788 500 999])))
"Elapsed time: 1602.424627 msecs"
(9808 10027 9825 10090 9963 10096 9984)
```

That's a lot faster! This is good in case the analyst asks for an even bigger sample size.

In this example, **pmap** came to the rescue and sped things up significantly. The beauty of **pmap** is that no extra coding is necessary. It's simple enough to write **pmap** instead of **map**. However, like many tools, the most important part is knowing when not to use it. This example was particularly well suited for parallelization because of the large size of the dataset. **pmap** should only be used in situations where you know that the calculation will generally be slow.

Futures

With **pmap**, Clojure takes care of all the thread management for you, which makes things easy. A lot of times, however, you need more control over your threads than what **pmap** provides. Clojure's **futures** do just this. They are a mechanism for spawning and waiting for new threads.

Consider a situation where two expensive calculations are needed to perform a third operation, such as adding the two results together. In a single-threaded context, we would just write this:

```
(+ (expensive-calc-1 5) (expensive-calc-2 19))
```

Written this way, the call to **expensive-calc-1** needs to complete before **expensive-calc-2** can start. If the calculations could be run in parallel, we would cut the execution time nearly in half, in the best cases. Running the two threads in parallel creates some new problems, though. We need a way of coordinating the return values, especially since we don't know whether **expensive-calc-1** or **expensive-calc-2** will complete first. We need a way to wait for both before calling **+**.

Futures are designed for this type of situation. The **future** macro causes the code it contains to be run in a separate thread. It immediately returns a placeholder, which is a reference to the *future* result. When the code in the new thread has completed, the placeholder can be **dereferenced**.

In Clojure, dereferencing applies when a value is not immediately available and can only be accessed by taking an additional step. With a var or a let binding, the value is immediately available. There is no extra step to take. We just use it. With a future, as well as with reference types that we'll see later in the chapter, we don't know whether the value is available yet. Using the **deref** function with a future means that we are willing to wait for it to complete. **deref** is necessary because we need a way to indicate this special behavior. To make your code easier to read (and type), instead of writing **(deref my-future)**, you can just type **@my-future**. This is an example of a reader macro: Clojure immediately translates **@my-future** into **(deref my-future)** when it reads your code.

With this in mind, we can rewrite the preceding expression. First, though, we'll define an artificially slow function using the Java **Thread/sleep** method:

```
user> (defn expensive-calc-1 [i]
    (Thread/sleep (+ 500 (rand 1000)))
    (println "Calc 1")
    (+ i 5))
user> (defn expensive-calc-2 [i]
    (Thread/sleep (+ 500 (rand 1000)))
    (println "Calc 2")
    (+ i 5))
```

> **Note**
>
> The **Thread/sleep** method is a convenient piece of Java interop that is useful for simulating long-running computations or input/output operations that take time. While it's good for experimenting, you rarely need it in production code.

With these functions, the original expression evaluates them one after the other:

```
user> (+ (expensive-calc-1 10) (expensive-calc-2 25))
Calc 1
Calc 2
45
```

No matter how many times this function is run, **expensive-calc-1** will always return before **expensive-calc-2**. With futures, this will change:

```
user> (let [c1 (future (expensive-calc-1 10))
      c2 (future (expensive-calc-2 20))]
   (+ (deref c1) (deref c2)))
Calc 2
Calc 1
40
user> (let [c1 (future (expensive-calc-1 10))
      c2 (future (expensive-calc-2 20))]
   (+ (deref c1) (deref c2)))
Calc 1
Calc 2
40
```

First of all, you'll probably notice that this version is slightly faster. Sometimes **expensive-calc-1** returns first, sometimes **expensive-calc-2** wins the race. It doesn't matter which one is faster: the final addition only happens when both are complete. This is the work of the **deref** function, which blocks the evaluation until the computation started by the corresponding call to **future** has returned.

The **(deref c1)** or **(deref c2)** expressions can be replaced with **@c1** or **@c2**, thanks to the **@** reader macro.

Exercise 12.02: A Crowdsourced Spellchecker

Have you ever typed a word into a search engine just to see whether you've spelled it correctly? In this exercise, we'll build a command-line tool that improves on this way of using the internet to verify spellings.

The goal is to be able to write out a command followed by several possible spellings for a word. The spelling tool will then query Wikipedia and return the word that received the most hits. We will use futures so that the different search queries can be run in parallel.

1. Use Leiningen to create a new project using the **app** template. You can call it whatever you want. We'll use **packt-clj.crowdspell** in our examples:

```
lein new app packt-clj.crowdspell
```

2. Go to the new directory that Leiningen created and modify the dependencies in the `project.clj` file. We'll need three libraries: `org.clojure/tools.cli` for accepting user input, `clj-http` for making HTTP requests, and `org.clojure/data.json`.

    The `:dependencies` map should look like this:

    ```
    :dependencies [[org.clojure/clojure "1.10.1"]
                   [org.clojure/tools.cli "0.4.2"]
                   [clj-http "3.10.0"]
                   [org.clojure/data.json "0.2.6"]]
    ```

3. In the `src/packt_clj/` directory, create a `crowdspell` directory. We'll use this directory for any namespaces we need to create for the project. Create a file there called `fetch.clj` and insert the following namespace definition:

    ```
    (ns packt-clj.crowdspell.fetch
      (:require [clj-http.client :as http]
                [clojure.data.json :as json]))
    ```

    All of the fetching and parsing of results will happen in this namespace. The `clj-http` library will help us to perform our web requests to the Wikipedia endpoint and `clojure.data.json` will help us to parse the JSON data that we get back.

4. While you're there, create an empty function definition for `get-best-word`. This will be the key interface of the application: given a list of words, `get-best-word` will return the best one based on the data retrieved from Wikipedia. All we know at this point is that it takes a language code and a list of words as an argument:

    ```
    (defn get-best-word [language-code words])
    ```

    Because Wikipedia uses a separate URL for each language, such as https://ja.wikipedia.org/ or https://en.wikipedia.org/, we can use the language code parameter to internationalize our app.

5. The `packt-clj/crowdspell` namespace, defined in `src/packt_clj/crowdspell.clj`, will be the entry point into the application. There should already be a `-main` function there, created using the `lein new` command.

    Modify the `-main` function so that it calls `get-best-word`. This will also require updating the namespace declaration so that you'll have access to `clojure.tools.cli` and `packt-clj.crowdspell.fetch`.

The namespace declaration should now look like this:

```
(ns packt-clj.crowdspell
  (:require
    [clojure.tools.cli :as cli]
    [packt-clj.crowdspell.fetch :as fetch])
  (:gen-class))
```

The **-main** function should look like this:

```
(defn -main
  [& args]
  (println (fetch/get-best-word "en" args)))
```

For now, we'll just hardcode English as the language code. At this point, the application would theoretically compile and run at the command line but would not do anything.

6. Back in **src/packt_clj/crowdspell/fetch.clj**, write a skeleton for a **word-search** function. This function will search for a single word. The **get-best-word** function will coordinate several concurrent HTTP requests using futures. Each request will be run with **word-search**:

```
(defn word-search [word language-code]
  (try
    ;; TODO: the HTTP request
    (catch Exception e
      {:status :error})))
```

There's a **language-code** parameter because we want our application to be multilingual. We'll add that as a command-line parameter later.

We want to use a **try** block here since our request might fail for any number of reasons. We've already made a design decision: the function will return a map containing, among other things, a **:status** code.

7. Now it's time to write the HTTP request itself. The **clj-http.client** library makes this fairly painless. We just have to make sure that we use the proper Wikipedia-specific parameters: **srsearch** is our search term, and **srlimit** tells the API that we only want one item. Only one item is necessary because the metadata in the response includes a field indicating how many total items were found. Since we are only interested in counting them, this is all we need. You can try the request in the REPL first if you like:

```
packt-clj.crowdspell.fetch> (http/get (str "https://en.wikipedia.org/w/api.php")
                 {:query-params {"action" "query"
                                 "list" "search"
                                 "srlimit" 1
                                 "srsearch" "Clojure"
                                 "format" "json"}
                  :accept :json
                  :cookie-policy :none})
```

If all goes well, a map containing HTTP response, including all the headers, should fill your REPL. You should find a key that says **:status 200**, which means that the request was successful. Any status besides **200** means that something is wrong:

```
"Vary"
"Accept-Encoding,Treat-as-Untrusted,X-Forwarded-Proto,Cookie,Authorization",
"Content-Disposition" "inline; filename=api-result.json",
"Server-Timing" "cache;desc=\"pass\"",
"X-Powered-By"
"PHP/7.2.22-1+0~20190902.26+debian9~1.gbpd64eb7+wmf1",
"X-Search-ID" "8k38f38amugic2y5uagm8zy6s",
"Cache-Control" "private, must-revalidate, max-age=0"&},
 :orig-content-encoding nil,
 :status 200,
 :length -1,
 :body
"{\"batchcomplete\":\"\",\"continue\":{\"sroffset\":1,\"continue\":\"-||\"},\"query\":{\"s
searchinfo\":{\"totalhits\":319},\"search\":[{\"ns\":0,\"title\":\"Clojure\",\"pageid\":1656
1990,\"size\":46433,\"wordcount\":3770,\"snippet\":\"<span class=\\\"searchmatch\\\">Clojur
e</span> (/\\u02c8klo\\u028a\\u0292\\u0259r/, like closure) is a modern, dynamic, and funct
sional dialect of the Lisp programming language on the Java platform. Like other Lisps\",\"t
stimestamp\":\"2019-10-11T18:30:36Z\"}]}}",
 :trace-redirects []}
packt-clj.crowdspell.fetch>
```

Figure 12.4: REPL output of a successful HTTP request

8. Let's add this request as a **let** binding inside the **try** block. The only change needed is to insert the two parameters: the word we're searching for and the language. Start by making a **let** binding from the result of the HTTP request to the Wikipedia endpoint. We will need the entire request later:

```
(defn word-search [word language-code]
  (try
    (let [http-result (http/get (str "https://" language-code ".wikipedia.org/w/api.
php")
                        {:query-params {"action" "query"
                                        "list" "search"
                                        "srlimit" 1
                                        "srsearch" word
                                        "format" "json"}
                         :accept :json
                         :cookie-policy :none})]
      ;; TODO: do something with the result
      {:status :ok :total-hits total-hits :word word})
    (catch Exception e
      {:status :error})))
```

9. Now we just need to interpret the result of the HTTP request. There are really two steps: first, convert the raw JSON response into a Clojure map, then extract the data we're looking for. The Wikipedia API provides a **totalhits** field that we can use to decide which word is the most popular. We can combine these two steps into a brief code snippet:

```
(-> (json/read-str (:body http-result) :key-fn keyword)
    (get-in [:query :searchinfo :totalhits]))
```

The **json/read-str** does just that: it reads the body of the response and converts it into a map. The **:key-fn** option allows us to provide a function that will be called on all the keys. In nearly all cases, the **keyword** function is used here so that we can have the convenience of Clojure keywords.

All that's left is to grab the one piece of data that we need. The result map is a large, multiple-nested map, which is not a problem for **get-in**.

10. Once we have the number of hits, we wrap all the data we'll need for later in a map: the status, the number of hits, and the word itself:

```
{:status :ok :total-hits total-hits :word word}
```

We know the word from the original argument supplied to the function. We also know that the status is :ok: if the query resulted in an error, we would be in the catch **block** instead.

The final function looks like this:

```
(defn word-search [word language-code]
  (try
    (let [http-result (http/get (str "https://" language-code ".wikipedia.org/w/api.
php")
                      {:query-params {"action" "query"
                              "list" "search"
                              "srlimit" 1
                              "srsearch" word
                              "format" "json"}
                       :accept :json
                       :cookie-policy :none})
          total-hits (-> (json/read-str (:body http-result) :key-fn keyword)
                      (get-in [:query :searchinfo :totalhits]))]
      {:status :ok :total-hits total-hits :word word})
    (catch Exception e
      {:status :error})))
```

If you test **word-search** in the REPL, you should see something like this:

```
packt-clj.crowdspell.fetch> (word-search "Clojure" "en")
{:status :ok, :total-hits 324, :word "Clojure"}
packt-clj.crowdspell.fetch> []
```

Figure 12.5: The important data extracted from the HTTP request

11. Now we turn to **get-best-word**. Its job is to make parallel calls to **word-search**. Futures are exactly what we need for that. Since the words are supplied as a list, the first step will be to call **word-search** inside a future for each of the words. This is remarkably straightforward:

```
(defn get-best-word
  [language-code words]
  (let [results (map (fn [a] [a (future (word-search a language-code))]) words)]
    ;; TODO: decide which word is the best
    ))
```

The HTTP requests will run simultaneously and the responses become available as they complete. This expression will return a list of futures. We will need to dereference them before we can use them. Except for that difference, we can look at **results** as though it were a list of ordinary values. Clojure's **future** and **deref** function manage the asynchronicity for us.

12. The final step here will be to select the word with the most hits. We'll use **reduce** with a pattern we introduced in *Chapter 5, Many to One: Reducing*:

```
(reduce (fn [best-so-far [word result-future]]
      (let [{:keys [status total-hits] :as result} @result-future]
       (if (= status :ok)
        (if (> total-hits (:total-hits best-so-far))
         result
          best-so-far)
         best-so-far)))
     {:total-hits 0}
     results)
```

Obviously, dereferencing **@result-future** here is the first very important step. But once the value is dereferenced, all the data is available, and we can forget all about its asynchronous past.

The rest of the call to **reduce** follows the familiar pattern: we check whether the current item has a better score than **best-so-far**, and if so, it replaces **best-so-far**.

To make a very polished app, we would want to warn the user in case there were errors, but, for now, it will suffice to simply ignore the failed requests.

13. Once we've found the best word, all that's left is to extract the **:word** key from the best word. For that, we'll use a threading macro, **->**, and **:word**. Altogether, that leaves us with this function:

```
(defn get-best-word
  [language-code words]
  (let [results (map (fn [a] [a (future (word-search a language-code))]) words)]
   (->
    (reduce (fn [best-so-far [word result-future]]
        (let [{:keys [status total-hits] :as result} @result-future]
         (if (= status :ok)
          (if (> total-hits (:total-hits best-so-far))
           result
           best-so-far)
```

```
          best-so-far)))
      {:total-hits 0}
      results)
  :word)))
```

14. Test **get-best-word** in the REPL with some really bad spellings of "Clojure" alongside the correct one:

```
packt-clj.crowdspell.fetch> (get-best-word "en" ["Fortran" "Pascal"])
"Pascal"
packt-clj.crowdspell.fetch> (get-best-word "en" ["Clojur" "Clojure" "Clojrre"])
"Clojure"
```

It seems to work!

15. To make this into a useful application, we still need to package this behavior into a command-line utility. The **-main** function back in **src/packt_clj/crowdspell.clj** is almost ready, except that the language code parameter is still just hardcoded as **en**.

    The **clojure.tools.cli** library will make it easy to add the language code as an optional parameter at the command line. The goal is to be able to compile our code to an uberjar and then type this:

```
java -jar packt-clj.crowdspell-0.1.0-SNAPSHOT-standalone.jar --language en Clojur
Clojure Clojrre
```

16. The **clojure.tools.cli/parse-opts** function takes the **args** value from **-main** and a list of argument prefix descriptors. The best way to understand this is with an example, like our language code option:

```
(cli/parse-opts
        args
        [["-l" "--language LANG" "Two-letter language code for search"
         :default "en"]])
```

The nested vector is the configuration argument to **parse-opts**. **"-l"** and **"--language LANG"** define the short and long form of the command-line option. Remember that the long form of the option will be used, in keyword form, as the name of the argument in the nested **:options** map that **parse-opts** returns.

The next string is a documentation string that will be displayed if there is an error, for example, an unknown option prefix.

After these first three items, there can be additional keyword-tagged parameters. There are a lot of possibilities here that we won't explore. **:default** is enough for our purposes here. If the user doesn't supply a **--language** option (or the shorter **-l** option), they will get results from the English-language Wikipedia output.

17. To test the configuration of the command-line options, there's no need to actually use the command line. **parse-opts** can be run in the **REPL** with a list of strings masquerading as command-line arguments:

```
packt-clj.crowdspell> (cli/parse-opts ["--language" "fr" "Cloj" "Clojure"] [["-l"
"--language LANG" "Language code for search"]])
{:options {:language "fr"},
 :arguments ["Cloj" "Clojure"],
 :summary " -l, --language LANG Language code for search",
 :errors nil}
```

18. This is useful because it shows us the structure of the map that is returned. To finalize the **-main** function, we just need to know how to extract the language option and the arguments from the map:

```
(defn -main
  [& args]
  (let [parsed (cli/parse-opts
          args
          [["-l" "--language LANG" "Two-letter language code for search"
           :default "en"]])]
    (fetch/get-best-word (get-in parsed [:options :language])
          (:arguments parsed))))
          (System/exit))))
```

The call to **System/exit** guarantees that our program will exit immediately. Because we used **future**, the program otherwise would not exit until the threads created by **future** had terminated entirely.

And that should be all the code we need.

19. Before compiling, we can test our code in the **REPL** by simulating the command-line arguments in a list:

```
packt-clj.crowdspell> (-main "-l" "en" "Klojure" "Cloojure" "Clojure")
"Clojure"
```

20. To compile, simply run **lein uberjar** in the root directory of the project. Now we can finally test the entire application:

```
$ java -jar target/uberjar/packt-clj.crowdspell-0.1.0-SNAPSHOT-standalone.jar
--language en Clojur Clojure Clojrre
Clojure
```

All right, it works. But it's slow. Yes, the Java runtime takes a few seconds to get started and it's a problem for something that should be a fast, easy-to-use app. It's best to consider this version as a proof of concept. A ClojureScript version based on Node.js would have a much shorter startup time. Or this could be built as a web service. You'll learn about building an application server in *Chapter 14, HTTP with Ring*. For now, the fastest and easiest approach would be to use **fetch.clj** directly in the REPL, although this requirement might limit the number of potential customers.

In this exercise, we learned how to write a simple multithreaded application using Clojure futures. Futures are particularly well suited for situations where discreet tasks can be handed off to separate threads. Even more importantly, **future**, with **deref**, provides a way to coordinate the data as it returns from the separate threads.

Coordination

Futures work well for cases like the **crowdspell** example. Work is assigned to a thread; the thread performs its task independently and returns a result to the initial thread. The coordination is in the gathering of the results: evaluation is blocked until all the futures have completed. Thanks to immutability, there is a guarantee that simultaneous threads won't interfere with each other because nothing is shared.

This simple model is effective precisely because it is simple. Sometimes, however, more coordination is necessary, especially when communication between threads is required.

With a future, we fork, perform a computation, and return the data:

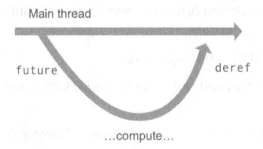

Figure 12.6: With a future, coordination occurs when the future is dereferenced

Message sending is one way to communicate among threads. Now, we imagine three threads that send messages to one another:

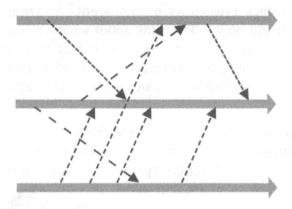

Figure 12.7: Complex interactions between multiple threads

To implement a communication model like this in Clojure, you could also use the **core. async** library, which is a sophisticated tool for creating channels between threads. The **core.async** library is widely used but would require its own chapter to cover it correctly:

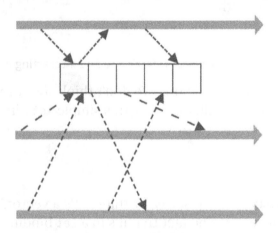

Figure 12.8: Threads referring to and modifying shared data

The fundamental challenge of concurrent programming stems from the fact that the timeline of a program is no longer linear. Threads in communication with each other do not know when they will receive new data or when the data they've sent will be processed on the receiving end. Unless the communication is carefully managed, accidents happen. If two threads try to update the same data simultaneously without coordination, the results become unpredictable. One update overwrites another. While a value is being updated, the original value is modified, and the update is suddenly obsolete. If more threads are involved, the interactions (and the possibilities for errors) are multiplied. In the **crowdspell** exercise, the futures coordinated the return value from the different threads. Instead of clobbering each other's data, the results were assembled into a coherent list that the rest of the program could use.

Clojure has several **reference types**: vars, atoms, agents, and refs. Before talking about each one separately, it might be good to think about what a *reference type* actually is. First of all, a reference type is not a data structure. In fact, you can use any of Clojure's data structures with any of these reference types. Instead, a reference type sits between your code and your data and provides a particular way of referring to your data.

It might help to visualize this relationship. The reference type as an interface allows your code to apply changes to the data and retrieve the current state of the data. Remember, the values that the reference type points to are still the familiar Clojure data types: integers, strings, vectors, maps, and so on:

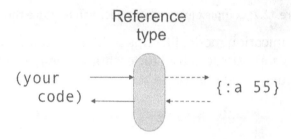

Figure 12.9: Reference type: a way of referring to and interacting with a piece of data

Most of the time, when coding in Clojure, we don't think about the difference between the name of a thing and thing itself. Consider this simple **let** binding:

```
(let [some-numbers [3 12 -1 55]]
  ;; TODO: do something
  )
```

What is **some-numbers**? Usually, we just say, or think, "it's a vector." Of course, it's really a symbol that points at a vector. The fact that it's in a **let** binding means that **some-numbers** will only point at **[3 12 -1 55]** inside that particular **let** expression. In other words, **let** defines a particular kind of pointing.

Now consider this **let** binding:

```
(let [some-atomic-numbers (atom [3 12 -1 55])]
  ;; TODO: do something with an atom
  )
```

This time, **some-atomic-numbers** is still just a symbol. It points at an atom (we'll explain what that means in a second), and the atom points at the vector:

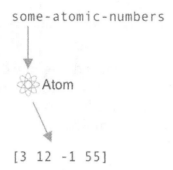

Figure 12.10: The binding points at the atom, and the atom points at the value

Immutability means that values don't change. An integer remains an integer, and a vector remains equal to itself. Immutability does not mean that a symbol always points at the same value, though. Clojure's reference types are a way to manage certain kinds of change while continuing to use immutable data.

One of the reference types is already very familiar to you by now: the var, which, among other roles, is how Clojure identifies functions. Up until now, we've treated the var as an immutable identity, and, for the most part, this is accurate. Generally, if you see **(def x 5)** in a program, that means that the value of **x** will not change.

However, at the REPL, you will quickly find that you can indeed redefine a var simply by calling **def** again:

```
user> (def x 5)
#'user/x
user> x
5
user> (def x 6)
#'user/x
user> x
6
```

While this is fine when experimenting with the REPL, clobbering a var like this in a program would be extremely unusual. That said, the var reference type does provide the **alter-var-root** function, which is a more graceful way to update a var. It takes a function and updates the value:

```
user> (def the-var 55)
#'user/the-var
user> (alter-var-root #'the-var #(+ % 15))
70
```

If you ever actually need to use this function, it will probably be to change some feature of your work environment. The point here is not to encourage you to start modifying vars, but rather to show how even vars have semantics for changing their values. **Vars** happen to be a reference type that strongly discourages change but does not prohibit it completely.

The other reference types—atoms, agents, and refs—are designed to give you much finer control over how to manage change and they do this by controlling what they point at. In the preceding diagram, we showed a **let** binding, **some-atomic-numbers**, pointing at an atom containing a vector. Now we can complete the picture by showing how the atom might evolve as different functions are called on it:

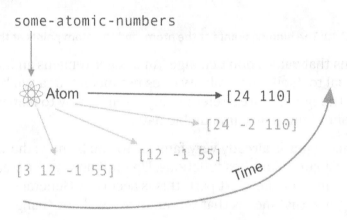

Figure 12.11: The atom points at different values over time

In this picture, the data (the vectors) is still immutable. The atom allows us to define some kind of identity that might have different values at different times. As we'll see, this turns out to be particularly useful in multithreaded programs, where one or more threads need to have access to stable identities in another thread.

So, what are atoms, refs, and agents? Let's take a quick look at each of these reference types.

Atoms

Atoms are the simplest and most commonly used reference type. They are also the only reference type that is currently available in ClojureScript, mostly due to the fact that the JavaScript runtime is single-threaded.

The life-cycle of an atom starts with an initial definition of the data with the **atom** function:

```
user> (def integer-atom (atom 5))
#'user/integer-atom
```

Just with like **future**, the underlying data can be accessed with **deref** (or the
@ reader macro):

```
user> (deref integer-atom)
5
```

Changing the data is done with **swap!**, which updates the atom by applying the function
you supply to the current value that the atom points to:

```
user> (swap! integer-atom inc)
6
user> (deref integer-atom)
6
```

The **swap!** function doesn't assign a value to the atom. Instead, it applies a function. This
way, if the value of the atom has changed since the last time we dereferenced it, the
function will simply be applied to the new value, whatever it is.

Let's see this in action. Here is the code we are going to execute in the REPL, once again
using **Thread/sleep** to simulate some long-running task:

```
user> (do
    (future (do (Thread/sleep 500) (swap! integer-atom + 500)))
    (future (swap! integer-atom * 1000))
    (deref integer-atom))
6000
```

What's going on here? The first future waits half a second before calling **swap!**. The
second future executes right away, multiplying the current value of the atom, **6**, by **1000**.
Now try dereferencing **integer-atom** again:

```
user> @integer-atom
6500
```

If we change the timing by modifying the durations of the **Thread/sleep** calls, the results
change too:

```
user> (do
    (def integer-atom (atom 6))
    (future (swap! integer-atom + 500))
    (future (do (Thread/sleep 500) (swap! integer-atom * 1000)))
    (deref integer-atom))
506
user> @integer-atom
506000
```

When calling **swap!**, you can't be sure ahead of time what the value of the atom will be. But you know that your function will be called on whatever the value happens to be at that point in time.

> **Note**
>
> There is also a more rarely used **compare-and-set!** function that provides finer grained control. It takes an additional value, usually the current value of the atom, and will only modify the atom if it still matches that. In other words, if another thread has already done something to your atom, **compare-and-set!** will leave it alone.

Concept: Retries

Changes to an atom are not instantaneous. Remember, we're sending a function to the atom. Depending on the work being done, some functions may take more time to complete. In a busy environment, it might mean that several threads try to make changes to an atom at the same time.

The following diagram shows a naïve implementation of an atom being modified by two threads, **Thread A** and **Thread B**. Even though they are just multiplying the value of the atom by 3 or by 4, let's imagine that this operation takes a few milliseconds:

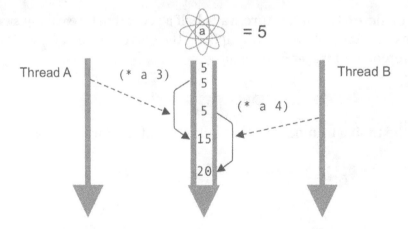

Figure 12.12: Overlapping updates to a naive implementation of a Clojure atom

The initial value of the atom is 5. Then **Thread A** intervenes to multiply by 3. As it is starting to perform its operation, **Thread B** starts as well. The input to the function of **Thread B**'s is still **5**. The function of **Thread A** completes, and the value of the atom is set to **15**. Then Thread B's function completes its calculation without having seen the new value of the atom. This result is based on a "stale" version of the initial value, but it overwrites the result of the first calculation. In the end, it's as if Thread A's update had never happened.

Clojure does not want this to happen to you! Here's what would take place with a real Clojure atom:

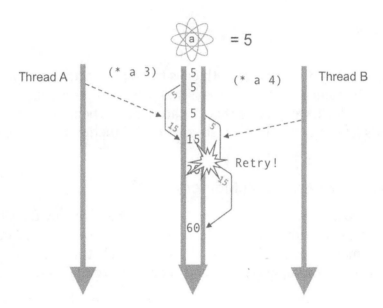

Figure 12.13: A real Clojure atom retries when a conflict occurs

This time, when the atom tries to apply the update from **Thread B**, it detects that the underlying value has changed and reapplies the function with the new value.

We can observe this in the REPL, using one slow-acting (long-sleeping) function and a quick function in two separate threads:

```
user> (do
    (def integer-atom (atom 5))
    (future (swap! integer-atom (fn [a] (Thread/sleep 2000)(* a 100))))
    (future (swap! integer-atom (fn [a] (Thread/sleep 500) (+ a 200))))
    @integer-atom)
5
user> @integer-atom
205
user> @integer-atom
20500
```

In this scenario, we can consider that both calls to **swap!** execute at approximately the same time, when the value of **integer-atom** is still 5. By dereferencing **integer-atom** at the end of the **do** block, we can see that the atom hasn't been updated yet. Yet, a couple of seconds later, the results indicate that both functions were applied, and in the correct order.

Refs and Software Transactional Memory

Refs are Clojure's most sophisticated reference type. They are why the Clojure language, when it was first introduced, became known for its advanced concurrency management and, more specifically, for STM. STM is an abstraction that guarantees that changes can be made to multiple *refs* in a safe, coordinated manner.

Behind STM, there is a fundamental concept: the transaction. If you have worked with database transactions, you are already familiar with the basic idea. A database transaction might consist of several related operations. If, during the transaction, any individual operation fails, the entire transaction is "rolled back" to the initial state, as if nothing had happened. Transactions are a way of avoiding invalid states where only part of an action is performed.

> **Note**
>
> In *Chapter 13, Database Interaction and the Application Layer,* we will take a closer look at database transactions.

The classic example for explaining database transactions also applies here: imagine a bank transaction where money moves from one account to another. To do this, at least two actions need to occur: an amount of money is removed from one account and added to another. If for some reason one of those operations fails, we don't want the other to succeed. If the second account was deleted after the funds are debited from the first account, those funds should return to the original account; otherwise, they would vanish into thin air. In a database transaction, if the second step is not completed, the first step is canceled as well. This way, the system returns automatically to a known, correct state.

Clojure's software transactional memory is conceptually similar to database transactions but works with data inside your program. A transaction in Clojure is managed by the **dosync** macro, which creates a space in which actions on refs will be coordinated. Imagine that the preceding banking scenario was implemented using Clojure reference types instead of a database. If you are drawing from one bank account ref and depositing to another, then both operations will succeed or the entire **dosync** block will be retried. Like database transactions, the purpose of refs is to make sure that your system remains in a coherent state. This is one of the first key differences between refs and atoms: unlike atoms, refs can provide coordination. When two atoms are updated, there is no such guarantee.

Refs actually offer even more fine-grained control over how they are modified. There are several functions that can update a ref, each with different semantics. The two most common are **alter** and **commute**. **alter** is the most restrictive: if the underlying value has changed outside the **dosync** block, then the entire transaction will be retried. The **commute** function can be used when this kind of guarantee is not necessary. When adding or subtracting from a total, for example, the order of operations does not affect the result, so these operations can accept changes to the underlying value without a retry. And when accessing the data, the **ensure** function can be used instead of **deref**. In this case, if a ref that is being read from has changed, a retry will be triggered.

Exercise 12.03: Stock Trading

In this exercise, we will observe refs in the REPL to get a better sense of their behavior.

Your current project is a prototype for a stock trading application. You need to write a function that will simulate a client buying some numbers of stocks at a given price. For the purchase to succeed, four things must happen:

- The client account is debited for the amount of the transaction.
- The broker account is credited for the same amount.

- The broker stock account (for that particular stock) is debited, that is, there are now n fewer stocks in that account.

- The client stock account (for that particular stock) is credited: there are now n more stocks.

However, if the price of the stock changes while this is happening, the entire purchase must be invalidated and retried.

Also, since this is a simulation, we will use **Thread/sleep** to slow the functions down:

1. In the REPL, set up some refs for the five different values we'll need. The first three will have integer values, representing account balances in whatever currency is being used:

```
user> (def client-account (ref 2100))
#'user/client-account
user> (def broker-account (ref 10000))
#'user/broker-account
user> (def acme-corp-share-price (ref 22))
#'user/acme-corp-share-price
```

2. Because the client and the broker would probably own stocks for various firms, we'll use maps for that:

```
user> (def broker-stocks (ref {:acme-corp 50}))
#'user/broker-stocks
user> (def client-stocks (ref {:acme-corp 0}))
#'user/client-stocks
```

The client starts off with zero **Acme Corp** stocks and a currency balance of **2100** in her account. The broker has **50** stocks and a balance of **10000**.

3. Write a function that describes a complete transaction:

```
user> (defn buy-acme-corp-shares [n]
    (dosync
      (let [purchase-price (* n @acme-corp-share-price)]
        (alter client-account #(- % purchase-price))
        (alter broker-account #(+ % purchase-price))
        (alter client-stocks update :acme-corp #(+ % n))
        (alter broker-stocks update :acme-corp #(- % n)))))
```

4. All our code here is wrapped in a **dosync** macro. Beyond that, the code is quite simple. Even in a **dosync** environment, it is necessary to dereference other refs when accessing their value, which is why we write **@acme-corp-share-price**. The syntax for updating the **client-stocks** and **broker-stocks** maps might look a little bit strange. The second argument to **alter** is always a function, and in this case it's the **update** function we've already used for updating maps. The remaining arguments to **alter** will be simply passed on to **update**, after the initial argument, which will be the map contained in the ref. All told, the final call to **update** will be as follows:

```
(update {:acme-corp 0} :acme-corp #(+ % n))
```

5. Because **update** behaves in the same way as **alter** and passes any additional arguments on to the provided function, our calls to **alter** could be rewritten like this:

```
(alter client-stocks update :acme-corp + n)
(alter broker-stocks update :acme-corp - n)
```

6. And likewise, the previous lines could use the same syntax:

```
(alter client-account - purchase-price)
(alter broker-account + purchase-price)
```

These forms are more concise and might be easier to read for experienced Clojure programmers. The forms using anonymous functions have the advantage of explicitly reminding us that we are providing functions as well as clearly laying out the order of the arguments.

7. Let's try our new function:

```
user> (buy-acme-corp-shares 1)
{:acme-corp 49}
```

The **dosync** block returns the last value, which, in this case, is the in-transaction value of **broker-account**. That might be useful sometimes, but the data we're really interested in is in the refs:

```
user> @client-account
2078
user> @broker-account
10022
user> @broker-stocks
{:acme-corp 49}
user> @client-stocks
{:acme-corp 1}
```

Here, we see that the balances of the two accounts have been correctly updated and that one stock has moved from **broker-stocks** to **client-stocks**.

This means that our best-case scenario works: none of the refs are changed outside of the current thread and the transactions are instantaneous. In these conditions, atoms would work just as well. Now it's time to simulate a more demanding environment for the purchase!

8. Modify **buy-acme-corp-shares** to make the transaction slower and print some information:

```
user> (defn buy-acme-corp-shares [n]
        (dosync
         (let [purchase-price (* n @acme-corp-share-price)]
           (println "Let's buy" n "stock(s) at" purchase-price "per stock")
           (Thread/sleep 1000)
           (alter client-account #(- % purchase-price))
           (alter broker-account #(+ % purchase-price))
           (alter client-stocks update :acme-corp #(+ % n))
           (alter broker-stocks update :acme-corp #(- % n)))))
#'user/buy-acme-corp-shares
```

With **Thread/sleep**, the transaction will now last one second.

9. Reset all the accounts to their initial values. To make this easier, let's write a quick reset function using the **ref-set** function:

```
user> (defn reset-accounts []
        (dosync
         (ref-set acme-corp-share-price 22)
         (ref-set client-account 2100)
         (ref-set broker-account 10000)
         (ref-set client-stocks {:acme-corp 0})
         (ref-set broker-stocks {:acme-corp 50})))
#'user/reset-accounts
user> (reset-accounts)
{:acme-corp 50}
user> @acme-corp-share-price
22
```

All the accounts and the stock price should now be back at their initial values. This will make it easier to observe the behavior of the function.

10. Use two separate threads to change the client's account during the transaction. To do this, we'll use **future** and set a shorter wait time to the thread by changing **client-account**:

```
user> (do
    (reset-accounts)
    (future (buy-acme-corp-shares 1))
    (future (dosync
            (Thread/sleep 300)
            (alter client-account + 500))))
Let's buy 1 stocks at 22 per stock
#<Future@611d7261: :pending>Let's buy 1 stocks at 22 per stock
```

Notice that the **println** message appears twice. What happened? Let's look at the values:

```
user> @client-account
2578
```

Both transactions were correctly recorded: +500 and -22. Here's what happened: first, **buy-acme-corp-shares** tried to complete the transaction but when it was time to write the new account balance to **client-account**, the underlying value had changed due to the deposit from the other thread. Without this, **buy-acme-corp-shares** would have overwritten the account balance, ignoring the recent deposit. The client would not have been pleased.

11. Simulate a busy broker account. The broker account is probably much busier than the client's account. Let's add more transactions:

```
user> (do
    (reset-accounts)
    (future (buy-acme-corp-shares 1))
    (future (dosync
            (Thread/sleep 300)
            (alter client-account + 500)))
    (future (dosync
            (Thread/sleep 350)
            (alter broker-account - 200)))
    (future (dosync
            (Thread/sleep 600)
            (alter broker-account + 1200))))
Let's buy 1 stock(s) at 22 per stock
#<Future@2ffabed2: :pending>Let's buy 1 stock(s) at 22 per stock
Let's buy 1 stock(s) at 22 per stock
```

Dereference the atoms to see their final values:

```
user> @broker-account
11022
user> @client-account
2578
```

More changes to the refs cause more restarts, which we can see because the **Let's buy 1 stock(s) at 22 per stock** message is printed three times. Each modification of an account causes the entire transaction to be retried. This is what atoms cannot do: with refs inside a **dosync** block, a change to any of the refs causes the entire block to restart.

This exercise shows the basics of using refs to simplify the sharing of data across threads. Obviously, real-life uses would generally be much more complex, but even at this scale we can see some of the difficulties posed by concurrency and how Clojure provides tools for dealing with it.

There are a few things that we can observe. Like with atoms, the retry strategy used by refs prevents near-simultaneous operations from interfering with one another. But refs go further by making sure that even if one ref causes a retry, all the updates in the transaction will be retried. This guarantees data coherence. It also means that we give up some control of when changes to refs will be made. As programmers, we are used to thinking in a very linear fashion: "do this, then do that." Multithreaded applications break this way of thinking. Clojure's reference types, and refs in particular, can help us write better code, especially if we learn to think less in terms of the strict order of operations and more in terms of the correctness and coherence of the operations.

More Cohesion with refs

In the previous example, STM helped us to make sure that the updates were coherent: the buyer had less money in her account, but more stocks; the seller had more money, but fewer stocks. If any one of those four changes had failed, the system would have returned to the previous valid state. Either way, everyone ends up with the correct balances on their accounts. There is, however, one possibility we didn't consider. What if the price of the stock changes during the transaction? Let's take a look:

```
user> (do
    (reset-accounts)
    (future (buy-acme-corp-shares 1))
    (future (dosync
        (Thread/sleep 300)
        (alter acme-corp-share-price + 10))))
```

```
Let's buy 1 stocks at 22 per stock
#<Future@11e639bf: :pending>
user> @client-account
2078
```

The balance on the client's account indicates that the purchase price was 22. The sequence of events suggests that the client got a good deal. While **buy-acme-corp-shares** was waiting for 1,000 milliseconds, in the second future, the stock price was changed to 32. When the purchase was finally complete, the price was no longer 22 but 32. Why didn't the refs protect us from this?

The problem here is that the **buy-acme-corp-shares** function consults the value of the **acme-corp-share-price** atom but does not do anything with it. As a result, **dosync** does not track the changes made to that ref. In the next exercise, we'll explore two different solutions: the **ensure** function and a clever way to use **alter**.

Exercise 12.04: Keeping up with the Stock Price

The initial prototype for the stock purchase function seems to be working but the team has realized that it does not react correctly to variations in the stock price that occur while the transaction is completing. You've been asked to suggest some solutions.

1. In your REPL, use the same environment as in the previous exercise. If necessary, recreate the same five refs and make sure that the **reset-accounts** function is defined.

2. In **buy-acme-corp-shares**, use **ensure** to dereference **acme-corps-stock-price**:

```
user> (defn buy-acme-corp-shares [n]
  (dosync
    (let [price (ensure acme-corp-share-price)]
    (println "Let's buy" n "stock(s) at" price "per stock")
    (Thread/sleep 1000)
    (alter client-account #(- % price))
    (alter broker-account #(+ % price))
    (alter client-stocks update :acme-corp #(+ % n))
    (alter broker-stocks update :acme-corp #(- % n)))))
#'user/buy-acme-corp-shares
```

3. Run the same transaction as before. We'll add an extra **println** statement to see when the share price updates occur:

```
user> (do
    (reset-accounts)
    (future (buy-acme-corp-shares 1))
    (future (dosync
        (Thread/sleep 300)
        (println "Raising share price to " (+ @acme-corp-share-price 10))
        (alter acme-corp-share-price + 10))))
Let's buy 1 stock(s) at 22 per stock
#<Future@5410594c: :pending>Raising share price to 32
Raising share price to 32
Raising share price to 32
user> @client-account
2078
```

There are two noteworthy things in this output: **Raising share price…** was printed 3 times and the client account balance is still only down by 22. What happened?

As soon as **ensure** was called in **buy-acme-corp-shares**, the value of **acme-corp-share-price** was frozen until the **dosync** block had completed. The second **dosync** macro then kept retrying until the first had completed. When **buy-acme-corp-shares** had terminated, **acme-corp-share-price** could finally be raised.

At the very instant that **buy-acme-corp-shares** purchased the shares, the price was still 22. Data coherence was thus maintained. There is, however, a problem. In the real world, a single buyer cannot force the rest of the stock market to wait for a purchase to go through. This solution is correct in a way, but in this scenario it would not work.

4. Use **alter** to trigger a retry. This time, we'll go back to **deref** for accessing the current share price. We'll also call **alter** on **acme-corp-share-price** to trigger a retry if that ref has changed. You might think "we can't change the share price!" You're right, of course, but our call to **alter** won't actually do anything, since we will only provide the **identity** function as an argument. We call **alter**, but just as a way to say "stay the way you are":

```
user> (defn buy-acme-corp-shares [n]
    (dosync
      (let [price @acme-corp-share-price]
        (println "Let's buy" n "stock(s) at" price "per stock")
        (Thread/sleep 1000)
        (alter acme-corp-share-price identity)
```

```
        (alter client-account #(- % price))
        (alter broker-account #(+ % price))
        (alter client-stocks update :acme-corp #(+ % n))
        (alter broker-stocks update :acme-corp #(- % n)))))
    #'user/buy-acme-corp-shares
```

Let's see what happens:

```
user> (do
    (reset-accounts)
    (future (buy-acme-corp-shares 1))
    (future (dosync
        (Thread/sleep 300)
        (println "Raising share price to " (+ @acme-corp-share-price 10))
        (alter acme-corp-share-price + 10))))
Let's buy 1 stock(s) at 22 per stock
#<Future@2b64a327: :pending>Raising share price to 32
Let's buy 1 stock(s) at 32 per stock
```

This time, **Let's buy 1 stock(s)…** is printed twice, with two different prices. **Raising share price…** is printed only once. The share price is changed during the first call to **buy-acme-corp-shares**. Because of the change, a retry is triggered, now with the correct share price. The purchase finally completes, with the correct price:

```
user> @client-account
2068
```

This exercise demonstrates the power and the subtlety of Clojure's STM. Depending on the problem you need to solve and on the environment you're working in, you will need retries to happen in slightly different circumstances. In this example, it was obvious that we could not ask the stock market to wait even 1 second for our transaction to complete. Refs give you the ability to precisely define the retry behavior that you need. (In addition to **alter** and **ref-set**, there is **commute**, which provides yet another set of semantics for updating refs when less control is needed.) And of course, this degree of control also requires careful thought about the relationships between refs.

Agents

The primary difference between agents and the other reference types is that, while updates to atoms and refs are **synchronous**, updates to agents are **asynchronous**. Changes made to an agent are sent to a queue, a waiting list of changes, and the functions are run in a separate thread. Unlike refs and atoms, the calling thread is not blocked while waiting for the action to complete. So, while agents provide far less control over updates than refs, they do not slow down operations with retries. In atoms and refs, retries are necessary to solve the problem of simultaneous mutations; in agents, the same problem is solved by giving up on simultaneity and simply executing incoming functions in the order they are received.

We can observe the asynchronous nature of an agent by making changes that take a few seconds to complete, thanks to **Thread/sleep** again:

```
user> (def integer-agent (agent 5))
#'user/integer-agent
user> (send integer-agent (fn [a] (Thread/sleep 5000) (inc a)))
#<Agent@3c221047: 5>
user> (send integer-agent (fn [a] (Thread/sleep 5000) (inc a)))
#<Agent@3c221047: 5>
user> @integer-agent
5
user> @integer-agent
6
user> @integer-agent
7
```

First, we define the agent, setting its value to **5**. Then we **send** two identical modifications to increment the agent's value after 5 seconds. If we quickly type **@integer-agent** (or **(deref**

integer-agent), but that takes more time), we see that the value is still **5**. If we wait a little bit longer and type **@integer-agent** again, we see that the value has moved to **6**. And a few seconds later, it increments again to **7**.

If we replace the agent in the preceding example with an atom (and use **swap!** instead of **send**), the final result is the same but we are forced to wait for the operation to complete before we regain control of the REPL:

```
user> (def integer-atom (atom 5))
#'user/integer-atom
user> (swap! integer-atom (fn [a] (Thread/sleep 5000) (inc a)))
6
user> (swap! integer-atom (fn [a] (Thread/sleep 5000) (inc a)))
7
```

If you try this in your REPL, you will see that the REPL prompt is blocked for 5 seconds after each call to **swap!**.

Because they do not block, there are some situations where agents are preferable to atoms or refs. For example, suppose your main application divides a processor-intensive task into several parts that can be passed to separate threads. While these threads are working, you want to present a progress bar to the user. When a thread accomplishes one unit of work, it increments a counter in an agent. The advantage of an asynchronous agent is that this would not slow the worker thread down: control returns immediately to the thread, which can start working again right away, and the agent can handle the update on its own:

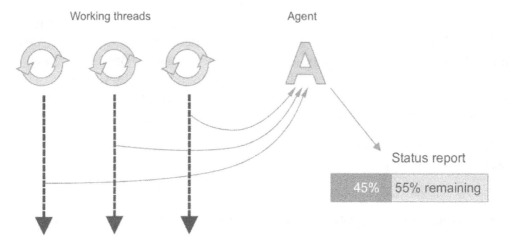

Figure 12.14: The worker threads send progress updates to the agent

Like refs and unlink atoms, agents also benefit from STM. Inside a **dosync** block, changes made to several agents benefit from the same retry semantics as refs. Because updates to agents are asynchronous, on the output side they do not provide as much control as refs, but they are less prone to deadlock from endless retries in very busy systems.

Atoms in ClojureScript

Vars and atoms are the only reference types available in ClojureScript. Even though JavaScript runtimes are not multithreaded, code execution is often non-linear. In the browser, a single-page application needs to be able to handle events that can come from every link or input, or from actions such as scrolling and hovering. Application state needs to be shared by the code triggered by these events, and atoms turn out to be a very good choice. (This is fortunate, since they are the only choice.)

The rest of this chapter will focus on atoms in the browser. The odds are that your first real-life experience of concurrency in Clojure won't be a complex multithreaded JVM application. There's a good chance that you'll take your first Clojure concurrency steps in a browser-based ClojureScript program. Many of the best-known ClojureScript frameworks for building browser applications, such as Reagent, Re-frame, and Om, use atoms to manage state.

Exercise 12.05: Rock, Scissors, Paper

In this exercise, we're going to implement the famous Rock, Scissors, Paper game in ClojureScript. The real game is played between two people who count to three and then simultaneously make a hand gesture, either a "rock," "scissors," or "paper." Each of the three choices can defeat one of the other two and be defeated by the other. Thus, "rock crushes scissors," "scissors cut paper," and "paper wraps rock". If both players choose the same object, it's a draw and they play again.

1. At the command-line prompt, create a new **figwheel** project using the following **Leiningen** command:

```
lein new figwheel packt-clj.rock-scissors-paper -- --rum
```

2. Move to the **packt-clj.rock-scissors-paper/** directory and type the following:

```
lein figwheel
```

After a few seconds, your browser should open to the default Figwheel page:

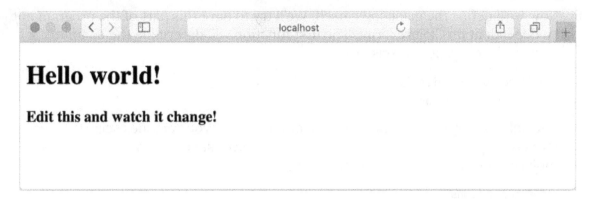

Figure 12.15: A fresh ClojureScript project waiting for your code

Open **packt-clj.rock-scissors-paper/src/packt_clj/rock_scissors_paper/core.cljs** and get ready to write some code.

3. Let's start by designing the underlying data. This is a very simple game, so it won't take much. We need to keep track of the computer's choice (rock, scissors, or paper) and the user's choice. We also need to have a game state, which will be one of three states: **:setup** (the game hasn't started yet), **:waiting** (waiting for the user to play), and **:complete** (we'll show who won and offer to play again).

    Replace the supplied **app-state** definition with the following:

    ```
    (defonce app-state (atom {:computer-choice nil
                :game-state :setup
                :user-choice nil}))
    ```

    We also want to make this our own app, so let's update some of the function names. Rename the **hello-world** component as **rock-scissors-paper**, for example.

4. All of the game logic will go in a **rock-paper-scissors** component. For now, we'll just have it display some text:

    ```
    (rum/defc rock-paper-scissors []
     [:div
      [:h1 "Rock, Paper, Scissors"]])
    ```

    While we're there, we can change the end of the file slightly to use the pattern that we used in *Chapter 9, Host Platform interoperability with Java and JavaScript*:

    ```
    (defn on-js-reload []
     (rum/mount (rock-paper-scissors)
          (. js/document (getElementById "app"))))

    (on-js-reload)
    ```

5. Now we'll define the game logic itself. We'll try to have this part of the program not be dependent on ClojureScript. The first function will determine the computer's choice of rock, paper, or scissors:

```
(defn computer-choice []
  (nth [:rock :scissors :paper] (rand-int 3)))
```

6. The only slightly complex problem is translating the "rock crushes scissors" rules into code. Of course, we could just write a long **cond** structure, but since this is Clojure, so we'll use a data structure instead:

```
(def resolutions
  {:rock {:paper :computer-wins
          :scissors :player-wins}
   :scissors {:rock :computer-wins
              :paper :player-wins}
   :paper {:scissors :computer-wins
           :rock :player-wins}})
```

In the **resolutions** map, the top-level keys correspond to the human player's choice. Each item contains two possible outcomes, based on the two non-tie choices the computer might make.

7. That means that if the player chooses **:rock** and the computer chooses **:scissors**, we can get the result like this:

```
packt-clj.rock-scissors-paper.core> (get-in resolutions [:rock :scissors])
:player-wins
```

8. This is how we'll write our **resolve-game** function. Checking for ties is easy with a simple equality check:

```
(defn resolve-game [player computer]
  (if (= player computer)
    :tie
    (get-in resolutions [player computer])))
```

9. We also want to tell the user why they won or lost by providing a message such as "Rock crushes scissors." These messages don't need to mention who won, so we only need associate pairs of objects with a message. :rock and :paper in any order should result in **Paper wraps rock**. Since order isn't important, **sets** might be a good choice. We can use the sets as map keys, like this:

```
(def object-sets->messages
  {#{:rock :scissors} "Rock crushes scissors."
   #{:scissors :paper} "Scissors cut paper."
   #{:paper :rock} "Paper wraps rock."})
```

Most of the time we use keywords as map keys, to the point that we forget sometimes that more complex data structures can also be used. This way, it doesn't matter if we write the following:

```
(get object-sets->messages #{:rock :scissors})
```

We can also write the following:

```
(get object-sets->messages #{:scissors :rock})
```

10. Let's wrap this logic into a function:

```
(defn result-messages [a b]
  (get object-sets->messages (hash-set a b)))
```

Here, **hash-set** builds the set to be used to look for the appropriate message. The **a** and **b** parameters can be, interchangeably, the player's choice or the computer's choice.

11. At this point, a game can be resolved with two function calls: one to know who won, the other to know why. Here, the player chooses **:scissors** and defeats the computer, who unwisely chose **:paper**:

```
packt-clj.rock-scissors-paper.core> (resolve-game :scissors :paper)
:player-wins
packt-clj.rock-scissors-paper.core> (result-messages :scissors :paper)
"Scissors cut paper."
```

12. The next step is to convert our gameplay into views. Let's break the game view out into its own component, which we'll call **game-view**. There are only three game states, so we can get away with a **case** expression. We'll start with just placeholders:

```
(rum/defc game-view < rum/reactive []
 (case (:game-state (rum/react app-state))
  :setup
  [:div "Ready to play?"
   [:div [:a {:href "#start"} "Start"]]]
  :waiting
  [:div "Choose one"
   [:div [:a {:href "#rock"} "Rock"]]
   [:div [:a {:href "#paper"} "Paper"]]
   [:div [:a {:href "#scissors"} "Scissors"]]]
  :complete
  [:div [:a {:href "#restart"} "Play again?"]]))
```

To see the output from this component, we can plug it into the **(rock-scissors-paper)** function we defined earlier:

```
(rum/defc rock-paper-scissors []
 [:div
  [:h1 "Rock, Paper, Scissors"]
  (game-view)])
```

At this point, the **game-view** component just shows some different markups depending on the game state, which is stuck at **:setup** because there is no code to make anything happen yet. Still, it's a good idea to make sure that everything is working as expected. The key here is how **app-state** is dereferenced using **rum/react**. The **rum** library adds a lot of built-in behavior that goes beyond just dereferencing. For now, though, we can think of **rum/react** as a fancy, framework-specific version of **deref**:

Figure 12.16: We have a start screen but no gameplay yet

13. To move on to the next game state, something needs to happen when the player clicks on **Start**. We need a function that will start the game.

   To start a new game, we need to do two things to **app-state**: set **:game-state** to **:waiting** and set **:computer-choice** to the output from our **computer-choice** function. It's also probably good practice to clean up the **:player-choice** field as well, since it is no longer valid. Our **start-game** function can look like this:

```
(defn start-game []
  (swap! app-state
      (fn [state]
        (assoc state
            :computer-choice (computer-choice)
            :game-state :waiting
            :player-choice nil))))
```

   Notice that we're using **swap!**. Since **app-state** is a real atom, this is how we have to interact with it, by providing a function. If we wanted to be more concise, our call to **swap!** could be rewritten like this:

```
(swap! app-state
    assoc
    :computer-choice (computer-choice)
    :game-state :waiting
    :player-choice nil)
```

14. Inside the **game-view** component, we can now add **start-game** as a click handler in both the **:setup** and **:complete** phases:

```
(rum/defc game-view < rum/reactive []
  (case (:game-state (rum/react app-state))
   :setup
   [:div "Ready to play?"
    [:div [:a {:href "#start"
          :onClick start-game} "Start"]]]
   :waiting
   [:div "Choose one"
    [:div [:a {:href "#rock"} "Rock"]]
    [:div [:a {:href "#paper"} "Paper"]]
    [:div [:a {:href "#scissors"} "Scissors"]]]
   :complete
   [:div [:a {:href "#restart"
          :onClick start-game} "Play again?"]]))
```

Let's check this new behavior. If you click on **Start**, you should now see this:

Figure 12.17: Starting the Rock, Paper, Scissors application

15. Now we need handlers for each of the choices. Since each handler will do essentially the same thing, just with a different value, let's write a function that returns a function using that value. We'll call it **player-choice**:

```
(defn player-choice [choice]
  (fn []
    (swap! app-state
        (fn [state]
          (assoc state
              :player-choice choice
              :game-state :complete)))))
```

The changes made to **app-state** here move the **:game-state** to the next phase and add in the **choice** parameter as a means of closure for the anonymous function.

16. Instead of writing three separate handlers, we can just call these functions in the view. Now our **game-view** component looks like this:

```
(rum/defc game-view < rum/reactive []
  (case (:game-state (rum/react app-state))
   :setup
   [:div "Ready to play?"
    [:div [:a {:href "#start"
          :onClick start-game} "Start"]]]
   :waiting
   [:div "Choose one"
    [:div [:a {:href "#rock"
          :onClick (player-choice :rock)} "Rock"]]
    [:div [:a {:href "#paper"
          :onClick (player-choice :paper)} "Paper"]]
    [:div [:a {:href "#scissors"
          :onClick (player-choice :scissors)} "Scissors"]]]
   :complete
   [:div [:a {:href "#restart"
              :onClick start-game} "Play again?"]]))
```

Notice that with the **start-game** handler, we supply the function itself, without parentheses. That's because **start-game** itself is the handler. With **player-choice**, we call the function when defining the view; it isn't the handler, instead it returns an anonymous handler, which is what will actually be called when the user clicks the link.

17. Now, when clicking on **Rock**, **Scissors**, or **Paper**, you should see the final screen:

Rock, Paper, Scissors

Play again?

Figure 12.18: Final screen of Rock, Paper, Scissors

18. The last step is to display the results. Since this is more complex than the other views, it's worth breaking it out into a new component, which we'll call **result-view**. Let's look at the code and then we'll go through the logic:

```
(rum/defc result-view < rum/reactive []
  (let [player (:player-choice (rum/react app-state))
        computer (:computer-choice (rum/react app-state))
        result (resolve-game player computer)]
    [:div
     [:div "You played " [:strong (name player)]]
     [:div "The computer played " [:strong (name computer)]]
     (if (= result :tie)
       [:div "It was a tie!"]
       [:div
        [:div (result-messages player computer)]
        [:div (if (= result :player-wins) "You won!" "Oops. The computer won.")]])
     [:div [:a {:href "#start"
                :onClick start-game} "Play again?"]]]))
```

We start off with some **let** bindings for the player choice, the computer choice, and the result, which is derived from the two choices.

Everything after that takes place in a single `:div` element. This is necessary because in React, and thus in all the React-based ClojureScript frameworks, a component can only return a single HTML element. Without this wrapping `:div` element, we would get an error.

After displaying both of the choices, using **name** to convert the keywords to strings, we get to the actual results. In case of a tie, there is not much to display, so we test for that first. The **result-messages** function provides a nice summary of what happened and then we can finally tell the player whether they won or lost, depending on the value of **result**. At the end, we've placed the "**Play again**?" link that was previously in the **game-view** component.

19. Now we just need to insert the **result-view** component into the **game-view** component:

```
(rum/defc game-view < rum/reactive []
  (case (:game-state (rum/react app-state))
    :setup
    [:div "Ready to play?"
     [:div [:a {:href "#start"
                :onClick start-game} "Start"]]]
    :waiting
    [:div "Choose one"
     [:div [:a {:href "#rock"
                :onClick (player-choice :rock)} "Rock"]]
     [:div [:a {:href "#paper"
                :onClick (player-choice :paper)} "Paper"]]
     [:div [:a {:href "#scissors"
                :onClick (player-choice :scissors)} "Scissors"]]]
    :complete
    (result-view)))
```

Note

The complete code for this exercise is available on the book's GitHub repository: https://packt.live/2uoDolF.

Now you should be able to play the game:

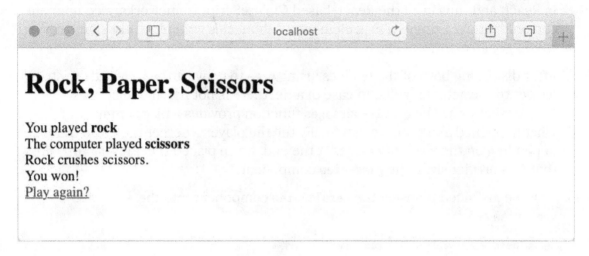

Figure 12.19: Prompt to play again

You won! By building this simple game, you've learned a basic template for stateful ClojureScript applications, using one of Clojure's reference types. Even though the JavaScript runtime is single-threaded, atoms are useful here because they allow event handlers to interact with shared program state in a safer way than simply overwriting data.

Watchers

In the previous exercise, we mentioned that when using the `Rum` library, writing `(rum/react app-state)` basically dereferences the `app-state` atom. There is, however, a little bit more going on, obviously, since otherwise we would use `deref` instead. In ClojureScript libraries such as Rum, atoms often serve as the application's "single source of truth." Rum and the Om framework both use plain atoms; Reagent and the popular `Re-frame` library, which is based on Reagent, both use a special `atom` implementation sometimes referred to as a "ratom" (from **r/atom**, if **r** is a namespace alias for Reagent). You'll learn more about Reagent in *Chapter 15, The Front End: A ClojureScript UI*.

Why are atoms so popular for ClojureScript libraries? First of all, atoms help manage concurrent updates. When there is a single source of truth, that means that many parts of the program may interfere with each other when they all try to update the same data source. As we've already seen, atoms, with their built-in retry logic, help avoid many of these issues.

Beyond this, however, Clojure (and ClojureScript) atoms have another important feature that makes them particularly useful as the single source of truth in a browser-based application. A common pattern in modern JavaScript architectures goes something like this:

- An event occurs and is handled by the application. In the previous exercise, these were the click handlers. There are, of course, many other kinds of events that might occur: scrolling events, timeouts, successful (or failed) network requests, and so on.

- In response to the event, the application state is modified. In the Rock, Paper, Scissors game, the player made their choice, and this was reflected in **app-state**, via **swap!**.

- The rest of the application reacts to this change in the application state. Views that reference the application state are updated automatically. Advancing the **:game-state** field in **app-state** caused the different phases of the game to be displayed. Once the appropriate views were defined, the framework seemed to take care of making sure that the views were updated.

When one part of the application updates the application states, the other parts respond. Atoms help with this because they accept "watcher" functions that are called when the atom changes. To "watch" an atom, we use the **add-watch** function:

```
user> (def observable-atom (atom 5))
#'user/observable-atom
user> (add-watch observable-atom :watcher-1
        (fn [k a old new]
          (println "The observable atom has gone from" old "to" new)))
#<Atom@14b35f8d: 5>
user> (swap! observable-atom inc)
The observable atom has gone from 5 to 6
6
```

We've provided an anonymous function that simply prints out a message when the atom is changed. When adding a **watch** function, a key such as **:watcher-1** is required so that, later, that particular watcher can be identified for removal by the **remove-watch** function. That key is then available as the first argument to the watcher function, **k** in this example. The **a** argument is the atom itself. Often, these two arguments will not be used; in most cases, what you really need is in the **old** and **new** arguments.

In the previous exercise, we defined our components using the **rum/reactive** mixin as follows:

```
(rum/defc game-view < rum/reactive []
  ;;
  )
```

rum/reactive then adds watchers as appropriate so that the component knows when to update. This way, multiple components can reference the same data in **app-state**; when the data changes, the components are watching, and they can update accordingly. This pattern happens to mesh nicely with some of the common patterns used with React.js, which is why it is seen so often in ClojureScript libraries and applications. Generally, when using these frameworks, you will not need to define your own watchers. The frameworks take care of that for you.

Validators are another feature of atoms that you could actually use in your ClojureScript app. Like watchers, validators are functions that can be added to Clojure reference types. When an atom, for example, is about to be modified by a call to **swap!**, if any validators have been set on the atom, they will be called. If any of them do not return **true**, the update will fail and an exception (or an error, if this is on the JavaScript runtime) will be thrown:

```
user> (def integer-atom (atom 5))
#'user/integer-atom
user> (set-validator! integer-atom #(< % 6))
nil
user> (swap! integer-atom inc)
Execution error (IllegalStateException) at user/eval12624 (REPL:612).
Invalid reference state
user>
```

Figure 12.20: Execution error

When an update fails validation, an exception is thrown.

Here, the validator enforces a "less than 6" rule on **integer-atom**. The call to **swap!** tries to increment the value to **6** but an exception is thrown instead. In the next exercise, we will incorporate some validation.

Exercise 12.06: One, Two, Three... "Rock!"

Your in-browser Rock, Paper, Scissors game is starting to generate some interest. You've created a start-up around it and now your investors want an improved version that is more like the original. Your plan is to introduce a countdown before the user can make their choice, just like in the original version of the game, where the two players coordinate their moves before revealing their choices: "One, two, three...Rock!"

To do this, we'll use JavaScript intervals to provide some timing for the countdown. In the browser, intervals are how JavaScript developers can cause a function to be called repeatedly after a certain number of milliseconds. We will use intervals to simulate a ticking clock, where each tick of the clock will be an event that the application reacts to. This will show how application state can be used to coordinate and react to events.

> **Note**
>
> This exercise builds on your code from the previous exercise. Either use the same project or make a copy.

1. At the command-line prompt, start the ClojureScript REPL:

```
lein figwheel
```

A browser window should open, inviting you to play a game of Rock, Paper, Scissors.

2. Add a `:countdown` field to the **app-state** atom:

```
(defonce app-state (atom {:computer-choice nil
                          :game-state :setup
                          :player-choice nil
                          :countdown 3}))
```

3. Add a validator to the **app-state** to make sure that the **:game-state** field always contains a game phase keyword and that the countdown never goes beyond 3 or below 0:

```
(set-validator! app-state #(and
                (>= 3 (:countdown %) 0)
                (#{:setup :waiting :complete} (:game-state %))))
```

> **Note**
>
> The greater-than and less-than family of functions all take more than two arguments. This is a convenient way of testing whether a value is between two other values.

4. Most of the improvements we want to make are going to affect the **:waiting** phase of the game. Let's make a dedicated view, which we'll call the **choices-view** function. It will show two things: the countdown and the list of choices.

    As a first step, set up the view with the same list of choices as before:

```
(rum/defc choices-view < rum/reactive []
  [:div.choices-view
   [:div.choices
   [:div "Choose one"
    [:div [:a {:href "#rock"
          :onClick (player-choice :rock)} "Rock"]]
    [:div [:a {:href "#paper"
          :onClick (player-choice :paper)} "Paper"]]
    [:div [:a {:href "#scissors"
          :onClick (player-choice :scissors)} "Scissors"]]]]])
```

At the same time, add this new view to **game-view**, instead of the previous list corresponding to the **:waiting** game state:

```
(rum/defc game-view < rum/reactive []
  (case (:game-state (rum/react app-state))
   :setup
   [:div "Ready to play?"
    [:div [:a {:href "#start"
          :onClick start-game} "Start"]]]
   :waiting
```

```
(choices-view)
:complete
(result-view)))
```

At this point, the game should still work exactly as before.

5. Before the countdown reaches zero, the links in the list of choices should be inactive to prevent the player from clicking too soon. Since each link needs to handle two different states, it makes sense to encapsulate that behavior in a component, like this:

```
(rum/defc choice-link-view [kw label countdown]
  (if (zero? countdown)
    [:div [:a {:href (str "#" (name kw))
               :on-click (player-choice kw)}
           label]]
    [:div label]))
```

> **Note**
>
> Remember to place **choice-link-view** before **choices-view** in the source file.

The first two arguments simply supply the keyword and the text label necessary for building the links, as before. The **countdown** argument, however, will allow us to determine what should be displayed. If the countdown has reached zero, we display the link. If not, we simply display the label.

6. We need to update **choices-view** as well:

```
(rum/defc choices-view < rum/reactive []
  (let [ready? (= :waiting (:game-state (rum/react app-state)))
        countdown (:countdown (rum/react app-state))]
    [:div.choices-view
     [:div.choices
      [:h3 "Choose one"]
      (choice-link-view :rock "Rock" countdown)
      (choice-link-view :paper "Paper" countdown)
      (choice-link-view :scissors "Scissors" countdown)]]))
```

When you try to play the game now, if you click on **Start**, you should see this:

Figure 12.21: Options available on clicking Start

7. We also want to display the countdown in this view. Let's make a new component for that too so that we can add a little bit of display logic:

```
(rum/defc countdown-view < rum/reactive [countdown]
  [:div.countdown
   [:div.countdown-message
    (if (> countdown 0)
      "Get ready to make your choice..."
      "Go!")]
   [:h1 countdown]])
```

And this view can be called from **choices-view** as well:

```
(rum/defc choices-view < rum/reactive []
  (let [countdown (:countdown (rum/react app-state))]
    [:div.player-choices-view
     (countdown-view countdown)
     [:div.choices
      [:h3 "Choose one"]
      (choice-link-view :rock "Rock" countdown)
      (choice-link-view :paper "Paper" countdown)
      (choice-link-view :scissors "Scissors" countdown)]]))
```

If you try to play the game at this point, you should see **3** displayed above the inactive links:

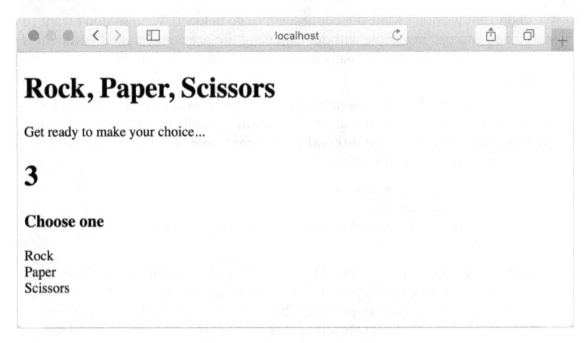

Figure 12.22: The countdown is there but it's not moving yet

8. For the timing of the countdown, we'll use **setInterval**, which means that we need some JavaScript interop. This function will cause the :**countdown** field to decrement every second:

```
(defn start-countdown []
  (js/setInterval #(swap! app-state update :countdown dec) 1000))
```

9. The **setInterval** function returns an identifier that we'll need later for canceling the interval. Each time a new game starts, we need to start the interval and record its identifier. These things can be done by the **start-game** function, which we'll update. (For this reason, **start-countdown** will need to be placed before the **start-game** function in your source file.):

```
(defn start-game []
  (let [interval (start-countdown)]
    (swap! app-state
        (fn [state]
          (assoc state
              :computer-choice (computer-choice)
              :game-state :waiting
              :countdown 3
              :interval interval)))))
```

The **interval** goes into the app-state for later use.

10. We know that we don't want the countdown to go below 0. We also don't want to start a new interval in a game without canceling the previous interval. After a few games, we would end up with many intervals all trying to update the :countdown field.

Stopping the interval is easy enough with the **clearInterval** function. But how do we know when it should be called? One solution would be to add a check in the function we passed to **setInterval** in the **start-countdown** function. For this exercise, though, we'll use a watcher:

```
(add-watch app-state :countdown-zero
    (fn [_k state old new]
      (when (and (= 1 (:countdown old)) (= 0 (:countdown new)))
        (js/clearInterval (:interval new)))))
```

We won't ever remove this watcher, but we still need to give it an identifier, for which we use a descriptive keyword. The interesting part of this call to **add-watch** is the anonymous function we provide. This function will be called every time a change occurs in the **app-state** atom. Most of the time, this function will do nothing. The exception, of course, is when the countdown is about to go to zero. In that case, **clearInterval** is called with the interval identifier stored in the atom.

Now the countdown should work as planned. When it reaches zero, the message changes to **Go!** and the links become active:

Figure 12.23: A successful countdown

This exercise showed us how watchers and validators work. Remember, in Clojure they can be used on all the different kinds of reference types.

Activity 12.01: A DOM Whack-a-mole Game

After the amazing success of your Rock, Paper, Scissors browser game, you've decided to create an even more ambitious product, based on the classic Whack-a-mole game. Whack-a-mole is an early arcade game. Moles pop up at random from several holes in a table. The player holds a mallet and tries to whack the moles as soon as they appear. When hit, the mole disappears back into its hole until it pops back up again.

Your version of Whack-a-mole will use DOM elements in a web browser. It might look something like this (if you know some CSS, you're free to make it look a little better):

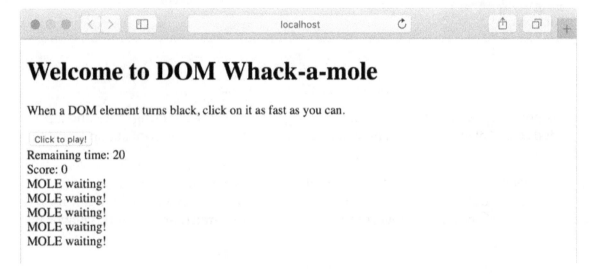

Figure 12.24: Before the game starts

Once the player clicks on the `Click to play!` button, the clock starts and the moles, who are actually just HTML `<div>` elements, start to randomly activate:

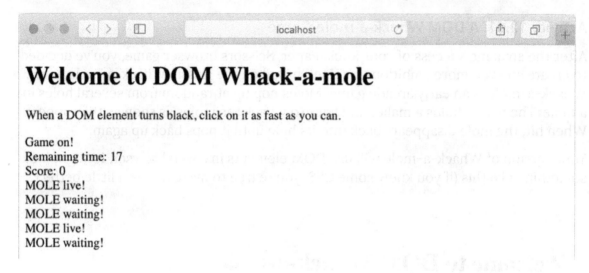

Figure 12.25: Click on the moles!

At this point, if the player clicks on a mole, it goes back to the waiting state and a point is added to the player's score. The game stops after a fixed number of seconds, probably 20 or so.

The behavior of the moles follows these rules: Only two moles are visible at a time. The moles to be made visible are selected randomly. A mole is visible for a fixed duration (2 or 3 seconds, probably) and reverts to the hidden state after that time if the player has not clicked on it.

To build this game, you should take these basic steps:

1. Use the same basic ClojureScript and Rum setup used in the Rock, Paper, Scissors exercises.

2. As in the last exercise, use `setInterval` to count down the seconds after the game starts. For more fluidity, it's probably best to use an interval smaller than 1 second. 100 milliseconds is probably about right.

3. Use multiple atoms for the various counters that you'll need: the countdown clock (the interval itself), the number of milliseconds remaining in the game, the game state (`:waiting` or `:playing`), and a vector of moles.

4. The moles themselves should have two values: their status (`:waiting` or `:live`) and the number of remaining milliseconds remaining if they are in the `:live` state. These values could be contained in a map or a two-item vector tuple.

5. Write event handlers for clicks on the **Start** button and on the active moles.

6. If you know some CSS, feel free to make the game look better by adding some definitions to **resources/public/css/style.css**.

> **Note**
>
> The solution for this activity can be found on page 738.

Summary

Concurrency, by its very nature, is a complex problem. While it's impossible to cover all the techniques you might need, hopefully, this chapter will provide you with the tools to get started. We covered the usage of **pmap** and **future** for using multiple threads. We also saw Clojure's reference types: var, atoms, agents, and refs. We used atoms to manage state in a browser-based ClojureScript application.

For each of these topics, there is a lot more that can be said. What you learn further down the road will depend on the kinds of problems you need to solve. Concurrency is one of the areas where the problems will be more diverse than almost any other. Familiarity with Clojure's basic approach to these questions will start you in the right direction when you search for solutions.

In the next chapter, we will take another big step toward real-world Clojure by learning how to interact with databases.

13

Database Interaction and the Application Layer

Overview

In this chapter we will create and connect to an Apache Derby instance on your local machine. We will also create and use a connection pool for efficient database interactions, and create and load a database schema. We will then create, read, update, and delete data using `clojure.java.jdbc`.

By the end of this chapter, you will be able to implement an application layer sitting on top of a database instance, ingest data from a CSV file on disk, and write it to the database via an application layer API.

Introduction

So far, we have been interacting with **Comma-Separated Values (CSV)** files from disk and in memory with no persistence. Each time we restart our REPL, we lose all the data manipulation or ELO calculations we've made up to that point and must restart from scratch. If there were a means of persisting this state each time, we could begin where we left off last time. Indeed, we could imagine building an ELO calculation application with a web interface or even a ClojureScript frontend once we've established a means of persistent storage so that our progress is maintained from session to session.

When considering persistence, most applications will reach for a relational database implementation (for example, MySQL, Oracle, or PostgreSQL). There are many implementations to choose from, each with their own strengths and weaknesses.

We'll use Apache Derby as an on-disk **Relational Database Management System (RDBMS)**. It is implemented entirely in Java, meaning there is minimal setup required for our use case, giving us more time to focus on the topics of data modeling, persistence, and retrieval. The function of the RDBMS is to manage the storage of our data across our user-defined tables, allowing queries to be executed across them. It is relational as it supports relations across these tables. For example, a driver owning one or more cars could be represented as a `Driver` table and a `Car` table, with a reference linking them. We'll cover the means of describing this relation in the *Creating Database Schemas* section later.

Going into a little more detail about our potential ELO calculation application, there are numerous topics to consider when it comes to persistence. We'll need to determine what data we want to store, and then determine the model that best describes that data and any relations between different parts of the model. There are constraints we'll have to consider; for example, how will we uniquely identify the entities we're persisting? This will be codified in our database schema using the **Data Definition Language (DDL)**.

With a schema defined, we need a means of inserting, retrieving, updating, and deleting data. Since Apache Derby is a **Structured Query Language (SQL)**-based RDBMS, this is the most appropriate means of interacting with the database for these purposes. We'll construct SQL commands that cover each of the preceding requirements. These commands will understand the underlying data model, how the relations are constructed, and how to access the relevant parts of the model we're interested in. Apache Derby will execute the SQL commands for us and return the result.

In terms of interacting with this database from Clojure, we'll primarily use `clojure.java.jdbc`, which is a longstanding, stable, low-level library for talking to databases using **Java Database Connectivity (JDBC)**.

It should be noted that the maintainers of this library have created a successor, **next. jdbc**, with a focus on simplicity and performance. An interesting task for you would be to take the examples provided here and rework them to conform to the **next.jdbc** API.

Connecting to a Database

As alluded to previously, we'll be leveraging JDBC for all our database interactions. JDBC allows a Java client to connect to an RDBMS using a well-defined **Application Programming Interface (API)**. This API gives us a clear contract between ourselves (the client) and our database (the server). Since Clojure sits atop the **Java Virtual Machine (JVM)**, JDBC is the natural choice for us.

For those familiar with JDBC, you'll have encountered the (occasionally unwieldy) JDBC URL. These URLs vary depending on the RDBMS, where the database is located, and how it is secured, among other things. In essence, they are a database connection descriptor.

Fortunately, **clojure.java.jdbc** abstracts this away with its concept of **db-spec** (a database specification). **db-spec** is a simple map structure holding details pertinent to the connection we're looking to make. This **db-spec** structure can then be passed to any **clojure.java.jdbc** API call and it will build the connection for us behind the scenes. This specification is fairly broad and can take many different forms. We'll touch on a few as we progress.

An important point to note is that **clojure.java.jdbc** expects the driver of your target database to be available on the classpath prior to making an API call. The driver acts as a means of converting your JDBC-based API calls into something your RDBMS understands. Each RDBMS will, therefore, have its own specific driver. Without this, any database operations will throw an exception.

For example, if we were to define a **deps.edn** with only the **clojure.java.jdbc** dependency, and then attempt a **jdbc/query** operation, this would be the result:

```
{:deps {org.clojure/java.jdbc {:mvn/version "0.7.9"}}}
(require '[clojure.java.jdbc :as jdbc])
```

Here, we encounter our first concrete **db-spec** definition. This is the **DriverManager** form of **db-spec** and is the preferred format for **clojure.java.jdbc**:

```
(def db {:dbtype "derby" ;; the type of RDBMS
         :dbname "derby-local" ;; the DB as it will be stored on disk
         :create true        ;; essential on first interaction
         })
```

Breaking down our **db-spec** definition, we're interacting with an Apache Derby database (this is the driver we're looking for). We're naming our database **derby-local** in the current working directory. The **:create true** flag will create the database file if it does not already exist:

```
user=> (jdbc/get-connection db)
```

The output is as follows:

```
Execution error (SQLException) at java.sql.DriverManager/getConnection (DriverManager.java:702).
No suitable driver found for jdbc:derby:derby-local
```

Figure 13.1: Error due to no driver being added

Encountering this is generally an indication that you have not added the driver to your **deps.edn** file or equivalent.

The *Releases and Dependencies* section of the **clojure.java.jdbc** GitHub page contains links to drivers for popular RDBMSes. Once the appropriate driver version has been located, add it to your **deps.edn** file. Consider the following example:

```
{:deps {org.apache.derby/derby {:mvn/version "10.14.2.0"}}}
```

As you can see, Apache Derby provides a package containing its database implementation alongside an embedded driver, meaning we don't need an explicit driver dependency in our project.

Exercise 13.01: Establishing a Database Connection

In this exercise, we will connect to a local on-disk database:

1. We'll begin by setting up our dependencies. Create a file named **deps.edn** in your current working directory and paste in the following content:

```
{:deps
  {org.apache.derby/derby {:mvn/version "10.14.2.0"}
   org.clojure/java.jdbc {:mvn/version "0.7.9"}}}
```

It should be noted, at the time of writing, that Apache Derby version 10.15.1.3 is available. This should *not* be used with **clojure.java.jdbc 0.7.9**! The maintainer of **clojure.java.jdbc** advises that it is untested against 10.15.x.

2. Require **clojure.java.jdbc** and alias (a temporary name) it as **jdbc** for convenience:

```
user=> (require '[clojure.java.jdbc :as jdbc])
nil
```

3. Here, we use the **db-spec** definition from the preceding introduction. Introduce a concrete instance of a **db-spec** definition:

```
user=> (def db {:dbtype "derby"
                :dbname "derby-local"
                :create true})
=> #'user/db
```

4. Test that we can obtain a connection to this database:

```
user=> (jdbc/get-connection db)
```

The output is as follows:

```
#object[org.apache.derby.impl.jdbc.EmbedConnection 0x4116f66a "org.apache.derby.impl.jdbc.EmbedCon
nection@1092023914 (XID = 159), (SESSIONID = 1), (DATABASE = derby-local), (DRDAID = null) "]
```

Figure 13.2: Obtaining a connection to the database

> **Note**
>
> The preceding output is the **toString** representation of our connection. The content is of no real consequence as we are not concerned with the internal representation of the connection object.

Great! We have a means of creating an Apache Derby instance on disk and have established a connection successfully. This **db-spec** definition is, therefore, valid and can be used anywhere the **db-spec** definition is accepted.

> **Note**
>
> Any time we wish to remove our local database and start over, we can do so by removing the directory matching our database name in our current working directory.

Introduction to Connection Pools

Although it's convenient for `clojure.java.jdbc` to create our database connections for us (it does this on each API call when we pass it a **db-spec** definition), there is a resulting performance overhead we should be aware of. This can become burdensome as establishing a connection (particularly to a remote machine) can often take many times longer than our query will actually take to execute! This is, therefore, an expensive operation that we'd like to avoid. Connection pooling is one such way of avoiding this overhead.

When we talk of a connection pool, we're essentially talking about establishing one or more connections ahead of time and making them available to our application anytime a database connection is required. In this way, we deal with the connection overhead once on application startup and benefit from connection reuse from that point onward.

`clojure.java.jdbc` does not itself offer a connection pooling implementation, but it does integrate well with a number of pooling libraries, including **c3p0** and **hikari-cp**. We'll focus on **hikari-cp** as it is a Clojure wrapper for the lightning-quick **hikariCP** connection with a super-simple API.

hikari-cp provides an API that allows us to construct a connection-pooled data source; we can use this to construct an alternative **db-spec** definition to use in place of our **DriverManager** based **db-spec** with no other changes required. **hikari-cp** will manage the pool of connections for us.

Exercise 13.02: Creating a Connection Pool

In this exercise, we will create an alternative **db-spec** definition that can be used in place of the one created in *Step 3* of *Exercise 13.01, Establishing a Database Connection*. The benefit will be an increase in the speed of database interactions since a connection does not need to be established afresh for each interaction:

1. Add the **hikari-cp** dependency into our application:

```
{:deps
 {hikari-cp {:mvn/version "2.8.0"}
  org.apache.derby/derby {:mvn/version "10.14.2.0"}
  org.clojure/java.jdbc {:mvn/version "0.7.9"}}}
```

2. Now, depending on our precise needs, we have a few different means of constructing a valid data source. When we are starting from scratch and are expected to create the database as well as establish a connection, then we will need to reach for the appropriate JDBC URL. The Apache Derby URLs are less troublesome than others to construct and follow this simple syntax:

```
jdbc:derby:[subprotocol:][databaseName][;attribute=value]
```

> **Note**
>
> More details on Derby JDBC database connection URL can be found at https://packt.live/2Fnnx9f.

3. Given this, we can define our **db-spec** definition (using the **datasource** format) like so:

```
user=> (require '[clojure.java.jdbc :as jdbc]
                '[hikari-cp.core :as hikari])
nil
user=> (def db {:datasource (hikari/make-datasource {:jdbc-url "jdbc:derby:derby-
local;create=true"})})
=> #'user/db
```

To break this down, we're connecting to an Apache Derby instance where the database is named **derby-local**. You will recall that **create=true** instructs the database to be created if not already present.

4. Alternatively, if we know the database already exists, then the **create=true** flag will not be required. We could amend the JDBC URL or allow **hikari-cp** to build it for us:

```
(def db {:datasource
  (hikari/make-datasource {:database-name "derby-local"
                           :datasource-class-name "org.apache.derby.jdbc.
EmbeddedDataSource"})})
```

Note that, here, we are required to specify the **datasource-class-name**, which, in this case, is the embedded version, since we're running locally.

5. Regardless of the means we've used to construct our data source, we can pass this to the **clojure.java.jdbc** library as an alternative **db-spec** definition:

```
(jdbc/get-connection db)
```

The output is as follows:

```
#object[com.zaxxer.hikari.pool.HikariProxyConnection 0x49f3ff41 "HikariProxyConnection@1240727361
wrapping org.apache.derby.impl.jdbc.EmbedConnection@1828438007 (XID = 160), (SESSIONID = 1), (DATA
BASE = derby-local), (DRDAID = null) "]
```

Figure 13.3: Printing the output

We've now defined and tested two different **db-spec** formats successfully, demonstrating the flexibility offered by **clojure.java.jdbc**. It should be noted that a considerable number of alternatives are also acceptable, including **:connection-uri** (a JDBC URL) and **:connection** (an already established connection, rarely required).

> **Note**
>
> You can refer to http://clojure.github.io/java.jdbc/#clojure.java.jdbc/get-connection for full details of the supported **db-spec** definition.

To summarize, **clojure.java.jdbc** is flexible in what it consumes. Therefore, we'll be working with a connection-pooled data source as we start to interact more seriously with our newly created database.

Creating Database Schemas

We have our database connection. Before we begin to persist and query data, we must define our database model, or "schema" as it is more commonly known. This will take the form of the following:

- Tables
- Fields/columns within tables
- Relationships across tables

Let's consider the example of a sports activity tracker, which our tennis superstars might use in their spare time. We'd like to store application users and activities. Let's look at how we could model those using two tables.

The **app_user** table will store the first name, surname, height, and weight. The activity table will store the date, activity type, distance, and duration.

Primary Keys

It's important to note that there is nothing unique in the information we're storing. How would we correctly load a user's height and weight when we only have their name to query on? For example, multiple users could be created with the same name, and then we'd run into issues regarding correct ownership of activities.

We need to introduce **primary keys** to each of our tables. These are unique to each row and could be constructed and added to our `insert` statements; however, it is useful to leverage a feature of Apache Derby where it can allocate a unique ID on our behalf, and then communicate that back to us on insertion.

Adding `GENERATED ALWAYS AS IDENTITY` to a column definition will instruct Apache Derby to auto-allocate a monotonically increasing integer ID on the insertion of each new row in our table. This removes any overhead we might have in constructing one and guarantees its uniqueness.

Foreign Keys

When considering an activity, we can observe that one cannot exist without the prior existence of an `app_user`; that is, an activity must reference an existing entry in the `app_user` table. This is where the concept of a **foreign key** comes in.

A foreign key is a means of creating a relationship between a parent table and a child table. We can define a foreign key in our activity table, which references the primary key of our `app_user` table. When we create an activity, we must have the primary key of the `app_user` table available to us such that we can add it to our activity. With this linkage/relationship in place, we can then construct a query for all activities belonging to a user, for example.

The definition of a simple foreign key would look like this:

```
<foreign key field name> <foreign key type> REFERENCES <parent table>
```

Additionally, we generally add `ON DELETE CASCADE` to this definition, indicating that entries in the child table should be deleted when the corresponding entries are deleted from the parent table. This is important if the entry in the activity table cannot exist as a standalone entity; that is, it only makes sense in the context of its association with an `app_user`.

Exercise 13.03: Defining and Applying a Database Schema

Given our table requirements mentioned previously, we'll now codify those using DDL (that is, the actual SQL commands we'll use to create these structures):

1. Representing this in DDL, we will have something like this:

```
(def create-app-user-ddl "CREATE TABLE app_user (
id INT GENERATED ALWAYS AS IDENTITY CONSTRAINT USER_ID_PK PRIMARY KEY,
first_name VARCHAR(32),
surname VARCHAR(32),
height SMALLINT,
weight SMALLINT)")
=> #'user/create-app-user-ddl
(def create-activity-ddl "CREATE TABLE activity (
  id INT PRIMARY KEY GENERATED ALWAYS AS IDENTITY,
  activity_type VARCHAR(32),
  distance DECIMAL(5,2),
  duration INT,
  user_id INT REFERENCES app_user ON DELETE CASCADE)")
#'user/create-activity-ddl
```

> **Note**
>
> Each of our preceding symbols is suffixed with **-ddl**. This is the syntax that's typically used for describing database schemas.

2. **clojure.java.jdbc** provides a helper function of sorts that can construct a DDL statement for us. Although, the only real benefits for our use case are the ability to switch the format of the entities (table names, column names, and types) as well as the usage of keywords in place of parts of the manually constructed string. The equivalent function execution that would generate the **create-app-user-ddl** is as follows:

```
(def create-app-user-ddl-2 (jdbc/create-table-ddl :app_user
  [[:id :int "GENERATED ALWAYS AS IDENTITY CONSTRAINT USER_ID_PK PRIMARY KEY"]
  [:first_name "varchar(32)"]
  [:surname "varchar(32)"]
  [:height :smallint]
  [:weight :smallint]]
  {:entities clojure.string/lower-case}))
```

3. Looking at the **clojure.java.jdbc** API, we may intuitively expect that we can execute these DDL statements using the **jdbc/execute!** function. We can (this approach will work for the creation of single tables), however, if we wish to create more than one table, make use of **db-do-commands**, which accepts one or more command statements to be executed within a transaction:

```
user=> (jdbc/db-do-commands db [create-app-user-ddl create-activity-ddl])
=> (0 0)
```

> **Note**
>
> Rerunning the preceding command results in an error indicating the table already exists.

The output is as follows:

```
Execution error (StandardException) at org.apache.derby.iapi.error.StandardException/newException
(REPL:-1).
Table/View 'APP_USER' already exists in Schema 'APP'.
```

Figure 13.4: The execution error

It should be noted that, in general, using **CREATE TABLE IF NOT EXISTS** is sufficient to avoid this. However, Apache Derby does not support this syntax. Avoidance of this error would involve writing custom code to do the following:

- Attempt a **SELECT** statement from said table and detect a **table does not exist** error before performing the creation of the table.

- Attempt the creation and gracefully handle the **table already exists** error message.

- Leverage a migration library such as **Migratus** to keep track of the schema updates that we've applied up to this point, and automatically apply new changes as we introduce them.

In summary, we now have the ability to define our database schema using DDL and can apply this schema to our database, ready for data ingestion.

Managing Our Data

When dealing with persistent storage, and services that interact with them, we usually encounter the term **CRUD**, which stands for **Create**, **Read**, **Update**, and **Delete**. These are the four primary operations we can expect to perform against our database. **clojure.java.jdbc** exposes an API that directly maps to each of those operations, as we'd expect any good database library to do.

The following commands describe each of the CRUD operations and the appropriate API call to use in `clojure.java.jdbc`. Note that the tables, columns, and values are arbitrary and only serve to show the format of the call.

For creating an entry in the **example** table, we will set **col1** to the numeric value **42** and **col2** to the string value **"123"**:

```
(jdbc/insert! db-spec :example {:col1 42 :col2 "123"})
```

We can read or extract an entry from the example table where the **id** value of the row is **13**:

```
(jdbc/query   db-spec ["SELECT * FROM example WHERE id = ?" 13])
```

To update the row with an ID of 13, we will set **col1** to the numeric value **77** and **col2** to the string value **"456"**:

```
(jdbc/update! db-spec :example {:col1 77 :col2 "456"} ["id = ?" 13])
```

Delete or remove an entry from the example table with ID **13**:

```
(jdbc/delete! db-spec :example ["id = ?" 13])
```

It should be noted that these functions have multiple arities, where the optional last argument is a map of SQL options. We'll cover these options as we are introduced to each function in turn.

Also of note is the **!** suffix on three of the API calls. This is conventionally (but not always!) used to indicate that the function itself will perform a side effect. In the functional programming world, this can be deemed important enough to draw extra attention to.

Inserting, updating, and deleting will indeed result in a side effect – that of changing the persistent storage in some way. A query, by contrast, is a simple read function and will have no effect besides data retrieval.

Inserting Data

We'll cover the **C** in **CRUD** first. Indeed, we can't do anything exciting with our database until it's populated with some data.

Recall our two database tables, **app_user** and **activity**, and the relationship between them. Our foreign key reference stipulates that an activity cannot exist without the prior existence of an **app_user**. The creation of an activity must, therefore, reference an entity in the **app_user**.

Inserting Single Rows

`jdbc/insert!` operates in two modes, accepting either a map of column-value pairs or accepting a vector of columns and a vector of values. Let's explore the differences between both modes.

Firstly, using map mode, the structure of our **insert** command and the associated return value will be:

```
user=> (jdbc/insert!
          <db-spec>
          table name keyword>
          {<column_name> <column_value>
           ..})
({:1 1M})
```

The equivalent in vector mode is as follows:

```
user=> (jdbc/insert!
          <db-spec>
          <table name keyword>
          [<column name> ..]
          [<column value> ..])
(1)
```

> **Note**
>
> It is possible to omit the vector describing the column names. This would require us to insert values using the column order of the table as it was created. However, it is not possible to do this with Apache Derby when one or more of the columns is autogenerated.

Although entirely equivalent in terms of the rows created in the database, you'll notice the return values differ.

In the first case, we are returned a single-element sequence containing a map. The value associated with the :1 key is the ID that's been generated and persisted along with the row that we've just inserted. That's handy; we can use that when persisting any further rows in tables that require this as a foreign key. Without the automatic return of the generated ID, we'd need to submit a separate query to the database to retrieve it.

In the second case, we again get a single-element sequence – this time containing an integer. It may be tempting to assume that the integer corresponds to a generated ID; this would be incorrect – the integer instead tells us the number of rows affected. **jdbc/insert!** only supports the insertion of a single row; this integer will always be 1 and is, therefore, of little use.

A few important points should be noted here. The "generated ID" or "generated key" format is RDBMS-specific. If we were to swap in MySQL instead, we'd find our return value would be of the following form:

```
({:generated_key 1})
```

We should, therefore, be careful about how we process these return values and be cognizant that a change of database could result in broken code.

The **({:1 1M})** return value looks a little curious. Keywordized integers are perfectly valid – they're just not encountered particularly often. Apache Derby obviously has no concept of Clojure keywords; **clojure.java.jdbc** is (helpfully) keywordizing our return keys by default.

This segues nicely into some of the options we can pass to any of the CRUD API calls, namely:

- **keywordize?** (Boolean, defaults to **true**)
- identifiers (function, defaults to **identity**)

If we are happy to receive our keys as is, then we can switch keywordization off:

```
user=> (jdbc/insert! db :app_user {:first_name "Andre" :surname "Agassi" :height 180
:weight 80} {:keywordize? false})
({"1" 1M})
```

Inserting Multiple Rows

insert-multi! (like **insert!**) works in two different modes. It accepts a collection of maps or a collection of vectors. The overall result of calling either is identical, but there are key differences that you need to be aware of.

We've already covered the "generated ID" (when working with maps) versus "rows affected" (when working with vectors) return values. This also holds true when working with **insert-multi!**.

In addition, we should be aware that doing multiple inserts in vector mode will execute the inserts in batched transactions. This is more performant when doing a large number of inserts.

The following code demonstrates **insert-multi!** in map and vector mode:

```
user=> (jdbc/insert-multi!
  <db-spec>
  <table name keyword>
  [{<column name> <column value> ..}
   {<column name> <column value> ..}])
({:1 1M} {:1 2M})
(jdbc/insert-multi!
  <db-spec>
  <table name keyword>
  [<column name> ..]
  [[<column value> ..] [<column value> ..]])
=> (1 1)
```

Again, note the return values indicating that we've allocated IDs **1** and **2** to the inserted rows.

We can insert partial records using either map or vector mode. When working with map mode, we simply omit any unwanted key-value pairs. In vector mode, we must specify the column names, and then insert nil values as required.

Exercise 13.04: Data Insertion

Let's begin by creating entries in each of the tables we've defined, ensuring we respect the foreign key constraint:

1. Inserting our favorite tennis player of the 1990s as an **app_user** can be achieved with either of the following function calls. We recommend choosing one of these to avoid spurious duplicates in our data:

```
user=> (jdbc/insert!
        db
        :app_user
        {:first_name "Andre"
         :surname    "Agassi"
         :height     180
         :weight     80})
({:1 1M})
user=> (jdbc/insert!
        db
```

```
            :app_user
            [:first_name :surname :height :weight]
            ["Andre" "Agassi" 180 80])
  (1)
```

> **Note**
>
> When considering the existing state of the database, the **1M** value for our generated key can differ since it represents the next unique integer value.

2. We've inserted our first record successfully. Let's now create several activities and associate them with our **app_user**, Andre. This will allow us to exercise the **jdbc/insert-multi!** API call:

```
user=> (jdbc/insert-multi!
  db
  :activity
  [{:activity_type "run" :distance 8.67 :duration 2520 :user_id 1}
   {:activity_type "cycle" :distance 17.68 :duration 2703 :user_id 1}])
({:1 1M} {:1 2M})
```

When inserting data, there are several considerations to keep in mind. If inserting a single row, use **insert!**. If inserting multiple rows, use **insert-multi!**. If we are interested in the generated keys, then we should favor map insertion mode. If, on the other hand, performance is critical, we may favor vector insertion mode. When inserting a mixture of full and partial rows, then the reader may use their personal preference of map versus vector mode.

Querying Data

In order to view what we've persisted in our database thus far, we'll consider the **R** in **CRUD**. Reading, or querying, data is very simple. At its most basic, we just need our **db-spec** definition along with a vector containing a SQL string.

Exercise 13.05: Querying Our Database

Here, we'll cover the variety of options that we have available to us when querying the data we inserted as part of the prior exercise:

1. To find what we have in our **app_user** and activity tables, the following will suffice:

```
user=> (jdbc/query db ["select * from app_user"])
({:id 1, :first_name "Andre", :surname "Agassi", :height 180, :weight 80})
user=> (jdbc/query db ["select * from activity"])
({:id 1, :activity_type "run", :distance 8.67M, :duration 2520, :user_id 1}
 {:id 2, :activity_type "cycle", :distance 17.68M, :duration 2703, :user_id 1})
```

As alluded to in the *Managing Our Data* introduction, there is a 3-arity definition of **jdbc/query**, accepting a map of options. Since we have not provided that (we used the 2-arity version here) we have accepted all the default options. We'll now explore those options and how they can be used to manipulate the result set.

Consider the preceding return values. We're returned a sequence of maps by default, where the keys are lowercase keywords.

Of the options that are supported, the first three we'll cover are trivial and allow us to control the format of the keys returned are **keywordize?**, **identifiers**, and **qualifier**.

2. Setting **keywordize?** to **false** gives us string keys. Identifiers can be overridden by providing a single-arity function that converts the key to our chosen format. For example, retrieving data where the keys are uppercase strings can be achieved using these options (and **clojure.string**):

```
{:keywordize? false :identifiers str/upper-case}
user=> (require '[clojure.string :as str])
=> nil
user=> (jdbc/query db ["select * from app_user"] {:keywordize? false :identifiers
str/upper-case})
({"ID" 1, "FIRST_NAME" "Andre", "SURNAME" "Agassi", "HEIGHT" 180, "WEIGHT" 80})
```

qualifier only works when **keywordize?** is true (the default) and allows us to specify a namespace for our keywords. Our keys are then returned in the form:

```
:<qualifier>/<column name>
user=> (jdbc/query db ["select * from app_user"] {:identifiers str/upper-case
:qualifier "app_user"})
(#:app_user{:ID 1, :FIRST_NAME "Andre", :SURNAME "Agassi", :HEIGHT 180, :WEIGHT 80})
```

3. For those not familiar with the preceding format, this indicates that we have a map where our keyword namespace is homogenous (every key has the same **app_user** namespace). More explicitly, we can see the individual keys from that query:

```
user=> (-> (jdbc/query db ["select * from app_user"] {:identifiers str/upper-case
:qualifier "app_user"})
      first
      keys)
=> (:app_user/ID :app_user/FIRST_NAME :app_user/SURNAME :app_user/HEIGHT :app_user/
WEIGHT)
```

4. In the same way, we can insert data using (sequences of) maps or (sequences of) vectors. We can control the maps versus vectors result format in our queries as well. In the preceding code, we see maps as the default and can alter this by passing the following options map:

```
{:as-arrays? true}
```

The output is as follows:

```
user=> (jdbc/query db ["select * from activity"] {:as-arrays? true})
[[:id :activity_type :distance :duration :user_id]
 [1 "run" 8.67M 2520 1]
 [2 "cycle" 17.68M 2703 1]]
```

Thinking back to the chapter where we first interacted with CSV files, you may recognize this as the same data structure used for reading from or writing to a CSV file; that is, a sequence of vectors where the first vector corresponds to the columns of the file and subsequent vectors are the data entries of the file.

Manipulating Query Return Values

Besides manipulating the format of the return values, there are two additional options that give us complete control over each individual row returned by the query, or over the result set as a whole. We provide these using the **:row-fn** or **:result-set-fn** options; these *can* be combined if required.

The **row-fn** option should be a single-arity function, where the sole argument is a map representation of the current row. Similarly, the **result-set-fn** option should be a single-arity function where the sole argument is a sequence of maps representing the entirety of the query result. Consider the following example.

```
(defn custom-row-fn [row]
)
(defn custom-result-set-fn [result-set]
)
```

There are no constraints in what our functions can do, besides returning a value in the same data structure we received as input.

It should be noted that the **result-set-fn** option you pass should *not* be lazy; otherwise, the connection could be closed before the function completes. **reduce** (or a function that calls **reduce** under the hood) is a good choice here.

Exercise 13.06: Controlling Results with Custom Functions

Examples, where the **row-fn** would be applicable, include performing some calculation or aggregation that would be clumsy to achieve in raw SQL, formatting values, and enriching each row with computed values.

Combining all three of these use cases, let's consider our activity table, specifically the duration column. This is an integer value measuring the number of seconds of the activity in question. For the purposes of display or reporting to a user, we may find it more user-friendly to quote this in hours, minutes, and seconds:

1. Defining a **row-fn** where the sole argument is a map representation of a row and that generally speaking the row should be returned, with any manipulation applied:

```
(defn add-user-friendly-duration
  [{:keys [duration] :as row}]
  (let [quot-rem (juxt quot rem)
        [hours remainder] (quot-rem duration (* 60 60))
        [minutes seconds] (quot-rem remainder 60)]
    (assoc row :friendly-duration
           (cond-> ""
                   (pos? hours) (str hours "h ")
                   (pos? minutes) (str minutes "m ")
                   (pos? seconds) (str seconds "s")
                   :always str/trim))))
#'user/add-user-friendly-duration
```

2. Now adding that to our SQL options map and re-running the activity query from *Exercise 13.05, Querying Our Database*:

```
user=> (jdbc/query db ["select * from activity"]
           {:row-fn add-user-friendly-duration})
({:id 1, :activity_type "run", :distance 8.67M, :duration 2520, :user_id 1,
  :friendly-duration "42m"}
 {:id 2, :activity_type "cycle", :distance 17.68M, :duration 2703, :user_id 1,
  :friendly-duration "45m 3s"})
```

3. Let's now calculate the total distance traveled across all activities in the database. This could trivially be achieved via raw SQL, but nevertheless will give us an opportunity to explore alternatives.

   We'll define our function as follows:

```
(fn [result-set]
  (reduce (fn [total-distance {:keys [distance]}]
            (+ total-distance distance))
          0
          result-set))
```

4. When used along with our query, we predictably retrieve a single number representing total distance across all activities:

```
user=> (jdbc/query db ["select * from activity"]
                  {:result-set-fn (fn [result-set]
                                    (reduce (fn [total-distance {:keys [distance]}]
                                              (+ total-distance distance))
                                            0
                                            result-set))})
26.35M
```

5. To demonstrate how **row-fn** and **result-set-fn** can work together, we could use a **row-fn** to extract the distance, then a much simpler **result-set-fn** to sum those numbers like so:

```
(jdbc/query db ["select * from activity"]
            {:row-fn       :distance
             :result-set-fn #(apply + %)})
=> 26.35M
```

Through these last two exercises, we see **clojure.java.jdbc** gives us complete control over our query results, directly within the API call. Regardless of our requirements, we can leverage the options to the **jdbc/query** function to achieve the result we want, with custom formatting.

Updating and Deleting Data

Finally, we come to the **U** and **D** in CRUD; updates and deletes. These are simpler operations than the previous two and can be covered much more concisely.

When the state of the world we're modeling has changed, we'll want to reflect that in our persisted data. Before we perform our update, we determine the following:

- The table(s) affected

- The new values we wish to set

- The subset of data we want to have those values

The signature of **jdbc/update!** gives us these pointers if we were not already aware:

```
(update! db table set-map where-clause opts)
```

Exercise 13.07: Updating and Removing Existing Data

Let's assume we discover that Andre Agassi has lost 2 kg. We can surmise that we'll be updating the **app_user** table, setting the weight to 78 kg where the first name and last names are **Andre** and **Agassi** (or where the ID is **1**; we may have this available to us from earlier queries):

1. Construct the **update!** function call as follows:

```
user=> (jdbc/update! db :app_user {:weight 78} ["first_name = 'Andre' and surname =
'Agassi'"])
=> (1)
```

> **Note**
>
> Updates (and deletes), when successful, will only ever return the number of rows affected.

2. If we query the **app_user** table, we expect this new fact to be persisted:

```
user => (jdbc/query db ["select * from app_user"])
=> ({:id 1, :first_name "Andre", :surname "Agassi", :height 180, :weight 78})
```

3. Now, we could imagine a case where **Agassi** has removed his account from our activity tracking service and requested that his data be deleted. We have a function signature as follows:

```
(delete! db table where-clause opts)
```

4. We can construct a function call that will remove **Agassi** and all his activities from our database:

```
user=> (jdbc/delete! db :app_user ["first_name = 'Andre' and surname = 'Agassi'"])
=> [1]
```

Interestingly, the number of rows affected is reported as **1**. Since we set an **ON DELETE CASCADE** option, we expected that all Andre's activities would also be removed. Let's verify that is indeed the case:

```
user=> (jdbc/query db ["select * from activity"])
=> ()
```

As we can see, Andre's activities have been removed. We can, therefore, conclude that the rows affected will only ever correspond to those removed from the target table.

Introduction to the Application Layer

Until now, we've been creating ad hoc functions, testing them out at the REPL, occasionally creating a namespace or two that brings them together. We can think of the application layer as bringing all those namespaces and functions together into a working, coherent application with an associated API. In essence, we are designing the backend of our application in this step. We will then learn how to expose that API via REST in the next chapter; it will be useful to bear that in mind as we design our application.

When designing our application layer, it makes sense to take a step back and ask what our requirements are. If we consider the activity tracking application, we might realistically have the following high-level requirements:

- Create a new user.

- Create an activity for a given user.

- Query users and activities.

- Run reports across individual users (that is, by activity or time period).

Implementing the preceding requirements would give us a functional (albeit limited) application that users could begin interacting with to track activities and measure their fitness.

Since we've already demonstrated most of this functionality as we learned how to interact with a database, we can leverage a lot of the code we've already written, making it more generic as we go.

We could structure the preceding application in a number of different ways, depending on our own individual views on the logical split that makes the most sense. We could spend a number of hours in the design phase, working out the exact project structure before we write any code; however, we would prefer to propose a starting structure, begin fleshing it out, and take an agile/evolutionary approach to develop this simple application.

Exercise 13.08: Defining the Application Layer

We'll look to create our backend/application layer here; defining our namespaces and exposing an appropriate API.

Looking at the requirements we have, I'd suggest the following namespaces:

- **schema**: Our data models

- **ingest**: Single user and activity ingestion

- **query**: General queries for users and activities, plus more complex report queries

Again, remembering that we'd ideally layer on a REST service on top, imagine a top-level **web** or **api** namespace that will be interacting with the preceding namespaces and the public functions within.

Before proceeding with this exercise, add the following to your **deps.edn** file or similar:

```
{:deps {..
        semantic-csv {:mvn/version "0.2.1-alpha1"}
        org.clojure/data.csv {:mvn/version "0.1.4"}}}
```

Starting with a clean database, we'll begin by defining our **ns** schema, containing our DDL definitions that we'll expand slightly to support our reporting requirement. Notably, we've added an **activity_date** field to the activity table, allowing us to report on activities across time:

1. Define our namespace, including our **jdbc** and **hikari** requirements:

```
(ns packt-clj.fitness.schema
  (:refer-clojure :exclude [load])
  (:require
    [clojure.java.jdbc :as jdbc]
    [hikari-cp.core :as hikari]))
```

Note the use of (:refer-clojure :exclude [load]) in the previous code. This is not essential, but will suppress a warning that we're replacing a function from clojure. core when we come to define our own load function next. The warning we'd experience without this line would be as follows:

```
WARNING: load already refers to: #'clojure.core/load in namespace: packt-clj.fitness.
schema, being replaced by: #'packt-clj.fitness.schema/load
```

2. Now, define our jdbc-url parameter and create a hikari connection-pooled data source. This db variable will be referenced and used throughout this exercise whenever we load our schema, insert rows, or query rows from our database:

```
(def ^:private jdbc-url "jdbc:derby:derby-local;create=true")
(def db {:datasource (hikari/make-datasource {:jdbc-url jdbc-url})})
```

3. We'll now create our app_user and activity DDL:

```
(def ^:private create-app-user-ddl "CREATE TABLE app_user (
  id int GENERATED ALWAYS AS IDENTITY CONSTRAINT USER_ID_PK PRIMARY KEY,
  first_name varchar(32),
  surname varchar(32),
  height smallint,
  weight smallint)")
(def ^:private create-activity-ddl "CREATE TABLE activity (
  id INT PRIMARY KEY GENERATED ALWAYS AS IDENTITY,
  activity_type VARCHAR(32),
  distance DECIMAL(7,2),
  duration INT,
  activity_date DATE,
  user_id INT REFERENCES app_user ON DELETE CASCADE)")
```

4. Finally, we'll bring this all together under a load function, which will apply our database schema (that is, our DDL) to the database referenced by our JDBC URL, via a connection pool:

```
(defn load
  []
  (jdbc/db-do-commands db [create-app-user-ddl create-activity-ddl]))
```

Notice that some of our variables are defined as private, meaning that referencing them outside of the schema namespace is not required (or permitted). We make reference to them indirectly by calling the public load function. Note that schema/ load is the only function in this ns that makes up our public API. The db var is public and we'd expect to reference it when making any queries or ingesting data.

5. Now for our ingestion code, where we'll allow the creation of individual users and activities:

```clojure
(ns packt-clj.fitness.ingest
  (:require
    [clojure.java.jdbc :as jdbc]))
(defn user
  [db app_user]
  (first (jdbc/insert! db :app_user app_user)))
(defn activity
  [db activity]
  (first (jdbc/insert! db :activity activity)))
```

> **Note**
>
> **jdbc/insert!** returns a one-element sequence. We can, therefore, call first on the result of each **insert** statement to save our callers some work.

6. This is our query code where we'll expand a little on what we've written before:

```clojure
(ns packt-clj.fitness.query
  (:require
    [clojure.java.jdbc :as jdbc]))
(defn all-users
  [db]
  (jdbc/query db ["select * from app_user"]))
(defn user
  [db user-id]
  (jdbc/query db [(str "select * from app_user where id = " user-id)]))
```

7. Expand on the **all-activities** function as follows:

```clojure
(defn all-activities
  [db]
  (jdbc/query db ["select * from activity"]))
(defn activity
  [db activity-id]
  (jdbc/query db [(str "select * from activity where id = " activity-id)]))
(defn activities-by-user
  [db user-id]
  (jdbc/query db [(str "select * from activity where user_id = " user-id)]))
```

8. Now, let's add our more advanced query definitions to the **query** namespace. We'll introduce the **medley** and **java-time** dependencies into our project and require them in our **ns** query before creating a function that determines the most active user:

```clojure
{:deps {..
         clojure.java-time {:mvn/version "0.3.2"}
         medley {:mvn/version "1.2.0"}}
(ns packt-clj.fitness.query
  (:require
    [clojure.java.jdbc :as jdbc]
    [java-time :as t]
    [medley.core :as medley]))
```

medley is a third-party convenience library that provides commonly required functions that would otherwise be constructed using components of **clojure.core**:

9. The **most-active-user** function would look as follows:

```clojure
(defn most-active-user
  [db]
  (jdbc/query
    db
    ["select au.first_name, au.surname, a.duration from app_user au, activity a where au.id = a.user_id "]
    {:row-fn        (fn [{:keys [first_name surname duration]}] {:name        (str first_name " " surname)
                                                                 :duration duration})
     :result-set-fn (fn [rs]
                      (->> rs
                           (group-by :name)
                           (medley/map-vals #(apply + (map :duration %)))
                           (sort-by val)
                           last))}))
```

10. Finally, we'll create a function that will calculate our single-user activity report by month:

query.clj

```
41 (defn monthly-activity-by-user
42   [db user-id]
43   (jdbc/query
44     db
45     [(str "select au.first_name, au.surname, a.duration, a.activity_type, a.distance, a.activity_
date from app_user au, activity a where au.id = a.user_id and a.user_id = " 1)]
46     {:row-fn        (fn [row] (update row :activity_date t/local-date))
47      :result-set-fn (fn [rs]
48                       (reduce
49                         (fn [acc {:keys [activity_date activity_type distance duration first_name
surname] :as row}]
50                           (let [month-year (t/as activity_date :month-of-year :year)]
```

The complete code can be referred at: https://packt.live/37G4naC

11. Now that we have an application layer defined, we can begin interacting with the functions we've exposed in each of our namespaces. We should see they read and return results in an intuitive manner. In order to make use of our API, require and alias each of our namespaces:

```
(require '[packt-clj.fitness.ingest :as ingest]
         '[packt-clj.fitness.schema :as schema]
         '[packt-clj.fitness.query :as query])
```

12. We must load our schema to our empty database, being careful to drop any child tables before their parents:

```
user=> (jdbc/execute! schema/db ["drop table activity"])
[0]
user=> (jdbc/execute! schema/db ["drop table app_user"])
[0]
user=> (schema/load)
(0 0)
```

13. Now, let's define a handful of users and persist them to the database:

```
user=> (def users [{:first_name "Andre"
            :surname    "Agassi"
            :height     180
            :weight     80}
          {:first_name "Pete"
            :surname    "Sampras"
            height      185
            :weight     77
          }
          {:first_name "Steffi"
            surname     "Graff"
            :height     176
            :weight     64}])
#'user/users
user=> (doseq [user users]
   (ingest/user schema/db user))
nil
```

Note our use of **doseq** in the preceding code. **doseq** can be used to iterate over a collection when we are not interested in the result (as we are when using **map**). Since we are iterating over a collection purely for side effects, we cannot be lazy about this operation as there is no guarantee we'd ever persist every user.

Familiarize yourself with the **sample-activities.csv** file, which contains 20 randomly generated activities for each of the three users we've just persisted. Note how the structure of the file does not map perfectly to our schema and consider potential methods we could use to parse the CSV file into a format that our **ingest/ activity** function would support.

One method would be to define a map where the keys are precisely those that meet our schema requirements. If the values were then single-arity functions that would extract the relevant data from a given row, we could apply each of these in turn, generating a map that conforms to our schema.

14. Define the accessor map as follows:

```
user=> (def accessors
   {:activity_type :type
    :distance :distance_metres
    :duration :duration_seconds
    :user_id :userid
    :activity_date (fn [{:keys [day month year]}] (str year "-" month "-" day))})
user=> #'user/accessors
```

Note how all but the **activity_date** accessor is performing a simple rename. **activity_date** is doing a (very slightly!) more complex operation, extracting multiple fields from a row and combining them into one. We could imagine extending this to perform arbitrarily complex parsing and data extraction.

15. An **apply-accessors** function is required to actually take a row, an accessor map, and return the schema-conforming map:

```
user=> (defn apply-accessors
  [row accessors]
  (reduce-kv
    (fn [acc target-key accessor]
      (assoc acc target-key (accessor row)))
    {}
    accessors))
=> #'user/apply-accessors
```

reduce-kv can be used to iterate over the key-value pairs in our accessor map.

16. With our accessors and our **apply-accessors** functions defined, we can now read our CSV file and parse to a form that matches our activity table schema:

```
user=> (require '[semantic-csv.core :as sc]
                '[clojure.data.csv :as csv]
                '[clojure.java.io :as io])
=> nil
user=> (def activities
  (->> (csv/read-csv (io/reader "resources/sample-activities.csv"))
       sc/mappify
       (map #(apply-accessors % accessors))))
user=> #'user/activities
```

Inspecting our first entry, we see that it does indeed look as we expect:

```
user=> (first activities)
=> {:activity_type "swim", :distance "5100.00", :duration "9180", :user_id "1",
:activity_date "2019-01-22"}
```

17. We can now persist these activities in the same manner that we did for persisting our users:

```
user=> (doseq [activity activities]
  (ingest/activity schema/db activity))
=> nil
```

18. Finally, let's exercise our queries in turn and verify the results:

```
user=> (count (query/all-users schema/db))
=> 3
user=> (count (query/all-activities schema/db))
=> 60
user=> (query/user schema/db 1)
=> ({:id 1, :first_name "Andre", :surname "Agassi", :height 180, :weight 80})
user=> (query/activity schema/db 1)
=>
({:id 1,
  :activity_type "swim",
  :distance 5100.00M,
  :duration 9180,
  :activity_date #inst"2019-01-22T00:00:00.000-00:00",
  :user_id 1})
user=> (count (query/activities-by-user schema/db 1))
=> 20
user=> (query/most-active-user schema/db)
=> ["Pete Sampras" 136680]
user=> (clojure.pprint/pprint (query/monthly-activity-by-user schema/db 3))
```

The output will look as follows:

```
{[1 2019]
 {"swim" {:distance 15050.00M, :duration 21120},
  "run" {:distance 37466.67M, :duration 10080}},
 [2 2019]
 {"swim" {:distance 1700.00M, :duration 3060},
  "cycle" {:distance 60533.33M, :duration 9300}},
 [3 2019]
 {"run" {:distance 77683.33M, :duration 23520},
  "swim" {:distance 5866.67M, :duration 7920}},
 [4 2019]
 {"cycle" {:distance 153233.34M, :duration 25440},
  "swim" {:distance 12000.00M, :duration 14400}}}
```

Figure 13.5: Output on verifying the results

We've now created the backend of our application, logically separating the various functions our application comprises. We've created a database, loaded our schema, and then ingested and retrieved data. This demonstrates a typical application life cycle, and hopefully we could imagine a REST service or mobile app sitting on top of this API we've constructed.

Activity 13.01: Persisting Historic Tennis Results and ELO Calculations

Given your experience with historic tennis results and ELO calculations, you've been hired by Tennis Analytics Ltd. They have a large CSV file that is difficult to work with; they'd like the competitor data to be modeled and persisted to a database. Once ingested, they would like to perform ELO calculations across the entire dataset maintaining a full ELO history. The ultimate goal is to find the competitor with the best ELO rating for a historic dataset.

These steps will help you complete the activity:

1. Add the required dependencies to your **deps.edn** file or equivalent.

2. Create the **packt-clj.tennis.database**, **packt-clj.tennis.elo**, **packt-clj.tennis. ingest**, **packt-clj.tennis.parse**, and **packt-clj.tennis.query** namespaces.

3. In the **database** namespace, define a connection pool, referencing a new **tennis** database on disk, and store it in the **db** var.

4. Define a database **player** table using DDL consisting of the **id** (provided in the CSV file) and **full_name** fields.

5. Define a **tennis_match** table consisting of the **id** (a composite ID can be constructed from the CSV file), **tournament_year**, **tournament**, **tournament_order**, **round_order**, **match_order**, and **winner_id** (a foreign key referencing the player ID from the table in *Step* 4) fields.

6. Define an **elo** table consisting of the **id** (can be autogenerated), **player_id** (foreign key referencing the player ID from the table in *Step* 4), and **rating** fields.

7. Create (and execute) a **load** function that will apply the DDL from *Steps* 4-6 to our database defined in *Step* 3.

   In the **parse** namespace, define a **historic** function that accepts a string representing a file path on the local disk. This function should read the CSV file from disk; convert the file to a sequence of maps; iterate over each row in turn; extract the fields pertinent for our **players** and **matches** data structures (fields will not necessarily be extracted exactly as-is; that is, some additional parsing or formatting will be required); and build up a data structure, ultimately returning a map of the following form:

```
{:players [<player 1> ...]
 :matches [<match 1> ...]}
```

   Here, **players** and **matches** are maps that conform to the schema we've created.

Helper functions should be defined as required. Some suggestions of functions that could prove helpful include being a means of parsing a row into a **winning-player**, **losing-player**, and **match** column, and being a means of defining the mapping of **target-key** function to the **row-extraction** function for each of the preceding structures.

> **Note**
>
> We should be cautious to avoid defining unique players multiple times. We should also be aware that the **match_id** column in the CSV file *is not unique!* An appropriate composite should be constructed.

8. In the **ingest** namespace, define a **historic** function that accepts a **db-spec** definition and a string representing a path/filename on the local disk. This function should pass the file path to the function defined in *step 8*, destructure the players and matches, and then perform **insert-multi!** on each in turn.

> **Note**
>
> Players must be ingested prior to matches to ensure we satisfy our foreign key constraints.

9. Copy the **match_scores_1991-2016_unindexed_csv.csv** CSV file into the **resources** directory, and then ingest all **player** and **match** data from this file using the **historic** function from *Step 8*.

> **Note**
>
> The **match_scores_1991-2016_unindexed_csv.csv** CSV file can be found on GitHub at https://packt.live/30291NO.

10. Now we have our data ingested, we'd like to calculate the ELO value for all historic matches, storing the ELO rating as we go. In the **query** namespace, define an **all-tennis-matches** function that accepts **db-spec** and returns the contents of the **tennis_match** table. This should be sorted appropriately by **tournament_year**, **tournament_order**, **reverse round_order**, and **match_order** to ensure we're calculating ratings chronologically.

11. We'll now leverage two of the functions we've already met in *Chapter 5, Many to One: Reducing*, namely **match-probability** and **recalculate-rating**. Introduce those to the **elo** namespace.

12. In the **elo** namespace, define a new **calculate-all** function that accepts **db-spec** and retrieves all tennis matches using **query/all-tennis-matches** (ordered chronologically, as described in *Step* 10), and then iterates over this dataset, calculating the ELO rating for each match, returning a collection of **elo** ratings that conform to the schema of the **elo** table.

13. Define a simple function that takes the result of the **calculate-all** function call and persists it into the **elo** table. Call this function to persist our ELO calculations.

14. Finally, define a **select-max-elo** function (we are interested in the player who has the highest ELO rating) in the **query** namespace, which returns a result in the following form:

```
{:max-rating …
 :player-name …}
```

On executing this, we should see a familiar name!

> **Note**
>
> The solution for this activity can be found on page 745.

Summary

This chapter gave us an introduction to the Apache Derby RDBMS, creating a locally hosted instance with minimal setup. We then explored data models and how to codify them into a schema using DDL. We used **clojure.java.jdbc** to load this schema before investigating how the API allows us to perform CRUD operations, spending time on how to control the results from our query executions.

We then built an application layer for our ELO calculation application. In doing so, we learned which functions to expose as part of our API and which are internal to our application and should be kept private from a user.

In the next chapter, we'll take the public API of our application layer and learn how to build a REST-based web service to expose that API over HTTP. In this way, we can make calls from a REST client and interact with our application over a network, rather than via a locally hosted REPL.

Subsequently, we'll improve this RESTful interaction by adding a higher-level UI layer so that a user can interact with our service via a web browser.

14

HTTP with Ring

Overview

In this chapter, we will process requests and generate responses, route incoming requests and manipulate requests via middleware. We will also serve up responses using various content types including **JavaScript Object Notation** (**JSON**) and **Extensible Data Notation** (**EDN**), create a web application using Ring and Compojure, and serve static resources via HTTP.

By the end of this chapter, you will be able to expose CRUD operations via HTTP.

Introduction

In the last chapter, we built our application layer and interacted with it via the REPL. This works sufficiently well for a single user performing ad hoc interactions, but it does not scale. Indeed, we could imagine a scenario where a third party or even another of our own services wants to make use of the data stored in our database, perform calculations, and persist updates. This interaction would be programmatic and would, therefore, benefit from being exposed over **HyperText Transfer Protocol (HTTP)** or similar.

We can achieve this by exposing our application layer via a web service. A web service allows interaction with our application layer over a network (most typically the internet, although it could be over an intranet for private applications).

To build our web service, we'll need a web application library to build our API, a web server to serve it up over HTTP, and a routing library to route incoming requests to the appropriate handler. Clojure has numerous implementations of each; however, for this chapter, we'll focus on using **Ring** to build our application, `Compojure` for routing, and Jetty to serve it all up.

An extension to this chapter could involve you taking the examples and exercises provided and implementing them using an alternative web app library, such as `Pedestal`.

HTTP, Web Servers, and REST

Before we dive into building a web service, let's cover the basics. HTTP is one of the primary protocols for communicating across the internet, particularly when working in a web browser. This protocol provides a contract for a client (typically a web browser) to communicate with a (web) server. In this example, the browser will construct a request containing a Uniform Resource Identifier (URI), which it will use to communicate to the server. The server will interpret the request, using the URI string to determine which resource the client is interested in retrieving/manipulating, then constructing a response containing information indicating that the request has completed, or containing a payload in the form of the response body.

Typically, when building a web service, we want to conform to the **REpresentational State Transfer (REST)** architecture. This architecture prescribes a set of operations we can choose to perform against a resource, allowing us to transition that resource through a number of valid states.

For example, let's assume we're interacting with our profile on our favorite online retailer's website. First, we'll retrieve our profile, then perhaps we'll retrieve our current address. We'll make a change to this address, then save our changes. In terms of REST interactions over HTTP, this may look as follows:

- GET https://packt.live/30NL9hm
- GET https://packt.live/2U026Ur
- PUT https://packt.live/2U026Ur

123 in the preceding example is our unique user ID.

The GET/PUT method preceding the URI is known as the HTTP method. GET indicates that we wish to read the content associated with the resource in the URI provided. The PUT method has an associated body containing the updated address; we're instructing the server to create/update the address resource with that provided.

An important distinction to make between PUT and POST is that PUT should be used when updating an existing resource or when we happen to know the unique ID of the entity we're creating. POST is used solely for the creation of resources and does not require us to know its unique ID. Instead, this ID will be allocated by the web service itself and communicated back to the client via the response headers.

The full set of supported methods are GET, POST, PUT, DELETE, HEAD, PATCH, CONNECT, OPTIONS, and TRACE. The first four of which are most typically encountered.

Request and Response

For those completely new to building web services, we will be covering a number of new concepts. These are not necessarily complex subjects, but sufficient detail to understand each of the building blocks will be given. As mentioned previously, we will use Ring (Clojure's most widely used web application library) to build our web service. A Ring application consists of only four components: requests, handlers, responses, and middleware.

We understand the concept of a request and response; we'll now cover them in detail, including how to parse the former and how to construct the latter, as well as the form that each typically takes.

In the most simple terms, the function of our web service should be to take an incoming request represented as a map, perform some operations based on the content of that map (for example, fetch a user's profile or update their address), and produce an appropriate response map ready to be rendered by a browser or interpreted by the client more generally. In Ring, the function that performs this conversion of a request to a response is referred to as a handler.

The most basic operation would follow this process:

Figure 14.1: Representation of the request-response process

A Ring handler is, therefore, a single-arity function, accepting a **request** map, and returning a **response** map:

```
(defn handler [request]
  ..
<response-map>)
```

What does a **request** map look like? At a minimum, a **request** map will contain the following top-level keys (sample values included):

```
{:remote-addr "0:0:0:0:0:0:0:1",
 :headers {"user-agent" "Mozilla/5.0 (X11; Linux x86_64) AppleWebKit/537.36 (KHTML, like Gecko) Chrome/77.0.3865.90 Safari/537.36",
           "cookie" "phaseInterval=120000; previewCols=url%20status%20size%20timeline; stats=true",
           "connection" "keep-alive",
           "accept" "text/html,application/xhtml+xml"},
 :server-port 8080,
 :uri "/request-demo",
 :server-name "localhost",
 :query-string nil,
 :body #object[org.eclipse.jetty.server.HttpInputOverHTTP 0x4a7d22dd
"HttpInputOverHTTP@4a7d22dd[c=0,q=0,[0]=null,s=STREAM]"],
 :scheme :http,
 :request-method :get}
```

Here's the meaning of each attribute:

- **:remote-addr**: The calling client's IP address
- **:headers**: Additional information sent along with the request, relating to security, content negotiation, cookies, and so on
- **:server-port**: The port of the server servicing the request

- `:uri`: The URI pointing to the resource the client wishes to interact with (used in routing)
- `:query-string`: A string that can be used to filter the resource content returned
- `:body`: A stream containing an optional payload (can only be read once!)
- `:request-method`: An HTTP request method (used in routing)

An important point worth highlighting is that this list is *not exhaustive*. Third-party and custom middleware can often add their own keys with their own special meaning and uses.

At the point at which our handler is invoked, the **request** map contains only a couple of keys of interest: the **query-string** and the **body**. The remaining keys have already been inspected and used to route the request to the appropriate handler, for example.

Response maps are much simpler and will consist of only three keys: status, headers, and body. The **status** key is a three-digit number indicating the outcome of the request. There are a large number of these, grouped into five different categories:

- 1xx: Informational
- 2xx: Success
- 3xx: Redirect
- 4xx: Client Error
- 5xx: Server Error

Generally, we'll encounter a **200** status indicating **OK**, or perhaps a **404** "**Not Found**" or **500** "**Internal Server Error**" error message.

The headers provide additional information about the generated response – most commonly, how to interpret the body. The body (sometimes called the payload) will contain any data retrieved or generated that will be of interest to the client.

We can easily construct this response map manually, as we'll see in *Exercise 14.01, Creating a Hello World Web Application*.

We've now encountered three of the four Ring components (with middleware being more complex and covered separately).

Jetty is the web server that will serve up our Ring application. It is software that allows interaction with our application over a network, in the same way your favorite websites are made available over the internet.

Exercise 14.01: Creating a Hello World Web Application

This exercise will see us make use of Ring and Jetty, where we'll create a trivial web application with a static **Hello World** response:

1. Begin with the following dependencies in **deps.edn** or similar:

```
{:deps {ring/ring-core {:mvn/version "1.7.1"}
        ring/ring-jetty-adapter {:mvn/version "1.7.1"}}}
```

2. Now define our Ring handler, remembering it's a single-arity function accepting a **request** map and returning a **response** map. Our **response** map contains an **ok 200** status code and a string response in the **body**:

```
user=> (defn handler [request]
  {:status 200
   :body "Hello World"})
=>#'user/handler
```

3. Now we'll start a Jetty web server, passing our handler and a couple of options:

```
user=> (require '[ring.adapter.jetty :refer [run-jetty]])
=> nil
user=> (def app (run-jetty handler {:port 8080
                           :join? false}))
=>#'user/app
```

By default, Jetty will spin up on port 80; we've overridden that to use **8080**. Notice that we've also passed :join? false. This ensures that our web server will not block the current thread that the REPL is running on, meaning we can interact with it and perform other REPL-based operations in the meantime. We now have a web server running, exposing our single handler over HTTP.

> **Note**
>
> We can stop the currently running server using Java interop:
>
> **user=> (.stop app)**
>
> **=> nil**
>
> If, at any point, an error such as **Address already in use** is encountered, be sure to stop your existing app before starting a new one.

This will prove useful going forward as we make changes to our application and test them out in the browser. If you have stopped the app, be sure to restart it by rerunning *Step 3* before proceeding.

4. Navigate to localhost:8080 in a browser:

Hello World

Figure 14.2: Printing Hello Word in a browser

Success! We have created our first handler and our web server is up and running with only a few lines of code. Be sure to stop our running app.

Request Routing

In the previous example, notice that run-jetty only accepts a single handler. We'll more than likely want our service to provide the ability to store, view, and otherwise manipulate numerous resources. For this, we'll need to support an arbitrary number of handlers to cater to each of our resources, plus a means of finding the correct handler to service our request. This is where request routing comes in.

Revisiting the request object, we find that it contains (among other things) the following keys:

- URI

- Request-method

We could enhance our handler to inspect the incoming request, extract the content of those keys, then determine the appropriate function to call to satisfy the request and generate a response. We'd probably call this handler our dispatcher or router. As we consider this approach, we should recall the chapter introduction where we mentioned Compojure, which bills itself as a small routing library for Ring that allows web applications to be composed of small, independent parts.

That's exactly what we're looking for. We'll now learn how to make use of `Compojure` to perform request routing and expand our application a little further.

Using Compojure

If routing requests manually sounded fairly tedious, breathe a sigh of relief as Compojure takes all the strain out of request routing. We define pairs of HTTP methods and resource paths we want to match and Compojure takes care of the rest.

A trivial route method is defined as follows, using the GET macro from the compojure. core namespace:

```
(def route
  (GET "/hello" request "Hello World"))
```

GET (and all other HTTP method macros) expect a path representing the resource we want to match against. In the preceding example, we match the hello path at the root of the web service. Compojure gives us a great deal of control over the path, allowing us to expect path parameters or match using a regular expression if we need to.

The next argument to the macro actually binds the incoming request map (or parts thereof) to the local symbol(s) we specify. In the preceding example, the entire incoming request map has been bound to the **request** symbol. We can choose to destructure elements of the map if we so wish.

The final argument to the macro is the body of our route. Here, we can add any logic we require, with the final expression being returned as the response. In this case, we simply return the string Hello world. Compojure will interpret a plain string as an implicit 200 response (that is, success) meaning we don't need to construct a map with an explicit :status key as we did in *Exercise 14.01, Creating a Hello World Web Application*.

Now we're likely to have more than a single route in our application, but Jetty only accepts a single handler. We can now reach for the **routes** function or the defroutes macro provided by Compojure; either of these can be used to combine one or more routes into a single handler. Using the macro, we bring our routes together, binding them to the **routes** variable, which we can then pass to Jetty:

```
(defroutes routes
          <route-1>
          <route-2>
          ..)
```

What if a user navigates to a route that we have not defined? When we define the routes and their unique paths, we're asking the routing library to inspect the incoming request and attempt to match it to each of our routes in turn. If this list of routes is exhausted before finding a match, an exception is thrown. In a browser, we'll receive the following (not particularly useful!) error message:

This page isn't working

localhost is currently unable to handle this request.

HTTP ERROR 500

Figure 14.3: Page not working error

We can avoid this by providing a catch-all, ensuring this is the *last* route defined. Compojure offers us a not-found route, which we can incorporate into our routes definition. It allows us to gracefully handle a request for a resource we cannot find a match for. The inclusion of this **not-found** route would look as follows:

```
(require '[compojure.route :as route])


(defroutes routes
          <route-1>
          <route-2>
          (route/not-found "Not the route you are looking for"))
```

Exercise 14.02: Introducing Routing with Compojure

Let's begin by tweaking our **Hello World** application by replacing the handler with a Compojure route definition:

1. Add the **compojure** dependency:

```
{:deps {compojure {:mvn/version "1.6.1"}
        ring/ring-core {:mvn/version "1.7.1"}
        ring/ring-jetty-adapter {:mvn/version "1.7.1"}}
```

2. Taking our original hello world handler, we'll convert this to the **compojure** route definition format using the **GET** macro from **compojure.core**:

```
(defn handler [request]
  {:status 200
   :body "Hello World"})
```

This will look as follows if we use Compojure:

```
(require '[compojure.core :refer [GET]])
(def route
  (GET "/" request "Hello World"))
```

3. Replace **handler** with **route** in our call to **run-jetty**, start the app (stopping any existing apps first!), and point your browser to **localhost:8080** once again:

```
(require '[ring.adapter.jetty :refer [run-jetty]])
(defn run
  []
  (run-jetty route
             {:port  8080
              :join? false}))
(.stop app)
(def app (run))
```

The output is as follows:

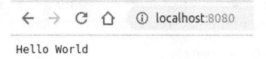

Hello World

Figure 14.4: Printing the output to the browser

There will be no material change; however, we have paved the way for rolling out Compojure and supporting an arbitrary number of routes in our application.

4. Let's define multiple routes, combining them under a single handler to exercise Compojure's routing ability:

```
(require '[compojure.core :refer [defroutes]])
(defroutes routes
           (GET "/route-1" request "Hello from route-1")
           (GET "/route-2" request "Hello from route-2"))
```

5. Pass these routes to our **run-jetty** call:

```
(defn run
  []
  (run-jetty routes {:port  8080
                     :join? false}))
(.stop app)
(def app (run))
```

We can now navigate to each of our routes in turn via the browser. Browse to our first route, **http://localhost:8080/route-1**:

Hello from route-1

Figure 14.5: Browsing to the first route

Browse to our second route, **http://localhost:8080/route-2**:

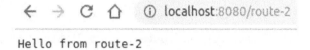

Hello from route-2

Figure 14.6: Browsing to the second route

6. While we're here, let's attempt to navigate to a non-existent route, **localhost:8080/nothing-to-see-here**. Your browser should inform you of localhost's inability to service this request, possibly indicating a **500** error:

This page isn't working

localhost is currently unable to handle this request.

HTTP ERROR 500

Figure: 14.7: Browsing to a non-existent route

7. Recalling our discussion of Compojure's **not-found** route definition, let's introduce that as a fallback for cases where no other route matches our request:

```
user=> (require '[compojure.route :as route])
nil
user=> (defroutes routes
          (GET "/route-1" request "Hello from route-1")
          (GET "/route-2" request "Hello from route-2")
          (route/not-found "Not the route you are looking for"))
=> #'user/routes
```

8. Restarting our web server and again browsing to **http://localhost:8080/nothing-to-see-here**, we now receive a much friendlier message:

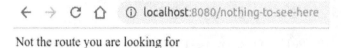

Not the route you are looking for

Figure 14.8: Navigating to nothing-to-see-here again

9. Finally, let's (temporarily) move our **not-found** route to the beginning of our routes definition, restart the app, and browse to **http://localhost:8080/route-1**:

```
(defroutes routes
        (route/not-found "Not the route you are looking for")
        (GET "/route-1" request "Hello from route-1")
        (GET "/route-2" request "Hello from route-2"))
```

The output is as follows:

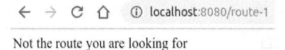

Not the route you are looking for

Figure 14.9: Navigating to route-1

This demonstrates the care required when defining and combining multiple routes. The web server will serve up the response for the *first* matching route it encounters. We can think of this as a simple order of precedence, with routes earlier in the definition being preferred over those following.

Excellent – we now understand how to define a route using Compojure, combine it with other Compojure route definitions, and provide a sensible not-found message in the event that someone navigates to a non-existent resource.

Response Formats and Middleware

The preceding trivial route definitions have all returned a string as the response body, which is perfectly acceptable for a human interacting with our service via a web browser. When we start to have other web services or a frontend interacting with our service, we may well have to serve up alternative response formats. A JavaScript frontend is likely to want a JSON response, whereas a ClojureScript frontend would likely prefer EDN. EDN is a data format favored in the Clojure ecosystem; indeed, Clojure itself is written in this format, meaning you will already be familiar with it by this stage!

The client can indicate which formats it accepts by providing an accept header as part of the request. The **accept** header takes the form of a string describing the **Multipurpose Internet Mail Extensions (MIME)** type, which the client is interested in receiving. A couple of examples of MIME types that we'll use are **application/json** and **application/edn**. The server can inspect this header and render the response in accordance with the formats accepted by the client. The server will assist the client by returning a **content-type** header in the response indicating which format it has selected.

> **Note**
>
> The client is in no way obligated to return data in the format requested but should do so if it is able.

Intuitively, we may be tempted to inspect the accept header manually within each of our routes and encode the response before we return it. While this would work, it would introduce a great deal of duplicative code into our application and distract from the core work of the route itself. For example, we may have a **render-response** function that determines which format to render based on the **accept** header. We would be obligated to include this call in every one of our routes. Much more preferable would be the ability to define this once and have it applied across all of our routes.

This is where the concept of middleware comes in. In simple terms, middleware is a function that wraps our route, allowing us to execute code before and/or after generating our response.

A middleware function for a synchronous response (that is, where the client will wait for the response using the same connection) typically takes the following format:

```
(defn custom-middleware
  [handler]
  (fn [request]
    (->> request
         ;; manipulate request before
         handler
         ;; manipulate response after
         )))
```

In essence, it is a function that accepts a handler, then returns a new function that calls the original handler. Besides that requirement, it is free to manipulate the request before passing it to the handler call, or it could manipulate the response generated by calling the handler, or both.

It should now be obvious that we could define a piece of middleware to handle the response rendering. Before we do that, let's take a look at **muuntaja**, which has been written specifically with this task in mind. Indeed, it supports JSON and EDN out of the box simply by wrapping our handler in a call to **muuntaja.middleware/wrap-format**. For example, the following tweak to our **run** function would automatically negotiate the incoming request body and outgoing response body formatting:

```
(require '[muuntaja.middleware :as middleware])
(defn run
  []
  (run-jetty
    (middleware/wrap-format routes)
    {:port  8080
     :join? false}))
```

Exercise 14.03: Response Rendering with Muuntaja

In this exercise, we'll cover middleware and how it can be used to render a response by taking the **accept** header into consideration. Our goal is to respect the **accept** header provided by the caller such that we can return JSON, EDN, or a plain string as required. We'll also look at how to interact with our route using **curl**, a popular tool used to make calls to web services.

By leveraging **muuntaja middleware**, our route code can remain completely agnostic of the response format requested by the client:

1. We'll begin by introducing the muuntaja dependency and requiring it:

```
{:deps {compojure {:mvn/version "1.6.1"}
metosin/muuntaja {:mvn/version "0.6.4"}
        ring/ring-core {:mvn/version "1.7.1"}
        ring/ring-jetty-adapter {:mvn/version "1.7.1"}}}
user=> (require '[muuntaja.middleware :as middleware])
=>nil
```

2. Now let's define a new set of routes, one of which returns a string, and another returning a nested data structure that can vary depending on the value of the **accept** header passed by the client:

```
(defroutes routes
          (GET "/string" request "a simple string response")
          (GET "/data-structure" request
            {:body {:a 1
                    :b #{2 3 4}
                    :c "nested data structure"}})
          (route/not-found "Not found"))
```

> **Note**
>
> Out of the box, Compojure does not know how to render a map, regardless of whether an accept header is specified.

Of interest will be how the middleware handles the keywords and sets depending on the response format we're interested in.

3. Recall that middleware wraps a handler; therefore, introducing **wrap-format** middleware of muuntaja is as simple as altering our **run** function like so:

```
(defn run
  []
  (run-jetty
    (middleware/wrap-format routes)
    {:port 8080
     :join? false}))
```

4. Now restart our app and request our **string** resource by expressing no preference for the response format, then stipulating we'd prefer **application/edn**. We're using **curl** here via Terminal or Command Prompt depending on your operating system:

```
$ curl -i http://localhost:8080/string
```

The output is as follows:

```
HTTP/1.1 200 OK
Date: Fri, 04 Oct 2019 13:22:12 GMT
Content-Type: text/html;charset=utf-8
Content-Length: 24
Server: Jetty(9.4.12.v20180830)

a simple string response
```

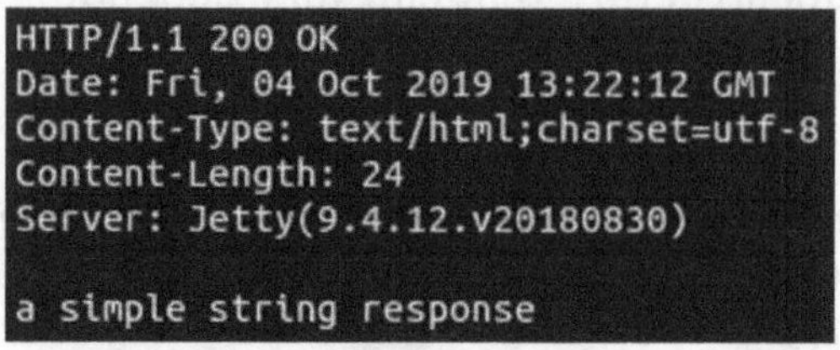

Figure 14.10: Printing the output of the curl command

Now, try the following:

```
$ curl -i -H "accept: application/edn" http://localhost:8080/string
```

The output is as follows:

```
HTTP/1.1 200 OK
Date: Fri, 04 Oct 2019 13:23:23 GMT
Content-Type: text/html;charset=utf-8
Content-Length: 24
Server: Jetty(9.4.12.v20180830)

a simple string response
```

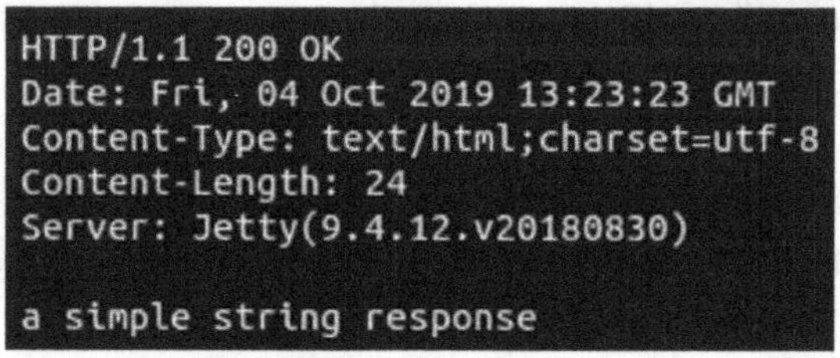

Figure 14.11: Printing the output of the curl command

Notice the response format is identical in both cases, which can be confirmed by checking the preceding **content-type** header. This shows that our server is unable to render the response as **EDN** and has chosen to ignore the **accept** header directive.

5. Our **data-structure** route is a little more interesting. Let's submit three different requests and compare them. Here's the first request:

```
curl -i http://localhost:8080/data-structure
```

The output is as follows:

```
HTTP/1.1 200 OK
Date: Fri, 04 Oct 2019 13:36:30 GMT
Content-Type: application/json;charset=utf-8
Content-Length: 47
Server: Jetty(9.4.12.v20180830)

{"a":1,"b":[4,3,2],"c":"nested data structure"}
```

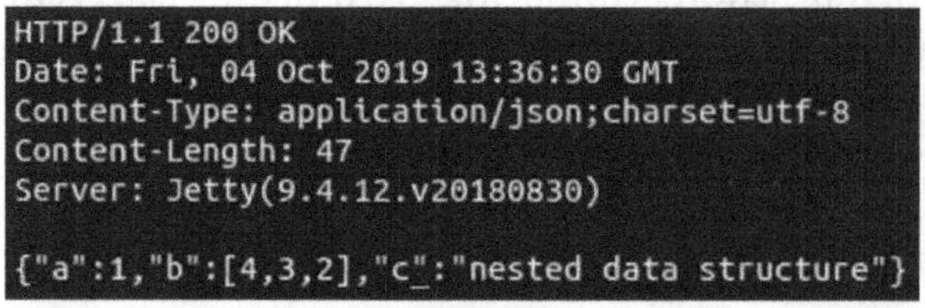

Figure 14.12: Output of the first request

Here's the second request:

```
curl -i -H "accept: application/json" http://localhost:8080/data-structure
```

The output is as follows:

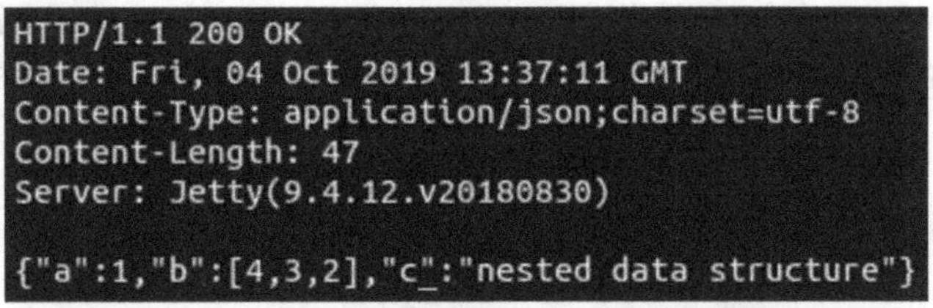

```
HTTP/1.1 200 OK
Date: Fri, 04 Oct 2019 13:37:11 GMT
Content-Type: application/json;charset=utf-8
Content-Length: 47
Server: Jetty(9.4.12.v20180830)

{"a":1,"b":[4,3,2],"c":"nested data structure"}
```

Figure 14.13: Output of the second request

Here's the third request:

```
curl -i -H "accept: application/edn" http://localhost:8080/data-structure
```

The output is as follows:

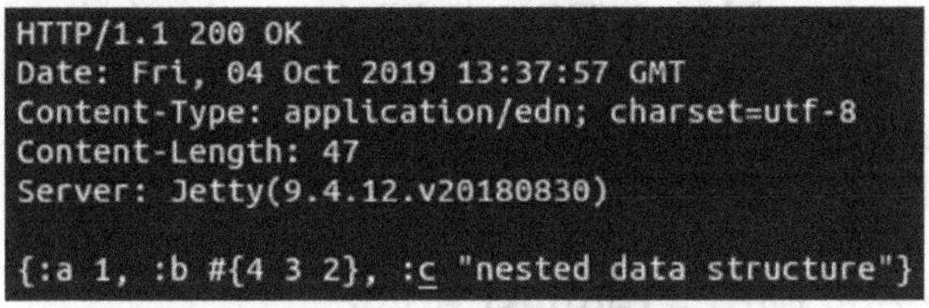

```
HTTP/1.1 200 OK
Date: Fri, 04 Oct 2019 13:37:57 GMT
Content-Type: application/edn; charset=utf-8
Content-Length: 47
Server: Jetty(9.4.12.v20180830)

{:a 1, :b #{4 3 2}, :c "nested data structure"}
```

Figure 14.14: Output of the third request

In this case, omitting the **accept** header gives us a JSON response by default. Requests for JSON and EDN are respected.

This demonstrates how remarkably simple (and powerful) content negotiation can be using middleware.

Handling a Request Body

So far, we have implemented a number of straightforward **GET** operations serving up static responses. Thinking back to our **Create Read Update Delete (CRUD)** tennis and fitness applications in *Chapter 13, Database Interaction and the Application Layer*, the **GET** method is how we read data. When creating (**PUT/POST**) or updating (**PUT**), we should provide a body along with our request. This body is the entity we wish to create or update.

> **Note**
>
> A **body** can be provided along with a **GET** request; however, this is uncommon and the content of the body should *not* have any material impact on the value returned.

The body, particularly when storing an entity, will often take the form of a map. The map could, therefore, be provided as JSON or EDN and should be parsed accordingly. The code we write as part of our route is again agnostic of the incoming format since the middleware will handle the formatting for us and provide an EDN representation for us to work with.

Exercise 14.04: Working with a request Body

In this exercise, we'll learn how the **wrap-formats** middleware is applied to the incoming request body, not just the outgoing response body. We'll also learn which part of the request will contain the content of the body, how to implement a quick in-memory database, and how to interact with a route via **clj-http** (a Clojure HTTP client library) rather than **curl**. We'll use this knowledge to perform basic CRUD operations on our in-memory database:

1. Let's introduce **clj-http** as a dependency, to demonstrate a native Clojure means of interacting with our web server. We'll also need a means of constructing a JSON payload, hence the inclusion of **clojure.data.json**:

```
{:deps {clj-http {:mvn/version "3.10.0"}
        compojure {:mvn/version "1.6.1"}
        metosin/muuntaja {:mvn/version "0.6.4"}
        org.clojure/data.json {:mvn/version "0.2.6"}
        ring/ring-core {:mvn/version "1.7.1"}
        ring/ring-jetty-adapter {:mvn/version "1.7.1"}}}
```

2. We'll define an atom to act as a cheap in-memory database for our server. Our **GET**, **PUT**, and **DELETE** routes will then use it as storage to demonstrate working with a **request** body:

```
(require '[compojure.core :refer [defroutes DELETE GET PUT]]
         '[compojure.route :as route])
(def db (atom {}))
(defroutes routes
        (GET "/data-structure" request
          (when-let [data-structure (@db :data)]
            {:body data-structure}))
        (PUT "/data-structure" request
          (swap! db assoc :data (:body-params request))
          {:status 201})
        (DELETE "/data-structure" request
          (swap! db dissoc :data))
        (route/not-found "Not found"))
```

Our **GET** method will read the value associated with the **:data** key; our **PUT** method will store the content of the **:body-params** key in our incoming request under the **:data** key in our atom, allowing us to roundtrip the data structure. Finally, our **DELETE** will remove the structure we have stored.

3. Our **run** function remains unchanged since **muuntaja wrap-format** works for both the incoming request body and the outgoing response body:

```
(defn run
  []
  (run-jetty
    (middleware/wrap-format routes)
    {:port  8080
     :join? false}))
```

4. After restarting our server, use **clj-http** to persist a JSON data structure:

```
(require '[clj-http.client :as http]
         '[clojure.data.json :as json]
         '[clojure.edn :as edn])
(-> (http/put "http://localhost:8080/data-structure"
              {:content-type :application/json
               :body         (json/write-str {:a 1
                                              :b #{2 3 4}})})
    :status)
=> 201
```

> **Note**
>
> The request body *must* be a string, hence our **json/write-str** call against our Clojure data structure. We must also provide a **content-type** header to aid our web service in formatting the incoming data correctly.

5. Now retrieve the persisted data in EDN format:

```
user=> (-> (http/get "http://localhost:8080/data-structure"
                     {:accept :application/edn})
           :body
           edn/read-string)
=> {:b [4 3 2], :a 1}
```

Notice that we attempted to persist a set as part of our payload; however, it has been returned as a vector. This is an important point to note: JSON to EDN conversion leads to a loss of data. This is due to EDN having more built-in type support than JSON (for example, sets and keywords).

This is particularly dangerous if we have several clients interacting with our service; one that persists/consumes JSON and another that persists/consumes EDN. There is a workaround where we can define a schema and coerce the incoming request body.

> **Note**
>
> **wrap-format** *does* coerce string keys to keywords as we saw in the preceding steps.

6. Now, let's confirm our EDN persistence and the retrieval behaves as expected:

```
(-> (http/put "http://localhost:8080/data-structure"
              {:content-type :application/edn
               :body         (pr-str {:a 1
                                      :b #{2 3 4}})})
    :status)
=> 201
(-> (http/get "http://localhost:8080/data-structure"
              {:accept :application/edn})
    :body
    edn/read-string)
=> {:a 1, :b #{4 3 2}}
```

7. We're now done with our **data-structure** resource; let's delete it from the server:

```
(-> (http/delete "http://localhost:8080/data-structure")
    :status)
=> 200
```

8. The preceding **200** status indicates that the deletion was successful; we can confirm this by attempting one more retrieval:

```
(http/get "http://localhost:8080/data-structure"
          {:accept :application/edn})
Execution error (ExceptionInfo) at slingshot.support/stack-trace (support.clj:201).
clj-http: status 404
```

We receive a **404** exception, since the resource is **not found**, as we expected.

Great – we have learned that the **wrap-format** middleware will assist us in formatting JSON and EDN request bodies as well as response bodies as we noted earlier. We know that the request body will be consumed by the **wrap-format** middleware and the EDN-formatted result placed in the **body-params** of the incoming request. We have also picked up a few tips on interacting with a Clojure service using **clj-http**.

Static Files

In the early days of the internet, web servers were used to serve up static HTML pages and images. Although technology has progressed a great deal since then, serving up static resources is still very much a requirement of today's web servers.

Thinking back to our CSV file of tennis matches from *Chapter 5, Many to One: Reducing*, we may wish to make this available to download via our web service.

compojure.route, which we previously used to provide a **not-found** route, also provides a means of easily serving static files from a custom location on disk. **compojure.route/ files** accepts a path where the files will be exposed as well as an options map where we can override the directory that our files are served from.

The following code would allow us to access any files located under the **/home/<user>/packt-http/resources/** directory by browsing to our web server's **/files/<filename>** route:

```
(route/files "/files/" {:root "/home/<user>/packt-http/resources/"})
```

Exercise 14.05: Serving Static Files

In this exercise, we'll make several files available via our web service, observing how the file-type determines the response of the web browser. We'll create a text file with the **.txt** file extension and see the contents displayed in our browser. We'll then see how requesting a CSV file results in the file being downloaded to our local machine:

1. Create a **resources** subdirectory containing a text file named **sample.txt** with the content **This is only a sample**, along with the **match_scores_1991-2016_unindexed_ csv.csv** file we are familiar with from https://packt.live/2NT96hM.

2. Now we'll use the **compojure.route/files** function to serve these up behind a **files** route:

```
(defroutes routes
           (route/files "/files/" {:root "./resources/"})
           (route/not-found "Not found"))
```

Restart the web server, then browse to **http://localhost:8080/files/sample.txt**, expecting an output similar to the following:

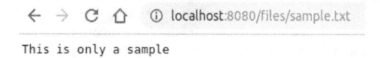

Figure 14.15: Output of the sample.txt file

3. Now browse to **http://localhost:8080/files/match_scores_1991-2016_unindexed_
    csv.csv**, expecting the file to be downloaded as follows:

Today

match_scores_1991-2016_unindexed_csv.csv   ×

http://localhost:8080/files/match_scores_1991-2016_unindexed_csv.csv

Show in folder

Figure 14.16: Downloading the CSV file

> **Note**
>
> The browser has inspected the **content-type** header in the response headers; in
> the **sample.txt** case, it is reported as **text/plain** and is rendered in the browser.
> In the CSV case, the **content-type** header is reported as **text/csv**, which generally
> is not rendered and is instead downloaded to disk. It may, however, be opened
> by spreadsheet software depending on your default application launch settings in
> your browser.

Excellent! We have seen how straightforward it is to expose local files via our web
service for display or download.

Integrating with an Application Layer

Recall the Activity Tracker database from *Activity 13.01, Persisting Historic Tennis Results
and ELO Calculations*, of *Chapter 13, Database Interaction and the Application Layer*,
and how it was mentioned that we could envisage a web service sitting on top of the
application layer. Our public functions in each of our namespaces were candidates for
exposing over HTTP.

Recall that what we're exposing over REST is access to read or manipulate a given
resource. Considering our **users** and **activities** as resources, we may want to retrieve
all of our **users** resources, all of our **activities** resources, a single user by ID, or all
activities for a given user. We start by constructing the paths that we would navigate to
reach each intended resource.

Let's consider the **users** resource. This is the collection of all users in the system and is sensibly located at the **/users** path. In terms of the route we'd create, our starting point would be the following:

```
(def route
  (GET "/users" [] (query/all-users db)))
```

Now, to access a single user within that collection, we'd require some means of keying into the **users** resource. Since we have defined an **ID** field associated with our **users** resource, we can uniquely identify a given user by their ID.

As such, we could envisage our **user-by-id** route looking very similar to the preceding route, with an additional parameter being passed. Our options for parameters are path parameters or query parameters. The distinction between the two being that **path** parameters are used when they uniquely identify a resource within a collection; **query** parameters are used to filter a resource by a property. As examples, we could have the following:

```
"/users/123"
"/users?first-name=David"
```

In the first instance, we're requesting a single user having ID 123. In the latter, we're filtering our **users** collection down to those whose first name is **David**.

With this knowledge in mind, we can take our public API and map each function to a **path** parameter where we'll expose it in our web service:

```
ingest/user                    POST /users
ingest/activity                POST /activities
query/all-users                GET /users
query/user                     GET /users/:id
query/activities-by-user       GET /users/:id/activities
query/all-activities           GET /activities
query/activity                 GET /activities/:id
query/most-active-user         GET /reports?report-type=most-active-user
query/monthly-activity-by-user GET /reports?report-type=monthly-activity-by-user
```

Now that we've described each of the paths, we can see a natural grouping of **users**, **activities**, and **reports**. Compojure offers us a means of reflecting this grouping when we define our routes by using the **compojure.core/context** macro. For example, to group the **GET** and **POST /users** routes, we can do the following:

```
(context "/users" []
  (GET "/" []
  ..
  (POST "/" request
  ..)
```

Not only have we created a shared path prefix for both routes, we also have the ability to destructure the request at the context level as well as the route level. If we had a shared query parameter, we could destructure it when we define the context, then make reference to it from any route within that context.

Accessing path and query Parameters in Compojure

A request map is structured such that the **path** and **query** parameters are available via the :params key. We can, therefore, destructure the parameters we're interested in as follows:

```
(def route
  (GET "/users/:id/activity" {:keys [id] :params} (query/all-users db))
```

However, Compojure offers some enhanced destructuring ability since parameters are some of the most common items to access within an incoming request. Using Compojure's destructuring, we could rewrite the preceding route as follows:

```
(def route
  (GET "/users/:id/activity" [id] (query/all-users db))
```

Notice that we've simply provided a vector containing the **id** symbol. Compojure then looks for an **id** key inside the **params** key of the incoming request map and makes the value available to us. Anything within the vector is automatically extracted from the value associated with the :**params** key and bound for use within the body of the route.

Exercise 14.06: Integrating with an Application Layer

In this exercise, we'll take the **packt-clj.fitness** backend along with the fitness database from the previous chapter and expand it such that we can ingest and query users and activities via a REST web service. We'll be reading data from an incoming body that is represented as an input stream. **slurp** is ideal in this case as it will open a reader on the stream and return the stream contents as a string. **slurp** also works on files, URIs, and URLs.

1. Add the following dependencies to **packt-clj.fitness** in the **deps.edn** file:

```
{:deps {..
        clj-http {:mvn/version "3.10.0"}
        compojure {:mvn/version "1.6.1"}
        metosin/muuntaja {:mvn/version "0.6.4"}
        org.clojure/data.json {:mvn/version "0.2.6"}
        ring/ring-core {:mvn/version "1.7.1"}
        ring/ring-jetty-adapter {:mvn/version "1.7.1"}}
```

2. Create a new namespace, **packt-clj.fitness.api**, with the following **requires** route:

```
(ns packt-clj.fitness.api
  (:require
    [clojure.edn :as edn]
    [compojure.core :refer [context defroutes DELETE GET PUT POST]]
    [compojure.route :as route]
    [muuntaja.middleware :as middleware]
    [packt-clj.fitness.ingest :as ingest]
    [packt-clj.fitness.query :as query]
    [packt-clj.fitness.schema :as schema]
    [ring.adapter.jetty :refer [run-jetty]]
    [ring.middleware.params :as params]))
```

3. Define our four routes for querying and persisting users, recalling that we can use a **context** to group routes that share a path prefix and/or reference the same **query** parameters:

```
(defroutes routes
            (context "/users" []
              (GET "/" []
                {:body (query/all-users schema/db)})
              (POST "/" req
                (let [ingest-result (ingest/user schema/db (edn/read-string (slurp
(:body req))))]
                    {:status  201
                     :headers {"Link" (str "/users/" (:1 ingest-result))}}))
```

```
(GET "/:id" [id]
  (when-first [user (query/user schema/db id)]
    {:body user}))
(GET "/:id/activities" [id]
  {:body (query/activities-by-user schema/db id)}})))
```

4. Define the three activity-related routes within the preceding **defroutes** definition:

```
(defroutes routes

  ..

  (context "/activities" []
    (GET "/" []
      {:body (query/all-activities schema/db)})
    (POST "/" req
      (let [ingest-result (ingest/activity schema/db (edn/read-string
(slurp (:body req))))]
        {:status  201
         :headers {"Link" (str "/activities/" (:1 ingest-result))}}}))
    (GET "/:id" [id]
      (when-first [activity (query/activity schema/db id)]
        {:body activity})))
```

> **Note**
>
> It is important to remember that our **body** is represented as a stream, meaning that it can only be read once. Any subsequent attempts to read from it will find it is already exhausted. Particular care should be taken when debugging not to read the body before it is actually utilized by the route. The same consideration should be made when writing middleware that interacts with the body.

5. Now add our reporting route along with our catch-all **not-found** route:

```
(defroutes routes

  ..

  (context "/reports" [report-type id]
    (GET "/" []
      {:body (case report-type
               "most-active-user" (query/most-active-user schema/db)
               "monthly-activity-by-user" (query/monthly-activity-by-user
schema/db id)
               nil)}))
  (route/not-found "Not found")
```

6. Create our **run** function, which will start our Jetty server, serving up the routes we've defined:

```
(defn run
  []
  (run-jetty
    (-> routes
        middleware/wrap-format
        params/wrap-params)
    {:port 8080
     :join? false}))
```

7. Now let's start the server and explore some of the endpoints we've created. Retrieve all users, then verify that we can retrieve a single user resource:

```
(require '[packt-clj.fitness.api :as api])
(def app (api/run))
```

The output is as follows:

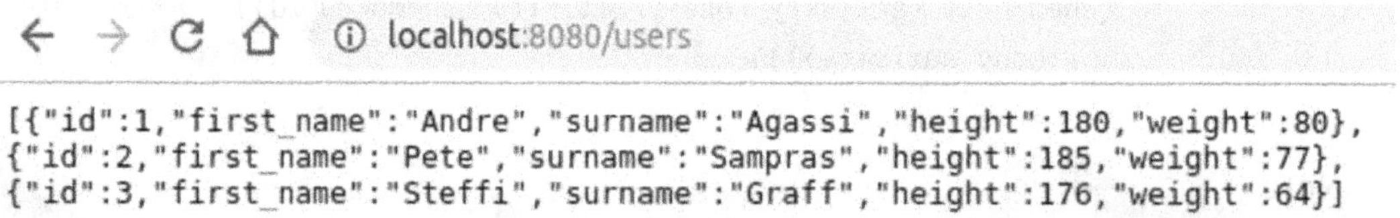

← → C ⌂ ⓘ localhost:8080/users

```
[{"id":1,"first_name":"Andre","surname":"Agassi","height":180,"weight":80},
{"id":2,"first_name":"Pete","surname":"Sampras","height":185,"weight":77},
{"id":3,"first_name":"Steffi","surname":"Graff","height":176,"weight":64}]
```

Figure 14.17: Retrieving all the users

Here is the output for retrieving a single user:

← → C ⌂ ⓘ localhost:8080/users/3

```
{"id":3,"first_name":"Steffi","surname":"Graff","height":176,"weight":64}
```

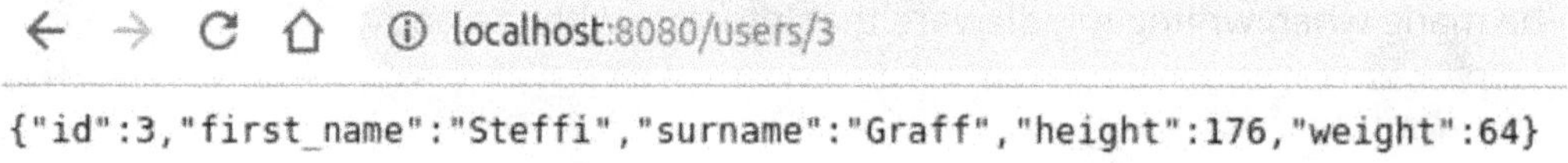

Figure 14.18: Retrieving a single user

8. Add a new user, an associated activity, then retrieve the list of activities that the user has taken part in:

```
(require '[clj-http.client :as http])
(-> (http/post "http://localhost:8080/users"
               {:body (pr-str {:first_name "Boris"
                               :surname    "Becker"
                               :height     191
                               :weight     85})})
    :headers
    (get "Link"))
```

```
user=> "/users/4"
(-> (http/post "http://localhost:8080/activities"
                {:body (pr-str {:user_id       4
                                :activity_type "run"
                                :activity_date "2019-03-25"
                                :distance      4970
                                :duration      1200})})
     :headers
     (get "Link"))
user=> "/activities/61"
```

Browsing to **http://localhost:8080/users/4/activities**, the output is as follows:

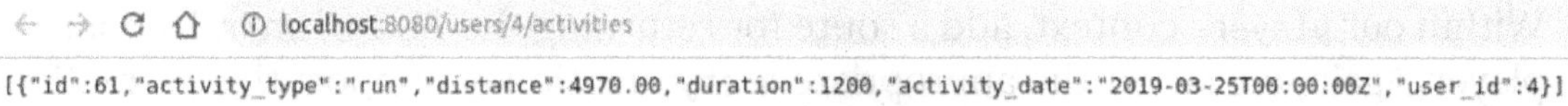

← → C ⌂   ⓘ localhost:8080/users/4/activities

[{"id":61,"activity_type":"run","distance":4970.00,"duration":1200,"activity_date":"2019-03-25T00:00:00Z","user_id":4}]

Figure 14.19: Printing the final output

> **Note**
>
> The preceding user and activity IDs (**4** and **61**) are autogenerated and *will* vary if you have persisted any additional data before writing the two preceding records.

Excellent. We've successfully taken our existing application layer and, with a small amount of code, made it accessible via a web browser or any other web client.

Activity 14.01: Exposing Historic Tennis Results and ELO Calculations via REST

The application layer delivered as part of **packt-clj.tennis** from *Chapter 13, Database Interaction and the Application Layer*, has been well received. You have now been asked to make this more widely available via a REST web service. Of most interest is the ability to browse player data, tennis matches, and ELO changes over time. The ability to persist new tennis matches and recalculate the ELO has also been requested. The historic data should be assumed to be already available in our database.

Consider the public API of your application layer, determine the resources that you'd like to expose, then build your web service to expose those resources via a web client (either a browser or another HTTP client). Additional application layer functions will be required to support the routes we'll create.

These steps will help you to perform the activity:

1. Add the required dependencies to your **deps.edn** file or equivalent.

2. Create the namespace, **packt-clj.tennis.api**.

3. Define our **routes** parameters, adding a **players** context containing routes that expose all our player resources, an individual player using their unique ID, and all of the tennis matches that the player took part in. Wire these routes up to appropriate functions in the **query** namespace.

4. Create a **run** function that will start up a Jetty server on port **8080**, exposing our **routes** parameter, ensuring we use middleware to help us with content negotiation and rationalizing the location of parameters within our request map.

5. Within our **players** context, add a route for returning the ELO of an individual player. Again, construct the appropriate **query** function to support this extraction.

6. Now add a **tennis-matches** context containing a route that exposes all matches, as well as individual matches by their unique ID.

7. Retrieve the current ELO of **Pete Sampras** (ID: **s402**) and **Novak Djokovic** (ID: **d643**).

8. Within the **tennis-matches** context, add a route to create a new match using existing players. The persistence of the new match should recalculate the ELO of the players involved.

9. Construct and persist a fictitious match between **Sampras** and **Djokovic** where **Djokovic** takes the win:

```
{:id "2019-1-d643-s402-5"
 :tournament_year   2019,
 :tournament        "umag",
 :tournament_order  1,
 :round_order       5,
 :match_order       1,
 :winner_id         "d643",
 :loser_id          "s402"}
```

10. Retrieve the updated ELO of **Sampras (s402)** and **Djokovic (d643)**, expecting ELO of **Sampras** to decrease, while Djokovic's will have increased.

Here is the expected output:

{"rating":1767.69,"id":190720}

Figure 14.20: Printing Sampras' rating

{"rating":2857.67,"id":190719}

Figure 14.21: Printing Djokovic's rating

> **Note**
>
> The solution for this activity can be found on page 753.

Summary

This chapter introduced us to HTTP, web servers, and the request-response interaction between a web server and a client. Multiple clients were introduced, including the most typical (the web browser) as well as **curl** and **clj-http**. We learned how a web server takes an incoming request and routes it according to key elements of the incoming request map, before constructing a response map, which is then presented to the requesting client.

We learned about middleware and how it intercepts our request and/or response map. We then used **muuntaja** to format the content we generated for the client, as well as to format incoming data from the client as JSON or EDN.

After considering the content of our database in the context of groups of related resources, we learned how to construct appropriate paths to address them using a REST architecture. This paved the way for integrating our existing application layers with a web service that would allow any web client to interact with them over HTTP.

We can now imagine a frontend (user interface) pulling resources from our web service, formatting them, and presenting them to a user who is then capable of manipulating those resources. In this case, the IDs (which are not particularly user-friendly) could be tracked by the UI and kept hidden from the users.

We'll explore how to interact with our new service via ClojureScript in the next chapter.

15

The Frontend: A ClojureScript UI

Overview

In this chapter, we will go over the basics of React's virtual DOM and lifecycle and then provide the tools necessary to build a rich user interface for the data application outlined in the previous chapters. We will see how to call JavaScript code from ClojureScript and how to convert between JavaScript and ClojureScript objects.

By the end of this chapter, you will be able to build a rich user interface for a data application.

Introduction

Clojure is a hosted language, which means that it runs on top of another language. In the same way that Clojure runs on top of the JVM, ClojureScript runs on top of JavaScript. More precisely, a ClojureScript program is transpiled into a JavaScript program that can run in the browser, on the server side, and in any environment where JavaScript is supported. For example, consider Node.js, an open source JavaScript server environment that allows us to execute JavaScript programs.

In this chapter, we will learn the basics of ClojureScript and how to create a ClojureScript program that runs in the browser. We will build a small frontend application on top of the Reagent framework that connects to an HTTP endpoint and displays **User Interface (UI)** components that the user can interact with. We will use Hiccup as a markup language for the UI components and discover how to execute JavaScript code from ClojureScript.

We will build an application using Figwheel, which supports hot code reloading. When your application is up, you will modify it either by changing its code or by evaluating code in the REPL. Your application will be magically updated without ever needing to refresh the page.

We will learn how to organize the different components of a Reagent application: the CSS, the HTML, and the `cljs` files. We will build several Reagent components that access and modify the state of the app and fetch data from the network.

Hiccup instead of HTML

Hiccup is a library for representing HTML in Clojure. In *Activity 6.01, Generating HTML from Clojure Vectors*, you implemented a simplified version of Hiccup. As you'll remember, Hiccup uses:

- Vectors to represent elements
- Maps to represent an element's attributes (including styles)

In a Hiccup vector, the first element is a keyword that specifies the corresponding HTML element:

- `:div` for a `<div>` tag
- `:span` for a `<span>` tag
- `:img` for a `<img>` tag

In Hiccup, an empty `<div>` is represented by `[:div]`.

The second element is an optional map that represents the element's attributes where the names of the attributes follow the kebab-case convention: we separate the words with one underscore character (**on-click** instead of **onClick**).

For example, **[:div {:class "myDiv"}]** represents **<div class="myDiv"></div>**.

Notice that in HTML, the **style** attribute is a string while in Hiccup it is a map where the keys follow the kebab-case convention. For example, consider the following example:

```
[:div
  {:style {:color "white"
           :background-color "blue" }}
  "Hello Hiccup"]
```

This represents the following in HTML:

```
<div style="color: white; background-color: blue;">Hello Hiccup</div>
```

Here, color: white denotes that the color of the **Hello Hiccup** text and **background-color** will be blue within the **div** tag.

Following the optional map of attributes, we have the children—as many as we want. For example, consider the following:

```
[:div "Hello " "my " "friends!"]
```

It represents the following:

```
<div>Hello my friends</div>
```

We can nest Hiccup elements as children of Hiccup elements. For instance, consider the following:

```
[:div

    [:img {:src "https://picsum.photos/id/10/2500/1667"}]

  [:div "A beautiful image"]]
```

This represents the following HTML code:

```
<div>

      <img src="https://picsum.photos/id/10/2500/1667"> </img>

  <div>A beautiful image </div>
</div>
```

In Hiccup, we can specify the class of an element in two ways:

- Specifying an element's attributes:

```
[:div {:class "myClass"} "Life is beautiful"]
```

- Using Hiccup shorthand, by appending a dot and the name of the class:

```
[:div.myClass "Life is beautiful"]
```

Compared to HTML, Hiccup is more compact and more readable.

In addition, we can blend code and data in Hiccup to generate UI components dynamically without requiring an additional template language, like we usually do in JavaScript.

For instance, let's say we want to create a list of 10 **todo** items. We would usually write them down manually as follows:

```
[:ul
 [:li "todo 1"]
 [:li "todo 2"]
 [:li "todo 3"]
 ...]
```

However, we can generate the exact same Hiccup element with **map** and **into**:

```
(into [:ul]
    (map (fn [num] [:li (str "todo " num)]) (range 10)))
```

Getting Started with Reagent

Reagent is a minimalistic ClojureScript wrapper for React.js. React.js is a JavaScript library for building a UI.

A Reagent component is similar to a Hiccup component except that the first element can be either a keyword or a function. When it's a keyword, it is a Hiccup component and when it's a function, Reagent calls the function in order to render the component and passes to the function the remaining parts of the vector.

A Reagent app is made of three parts: the ClojureScript code, the HTML page, and the CSS rules.

In Reagent, like in React, the HTML page is minimalistic: it is mainly a **\<div\>** element with an ID, usually **\<div id="app"\>**.

The CSS rules work the same as in any JavaScript application. The ClojureScript code usually starts at the core.cljs file, which renders the main component of the application. In the exercises and the activities of this chapter, the app will be made of a single namespace, but in a production application, the application is split into several namespaces, like in Clojure.

In Reagent, the state of the application is stored in a ratom (shorthand for reagent/atom), which has the same interface as regular Clojure atoms. The difference between a ratom and a Clojure atom is that when a ratom changes, the UI is rerendered.

React.js embraces the functional programming approach and encourages the developer to build their frontend application from components that manipulate data structures. The data structures are rendered by React in the browser's **Document Object Model (DOM)** in a very efficient way. React keeps the developer's mind free from having to deal with the DOM at a low level, enabling them to focus on the business logic.

Clojure's data-oriented approach, its immutable data structures, and the way it manages changes via atoms make React and ClojureScript a powerful combination.

The Virtual DOM and Component Lifecycle

When we build an application in React.js, we don't deal directly with the DOM, which is the browser's rendering mechanism and object model. Instead, React exposes a virtual DOM to the developer and keeps the implementation details hidden from them. This is what makes React so powerful. In a nutshell, when developing a React application, the developer writes React components that return data structures and the React frameworks automatically update the DOM and render the component on the UI.

Moreover, React is smart enough to calculate the smallest amount of DOM changes that are required in order to update the state of the UI, which makes React applications highly performant.

If a complex component's behavior is required by the application, such as doing something special as soon as the component is mounted or just before the component is updated, React provides lifecycle methods that the component can interact with.

Exercise 15.01: Creating a Reagent Application

In this exercise, we're going to create a very simple Hiccup component in Reagent: an image with a couple of CSS properties. The CSS properties that we are going to use through the chapter are:

- Padding: 7px; // the inner padding

- Cursor: pointer; // the type of cursor

- Margin-left: 10px; // horizontal spacing between elements

- Margin-bottom: 10px; // vertical spacing between elements

- Border: 1px solid gray; // a 1px solid border of color gray

- Border-radius: 10px; // the radius of the corners

- Color: gray; // the text color

- Font-size: 15px; // the size of the font

- Float: left; horizontal alignment instead of the default vertical alignment

1. At the command-line prompt, create a new Figwheel project using the following Leiningen command:

```
lein new figwheel packt-clj.reagent-sandbox -- --reagent
```

2. Change folder to the **packt-clj.reagent-sandbox/** directory and type the following command to launch the application:

```
lein figwheel
```

After a few seconds, your browser should open to the default Figwheel page:

Hello world!

Edit this and watch it change!

Figure 15.1: A fresh ClojureScript project waiting for your code

3. Under the current folder, open the **src/packt_clj/reagent_sandbox/core.cljs** file in your preferred editor and take a look at the following expression:

```
(reagent/render-component [hello-world]
                          (. js/document (getElementById "app")))
```

This code renders the UI by calling the **reagent/render-component** function with two arguments. The first is the Reagent component to render **[hello-world]** and the HTML element where the component is going to be rendered – in our case, the element whose ID is **app**.

4. Let's look now at the **hello-world** function that renders the main component of the application:

```
(defn hello-world []
  [:div
   [:h1 (:text @app-state)]
   [:h3 "Edit this and watch it change!"]])
```

hello-world returns a vector, a Hiccup component of type **:div**, with two children. The first child is **[:h1 (:text @app-state)]**, which is an **:h1** component with text that comes from the **:text** value of the dereferencing of the **app-state** atom (see *Chapter 12, Concurrency*, about atoms). The second child is **[:h3 "Edit this and watch it change!"]**, which is an **:h3** component with fixed text. Let's see that in action!

5. Go back to the Terminal window where you ran lein figwheel. You are in a Figwheel REPL. You should see a prompt like this:

```
dev:cljs.user =>
```

6. Now, let's switch to the packt-clj.reagent-sandbox.core namespace by typing the following in the REPL:

```
dev:packt-clj.reagent-sandbox.core=> (require 'packt-clj.reagent-sandbox.core)
nil
dev:packt-clj.reagent-sandbox.core=> (in-ns 'packt-clj.reagent-sandbox.core)
dev:packt-clj.reagent-sandbox.core=>
```

7. Now, let's inspect the state of our app:

```
dev:packt-clj.reagent-sandbox.core!{:conn 2}=> app-state
#<Atom: {:text "Hello world!"}>
```

8. And let's modify the value of `:text` in the atom:

```
dev:packt-clj.reagent-sandbox.core=> (swap! app-state assoc-in [:text] "Hello
Reagent!")
{:text "Hello Reagent!"}
```

The application immediately updates with the new text:

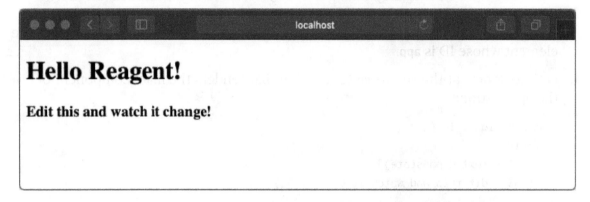

Figure 15.2: Printing the updated text

As we mentioned before, **app-state** is a ratom; therefore, when it changes, Reagent rerenders the UI.

Exercise 15.02: Displaying an Image with Style

Let's render an image with a couple of CSS properties:

1. Edit **src/packt_clj/reagent_sandbox/core.cljs**:

```
(defn image [url]
  [:img {:src url
         :style {:width "500px"
                 :border "solid gray 3px"
                 :border-radius "10px"}}])
(defn hello-world []
  [:div
   [:h1 (:text @app-state)]
   [:div [image «https://picsum.photos/id/0/5616/3744»]]
   [:h3 "Edit this and watch it change!"]])
```

The first part creates an image component and the second part includes an instance of the image component as part of the main component of the app. The moment you save the file, your app should look like this:

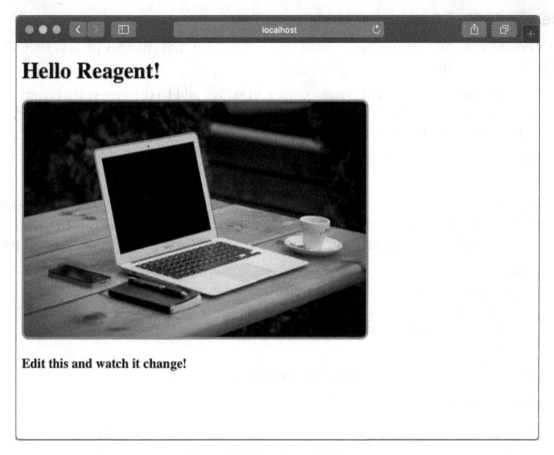

Figure 15.3: Rendering the image

This is what we call hot code reloading: you change the code and the app updates immediately without refreshing the page.

Managing Component State

In Reagent, the behavior of a component depends on the state of the component. The state is stored in two places:

- The arguments passed to the component when the component is instantiated

- A ratom

Arguments passed to the component cannot be modified by the component but a ratom can be modified. This is useful when we want to allow a component to change the state of itself (or of another component) upon user interaction (for example, a click).

To build real-life production applications with complex application state, we use a framework on top of Reagent, for instance, Reframe, a popular framework for writing single-page applications on top of Reagent.

Exercise 15.03: A Button that Modifies Its Text

Let's create a toggle button whose initial text is "ON" and that changes its text to "OFF" when we click on it:

1. Edit **src/packt_clj/reagent_sandbox/core.cljs**. We add to the **app-state** ratom information about whether the button is on or off by including a **:button-on?** key whose initial value is **true**:

    ```
    (defonce app-state (atom {:text "Hello world!"
                              :button-on? true}))
    ```

2. Now we create the **button** component with the text of the button depending on the value of **:button-on?** and the click handler toggles the value of **:button-on?**. Notice that the click handler is referenced by **:on-click** (while in plain HTML, it's **onClick**):

    ```
    (defn button []
      (let [text (if (get-in @app-state [:button-on?]) "ON" "OFF")]
        [:button
         {:on-click #(swap! app-state update-in [:button-on?] not)}
         text]))
    ```

3. Finally, we instantiate the button as part of our app:

    ```
    (defn hello-world []
      [:div
       [:h1 (:text @app-state)]
       [button]
       [:div [image "https://picsum.photos/id/0/5616/3744"]]
       [:h3 "Edit this and watch it change!"]])
    ```

    Switch to your browser window, **refresh the page**, click on the button, and see how the text modifies itself. In this case, we have to refresh the page because we have changed the initial state of the app.

4. You can also change the state of the button via the REPL:

    ```
    dev:packt-clj.reagent-sandbox.core=> (swap! app-state assoc-in [:button-on?] true)
    {:text "Hello world!", :button-on? true}
    ```

    The UI is updated immediately. We don't need to refresh the page due to hot reload. Clicking on the button or swapping the ratom are two equivalent ways to update the state of the app.

Components with Children Components

As we saw when we introduced Hiccup, we can programmatically generate child components inside a Reagent component. For instance, we can start from an array of image URLs and convert each URL into an image component. This way, we are able to programmatically generate a grid of images.

Exercise 15.04: Creating a Grid of Images

Let's create a component that renders a collection of images in a grid:

1. Edit **src/packt_clj/reagent_sandbox/core.cljs**. First, we create an **image-with-width** component that receives the image width as an argument:

```
(defn image-with-width [url width]
  [:img {:src url
         :style {:width width
                 :border "solid gray 3px"
                 :border-radius "10px"}}])
```

2. Create a grid component as follows:

```
(defn image-grid [images]
  (into [:div]
        (map (fn [image-data]
               [:div {:style {:float "left"
                              :margin-left "20px"}}
                [image-with-width image-data "50px"]])
             images)))
```

3. Now, we create a vector of image URLs:

```
(def my-images
  ["https://picsum.photos/id/0/5616/3744"
   "https://picsum.photos/id/1/5616/3744"
   "https://picsum.photos/id/10/2500/1667"
   "https://picsum.photos/id/100/2500/1656"
   "https://picsum.photos/id/1000/5626/3635"
   "https://picsum.photos/id/1001/5616/3744"
   "https://picsum.photos/id/1002/4312/2868"
   "https://picsum.photos/id/1003/1181/1772"
   "https://picsum.photos/id/1004/5616/3744"
   "https://picsum.photos/id/1005/5760/3840"])
```

4. Finally, we instantiate the image grid with **my-images**:

```
(defn hello-world []
  [:div
   [:h1 (:text @app-state)]
   [image-grid my-images]])
```

Now, when we switch to the browser window, we see the following:

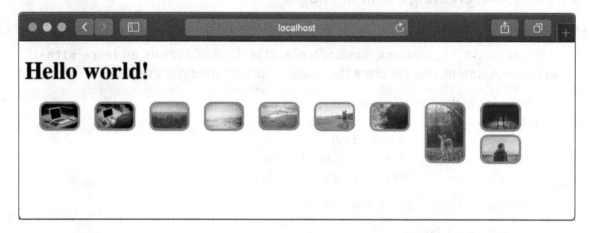

Figure 15.4: The image grid

5. In order to get a better understanding of **image-grid**, let's inspect the **Hiccup** vector returned by the **image-grid** function in the REPL when we pass to it the first three elements of **my-images**:

```
dev:packt-clj.reagent-sandbox.core=> (image-grid (take 3 my-images))
```

This will return the following:

```
[:div
 [:div
  {:style {:float "left", :margin-left "20px"}}
  [#object[packt_clj$reagent_sandbox$core$image_with_width]
   «https://picsum.photos/id/0/5616/3744»
   «50px»]]
 [:div
  {:style {:float "left", :margin-left "20px"}}
  [#object[packt_clj$reagent_sandbox$core$image_with_width]
   «https://picsum.photos/id/1/5616/3744»
   «50px»]]
 [:div
  {:style {:float "left", :margin-left "20px"}}
```

```
[#object[packt_clj$reagent_sandbox$core$image_with_width]
  «https://picsum.photos/id/10/2500/1667»
  «50px»]]]
```

It's a `:div` component with three children, where each child is a `:div` element with a `style` map and a nested `image-with-width-component`.

Hot Reload

Have you noticed that **app-state** is defined via **defonce** and not via **def**, like we usually define vars in Clojure?

The difference between **defonce** and **def** is that when **defonce** is called twice, the second call has no effect.

Let's take a look at a simple example:

```
(defonce a 1)
(defonce a 2)
```

The value of **a** is now **1**. In the context of hot reloading, defonce is crucial. The reason is that with hot code reloading, we want:

- The code to be reloaded
- The state of the app to remain the same

Those two desires seem contradictory because the initial state of the **app** is defined in the code. As a consequence, reloading the code seems to imply re-initializing the state of the **app**. Here, **defonce** comes to the rescue. The code that sets the initial state of the **app** is called only once!

If you are curious, you can, just for the sake of understanding the difference between **defonce** and **def**, replace **defonce** with **def** in the code of the app you built and see how the app comes back to its initial state each time we save a code change.

JavaScript Interop

Now it's time to learn how in ClojureScript, we can interop with the underlying JavaScript language. By interop, we mean mainly:

- Accessing the window global object from ClojureScript
- Calling a JavaScript function from ClojureScript code
- Converting between JavaScript and ClojureScript objects

In order to access the window scope, we use the **js/** prefix. For instance, **js/document** represents the document object and **js/Math.abs** represents the **abs** function in the **Math** scope. In order to call a method on a JavaScript object, we use dot notation, as follows:

- **(. js/Math abs -3)** is equivalent to **Math/abs(3)**.

- **(. js/document (getElementById "app"))** corresponds to **document. getElementById("app")**.

Now, you can fully understand the expression in **src/packt_clj/reagent_sandbox/core. cljs** that renders the UI:

```
(reagent/render-component [hello-world]
                          (. js/document (getElementById "app")))
```

When we want to convert between JavaScript and ClojureScript objects, we use the js->clj and clj->js functions.

Consider the following example:

```
(clj->js {"total" 42})
```

This returns the JavaScript object {total: 42}, represented in the REPL as #js {:total 42}.

Notice that ClojureScript keywords are converted into strings:

```
(clj->js {:total 42})
```

This returns the JavaScript object **{total: 42}**.

clj->js works recursively, which means that nested objects are also converted to JavaScript objects. Consider the following example:

```
(clj->js {"total" 42
          "days" ["monday" "tuesday"]})
```

This will return the following:

```
{total: 42,
  days: ["monday" "tuesday"]}
```

You can also use the **#js** notation to generate a JavaScript object, but note that it is not recursive. **#js {:total 42}** in ClojureScript generates **{total: 42}** in JavaScript.

What about the other direction, from JavaScript to ClojureScript? You use the **js->clj** function. **(js->clj #js {"total" 42})** returns the ClojureScript object **{"total" 42}**.

If you want JavaScript strings to be converted to ClojureScript keywords, you need to keywordize the keys by passing extra args to **js->clj**:

```
(js->clj #js {"total" 42} :keywordize-keys true)
```

This returns the ClojureScript object **{:total 42}**.

Exercise 15.05: Fetching Data from an HTTP Endpoint

Let's use our JavaScript interop knowledge to fetch data from an HTTP endpoint that returns JSON, namely https://packt.live/2RURzar. This endpoint returns a JSON array made of three objects with data about images:

1. In JavaScript, we would fetch the JSON by using the JavaScript **fetch** function and two promises to convert the server response into a JSON object:

```
fetch("https://picsum.photos/v2/list?limit=3")
.then((function (response){
  return response.json();
}))
.then((function (json){
  return console.log(json);
}))
```

2. In ClojureScript, the preceding code translates to the following:

```
(-> (js/fetch "https://picsum.photos/v2/list?limit=3")
    (.then (fn [response] (.json response)))
    (.then (fn [json] (println (js->clj json :keywordize-keys true)))))
```

It prints a ClojureScript vector to the console with three ClojureScript objects:

```
[{:id "0",
  :author "Alejandro Escamilla",
  :width 5616,
  :height 3744,
  :url "https://unsplash.com/photos/yC-Yzbqy7PY",
  :download_url "https://picsum.photos/id/0/5616/3744"}
 {:id "1",
  :author "Alejandro Escamilla",
  :width 5616,
  :height 3744,
  :url "https://unsplash.com/photos/LNRyGwIJr5c",
```

```
      :download_url "https://picsum.photos/id/1/5616/3744"}
     {:id "10",
      :author "Paul Jarvis",
      :width 2500,
      :height 1667,
      :url "https://unsplash.com/photos/6J--NXulQCs",
      :download_url "https://picsum.photos/id/10/2500/1667"}]
```

All the pieces are now in place to build a small frontend application that displays a grid of images from the internet.

Activity 15.01: Displaying a Grid of Images from the Internet

You are asked to write a frontend application for a freelancer graphics editor that displays a grid of six images from and two buttons:

- A button that clears the images

- A button that hides the authors' names

This button can be used by the graphics editor to see the author names to add to the images.

These steps will help you complete the activity:

1. Create a new Figwheel project.

2. Create two buttons; one will clear images and the other will hide author names.

3. Add the images.

Upon completing the activity, you should be able to see something like this:

Figure 15.5: Expected outcome

Note

The solution for this activity can be found on page 758.

Activity 15.02: Tennis Players with Ranking

Let's wrap up this chapter by combining the knowledge gained from it with the material we covered in *Chapter 14, HTTP with Ring*. In the activity of *Chapter 14, HTTP with Ring*, we built an HTTP API server that returned data about tennis players. In the current activity, you are asked to build a frontend for this HTTP server.

You have to build a web app that:

- Displays the names of all the tennis players
- Displays the ranking of any tennis player when the user clicks on their name

Before starting, you need to perform the activity from *Chapter 14, HTTP with Ring*, with a slight change in the code of the server to support API requests from the web app we are going to build. The current activity is going to request data from this server. By default, web servers don't allow requests that come from another host. In our case, the API server runs on port **8080** while the frontend server runs on port **3449**. In order to allow requests that come from the frontend app to be served by the API server, we need to configure the API server so that it allows **Cross-Origin Resource Sharing (CORS)**.

Before starting the activity, you'll need to make the following changes:

1. Open the folder that contains the code of *Activity 14.01, Exposing Historic Tennis Results and ELO Calculations via REST*.

2. Add the following dependency to the **deps.edn** file:

```
jumblerg/ring-cors {:mvn/version "2.0.0"}
```

3. Open the **packt-clj/src/packt_clj/tennis/api.clj** file and add the following line in the **require** expression at the top of the file:

```
[jumblerg.middleware.cors :refer [wrap-cors]]
```

4. Open the **packt-clj/src/packt_clj/tennis/api.clj** file and add the following two lines in the definition of the **run** function at the end of the file:

```
(wrap-cors ".*")
(wrap-cors identity)
```

The **run** function should now look like this:

```
(defn run
  []
  (run-jetty
    (-> routes
        middleware/wrap-format
        params/wrap-params
        (wrap-cors ".*")
        (wrap-cors identity))
     {:port  8080
      :join? false})))
```

5. Now, run the server as explained in *Activity* 14.01, Exposing Historic Tennis Results and ELO Calculations via REST.

Follow these steps to complete this activity:

1. Set up a new Figwheel project that uses Reagent.

2. Write code that fetches tennis player data from the server from *Chapter* 14, HTTP with Ring, and inserts it into the application state of your new ClojureScript app. You'll also want a field in the application state for the current player when a player has been selected.

3. Write views for displaying the list of players and for displaying a single player with their data.

4. Incorporate handlers for the links that select the player to view, and for the buttons that load and clear the list of players.

Upon completing the current activity, you should see something like this in your browser:

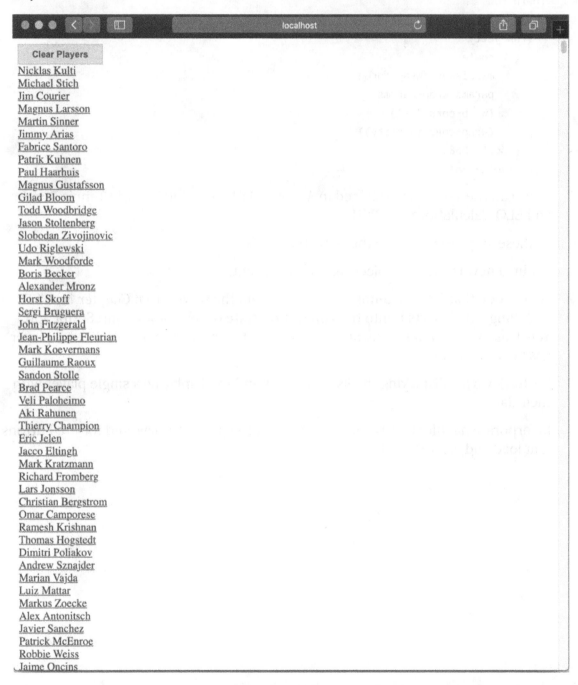

Figure 15.6: List of players

And when the user clicks on Michael Stich, the app looks like this:

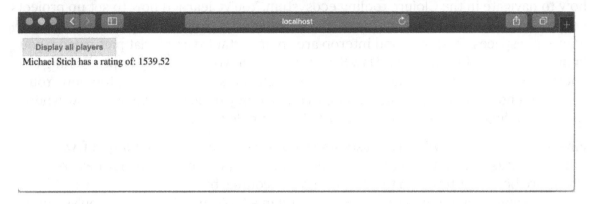

Display all players

Michael Stich has a rating of: 1539.52

Figure 15.7: The rating of a player

> **Note**
>
> The solution for this activity can be found on page 762.

Summary

In this chapter, you have learned the basics of how to build a frontend application in ClojureScript using Reagent, a wrapper around React.js.

We built a couple of Reagent components using the Hiccup markup language, which uses Clojure collections to define the HTML structure and properties. The state of the application is stored in a Reagent atom that you interacted with through the REPL.

We saw how to call JavaScript code from ClojureScript and how to convert between JavaScript and ClojureScript objects. You used these interop features to fetch image data from an HTTP server and convert the data into a ClojureScript object.

We've reached the end of the book. You've seen a lot of new things since the first pages of *Chapter 1, Hello REPL!*. Beyond the syntactic basics, you've learned a lot about functional programming and, even more importantly, how to think in a functional way. It's one thing to know what immutability is and something else entirely to know how to accomplish tasks using immutable data. By focusing intensively on collections, we were able to show you some of Clojure's most distinctive features, such as lazy sequences, while building up your mental library of useful patterns for solving problems. Clojure is often considered a data-centric language, so collections are a key part of that. Programming is more than just mastering language features.

Our other focus has been on getting things done with Clojure, and that means knowing how to navigate in the Clojure tooling ecosystem. You've learned how to set up projects, how to use Leiningen for both Clojure and ClojureScript projects, and how to organize your namespaces. Platforms and interop are an important part of that picture too: you know the basics of using Java or JavaScript features in your Clojure(Script). Testing is another necessary skill for any real-world project. You know about that too now. You've also seen enough of macros and Clojure's concurrency tools that you will know where to start the first time you need them to solve a complex problem.

Finally, you've worked with databases and web servers. On just about any software project, at least one of those two technologies will be present. Often, both will be. These are both vast topics in their own right, of course, but by now you have an idea of how to approach them in a Clojure way—and in a ClojureScript way, as you've done in this chapter. And beyond the details, we hope that your first steps in Clojure have opened your eyes to new ways of thinking about programming. That way, you'll be able to learn whatever you need down the road.

Appendix

About

This section is included to assist the students to perform the activities present in the book. It includes detailed steps that are to be performed by the students to complete and achieve the objectives of the book.

Chapter 1: Hello REPL!

Activity 1.01: Performing Basic Operations

Solution:

1. Open the REPL.

2. Print the message **"I am not afraid of parentheses"** to motivate yourself:

```
user=> (println "I am not afraid of parentheses")
I am not afraid of parentheses
nil
```

3. Add 1, 2, and 3 and multiply the result by 10 minus 3, which corresponds to the following **infix** notation: (1 + 2 + 3) * (10 – 3):

```
user=> (* (+ 1 2 3) (- 10 3))
42
```

4. Print the message **"Well done!"** to congratulate yourself:

```
user=> (println "Well done!")
Well done!
Nil
```

5. Exit the REPL by pressing *Ctrl + D* or typing the following command:

```
user=> (System/exit 0)
```

By completing this activity, you have written code that prints a message to the standard output. You have also performed some mathematical operations using the *prefix* notation and nested expressions.

Activity 1.02: Predicting the Atmospheric Carbon Dioxide Level

Solution:

1. Open your favorite editor and a REPL window next to it.

2. In your editor, define two constants, **base-co2** and **base-year**, with the values 382 and 2006, respectively:

```
(def base-co2 382)
(def base-year 2006)
```

3. In your editor, write the code to define the **co2-estimate** function without forgetting to document it with the **doc-string** parameter.

4. You may be tempted to write the function body in a single line, but nesting a lot of function calls decreases the readability of the code. It is also easier to reason about each step of the process by decomposing them in a **let** block. Write the body of the function using **let** to define the local binding, **year-diff**, which is the subtraction of 2006 from the **year** parameter:

```
(defn co2-estimate
  "Returns a (conservative) year's estimate of carbon dioxide parts per million in
the atmosphere"
  [year]
  (let [year-diff (- year base-year)]
  (+ base-co2 (* 2 year-diff))))
```

5. Test your function by evaluating **(co2-estimate 2050)**. You should get **470** as the result:

```
user=> (co2-estimate 2050)
470
```

6. Look up the documentation of your function with **doc** and make sure that it has been defined correctly:

```
user=> (doc co2-estimate)
-------------------------
user/co2-estimate
([year])
  Returns a (conservative) year's estimate of carbon dioxide parts per million in
the atmosphere
nil
```

In this activity, we calculated the estimated level of CO2 parts per million for a given year.

Activity 1.03: The meditate Function v2.0

Solution:

1. Open your favorite editor and a REPL window next to it.

2. In your editor, define a function with the name **meditate**, taking two arguments, **calmness-level** and **s**, without forgetting to write its documentation.

3. In the function body, start by writing an expression that prints the string, **"Clojure Meditate v2.0"**:

```
(defn meditate
  "Return a transformed version of the string 's' based on the 'calmness-level'"
  [s calmness-level]
  (println "Clojure Meditate v2.0"))
```

4. Following the specification, write the first condition to test whether the calmness level is strictly inferior to 5. Write the first branch of the conditional expression (the "then").

5. Write the second condition, which should be nested in the second branch of the first condition (the "else").

6. Write the third condition, which should be nested in the second branch of the second condition. It will check that **calmness-level** is exactly 10 and return the reverse of the **s** string when that is the case:

```
(defn meditate
  "Return a transformed version of the string 's' based on the 'calmness-level'"
  [s calmness-level]
  (println "Clojure Meditate v2.0")
  (if (< calmness-level 4)
    (str (clojure.string/upper-case s) ", I TELL YA!")
    (if (<= 4 calmness-level 9)
        (clojure.string/capitalize s)
        (if (= 10 calmness-level)
          (clojure.string/reverse s)))))
```

7. Test your function by passing a string with different levels of calmness. The output should be similar to the following:

```
user=> (meditate "what we do now echoes in eternity" 1)
Clojure Meditate v2.0
"WHAT WE DO NOW ECHOES IN ETERNITY, I TELL YA!"


user=> (meditate "what we do now echoes in eternity" 6)
```

```
Clojure Meditate v2.0
"What we do now echoes in eternity"

user=> (meditate "what we do now echoes in eternity" 10)
Clojure Meditate v2.0
"ytinrete ni seohce won od ew tahw"

user=> (meditate "what we do now echoes in eternity" 50)
Clojure Meditate v2.0
nil
```

If you have been using the **and** operator to find out whether a number was between two other numbers, rewrite your function to remove it and only use the **<=** operator. Remember that **<=** can take more than two arguments.

8. Look up the **cond** operator in the documentation and rewrite your function to replace the nested conditions with **cond**:

```
user=> (doc cond)
-------------------------
clojure.core/cond
([& clauses])
Macro
  Takes a set of test/expr pairs. It evaluates each test one at a
  time.  If a test returns logical true, cond evaluates and returns
  the value of the corresponding expr and doesn't evaluate any of the
  other tests or exprs. (cond) returns nil.
nil

user=>
(defn meditate
  "Return a transformed version of the string 's' based on the 'calmness-level'"
  [s calmness-level]
  (println "Clojure Meditate v2.0")
  (cond
    (< calmness-level 4)  (str (clojure.string/upper-case s) ", I TELL YA!")
    (<= 4 calmness-level 9) (clojure.string/capitalize s)
    (= 10 calmness-level) (clojure.string/reverse s)))
```

By completing this activity, you have written a documented function that takes multiple parameters, prints a message, and conditionally returns a transformation of a string.

Chapter 2: Data Types and Immutability

Activity 2.01: Creating a Simple In-Memory Database

Solution:

1. First, create the helper functions. You can get the Hash Map by executing the **read-db** function with no arguments, and write to the database by executing the **write-db** function with a Hash Map as an argument:

```
user=>
(def memory-db (atom {}))
#'user/memory-db
(defn read-db [] @memory-db)
#'user/read-db
user=> (defn write-db [new-db] (reset! memory-db new-db))
#'user/write-db
```

2. Start by creating the **create-table** function. This function should take one parameter: the table name. It should add a new key (the table name) at the root of our Hash Map database, and the value should be another Hash Map containing two entries – an empty vector at the **data** key and an empty Hash Map at the **indexes** key:

```
user=>
(defn create-table
  [table-name]
  (let [db (read-db)]
    (write-db (assoc db table-name {:data [] :indexes {}}))))
#'user/create-table
```

3. Test that your **create-table** function works. The output should be as follows:

```
user=> (create-table :clients)
{:clients {:data [], :indexes {}}}
user=> (create-table :fruits)
{:clients {:data [], :indexes {}}, :fruits {:data [], :indexes {}}}
```

4. Let's create the next function: **drop-table**. The function should take one parameter as well: the table name. It should remove a table, including all its data and indexes from our database:

```
user=>
(defn drop-table
  [table-name]
  (let [db (read-db)]
```

```
      (write-db (dissoc db table-name)))))
  #'user/drop-table
```

5. Test that your **drop-table** function works. The output should be as follows:

```
user=> (create-table :clients)
{:clients {:data [], :indexes {}}}
user=> (create-table :fruits)
{:clients {:data [], :indexes {}}, :fruits {:data [], :indexes {}}}
user=> (drop-table :clients)
{:fruits {:data [], :indexes {}}}
```

6. Let's move on to the **insert** function. This function should take three parameters: **table**, **record**, and **id-key**. The **record** parameter is a Hash Map, and **id-key** corresponds to a key in the record map that will be used as a unique index. For example, inserting a record in the **fruits** table would look like this:

```
user=> (insert :fruits {:name "Pear" :stock 3} :name)
{:fruits {:data [{:name "Pear", :stock 3}], :indexes {:name {"Pear" 0}}}}
```

For now, we will not handle cases where a table does not exist or when an index key already exists in a given table.

Try to use a **let** block to divide the work of the **insert** function into multiple steps.

In a **let** statement, create a binding for the value of the database, retrieved with **read-db**:

```
(defn insert
  [table-name record id-key]
  (let [db (read-db)
```

In the same **let** statement, create a second binding for the new value of the database (after adding the record in the **data** vector):

```
(defn insert
  [table-name record id-key]
  (let [db (read-db)
        new-db (update-in db [table-name :data] conj record)
```

In the same **let** statement, retrieve the index at which the record was inserted by counting the number of elements in the **data** vector:

```
(defn insert
  [table-name record id-key]
  (let [db (read-db)
        new-db (update-in db [table-name :data] conj record)
        index (- (count (get-in new-db [table-name :data])) 1)]
```

In the body of the **let** statement, update the index at **id-key** and write the resulting map to the database with **write-db**:

```
user=>
(defn insert
  [table-name record id-key]
    (let [db (read-db)
          new-db (update-in db [table-name :data] conj record)
          index (- (count (get-in new-db [table-name :data])) 1)]
      (write-db
        (update-in new-db [table-name :indexes id-key] assoc (id-key record)
index))))
#'user/insert
```

7. To verify that your **insert** function works, try to use it multiple times to insert new records. The output should look like this:

```
user=>  (insert :fruits {:name "Apricot" :stock 30} :name)
{:fruits {:data [{:name "Pear", :stock 3} {:name "Apricot", :stock 30}], :indexes
{:name {"Pear" 0, "Apricot" 1}}}}
user=>  (insert :fruits {:name "Grapefruit" :stock 6} :name)
{:fruits {:data [{:name "Pear", :stock 3} {:name "Apricot", :stock 30} {:name
"Grapefruit", :stock 6}], :indexes {:name {"Pear" 0, "Apricot" 1, "Grapefruit" 2}}}}
```

8. Create a **select-*** function that will return all the records of a table passed as a parameter. Given the three preceding records, the output should be similar to this:

```
user=> (select-* :fruits)
[{:name "Pear", :stock 3} {:name "Apricot", :stock 30} {:name "Grapefruit", :stock
6}]
user=>
(defn select-*
  [table-name]
  (get-in (read-db) [table-name :data]))
#'user/select-*
```

9. Create a **select-*-where** function that takes three arguments: **table-name**, **field**, and **field-value**. The function should use the index map to retrieve the index of the record in the data vector and return the element. Given the three preceding records, the output should be similar to this:

```
user=> (select-*-where :fruits :name "Apricot")
{:name "Apricot", :stock 30}
user=>
(defn select-*-where
  [table-name field field-value]
  (let [db (read-db)
```

```
        index (get-in db [table-name :indexes field field-value])
        data (get-in db [table-name :data])]
    (get data index)))
#'user/select-*-where
```

10. Modify the **insert** function to reject any index duplicate. When a record with **id-key** already exists in the **indexes** map, we should not modify the database and print an error message to the user. The output should be similar to this:

```
user=>  (insert :fruits {:name "Pear" :stock 3} :name)
Record with :name Pear already exists. Aborting
user=> (select-* :fruits)
[{:name "Pear", :stock 3} {:name "Apricot", :stock 30} {:name "Grapefruit", :stock
6}]
user=>
(defn insert
  [table-name record id-key]
  (if-let [existing-record (select-*-where table-name id-key (id-key record))]
    (println (str "Record with " id-key ": " (id-key record) " already exists.
      Aborting"))
    (let [db (read-db)
          new-db (update-in db [table-name :data] conj record)
          index (- (count (get-in new-db [table-name :data])) 1)]
      (write-db
        (update-in new-db [table-name :indexes id-key] assoc (id-key record)
          index)))))
#'user/insert
```

The final output should be similar to this:

```
user=> (create-table :fruits)
{:clients {:data [], :indexes {}}, :fruits {:data [], :indexes {}}}
user=> (insert :fruits {:name "Pear" :stock 3} :name)
Record with :name Pear already exists. Aborting
user=> (select-* :fruits)
[{:name "Pear", :stock 3} {:name "Apricot", :stock 30} {:name "Grapefruit", :stock
6}]
user=> (select-*-where :fruits :name "Apricot")
{:name "Apricot", :stock 30}
```

In this activity, we have used our new knowledge about reading and updating both simple and deeply nested data structures to implement a simple in-memory database.

Chapter 3: Functions in Depth

Activity 3.01: Building a Distance and Cost Calculator

Solution:

1. Start by defining the **walking-speed** and **driving-speed** constants:

```
(def walking-speed 4)
(def driving-speed 70)
```

2. Create two other constants representing two locations with the coordinates **:lat** and **:lon**. You can use the previous example with Paris and Bordeaux or look up your own. You will be using them to test your distance and itinerary functions:

```
(def paris {:lat 48.856483 :lon 2.352413})
(def bordeaux {:lat 44.834999  :lon -0.575490})
```

3. Create the distance function. It should take two parameters representing the two locations for which we need to calculate the distance. You can use a combination of sequential and associative destructuring right in the function parameters to disassemble the latitude and longitude from both locations. You can decompose the steps of the calculation in a **let** expression and use the **Math/cos** function to calculate the cosine and **Math/sqrt** to calculate the square root of a number:

```
(defn distance
  "Returns a rough estimate of the distance between two coordinate points, in
    kilometers. Works better with smaller distance"
  [{lat1 :lat lon1 :lon} {lat2 :lat lon2 :lon}]
  (let [deglen 110.25
        x (- lat2 lat1)
        y (* (Math/cos lat2) (- lon2 lon1))]
    (* deglen (Math/sqrt (+ (* y y) (* x x))))))
```

4. Create a multimethod called **itinerary**. It will offer the flexibility of adding more types of transport in the future. It should use the value at **:transport** as a dispatch *value*:

```
(defmulti itinerary
  "Calculate the distance of travel between two location, and the cost and
    duration based on the type of transport"
  :transport)
```

5. Create the itinerary function for the :**walking** dispatch value. You can use associative destructuring in the function parameters to retrieve the :**from** and :**to** keys from the **HashMap** parameter. You can use a **let** expression to decompose the calculations of the distance and duration. The distance should simply use the **distance** function you created before. To calculate the duration, you should use the **walking-speed** constant that you defined in *Step 1*:

```
(defmethod itinerary :walking
  [{:keys [:from :to]}]
  (let [walking-distance (distance from to)
    duration (/ (distance from to) walking-speed)]
    {:cost 0 :distance walking-distance :duration duration}))
```

6. For the :**driving** itinerary function, you could use a *dispatch table* that contains the vehicle associated with their costing function. Create a **vehicle-cost-fns** dispatch table. It should be a **HashMap** with the keys being the types of vehicles, and the values being cost calculation functions based on the distance:

```
(def vehicle-cost-fns
  {
    :sporche (partial * 0.12 1.3)
    :tayato (partial * 0.07 1.3)
    :sleta (partial * 0.2 0.1)
  })
```

7. Create the itinerary function for the :**driving** dispatch value. You can use associative destructuring in the function parameters to retrieve the :**from**, :**to**, and :**vehicle** keys from the **HashMap** parameter. The driving distance and duration can be calculated similarly to the walking distance and duration. The cost can be calculated by retrieving the **cost** function from the dispatch table using the :**vehicle** key:

```
(defmethod itinerary :driving
  [{:keys [:from :to :vehicle]}]
  (let [driving-distance (distance from to)
        cost ((vehicle vehicle-cost-fns) driving-distance)
        duration (/ driving-distance driving-speed)]
    {:cost cost :distance driving-distance :duration duration}))
```

Now try the following:

```
user=> (def london {:lat 51.507351, :lon -0.127758})
#'user/london
user=> (def manchester {:lat 53.480759, :lon -2.242631})
#'user/manchester
user=> (itinerary {:from london :to manchester :transport :walking})
{:cost 0, :distance 318.4448148814284, :duration 79.6112037203571}
user=> (itinerary {:from manchester :to london :transport :driving :vehicle :sleta})
{:cost 4.604730845743489, :distance 230.2365422871744, :duration 3.2890934612453484}
```

In this activity, we've put in practice the destructuring and multimethod techniques that we have learned in this chapter by building a distance and cost calculator between two locations. In the future, you could imagine putting this code behind a web server and finishing building a fully blown itinerary calculation app!

Chapter 4: Mapping and Filtering

Activity 4.01: Using map and filter to Report Summary Information

Solution:

1. To start, set up a simple framework using the -`>>` threading macro:

```
(defn max-value-by-status [field status users]
      (->>
          users
          ;; code will go here
      ))
```

This defines the fundamental structure of our function, which we can sum up as follows: start with **users** and send it through a series of transformations.

2. The first of these transformations will be to filter out all the users that don't have the status we are looking for. We'll use **filter** for that, naturally, and we'll include a predicate that compares the :**status** field from each user with the **status** parameter that was passed into the function: **(filter #(= (:status %) status))**.

With that, our function now looks like this:

```
(defn max-value-by-status [field status users]
      (->>
          users
          ;; step 1: use filter to only keep users who
          ;; have the status we are looking for
          (filter #(= (:status %) status))
          ;; More to come!
      ))
```

We know that we have the correct set of users. Now, we need to extract the field we're interested in. The **field** parameter is a keyword, so we can use it as a function to extract the necessary data as we map over each user, like this: **(map field)**.

Now, our function looks like this:

```
(defn max-value-by-status [field status users]
            (->>
              users
              ;; step 1: use filter to only keep users who
              ;; have the status we are looking for
              (filter #(= (:status %) status))
              ;; step 2: field is a keyword, so we can use it as
              ;; a function when calling map.
              (map field)
              ;; Watch this space!
              ))
```

3. In the final step, we use **(apply max)** to find the needle in this haystack: the maximum value corresponding to **field**.

   The complete function looks like this:

```
(defn max-value-by-status [field status users]
            (->>
              users
              (filter #(= (:status %) status))
              (map field)
              (apply max 0)))

(defn min-value-by-status [field status users]
            (->>
              users
              (filter #(= (:status %) status))
              (map field)
              (apply min 0)))
```

Activity 4.02: Arbitrary Tennis Rivalries

Solution:

1. The first step will be to set up the function and the **with-open** macro:

```
(defn rivalry-data [csv player-1 player-2]
  (with-open [r (io/reader csv)]
    ))
```

2. Inside that, set up a **let** binding. The first binding will be to the **lazy-seq** returned by **csv/read-csv**:

```
(let [rivalry-seq (->> (csv/read-csv r)
                    sc/mappify
                    (sc/cast-with {:winner_sets_won sc/->int
                                   :loser_sets_won sc/->int
                                   :winner_games_won sc/->int
                                   :loser_games_won sc/->int}))]
  ;; more to come
  )
```

3. In the same **->>** chain, we also want to keep only the matches where our players are actually against each other. Like we did previously, we'll use the set pattern to see whether the set "winner and loser in the match" is equal to the set of the two players we are looking for. We'll also use **map** and **select-keys** to only keep the fields we want:

```
(filter #(= (hash-set (:winner_name %) (:loser_name %))
            #{player-1 player-2}))
(map #(select-keys % [:winner_name
                      :loser_name
                      :winner_sets_won
                      :loser_sets_won
                      :winner_games_won
                      :loser_games_won
                      :tourney_year_id
                      :tourney_slug]))
```

4. We can already start gathering some data here, so we'll make some more bindings in the same **let** statement:

```
player-1-victories (filter #(= (:winner_name %) player-1) rivalry-seq)
        player-2-victories (filter #(= (:winner_name %) player-2) rivalry-
          seq)
```

These are simple filter calls that give us two lists of victories.

5. We have all the bindings we need, so now it's time to do some work with them inside the scope of the **let** statement. Everything can happen inside the map that we are going to return. Now that we have our three sequences, that is, **player-1-victories**, **player-2-victories**, and the overall **rivalry-seq**, it becomes easier to grab some of our summary data with calls to **count** and **first**. We'll also write one more call to **filter** that inspects the score difference in the rivalry:

```
{:first-victory-player-1 (first player-1-victories)
 :first-victory-player-2 (first player-2-victories)
 :total-matches (count rivalry-seq)
 :total-victories-player-1 (count player-1-victories)
 :total-victories-player-2 (count player-2-victories)
 :most-competitive-matches (->> rivalry-seq
                                (filter #(= 1 (- (:winner_sets_won %)
                                                 (:loser_sets_won %)))))}
```

> **Note**
>
> You may be surprised that we did not need to call **doall** in this solution. This is because **rivalry-seq** is fully realized by the call to **count**. The final code can be found at https://packt.live/2Ri3904.

By completing this activity, we have produced the summary data for any two players who have actually played against each other.

Chapter 5: Many to One: Reducing

Activity 5.01: Calculating Elo Ratings for Tennis

Solution:

1. Here is the minimal **deps.edn** file you'll need:

```
{:deps
 {org.clojure/data.csv {:mvn/version "0.1.4"}
  semantic-csv {:mvn/version "0.2.1-alpha1"}
  org.clojure/math.numeric-tower {:mvn/version "0.0.4"}}}
```

2. Here is the corresponding namespace declaration:

```
(ns packt-clj.elo
  (:require [clojure.math.numeric-tower :as math]
            [clojure.java.io :as io]
            [clojure.data.csv :as csv]
            [semantic-csv.core :as sc])
```

3. For the overall structure of your function, we will follow the same patterns we've used so far: a **with-open** macro with some pre-processing code:

```
(defn elo-world
  ([csv k]
   (with-open [r (io/reader csv)]
     (->> (csv/read-csv r)
          sc/mappify
          (sc/cast-with {:winner_sets_won sc/->int
                         :loser_sets_won sc/->int
                         :winner_games_won sc/->int
                         :loser_games_won sc/->int})
          ;; TODO: just getting started
          ))))
```

4. The next step is to outline the call to **reduce**. The **:match-count**, **:predictable-match-count**, and **:correct-predictions** fields are just counters that will need to be updated depending on whether each match is correctly predicted. The **:players** map will contain a key for each player; the values will be their Elo ratings:

```
(defn elo-world
  ([csv k]
   (with-open [r (io/reader csv)]
     (->> (csv/read-csv r)
          sc/mappify
          (sc/cast-with {:winner_sets_won sc/->int
                         :loser_sets_won sc/->int
                         :winner_games_won sc/->int
                         :loser_games_won sc/->int})
          (reduce (fn [{:keys [players] :as acc} {:keys [:winner_name :winner_slug
                                                         :loser_name :loser_slug]
:as match}]
                    ;; TODO: more code
                    )
                  {:players {}
                   :match-count 0
                   :predictable-match-count 0
                   :correct-predictions 0})))))
```

5. From here, it is just a question of applying logic that we've already developed. First, we extract and calculate, and then we update the accumulator. The body of the reducing function starts with some **let** bindings:

```
(let [winner-rating (get players winner_slug 400)
      loser-rating (get players loser_slug 400)
      winner-probability (match-probability winner-rating loser-rating)
      loser-probability (- 1 winner-probability)
      predictable-match? (not= winner-rating loser-rating)
      prediction-correct? (> winner-rating loser-rating)
      correct-predictions (if (and predictable-match? prediction-correct?)
                            (inc (:correct-predictions acc))
                            (:correct-predictions acc))
      predictable-matches (if predictable-match?
                            (inc (:predictable-match-count acc))
                            (:predictable-match-count acc))]

  ;; TODO: update the accumulator
  )
```

winner-rating and **loser-rating** are extracted from the **:players** map in the accumulator. After we make our prediction regarding the match winner by calling **match-probability**, the remainder of the operations simply apply the consequences of whether our prediction was correct.

6. Now, we can finally update the accumulator. The following code goes inside the **let** expression above. This is what the reducing function will return. We use the **->** macro to thread the existing **acc** through a series of changes:

```
(-> acc
    (assoc :predictable-match-count predictable-matches)
    (assoc :correct-predictions correct-predictions)
    (assoc-in [:players winner_slug] (recalculate-rating k winner-rating winner-
probability 1))
    (assoc-in [:players loser_slug] (recalculate-rating k loser-rating loser-
probability 0))
    (update :match-count inc))
```

7. Here is the entire function, when we put everything back together:

tennis.clj

```
16   (defn elo-world-simple
17    ([csv k]
18    (with-open [r (io/reader csv)]
19      (->> (csv/read-csv r)
20           sc/mappify
21           (sc/cast-with {:winner_sets_won sc/->int
22                          :loser_sets_won sc/->int
23                          :winner_games_won sc/->int
24                          :loser_games_won sc/->int})
25           (reduce (fn [{:keys [players] :as acc} {:keys [:winner_name
                  :winner_slug
26                                                          :loser_name
                                                           :loser_slug] :as match}]
```

The complete code for this snippet can be found at: https://packt.live/38wSCUn

It might be interesting to experiment with different values of **k** to see whether the precision of the predictions can be improved. This is why we keep track of **:correction-predictions** and **:predictable-match-count**. There are many other kinds of improvements that could be made: modifying the function to run on multiple CSV files (if the ratings started at the very beginning of the dataset, in 1877, we would expect the quality to improve); perhaps contextually adjusting **k** depending on the relative strength of the two players, or based on current winning and losing streaks; or attributing bonuses to players who win more in certain locations. You now have a framework for experimentation.

Chapter 6: Recursion and Looping

Activity 6.01: Generating HTML from Clojure Vectors

Solution:

1. We'll use **clojure.string** in our solution. It is not strictly necessary, but **clojure.string/join** is a very convenient function. Because **clojure.string** is a standard Clojure namespace, a **deps.edn** file containing only an empty map is sufficient for this activity:

```
(ns my-hiccup
  (:require [clojure.string :as string]))
```

2. Here are the smaller functions that we'll use later in the main HTML-producing function:

```
(defn attributes [m]
  (clojure.string/join " "
              (map (fn [[k v]]
                 (if (string? v)
                   (str (name k) "=\"" v "\"")
                   (name k)))
               m)))
```

The first one, **attributes**, takes **map** attribute names and values. We treat the map like a sequence and map over the **[key value]** pairs. The keys are Clojure keywords, so they need to be converted to strings with the name function. The key-value pair becomes a string, **key="value"**. Then, we use **clojure.string/join** to combine all the substrings into a single string, making sure that each attribute is separated from the others by some whitespace. If the input map, **m**, is empty, **clojure.string/join** will return an empty string.

3. The next functions are simple formatting tools for building different kinds of tags:

```
(defn keyword->opening-tag [kw]
  (str "<" (name kw) ">"))
(defn keyword-attributes->opening-tag [kw attrs]
  (str "<" (name kw) " " (attributes attrs) ">"))
(defn keyword->closing-tag [kw]
  (str "</" (name kw) ">"))
```

The next set of helper functions are predicates that we will need since the main recursive function walks the tree of nested vectors. They all take the same kind of argument: the tree or subtree that we are analyzing.

4. We need to be able to distinguish between input vectors that have attributes and those that don't. We do this by looking at the type of the second item in the vector:

```
(defn has-attributes? [tree]
  (map? (second tree)))
```

5. The second item of a simple element like [:h1 "Hello world"] is a string, so has-attributes? would return nil. If the second item was another vector, the result would be the same. On [:h1 {:class "title"} "Hello Universe"], has-attributes? would return true. Because (map? nil) returns nil, we don't need to have a special case for single-item vectors. (has-attributes? [:br]) simply returns nil:

```
(defn singleton? [tree]
  (and (vector? tree)
       (#{:img :meta :link :input :br} (first tree))))
```

6. The singleton? function tests whether an element is a member of a small set of HTML elements that are not allowed to have closing tags. Naturally, we use a Clojure set to test this. First, though, we make sure that the current item is a vector because, sometimes, the current item will be a string (such as the second item in [:h1 "Hello world"]):

```
(defn singleton-with-attrs? [tree]
  (and (singleton? tree) (has-attributes? tree)))
(defn element-with-attrs? [tree]
  (and (vector? tree) (has-attributes? tree)))
```

These two predicates follow the same basic logic but build on the function we've already defined.

7. Now it's time for the main recursive function. Like the predicates, it will take a tree as an argument, which can, of course, be the entire vector tree or a subtree. Like most recursive functions, there is a cond with several branches.

Here is the basic structure:

```
(defn my-hiccup [tree]
  (cond


  ))
```

8. Let's go through the various conditions one by one, before putting them all back together:

```
(not tree) tree
```

9. If **tree** is not truthy, it means there is nothing we can do, so we simply return **nil**. For the rest of the inputs, we won't have to worry about getting **nil**:

```
(string? tree) tree
```

10. If **tree** is a string, we don't want to transform it. It can be integrated into the output string as is:

```
(singleton-with-attrs? tree)
(keyword-attributes->opening-tag (first tree) (second tree))
```

11. This is why we needed the **singleton-with-attrs?** predicate. Now, all we need to do is match the singleton tree with the corresponding formatting function. Because singleton elements don't have any content, no recursion is possible here:

```
(singleton? tree)
(keyword->opening-tag (first tree))
```

12. This is a simpler version of the previous condition:

```
(element-with-attrs? tree)
(apply str
    (concat
      [(keyword-attributes->opening-tag (first tree) (second tree))]
      (map my-hiccup (next (next tree)))
      [(keyword->closing-tag (first tree))]))
```

13. Now, we finally get to do some recursion! If an element has attributes, start making a string out of a list. That's what **(apply str...)** is for. We'll use **concat** to prepend the opening tag and the attributes, now formatted as a string, to a list that will be produced by **next** calls to **my-hiccup**, which will happen with the call to **map**. And, at the end of the list, we have the formatted closing tag. This is the classic case where we cannot use **recur**: the call to **(apply str (concat...))** cannot complete until all the underlying calls to **my-hiccup** have completed:

```
(vector? tree)
(apply str
    (concat
      [(keyword->opening-tag (first tree))]
      (map my-hiccup (next tree))
      [(keyword->closing-tag (first tree))]))
```

14. The last condition follows the same pattern as the previous pattern. We could have made this a default condition instead of testing with **vector?**. If our input vector tree is malformed, the error indicating no matching case should put us on the right track for debugging. In production code, we could add an **:otherwise** condition that would throw an exception. You'll learn about exceptions in *Chapter 9, Host Platform Interoperability with Java and JavaScript*.

If we reassemble **my-hiccup**, it looks like this:

```
(defn my-hiccup [tree]
 (cond
  (not tree) tree
  (string? tree) tree
  (singleton-with-attrs? tree)
  (keyword-attributes->opening-tag (first tree) (second tree))
  (singleton? tree)
  (keyword->opening-tag (first tree))
  (element-with-attrs? tree)
  (apply str
      (concat
       [(keyword-attributes->opening-tag (first tree) (second tree))]
       (map my-hiccup (next (next tree)))
       [(keyword->closing-tag (first tree))]))
  (vector? tree)
  (apply str
      (concat
       [(keyword->opening-tag (first tree))]
       (map my-hiccup (next tree))
       [(keyword->closing-tag (first tree))]))))
```

If you try the **my-hiccup** function in the REPL, you should be able to produce the string for a complete HTML page:

```
packt-clj.my-hiccup> (my-hiccup
                       [:html
                        [:head
                         [:title "HTML output from vectors!"]]
                        [:body
                         [:h1 {:id "page-title"} "HTML output from vectors!"]
                         [:div {:class "main-content"}
                          [:p "Converting nested lists into HTML is an old Lisp trick"]
                          [:p "But Clojure uses vectors instead."]]]])
"<html><head><title>HTML output from vectors!</title></head><body><h1 id=\"page-title\">HTM
L output from vectors!</h1><div class=\"main-content\"><p>Converting nested lists into HTML
 is an old Lisp trick</p><p>But Clojure uses vectors instead.</p></div></body></html>"
packt-clj.my-hiccup> []
```

Figure 6.10: Final output

> **Note**
>
> Feel free to try different inputs and page structures. You can even copy the output string into a text file to load into your browser.

By completing this activity, we are now able to take any vector written with this syntax, including an arbitrary number of descendant vectors, and produce a single string containing correctly structured HTML.

Chapter 7: Recursion II: Lazy Sequences

Activity 7.01: Historical, Player-Centric Elo

Solution:

1. Set up your project, which should be based on the code written for the last exercises in this chapter.

2. The solution follows the pattern established with **take-matches**. Let's start with the parameters. We need to define separate behaviors for matches played by the "focus player" and matches played between other players. The first thing we need is, of course, a way to identify the player, so we'll add a **player-slug** argument. This wasn't necessary in **take-matches** because there we treated all the matches the same, regardless of who played in them.

    In **take-matches**, we had a **limit** argument to control how deeply we walked the tree. In this case, we need two different parameters, which we will call **focus-depth** and **opponent-depth**. Together, that gives us the following parameters for our new **focus-history** function:

    ```
    (defn focus-history [tree player-slug focus-depth opponent-depth f]
    ;;...
    )
    ```

    The **tree** parameter is, of course, the result of a call to **match-tree-by-player**, as before.

    Finally, the **f** argument will work the same way as in **take-matches**.

3. Controlling the function's movement through the tree will end up being a challenge. As usual, we will set up a **cond** form that will determine how the function reacts to the incoming data. The first two conditions are quite simple, and in fact, are nearly identical to the code in **take-matches**:

    ```
    (defn focus-history [tree player-slug focus-depth opponent-depth f]
      (cond
        (zero? focus-depth)
        '()
        (= 1 focus-depth)
        (f (first tree))))
    ```

    The only change from **take-matches** is that now we are using **focus-depth** instead of **limit**. The fact that we are using **focus-depth** here is important nonetheless. We are only concerned about **focus-depth** at this stage, and not **opponent-depth**, because if **focus-depth** is zero or one, the entire operation stops and in this case we no longer care about **opponent-depth**.

4. The final condition is where this function behaves differently from **take-matches**. It is also more complex, though perhaps not as much as you might think at first glance. To understand this, let's look at the equivalent part of **take-matches**:

```
:otherwise-continue
      (cons
        (f (first tree))
        (cons
          [(take-matches (dec limit) (first (second tree)) f)
           (take-matches (dec limit) (second (second tree)) f)]
          '())))
```

5. At this point, we are placing **(f (first tree))** at the head of the current lazy seq. As such, we are connecting it onto the rest of the sequence, whose first item will be a vector containing the starting point for two more branch lazy seqs.

All we need to do here, in order to introduce separate behaviors for the two possible cases, is to replace the calls to **take-matches** inside the two-item vector. Those two matches are the "parent" matches of the current match; that is, they are the matches played by the winner and loser before the current match. We need to test first to find which "parent" matches belong to the focus player and which belong to an opponent. For the focus player's previous match, we call **focus-history**. For the opponent's previous match we call **take-matches**. In other words, instead of just having two calls to **take-matches**, as above, we have two branching conditions:

```
:otherwise
(cons
  (f (first tree))
  (cons [(if (player-in-match? (ffirst (second tree)) player-slug)
            (focus-history (first (second tree)) player-slug (dec focus-depth)
opponent-depth f)
            (take-matches opponent-depth (first (second tree))  f))
         (if (player-in-match? (first (second (second tree))) player-slug)
            (focus-history (second (second tree)) player-slug (dec focus-depth)
opponent-depth f)
            (take-matches opponent-depth (second (second tree)) f))]
    '())))
```

6. In both of these cases, whether we call **focus-history** or **take-matches**, we have to be careful to adjust the **tree** argument and the **focus-depth** arguments correctly. Remember that **tree** is always relative to the current two-item sequence composed of a match and a two-item vector, which is why we use **(first (second tree))** and **(second (second tree))**, that is, the first and the second of the two lazy sequences in the vector. While it would be tempting to assign these to **let** bindings to avoid repeating **(second tree)**, it is generally better in these cases to avoid "holding onto the head."

    Here's the complete function:

```
(defn focus-history [tree player-slug focus-depth opponent-depth f]
    (cond
        (zero? focus-depth)
        '()
        (= 1 focus-depth)
        (f (first tree))
        :otherwise
        (cons
            (f (first tree))
            (cons [(if (player-in-match? (ffirst (second tree)) player-slug)
                        (focus-history (first (second tree)) player-slug (dec focus-depth)
                            opponent-depth f)
                        (take-matches opponent-depth (first (second tree))  f))
                    (if (player-in-match? (first (second (second tree))) player-slug)
                        (focus-history (second (second tree)) player-slug (dec focus-depth)
                            opponent-depth f)
                        (take-matches opponent-depth (second (second tree)) f))]
                '())))))
```

7. It's worth noting that this function is only slightly more complex than **take-matches**. As is often the case with recursive solutions, the code itself is rather simple. The difficulty is in choosing the best strategy.

Here is the function in action, from start to finish. First, we read in the data and generate the ratings:

```
packt-clojure.lazy-tennis> (def ratings (elo-db
    "match_scores_1991-2016_unindexed_csv.csv" 35))
```

Then we build the lazy match tree for the player we're interested in:

```
#'packt-clojure.lazy-tennis/ratings
packt-clojure.lazy-tennis> (def federer (match-tree-by-player ratings
    "roger-federer"))
#'packt-clojure.lazy-tennis/federer
```

And now we call our new function:

```
packt-clojure.lazy-tennis> (focus-history federer
                                          "roger-federer"
                                          4
                                          2
                                          #(select-keys % [:winner_name :loser_name
                                            :winner_rating :loser_rating]))
```

The indentation in the results reveals a tree structure:

```
({:winner_name "Roger Federer",
  :loser_name "Guido Pella",
  :winner_rating 1129.178155312036,
  :loser_rating 625.3431873490674}
 [({:winner_name "Roger Federer",
    :loser_name "Marcus Willis",
    :winner_rating 1128.703390288765,
    :loser_rating 384.0402195770708}
   [({:winner_name "Roger Federer",
      :loser_name "Daniel Evans",
      :winner_rating 1127.06735832767,
      :loser_rating 603.2729932046952}
     [{:winner_name "Roger Federer",
       :loser_name "Steve Johnson",
       :winner_rating 1122.7516522815502,
       :loser_rating 782.0059408768791}
      ({:winner_name "Daniel Evans",
        :loser_name "Liam Broady",
        :winner_rating 595.9600755434737,
        :loser_rating 364.68547206909847}
       [{:winner_name "Daniel Evans",
         :loser_name "Ricardas Berankis",
         :winner_rating 579.3218764693715,
         :loser_rating 562.1982931522488}
        {:winner_name "Inigo Cervantes",
         :loser_name "Liam Broady",
         :winner_rating 470.1485260098959,
         :loser_rating 377.6326375223018}])])
    ({:winner_name "Pierre-Hugues Herbert",
      :loser_name "Marcus Willis",
      :winner_rating 587.634881154115,
      :loser_rating 392.63430666689504}
     [{:winner_name "Pierre-Hugues Herbert",
       :loser_name "Daniil Medvedev",
       :winner_rating 578.8847540928984,
       :loser_rating 388.03961566213536}
      {:winner_name "Daniel Kosakowski",
       :loser_name "Marcus Willis",
       :winner_rating 475.1397044731464,
       :loser_rating 406.73254794551923}])])
  ({:winner_name "Benjamin Becker",
    :loser_name "Guido Pella",
    :winner_rating 638.7921462877312,
    :loser_rating 643.0580458561587}
   [{:winner_name "Dudi Sela",
     :loser_name "Benjamin Becker",
     :winner_rating 560.0126295247488,
     :loser_rating 661.2518854789847}
    {:winner_name "Guido Pella",
     :loser_name "Diego Schwartzman",
     :winner_rating 623.4399911176613,
     :loser_rating 665.6978632936225}])])
```

Figure 7.10: The results of focus-history

Matches played by Federer contain deeper sub-trees of the preceding matches. The data is ready to be passed to the frontend team, who will translate it into a beautiful visualization.

Chapter 8: Namespaces, Libraries and Leiningen

Activity 8.01: Altering the Users List in an Application

Solution:

1. Import the **clojure.string** namespace with **use** and the **:rename** keyword for the **replace** and **reverse** functions:

```
(use '[clojure.string :rename {replace str-replace, reverse str-reverse}])
```

2. Create a set of users:

```
(def users #{"mr_paul smith" "dr_john blake" "miss_katie hudson"})
```

3. Replace the underscore between honorifics and first names:

```
(map #(str-replace % #"_" " ") users)
```

This will return the following:

```
("mr paul smith" "miss katie hudson" "dr john blake")
```

4. Use the **capitalize** function to capitalize each person's initials in the user group:

```
(map #(capitalize %) users)
```

This will return the following:

```
("Mr_paul smith" "Miss_katie hudson" "Dr_john blake")
```

5. Update the user list by using the string's **replace** and **capitalize** functions:

```
(def updated-users (into #{}
                     (map #(join " "
                            (map (fn [sub-str] (capitalize sub-str))
                                 (split (str-replace % #"_" " ") #" ")))
                       users)))
updated-users
```

The output is as follows:

```
#{"Mr Paul Smith" "Dr John Blake" "Miss Katie Hudson"}
```

6. Import only the **print-table** function from the **clojure.pprint** namespace:

```
(use '[clojure.pprint :only (print-table)])
```

7. Print a table with users:

```
(print-table (map #(hash-map :user-name %) updated-users))
```

The output is as follows:

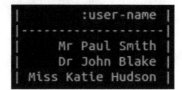

Figure 8.23: Printing the table of users

8. Import the **clojure.set** namespace, excluding the **join** function:

```
(use '[clojure.set :exclude (join)])
```

9. Create and display a set of admins:

```
(def admins #{"Mr Paul Smith" "Miss Katie Hudson" "Dr Mike Rose" "Mrs Tracy Ford"})
```

The output is as follows:

```
#'user/admins
```

10. Now execute the following:

```
admins
```

The output is as follows:

```
#{"Mr Paul Smith" "Dr Mike Rose" "Miss Katie Hudson" "Mrs Tracy Ford"}
```

11. Call the **subset?** function on two sets:

```
(subset? users admins)
```

The output is as follows:

```
false
```

12. To print the final output, execute the following:

```
(print-table (map #(hash-map :user-name %) updated-users))
```

The output is as follows:

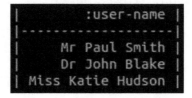

Figure 8.24: Printing the final user table

In this activity, we worked on two features. With the first feature, we capitalized usernames. With the second feature, we used **Clojure.set** functions to check whether any users were also admins.

Activity 8.02: Summing Up Numbers

Solution:

1. Create a Leiningen application:

```
lein new app hello-leiningen
```

2. Convert string arguments to integers:

```
(map #(Integer/parseInt %) args)
```

3. Add integers to calculate the sum:

```
apply +
```

4. Print the result as follows:

```
println
```

The output will look like the following:

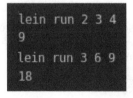

```
lein run 2 3 4
9
lein run 3 6 9
18
```

Figure 8.25: Printing the sum

The complete solution should look as follows:

```
(ns hello-leiningen.core)
(defn -main
  "Sum integers passed as arguments."
  [& args]
  (println (apply + (map #(Integer/parseInt %) args))))
```

In this activity, we created a new Leiningen project. This application accepted parameters from the command line. Numbers input into the command line were summed and the result was displayed.

Activity 8.03: Building a Format-Converting Application

Solution:

1. Inside **project.clj**, add the **cheshire** dependency:

```
(defproject json-parser "0.1.0-SNAPSHOT"
;;; code committed
   :dependencies [[org.clojure/clojure "1.10.0"]
                             [cheshire "3.0.0"]]
;;; code ommited
)
```

2. Create a function to convert from hash to JSON. Inside the core namespace, add the following:

```
(ns json-parser.core
    (:require [cheshire.core :as json])
    (:gen-class))


(defn generate-json-from-hash [hash]
      (json/generate-string hash))
```

Testing the **generate-json-from-hash** function in the REPL should give us the following result:

```
json-parser.core=> (in-ns 'json-parser.core)
#object[clojure.lang.Namespace 0x164d1490 "json-parser.core"]
json-parser.core=> (generate-json-from-hash {:name "John" :occupation "programmer"})
"{\"name\":\"John\",\"occupation\":\"programmer\"}"
```

Figure 8.26: Generating JSON from hash

3. Create a function to convert from JSON to hash:

```
(defn generate-hash-from-json [json]
      (json/parse-string json))
```

Testing **generate-hash-from-json** in the REPL should give us the following result:

```
json-parser.core=> (generate-hash-from-json "{\"name\":\"Mike\",\"occupation\":\"carpenter\"}")
{"name" "Mike", "occupation" "carpenter"}
```

Figure 8.27: Generating hash from JSON

4. Add the **expectations** library to the testing profile defined for the project. In **project.clj**, add the following:

```
(defproject json-parser "0.1.0-SNAPSHOT"
  ;;; code ommited
   :profiles {:qa  {:dependencies [[expectations "2.1.10"]]}
  ;;; code ommited
})
```

5. Add the **lein-expectations** plugin for the project:

```
(defproject json-parser "0.1.0-SNAPSHOT"
  ;;; code ommited
   :profiles {:qa  {:plugins      [[lein-expectations "0.0.8"]]}
  ;;; code ommited
})
```

6. Write the test for the JSON functions. Inside the **json-parser/test/json_parser/ core_test.clj** files, add the following:

```
(ns json-parser.core-test
  (:require [expectations :refer [expect]]
            [json-parser.core :refer :all]))
(expect (generate-json-from-hash {:name "John" :occupation "programmer"})
        "{\"name\":\"John\",\"occupation\":\"programmer\"}")
(expect (generate-hash-from-json "{\"name\":\"Mike\",\"occupation\":\"carpenter\"}")
        {"name" "Mike", "occupation" "carpenter"})
```

Calling tests with the **qa** profile should give us the following:

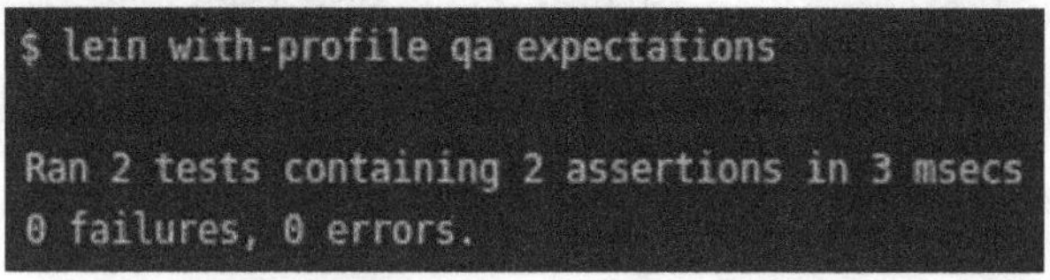

```
$ lein with-profile qa expectations

Ran 2 tests containing 2 assertions in 3 msecs
0 failures, 0 errors.
```

Figure 8.28: Executing the test profile

7. Add **lein-ancient** to user-wide profiles. In **~/.lein/profiles.clj**, add the following:

```
{:user {:plugins [[lein-ancient "0.6.15"]]
        :dependencies [[clojure-humanize "0.2.2"]]}}
```

Checking for outdated dependencies should show the following:

```
$ lein ancient
[org.clojure/clojure "1.10.1"] is available but we use "1.10.0" (use :check-clojure to upgrade)
[cheshire "5.9.0"] is available but we use "3.0.0"
```

Figure 8.29: Checking for outdated dependencies

In this activity, we have created an application that performs a conversion from JSON format to Clojure data and back. In order to make sure that our application runs correctly, we created a testing profile where we included dependencies on the **expectations** library and a plugin. To make sure that the libraries in all our projects are not outdated, we included the **lein-ancient** plugin in our user-wide profile.

Chapter 9: Host Platform Interoperability with Java and JavaScript

Activity 9.01: Book-Ordering Application

Solution:

1. Create a new project:

```
lein new app books-app
```

2. Import the necessary namespaces:

```
(ns books-app.core
  (:require [books-app.utils :as utils])
  (:import [java.util Scanner])
  (:gen-class))
```

3. Create a map to hold books by year:

```
(def ^:const books {:2019 {:clojure {:title "Hands-On Reactive Programming with
Clojure" :price 20}
                           :go      {:title "Go Cookbook" :price 18}}
                    :2018 {:clojure {:title "Clojure Microservices" :price 15}
                           :go {:title "Advanced Go programming" :price 25}}})
```

4. Create a variable for a file that stores orders:

```
(def ^:const orders-file "orders.edn")
```

5. Create the initial menu with options to order a book and list orders:

```
(def input (Scanner. System/in))
(defn- start-app []
       "Displaying main menu and processing user choices."
       (let [run-application (ref true)]
            (while (deref run-application)
                   (println "\n|      Books app         |")
                   (println "| 1-Menu 2-Orders 3-Exit |\n")
                   (let [choice (.nextInt input)]
                        (case choice
                              1 (show-menu)
                              2 (show-orders)
                              3 (dosync (alter run-application (fn [_]
                                  false)))))))))
```

The output is as follows:

Figure 9.53: Output for the initial menu

6. Create a menu to display books by year:

```
(defn- show-menu []
       (println "| Available books by year |")
       (println "|1. 2019   2. 2018 |")
       (let [choice (.nextInt input)]
            (case choice
                  1 (show-year-menu :2019)
                  2 (show-year-menu :2018))))
```

The output is as follows:

Figure 9.54: Output for available books by the year

7. Create the application's **main** method:

```
(defn -main
   "Main function to run the app."
   [& args]
   (start-app))
```

8. Create a function to save data to a file:

```
(ns books-app.utils
    (:require [clojure.java.io :as io])
    (:import [java.io PushbackReader]))
(defn save-to [location data]
      (spit location data :append true))
```

9. Create a function to save an order:

```
(defn save-book-order [orders-file year prog-lang number price]
      (save-to orders-file {:year year :prog-lang prog-lang :number number :price
price}))
```

10. Create a function to calculate the price of a book:

```
(defn calculate-book-price [books title number]
    (->
      (get books title)
      :price
      (* number)
      float))
```

11. Create a function to display an order confirmation message:

```
(defn display-bought-book-message [title number total]
    (println "Buying" number title "for total:€" total))
```

The output is as follows:

```
Buying 2 Hands-On Reactive Programming with Clojure for total:€ 40.0
```

Figure 9.55: Order confirmation message

12. Create a function to display the bought order:

```
(defn display-order [order books]
    (str "Bought " (:number order) ": " (:title (get (get books (:year order))
(:prog-lang order))) " published in " (name (:year order)) " for €" (:price order)))
```

The output is as follows:

```
Bought 2: Hands-On Reactive Programming with Clojure published in 2019 for €40.0
Bought 3: Go Cookbook published in 2019 for €54.0
```

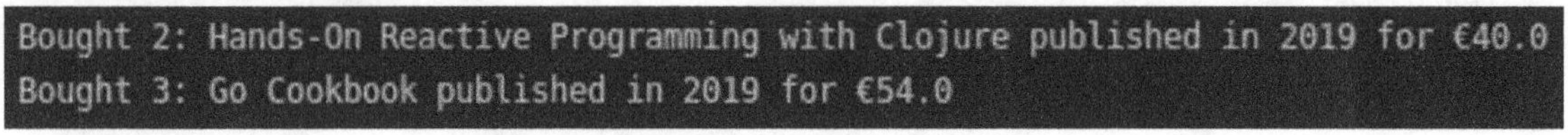

Figure 9.56: Displaying the purchased order

13. Create a function to read a single order:

```
(defn read-one-order
    [r]
    (try
      (read r)
      (catch java.lang.RuntimeException e
        (if (= "EOF while reading" (.getMessage e))
          ::EOF
          (throw e)))))
```

14. Create a function to check whether a file exists:

```
(defn file-exists [location]
      (.exists (io/as-file location)))
```

15. Create a function to load orders from a file:

```
(defn load-orders
      "Reads a sequence of orders in file at path."
      [file]
      (if (file-exists file)
        (with-open [r (PushbackReader. (io/reader file))]
                   (binding [*read-eval* false]
                            (doall (take-while #(not= ::EOF %) (repeatedly
                                #(read-one-order r))))))
        []))
```

16. Create a submenu to order a book:

```
(ns coffee-app.core)
(defn- show-year-menu [year]
       (let [year-books (get books year)]
            (println "| Books in" (name year) "|")
            (println "| 1. " (:title (:clojure year-books)) " 2. " (:title
                (:go year-books))  "|")
            (let [choice (.nextInt input)]
                 (case choice
                       1 (buy-book year :clojure)
                       2 (buy-book year :go)))))
```

The output is as follows:

```
| Books in 2019 |
| 1.  Hands-On Reactive Programming with Clojure  2.  Go Cookbook |
```

Figure 9.57: Submenu for book order

17. Create a function to buy a book by year:

```
(defn- buy-book [year prog-lang]
       (println "How many books do you want to buy?")
       (let [choice (.nextInt input)
             price (utils/calculate-book-price (get books year) prog-lang
                 choice)]
            (utils/save-book-order orders-file year prog-lang choice price)
            (utils/display-bought-book-message (:title (get (get books year)
                prog-lang)) choice price)))
```

The output is as follows:

```
How many books do you want to buy?
```

Figure 9.58: Function to buy books by year

18. Create a function to show orders by year:

```
(defn- show-orders-by-year [year]
      (println "\n")
      (doseq [order (filter #(= year (:year %)) (utils/load-orders orders-
        file))]
            (println (utils/display-order order books))))
```

19. Create a submenu to list orders:

```
(defn show-orders []
      (println "| Books by publish year |")
      (println "|1. 2019   2. 2018 |")
      (let [choice (.nextInt input)]
           (case choice
                 1 (show-orders-by-year :2019)
                 2 (show-orders-by-year :2018))))
```

The output is as follows:

```
| Books by publish year |
|1. 2019   2. 2018 |
```

Figure 9.59: Creating submenu

In this activity, we created an application for ordering books and displaying orders. We used our new knowledge about I/O and Java to complete this activity.

Once you complete the activity, you should have an output similar to the following.

Initial menu:

```
|      Books app         |
| 1-Menu 2-Orders 3-Exit |
```

Figure 9.60: Initial menu

Listing years:

| Available books by year |
|1. 2019   2. 2018 |

Figure 9.61: Listing years

Books in one year:

| Books in 2019 |
| 1.   Hands-On Reactive Programming with Clojure   2.   Go Cookbook |

Figure 9.62: Books purchased in 2019

Asking how many books to buy:

How many books do you want to buy?

Figure 9.63: Asking for the numbers of books to be bought

Order confirmation message:

Buying 2 Hands-On Reactive Programming with Clojure for total:€ 40.0

Figure 9.64: Order confirmation message

Listing purchased books:

Bought 2: Hands-On Reactive Programming with Clojure published in 2019 for €40.0
Bought 3: Go Cookbook published in 2019 for €54.0

Figure 9.65: Listing purchased books

In this section, we used our knowledge of Java interoperability to create a command-line application. In the next section, we will learn how to use JavaScript in ClojureScript.

Activity 9.02: Creating a Support Desk

Solution:

1. Create a new project:

```
lein new figwheel-main support-desk
```

2. Add the **jayq** and **cuerdas** libraries as dependencies in **project.clj**:

```
:dependencies [[org.clojure/clojure "1.9.0"]
               [org.clojure/clojurescript "1.10.520"]
               [funcool/cuerdas "2.2.0"]
               [jayq "2.5.4"]
               [rum "0.11.2"]]
```

3. Create the **utils** function to filter the issues list by priority:

```
(ns support-desk.utils)
(defn get-priorities-list [list priority]
      (filter #(<= (:priority %) priority) list))
```

4. Create the **utils** function to get the sorted issues list:

```
(defn get-sorted-priorities-list [list]
      (sort-by :priority list))
```

5. Create the **utils** function to get the sort message by issues count:

```
(defn get-sort-message [items-count]
      (str (cond
             (< items-count 3) "little"
             (< items-count 6) "medium"
             :else "many") " (" items-count ")"))
```

For **0** issues, the output is as follows:

```
Sorting done: little (0) times
```

For **3** issues, the output is as follows:

```
Sorting done: medium (3) times
```

6. Create the **utils** function to delete issue from a list:

```
(defn delete-item-from-list-by-title [title list]
      (remove #(= title (:title %)) list))
```

7. Create the **utils** function called when sorting is finished:

```
(defn handle-sort-finish [state]
       (fn [ev ui]
            (swap! state update-in [:sort-counter] inc)))
```

8. Add jQuery and jQuery UI to **index.html**:

```
<script src="https://code.jquery.com/jquery-3.4.1.min.js" integrity="sha256-CSXorXvZ
cTkaix6Yvo6HppcZGetbYMGWSFlBw8HfCJo=" crossorigin="anonymous"></script>
<script src="https://code.jquery.com/ui/1.12.1/jquery-ui.min.js" integrity="sha256-
VazP97ZCwtekAsvgPBSUwPFKdrwD3unUfSGVYrahUqU=" crossorigin="anonymous"></script>
```

9. Import **jayq**, **cuerdas**, and **utils** to the core namespace:

```
(ns ^:figwheel-hooks support-desk.core
  (:require [cuerdas.core :as str]
            [goog.dom :as gdom]
            [jayq.core :as jayq :refer [$]]
            [rum.core :as rum]
            [support-desk.utils :as utils]))
```

10. Define the priorities list as follows:

```
(def priorities-list [{:title "IE bugs" :priority 2} {:title "404 page" :priority 1}
{:title "Forgotten username" :priority 2}
                        {:title "Login token" :priority 1} {:title "Mobile version"
:priority 3} {:title "Load time" :priority 5}])
```

11. Define **app-state** as follows:

```
(defonce app-state (atom {:sort-counter 0
                          :items       (utils/get-sorted-priorities-list (utils/
get-priorities-list priorities-list 3))}))
```

12. Define the **counter** Rum component:

```
(rum/defc counter [number]
          [:div
            (str/format "Sorting done: %s times" (utils/get-sort-message number))])
```

13. Create the issue on **click** function:

```
(defn done-button-click [item]
       (swap! app-state update-in [:items] #(utils/delete-item-from-list-by-
          title (:title item) %)))
```

14. Define the issue item in the Rum component:

```
(rum/defc item [item]
          [:li.ui-state-default {:key (:title item)}
           (str/format "Priority %s for: %s " (:priority item) (:title
              item))
           [:button.delete
            {:on-click #(done-button-click item)}
            "Done"]])
```

The output is as follows:

Priority 1 for: 404 page [Done]

Figure 9.66: Defining an issue item in a Rum component

15. Define the **reactive** issue items component:

```
(rum/defc items < rum/reactive [num]
          [:ul#sortable (vec (for [n num]
                               (item n)))])
```

16. Define the reactive page **content** component:

```
(rum/defc content < rum/reactive []
          [:div {}
           (items (:items (deref app-state)))
           (counter (:sort-counter (rum/react app-state)))])
```

17. Make the item components sortable:

```
(defn attrs [a]
      (clj->js (sablono.util/html-to-dom-attrs a)))
(defn make-sortable []
      (.sortable ($ (str "#sortable"))
                 (attrs {:stop (utils/handle-sort-finish app-state)})))
```

18. Mount the page component:

```
(defn mount [el]
  (rum/mount (content) el))
(defn mount-app-element []
  (when-let [el (get-app-element)]
    (mount el)))
```

19. Call the **mount** function:

```
(mount-app-element)
```

20. Call the **sortable** function:

```
(make-sortable)
```

21. Run the application:

```
lein fig:build
```

The initial issues list will look as follows:

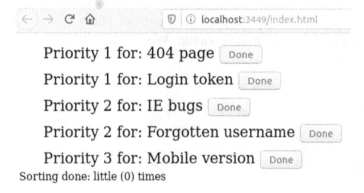

Figure 9.67: Initial issue list

The issues list after sorting will look as follows:

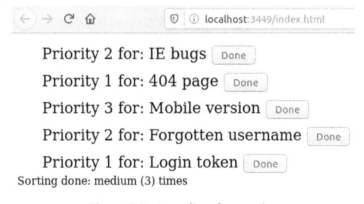

Figure 9.68: Issue list after sorting

The issues list after resolving three issues will look as follows:

Figure 9.69: Issue list after resolving issues

In this activity, we created a support desk application. The application displays a list of issues. The issues can be sorted and resolved. We used JavaScript interoperability to add a sorting feature.

Chapter 10: Testing

Activity 10.01: Writing Tests for the Coffee-Ordering Application

Solution:

1. Import the testing namespaces:

```
(ns coffee-app.utils-test
    (:require [clojure.test :refer :all]
              [coffee-app.core :refer [price-menu]]
              [coffee-app.utils :refer :all]))
```

2. Create tests using the **clojure.test** library to display the orders messages.

3. Test the application using the **is** macro:

```
(deftest display-order-test
        (testing "Multiple tests with is macro"
                (is (= (display-order {:number 4 :price 3.8 :type :latte}) "Bought
    4 cups of latte for €3.8"))
                (is (= (display-order {:number 7 :price 6.3 :type :espresso})
    "Bought 7 cups of espresso for €6.3"))))
```

4. Tests using the **are** macro:

```
(deftest display-order-test
        (testing "Multiple tests with are macro"
                (are [order result]
                    (= (display-order order) result)
                    {:number 2 :price 1.5 :type :latte} "Bought 2 cups of
                        latte for €1.5"
                    {:number 3 :price 6.3 :type :mocca} "Bought 3 cups of
                        mocca for €6.3"
                    {:number 8 :price 10 :type :espresso} "Bought 8 cups
                        of espresso for €10")))
```

5. Create tests using the **clojure.test** library to check whether the file exists.

Test whether the file does not exist:

```
(deftest file-exists-test
    (testing "File does not exist"
                (testing "Multiple tests with is macro"
                        (is (false? (file-exists "no-file")))
                        (is (false? (file-exists "missing-file"))))
                (testing "Multiple tests with are macro"
                        (are [file] (false? (file-exists file))
                                "eettcc"
                                "tmp-tmp"
                                "no-file-here"))))
```

Test whether the file does exist:

```
(deftest file-exists-test
        (testing "File does exist"
                (testing "Multiple tests with is macro"
                        (is (file-exists "/etc"))
                        (is (file-exists "/lib")))
                (testing "Multiple tests with are macro"
                        (are [file] (true? (file-exists file))
                                "/etc"
                                "/var"
                                "/tmp"))))
```

6. Create tests using the **clojure.test** library to save and load orders.

Save orders:

```
(defn uuid [] (str (java.util.UUID/randomUUID)))
(deftest saves-coffee-order
        (testing "Saves cofee order"
                (let [test-file (str "/tmp/" (uuid) ".edn")
                        test-data {:type :latte, :number 2, :price 2.6}]
                        (save-coffee-order test-file :latte 2 2.6)
                        (is (= (list test-data) (load-orders test-file))))))
```

Load empty orders:

```
(deftest loads-empty-vector-from-not-existing-file
        (testing "saving and loading"
                (let [test-file (str "/tmp/" (uuid) ".edn")]
                        (is (= [] (load-orders test-file))))))
```

Load coffee orders:

```
(deftest can-save-and-load-some-data
         (testing "saving and loading"
                  (let [test-file (str "/tmp/" (uuid) ".edn")
                        test-data {:number 1 :type :latte}]
                    (save-to test-file test-data)
                    (is (= (list test-data) (load-orders test-file))))))))
```

The output is as follows:

```
$ lein test

lein test coffee-app.utils-test

lein test coffee-app.utils-test-expectations

Ran 9 tests containing 26 assertions.
0 failures, 0 errors.

Ran 13 tests containing 13 assertions in 15 msecs
0 failures, 0 errors.
```

Figure 10.57: Output after saving and loading orders

7. Create tests using the expectations library to display the orders message:

```
(ns coffee-app.utils-test-expectations
    (:require [coffee-app.utils :refer :all]
              [expectations :refer [expect side-effects]]))
(expect "Bought 4 cups of latte for €3.8" (display-order {:number 4 :price 3.8 :type
:latte}))
(expect "Bought 7 cups of espresso for €6.3" (display-order {:number 7 :price 6.3
:type :espresso}))
(expect String (display-order {:number 7 :price 6.3 :type :espresso}))
(expect #"Bought 7 cups" (display-order {:number 7 :price 6.3 :type :espresso}))
(expect #"cups of espresso" (display-order {:number 7 :price 6.3 :type :espresso}))
(expect #"for €6.3" (display-order {:number 7 :price 6.3 :type :espresso}))
```

8. Create tests using the **Expectations** library to check whether the file exists:

```
(expect true (file-exists "/tmp"))
(expect false (file-exists "no-file"))
(expect Boolean (file-exists "etc"))
```

9. Create tests using the **Expectations** library to save and load orders.

Save data to a file:

```
(expect [["/tmp/menu.edn" {:type :latte :number 1 :price 2.4} :append true]
         ["/tmp/menu.edn" {:type :latte :number 3 :price 4.7} :append true]]
        (side-effects [spit]
                      (save-to "/tmp/menu.edn" {:type :latte :number 1 :price 2.4})
                      (save-to "/tmp/menu.edn" {:type :latte :number 3 :price
4.7})))
```

Save coffee orders:

```
(expect [["/tmp/orders.edn" :latte 1 2.4]
         ["/tmp/orders.edn" :latte 2 3.9]]
        (side-effects [save-coffee-order]
                      (save-coffee-order "/tmp/orders.edn" :latte 1 2.4)
                      (save-coffee-order "/tmp/orders.edn" :latte 2 3.9)))
```

Save coffee data:

```
(expect [["/tmp/coffees.edn" {:type :latte :number 1 :price 2.4}]
         ["/tmp/coffees.edn" {:type :latte :number 2 :price 3.9}]]
        (side-effects [save-to]
                      (save-coffee-order "/tmp/coffees.edn" :latte 1 2.4)
                      (save-coffee-order "/tmp/coffees.edn" :latte 2 3.9)))
Load orders:
(expect [] (load-orders "/tmp/data.edn"))
```

The output is as follows:

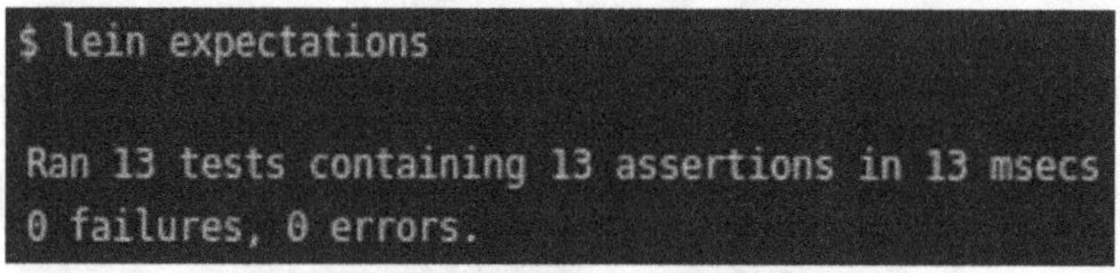

Figure 10.58: Testing using the Expectations library

10. Create tests using the **Midje** library to display the orders messages:

```clojure
(ns coffee-app.utils-test-midje
    (:require [coffee-app.utils :refer :all]
              [midje.sweet :refer :all]))


(facts "Passing an order should return display message"
       (fact (display-order {:number 4 :price 3.8 :type :latte}) => "Bought 4 cups
of latte for €3.8")
       (fact (display-order {:number 7 :price 6.3 :type :espresso}) => "Bought 7
cups of espresso for €6.3"))

(facts "Returned message should match regular expression"
       (fact (display-order {:number 7 :price 6.3 :type :espresso}) => #"Bought 7
cups")
       (fact (display-order {:number 7 :price 6.3 :type :espresso}) => #"cups of
espresso")
       (fact (display-order {:number 7 :price 6.3 :type :espresso}) => #"for €6.3"))
```

11. Create tests using the **Midje** library to checking whether the file exists:

```clojure
(facts "True should be returned when a file exists"
       (fact (file-exists "/tmp") => true)
       (fact (file-exists "/etc") => true))
(facts "False should be returned when a file does not exist"
       (fact (file-exists "no-file") => false)
       (fact (file-exists "missing-file") => false))
```

12. Create tests using the **Midje** library to load orders:

```clojure
(facts "Empty vector should be returned when there is no orders file"
       (fact (load-orders "/tmp/data.edn") => [])
       (fact (load-orders "/tmp/no-data.edn") => []))
```

The output is as follows:

```
$ lein repl
nREPL server started on port 35131 on host 127.0.0.1 - nrepl://127.0.0.1:35131
coffee-app.core=> (use 'midje.repl)
Run `(doc midje)` for Midje usage.
Run `(doc midje-repl)` for descriptions of Midje repl functions.
nil
coffee-app.core=> (autotest)


============================================================================
Loading (coffee-app.utils coffee-app.core coffee-app.utils-test-midje coffee-app.utils-test)
>>> Midje summary:
All checks (11) succeeded.

>>> Output from clojure.test tests:

Ran 9 tests containing 26 assertions.
0 failures, 0 errors.
[Completed at 19:33:21]
```

Figure 10.59: Test for loading orders using the Midje library

13. Create tests using **test.check** to displaying the orders messages. Import the **test. check** namespaces:

```
(ns coffee-app.utils-test-check
   (:require [coffee-app.utils :refer :all]
      [clojure.test.check :as tc]
      [clojure.test.check.generators :as gen]
      [clojure.test.check.properties :as prop]
      [clojure.test.check.clojure-test :refer [defspec]]))
```

14. Test displaying the order function:

```
(defspec display-order-test-check 1000
        (prop/for-all [order (gen/fmap (fn [[number type price]]
                                  {:number number
                                   :type type
                                   :price price})
                              (gen/tuple (gen/large-integer* {:min
                                 0})
```

```
                                              gen/keyword
                                              (gen/double* {:min 0.1 :max 999
  :infinite? false :NaN? false} )))]
                        (= (str "Bought " (:number order) " cups of " (name (:type
  order)) " for €" (:price order)) (display-order order))))
```

15. Create tests using **test.check** to check whether the file exists:

```
(defspec file-exists-test-check 1000
        (prop/for-all [file gen/string-alphanumeric]
                      (false? (file-exists file))))
```

16. Create tests using **test.check** to load orders:

```
(defspec load-orders-test-check 1000
        (prop/for-all [file gen/string-alphanumeric]
                      (vector? (load-orders file))))
```

The output is as follows:

```
$ lein test

lein test coffee-app.utils-test

lein test coffee-app.utils-test-check
{:result true, :num-tests 1000, :seed 1571837004058, :time-elapsed-ms 262, :test-var "load-orders-test-check"}
{:result true, :num-tests 1000, :seed 1571837004324, :time-elapsed-ms 214, :test-var "display-order-test-check"}
{:result true, :num-tests 1000, :seed 1571837004539, :time-elapsed-ms 221, :test-var "file-exists-test-check"}

Ran 12 tests containing 29 assertions.
0 failures, 0 errors.

Ran 0 tests containing 0 assertions in 0 msecs
0 failures, 0 errors.
```

Figure 10.60: Using test.check to create tests for loading orders

In this activity, we created a test suite for the coffee-ordering application. We wrote tests for utility functions using four unit testing libraries. We started with tests using **clojure.test**, followed by tests with **Expectations** and **Midje**. Finally, we wrote property-based tests using the **test.check** library.

Activity 10.02: Support Desk Application with Tests

Solution:

1. Add the testing dependencies to the **project.clj** file:

```
:dependencies [[org.clojure/test.check "0.10.0"]]
```

2. Import the namespaces to the **core_test.cljs** file:

```
(ns support-desk.core-test
  (:require
    [cljs.test :refer-macros [are deftest is testing use-fixtures]]
    [clojure.test.check.generators :as gen]
    [clojure.test.check.properties :refer-macros [for-all]]
    [clojure.test.check.clojure-test :refer-macros [defspec]]
    [cuerdas.core :as str]
    [support-desk.utils :refer [delete-item-from-list-by-title get-priorities-list
get-sort-message get-sorted-priorities-list handle-sort-finish]]))
```

3. Create fixtures with issues in the application state:

```
(ns support-desk.core-test)
(use-fixtures :each
              {:before (fn [] (do
                                (def priorities-list [{:title "IE bugs" :priority 2}
{:title "404 page" :priority 1} {:title "Forgotten username" :priority 2}
                                                      {:title "Login token"
:priority 1} {:title "Mobile version" :priority 3} {:title "Load time" :priority
5}])
                                (def app-state (atom {:sort-counter 0}))))})
```

4. Write tests for the sort message function using **cljs.test**:

```
(deftest get-sort-message-test
        (testing "Using is macro"
                (is (= "little (1)" (get-sort-message 1)))
                (is (= "medium (4)" (get-sort-message 4)))
                (is (= "many (8)" (get-sort-message 8))))
        (testing "Using are macro"
                (are [result number] (= result (get-sort-message number))
                        "little (1)" 1
                        "little (2)" 2
                        "medium (3)" 3
                        "medium (4)" 4
                        "medium (5)" 5
                        "many (6)" 6)))
```

5. Write tests for the sort message function using **test.check**:

```
(defspec get-sort-message-test-check 10
    (for-all [count gen/nat]
        (= (str/format "%s (%s)"
                    (cond
                        (< count 3) "little"
                        (< count 6) "medium"
                        :else "many")
                    count)
            (get-sort-message count))))
```

6. Write tests for the filter issues by priority function using **cljs.test**:

```
(deftest get-priorities-list-test
    (testing "Testing filtering priorities based on priority number"
        (is (= []
                (get-priorities-list priorities-list 0)))
        (is (= [{:title "404 page", :priority 1} {:title "Login token",
            :priority 1}]
                (get-priorities-list priorities-list 1)))
        (is (= [{:title "IE bugs", :priority 2}
                {:title "404 page", :priority 1}
                {:title "Forgotten username", :priority 2}
                {:title "Login token", :priority 1}]
                (get-priorities-list priorities-list 2)))
        (is (=
                [{:title "IE bugs", :priority 2}
                {:title "404 page", :priority 1}
                {:title "Forgotten username", :priority 2}
                {:title "Login token", :priority 1}
                {:title "Mobile version", :priority 3}]
                (get-priorities-list priorities-list 3)))))
```

7. Write tests to sort the issues list using **cljs.test**:

```
(deftest get-sorted-priorities-list-test
    (testing "Sorting priorities list"
        (is (= [{:title "404 page", :priority 1}
                {:title "Login token", :priority 1}
                {:title "IE bugs", :priority 2}
                {:title "Forgotten username", :priority 2}
                {:title "Mobile version", :priority 3}
                {:title "Load time", :priority 5}]
                (get-sorted-priorities-list priorities-list)))))
```

8. Write tests to delete issues from the list using `cljs.test`:

```
(deftest delete-item-from-list-by-title-test
        (testing "Passing empty list"
                (is (= []
                        (delete-item-from-list-by-title "Login token" [])))
                (is (= []
                        (delete-item-from-list-by-title "Login token" nil))))
        (testing "Passing valid list"
                (is (= (delete-item-from-list-by-title "Login token"
                        priorities-list)))))
```

9. Write tests for the handle the sort function using `cljs.test`:

```
(deftest handle-sort-finish-test
        (testing "Calling fn once"
                (is (= {:sort-counter 1}
                        ((handle-sort-finish app-state) "event"
                                "object"))))
        (testing "Calling fn twice"
                (is (= {:sort-counter 2}
                        ((handle-sort-finish app-state) "event"
                                "object")))))
```

10. We will use the command line to run the tests:

```
lein fig:test
```

When the tests are run, they should show the following:

```
$ lein fig:test
2019-11-20 12:12:55.301:INFO::main: Logging initialized @5773ms to org.eclipse.jetty.util.log.StdErrLog
[Figwheel] Validating figwheel-main.edn
[Figwheel] figwheel-main.edn is valid \(ツ)/
[Figwheel] Compiling build test to "resources/public/cljs-out/test-main.js"
[Figwheel] Successfully compiled build test to "resources/public/cljs-out/test-main.js" in 4.577 seconds.
Opening URL http://localhost:9500/test.html

Testing support-desk.utils-test
{:result true, :num-tests 10, :seed 1574248386648, :time-elapsed-ms 18, :test-var "get-sort-message-test-check"}

Ran 6 tests containing 20 assertions.
0 failures, 0 errors.
:figwheel.main.testing/success
```

Figure 10.61: Output after running the tests

In this activity, we added ClojureScript tests to a support desk application. We wrote unit tests using `cljs.test` and property-based tests using the `test.check` library.

Chapter 11: Macros

Activity 11.01: A Tennis CSV Macro

Solution:

1. Here is one possibility for the expanded code:

```clojure
(with-open [reader (io/reader csv)]
  (->> (csv/read-csv reader)
       sc/mappify
       (sc/cast-with {:winner_games_won sc/->int
                      :loser_games_won sc/->int})
       (map #(assoc % :games_diff (- (:winner_games_won %) (:loser_games_won %))))
       (filter #(> (:games_diff %) threshold))
       (map #(select-keys % [:winner_name :loser_name :games_diff]))
       doall))
```

This should be taken as a rough sketch for the final output.

2. Set up your project. The **deps.edn** file should look like this:

```clojure
{:deps
 {org.clojure/data.csv {:mvn/version "0.1.4"}
  semantic-csv {:mvn/version "0.2.1-alpha1"}
  org.clojure/math.numeric-tower {:mvn/version "0.0.4"}}}
```

The namespace declaration of the **tennis_macro.clj** file should look like this:

```clojure
(ns packt-clj.tennis-macro
    (:require [clojure.java.io :as io]
              [clojure.data.csv :as csv]
              [semantic-csv.core :as sc]))
```

3. The macro's call signature should look like this:

```clojure
(defmacro with-tennis-csv [csv casts fields & forms])
```

Because the macro needs to be able to handle a variable number of forms, we use **& forms**, which will provide us with a list of forms inside the body of the macro.

4. Add the **with-open** and **->>** expressions and add the threaded function calls that never change. Don't forget to use a gensym for the **reader** binding:

```
(defmacro with-tennis-csv [csv casts fields & forms]
  '(with-open [reader# (io/reader ~csv)]
     (->> (csv/read-csv reader#)
          sc/mappify
          (sc/cast-with ~casts)
          ;; TODO: what goes here?
          doall)))
```

It turns out that if **sc/cast-with** is supplied with an empty **map**, that is, no fields to change, it simply changes nothing. On the other hand, **select-keys** does the opposite: with no keys to preserve, it returns an empty **map**. It will require some more logic so that when no fields are provided, we get all the fields, rather than no fields at all. That's why we haven't included it yet.

5. Use unquote-splice (**~@**) to insert the threaded forms:

```
(defmacro with-tennis-csv [csv casts fields & forms]
  '(with-open [reader# (io/reader ~csv)]
     (->> (csv/read-csv reader#)
          sc/mappify
          (sc/cast-with ~casts)
          ~@forms
          ;; TODO: select-keys
          doall)))
```

6. We need a way to conditionally apply **select-keys**, depending on whether or not there are fields to select or not. There are a lot of ways to solve this, but perhaps the simplest is to define a specialized version of **select-keys**. We'll call it **maybe-select-keys**:

```
(defn maybe-select-keys [m maybe-keys]
  (if (seq maybe-keys)
    (select-keys m maybe-keys)
    m))
```

This allows us to add a call to **map** that can be the same, regardless of the presence of fields to select or not:

```
(defmacro with-tennis-csv [csv casts fields & forms]
  '(with-open [reader# (io/reader ~csv)]
     (->> (csv/read-csv reader#)
          sc/mappify
          (sc/cast-with ~casts)
          ~@forms
          (map #(maybe-select-keys % ~fields))
          doall)))
```

Many other solutions to this part of the problem probably involve referring to fields more than once. In these cases, a gensym should be used:

```
(let [fields# ~fields]

  )
```

7. Test the macro. Let's try it with the **blowouts** function (this assumes that the CSV file has been copied into the project directory):

```
user> (blowouts "match_scores_1991-2016_unindexed_csv.csv" 16)
({:winner_name "Jean-Philippe Fleurian",
  :loser_name "Renzo Furlan",
  :games_diff 17}
 {:winner_name "Todd Witsken",
  :loser_name "Kelly Jones",
  :games_diff 17}
 {:winner_name "Nicklas Kulti",
  :loser_name "German Lopez",
  :games_diff 17}
 {:winner_name "Jim Courier",
  :loser_name "Gilad Bloom",
  :games_diff 16}
 {:winner_name "Andrei Medvedev",
  :loser_name "Lars Koslowski",
  :games_diff 17}
 ;;; etc.
 )
```

These are the most lopsided victories in the dataset. Our macro seems to work.

Here, we've obtained a list of all the players who have defeated Roger Federer (from 1991 to 2016):

```
user> (with-tennis-csv "match_scores_1991-2016_unindexed_csv.csv"
    {}
    [:winner_name]
    (filter #(= "Roger Federer" (:loser_name %))))
({:winner_name "Lucas Arnold Ker"}
 {:winner_name "Jan Siemerink"}
 {:winner_name "Andre Agassi"}
 {:winner_name "Arnaud Clement"}
 {:winner_name "Yevgeny Kafelnikov"}
 {:winner_name "Kenneth Carlsen"}
 {:winner_name "Vincent Spadea"}
 {:winner_name "Patrick Rafter"}
 {:winner_name "Byron Black"}
;; .... etc.
)
```

There is one question that should always be asked when writing a macro: could this be a function instead? The answer here is probably somewhere between "yes" and "maybe."

One approach might be to write a function that simply extracts all the data from the CSV file. After passing through **doall**, any kind of transformation would be possible. With this solution, however, the benefits of lazy evaluation would be lost, which means that the entire CSV file would need to be loaded into memory. If one of the processing steps involves filtering out some of the matches, the macro solution would be more efficient because the filtering would occur before the entire file was read.

Another approach would be to use functional composition. The user would supply a series of functions that would be wrapped inside a single function called from inside the **with-open** macro. This approach would preserve the advantages of lazy evaluation. However, the supplied functions would have to be written in a precise way that might not be as clear. Here, we've been writing the following:

```
(filter #(> (:games_diff %) threshold))
```

Instead, we would have to define a function:

```
(fn [ms] (filter #(> (:games_diff %)) threshold))
```

This might not be a deal-breaker. Everything depends on the intended use and the intended audience. Macros can often provide a very flexible interface, which can be an important factor in choosing to use them.

When you find yourself repeating code that cannot be easily encapsulated with functions, for whatever reason, writing a macro can often be the solution. In this case, as in *Exercise 11.04, Monitoring Functions* writing a macro is probably the least obtrusive way to simplify your code. Writing a macro is always a trade-off in terms of added complexity: as we said at the beginning of this chapter, macro code is hard to debug, and it can make the rest of your code harder to debug as well. But, as is often said, code you never need to debug is code you don't have to write. So, if a solid macro can help you avoid writing many lines of code, it might be worth it.

Chapter 12: Concurrency

Activity 12.01: A DOM Whack-a-mole Game

Solution:

1. Create a project with **lein figwheel**:

```
lein new figwheel packt-clj.dom-whackamole -- --rum
```

2. Move to the new **packt-clj.dom-whackamole** directory and start a ClojureScript REPL:

```
lein figwheel
```

   In your browser, at **localhost:3449/index.html**, you should see the default Figwheel page:

Figure 12.26: Default Figwheel page

3. Open **dom-whackamole/src/packt-clj/dom-whackamole/core.cljs** in your editor or IDE. This is where you will write all the remaining code.

4. Define the atoms that will determine the game's state:

```
(def game-length-in-seconds 20)

(def millis-remaining (atom (* game-length-in-seconds 1000)))
(def points (atom 0))
(def game-state (atom :waiting))
(def clock-interval (atom nil))

(def moles (atom (into []
              (repeat 5 {:status :waiting
                   :remaining-millis 0}))))
```

Most of these are fairly self-explanatory. The **clock-interval** atom will be set to a JavaScript interval when the game starts. Defining **game-length-in-seconds** and then multiplying by 1,000 isn't necessary but it helps to make our code more readable.

The **moles** atom will be a vector of maps with **:status** and **:remaining-millis** fields. Why type out five identical maps when **repeat** can do the work for us? Later, we'll update the moles using their index in the vector, which is why we really want to have a vector here, and not a list. By itself, **repeat** would return a simple list. To avoid that, we use **(into [] …)** to be sure we have a real vector.

5. Another equally valid approach would be to wrap all of these items in a single atom that could be structured like this:

```
(def app-state
  (atom
   {:points 0
    :millis-remaining (* game-length-in-seconds 1000)
    :game-state :waiting
    :clock-interval nil
    :moles (into []
             (repeat 5 {:status :waiting
                        :remaining-millis 0}))}))
```

This approach would mean changing most of the functions involving data access but would not fundamentally change how the game is built.

> **Note**
>
> Generally, in more complex applications, the single atom approach would be preferable. The downside to this is that any change to the atom would cause all the components to update. If only one part of the multi-level map contained in the atom has changed, many of these updates would be useless. To avoid this, React-based ClojureScript frameworks all have some means for tracking changes to only one part of the application state atom. Rum, as well as Om and Reagent, calls these cursors. A cursor allows a component to listen to a particular part of the atom state, thus avoiding unnecessary re-renders when unrelated parts of the atom change.

6. Define functions for making changes to the application state atoms:

```
(defn activate-mole [mole-idx]
  (swap! moles
    (fn [ms]
      (update ms mole-idx
        #(if (= :waiting (:status %))
          {:status :live :remaining-millis 3000}
          %)))))
(defn deactivate-mole [mole-idx]
  (swap! moles
    (fn [ms]
      (assoc ms mole-idx
        {:status :waiting :remaining-millis 0})))))
```

7. The first two functions are fairly straightforward. **activate-mole** uses **update** instead of **assoc** in order to test whether the mole is already activated or not. If it is already **:live**, we don't want to change the number of remaining milliseconds back to 3,000:

core.cljs

```
43 (defn mole-countdown []
44   (swap! moles
45     (fn [ms]
46       (into []
47         (map (fn [m]
48           (if (= (:status m) :live)
49             (let [new-remaining (max (- (:remaining-millis m) 100)
               0)]
50               (if (pos? new-remaining)
51                 (assoc m :remaining-millis new-remaining)
52                 {:status :waiting :remaining-millis 0}))
53               m))
54           ms)))))
```

The full code for this step is available at https://packt.live/2Rmq8aq.

These functions are the heart of the game's logic.

The first function, **mole-countdown**, removes 100 from the **:remaining-millis** field of any active moles. To do this, it maps over the list of moles. If a mole is not **:live**, it is left alone. (We can't use **filter** here because we don't want to eliminate the inactive moles; we only want to ignore them.) If the mole is **:live**, we subtract 100 from the remaining time. If there is still time left, we just update the remaining time in the mole. If we've reached zero, though, we set the status back to **:waiting**. This is the case when the player has not clicked on the mole after 3 seconds.

The next function, **update-moles**, will be called on each 100-millisecond tick of the game clock. It calls **mole-countdown** and then checks whether there are enough active moles in the list. If there aren't two active moles, **activate-mole** is called with a random index between 0 and 4.

You might be surprised that we don't check to see whether the mole we are activating here is already :**live** or not. Because this check will happen every 100 milliseconds (and because the gameplay of Whack-a-mole doesn't require extreme precision), we can avoid doing so. If we try to activate an already active mole, nothing will happen (thanks to how we wrote **activate-mole**) and we can try again on the next clock tick.

The **reset-moles** function will be called when the game clock gets to zero. All the moles hide when the game is over.

Finally, the **whack!** function will actually be the click handler. It looks up the mole by its index and then calls **deactivite-mole** if the mole happens to be :**live**, in which case it also adds a point to the player's score.

It's important to note here that all of these functions interact directly with the atoms. They all use **deref** (via the @ reader macro) and not **rum/react**. All of this logic, so far, is independent of the Rum components.

8. Write the game clock functions:

```
(defn clock-tick []
  (if (= @millis-remaining 0)
    (do
      (reset! game-state :waiting)
      (reset-moles))
    (do
      (update-moles)
      (swap! millis-remaining #(- % 100)))))

(defn start-clock []
  (when @clock-interval
    (js/clearInterval @clock-interval))
  (swap! clock-interval
      (fn [] (js/setInterval clock-tick 100))))
```

The **clock-tick** function determines what happens every 100 milliseconds. Either the game is over (**millis-remaining** has reached zero) or it is still going. If the game is over, we reset the moles and change the game state back to :**waiting**. If not, we call **update-moles** to advance their internal time counters and then we advance the global **millis-remaining** atom.

The **start-clock** function does just that. The first step here is to check for an existing interval and stop it. We definitely don't want more than one interval running at the same time. (If you notice the clock running at a very fast rate, that is probably what is happening.)

Our call to **swap!** is then just a call to **setInterval** with the **clock-tick** function and the 100-millisecond interval.

9. Now we're ready to write our **start-game** function that will be called when the user clicks on the **Start** button:

```
(defn start-game []
 (start-clock)
 (reset! game-state :playing)
 (reset! points 0)
 (reset! millis-remaining (* game-length-in-seconds 1000)))
```

10. Let's start writing some simple Rum components that just display the current state:

```
(rum/defc clock < rum/reactive []
 [:div.clock
  [:span "Remaining time: "]
  [:span.time
   (Math/floor (/ (rum/react millis-remaining) 1000))]])

(rum/defc score < rum/reactive []
 [:div.score
  [:span "Score: "]
  [:span (rum/react points)]])
```

The **clock** and **score** views simply display those values. Since we don't want to actually display milliseconds on the clock, we divide by 1,000. And since we don't want show times like 5.034, we round down using the **floor** method from the JavaScript **Math** library. (Don't worry if you don't know about this JavaScript library: displaying milliseconds works fine for this exercise.)

11. Write a component for the **start-game** button:

```
(rum/defc start-game-button < rum/reactive []
 (if (= (rum/react game-state) :waiting)
  [:button
   {:onClick start-game}
   "Click to play!"]
  [:div "Game on!"]))
```

The **start-game-button** view observes the **game-state** atom and shows either a **Click to play!** button or an encouraging message.

12. Write the mole views:

```
(rum/defc single-mole-view [mole-idx {:keys [status remaining-millis]}]
  [:div {:class [(str "mole " (name status))]}
   [:a {:onClick (partial whack! mole-idx)}
   (str "MOLE " (name status) "!")]])


(rum/defc moles-view < rum/reactive []
  (let [ms (rum/react moles)]
   [:div {:class "game moles"}
    (single-mole-view 0 (first ms))
    (single-mole-view 1 (second ms))
    (single-mole-view 2 (nth ms 2))
    (single-mole-view 3 (nth ms 3))
    (single-mole-view 4 (nth ms 4))]))
```

A lot of important game logic is related to the moles, so we split out a separate **mole** component. Notice that **single-mole-view** does not have the **< rum/reactive** mixin. These views will get all of their props from their parent view. As a result, they do not need to react directly to changes in the atoms; they will receive the changes through their arguments.

The **single-mole-view** displays the state of the mole, **:waiting** or **:live**, and sets up the click handler. We've set up the **whack!** function to do nothing if the mole's status is **:waiting**, so we don't have to add any logic about that here.

The **moles-view** simply wraps the calls to **single-mole-view** in a **<div>** element and provides them with the appropriate data from the **moles** atom.

13. Write the base view:

```
(rum/defc app []
  [:div#main
   [:div.header
   [:h1 "Welcome to DOM Whack-a-mole"]
   [:p "When a MOLE goes goes 'live', click on it as fast as you can."]
   (start-game-button)
   (clock)
   (score)]
   (moles-view)])
```

The **app** view simply reunites all the previous views in a single while providing some additional presentation.

14. Make sure that you the **app** view is mounted at the end of your file:

```
(defn on-js-reload []
  (rum/mount (app) (.getElementById js/document "app")))


(on-js-reload)
```

The call to **on-js-reload** ensures that your code is read again when the browser reloads.

Now you can play the game!:

Welcome to DOM Whack-a-mole

When a MOLE goes goes 'live', click on it as fast as you can.

Game on!
Remaining time: 11
Score: 7
MOLE waiting!
MOLE live!
MOLE live!
MOLE waiting!
MOLE waiting!

Figure 12.27: Playing DOM Whack-a-mole

Chapter 13: Database Interaction and the Application Layer

Activity 13.01: Persisting Historic Tennis Results and ELO Calculations

Solution:

1. In a new project, begin with the following dependencies:

```
{:deps {clojure.java-time {:mvn/version "0.3.2"}
        hikari-cp {:mvn/version "2.8.0"}
        org.apache.derby/derby {:mvn/version "10.14.2.0"}
        org.clojure/data.csv {:mvn/version "0.1.4"}
        org.clojure/java.jdbc {:mvn/version "0.7.9"}
        semantic-csv {:mvn/version "0.2.1-alpha1"}}}
```

2. In our **src** directory, create the following namespaces:

```
packt-clj.tennis.database
packt-clj.tennis.elo
packt-clj.tennis.ingest
packt-clj.tennis.parse
packt-clj.tennis.query
```

3. Creating our connection pool in the database namespace is straightforward using **hikari**:

```
(ns packt-clj.tennis.database
  (:require
    [hikari-cp.core :as hikari]))
(def db {:datasource (hikari/make-datasource {:jdbc-url
"jdbc:derby:tennis;create=true"})})
```

4. Our DDL should look similar to the following. Field data types may vary, although not significantly:

```
(def ^:private create-player-ddl "CREATE TABLE player (
  id varchar(4) CONSTRAINT PLAYER_ID_PK PRIMARY KEY,
  full_name varchar(128))")
(def ^:private create-tennis-match-ddl "CREATE TABLE tennis_match (
  id varchar(32) CONSTRAINT MATCH_ID_PK PRIMARY KEY,
  tournament_year int,
  tournament varchar(32),
  tournament_order int,
  round_order int,
  match_order int,
  winner_id varchar(4) REFERENCES player(id) ON DELETE CASCADE,
```

```
    loser_id varchar(4) REFERENCES player(id) ON DELETE CASCADE)")
(def ^:private create-elo-ddl "CREATE TABLE elo (
    id int GENERATED ALWAYS AS IDENTITY CONSTRAINT ELO_ID_PK PRIMARY KEY,
    player_id varchar(4) REFERENCES player(id) ON DELETE CASCADE,
    rating DECIMAL(6,2))")
```

5. Leveraging **clojure.java.jdbc**, we can apply the schema, taking care of the ordering:

```
(ns packt-clj.tennis.database
  (:require
    [clojure.java.jdbc :as jdbc]
    [hikari-cp.core :as hikari]))
(defn load []
  (jdbc/db-do-commands db [create-player-ddl create-tennis-match-ddl create-elo-
ddl]))
(require '[packt-clj.tennis.database :as database])
user=> (database/load)
(0 0 0)
```

6. This is perhaps one of the more creative aspects of the activity, meaning that there are many ways to solve the problem, with the following only being one of them.

   In the **parse** namespace, we begin by defining the accessors required to extract each of the fields we're interested in:

```
(ns packt-clj.tennis.parse
  (:require
    [clojure.string :as str]))
(def ^:private winning-player-accessors
  {:id         :winner_player_id
   :full_name :winner_name})
(def ^:private losing-player-accessors
  {:id         :loser_player_id
   :full_name :loser_name})
(def ^:private match-accessors
  {:id                 #(str (:match_id %) "-" (:round_order %))
   :tournament_year   (comp first #(str/split % #"-") :tourney_year_id)
   :tournament        :tourney_slug
   :tournament_order  :tourney_order
   :round_order       :round_order
   :match_order       :match_order
   :winner_id         :winner_player_id
   :loser_id          :loser_player_id})
```

Each preceding definition is a map of **target-key** (that is, where we want to store the value in our data structure) to **accessor** (that is, a single-arity function that, given a row, will extract, format, and aggregate fields as required).

7. We can then define a function that will perform the application of these accessors on any given row:

```
(defn apply-accessors
  [row accessors]
  (reduce-kv
    (fn [acc target-key accessor]
      (assoc acc target-key (accessor row)))
    {}
    accessors))
```

8. Some well-named helper functions can be defined to perform the extraction for each of our target structures, which are combined in a simple **parse-row** function:

```
(defn extract-winning-player
  [row]
  (apply-accessors row winning-player-accessors))
(defn extract-losing-player
  [row]
  (apply-accessors row losing-player-accessors))
(defn extract-match
  [row]
  (apply-accessors row match-accessors))
(defn parse-row
  [row]
  {:winning-player (extract-winning-player row)
   :losing-player  (extract-losing-player row)
   :match          (extract-match row)})
```

9. Finally, we can combine these into our historic function as follows, adding the relevant requires:

```
(ns packt-clj.tennis.parse
  (:require
    [clojure.data.csv :as csv]
    [clojure.java.io :as io]
    [clojure.string :as str]
    [semantic-csv.core :as sc]))
(defn new-player?
  [seen candidate]
  (not (seen (:id candidate))))
```

```
(defn historic
  [file-path]
  (->> (io/reader file-path)
       (csv/read-csv)
       sc/mappify
       (reduce (fn
                 [{:keys [player-ids-seen] :as acc} row]
                 (let [{:keys [winning-player losing-player match]} (parse-row row)
                       new-players (filter #(new-player? player-ids-seen %) [winning-
player losing-player])]
                   (-> acc
                       (update-in [:data :players] into new-players)
                       update-in [:data :matches] conj match)
                       (update :player-ids-seen into (map :id new-players)))))
               {:player-ids-seen #{}
                :data            {:players []
                                  :matches []}})
       :data))
```

The **reduce** function we've defined here begins by parsing the incoming row into the three target data structures we're interested in: the players (**winning** and **losing**) as well as the match itself. We then check to ensure we're only going to persist a player if we've not already seen it. We do this by checking against the **player-ids-seen** set using the appropriately named **helper** function.

Finally, we use the thread-first macro to maintain our accumulator, adding new players/matches and maintaining the set of player IDs we've already processed, before extracting the **:data** portion of the map and returning.

10. In the **ingest** namespace, a simple call to **parse/historic**, along with a destructure in our **let** binding, is enough to extract the players and matches we are going to insert into the **db** variable:

```
(ns packt-clj.tennis.ingest
  (:require
    [packt-clj.tennis.parse :as parse]
    [clojure.java.jdbc :as jdbc]))
(defn historic
  [db file-path]
  (let [{:keys [players matches]} (parse/historic file-path)]
    (jdbc/insert-multi! db :player players)
    (jdbc/insert-multi! db :tennis_match matches)))
```

11. Having taken the **match_scores_1991-2016_unindexed_csv.csv** file and placed it in the **resources** directory, we can now ingest our historic data and perform a few sanity checks to see whether our **player** and **tennis_match** counts match those as follows:

```
(require '[packt-clj.tennis.ingest :as ingest]
         '[clojure.java.jdbc :as jdbc]
         '[clojure.java.io :as io]
          '[packt-clj.tennis.database :as database])
user=> (ingest/historic database/db (io/file "packt-clj/resources/match_scores_1991-
2016_unindexed_csv.csv"))
user=> (jdbc/query database/db ["select count(*) from player"])
=> ({:1 3483})
user=> (jdbc/query database/db ["select count(*) from tennis_match"])
=> ({:1 95359})
```

12. The SQL to extract all tennis matches in the **query** namespace is fairly straightforward; however, attention should be drawn to the **round_order desc**. Since **round_order** *decreases* as the tournament progresses, we must sort this into reverse order:

```
(ns packt-clj.tennis.query
  (:require
    [clojure.java.jdbc :as jdbc]))
(defn all-tennis-matches
  [db]
  (jdbc/query db ["select *
              from tennis_match
                  order by tournament_year, tournament_order, round_order desc,
match_order"]))
```

13. Leveraging our functions from *Chapter 5*, *Many to One: Reducing*, our **elo** namespace starts off as follows:

```
(ns packt-clj.tennis.elo
  (:require
    [clojure.java.jdbc :as jdbc]
    [packt-clj.tennis.query :as query]))=
(def k-factor 32)
(defn match-probability [player-1-rating player-2-rating]
  (/ 1
      (+ 1 (Math/pow 10 (/ (- player-2-rating player-1-rating) 1000)))))
(defn recalculate-rating [previous-rating expected-outcome real-outcome]
  (+ previous-rating (* k-factor (- real-outcome expected-outcome))))
```

14. Calculating the ELO rating for all matches can be achieved as follows. First, we can define two helper functions, the first of which yields a tuple of expected outcomes. Since probabilities must sum to 1, we can calculate one probability and then subtract it from 1 to get the other probability:

```
(defn- expected-outcomes
  [winner-rating loser-rating]
  (let [winner-expected-outcome (match-probability winner-rating loser-rating)]
    [winner-expected-outcome (- 1 winner-expected-outcome)]))
```

15. We then destructure the tuple in the body of our second helper function, which allows us to calculate the new ratings for each player returning an updated player data structure that is destructured in **calculate-all**:

```
(defn- calculate-new-ratings [current-player-ratings {:keys [winner_id loser_id]}]
  (let [winner-rating (get current-player-ratings winner_id 1000)
        loser-rating  (get current-player-ratings loser_id 1000)
        [winner-expected-outcome loser-expected-outcome] (expected-outcomes winner-
rating loser-rating)]
    [{:player_id winner_id
      :rating    (recalculate-rating winner-rating winner-expected-outcome 1)}
     {:player_id loser_id
      :rating    (recalculate-rating loser-rating loser-expected-outcome 0)}]))
```

16. Finally, we destructure the result of the call to **calculate-new-ratings**, extracting the **winner** and **loser** IDs so that we can update the **current-player-ratings** data structure for the next iteration:

```
(defn calculate-all
  [db]
  (->> (query/all-tennis-matches db)
       (reduce
         (fn [{:keys [current-player-ratings] :as acc} match]
           (let [[[{winner-id :player_id :as new-winner-rating} {loser-id :player_id
:as new-loser-rating}] (calculate-new-ratings current-player-ratings match)]
             (-> acc
                 (update :elo-ratings into [new-winner-rating
                                            new-loser-rating])
                 (assoc-in [:current-player-ratings winner-id] (:rating new-winner-
rating))
                 (assoc-in [:current-player-ratings loser-id] (:rating new-loser-
rating)))))
         {:elo-ratings            []
          :current-player-ratings {}})
       :elo-ratings))
```

Using **winner_id** and **loser_id** for the current match, we can look up their existing ratings in our accumulator (defaulting to **1000**) if they're not found. Next, we determine the expected outcomes using the function described previously. Once we have that, we can plug this into the **recalculate-rating** function and store the updated values in our accumulator for the next iteration.

current-player-rating is effectively an in-memory cache; we would not want to persist ratings to the database only to look them up again.

17. It is also more performant to do a single call to **jdbc/insert-multi!** in the **persist-all** function than it is to persist as we go:

```
(defn persist-all
  [db]
  (let [elo-ratings (calculate-all db)]
    (jdbc/insert-multi! db :elo elo-ratings)))


user=>(require '[packt-clj.tennis.elo :as elo]
               '[packt-clj.tennis.query :as query])
nil
user=> (elo/persist-all database/db)
```

18. The SQL required to extract all names and ratings is straightforward. Bolting on a **result-set-fn** function that iterates over the results one at a time is straightforward and intuitive, if less performant than a raw SQL approach:

```
(defn select-max-elo
  [db]
  (jdbc/query db ["select p.full_name, e.rating
                   from player p, elo e
                   where p.id = e.player_id"]
              {:result-set-fn (fn [rs]
                                (reduce (fn [{:keys [max-rating] :as acc} {:keys
                                         [full_name rating]}]
                                          (cond-> acc

                                            (< max-rating rating) (assoc
                                             :max-rating rating
                                             :player-name full_name)))
                                        {:max-rating Integer/MIN_VALUE
                                         :player-name nil}
                                        rs))}))
```

We begin by defining the maximum rating as the smallest integer, guaranteeing that it won't end up featuring in our final result! A simple comparison of the existing highest rating with the candidate rating allows us to determine whether we update our accumulator using the conditional thread-first macro.

19. Finally, let's confirm that the player with the highest ELO value matches what was expected:

```
user => (query/select-max-elo database/db)
=> {:max-rating 2974.61M, :player-name "Novak Djokovic"}
```

Excellent! We've successfully built an application layer allowing us to ingest, query, and perform calculations on our large tennis results CSV dataset. Anyone new to the application should be able to grasp the purpose of it from the namespaces alone. The intention of each individual function, when taken in the context of the namespace, should also be clear.

Chapter 14: HTTP with Ring

Activity 14.01: Exposing Historic Tennis Results and ELO Calculations via REST

Solution:

1. Add the following dependencies to **packt-clj.tennis** in the **deps.edn** file:

```
{:deps {..
        clj-http {:mvn/version "3.10.0"}
        compojure {:mvn/version "1.6.1"}
        metosin/muuntaja {:mvn/version "0.6.4"}
        org.clojure/data.json {:mvn/version "0.2.6"}
        ring/ring-core {:mvn/version "1.7.1"}
        ring/ring-jetty-adapter {:mvn/version "1.7.1"}}}
```

2. Create our namespace with the following **require** route:

```
(ns packt-clj.tennis.api
  (:require
    [clojure.edn :as edn]
    [compojure.core :refer [context defroutes GET PUT]]
    [compojure.route :as route]
    [muuntaja.middleware :as middleware]
    [packt-clj.tennis.database :as database]
    [packt-clj.tennis.elo :as elo]
    [packt-clj.fitness.ingest :as ingest]
    [packt-clj.tennis.query :as query]
    [ring.adapter.jetty :refer [run-jetty]]
    [ring.middleware.params :as params]))
```

3. The routes required to expose our player resources and the tennis matches they've taken part in are as follows:

```
(defroutes routes
        (context "/players" []
          (GET "/" []
            {:body (query/all-players database/db)})
          (GET "/:id" [id]
            (when-first [user (query/player database/db id)]
              {:body user}))
          (GET "/:id/tennis-matches" [id]
            {:body (query/tennis-matches-by-player database/db id)}))
        (route/not-found "Not found"))
```

4. The **query** functions referenced are defined in the **query** namespace like so:

```
(defn all-players
  [db]
  (jdbc/query db ["select * from player"]))
(defn player
  [db id]
  (jdbc/query db [(str "select * from player where id = '" id "'")]))
(defn tennis-matches-by-player
  [db id]
  (jdbc/query db [(str "select * from tennis_match
                  where winner_id = '" id "' or loser_id = '" id "'")]))
```

5. Our **run** function looks similar to that we've used before, leveraging the **wrap-format** and **wrap-params** middleware:

```
(defn run
  []
  (run-jetty
    (-> routes
        middleware/wrap-format
        params/wrap-params)
    {:port  8080
     :join? false}))
```

6. We can add the following route to our **players** context for ELO retrieval, along with the means to extract it from our **query** namespace:

```
(GET "/:id/elo" [id]
              (when-first [elo (query/player-elo database/db id)]
                {:body elo}))
(defn player-elo
  [db id]
  (jdbc/query db [(str "select e.rating, e.id
                   from elo e, player p
                   where e.player_id = p.id and
                   p.id = '" id "' and
                   e.id in (select max(e2.id)
                            from elo e2
                            where e2.player_id = '" id "')")]))
```

7. Define a new **tennis-matches** context, along with the new **query/tennis-match** function:

```
(context "/tennis-matches" []
          (GET "/" []
            {:body (query/all-tennis-matches database/db)})
          (GET "/:id" [id]
            (when-first [tennis-match (query/tennis-match database/db id)]
              {:body tennis-match})))

(defn tennis-match
  [db id]
  (jdbc/query db [(str "select * from tennis_match where id = '" id "'")]))
```

Optionally, if starting from a clean database, we can populate it with relevant data using the following:

```
(require '[packt-clj.tennis.database :as database]
         '[packt-clj.tennis.ingest :as ingest]
         '[packt-clj.tennis.elo :as elo])
(database/load)
(ingest/historic database/db "./resources/match_scores_1991-2016_unindexed_csv.csv")
(elo/persist-all database/db)
```

8. After starting the web server, we can use a browser to retrieve the current ELOs for reference:

```
(require '[packt-clj.tennis.api :as api])
(def app (api/run))
```

The output is as follows:

← → C ⌂   ⓘ localhost:8080/players/s402/elo

{"rating":1770.13,"id":77743}

Figure 14.22: Printing Sampras' current rating

Printing the current rating of **Djokovic**:

`{"rating":2855.24,"id":190718}`

Figure 14.23: Printing Djokovic's current rating

9. We define our **tennis-match** creation route using **PUT** since we know the ID ahead of time. This is added to the **tennis-matches** context. We must query the ELO of the two players involved in the match, then create a new record for each of them with their updated ELO. This requires a new **ingest/tennis-match** and **elo/persist** functions, as shown. Note that the **elo/calculate-new-ratings** function should now be marked as public (**defn** rather than **defn-**) now that we require it outside of the **elo** namespace:

```clojure
(defn tennis-match
  [db tennis-match]
  (first (jdbc/insert! db :tennis_match tennis-match)))
(defn persist
  [db elo-ratings]
  (jdbc/insert-multi! db :elo elo-ratings))
(PUT "/:id" req
                (let [id (-> req :params :id)
                        {:keys [winner_id loser_id] :as tennis-match} (assoc (edn/read-
  string (slurp (:body req)))
                                                                             :id id)
                        [{winner-elo :rating}] (query/player-elo database/db
                          winner_id)
                        [{loser-elo :rating}] (query/player-elo database/db
                          loser_id)
                        new-player-ratings (elo/**calculate-new-ratings**
                                          {winner_id winner-elo
                                           loser_id  loser-elo}
                                          tennis-match)]
                  (ingest/tennis-match database/db tennis-match)
                  (elo/persist database/db new-player-ratings)
                  {:status  201
                   :headers {"Link" (str "/tennis-matches/" id)}}))
```

After restarting our app, we can use **clj-http** to submit a **PUT** instruction to our web service as follows:

```
(.stop app)
(def app (api/run))
(require '[clj-http.client :as http])
(http/put "http://localhost:8080/tennis-matches/2019-1-d643-s403-5"
          {:body (pr-str {:tournament_year  2019,
                          :tournament       "umag",
                          :tournament_order 1,
                          :round_order      5,
                          :match_order      1,
                          :winner_id        "d643",
                          :loser_id         "s402"})})
```

10. Since Sampras lost our fictitious match, we see his ELO decrease slightly, while Djokovic's has increased:

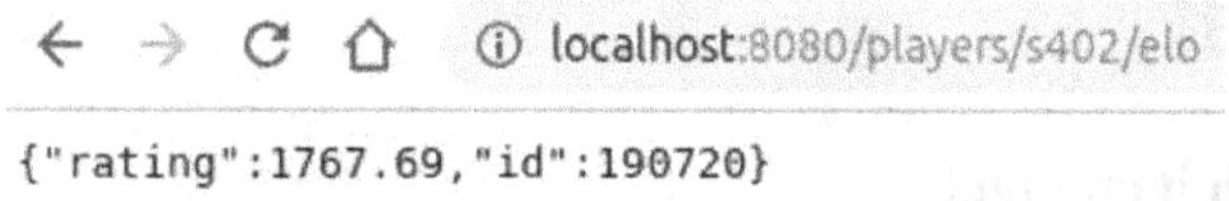

```
{"rating":1767.69,"id":190720}
```

Figure 14.24: Printing Sampras' rating

Following are Djokovic's ratings:

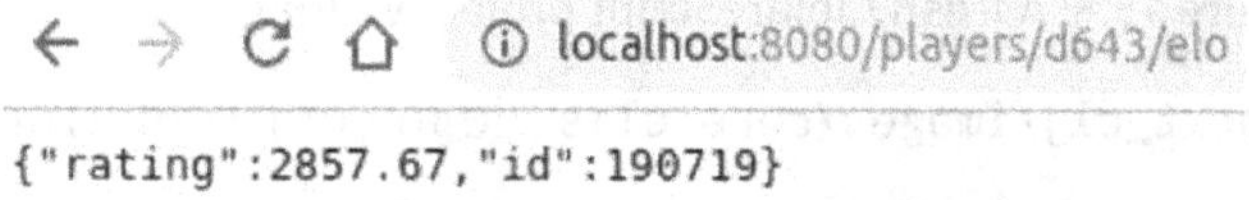

```
{"rating":2857.67,"id":190719}
```

Figure 14.25: Printing Djokovic's current rating

Thus, by completing this activity, we have made our application layer more widely available via a REST web service.

Chapter 15: The Frontend: A ClojureScript UI

Activity 15.01: Displaying a Grid of Images from the Internet

Solution:

1. At the command-line prompt, create a new Figwheel project using the following Leiningen command:

```
lein new figwheel packt-clj.images -- --reagent
```

2. Move to the **packt-clj.images/** directory and type:

```
lein figwheel
```

After a few seconds, your browser should open to the default Figwheel page:

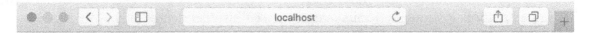

Hello world!

Edit this and watch it change!

Figure 15.8: A fresh ClojureScript project waiting for your code

3. Open the **src/packt_clj/images/core.cljs** file in your preferred editor and modify the code:

```
(ns packt-clj.images.core
    (:require [reagent.core :as r]))
```

4. The commonly used alias for Reagent is **r** instead of Reagent:

```
(defonce app-state (r/atom {:images []
                            :author-display true}))
```

The **app-state** is made of two pieces of data: a vector of images that we fetched, initially an empty vector, and whether to display the author's name, initially true.

5. Let's create a button that fetches images from the HTTP endpoint and updates the `:images` value of the **app-state**. We need two handlers: **fetch-images**, which updates `:images` in the **app** state with a vector of images, and **clear-images**, which updates `:images` in the **app** state with an empty vector:

```
(defn fetch-images []
  (-> (js/fetch "https://picsum.photos/v2/list?limit=6")
        (. then (fn [response] (.json response)))
        (. then (fn [json] (swap! app-state assoc-in [:images] (js->clj json
:keywordize-keys true))))))
(defn clear-images []
      (swap! app-state assoc-in [:images] []))
```

6. And here is the code for the **fetch-or-clear-button** component:

```
(defn fetch-or-clear-button []
    (let [handler (if (empty? (:images @app-state)) fetch-images clear-images)
          text    (if (empty? (:images @app-state)) "Fetch Images" "Clear Images")]
        [:button.btn {:on-click handler} text]))
```

7. We apply the **btn** class to the button by using the **:button.btn** short Hiccup syntax. The **btn** class is defined in **resources/public/css/style.css**:

```
.btn {
  padding: 7px 20px;
  cursor: pointer;
  margin-left: 10px;
  margin-bottom: 10px;
  border: 1px solid gray;
}
```

8. Let's build an **image** component and an **image-grid** component:

```
(defn image [{:keys [download_url author]}]
  [:div
   [:img {:src download_url
              :height "130px"
              :style {:border "solid gray 3px"
                           :border-radius "10px"}}]
     (when (:author-display @app-state)
       [:div {:style {:font-size "15px"
                           :color "gray" }}
         (str "Image by ") author])])

(defn image-grid [images]
    (if (empty? images)
```

```
            [:div "Click the button to fetch images"]
            (into [:div] (map (fn [image-data] [:div {:style {:float "left"
                                                               :margin-left "20px"}}
        [image image-data]])
                                              images))))
```

9. The last component is a button that hides or displays author names:

```
(defn author-display-button []
  (let [text (if (:author-display @app-state)
                "Hide author"
                "Show author")]
    [:button.btn {:on-click #(swap! app-state update-in [:author-display] not)}
       text]))
```

10. Now, we add all the components as children of the **main** component. We renamed the **hello-world** function **app**:

```
(defn app []
  [:div
   [fetch-or-clear-button]
   [author-display-button]
   [image-grid (:images @app-state)]])
```

11. Finally, we render the main component (named **app** instead of **hello-world**):

```
(r/render-component [app] (. js/document (getElementById "app")))
```

If everything went well, you should see a screen like this:

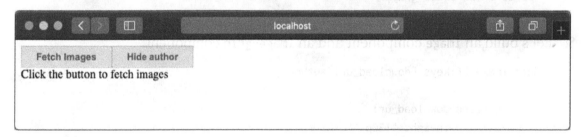

Figure 15.9: Buttons to fetch and clear images

When you click on the **Fetch Images** button, the images appear with authors' names:

Figure 15.10: Fetching the images

Finally, when you click on the **Hide author** button, the authors' names disappear:

Figure 15.11: Hiding the authors

Here, we have created a single-page application that can load and clear images and text as required.

Activity 15.02: Tennis Players with Ranking

Solution:

1. At the command-line prompt, create a new Figwheel project using the following Leiningen command:

```
lein new figwheel packt-clj.tennis -- --reagent
```

2. Move to the **packt-clj.tennis/** directory and type the following:

```
lein figwheel
```

   After a few seconds, your browser should open to the default Figwheel page:

Hello world!

Edit this and watch it change!

Figure 15.12: A fresh ClojureScript project waiting for your code

3. Open the **src/packt_clj/tennis/core.cljs** file in your preferred editor and modify the code:

```
(ns packt-clj.tennis.core
    (:require [reagent.core :as r]))
```

   app-state consists of the list of players and the details about the currently selected player.

4. We start with an empty list of players:

```
(defonce app-state (r/atom {:players []
                            :current-player nil}))
```

5. Here is the code that fetches the ranking data from the server about a specific player:

```
(defn fetch-player [id full_name]
  (-> (js/fetch (str "http://localhost:8080/players/" id "/elo"))
      (.then (fn [response] (.json response)))
      (.then (fn [json] (swap! app-state assoc-in [:current-player] (assoc (js->clj
json :keywordize-keys true)
                                                                          :full_name
full_name))))))
```

6. Here is a player component that displays the name of a player and their ranking:

```
(defn player-alone [{:keys [rating full_name]}]
  [:div
   (str full_name " has a rating of: " rating)])
```

7. Let's create a button that clears the current player and goes back to the list of all the players:

```
(defn player-list-button []
  [:button.btn {:on-click #(swap! app-state assoc-in [:current-player] nil)}
"Display all players"])
```

8. Let's write the code for the list of players. We start by writing a component for an element of the list. The content is the name of the player. When we click on it, it fetches the ranking data about the selected player:

```
(defn player [{:keys [id full_name]}]
  [:div [:span
         [:a
          {:href "#"
           :on-click (partial fetch-player id full_name)}
          full_name]]])
```

9. We now build the **player-list** component. It receives a vector of players and returns a **:div** that contains a player component for each player:

```
(defn player-list [players]
  (if (empty? players)
    [:div "Click the button to fetch players"]
    (into [:div] (map player players))))
```

10. This is the code for the function that fetches the players data from the server:

```
(defn fetch-players []
  (-> (js/fetch "http://localhost:8080/players/")
      (.then (fn [response] (.json response)))
      (.then (fn [json] (swap! app-state assoc-in [:players] (js->clj json
        :keywordize-keys true))))))
```

11. We also need a function that clears the list of players by modifying **app-state**:

```
(defn clear-players []
  (swap! app-state assoc-in [:players] []))
```

12. Now we add a button that either clears or fills the list of players:

```
(defn fetch-or-clear-button []
  (let [handler (if (empty? (:players @app-state)) fetch-players clear-players)
        text    (if (empty? (:players @app-state)) "Fetch Players" "Clear Players")]
    [:button.btn {:on-click handler} text]))
```

13. Now, we write the **main** component. When the value associated to **:current-player** is not **nil**, we display the currently selected player. Otherwise, we display a list of players. This is the code for the main **app** component:

```
(defn app []
  (if (:current-player @app-state)
    [:div
     [player-list-button]
     [player-alone (:current-player @app-state)]]
    [:div
     [fetch-or-clear-button]
     [player-list (:players @app-state)]]))
```

14. Finally, we render the main component:

```
(r/render-component [app] (. js/document (getElementById "app")))
```

By completing the activities, we have seen how to organize the different components of a Reagent application: the CSS, HTML, and **cljs** files. Being able to iteratively modify the code and have the web page immediately update without any page refresh was helpful and time-saving. We learned how to store the state of the app in a ratom and access the state for the code of the Reagent components.

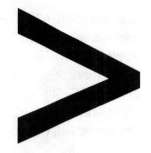

Index

About

All major keywords used in this book are captured alphabetically in this section. Each one is accompanied by the page number of where they appear.